The

Bessie Parmet Kannerstein '32

𝔐emorial 𝔉und

Established by

MR. JOSEPH PARMET

for the purchase of

REFERENCE BOOKS

for the

CEDAR CREST COLLEGE

LIBRARY

Twentieth-Century Short Story Explication

Supplement III to Third Edition

With Checklists of Books and Journals Used

WARREN S. WALKER
Horn Professor Emeritus of English
Texas Tech University

THE SHOE STRING PRESS, INC.
1987

Third Edition, Supplement III
© 1987 The Shoe String Press, Inc.
Hamden, Connecticut 06514

Printed in the United States of America

First edition published 1961
Supplement I to first edition published 1963
Supplement II to first edition published 1965
Second edition published 1967
Supplement I to second edition published 1970
Supplement II to second edition published 1973
Third edition published 1977
Supplement I to third edition published 1980
Supplement II to third edition published 1984

The paper in this book meets the guidelines for permanence
and durability of the Committee on Production Guidelines
for Book Longevity of the Council on Library Resources.
∞
Printed in the United States of America

Library of Congress Cataloging-in-Publication Data
(Revised for vol. 3)

Walker, Warren S.
Twentieth-century short story explication.
Includes index.
1. Short story—Indexes. I. Title.
Z5917.S5W33 1977, Suppl. [PN3373] 016.8093'1 80–16175
ISBN 0–208–02122–1 (3rd Ed. S. III)
ISBN 0–208–01813–1 (vol. 1)

CONTENTS

PREFACE

More than 6,000 entries are included in this tenth volume of *Twentieth-Century Short Story Explication*. Of the 957 short story writers represented, 469 appear for the first time in this volume, increasing to 1,767 the total number of authors covered in the Third Edition and its three Supplements. The newcomer authors are from many different parts of the world, the three largest groups coming from Latin America, Asia, and the wondrous realm of science fiction and fantasy.

Whatever the original languages of the stories themselves, their explications are here limited to those published in the major languages of Western Europe. Although these parameters may seem unduly restrictive, the fact of the matter is that they encompass the vast majority of critical studies of the genre. The growing numbers of competent Indian writers, for example, are far more frequently discussed in English than they are in Hindi or Bengali or Tamil. Similarly, despite the emphasis on indigenous languages among African states that were once colonies, their literary journals are usually printed in French or English.

Twentieth-Century Short Story Explication is a bibliography of interpretations that have appeared since 1900 of short stories published since 1800. The term *short story* here has the same meaning it carries in the Wilson Company's *Short Story Index*: "A brief narrative of not more than 150 average-sized pages." By *explication* I suggest simply interpretation or explanation of the meaning of a story, including observations on theme, symbol, and sometimes structure. This excludes from the bibliography what are essentially studies of sources, biographical data, and background materials. Occasionally there are explicatory passages cited in works otherwise devoted to these external considerations. All page numbers refer strictly to interpretive passages, not to the longer works in which they occur.

The profusion of interpretations generated in the "knowledge explosion" of recent decades required that, beginning with the Third Edition (1977), we adopt a system of coding and consequently a format different from that used in the first two editions and their Supplements. Each book is cited by author or editor and a short title; the full title and publication data are provided in A Checklist of Books Used. For an article in a journal or an essay in a critical collection, the full publication information is provided in the text the first time the study is cited. In subsequent entries only the critic's or scholar's name and a short title are used as long as these entries appear under the name of the same short story author; if an article or essay explicates stories by two or more authors, a complete initial entry is made for each author. As in Supplements I and II, we have again included A Checklist of Journals Used. This should be especially helpful to students who may not be familiar with titles of professional journals, much less the abbreviations for such titles.

Supplement II to the Third Edition carried forward the coverage of short story interpretation from January 1, 1979, through December 31, 1981. The present volume, Supplement III, extends that coverage through December 31, 1984. Both volumes include a few earlier explications that had been overlooked previously, as well as reprintings of earlier studies. An asterisk preceding an entry indicates that the item is a reprinting of an explication listed in the Third Edition.

In the preparation of this book I have been indebted to the editors of such journals as *PMLA, Modern Fiction Studies, Studies in Short Fiction,* and *Journal of*

Modern Literature. I wish to extend thanks to the Interlibrary Loan Department of Texas Tech University Library, especially to its chairperson, Gloria Lyerla, and her assistant, Valerie Warwick. As usual, I am most grateful to my wife, Barbara K. Walker, for her continuous encouragement and assistance.

Warren S. Walker
Texas Tech University

SUFI 'ABD ALLAH

"The Empty Seat"
Accad, Évelyne. *Veil of Shame* . . . , 120–121.

"A Girl's School"
Accad, Évelyne. *Veil of Shame* . . . , 117–118.

"I Am a Murderess"
Accad, Évelyne. *Veil of Shame* . . . , 119–120.

"I Chose My Husband"
Accad, Évelyne. *Veil of Shame* . . . , 118–119.

WALTER ABISH

"The English Garden"
Karl, Frederick R. *American Fictions* . . . , 551–552.

"In So Many Words"
Klinkowitz, Jerome. *The Self-Apparent Word* . . . , 93–94.

"This Is Not a Film, This Is a Precise Act of Disbelief"
Klinkowitz, Jerome. *The Self-Apparent Word* . . . , 91–92.

SHOLEM YANKEV ABRAMOVITSH
[MENDELE MOKHER SEFORIM]

"Burned-Out Beggars"
Mintz, Alan. *Hurban* . . . , 119–123.

"Secret Thunder"
Mintz, Alan. *Hurban* . . . , 117–118.

"Shem and Japhet on the Train"
Roskies, David G. *Against the Apocalypse* . . . , 70–72.

CHINUA ACHEBE

"Beginning of the End" [originally titled "The Old Order in Conflict with
    the New"]
Lindfors, Bernth. *Early Nigerian Literature*, 100–101.

"Dead Men's Path"
Lindfors, Bernth. *Early Nigerian Literature*, 102–106.

"In a Village Church"
Lindfors, Bernth. *Early Nigerian Literature*, 98–100.

"The Madman"
Balogun, F. Odun. "Achebe's 'The Madman': A Poetic Realization of Irony,"
  Okike, 23 (August, 1983), 72–79.
Ogu, Julius N. "The Concept of Madness in Chinua Achebe's Writing," *J Commonwealth Lit*, 18, i (1983), 48–54.

"Vengeful Creditor"
Balogun, F. Odun. "Russian and Nigerian Literatures," *Comp Lit Stud*, 21
  (1984), 487–494.

BILL ADAMS

"God Rest You Merry, Gentlemen"
Perrine, Laurence, and Thomas R. Arp. *Instructor's Manual . . .* , 6th ed., 32–
  35.

ALEKSANDER ADMIRALSKII

"The Genius"
Smyrniw, Walter. "Satirical Trends in Recent Soviet Science Fiction," in Bristol,
  Evelyn, Ed. *Russian Literature . . .* , 195.

JAMES AGEE

"A Mother's Tale"
Perrine, Laurence, and Thomas R. Arp. *Instructor's Manual . . .* , 6th ed., 37–
  39.

SHMUEL [SHAY] YOSEF AGNON [SHMUEL YOSEF CZACZKES]

"The Betrothed"
Fisch, Harold. *A Remembered Future . . .* , 36–37.

"The Covering of the Blood"
Fisch, Harold. *A Remembered Future . . .* , 170–172.

"Edo and Enam" [same as "Iddo and Aynam"]
Fisch, Harold. *A Remembered Future . . .* , 53–56.
Fuchs, Esther. "'Edo and Enam': The Ironic Perspective," *Mod Lang Stud*, 13,
  i (1983), 85–100.
Rosenberg, Israel. *Shay Agnon's World . . .* , 3–143.

"The Face and the Image"
Baumgarten, Murray. *City Scriptures . . .* , 106–109.

"In the Heart of the Seas"
Yudkin, Leon I. *Jewish Writing . . .* , 82–83.

"The Scribe"
Baumgarten, Murray. *City Scriptures* . . . , 95–97.

DEMETRIO AGUILERA-MALTA

"The *Cholo*'s Vengeance"
Brushwood, John S. "The Spanish American Short Story from Quiroga to
    Borges," in Peden, Margaret S., Ed. *The Latin American Short Story* . . . , 82–
    83.

ILSE AICHINGER

"Ghost Ship"
Corkhill, Alan. "Ilse Aichinger's 'Seegeister' und Christa Reinigs 'Drei Schiffe,'"
    Colloquia Germanica, 15 (1982), 122–131.

CONRAD AIKEN

"Mr. Arcularis"
Butscher, Edward. "Conrad Aiken's Short Fiction: The Poet's Story," *Southern
    Q*, 21, i (1982), 107–111.

"Silent Snow, Secret Snow"
Butscher, Edward. "Conrad Aiken's Short Fiction . . . ," 104–107.
Kloss, Robert. "The Secret of Aiken's Snow," *Hartford Stud Lit*, 12 (1980), 29–
    38.
Tebeaux, Elizabeth. "'Silent Snow, Secret Snow': Style as Art," *Stud Short Fiction*,
    20 (1983), 105–114.

"Strange Moonlight"
Butscher, Edward. "Conrad Aiken's Short Fiction . . . ," 111–117.

CHINGIZ AITMATOV

"The Rivals"
Ponomareff, Constantin V. "A Poetic Vision in Conflict: Chingiz Aitmatov's
    Fiction," in Bristol, Evelyn, Ed. *Russian Literature* . . . , 162–163.

"Skewbald Dog Running at the Edge of the Sea"
Ponomareff, Constantin V. "A Poetic Vision . . . ," 163–164.

VASILY AKSENOV [VASILY AKSYONOV]

"Halfway to the Moon"
Brown, Edward J. . . . *Since the Revolution*, 3rd ed., 365.

AKUTAGAWA RYŪNOSUKE

"The Ball"
Keene, Donald. *Dawn to the West* . . . , 570–571.

"A Clod of Earth"
Keene, Donald. *Dawn to the West* . . . , 577–578.

"Death of a Martyr"
Keene, Donald. *Dawn to the West* . . . , 568–569.

"Death Register"
Keene, Donald. *Dawn to the West* . . . , 582–583.

"The Early Life of Daidōji Shinsuke"
Keene, Donald. *Dawn to the West* . . . , 581–582.

"Genkaku's Villa"
Keene, Donald. *Dawn to the West* . . . , 578–579.

"The Handkerchief"
Keene, Donald. *Dawn to the West* . . . , 569.

"A Life Spent at Frivolous Writing"
Keene, Donald. *Dawn to the West* . . . , 566–568.

"Rashōmon"
Miller, James E., and Bernice Slote. *Instructor's Manual* . . . , 2nd ed., 14.

"The Spider's Thread"
Keene, Donald. *Dawn to the West* . . . , 563.

"Within a Grove"
Keene, Donald. *Dawn to the West* . . . , 571–572.

LEOPOLDO ALAS

"The Conversion of Chiripa"
Abellan, Manuel L. "Clarín: La inversión de paradigmas ideologicos como recurso literario: A propósito de 'La conversión de Chiripa,'" *Diálogos*, 4 (1984), 97–108.

"Madrid, June 1882"
Richmond, Carolyn. "Un documento (vivo, literario y critico): Análisis de un cuento de Clarín," *Boletín del Instituto de Estudios Asturianos*, 36 (1982), 367–384.

BOZORG [BUZURG] ALAVI

"The Bride of a Thousand Husbands"
Wickens, G. M. "Bozorg Alavi's Portmanteau," in Ricks, Thomas M., Ed. *Critical Perspectives* . . . , 229–301.

"Dance of Death"
Alvi, Sajida. "Bozorg Alavi's Writing from Prison," in Ricks, Thomas M., Ed. *Critical Perspectives* . . . , 280–282.

"Expectation"
Alvi, Sajida. "Bozorg Alavi's Writing . . . ," 277–279.

"General Amnesty"
Alvi, Sajida. "Bozorg Alavi's Writing . . . ," 282–283.

"The Lead Soldier"
Wickens, G. M. "Bozorg Alavi's Portmanteau," 303–306.

"Pestle"
Alvi, Sajida. "Bozorg Alavi's Writing . . . ," 279–280.

"The Portmanteau"
Wickens, G. M. "Bozorg Alavi's Portmanteau," 296–298.

"The Sacrifice"
Wickens, G. M. "Bozorg Alavi's Portmanteau," 298–299.

"The Story of My Room"
Wickens, G. M. "Bozorg Alavi's Portmanteau," 301–303.

"The Thresher"
Shojai, D. A. "The Fatal Rage: Heroic Anger in Modern Iranian Fiction," *Iranian Stud,* 8, iv (1975), 226–227.

A. ALBERTS

"The Car and the Nuns"
Nieuwenhuys, Rob. *Mirror of the Indies* . . . , 291–292.

"Chase"
Nieuwenhuys, Rob. *Mirror of the Indies* . . . , 294–295.

"Green"
Nieuwenhuys, Rob. *Mirror of the Indies* . . . , 295–296.

LOUISA MAY ALCOTT

"The Abbot's Ghost; or, Maurice Trehearne's Temptation"
Stern, Madeleine B. "Introduction," in Stern, Madeleine B., Ed. *Behind a Mask* . . . , xvi–xvii; rpt. Stern, Madeleine B., Ed. *Critical Essays* . . . , 56–57.

"Behind a Mask; or, A Woman's Power"
Stern, Madeleine B. "Introduction," xvii–xix; rpt. Stern, Madeleine B., Ed. *Critical Essays* . . . , 58–59.

"The Children's Joke"
Marsella, Joy A. *The Promise of Destiny* . . . , 123–124.

"Cupid and Chow-Chow"
Marsella, Joy A. *The Promise of Destiny* . . . , 93–99.

"A Curious Call"
Marsella, Joy A. *The Promise of Destiny* . . . , 20–21.

"Dandelion"
Marsella, Joy A. *The Promise of Destiny* . . . , 36–38.

"Fancy's Friend"
Marsella, Joy A. *The Promise of Destiny* . . . , 145–148.

"An Hour"
Cohn, Jan. "The Negro Character in Northern Magazine Fiction of the 1860's," *New England Q,* 43 (1970), 588–590; rpt. Stern, Madeleine B., Ed. *Critical Essays* . . . , 30–32.

"Marjorie's Three Gifts"
Marsella, Joy A. *The Promise of Destiny* . . . , 37–39.

"The Moss People"
Marsella, Joy A. *The Promise of Destiny* . . . , 106–109.

"My Contraband"
Cohn, Jan. "The Negro Character . . . ," 591–592; rpt. Stern, Madeleine B., Ed. *Critical Essays* . . . , 32–33.

"Pauline's Passion and Punishment"
Stern, Madeleine B. "Introduction," xv–xvi; rpt. Stern, Madeleine B., Ed. *Critical Essays* . . . , 55–56.

"Roses and Forget-Me-Nots"
Marsella, Joy A. *The Promise of Destiny* . . . , 42–43.

"Shadow-Children"
Marsella, Joy A. *The Promise of Destiny* . . . , 72–75.

"Tessa's Surprises"
Marsella, Joy A. *The Promise of Destiny* . . . , 44–46.

"V. V.; or, Plots and Counterplots"
Stern, Madeleine B. "Introduction," xvii; rpt. Stern, Madeleine B., Ed. *Critical Essays* . . . , 57.

BRIAN W. ALDISS

"An Appearance of Life"
Griffin, Brian, and David Wingrove. *Apertures* . . . , 195–196.
Wingrove, David. "Thinking in Fuzzy Sets—The Recent SF of Brian W. Aldiss," *Pacific Q*, 4 (1979), 290.

"The Circulation of the Blood"
Griffin, Brian, and David Wingrove. *Apertures* . . . , 95–96.

"Man in His Time"
Griffin, Brian, and David Wingrove. *Apertures* . . . , 84–85.

"The Saliva Tree"
Griffin, Brian, and David Wingrove. *Apertures* . . . , 98–100.

"Segregation"
Griffin, Brian, and David Wingrove. *Apertures* . . . , 31–34.

"The Source"
Griffin, Brian, and David Wingrove. *Apertures* . . . , 81–83.

"T"
Griffin, Brian, and David Wingrove. *Apertures* . . . , 20–22.

"The Worm That Flies"
Griffin, Brian, and David Wingrove. *Apertures* . . . , 97–98.

THOMAS BAILEY ALDRICH

"Mlle. Olympe Zabriski"
Habegger, Alfred. *Gender, Fantasy* . . . , 31–32.

SHOLEM ALEICHEM [SHOLOM RABINOWITZ]

"Geese"
Baumgarten, Murray. *City Scriptures* . . . , 80–82.

"Happy New Year"
Baumgarten, Murray. *City Scriptures* . . . , 84–87.

"A Hundred and One"
Roskies, David G. *Against the Apocalypse* . . . , 165–167.

"On Account of a Hat"
Baumgarten, Murray. *City Scriptures* . . . , 46–47.
Greenspan, Ezra. *The "Schlemiel"* . . . , 14–16.

"The Penknife"
Liptzin, Sol. *The Flowering* . . . , 94–95.

"Tales of a Thousand and One Nights"
Roskies, David G. *Against the Apocalypse* . . . , 179–182.

"Tevye the Dairyman"
Liptzin, Sol. *The Flowering* . . . , 90–91.

"Three Widows"
Baumgarten, Murray. *City Scriptures* . . . , 74–75, 89–92.

"A Wedding Without Musicians"
Roskies, David G. *Against the Apocalypse* . . . , 173–176.

GRANT ALLEN [CHARLES GRANT BLAIRFINDIE ALLEN]

"The Child of the Phalanstery"
Morton, Peter. *The Vital Science* . . . , 141–144.

WOODY ALLEN

"The Kugelmass Episode"
Culler, Jonathan. "The Uses of *Madame Bovary*," in Schor, Naomi, and Henry Majewski, Eds. *Flaubert and Postmodernism*, 10–11.

JOÃO ALPHONSUS

"Sardanapalus"
Sadlier, Darlene J. "Compreendendo o Medo de Gatos no Narrador de 'Sardanapalo,'" *Minas Gerais*, 14 (Nov. 14, 1981), 6–7.

GHADAH AL-SAMMAN

"A Crime of Honour"
Awwad, Hanan A. *Arab Causes* . . . , 85–86.

"The Crossing"
Awwad, Hanan A. *Arab Causes* . . . , 86–87.

"The Crow and the Two Time Zones"
Awwad, Hanan A. *Arab Causes* . . . , 89–90.

"The Fear of Other Birds"
Accad, Évelyne. *Veil of Shame* . . . , 113–114.

"The Great Danube"
Awwad, Hanan A. *Arab Causes* . . . , 80–82.

"A Gypsy Without a Haven"
Accad, Évelyne. *Veil of Shame* . . . , 115–116.

"The Meowing"
Accad, Évelyne. *Veil of Shame* . . . , 114–115.

"Oh! Damascus"
Awwad, Hanan A. *Arab Causes* . . . , 67–69.

"The Sixth Finger"
Awwad, Hanan A. *Arab Causes* . . . , 64–65.

"That Summer's Fire"
Awwad, Hanan A. *Arab Causes* . . . , 79–82.

"The Thread of Red Pebbles"
Awwad, Hanan A. *Arab Causes* . . . , 60–61.

"The Virgin of Beirut"
Awwad, Hanan A. *Arab Causes* . . . , 87–89.

"The Widow of Joy"
Awwad, Hanan A. *Arab Causes* . . . , 82–85.

"A Wounded Serpent"
Awwad, Hanan A. *Arab Causes* . . . , 57–58.

JORGE AMADO

"How Porciúncula the Mulatto Got the Corpse Off His Back"
Foster, David W. "Major Figures in the Brazilian Short Story," in Peden, Margaret S., Ed. *The Latin American Short Story* . . . , 9–12.

ENRIQUE AMORIM

"Oxcart Stop"
Brushwood, John S. "The Spanish American Short Story from Quiroga to Borges," in Peden, Margaret S., Ed. *The Latin American Short Story* . . . , 84.

BENNY ANDERSEN

"The Bouncer"
Marx, Leonie. *Benny Andersen* . . . , 98–100.

"The Break-Up"
Marx, Leonie. *Benny Andersen* . . . , 79–81.

"Distinctive Mark"
Marx, Leonie. *Benny Andersen* . . . , 83–85.

"The Drowning"
Marx, Leonie. *Benny Andersen* . . . , 89–90.

"The Family Friend"
Marx, Leonie. *Benny Andersen* . . . , 88.

"Fats Olsen"
Marx, Leonie. *Benny Andersen* . . . , 104–111.

"A Happy Person"
Marx, Leonie. *Benny Andersen* . . . , 97–98.

"The Hot-Water Bottle"
Marx, Leonie. *Benny Andersen* . . . , 87–88.

"Ice-Floes in the Baltic"
Marx, Leonie. *Benny Andersen* . . . , 89.

"In the Course of Last Year"
Marx, Leonie. *Benny Andersen* . . . , 91.

"The Intercom"
Marx, Leonie. *Benny Andersen* . . . , 81–83.

"It Must Be Possible"
Marx, Leonie. *Benny Andersen* . . . , 100–102.

"Kill Those Bantam Chickens"
Marx, Leonie. *Benny Andersen* . . . , 85–86.

"The Matches"
Marx, Leonie. *Benny Andersen* . . . , 88.

"The Pants"
Marx, Leonie. *Benny Andersen* . . . , 92–93.

"The Passage"
Marx, Leonie. *Benny Andersen* . . . , 93–95.

"The Pillows"
Marx, Leonie. *Benny Andersen* . . . , 95–97.

"The Shoes"
Marx, Leonie. *Benny Andersen . . .* , 103.

"The Telephone Call"
Marx, Leonie. *Benny Andersen . . .* , 90–91.

"Ulla and Søren"
Marx, Leonie. *Benny Andersen . . .* , 102.

POUL ANDERSON

"Call Me Joe"
Tweet, Roald D. "Poul Anderson," in Bleiler, Everett F., Ed. *Science Fiction Writers . . .* , 262.

"The Faun"
Fredericks, Casey. *The Future of Eternity . . .* , 28–29.

"Goat Song"
Miesel, Sandra. *Against Time's Arrow . . .* , 37–43.

"Kyrie"
King, Betty. *Women of the Future . . .* , 108–109.
Meyers, Walter E. *Aliens and Linguists . . .* , 142–143.

"License"
Pierce, Hazel B. *A Literary Symbiosis . . .* , 157–158.

"The Longest Voyage"
Tweet, Roald D. "Poul Anderson," 261–262.

"The Queen of Air and Darkness"
Meyers, Walter E. *Aliens and Linguists . . .* , 141–142.
Miesel, Sandra. *Against Time's Arrow . . .* , 21–24.
Pierce, Hazel B. *A Literary Symbiosis . . .* , 229–230.

POUL ANDERSON and F. N. WALDROP

"Tomorrow's Children"
Miesel, Sandra. *Against Time's Arrow . . .* , 43–44.

SHERWOOD ANDERSON

"Another Wife"
Gado, Frank, Ed. . . . *Teller's Tales,* 10–11.

"Brother Death"
Gado, Frank, Ed. . . . *Teller's Tales,* 19–20.

"Daughters"
Gado, Frank, Ed. . . . *Teller's Tales,* 11–12.

"Death in the Woods"
Gado, Frank, Ed. . . . *Teller's Tales,* 17–19.
Sheidley, William E., and Ann Charters. *Instructor's Manual . . . ,* 65–66.
Watson, James G. "The American Short Story: 1930–1945," in Stevick, Philip, Ed. *The American Short Story, 1900–1945,* 123–124.

"The Egg"
Scott, Virgil, and David Madden. *Instructor's Manual . . . ,* 4th ed., 12–14; Madden, David. *Instructor's Manual . . . ,* 5th ed., 71–73; Madden, David, and Virgil Scott. *Instructor's Manual . . . ,* 6th ed., 79–82.
Sirlin, Rhoda, and David H. Richter. *Instructor's Manual . . . ,* 1–2.

"Hands"
Elledge, Jim. "Dante's Lovers in Sherwood Anderson's 'Hands,'" *Stud Short Fiction,* 21 (1984), 11–15.
Kimbel, Ellen. "The American Short Story: 1900–1920," in Stevick, Philip, Ed. *The American Short Story, 1900–1945,* 65–66.
Sheidley, William E., and Ann Charters. *Instructor's Manual . . . ,* 63.

"I Want to Know Why"
*Abcarian, Richard, and Marvin Klotz. *Instructor's Manual . . . ,* 2nd ed., 1; 3rd ed., 1.
Freese, Peter. "'Rising in the World' and 'Wanting to Know Why': The Socialization Process as Theme of the American Short Story," *Archiv,* 218, ii (1981), 294–296.
Gado, Frank, Ed. . . . *Teller's Tales,* 7–9.
Kimbel, Ellen. "The American Short Story . . . ," 77–78.

"In a Strange Town"
Gado, Frank, Ed. . . . *Teller's Tales,* 6–7.

"The Man Who Became a Woman"
Gado, Frank, Ed. . . . *Teller's Tales,* 15–17.

"Sophistication"
Miller, James E., and Bernice Slote. *Instructor's Manual . . . ,* 2nd ed., 11.

"The Strength of God"
Kimbel, Ellen. "The American Short Story . . . ," 67–68.

"There She Is—She Is Taking Her Bath"
Gado, Frank, Ed. . . . *Teller's Tales,* 9–10.

MARÍO RAUL DE MORAIS ANDRADE

"The Christmas Turkey"
Foster, David W. "Major Figures in the Brazilian Short Story," in Peden, Margaret S., Ed. *The Latin American Short Story . . . ,* 9–12.

HORACE T. ANDREWS

"The Cricket Pro of Halethorpe"
Oriard, Michael. *Dreaming of Heroes . . .* , 42–43.

MICHAEL ANTHONY

"Enchanted Alley"
Smyer, Richard I. "Enchantment and Violence in the Fiction of Michael Anthony," *World Lit Written Engl,* 21 (1982), 149–150.

A. APPELFELD

"After the Wedding"
Mintz, Alan. *Hurban . . .* , 233–234.

"Along the Shore"
Mintz, Alan. *Hurban . . .* , 212–215.

"Changing the Watch"
Mintz, Alan. *Hurban . . .* , 231–232.

"The Cold Heights"
Mintz, Alan. *Hurban . . .* , 228–230.

"Cold Spring"
Mintz, Alan. *Hurban . . .* , 208–210.

"The Escape"
Mintz, Alan. *Hurban . . .* , 223–227.

"The Expulsion"
Mintz, Alan. *Hurban . . .* , 216–220.

"The Inn"
Mintz, Alan. *Hurban . . .* , 232–233.

"The Merchant Bartfuss"
Mintz, Alan. *Hurban . . .* , 236–238.

"Regina"
Mintz, Alan. *Hurban . . .* , 235–236.

MAX APPLE

"Free Agents"
Wilde, Alan. *Horizons of Assent . . .* , 132–133.

"Vegetable Love"
Glausser, Wayne. "Spots of Meaning: Literary Allusions in Max Apple's 'Vegetable Love,'" *Stud Short Fiction*, 20 (1983), 255–263.

ARAHATA KANSON

"The Escapists"
Rubin, Jay. *Injurious to Public Morals . . .* , 184–188.

FRANCISCO ARCELLANA

"The Yellow Shawl"
San Juan, E. *Toward a People's Literature . . .* , 169–171.

JOSÉ MARÍA ARGUEDAS

"Puppy Love"
Brushwood, John S. "The Spanish American Short Story from Quiroga to Borges," in Peden, Margaret S., Ed. *The Latin American Short Story . . .* , 86.

ARISHIMA TAKEO

"The Death of Osue"
Anderer, Paul. *Other Worlds . . .* , 32.

"The Laboratory"
Anderer, Paul. *Other Worlds . . .* , 127–128.

[LUDWIG] ACHIM VON ARNIM

"Isabella von Ägypten"
Hoermann, Roland. *Achim von Arnim*, 90–103.
Lokke, Kari E. "Achim von Arnim and the Romantic Grotesque," *Germ R*, 58 (1983), 21–32.

"Die Majoratsherren"
Hoermann, Roland. *Achim von Arnim*, 115–138.

"The Matchmaker"
Menhennet, Alan. *The Romantic Movement*, 198–199.

"Mistris Lee"
Menhennet, Alan. *The Romantic Movement*, 195.

"Der Tolle Invalide auf dem Fort Ratonneau"
Hoermann, Roland. *Achim von Arnim*, 103–114.
Menhennet, Alan. *The Romantic Movement*, 200–201.

JUAN JOSÉ ARREOLA

"Baby H. P."
Washburn, Yulan M. *Juan José Arreola,* 42–43.

"The Bird Spider"
Washburn, Yulan M. *Juan José Arreola,* 46–48.

"The Convert"
Otero, José. "Religion moral y existencia en tres cuentos de Juan José Arreola,"
    Cuadernos Americanos, 234, i (1981), 222–231.
Washburn, Yulan M. *Juan José Arreola,* 107–108.

"Corrido"
Menton, Seymour. "Juan José Arreola and the Twentieth-Century Short Story,"
    Hispania, 42, iii (1959), 300–301.

"The Crow Catcher"
Washburn, Yulan M. *Juan José Arreola,* 116–117.

"The Disciple"
Washburn, Yulan M. *Juan José Arreola,* 68–69.

"Flash"
Gilgen, Read G. "Absurdist Techniques in the Short Stories of Juan José Ar-
    reola," *J Spanish Stud: Twentieth Century,* 8 (1980), 74–75.

"The Fraud"
Washburn, Yulan M. *Juan José Arreola,* 60–61.

"He Did Good While He Lived"
Washburn, Yulan M. *Juan José Arreola,* 112–115.

"In Memoriam"
Menton, Seymour. "Juan José Arreola . . . ," 298–299.

"The News"
Washburn, Yulan M. *Juan José Arreola,* 81–82.

"Parable of the Exchange"
Washburn, Yulan M. *Juan José Arreola,* 87–92.

"*Parturient Montes*"
Washburn, Yulan M. *Juan José Arreola,* 62–68.

"Paul"
Washburn, Yulan M. *Juan José Arreola,* 100–103.

"The Prodigious Milligram"
Newgard, Jerry. "Dos cuentos de Juan José Arreola," *Cuadernos Hispanoameri-
    canos,* 336 (1978), 527–533.
Washburn, Yulan M. *Juan José Arreola,* 38–42.

"The Silence of God"
Otero, José. "Religion moral . . . ," 222–231.
Washburn, Yulan M. *Juan José Arreola,* 103–107.

"El soñado"
Gilgen, Read G. "Absurdist Techniques . . . ," 73–74.

"The Switchman"
McMurray, George R. "The Spanish American Short Story from Borges to the
    Present," in Peden, Margaret S., Ed. *The Latin American Short Story . . . ,*
    106–107.
Menton, Seymour. "Juan José Arreola . . . ," 296–297.
Newgard, Jerry. "Dos cuentos . . . ," 527–533.
Otero, José. "Religion moral . . . ," 222–231.
Washburn, Yulan M. *Juan José Arreola,* 49–53.

"A Tamed Woman"
Washburn, Yulan M. *Juan José Arreola,* 94–96.

"Topos"
Menton, Seymour. "Juan José Arreola . . . ," 296.

"You and I"
Washburn, Yulan M. *Juan José Arreola,* 77.

SHOLEM ASCH

"In a Carnival Night"
Roskies, David G. *Against the Apocalypse . . . ,* 264–265.

"Kola Street"
Roskies, David G. *Against the Apocalypse . . . ,* 142.

"Reb Shlome Nagid"
Liptzin, Sol. *The Flowering . . . ,* 180–181.

"Sanctification of the Name"
Liptzin, Sol. *The Flowering . . . ,* 181–184.

"The Village"
Liptzin, Sol. *The Flowering . . . ,* 178–179.

"The Witch of Castile"
Liptzin, Sol. *The Flowering . . . ,* 184–185.

ISAAC ASIMOV

"Anniversary"
Pierce, Hazel B. *A Literary Symbiosis . . . ,* 64–65.

"Hostess"
Fiedler, Jean, and Jim Mele. *Isaac Asimov*, 16–17.
Gunn, James. *Isaac Asimov . . .* , 93–95.

"In a Good Cayse—"
Gunn, James. *Isaac Asimov . . .* , 96–97.

"The Last Question"
Allen, L. David. "Isaac Asimov," 271–272.

"Liar!"
Allen, L. David. "Isaac Asimov," 267.
Fiedler, Jean, and Jim Mele. *Isaac Asimov*, 31–32.
King, Betty. *Women of the Future . . .* , 64–65.

"The Life and Times of Multivac"
Gunn, James. *Isaac Asimov . . .* , 77.
Stableford, Brian. "Man-Made Catastrophes," in Rabkin, Eric S., Martin H.
     Greenberg, and Joseph D. Olander, Eds. *The End . . .* , 112–113.

"Little Lost Robot"
Fiedler, Jean, and Jim Mele. "Asimov's Robots," in Riley, Dick, Ed. *Critical
     Encounters*, 5.
Gunn, James. *Isaac Asimov . . .* , 62–63.

"Marooned Off Vesta"
Gunn, James. *Isaac Asimov . . .* , 87.

"The Martian Way"
Fiedler, Jean, and Jim Mele. *Isaac Asimov*, 20–23.
Gunn, James. *Isaac Asimov . . .* , 97.

"The Mayors" [originally titled "Bridle and Saddle"]
Gunn, James. *Isaac Asimov . . .* , 31–32.

"The Merchant Princes" [originally titled "The Wedge"]
Gunn, James. *Isaac Asimov . . .* , 32–33.

"Mirror Image"
Gunn, James. *Isaac Asimov . . .* , 72–73.

"Mother Earth"
Gunn, James. *Isaac Asimov . . .* , 90–91.

"The Mule"
Allen, L. David. "Isaac Asimov," 270.
Gunn, James. *Isaac Asimov . . .* , 34–35.

"Nightfall"
Allen, L. David. "Isaac Asimov," 268–269.
Fiedler, Jean, and Jim Mele. *Isaac Asimov*, 8–12.

Gunn, James. *Isaac Asimov . . .* , 79–86.
Hartwell, David. *Age of Wonders . . .* , 52–53.

"Profession"
Gunn, James. *Isaac Asimov . . .* , 100–101.

"The Psychohistorians"
Gunn, James. *Isaac Asimov . . .* , 30.

"Robbie" [originally titled "Strange Playfellow"]
Allen, L. David. "Isaac Asimov," 267.
Fiedler, Jean, and Jim Mele. "Asimov's Robots," 2–3.
Gunn, James. *Isaac Asimov . . .* , 57–58.
King, Betty. *Women of the Future . . .* , 62–64.

"Runaround"
Allen, L. David. "Isaac Asimov," 268.
Fiedler, Jean, and Jim Mele. "Asimov's Robots," 3–4.
Gunn, James. *Isaac Asimov . . .* , 60.

"Satisfaction Guaranteed"
Fiedler, Jean, and Jim Mele. "Asimov's Robots," 8–9.

"Search by Mule" [originally titled "Now You See It . . ."]
Gunn, James. *Isaac Asimov . . .* , 35–36.

"Search by the Fountain" [originally titled " . . . And Now You Don't"]
Gunn, James. *Isaac Asimov . . .* , 36–37.

"Someday"
Gunn, James. *Isaac Asimov . . .* , 71.

"Strangers in Paradise"
Fiedler, Jean, and Jim Mele. *Isaac Asimov,* 73–74.

"Sucker Bait"
Fiedler, Jean, and Jim Mele. *Isaac Asimov,* 19–20.
Gunn, James. *Isaac Asimov . . .* , 98–99.

"The Tercentenary Incident"
Gunn, James. *Isaac Asimov . . .* , 74–75.

"That Thou Art Mindful of Him"
Gunn, James. *Isaac Asimov . . .* , 73–74.

"The Traders" [originally titled "The Big and the Little"]
Gunn, James. *Isaac Asimov . . .* , 32.

"The Ugly Little Boy" [originally titled "Lastborn"]
Allen, L. David. "Isaac Asimov," 272.
Gunn, James. *Isaac Asimov . . .* , 101–102.

MIGUEL ANGEL ASTURIAS

"The Legend of the Tattooed Woman"
Brushwood, John S. "The Spanish American Short Story from Quiroga to
    Borges," in Peden, Margaret S., Ed. *The Latin American Short Story* . . . , 81–
    82.

A. A. ATTANASIO

"Interface"
Meyers, Walter E. *Aliens and Linguists* . . . , 63–64.

MARGARET ATWOOD

"Giving Birth"
Rosenberg, Jerome H. *Margaret Atwood*, 124–125.

"The Man from Mars"
Rosenberg, Jerome H. *Margaret Atwood*, 121–122.

"Polarities"
Rosenberg, Jerome H. *Margaret Atwood*, 122.

"Rape Fantasies"
Perrine, Laurence, and Thomas R. Arp. *Instructor's Manual* . . . , 6th ed., 69–
    71.

"The War in the Bathroom"
Rosenberg, Jerome H. *Margaret Atwood*, 120–121.

MARTIN AVERY

"Five-Cent Photograph"
Vauthier, Simone. "Copie non conforme: Regards sur une nouvelle de Martin
    Avery," *Fabula*, 4 (1984), 59–72.

RENÉ AVILÉS FABILA

"The Perfect Triangle"
Romero, Juan R. "La sátira en 'El triángulo perfecto' de René Avilés Fabila,"
    Mester, 13, i (1984), 73–84.

ISAAC EMMANUILOVICH BABEL

"The Father"
Mendelson, Danuta. *Metaphor* . . . , 56–80.

"Guy de Maupassant"
Nilsson, Nils A. "Babel: 'Guy de Maupassant,'" in Zelinsky, Bodo, Ed. *Die rus-
    sische Novelle*, 182–190.
———. "Isaac Babel's Story 'Guy de Maupassant,'" in Nilsson, Nils A., Ed.
    ... *Russian Prose*, 213–227.
Sheidley, William E., and Ann Charters. *Instructor's Manual* ... , 100.

"Italian Sunshine"
Avins, Carol. *Border Crossings* ... , 132–137.

"Justice in Parentheses"
Mendelson, Danuta. *Metaphor* ... , 92–96.

"Line and Color"
Mendelson, Danuta. *Metaphor* ... , 105–112.

"My First Goose"
Bergman, David, Joseph de Roche, and Daniel M. Epstein. *Instructor's Man-
    ual* ... , 38.
Sheidley, William E., and Ann Charters. *Instructor's Manual* ... , 98–99.

"Pan Apolek"
Sicher, Efraim. "Art as Metaphor, Epiphany, and Aesthetic Statement: The
    Short Stories of Isaac Babel," *Mod Lang R*, 77 (1982), 391–396.
———. "The Road to a Red Cavalry: Myth and Mythology in the Works of
    Isaak Babel of the 1920s," *Slavonic & East European R*, 60 (1982), 532–542.

INGEBORG BACHMANN

"Jugend in einer österreichischen Stadt"
Bartsch, Kurt. "Geschichtliche Erfalrungen in der Prosa von Bachmann: Am
    Beispiel der Erzählungen 'Jugend in einer österreichischen Stadt' und 'Un-
    ter Mördern und Irren,'" in Höller, Hans, Ed. *Der dunkle Schatten* ... , 111–
    124.

"A Place of Coincidences"
Penner, Dick, Ed. *Fiction of the Absurd* ... , 311–313.

"Ein Schritt nach Gomorrha"
Achberger, Karen. "Bachmann und die Bibel: 'Ein Schritt nach Gomorrha' als
    weibliche Schöpfungsgeschichte," in Höller, Hans, Ed. *Der dunkle Schat-
    ten* ... , 97–110.

"Unter Mördern und Irren"
Bartsch, Kurt. "Geschichtliche Erfalrungen ... ," 111–124.

YA'QUB BALBUL

"Sa'ida"
Accad, Évelyne. *Veil of Shame* ... , 145–146.

JAMES BALDWIN

"Going to Meet the Man"
Vickery, John B. *Myths and Texts* . . . , 141–143.

"Sonny's Blues"
Albert, Richard N. "The Jazz Blues Motif in Baldwin's 'Sonny's Blues,'" *Coll Lit*, 11 (1984), 178–185.
Bergman, David, Joseph de Roche, and Daniel M. Epstein. *Instructor's Manual* . . . , 45–46.
Byerman, Keith E. "Words and Music: Narrative Ambiguity in 'Sonny's Blues,'" *Stud Short Fiction*, 19 (1982), 367–372.
Mosher, Marlene. "Baldwin's 'Sonny's Blues,'" *Explicator*, 40, iv (1982), 59.
Ro, Sigmund. *Rage and Celebration* . . . , 12–27.
Sirlin, Rhoda, and David H. Richter. *Instructor's Manual* . . . , 3–4.

CLIFFORD BALL

"Duar the Accused"
De Camp, L. Sprague. *Literary Swordsmen* . . . , 277–278.

J. G. BALLARD

"The Assassination Weapon"
Pringle, David. *Earth* . . . , 30–31.

"The Day of Forever"
Pringle, David. *Earth* . . . , 42–43.

"The Drowned Giant"
Fredericks, Casey. *The Future of Eternity* . . . , 95–96.
Pringle, David. *Earth* . . . , 59.

"The Garden of Time"
Pringle, David. *Earth* . . . , 31.

"Having a Wonderful Time"
Pringle, David. *Earth* . . . , 43–44.

"Low-Flying Aircraft"
Pringle, David. *Earth* . . . , 57.
Wagar, W. Warren. *Terminal Visions* . . . , 202.

"The Question of Re-entry"
Pringle, David. *Earth* . . . , 32.

"The Terminal Beach"
Pringle, David. *Earth* . . . , 30.
Ricci, Vittorio. "Il delirio e i sogni: 'The Terminal Beach' di J. G. Ballard," *Quaderni di Filologia Germanica*, 1 (1980), 141–149.

"The Time-Tombs"
Pringle, David. *Earth . . .* , 34.

"The Venus Hunters"
Wagar, W. Warren. *Terminal Visions . . .* , 194–195.

"The Voice of Time"
Pringle, David. *Earth . . .* , 34–35.
Wagar, W. Warren. "The Rebellion of Nature," in Rabkin, Eric S., Martin H. Greenberg, and Joseph D. Olander, Eds. *The End . . .* , 172.

EDWIN BALMER

"The Private Bank Puzzle"
Pierce, Hazel B. *A Literary Symbiosis . . .* , 34–35.

HONORÉ DE BALZAC

"Facino Cane"
Brooks, Peter. *Reading for the Plot . . .* , 219–221.
Cesare, Raffaele de. "Balzac e i temi italiani di 'Facino Cane,'" in *Mélanges à la mémoire . . .* , 313–325.

"La Grande Bretèche"
Lock, Peter. "Text Crypt," *Mod Lang Notes*, 97 (1982), 872–889.
McCarthy, Mary S. *Balzac and His Reader . . .* , 74–92.

TONI CADE BAMBARA

"Broken Field Running"
Bambara, Toni Cade. "Salvation Is the Issue," in Evans, Mari, Ed. *Black Women . . .* , 46.

"Gorilla, My Love"
Hargrove, Nancy D. "Youth in Toni Cade Bambara's *Gorilla, My Love*," in Prenshaw, Peggy W., Ed. *Women Writers . . .* , 218–220.

"The Hammer Man"
Hargrove, Nancy D. "Youth . . . ," 225–227.

"Happy Birthday"
Hargrove, Nancy D. "Youth . . . ," 216–218.

"The Lesson"
Abcarian, Richard, and Marvin Klotz. *Instructor's Manual . . .* , 3rd ed., 1–2.
Hargrove, Nancy D. "Youth . . . ," 220–223.
Sundell, Roger H. "'The Lesson,'" in Dietrich, R. F., and Roger H. Sundell. *Instructor's Manual . . .* , 4th ed., 18–19.

"Maggie of the Green Bottle"
Hargrove, Nancy D. "Youth . . . ," 228–230.

"Medley"
Burks, Ruth E. "From Baptism to Resurrection: Toni Cade Bambara and the
    Incongruity of Language," in Evans, Mari, Ed. *Black Women* . . . , 54–55.

"My Man Bovanne"
Bergman, David, Joseph de Roche, and Daniel M. Epstein. *Instructor's Man-
    ual* . . . , 11.
Burks, Ruth E. "From Baptism . . . ," 49–50.

"Raymond's Run"
Hargrove, Nancy D. "Youth . . . ," 230–232.

"The Sea Birds Are Still Alive"
Traylor, Eleanor W. "Music as Theme: The Jazz Mode in the Works of Toni
    Cade Bambara," in Evans, Mari, Ed. *Black Women* . . . , 66–67.

"The Survivor"
Burks, Ruth E. "From Baptism . . . ," 52.

"Sweet Town"
Hargrove, Nancy D. "Youth . . . ," 223–225.

"A Tender Man"
Burks, Ruth E. "From Baptism . . . ," 53.

JOHN BANIN

"The Roman Merchant"
Schirmer, Gregory A. "Tales from Big House and Cabin: The Nineteenth Cen-
    tury," in Kilroy, James F., Ed. *The Irish Short Story* . . . , 29.

RUSSELL BANKS

"Searching for Survivors (I)"
Robinson, James C. "1968–1980: Experiment and Tradition," in Weaver, Gor-
    don, Ed. *The American Short Story, 1945–1980,* 90–91.
Werner, Craig H. *Paradoxical Resolutions* . . . , 47–48.

"Searching for Survivors (II)"
Robinson, James C. ". . . Experiment and Tradition," 91.

KHANATA BANNUDA

"Fire and Choice"
Accad, Évelyne. *Veil of Shame* . . . , 56–57.

IMAMU AMIRI BARAKA [formerly LE ROI JONES]

"Uncle Tom's Cabin: Alternate Ending"
Sheidley, William E., and Ann Charters. *Instructor's Manual* . . . , 182–183.

EVGENII BARATYNSKY

"Persten"
Grau, R. M. "'Persten': Baratynskii's Fantastic Tale," *Canadian Slavonic Papers*,
26 (1984), 296–306.

JULES-AMEDÉE BARBEY D'AUREVILLY

"A un dîner d'athées"
Bernheimer, Charles. "Female Sexuality and Narrative Closure: Barbey's 'La
Vengeance d'une femme' and 'A un dîner d'athées,'" *Romanic R*, 74 (1983),
335–340.

"Le Dessous de cartes d'une partie de whist"
Tranouez, Pierre. "Ricochets de fascination: Récit et narration dans 'Le Dessous
de cartes d'une partie de whist' de Barbey d'Aurevilly," *Francofonia*, 4, vi
(1984), 53–78.

"Le Rideau cramoisi"
Tranouez, Pierre. "L'Efficacité narrative: Études du 'Rideau cramoisi,'" *Poétique*, 11, iv (1980), 51–59.

"A Woman's Vengeance"
Bernheimer, Charles. "Female Sexuality . . . ," 330–335.

ARTHUR K. BARNES

"Hothouse Planet"
King, Betty. *Women of the Future* . . . , 39–41.

"Siren Satellite"
King, Betty. *Women of the Future* . . . , 65–66.

JOHN BARTH

"Anonymiad"
Harris, Charles B. *Passionate Virtuosity* . . . , 120–121.

"Autobiography: A Self-Recorded Fiction"
Bergman, David, Joseph de Roche, and Daniel M. Epstein. *Instructor's Manual* . . . , 33–34.

"Bellerophoniad"
Harris, Charles B. *Passionate Virtuosity* . . . , 146–155.
Karl, Frederick R. *American Fictions* . . . , 462–463.

"Dunyazadiad"
Harris, Charles B. *Passionate Virtuosity* . . . , 130–137.
Karl, Frederick R. *American Fictions* . . . , 458–460.

"Echo"
Harris, Charles B. *Passionate Virtuosity* . . . , 111–114.
Karl, Frederick R. *American Fictions* . . . , 479–480.

"Life-Story"
Marta, Jan. "John Barth's Portrait of the Artist as a Fiction: Modernism
    Through the Looking-Glass," *Canadian R Comp Lit*, 9 (1982), 218–219.

"Lost in the Funhouse"
Bašić, Sonja. "John Barth's Acrobatic Games: An Analysis of 'Lost in the Fun-
    house,'" in Thorson, James L., Ed. *Yugoslav Perspectives* . . . , 185–205.
Hipkiss, Robert A. *The American Absurd* . . . , 77–78.
Marta, Jan. "John Barth's Portrait . . . ," 219–220.
Miller, James E., and Bernice Slote. *Instructor's Manual* . . . , 2nd ed., 21–22.
Sheidley, William E., and Ann Charters. *Instructor's Manual* . . . , 170–172.
Sirlin, Rhoda, and David H. Richter. *Instructor's Manual* . . . , 4–5.
Waugh, Patricia. *Metafiction* . . . , 95.

"Menelaid"
Harris, Charles B. *Passionate Virtuosity* . . . , 116–117.
Karl, Frederick R. *American Fictions* . . . , 480.

"Night-Sea Journey"
Deer, Irving. "'Night-Sea Journey,'" in Dietrich, R. F., and Roger H. Sundell.
    Instructor's Manual . . . , 3rd ed., 78–81; 4th ed., 134–136.

"Perseid"
Harris, Charles B. *Passionate Virtuosity* . . . , 136–146.
Karl, Frederick R. *American Fictions* . . . , 460–462.

DONALD BARTHELME

"At the End of the Mechanical Age"
Bergman, David, Joseph de Roche, and Daniel M. Epstein. *Instructor's Man-
    ual* . . . , 34.
Molesworth, Charles. *Donald Barthelme's Fiction*, 24–29.

"At the Tolstoy Museum"
Achilles, Jochen. "Donald Barthelme's Aesthetic of Inversion: Calgari's Come-
    Back as Calgari's Leave-Taking," *J Narrative Technique*, 12 (1982), 109–110.
Hicks, Jack. *In the Singer's Temple* . . . , 66–69.

"The Balloon"
Miller, James E., and Bernice Slote. *Instructor's Manual* . . . , 2nd ed., 22–23.

"City Life"
Hicks, Jack. *In the Singer's Temple* . . . , 71–72.

"Daumier"
Wilde, Alan. *Horizons of Assent* . . . , 181–182.

"The Death of Edward Lear"
Wilde, Alan. *Horizons of Assent* . . . , 149–150.

"The Dolt"
Hicks, Jack. *In the Singer's Temple* . . . , 52–54.

"Engineer-Private Paul Klee Misplaces an Aircraft Between Milbertshofen and
    Cambrai, March 1916"
Achilles, Jochen. "Donald Barthelme's Aesthetic . . . ," 112.
Molesworth, Charles. *Donald Barthelme's Fiction,* 17–18.
Wilde, Alan. *Horizons of Assent* . . . , 184–186.

"A Film"
Karl, Frederick R. *American Fictions* . . . , 394–395.

"Games Are the Enemies of Beauty, Truth, and Sleep, Amanda Said"
Wilde, Alan. *Horizons of Assent* . . . , 174–175.

"Hiding Man"
Achilles, Jochen. "Donald Barthelme's Aesthetic . . . ," 107–108.

"The Indian Uprising"
Hicks, Jack. *In the Singer's Temple* . . . , 56–57.

"Kierkegaard Unfair to Schlegel"
Achilles, Jochen. "Donald Barthelme's Aesthetic . . . ," 114.
Hicks, Jack. *In the Singer's Temple* . . . , 59–60.

"Me and Miss Mandible"
Achilles, Jochen. "Donald Barthelme's Aesthetic . . . ," 108.
Karl, Frederick R. *American Fictions* . . . , 391–392.
Klinkowitz, Jerome. *The Self-Apparent Word* . . . , 14–15.

"Paraguay"
Hicks, Jack. *In the Singer's Temple* . . . , 63.

"The Phantom of the Opera's Friend"
Achilles, Jochen. "Donald Barthelme's Aesthetic . . . ," 114–115.

"A Picture History of the War"
Achilles, Jochen. "Donald Barthelme's Aesthetic . . . ," 108–109.

"Porcupines at the University"
Klinkowitz, Jerome. *The Self-Apparent Word* . . . , 30–31.

"Report"
Scott, Virgil, and David Madden. *Instructor's Manual* . . . , 4th ed., 41–43; Madden, David. *Instructor's Manual* . . . , 5th ed., 42–44; Madden, David, and Virgil Scott. *Instructor's Manual* . . . , 6th ed., 54–57.

"Robert Kennedy Saved from Drowning"
Hicks, Jack. *In the Singer's Temple* . . . , 36–37.
Molesworth, Charles. *Donald Barthelme's Fiction*, 64–70.

"The Sandman"
Abcarian, Richard, and Marvin Klotz. *Instructor's Manual* . . . , 2nd ed., 3; 3rd ed., 2.

"The School"
Warde, William B. "Barthelme's 'The School': Pedagogical Monologue and Social Commentary," *New Orleans R,* 8 (1981), 149–153.

"See the Moon?"
Hicks, Jack. *In the Singer's Temple* . . . , 58.

"A Shower of Gold"
Achilles, Jochen. "Donald Barthelme's Aesthetic . . . ," 111–112.
Hicks, Jack. *In the Singer's Temple* . . . , 35–36.
Sirlin, Rhoda, and David H. Richter. *Instructor's Manual* . . . , 6–7.

"Some of Us Had Been Threatening Our Friend Colby"
Perrine, Laurence, and Thomas R. Arp. *Instructor's Manual* . . . , 6th ed., 62–64.

"The Temptation of St. Anthony"
Wilde, Alan. *Horizons of Assent* . . . , 182–184.

"The Viennese Opera Ball"
Hicks, Jack. *In the Singer's Temple* . . . , 41–43.

"Views of My Father Weeping"
Achilles, Jochen. "Donald Barthelme's Aesthetic . . . ," 109.

H. E. BATES

"Alexander"
Vannatta, Dennis. *H. E. Bates,* 24–27.

"The Bridge"
Vannatta, Dennis. *H. E. Bates,* 55.

"Charlotte Esmond"
Vannatta, Dennis. *H. E. Bates,* 33–34.

"Colonel Julian"
Vannatta, Dennis. *H. E. Bates,* 77–78.

"The Cowslip"
Vannatta, Dennis. *H. E. Bates,* 84–85.

"The Easter Blessing"
Vannatta, Dennis. *H. E. Bates,* 18–19.

"Elaine"
Vannatta, Dennis. *H. E. Bates,* 81–82.

"The Frontier"
Vannatta, Dennis. *H. E. Bates,* 79–80.

"Harvest"
Vannatta, Dennis. *H. E. Bates,* 15–18.

"The Holiday"
Vannatta, Dennis. *H. E. Bates,* 21–22.

"The Kimono"
Vannatta, Dennis. *H. E. Bates,* 41–42.

"Love in a Wych Elm"
Baldwin, Dean R. "Atmosphere in the Stories of H. E. Bates," *Stud Short Fiction,*
    21 (1984), 219.

"The Mill"
Baldwin, Dean R. "Atmosphere . . . ," 219–220.
Vannatta, Dennis. *H. E. Bates,* 38–39.

"The Mower"
Baldwin, Dean R. "Atmosphere . . . ," 216–217.

"Now Sleeps the Crimson Petal"
Vannatta, Dennis. *H. E. Bates,* 87–88.

"The Old Eternal"
Vannatta, Dennis. *H. E. Bates,* 89–90.

"The Ox"
Baldwin, Dean R. "Atmosphere . . . ," 220–221.

"Something Short and Sweet"
Vannatta, Dennis. *H. E. Bates,* 40–41.

"The Station"
Baldwin, Dean R. "Atmosphere . . . ," 217–218.
Vannatta, Dennis. *H. E. Bates,* 37–38.

"The Watercress Girl"
Baldwin, Dean R. "Atmosphere . . . ," 218–219.

"The Wedding Party"
Vannatta, Dennis. *H. E. Bates,* 90–91.

"Where the Cloud Breaks"
Vannatta, Dennis. *H. E. Bates,* 86–87.

ANN BEATTIE

"A Clever-Kid Story"
Gelfant, Blanche H. *Women Writing . . . ,* 38–39.

"Dwarf House"
Gelfant, Blanche H. *Women Writing . . . ,* 36.

"Waiting"
Sheidley, William E., and Ann Charters. *Instructor's Manual . . . ,* 191.

CHARLES BEAUMONT

"Blood Brother"
Pierce, Hazel B. *A Literary Symbiosis . . . ,* 225–226.

SAMUEL BECKETT

"Afar a Bird"
Lawley, Paul. "Samuel Beckett's 'Art and Craft': A Reading of 'Enough,'" *Mod Fiction Stud,* 29 (1983), 33–35.

"Assumption"
Dearlove, J. E. *Accommodating the Chaos . . . ,* 18–19.

"The Calmative"
Butler, Lance S. *Samuel Beckett . . . ,* 90–92.

"A Case in a Thousand"
Dearlove, J. E. *Accommodating the Chaos . . . ,* 19–20.
Rabinovitz, Rubin. *The Development . . . ,* 64–66.

"Echo's Bones"
Rabinovitz, Rubin. *The Development . . . ,* 55–61.

"The End"
Hogan, Robert. "Old Boys, Young Bucks, and New Women: The Contemporary Irish Short Story," in Kilroy, James F., Ed. *The Irish Short Story . . . ,* 173.
Stewart, Garrett. *Death Sentence . . . ,* 329–330.

"Enough"
Brater, Enoch. "Why Beckett's 'Enough' Is More or Less Enough," *Comp Lit*,
    21 (1980), 252–266.
Company, Juan M. "Sobre el amor en Beckett," *Quimera*, 36 (March, 1984), 41–
    42.
Lawley, Paul. "Samuel Beckett's 'Art and Craft' . . . ," 25–41.
Murphy, Peter. "The Nature and Art of Love in 'Enough,'" *J Beckett Stud*, 4
    (Spring, 1979), 14–34.

"First Love"
Penner, Dick, Ed. *Fiction of the Absurd* . . . , 171–174.

"How It Is"
Butler, Lance S. *Samuel Beckett* . . . , 163–165.
Dearlove, J. E. *Accommodating the Chaos* . . . , 85–106.

"Imagination Dead Imagine"
Dearlove, J. E. *Accommodating the Chaos* . . . , 109–112.

"Lessness"
Butler, Lance S. *Samuel Beckett* . . . , 180–183.

"The Lost Ones"
Butler, Lance S. *Samuel Beckett* . . . , 171–173.
Dearlove, J. E. *Accommodating the Chaos* . . . , 132–138.

"Ping"
Dearlove, J. E. *Accommodating the Chaos* . . . , 112–118.

"Still"
Murphy, Peter. "Orpheus Returning: The Nature of Myth in Samuel Beckett's
    'Still' Trilogy," *Int'l Fiction R*, 11 (1984), 109–112.

WILLIAM BECKFORD

"The Vision" [originally titled "Long Story"]
Miyoshi, Masao. *The Divided Self* . . . , 16–18.

GUSTAVO ADOLFO BÉCQUER

"Los ojos verdes"
Boyer, H. Patsy. "A Feminist Reading of 'Los ojos verdes,'" in Mora, Gabriela,
    and Karen S. Van Hooft, Eds. *Theory and Practice* . . . , 188–200.

SAMAD BEHRANGI

"The Bald Pigeon Keeper"
Ricks, Thomas M. "Samad Behrangi and Contemporary Iran: The Artist in
    Revolutionary Struggle," in Ricks, Thomas M., Ed. *Critical Perspectives* . . . ,
    365–366.

"The Little Black Fish"
Ricks, Thomas M. "Samad Behrangi . . . ," 367.

"One Peach—A Thousand Peaches"
Ricks, Thomas M. "Samad Behrangi . . . ," 367–368.

"Twenty-Four Restless Hours"
Ricks, Thomas M. "Samad Behrangi . . . ," 368–369.

MARY BELL

"Sing Kee's Chinese Lily"
Wu, William F. *The Yellow Peril* . . . , 63–64.

SAUL BELLOW

"A Father-to-Be"
Braham, Jeanne. *A Sort of Columbus* . . . , 89–91.
Dietrich, R. F. "The Biological Draft-Dodger in Bellow's 'A Father-to-Be,'" *Stud Hum*, 9, i (1981), 45–51; rpt. Dietrich, R. F., and Roger H. Sundell. *Instructor's Manual* . . . , 4th ed., 102–109.
Fuchs, Daniel. *Saul Bellow* . . . , 289–292.
Madden, David. *Instructor's Manual* . . . , 5th ed., 95–96; Madden, David, and Virgil Scott. *Instructor's Manual* . . . , 6th ed., 117–119.
Weinstein, Ann. "A Toast to Life, *L'Chayim*: Saul Bellow's 'A Father-to-Be,'" *Saul Bellow J*, 2, i (1982), 32–35.

"Leaving the Yellow House"
Fuchs, Daniel. *Saul Bellow* . . . , 295–297.

"Looking for Mr. Green"
Fuchs, Daniel. *Saul Bellow* . . . , 287–289.
Sirlin, Rhoda, and David H. Richter. *Instructor's Manual* . . . , 7–8.

"The Mexican General"
Fuchs, Daniel. *Saul Bellow* . . . , 282–283.
Walsh, Thomas F. "Heroism in Bellow's 'The Mexican General,'" *Saul Bellow J*, 1, ii (1982), 31–33.

"Mosby's Memoirs"
Fuchs, Daniel. *Saul Bellow* . . . , 280–281.
Miller, James E., and Bernice Slote. *Instructor's Manual* . . . , 2nd ed., 20–21.

"The Old System"
Fuchs, Daniel. *Saul Bellow* . . . , 297–299.

"Seize the Day"
Bradbury, Malcolm. *Saul Bellow*, 53–56.
Cronin, Gloria L. "Saul Bellow's Quarrel with Modernism in 'Seize the Day,'" *Encyclia*, 57 (1980), 95–102.

Fuchs, Daniel. *Saul Bellow* . . . , 78–97.
Greenspan, Ezra. *The "Schlemiel"* . . . , 164–168.
Karl, Frederick R. *American Fictions* . . . , 329–331.
Lister, Paul A. " 'The Compleat Fool' in 'Seize the Day,' " *Saul Bellow J*, 3, ii (1984), 32–39.
Rodrigues, Eusebio L. *Quest for the Human* . . . , 81–107.

"A Sermon by Dr. Pep"
Fuchs, Daniel. *Saul Bellow* . . . , 280–285.

"The Trip to Galena"
Fuchs, Daniel. *Saul Bellow* . . . , 285–287.

"Two Morning Monologues"
Braham, Jeanne. *A Sort of Columbus* . . . , 13–14.
Fuchs, Daniel. *Saul Bellow* . . . , 280–282.

HANS BENDER

"Die Wölfe kommen zurück"
Koscielecki, Marek M. "Discussion of the Allegorical Significance of Hans Bender's Short Story 'Die Wölfe kommen zurück,' " *Lang Q*, 20, iii–iv (1982), 51–52.

JUAN BENET

"Afterwards"
Cabrera, Vicente. *Juan Benet*, 37–40.
Manteiga, Roberto C. "Time, Space, and Narration in Juan Benet's Short Stories," in Manteiga, Roberto C., David K. Herzberger, and Malcolm A. Compitello, Eds. *Critical Approaches* . . . , 124–127.

"Baalbec, A Stain"
Cabrera, Vicente. *Juan Benet*, 34–36.

"Catalysis"
Cabrera, Vicente. *Juan Benet*, 57–58.
Manteiga, Roberto C. "Time, Space . . . ," 132–133.

"Duel"
Manteiga, Roberto C. "Time, Space . . . ," 127–128.

"Evil of Parity"
Cabrera, Vicente. *Juan Benet*, 78–81.

"Final Nights of a Damp Winter"
Cabrera, Vicente. *Juan Benet*, 74–76.

"From Far Away"
Cabrera, Vicente. *Juan Benet*, 71–73.
Manteiga, Roberto C. "Time, Space . . . ," 129–131.

"Garet"
Cabrera, Vicente. *Juan Benet,* 62–64.

"An Incomplete Line"
Cabrera, Vicente. *Juan Benet,* 73–74.
Manteiga, Roberto C. "Time, Space . . . ," 128–129.

"It Was Ruined"
Cabrera, Vicente. *Juan Benet,* 64–67.

"Mourning"
Cabrera, Vicente. *Juan Benet,* 36–37.

"Numa: A Legend"
Cabrera, Vicente. *Juan Benet,* 47–50.

"Obiter Dictum"
Cabrera, Vicente. *Juan Benet,* 76–78.

"Reichenau"
Cabrera, Vicente. *Juan Benet,* 54–55.
Manteiga, Roberto C. "Time, Space . . . ," 124.

"Seemingly Empty Hours"
Cabrera, Vicente. *Juan Benet,* 69–71.

"Sub rosa"
Cabrera, Vicente. *Juan Benet,* 45–47.

"Syllabus"
Cabrera, Vicente. *Juan Benet,* 55–57.

"TLB"
Cabrera, Vicente. *Juan Benet,* 52–54.

"A Tomb"
Cabrera, Vicente. *Juan Benet,* 40–45.
Gullón, Ricardo. "Sobre espectros y tumbas," *Cuaderno de Norte,* [n.v.] (1976),
    83–95.

"Viator"
Cabrera, Vicente. *Juan Benet,* 58–60.

"The Way It Used to Be"
Cabrera, Vicente. *Juan Benet,* 67–69.

"You Will Never Get Anywhere"
Cabrera, Vicente. *Juan Benet,* 32–34.
Manteiga, Roberto C. "Time, Space . . . ," 133–135.

STEPHEN VINCENT BENÉT

"By the Waters of Babylon" [originally titled "The Place of the Gods"]
Wagar, W. Warren. *Terminal Visions . . .* , 163–164.

ARNOLD BENNETT

"The Artist's Model"
Bellamy, William. *The Novels . . .* , 85–86.

"The Death of Simon Fuge"
Batchelor, John. *The Edwardian Novelists*, 167–170.
Wain, John. "Remarks on the Short Story," *Les Cahiers de la Nouvelle*, 2 (January,
     1984), 49–66.

STELLA BENSON

"The Desert Island"
Bedell, R. Meredith. *Stella Benson*, 115–116.

"A Dream"
Bedell, R. Meredith. *Stella Benson*, 113.

"Hope Against Hope"
Bedell, R. Meredith. *Stella Benson*, 114.

"Story Coldly Told"
Bedell, R. Meredith. *Stella Benson*, 116–117.

"Submarine"
Bedell, R. Meredith. *Stella Benson*, 115.

OLES BERDNYK

"The Journey into the Antiworld"
Smyrniw, Walter. "Satiric Trends in Recent Soviet Science Fiction," in Bristol,
     Evelyn, Ed. *Russian Literature . . .* , 200–201.

THOMAS BERNHARD

"Die Verrückte Magdalena"
Dittmar, Jens. " 'Die Verrückte Magdalena'—An Early Short Story by Thomas
     Bernhard," *Germ Life & Letters*, 35 (1982), 266–271.

ALFRED BESTER

"Adam and No Eve"
Wendell, Carolyn. *Alfred Bester,* 51.

"The Biped, Reegan"
Wendell, Carolyn. *Alfred Bester,* 51.

"The Broken Axiom"
Wendell, Carolyn. *Alfred Bester,* 8–9.

"Disappearing Art"
Wendell, Carolyn. *Alfred Bester,* 47–48.

"Fondly Fahrenheit"
Riggenbach, Jeff. "Science Fiction as Will and Ideal: The World of Alfred
    Bester," *Riverside Q,* 5 (August, 1972), 170.
Wendell, Carolyn. *Alfred Bester,* 53–55.

"The Four-Hour Fugue"
Wendell, Carolyn. *Alfred Bester,* 52–53.

"Hell Is Forever"
Knapp, L. J. "Alfred Bester, *The Light Fantastic,*" *Sci Fiction R Monthly,* [n.v.]
    (July–August, 1976), 8–9.
Wendell, Carolyn. *Alfred Bester,* 44–45.

"Hobson's Choice"
Wendell, Carolyn. *Alfred Bester,* 46–47.

"Life for Sale"
Wendell, Carolyn. *Alfred Bester,* 42.

"The Men Who Murdered Mohammed"
Wendell, Carolyn. *Alfred Bester,* 45–46.

"Oddy and Id"
Wendell, Carolyn. *Alfred Bester,* 48–49.

"Of Time and Third Avenue"
Meyers, Walter E. *Aliens and Linguists . . . ,* 28–29.

"Out of This World"
Wendell, Carolyn. *Alfred Bester,* 51.

"The Pi-Man"
Wendell, Carolyn. *Alfred Bester,* 52–53.

"The Roller Coaster"
Wendell, Carolyn. *Alfred Bester,* 47.

"Something Up There Likes Me"
Wendell, Carolyn. *Alfred Bester,* 52.

"The Starcomber"
Riggenbach, Jeff. "Science Fiction as Will . . . ," 172, 174–176.

"They Don't Make Life Like They Used To"
Wendell, Carolyn. *Alfred Bester,* 51–52.

"Time Is the Traitor"
Wendell, Carolyn. *Alfred Bester,* 48.

"The Unseen Blushes"
Wendell, Carolyn. *Alfred Bester,* 43.

"Voyage to Nowhere"
Wendell, Carolyn. *Alfred Bester,* 42–43.

NIKOLAY BESTUZHEV

"Hugo von Bracht"
Mersereau, John. *Russian Romantic Fiction,* 63–64.

ALEXANDER BESTUZHEV-MARLINSKY

"Roman and Olga"
Mersereau, John. *Russian Romantic Fiction,* 53–56.

DORIS BETTS

"The Astronaut"
Holman, David M. "Faith and the Unanswerable Questions: The Fiction of
    Doris Betts," *Southern Lit J,* 15, i (1982), 16–18.

"The Mandarin"
Holman, David M. "Faith and the Unanswerable . . . ," 18–19.

"The Ugliest Pilgrim"
Holman, David M. "Faith and the Unanswerable . . . ," 19–20.

"The Very Old Are Beautiful"
Holman, David M. "Faith and the Unanswerable . . . ," 20.

DHARM VIR BHARATI

"The Son of Hirnakush"
Pande, Trilochan. "Folk Elements in the Modern Hindi Short Story," *Folklore*
    (Calcutta), 231 (1979), 148.

AMBROSE BIERCE

"An Affair of Outposts"
*Solomon, Eric. "The Bitterness of Battle: Ambrose Bierce's War Fiction," in
Davidson, Cathy N., Ed. *Critical Essays* . . . , 185–186.

"A Baby Tramp"
Davidson, Cathy N. *The Experimental Fiction* . . . , 118–119.

"A Bottomless Grave"
Davidson, Cathy N. *The Experimental Fiction* . . . , 19–20.

"Charles Ashmore's Trail"
Davidson, Cathy N. *The Experimental Fiction* . . . , 85–86.

"Chickamauga"
Davidson, Cathy N. *The Experimental Fiction* . . . , 36–44.
*Solomon, Eric. "The Bitterness . . . ," 193–194.

"The Coup de Grâce"
Davidson, Cathy N. *The Experimental Fiction* . . . , 94–98.

"The Damned Thing"
Stark, Cruce. "The Color of 'The Damned Thing': The Occult as the Supra-
sensational," in Kerr, Howard, John W. Crowley, and Charles L. Crow, Eds.
The Haunted Dusk . . . , 212–213.

"The Death of Halpin Frayser"
Davidson, Cathy N. *The Experimental Fiction* . . . , 103–114.
Stein, William B. "Bierce's 'The Death of Halpin Frayser': The Poetics of Gothic
Consciousness," *Emerson Soc Q,* 18, ii (1972), 115–122; rpt. Davidson,
Cathy N., Ed. *Critical Essays* . . . , 217–227.

"The Eyes of the Panther"
Davidson, Cathy N. *The Experimental Fiction* . . . , 75–81.

"The Famous Gilson Bequest"
Davidson, Cathy N. *The Experimental Fiction* . . . , 119–121.

"Haïta the Shepherd"
Davidson, Cathy N. *The Experimental Fiction* . . . , 117–118.

"A Jug of Sirup" [sic]
Davidson, Cathy N. *The Experimental Fiction* . . . , 86–88.

"Jupiter Doke, Brigadier General"
Davidson, Cathy N. *The Experimental Fiction* . . . , 72–75.

"The Man and the Snake"
Davidson, Cathy N. *The Experimental Fiction* . . . , 33–36.
*Grenander, M. E. "Bierce's Turn of the Screw: Tales of Ironical Terror," in
Davidson, Cathy N., Ed. *Critical Essays* . . . , 214–216.

"Mr. Masthead, Journalist"
Davidson, Cathy N. *The Experimental Fiction* . . . , 61–62.

"The Mocking-Bird"
Davidson, Cathy N. *The Experimental Fiction* . . . , 25–26.

"The Moonlit Road"
Davidson, Cathy N. *The Experimental Fiction* . . . , 88–94.

"Moxon's Master"
Davidson, Cathy N. *The Experimental Fiction* . . . , 62–66.

"My Favorite Murder"
Davidson, Cathy N. *The Experimental Fiction* . . . , 58–60.

"The Night-Doings at 'Dead-Man's' "
Wu, William F. *The Yellow Peril* . . . , 22–23.

"An Occurrence at Owl Creek Bridge"
*Abcarian, Richard, and Marvin Klotz. *Instructor's Manual* . . . , 2nd ed., 3–5;
   3rd ed., 2–3.
Cheatham, George and Judy. "Bierce's 'An Occurrence at Owl Creek Bridge,' "
   Explicator, 43, i (1984), 45–47.
Davidson, Cathy N. *The Experimental Fiction* . . . , 45–54.
Logan, F. J. "The Wry Seriousness of 'Owl Creek Bridge,' " *Am Lit Realism*, 10
   (1977), 101–113; rpt. Davidson, Cathy N., Ed. *Critical Essays* . . . , 195–208.
Powers, James G. "Freud and Farquhar: An Occurrence at Owl Creek Bridge,"
   Stud Short Fiction, 19 (1982), 278–281.
Sheidley, William E., and Ann Charters. *Instructor's Manual* . . . , 20–21.

"One of the Missing"
*Grenander, M. E. "Bierce's Turn of the Screw . . . ," 214–216.
Madden, David, and Virgil Scott. *Instructor's Manual* . . . , 6th ed., 30–32.

"One Officer, One Man"
Davidson, Cathy N. *The Experimental Fiction* . . . , 29–30.
*Grenander, M. E. "Bierce's Turn of the Screw . . . ," 214–216.

"Parker Adderson, Philosopher"
Davidson, Cathy N. *The Experimental Fiction* . . . , 66–69.

"A Son of the Gods"
*Solomon, Eric. "The Bitterness . . . ," 191–192.

"The Story of a Conscience"
Davidson, Cathy N. *The Experimental Fiction* . . . , 69–72.

"A Tough Tussle"
Davidson, Cathy N. *The Experimental Fiction* . . . , 26–27.

EANDO BINDER [pseudonym of BINDER BROTHERS]

"Rope Trick"
Franklin, H. Bruce. "America as Science Fiction: 1939," in Slusser, George E.,
     Eric S. Rabkin, and Robert Scholes, Eds. *Coordinates . . .* , 114–115.

ADOLFO BIOY CASARES

"El otro laberinto"
Meehan, Thomas C. "Temporal Simultaneity and the Theme of Time Travel
     in a Fantastic Story by Adolfo Bioy Casares," *Kentucky Romance Q,* 30 (1983),
     167–183.

MICHAEL BISHOP

"Death and Designation Among the Asadi"
Meyers, Walter E. *Aliens and Linguists . . .* , 78–79.

CLARK BLAISE

"Among the Dead"
Lecker, Robert. "Murals Deep in Nature: The Short Stories of Clark Blaise,"
     Essays Canadian Writing, 23 (1982), 65–66; rpt. in his *On the Line . . .* , 56–
     57.

"The Bridge"
Lecker, Robert. "Murals . . . ," 39–40; rpt. in his *On the Line . . .* , 30–31.

"Broward Dowdy"
Lecker, Robert. "Murals . . . ," 49–51; rpt. in his *On the Line . . .* , 40–42.

"A Class of New Canadians"
Lecker, Robert. "Murals . . . ," 28–30; rpt. in his *On the Line . . .* , 19–20.

"Extractions and Constructions"
Lecker, Robert. "Murals . . . ," 34; rpt. in his *On the Line . . .* , 25.

"Eyes"
Lecker, Robert. "Murals . . . ," 30–32; rpt. in his *On the Line . . .* , 21–24.

"The Fabulous Eddie Brewster"
Lecker, Robert. "Murals . . . ," 52–53; rpt. in his *On the Line . . .* , 43–44.

"Going to India"
Lecker, Robert. "Murals . . . ," 36–37; rpt. in his *On the Line . . .* , 27–29.

"Grids and Doglegs"
Lecker, Robert. "Murals . . . ," 53–57; rpt. in his *On the Line . . .* , 44–48.

"He Raises Me Up"
Davey, Frank. "Impressionable Realism: The Stories of Clark Blaise," *Open Letter,* 3 (Summer, 1976), 69–70.
Lecker, Robert. "Murals . . . ," 64–65; rpt. in his *On the Line . . . ,* 55–56.

"How I Became a Jew"
Lecker, Robert. "Murals . . . ," 62; rpt. in his *On the Line . . . ,* 53.

"I'm Dreaming of Rocket Richard"
Lecker, Robert. "Murals . . . ," 57–58; rpt. in his *On the Line . . . ,* 48–49.

"The March"
Lecker, Robert. "Murals . . . ," 63; rpt. in his *On the Line . . . ,* 54.

"A North American Education"
Lecker, Robert. "Murals . . . ," 42–44; rpt. in his *On the Line . . . , ,* 33–35.

"Notes Beyond a History"
Lecker, Robert. "Murals . . . ," 60–62; rpt. in his *On the Line . . . ,* 51–53.

"Relief "
Lecker, Robert. "Murals . . . ," 51–52; rpt. in his *On the Line . . . ,* 42–43.

"The Salesman's Son Grows Older"
Lecker, Robert. "Murals . . . ," 40–41; rpt. in his *On the Line . . . ,* 33.

"The Seizure"
Lecker, Robert. "Murals . . . ," 59; rpt. in his *On the Line . . . ,* 50–51.

"Snow People"
Lecker, Robert. "Murals . . . ," 44–48; rpt. in his *On the Line . . . ,* 35–39.

"The Street"
Lecker, Robert. "Murals . . . ," 34–35; rpt. in his *On the Line . . . ,* 25–26.

"Words for a Winter"
Lecker, Robert. "Murals . . . ," 32–33; rpt. in his *On the Line . . . ,* 21–23.

MEIR BLINKIN

"Card Game"
Wisse, Ruth R. "Introduction," in Blinkin, Meir. *Stories by Meir Blinkin,* xiii–xiv.

"Family Life: A Chapter"
Wisse, Ruth R. "Introduction," xiii.

JAMES BLISH

"Beanstalk"
Stableford, Brian M. *The Clash . . . ,* 20–21.

"Beep"
Stableford, Brian M. *The Clash* . . . , 30–31.

"Common Time"
Stableford, Brian M. *The Clash* . . . , 37–39.

"A Dusk of Idols"
Stableford, Brian M. *The Clash* . . . , 34–35.

"A Hero's Life" [revised as "A Style in Treason"]
Stableford, Brian M. *The Clash* . . . , 44–46.

"Let the Finder Beware"
Stableford, Brian M. *The Clash* . . . , 10–12.

"Testament of Andros"
Stableford, Brian M. *The Clash* . . . , 39–40.

"There Shall Be No Darkness"
Stableford, Brian M. *The Clash* . . . , 7–10.

"Tomb Tapper"
Stableford, Brian M. *The Clash* . . . , 33.

"We All Die Naked"
Stableford, Brian M. *The Clash* . . . , 36–37.

"A Work of Art" [originally titled "Art-Work"]
Stableford, Brian M. *The Clash* . . . , 31–32.

JAMES BLISH and VIRGINIA KIDD

"On the Wall of the Lodge"
Stableford, Brian M. *The Clash* . . . , 43–44.

ESTHER B. BOCK

"Ah Choo"
Wu, William F. *The Yellow Peril* . . . , 62–63.

LOUISE BOGAN

"Dove and Serpent"
Ridgeway, Jaqueline. *Louise Bogan*, 38–40.

"Journey Around My Room"
Ridgeway, Jaqueline. *Louise Bogan*, 37–38.

"Keramic"
Ridgeway, Jaqueline. *Louise Bogan,* 70–71.

"Letdown"
Ridgeway, Jaqueline. *Louise Bogan,* 73–74.

"The Long Walk"
Ridgeway, Jaqueline. *Louise Bogan,* 77–78.

"Sabbatical Summer"
Ridgeway, Jaqueline. *Louise Bogan,* 71–72.

"Summer Day"
Ridgeway, Jaqueline. *Louise Bogan,* 72.

"Whatever It Is"
Ridgeway, Jaqueline. *Louise Bogan,* 72–73.

"With Mirrors"
Ridgeway, Jaqueline. *Louise Bogan,* 74–75.

"Zest"
Ridgeway, Jaqueline. *Louise Bogan,* 76–77.

HEINRICH BÖLL

"Action Will Be Taken"
Conard, Robert C. *Heinrich Böll,* 62–64.

"The Adventure"
Conard, Robert C. *Heinrich Böll,* 69–72.

"At the Bridge"
Schwarz, Wilhelm J. *Heinrich Böll . . . ,* 42, 88.

"The Balek Scales"
Conard, Robert C. *Heinrich Böll,* 60–64.

"The Black Sheep"
Schwarz, Wilhelm J. *Heinrich Böll . . . ,* 57–58.

"Business Is Business"
Schwarz, Wilhelm J. *Heinrich Böll . . . ,* 44–45.

"Candles for the Madonna"
Schwarz, Wilhelm J. *Heinrich Böll . . . ,* 46–47.

"The Death of Elsa Baskoleit"
Conard, Robert C. *Heinrich Böll,* 58–60.
Schwarz, Wilhelm J. *Heinrich Böll . . . ,* 89–90.

"Unexpected Guest"
Conard, Robert C. *Heinrich Böll*, 64–68.

"We Broommakers"
Conard, Robert C. *Heinrich Böll*, 41–43.

MARÍA LUISA BOMBAL

"The New Islands"
Agosín, Marjorie. "'Las islas nuevas' o la violación de lo maravilloso," *Hispania*, 67 (1984), 577–584.

"The Tree"
Agosín, Marjorie. "La mimesis de la interiordad: 'Soledad de la sangre' de Marta Brunet y 'El árbol' de María Luisa Bombal," *Neophilologus*, 68 (1984), 380–388.
Brushwood, John S. "The Spanish American Short Story from Quiroga to Borges," in Peden, Margaret S., Ed. *The Latin American Short Story . . .* , 90–91.

NELSON BOND

"The Cunning of the Beast"
Fredericks, Casey. *The Future of Eternity . . .* , 8–10.

JORGE LUIS BORGES

"Abenjacán the Bojarí, Dead in His Labyrinth"
Wilson, Robert R. "Godgames and Labyrinths: The Logic of Entrapment," *Mosaic*, 15, iv (1982), 1–22.

"The Aleph"
Concha, Jaime. "'El Aleph': Borges y la historia," *Revista Iberoamericana*, 49 (1983), 471–485.
Earle, Peter G. "Dreams of Creation: Short Fiction in Spanish America," *Denver Q*, 12 (1977), 75.
Hayles, N. Katherine. *The Cosmic Web . . .* , 156–161.
King, Lloyd. "Antagonism, Irony, and Death in Two Stories by Borges," *Coll Lang Assoc J*, 23 (1980), 403–406.
McMurray, George R. "The Spanish American Short Story from Borges to the Present," in Peden, Margaret S., Ed. *The Latin American Short Story . . .* , 100–101.
Ortega, Julio. *Poetics of Change . . .* , 11–19.

"The Approach to Almotásim" [here Al-Mu'tasim]
Hayles, N. Katherine. *The Cosmic Web . . .* , 148–151.

"Averroes' Search"
Baumgarten, Murray. *City Scriptures . . .* , 95–97.

"The Babylonian Lottery"
Doxey, William S. "Culture as an Aspect of Style in Fantasy," *West Georgia Coll R*, 13 (May, 1981), 4–5.
Fragoso, Milton. "Jorge Luis Borges' *a-homo ludens*: 'The Lottery in Babylon,'" in Finke, Wayne H., and Enrique Ledesma, Eds. *Homenaje a Humberto Piñera* . . . , 69–75.

"The Circular Ruins"
Apter, T. E. *Fantasy Literature* . . . , 127–128.
Marini, Sergio. "Don Quisciotte contro i mulini a vento: Sogno e realtà in un racconto di Borges," *Humanitas*, 38, i (1983), 110–115.

"Death and the Compass"
Baumgarten, Murray. *City Scriptures* . . . , 109–111.
Fama, Antonio. "Análisis de 'La muerto y la brújula' de Jorge Luis Borges," *Bull Hispanique*, 85 (1983), 161–173.
King, Lloyd. "Antagonism . . . ," 400–403.
Knopka, Nancy C. "Jorge Luis Borges on the Nature of Man," in Finke, Wayne H., and Enrique Ledesma, Eds. *Homenaje a Humberto Piñera* . . . , 129.
McMurray, George R. ". . . Borges to the Present," 98–100.

"Deutsches Requiem"
Zuloaga, Nicomedes. "Borges: Origen y destino," *Zona Franca*, 6 (March–April, 1983), 34–37.

"The Dread Redeemer Lazarus Morell"
Martínez, María E. "Borges' Deconstruction of History in 'The Dread Redeemer Lazarus Morell,'" *Chircú*, 3, iii (1984), 9–18.

"Emma Zunz"
Aizenberg, Edna. "Emma Zunz: A Kabbalistic Heroine in Borges's Fiction," *Stud Am Jewish Lit*, 3 (1983), 223–235.
Alvarez, Nicolás E. "La realidad trascendida: Dualismo y rectangularidad en 'Emma Zunz,'" *Explicación de Textos Literarios*, 12, i (1983–1984), 27–36.
———. "La simplicidad de los hechos: Realidad e ironía en 'Emma Zunz,'" in Paolini, Gilbert, Ed. *LA CHISPA '83* . . . , 27–33.
Apter, T. E. *Fantasy Literature* . . . , 120–122.
Hall, J. B. "Deception or Self-Deception? The Essential Ambiguity of Borges' 'Emma Zunz,'" *Forum Mod Lang Stud*, 18 (1982), 258–265.

"The End of the Duel"
Sheidley, William E., and Ann Charters. *Instructor's Manual* . . . , 115–116.

"Examination of the Works of Herbert Quain"
Capobianco, Michael. "Mathematics in the *Ficciones* of Jorge Luis Borges," *Int'l Fiction R*, 9, i (1982), 51–54.

"Funes the Memorious"
Bruffee, Kenneth A. *Elegiac Romance* . . . , 202–206.

"The Garden of Forking Paths"
Apter, T. E. *Fantasy Literature* . . . , 114–115.
Baumgarten, Murray. *City Scriptures* . . . , 99–100.
Benevento, Joseph J. "An Introduction to the Realities of Fiction: Teaching
    Magic Realism in Three Stories by Borges, Fuentes, and Márquez," *Kansas
    Q,* 16, iii (1984), 126–128.
Brooks, Peter. *Reading for the Plot* . . . , 317–319.
Philmus, Roger M. "Wells and Borges and the Labyrinth of Time," *Sci Fiction
    Stud,* 1 (1974), 235–239.
Sirlin, Rhoda, and David H. Richter. *Instructor's Manual* . . . , 9–10.

"The God's Script"
Alvarez, Nicolás E. "Borges y Tzinacán," *Revista Iberoamericana,* 50 (1984), 459–
    473.
Apter, T. E. *Fantasy Literature* . . . , 115–116.
Lutes, Philip. "Cranial Imagery as Metaphor of Consciousness in Borges' 'La
    escritura del Dios,'" *Selecta,* 3 (1982), 122–126.

"The Gospel According to Mark"
McMurray, George R. ". . . Borges to the Present," 126–127.

"The Immortal"
Morgan, Sophia S. "Borges's 'Immortal': Metaritual, Metaliterature, Metaper-
    formance," in MacAloon, John J., Ed. *Rite, Drama* . . . , 79–101.
Río, Carmen M. de. "Borges la literatura y el tiempo: Hacia una estica para
    mortales," *Explicación de Textos Literarios,* 11, ii (1982–1983), 57–67.

"The Library of Babel"
Apter, T. E. *Fantasy Literature* . . . , 118–119.
Capobianco, Michael. "Mathematics . . . ," 51–54.
Hayles, N. Katherine. *The Cosmic Web* . . . , 151–152.
Sturrock, John. "Between Commentary and Comedy: The Satirical Side of
    Borges," in Rawson, Claude, Ed. *English Satire* . . . , 276–286.

"The Man at the Pink Corner"
Flores, Arturo C. "Una aproximación al cuento 'El hombre de la esquina rosada'
    de Jorge Luis Borges," *Káñina,* 5, ii (1981), 48–51.

"The Other Death"
Bruffee, Kenneth A. *Elegiac Romance* . . . , 202–205.
Fisch, Harold. *A Remembered Future* . . . , 48–50.

"Pierre Menard, Author of *Quixote*"
Doxey, William S. "Culture . . . ," 3–4.
Hayles, N. Katherine. *The Cosmic Web* . . . , 138–139.
McNair, Nora M. "'Pierre Menard, Autor del *Quijote*': Huellas y Sentido," in
    Finke, Wayne H., and Enrique Ledesma, Eds. *Homenaje a Humberto Pi-
    ñera* . . . , 159–165.

"The Secret Miracle"
Apter, T. E. *Fantasy Literature* . . . , 123–124.
Knopka, Nancy C. "Jorge Luis Borges . . . ," 127.

"The South"
Apter, T. E. *Fantasy Literature* . . . , 124–126.
Doxey, William S. "Culture . . . ," 1–3.
Friederich, Reinhard H. "Necessary Inadequacies: Poe's 'Tale of the Ragged Mountains' and Borges's 'South,'" *J Narrative Technique*, 12, i (1982), 155–166.
Neglia, Erminio G. "Fictional Death in Stephen Crane's 'The Blue Hotel' and Jorge Luis Borges' 'El Sur,'" *Chasqui*, 10, ii–iii (1981), 20–25.

"Tlön, Uqbar, Orbis Tertius"
Capobianco, Michael. "Mathematics . . . ," 51–54.
Graña, María C. "El once y el espejo, motivos de simetria en un relato de Borges," *Annali della Facultà*, 20 (1981), 169–175.
Hayes, Aden W. "*Orbis Tertius* and *Orbis Novus*: The Creation and Discovery of New Worlds," *Revista Canadiense de Estudios Hispánicos*, 8 (1984), 275–280.
Hayles, N. Katherine. *The Cosmic Web* . . . , 144–148.
Heiney, Donald. "Calvino and Borges: Some Implications of Fantasy," *Mundus Artium*, 2 (1968), 68–70.
Jaén, Didier T. "The Esoteric Tradition in Borges' 'Tlön, Uqbar, Orbis Tertius,'" *Stud Short Fiction*, 21 (1984), 25–39.
Kreuziger, Frederick A. *Apocalypse* . . . , 17–18.
McMurray, George R. ". . . Borges to the Present," 97–98.
Mosca, Stefania. "Borges: Antiutopía," *Zona Franca*, 6 (March–April, 1983), 29–33.
Philmus, Roger M. "Wells and Borges . . . ," 243–245.

"The Wait"
Lafontaine, Cécile A. "Waiting in Hemingway's 'The Killers' and Borges' 'La espera,'" *Revue de Littérature Comparée*, 57 (1983), 67–80.

"The Zahir"
Apter, T. E. *Fantasy Literature* . . . , 116–117.

TADEUSZ BOROWSKI

"Auschwitz, Our Home (A Letter)"
Langer, Lawrence L. *Versions of Survival* . . . , 118–120.

"A Day at Harmenz"
Langer, Lawrence L. *Versions of Survival* . . . , 111–116.

"The People Who Walked On"
Langer, Lawrence L. *Versions of Survival* . . . , 116–118.

"This Way for the Gas, Ladies and Gentlemen"
Karl, Frederick R. *American Fictions* . . . , 588.
Langer, Lawrence L. *Versions of Survival* . . . , 107–111.

F. VAN DEN BOSCH

"Disponent Andersson"
Nieuwenhuys, Rob. *Mirror of the Indies . . .* , 312–313.

"House of Rain"
Nieuwenhuys, Rob. *Mirror of the Indies . . .* , 310–311.

"Nom-de-Guerre"
Nieuwenhuys, Rob. *Mirror of the Indies . . .* , 311–312.

JUAN BOSCH

"Two Dollars' Worth of Water"
Brushwood, John S. "The Spanish American Short Story from Quiroga to Borges," in Peden, Margaret S., Ed. *The Latin American Short Story . . .* , 92.

ANTHONY BOUCHER

"Balaam"
Fredericks, Casey. *The Future of Eternity . . .* , 52–53.

"The Quest for St. Aquin"
Fredericks, Casey. *The Future of Eternity . . .* , 53–54.

ELIZABETH BOWEN

"Ann Lee's"
Meredith, David W. "Authorial Detachment in Elizabeth Bowen's 'Ann Lee's,'" *Massachusetts Stud Engl*, 8, ii (1982), 9–20.

"Breakfast"
Dunleavy, Janet E. "The Subtle Satire of Elizabeth Bowen and Mary Lavin," *Tulsa Stud Women's Lit*, 2, i (1983), 73–74.

"The Demon Lover"
Sirlin, Rhoda, and David H. Richter. *Instructor's Manual . . .* , 10–12.

"The Happy Autumn Fields"
Hooper, Brad. "Elizabeth Bowen's 'The Happy Autumn Fields': A Dream or Not," *Stud Short Fiction*, 21 (1984), 151–153.

"I Hear You Say So"
Medoff, Jeslyn. "'There Is No Elsewhere': Elizabeth Bowen's Perception of War," *Mod Fiction Stud*, 30 (1984), 79–80.

"Maria"
Dunleavy, Janet E. "The Subtle Satire . . . ," 77–78.

"Mysterious Kôr"
Medoff, Jeslyn. "'There Is No Elsewhere'...," 76–79.

"Summer Night"
Medoff, Jeslyn. "'There Is No Elsewhere'...," 74–76.

PAUL BOWLES

"At Paso Rojo"
Bertens, Johannes W. *The Fiction of Paul Bowles*..., 238–243.

"By the Waters"
Bertens, Johannes W. *The Fiction of Paul Bowles*..., 201–203.

"Call at Corazón"
Bertens, Johannes W. *The Fiction of Paul Bowles*..., 236–237.

"The Delicate Prey"
Bertens, Johannes W. *The Fiction of Paul Bowles*..., 194–195.

"A Distant Episode"
Bertens, Johannes W. *The Fiction of Paul Bowles*..., 195.

"The Echo"
Bertens, Johannes W. *The Fiction of Paul Bowles*..., 230–231.
Wells, Linda S. "Paul Bowles: 'Do not appropriate *my* object,'" *R Contemp Fiction*, 2, iii (1982), 75–84.

"The Frozen Field"
Bertens, Johannes W. *The Fiction of Paul Bowles*..., 231–235.
Stewart, Lawrence D. "Paul Bowles and 'The Frozen Field' of Vision," *R Contemp Fiction*, 2, iii (1982), 64–71.

"How Many Midnights"
Bertens, Johannes W. *The Fiction of Paul Bowles*..., 235–236.

"The Hyena"
Bertens, Johannes W. *The Fiction of Paul Bowles*..., 199–201.

"Pages from Cold Point"
Bertens, Johannes W. *The Fiction of Paul Bowles*..., 243–245.
Malin, Irving. "Drastic Points," *R Contemp Fiction*, 2, iii (1982), 30–32.
Wells, Linda S. "Paul Bowles...," 75–80.

"Pastor Dowe at Tacaté"
Bertens, Johannes W. *The Fiction of Paul Bowles*..., 209–218.

"Tapiama"
Bertens, Johannes W. *The Fiction of Paul Bowles*..., 195–197.

"A Thousand Days of Mokhtar"
Bertens, Johannes W. *The Fiction of Paul Bowles* . . . , 203–204.

"The Time of Friendship"
Bertens, Johannes W. *The Fiction of Paul Bowles* . . . , 218–230.

"Under the Sky"
Bertens, Johannes W. *The Fiction of Paul Bowles* . . . , 237–238.

KAY BOYLE

"Kroy Wren"
Watson, James G. "The American Short Story: 1930–1945," in Stevick, Philip, Ed. *The American Short Story, 1900–1945,* 116–117.

"The White Horse of Vienna"
Watson, James G. "The American Short Story . . . ," 116, 117–118.

LEIGH BRACKETT

"All the Colors of the Rainbow"
Arbur, Rosemarie. "Leigh Brackett: No 'Long Goodbye' Is Good Enough," in Staicar, Tom, Ed. *The Feminine Eye* . . . , 10–11.

"Enchantress of Venus"
Hansen, Terry J. "Myth-Adventure in Leigh Brackett's 'Enchantress of Venus,'" *Extrapolation,* 23, i (1982), 77–82.

"The Tweener"
Arbur, Rosemarie. "Leigh Brackett . . . ," 9–10.

RAY BRADBURY

"Boys, Raise Giant Mushrooms in *Your* Cellar!"
Johnson, Wayne L. "The Invasion Stories of Ray Bradbury," in Riley, Dick, Ed. *Critical Encounters [I]* . . . , 25–27.

"Dark They Were and Golden Eyed"
Johnson, Wayne L. "The Invasion Stories . . . ," 37–39.

"Downwind from Gettysburg"
Johnson, Wayne L. *Ray Bradbury,* 77–78.

"Embroidery"
Johnson, Wayne L. *Ray Bradbury,* 63–64.

"Fever Dream"
Johnson, Wayne L. "The Invasion Stories . . . ," 28–29.

"The Flying Machine"
Johnson, Wayne L. *Ray Bradbury*, 134.

"G.B.S.—Mark V"
Johnson, Wayne L. *Ray Bradbury*, 76–77.

"The Garbage Collector"
Johnson, Wayne L. *Ray Bradbury*, 59–61.

"Hail and Farewell"
Johnson, Wayne L. *Ray Bradbury*, 41–42.

"The Highway"
Johnson, Wayne L. *Ray Bradbury*, 62–63.
Wolfe, Gary K. "The Remaking of Zero: Beginning at the End," in Rabkin,
    Eric S., Martin H. Greenberg, and Joseph D. Olander, Eds. *The End . . .*,
    1–3.

"Homecoming"
Johnson, Wayne L. *Ray Bradbury*, 39–40.

"Jack-in-the-Box"
Johnson, Wayne L. *Ray Bradbury*, 44–45.

"The Jar"
Johnson, Wayne L. *Ray Bradbury*, 20–21.

"The Lost City of Mars"
Johnson, Wayne L. *Ray Bradbury*, 81–83.

"The Man Upstairs"
Pierce, Hazel B. *A Literary Symbiosis . . .*, 219–220.

"Marionettes, Inc."
Johnson, Wayne L. *Ray Bradbury*, 74.

"The Million-Year Picnic"
Wagar, W. Warren. *Terminal Visions . . .*, 145–146.

"The Next in Line"
Johnson, Wayne L. *Ray Bradbury*, 28–29.

"No Particular Night or Morning"
Johnson, Wayne L. *Ray Bradbury*, 53–54.

"The Off Season"
Johnson, Wayne L. "The Invasion Stories . . . ," 36.

"The One Who Waits"
Johnson, Wayne L. "The Invasion Stories . . . ," 34–35; rpt. in his *Ray Bradbury*,
    38–39.

"The Pedestrian"
Johnson, Wayne L. *Ray Bradbury*, 84–85.

"Perhaps We Are Going Away"
Johnson, Wayne L. "The Invasion Stories . . . ," 32–33.

"A Scent of Sarsaparilla"
Johnson, Wayne L. *Ray Bradbury*, 71–72.

"The Strawberry Window"
Johnson, Wayne L. *Ray Bradbury*, 22–23.

"The Summer Night"
Johnson, Wayne L. "The Invasion Stories . . . ," 33–34.

"There Will Come Soft Rains"
Bergman, David, Joseph de Roche, and Daniel M. Epstein. *Instructor's Manual . . .* , 30–31.

"To the Chicago Abyss"
Johnson, Wayne L. *Ray Bradbury*, 14–15.

"Tomorrow's Child"
Johnson, Wayne L. *Ray Bradbury*, 42–43.

"Uncle Einar"
Johnson, Wayne L. *Ray Bradbury*, 40–41.

"Usher II"
Guffey, George R. "*Fahrenheit 451* and the 'Cubby-Hole Editors' of Ballantine Books," in Slusser, George E., Eric S. Rabkin, and Robert Scholes, Eds. *Coordinates . . .* , 99–100.

"The Vacation"
Johnson, Wayne L. *Ray Bradbury*, 61–62.

"The Wind"
Johnson, Wayne L. *Ray Bradbury*, 35–36.

"The Women"
Johnson, Wayne L. *Ray Bradbury*, 36–38.

"Ylla"
Johnson, Wayne L. *Ray Bradbury*, 112–113.

"Zero Hour"
Johnson, Wayne L. "The Invasion Stories . . . ," 24–25.

MARION ZIMMER BRADLEY

"The Wind People"
King, Betty. *Women of the Future . . .* , 77–79.

WILLEM BRANDT

"The Candle"
Nieuwenhuys, Rob. *Mirror of the Indies* . . . , 228.

RICHARD BRAUTIGAN

"Homage to the San Francisco YMCA"
Dietrich, R. F. " 'Homage to the San Francisco YMCA,' " in Dietrich, R. F., and
  Roger H. Sundell. *Instructor's Manual* . . . , 4th ed., 137–139.

CLEMENS BRENTANO

"Brave Kasperl and Beautiful Annerl"
Gockel, Heinz. "Gestörte Ordnung: Überlegungen zu Brentanos 'Geschichte
  vom braven Kasperl und dem schönen Annerl,' " *Jahrbuch des Freien
  Deutschen Hochstifts*, [n.v.] (1984), 253–261.
Kittler, Wolf. "Familie, Geschlecht, und Poesie: Brentanos 'Geschichte vom
  braven Kasperl und dem schönen Annerl,' " in Peschel, Dietmar, Ed. *Germanistik in Erlangen* . . . , 231–237.
Menhennet, Alan. *The Romantic Movement*, 205–206.

"Gockel, Hinkel, und Gackeleia"
Menhennet, Alan. *The Romantic Movement*, 203–204.

MAX BROD

"Tod den Toten"
Habermann, Angela. " 'Indifferentism' in the Early Fiction of Max Brod: The
  Representation of Decadence in the Prague Circle," *Int'l Fiction R*, 11, i
  (1984), 49.

LOUIS BROMFIELD

"Death in Monte Carlo"
Anderson, David D. *Louis Bromfield*, 138–139.

"The End of the Road"
Anderson, David D. *Louis Bromfield*, 142.

"The Life of Vergie Winters"
Anderson, David D. *Louis Bromfield*, 63.

"Miss Mehaffy"
Anderson, David D. *Louis Bromfield*, 91–92.

"The Old House"
Anderson, David D. *Louis Bromfield*, 139–140.

"Up Ferguson Way"
Anderson, David D. *Louis Bromfield*, 140.

CHARLES BROCKDEN BROWN

"The Death of Cicero, A Fragment"
Axelrod, Alan. *Charles Brockden Brown . . .* , 81–82.

FREDRIC BROWN

"Answer"
Fabry, Heinz-Wilhelm, and Peter Wenzel. "Mythisch-religöse Themen in der
    Very Short Science Fiction Story: Eric Frank Russells 'Sole Solution' und
    Fredric Browns 'Answer,' " [sic] *Anglistik & Englischunterricht*, 23 (1984),
    129–140.

"Arena"
Huntington, James. "Impossible Love in Science Fiction," *Raritan*, 14, ii (1984),
    86–90.

MARTA BRUNET

"Soledad de la sangre"
Mora, Gabriela. "Una lectura de 'Soledad de la sangre' de Marta Brunet," *Es-
    tudios Filológicos*, 19 (1984), 81–90.

JOHN BRUNNER

"Nobody Axed You"
Pierce, Hazel B. *A Literary Symbiosis . . .* , 115–116.

WILLIAM CULLEN BRYANT

"A Border Tradition"
Ringe, Donald A. "Bryant's Fiction: The Problem of Perception," in Brodwin,
    Stanley, and Michael D'Innocenzo, Eds. *William Cullen Bryant . . .* , 169–
    170.

"The Indian Spring"
Ringe, Donald A. "Bryant's Fiction . . . ," 174–176.

"The Legend of the Devil's Pulpit"
Ringe, Donald A. "Bryant's Fiction . . . ," 169.

"Medfield"
Ringe, Donald A. *American Gothic . . .* , 126; rpt., expanded, in Brodwin, Stanley,
    and Michael D'Innocenzo, Eds. *William Cullen Bryant . . .* , 171–174.

JOHN BUCHAN

"The Grave of Ashtaroth"
Zahorski, Kenneth L., and Robert H. Boyer. "The Secondary Worlds of High
Fantasy," in Schlobin, Roger C., Ed. *The Aesthetics* . . . , 77–78.

"No-Man's Land"
Hunter, Jefferson. *Edwardian Fiction,* 113–114.

ALGIS BUDRYS [ALGIRDAS JONAS BUDRYS]

"All for Love"
Nicholls, Peter. "Algis Budrys," in Bleiler, Everett F., Ed. *Science Fiction Writ-*
ers . . . , 309–310.

MIKHAIL BULGAKOV

"Diaboliad"
Proffer, Ellendea. *Bulgakov* . . . , 105–108.

"Morphine"
Proffer, Ellendea. *Bulgakov* . . . , 94–95.

"Notes on the Cuff"
Proffer, Ellendea. *Bulgakov* . . . , 77–80.

"No. 13, The Elpit-Rabkommun Building"
Proffer, Ellendea. *Bulgakov* . . . , 118–119.

"The Raid"
Proffer, Ellendea. *Bulgakov* . . . , 142–143.

SILVINA BULLRICH

"Abnegation"
Lindstrom, Naomi. "Literary Convention and Sex-Role Analysis: Silvina Bull-
rich's 'Abnegation,'" *Denver Q,* 17, ii (1982), 98–104.

CARLOS BULOSAN

"The Americano from Luzon"
San Juan, E. *Toward a People's Literature* . . . , 130–131.

"Homecoming"
San Juan, E. *Toward a People's Literature* . . . , 136.

"I Would Remember"
San Juan, E. *Toward a People's Literature* . . . , 136–137.

"Silence"
San Juan, E. *Toward a People's Literature* . . . , 134.

IVAN BUNIN

"Antonov Apples"
Connolly, Julian W. *Ivan Bunin*, 31–34.

"Brethren"
Connolly, Julian W. *Ivan Bunin*, 80–83.

"By the Road"
Connolly, Julian W. *Ivan Bunin*, 68–71.

"Calling Cards"
Connolly, Julian W. *Ivan Bunin*, 127–128.

"Cold Autumn"
Connolly, Julian W. *Ivan Bunin*, 130–131.

"The Cup of Life"
Connolly, Julian W. *Ivan Bunin*, 74–75.

"The Dreams of Chang"
Connolly, Julian W. *Ivan Bunin*, 83–84.

"The Endless Spring"
Connolly, Julian W. *Ivan Bunin*, 92–93.

"An Epitaph"
Connolly, Julian W. *Ivan Bunin*, 33–34.

"A Gay Farmhouse"
Connolly, Julian W. *Ivan Bunin*, 51–52.

"The Gentleman from San Francisco"
Connolly, Julian W. *Ivan Bunin*, 84–90.

"The Gold Mine"
Connolly, Julian W. *Ivan Bunin*, 33–34.

"Gotami"
Connolly, Julian W. *Ivan Bunin*, 96–97.

"The Grammar of Love"
Connolly, Julian W. *Ivan Bunin*, 73–74.

"Ida"
Connolly, Julian W. *Ivan Bunin*, 110–111.

"The Yelagin Affair"
Connolly, Julian W. *Ivan Bunin,* 100–102.

YEHUDA BURLA

"Luna"
Yudkin, Leon I. *Jewish Writing . . . ,* 92–93.

EDGAR RICE BURROUGHS

"The Mouthpiece of Zitu"
Sampson, Robert. *Yesterday's Faces, II . . . ,* 196–197.

DINO BUZZATI

"A Drop"
Rawson, Judy. "Dino Buzzati," in Caesar, Michael, and Peter Hainsworth, Eds. *Writers and Society . . . ,* 195–196.

VASILY BYKOV

"Sotnikov"
Blum, Jakub. "Soviet Russian Literature," in Blum, Jakub, and Vera Rich. *The Image of the Jew . . . ,* 47–49.

GEORGE WASHINGTON CABLE

"Jean-ah Poquelin"
Christophersen, Bill. "'Jean-ah Poquelin': Cable's Place in Southern Gothic," *So Dakota R,* 20, ii (1982), 55–66.
Petry, Alice H. "A Fable of Love and Death: The Artistry of Cable's 'Jean-ah Poquelin,'" *Southern Lit R,* 15, ii (1983), 87–99.

LYDIA CABRERA

"The Devil's Treasurer"
Valdes-Cruz, Rosa. "The Short Stories of Lydia Cabrera: Transpositions or Creations?" in Miller, Yvette E., and Charles M. Tatum, Eds. *Latin American Women Writers . . . ,* 149–150.

"La Loma de Mambiala"
Hewitt, Julia Cuervo. "Yoruba Presence: From Nigerian Oral Literature to Contemporary Cuban Narrative," in Luis, William, Ed. *Voices from Under . . . ,* 76.

"The Sweet Potato Thief"
Valdes-Cruz, Rosa. "The Short Stories . . . ," 150–153.

GUILLERMO CABRERA INFANTE

"At the Great Echo"
McMurray, George R. "The Spanish American Short Story from Borges to the Present," in Peden, Margaret S., Ed. *The Latin American Short Story . . . ,* 116–117.

"Un rato de tenmealla"
Bockus Aponte, Barbara. "El niño como testigo: La visión infantil en el cuento hispanoamericano contemporáneo," *Explicación de Textos Literarios,* 11, i (1982), 19–23.

ABRAHAM CAHAN

"The Apostate of Chego-Chegg"
Kress, Susan. "Women and Marriage in Abraham Cahan's Fiction," *Stud Am Jewish Lit,* 3 (1983), 29–31.
Marovitz, Sanford E. "The Lonely New Americans of Abraham Cahan," *Am Q,* 20 (1968), 203.

"Circumstances"
Kress, Susan. "Women and Marriage . . . ," 33–34.

"The Daughter of Reb Avrom Leib"
Kress, Susan. "Women and Marriage . . . ," 31–33.
Marovitz, Sanford E. "The Lonely New Americans . . . ," 202–203.

"Dumitru and Sigrid"
Marovitz, Sanford E. "The Lonely New Americans . . . ," 203.

"A Ghetto Wedding"
Marovitz, Sanford E. "The Lonely New Americans . . . ," 200–201.

"The Imported Bridegroom"
Greenspan, Ezra. *The "Schlemiel" . . . ,* 33–36.
Kress, Susan. "Women and Marriage . . . ," 27–29.
Marovitz, Sanford E. "The Lonely New Americans . . . ," 201–202.

"A Providential Match"
Greenspan, Ezra. *The "Schlemiel" . . . ,* 31–33.

"Rabbi Eliezer's Christmas"
Marovitz, Sanford E. "The Lonely New Americans . . . ," 200.

"Tzinchadzi of the Catskills"
Marovitz, Sanford E. "The Lonely New Americans . . . ," 204.

ERSKINE CALDWELL

"August Afternoon"
Devlin, James E. *Erskine Caldwell*, 78–81.

MORLEY CALLAGHAN

"The Enchanted Pimp"
Morley, Patricia. "Morley Callaghan: Magician and Illusionist," in Staines, David, Ed. *The Callaghan Symposium*, 62–64.

"Getting on in the World"
Sirlin, Rhoda, and David H. Richter. *Instructor's Manual* . . . , 12–13.

ITALO CALVINO

"The Adventure of a Motorist"
Ricci, Franco. "Silence and the Loss of Self in Italo Calvino's *Gli amori difficili*," *Italianist*, 4 (1984), 58–60.

"The Adventure of a Poet"
Ricci, Franco. "Silence . . . ," 65–66.

"The Adventure of a Reader"
Ricci, Franco. "Silence . . . ," 63–65.

"The Adventure of a Soldier"
Ricci, Franco. "Silence . . . ," 56–58.

"Big Fish, Little Fish"
Woodhouse, J. R. "Fantasy, Alienation and the *Racconti* of Italo Calvino," *Forum Mod Lang Stud*, 6 (1970), 405.

"The Canary Prince"
Bergman, David, Joseph de Roche, and Daniel M. Epstein. *Instructor's Manual* . . . , 6–7.

"The Distance of the Moon"
Koelb, Clayton. *The Incredulous Reader* . . . , 169–170.

"A Goatherd at Lunch"
Woodhouse, J. R. "Fantasy . . . ," 406–407.

"The Hen of the Department"
Woodhouse, J. R. "Fantasy . . . ," 410–411.

"The Peasant"
Woodhouse, J. R. "Fantasy . . . ," 408–410.

"A Sign in Space"
Koelb, Clayton. *The Incredulous Reader* . . . , 171–173.

"The Spiral"
Andrews, Richard. "Italo Calvino," in Caesar, Michael, and Peter Hainsworth,
    Eds. *Writers and Society* . . . , 270–271.

JOHN W. CAMPBELL

"Atomic Power"
Cioffi, Frank. *Formula Fiction?* . . . , 123–125.

"Forgetfulness"
Bleiler, Everett F. "John W. Campbell," in Bleiler, Everett F., Ed. *Science Fiction
    Writers* . . . , 156.

"Islands of Space"
Bleiler, Everett F. "John W. Campbell," 153.

"The Machine"
Bleiler, Everett F. "John W. Campbell," 156.

"The Mightiest Machine"
Bleiler, Everett F. "John W. Campbell," 154.

"Night" [published under pseudonym Don A. Stuart]
Bleiler, Everett F. "John W. Campbell," 155.

"Rebellion"
Cioffi, Frank. *Formula Fiction?* . . . , 122–123.

"Twilight" [published under pseudonym Don A. Stuart]
Arbur, Rosemarie. "Teleology of Human Nature for Mentality?" in Myers,
    Robert E., Ed. *The Intersection* . . . , 83–84.
Bleiler, Everett F. "John W. Campbell," 154–155.
Cioffi, Frank. *Formula Fiction?* . . . , 90–94.

"Who Goes There?" [published under pseudonym Don A. Stuart]
Bleiler, Everett F. "John W. Campbell," 155.
Rawlins, Jack P. "Confronting the Alien: Fantasy and Anti-Fantasy in Science
    Fiction Film and Literature," in Slusser, George E., Eric S. Rabkin, and
    Robert Scholes, Eds. *Bridges to Fantasy,* 162–166.

MEG CAMPBELL

"Just Saying You Love Me Doesn't Make It So"
Scott, Virgil, and David Madden. *Instructor's Manual* . . . , 4th ed., 46–49; Mad-
    den, David. *Instructor's Manual* . . . , 5th ed., 5–7; Madden, David, and Vir-
    gil Scott. *Instructor's Manual* . . . , 6th ed., 3–6.

ALBERT CAMUS

"The Adulterous Woman"
Day, Loraine. "The Theme of Death in Camus's 'La Femme adultère' and 'Retour à Tipasa,'" *Essays French Lit*, 20 (1983), 67–94.
Showalter, English. *Exiles and Strangers . . .* , 19–34.
Suther, Judith D. "The Concept of 'Kingdom' in Camus' 'La Femme adultère' and Colette's *La Vagabonde*," in Martín, Gregorio C., Ed. *Selected Proceedings . . .* , 367–371.
Talmor, Avital. "Beyond 'Wedlock' and 'Hierogamy': Non-Marriage in Modern Fiction," *Durham Univ J*, 77 (1984), 79–85.

"The Fall"
Ellison, David R. "Camus and the Rhetoric of Dizziness: 'La Chute,'" *Contemp Lit*, 24 (1983), 322–348.
Fitch, Brian T. "Narcisse interprète: 'La Chute' comme modelé herméneutique," *La Revue des Lettres Modernes*, 632–636 (1982), 89–108.
———. *The Narcissistic Text . . .* , 69–88.
McCarthy, Patrick. *Camus*, 307–310.
Otten, Terry. *After Innocence . . .* , 114–133.
Weisberg, Richard H. *The Failure . . .* , 123–129.
Zepp, Evelyn H. "Dialogizing the Monologue: The Creation of the 'Double-Voiced' Word in Camus's 'La Chute,'" *Symposium*, 35 (1982), 357–371.
———. "The Generic Ambiguity of Albert Camus's 'La Chute,'" *French Forum*, 7 (1982), 252–260.

"The Growing Stone"
Feldmann, Helmut. "Le Thème du voyage dans l'au-delà dans la nouvelle 'La pierre qui pousse' d'Albert Camus," in Knabe, Peter-Eckhard, Jürgen Rolshoven, and Margarethe Stracke, Eds. *Le Sacré . . .* , 127–134.
Goodhand, Robert. "The Omphalos and the Phoenix: Symbolism of the Center in Camus' 'La Pierre Qui Pousse,'" *Stud Short Fiction*, 21 (1984), 117–126.
Showalter, English. *Exiles and Strangers . . .* , 107–129.
Walker, David H. "Image, symbole et signification dans 'La Pierre qui pousse,'" *R Lettres Modernes*, 648–651 (1982), 77–104.

"The Guest"
McDermott, John V. "Albert Camus' Flawed Guest," *Notes Contemp Lit*, 14, iii (1984), 5–7.
Madden, David. *Instructor's Manual . . .* , 5th ed., 96–98; Madden, David, and Virgil Scott. *Instructor's Manual . . .* , 6th ed., 109–111.
Perrine, Laurence. "Daru: Camus' Humane Host," *Notes Contemp Lit*, 14, v (1984), 11–12.
Showalter, English. *Exiles and Strangers . . .* , 73–87.
Sirlin, Rhoda, and David H. Richter. *Instructor's Manual . . .* , 14–15.

"Jonas, or The Artist at Work"
Fitch, Brian T. *The Narcissistic Text . . .* , 35–48.
Pasco, Allen H. "'And Seated Ye Shall Fall': Some Lexical Markers in Camus's 'Jonas,'" *Mod Fiction Stud*, 28 (1982), 240–242.
Showalter, English. *Exiles and Strangers . . .* , 89–106.

"The Renegade"
Showalter, English. *Exiles and Strangers* . . . , 35–52.

"The Silent Men"
Showalter, English. *Exiles and Strangers* . . . , 53–71.
Steinbach, Hansjörg. "'Les Muets': Überlegungen zur Interpretation von Albert Camus' Novelle in der Oberstufe," *Französisch Heute*, 4 (1982), 263–272.

"The Stranger"
Fitch, Brian T. *The Narcissistic Text* . . . , 49–67.
Lee, Dorothy H. "Denial of Time and the Failure of Moral Choice: Camus' 'The Stranger,' Faulkner's 'Old Man,' and Wright's 'The Man Who Lived Underground,'" *Coll Lang Assoc J*, 23 (1980), 364–368.
Le Hir, Jeanne. "De Meursault à Meursault: Une Lecture 'intertextuelle' de 'L'Étranger,'" *R Lettres Modernes*, 632–636 (1982), 29–52.
McCarthy, Patrick. *Camus*, 155–163.
Ohayon, Stephen. "Camus' 'The Stranger': The Sun-Metaphor and Patricidal Conflict," *Am Imago*, 40 (1983), 189–205.
Parr, Susan R. *The Moral* . . . , 137–145.
Van den Heuvel, Pierre. "Parole, mot et silence: Les avatars de l'enonciation dans 'L'Étranger' d'Albert Camus," *La Revue des Lettres Modernes*, 632–636 (1982), 53–88.
Weisberg, Richard H. *The Failure* . . . , 114–23.
Welch, David. "Paradox and the Poetry of Paradox in Albert Camus's 'L'Étranger,'" in Pickford, Cedric, Ed. *Mélanges* . . . , 275–288.

KAREL ČAPEK

"The Death of the Baron Granada"
Davydov, Sergej. *"Tales from One Pocket*: Detective and Justice Stories of Karel Čapek," in Steiner, P[eter], M[ironlav] Červenka, and R[onald] Vroom, Eds. *The Structure* . . . , 99.

"The Disappearance of Actor Benda"
Davydov, Sergej. *"Tales from One Pocket* . . . ," 102.

"The Farm Murder"
Davydov, Sergej. *"Tales from One Pocket* . . . ," 102–103.

"The Footprints"
Davydov, Sergej. *"Tales from One Pocket* . . . ," 104–106.

"The Fortune-Teller"
Davydov, Sergej. *"Tales from One Pocket* . . . ," 98–99.

"The Last Judgment"
Davydov, Sergej. *"Tales from One Pocket* . . . ," 103–104.

"The Post Office Crime"
Davydov, Sergej. *"Tales from One Pocket* . . . ," 102.

TRUMAN CAPOTE

"A Christmas Memory"
Perrine, Laurence, and Thomas R. Arp. *Instructor's Manual . . .* , 6th ed., 31–
    32.

"Jug of Silver"
Walker, Jeffrey. "1945–1956: Post-World War II Manners and Mores," in
    Weaver, Gordon, Ed. *The American Short Story, 1945–1980,* 22–23.

"Miriam"
Madden, David. *Instructor's Manual . . .* , 5th ed., 92–93; Madden, David, and
    Virgil Scott. *Instructor's Manual . . .* , 6th ed., 95–97.

WILLIAM CARLETON

"The Battle of the Factions"
Chesnutt, Margaret. *Studies . . .* , 119–121.
Hayley, Barbara. *Carleton's "Traits and Stories" . . .* , 5–7.
Sullivan, Eileen A. *William Carleton,* 55–56.

"The Broken Oath"
Chesnutt, Margaret. *Studies . . .* , 43–50.

"The Brothers"
Sullivan, Eileen A. *William Carleton,* 38–40.

"Condy Cullen; or, The Excisemen Defeated"
Chesnutt, Margaret. *Studies . . .* , 177–178.

"Confessions of a Reformed Ribbonman"
Chesnutt, Margaret. *Studies . . .* , 126–132.

"Denis O'Shaughnessy Going to Maynooth"
Chesnutt, Margaret. *Studies . . .* , 75–79, 156–162.
Hayley, Barbara. *Carleton's "Traits and Stories" . . .* , 88–108.
Meir, Colin. "Voice and Audience in Early Carleton," *Études Irlandaises,* 4
    (1979), 276–277.
Schirmer, Gregory A. "Tales from Big House and Cabin: The Nineteenth Cen-
    tury," in Kilroy, James F., Ed. *The Irish Short Story . . .* , 34–35.
Waters, Maureen. *The Comic Irishman,* 66–67.

"The Donagh, or The Horse Stealers"
Hayley, Barbara. *Carleton's "Traits and Stories" . . .* , 161–178.
Sullivan, Eileen A. *William Carleton,* 62–64.

"Father Butler"
Sullivan, Eileen A. *William Carleton,* 34–35.

"The Funeral and Party Fight"
Chesnutt, Margaret. *Studies . . .* , 121–126.

"The Geography of an Irish Oath"
Chesnutt, Margaret. *Studies . . .* , 99–100.

"The Hedge School"
Chesnutt, Margaret. *Studies . . .* , 162–165.
Hayley, Barbara. *Carleton's "Traits and Stories" . . .* , 11–14, 50–52.

"The Illicit Distiller, or The Force of Conscience"
Sullivan, Eileen A. *William Carleton*, 43–44.

"Larry M'Farland's Wake"
Sullivan, Eileen A. *William Carleton*, 54–55.

"A Legend of Knockmany"
Waters, Maureen. *The Comic Irishman*, 33–34.

"The Lianhan Shee"
Hayley, Barbara. *Carleton's "Traits and Stories" . . .* , 75–87.
Sullivan, Eileen A. *William Carleton*, 42–43.

"Lough Derg Pilgrim"
Hayley, Barbara. *Carleton's "Traits and Stories" . . .* , 334–340.

"Mary Murray the Irish Matchmaker"
Sullivan, Eileen A. *William Carleton*, 69–70.

"The Midnight Mass"
Hayley, Barbara. *Carleton's "Traits and Stories" . . .* , 179–193.

"Neal Malone"
Hayley, Barbara. *Carleton's "Traits and Stories" . . .* , 328–334.
Sullivan, Eileen A. *William Carleton*, 64–66.

"Phelim O'Toole's Courtship"
Chesnutt, Margaret. *Studies . . .* , 95–99.
Hayley, Barbara. *Carleton's "Traits and Stories" . . .* , 244–256.
Waters, Maureen. *The Comic Irishman*, 35–39.

"Phil Purcel the Pig-Driver"
Chesnutt, Margaret. *Studies . . .* , 178–181.
Hayley, Barbara. *Carleton's "Traits and Stories" . . .* , 194–203.

"A Pilgrimage to Patrick's Purgatory"
Chesnutt, Margaret. *Studies . . .* , 30–42.

"The Poor Scholar"
Chesnutt, Margaret. *Studies . . .* , 110–115.
Hayley, Barbara. *Carleton's "Traits and Stories" . . .* , 224–243.

"Shane Fadh's Wedding"
Hayley, Barbara. *Carleton's "Traits and Stories" . . .* , 43–46.

"The Station"
Hayley, Barbara. *Carleton's "Traits and Stories"* . . . , 15–23.
Sullivan, Eileen A. *William Carleton,* 35–37.

"Tom Gressiey the Irish Senachie"
Meir, Colin. "Voice and Audience . . . , " 280.

"Tubber Derg, or The Red Well" [expansion of story originally titled "The
    Landlord and the Tenant"]
Chesnutt, Margaret. *Studies* . . . , 100–110, 166–168.
Hayley, Barbara. *Carleton's "Traits and Stories"* . . . , 137–160.

"Wildgoose Lodge" [originally titled "Confessions of a Reformed Ribbonman"]
Hayley, Barbara. *Carleton's "Traits and Stories"* . . . , 123–136.
Schirmer, Gregory A. "Tales from Big House . . . ," 36–37.

ALEJO CARPENTIER

"El Camino de Santiago"
Benítez Rojo, Antonio. " 'El camino de Santiago' de Alejo Carpentier y el *Canon
    Perpetuus* de Juan Sebastián Bach: Paralelismo estructural," *Revista Ibero-
    americana,* 49, cxxiii–cxxiv (1983), 293–322.
Foster, David W. "The 'Everyman' Theme in Carpentier's 'El Camino de San-
    tiago,'" *Symposium,* 18, ii (1964), 229–240.
Magnarelli, Sharon. " 'El camino de Santiago' de Alejo Carpentier y la pica-
    resca," *Revista Iberoamericana,* 40 (1974), 65–86.
Rodríguez Alcalá, Hugo. "Sentido de 'El Camino de Santiago,'" *Humanities,* 5
    (1964), 245–254.
Verzasconi, Ray. "Juan and Sisyphus in Carpentier's 'El camino de Santiago,'"
    Hispania, 48, i (1965), 70–75.

"Histoire de Lunes"
Piedra, José. "A Return to Africa with a Carpentier Tale," *Mod Lang Notes,* 97
    (1982), 401–410.

ROSARIO CASTELLANOS

"Waltz Caprice"
Anderson, Heleme M. "Rosario Castellanos and the Structures of Power," in
    Meyer, Doris, and Margarite F. Olmos, Eds. *Contemporary Women* . . . , 27–
    28.

WILLA CATHER

"The Affair at Grover Station"
Arnold, Marilyn. . . . *Short Fiction,* 27–28.

"Ardessa"
Arnold, Marilyn. . . . *Short Fiction,* 102–103.

"Before Breakfast"
Arnold, Marilyn. . . . *Short Fiction*, 167–170.

"Behind the Singer Tower"
Arnold, Marilyn. . . . *Short Fiction*, 92–97.

"The Bohemian Girl"
Arnold, Marilyn. . . . *Short Fiction*, 86–89.

"The Bookkeeper's Wife"
Arnold, Marilyn. . . . *Short Fiction*, 102.

"The Clemency of the Court"
Arnold, Marilyn. . . . *Short Fiction*, 3.

"Coming, Aphrodite!" [same as "Coming, Eden Bower"]
Arnold, Marilyn. . . . *Short Fiction*, 112–119.

"Consequences"
Arnold, Marilyn. . . . *Short Fiction*, 99–101.

"The Count of Crow's Nest"
Arnold, Marilyn. . . . *Short Fiction*, 11–12.

"The Dance at Chevalier's"
Arnold, Marilyn. . . . *Short Fiction*, 26–27.

"A Death in the Desert"
Arnold, Marilyn. . . . *Short Fiction*, 54–56.
Kimbel, Ellen. "The American Short Story: 1900–1920," in Stevick, Philip, Ed.
    The American Short Story, 1900–1945, 52–54.

"The Diamond Mine"
Arnold, Marilyn. . . . *Short Fiction*, 107–109.

"El Dorado: A Kansas Recessional"
Arnold, Marilyn. . . . *Short Fiction*, 40–41.

"Double Birthday"
Arnold, Marilyn. . . . *Short Fiction*, 126–129.

"Eleanor's House"
Arnold, Marilyn. . . . *Short Fiction*, 78–81.

"The Elopement of Allen Poole"
Arnold, Marilyn. . . . *Short Fiction*, 8–9.

"The Enchanted Bluff"
Arnold, Marilyn. . . . *Short Fiction*, 82–83.

"Eric Hermannson's Soul"
Arnold, Marilyn. . . . *Short Fiction*, 20–25.

"The Fear That Walks by Noonday"
Arnold, Marilyn. . . . *Short Fiction,* 7.

"Flavia and Her Artists"
Arnold, Marilyn. . . . *Short Fiction,* 46–48.

"The Garden Lodge"
Arnold, Marilyn. . . . *Short Fiction,* 51–53.

"A Gold Slipper"
Arnold, Marilyn. . . . *Short Fiction,* 109–111.

"Her Boss"
Arnold, Marilyn. . . . *Short Fiction,* 103–106.

"Jack-a-Boy"
Arnold, Marilyn. . . . *Short Fiction,* 37–39.
Bruffee, Kenneth A. *Elegiac Romance . . . ,* 197–199.

"The Joy of Nelly Deane"
Arnold, Marilyn. . . . *Short Fiction,* 83–86.

"Lou, the Prophet"
Arnold, Marilyn. . . . *Short Fiction,* 5–6.

"The Marriage of Phaedra"
Arnold, Marilyn. . . . *Short Fiction,* 56–57.

"The Namesake"
Arnold, Marilyn. . . . *Short Fiction,* 75–78.

"Nanette: An Aside"
Arnold, Marilyn. . . . *Short Fiction,* 16–17.

"Neighbour Rosicky"
Arnold, Marilyn. . . . *Short Fiction,* 135–140.

"A Night at Greenway Court"
Arnold, Marilyn. . . . *Short Fiction,* 7–8.

"The Old Beauty"
Arnold, Marilyn. . . . *Short Fiction,* 158–165.

"Old Mrs. Harris"
Arnold, Marilyn. . . . *Short Fiction,* 141–152.

"On the Divide"
Arnold, Marilyn. . . . *Short Fiction,* 4–5.
Chadbourne, Richard. "Two Visions of the Prairie: Willa Cather and Gabrielle
    Roy," in Chadbourne, Richard, and Hallvard Dahlie, Eds. *The New
    Land . . . ,* 97–98.

"On the Gull's Road"
Arnold, Marilyn. . . . *Short Fiction*, 89–92.

"Paul's Case"
Arnold, Marilyn. . . . *Short Fiction*, 61–65.
Kimbel, Ellen. "The American Short Story . . . ," 55–57.
Madden, David, and Virgil Scott. *Instructor's Manual . . .* , 6th ed., 72–76.
Sheidley, William E., and Ann Charters. *Instructor's Manual . . .* , 54–56.

"Peter"
Arnold, Marilyn. . . . *Short Fiction*, 2–3.

"The Professor's Commencement"
Arnold, Marilyn. . . . *Short Fiction*, 41–42.

"The Profile"
Arnold, Marilyn. . . . *Short Fiction*, 69–72.

"A Resurrection"
Arnold, Marilyn. . . . *Short Fiction*, 10.

"Scandal"
Arnold, Marilyn. . . . *Short Fiction*, 111–112.

"The Sculptor's Funeral"
Arnold, Marilyn. . . . *Short Fiction*, 48–51.
Chadbourne, Richard. "Two Visions . . . ," 98.
Kimbel, Ellen. "The American Short Story . . . ," 54–55.
Miller, James E., and Bernice Slote. *Instructor's Manual . . .* , 10–11.

"The Sentimentality of William Tavener"
Arnold, Marilyn. . . . *Short Fiction*, 28–29.

"The Strategy of the Were-Wolf Dog"
Arnold, Marilyn. . . . *Short Fiction*, 12–13.

"The Treasure of Far Island"
Arnold, Marilyn. . . . *Short Fiction*, 39–40.

"Two Friends"
Arnold, Marilyn. . . . *Short Fiction*, 152–158.

"Uncle Valentine"
Arnold, Marilyn. . . . *Short Fiction*, 119–126.

"A Wagner Matinée"
Arnold, Marilyn. . . . *Short Fiction*, 57–60.

"The Way of the World"
Arnold, Marilyn. . . . *Short Fiction*, 17–20.

"The Willing Muse"
Arnold, Marilyn. . . . *Short Fiction*, 72–74.

ROBERT W. CHAMBERS

"The Maker of Moons"
Wu, William F. *The Yellow Peril* . . . , 88–92.

ADELBERT VON CHAMISSO

"Peter Schlemihls Wundersame Geschichte"
Fink, Gonthier-Louis. "'Peter Schlemihl' et la tradition du conte romantique,"
    Recherches Germanique, 12 (1982), 24–54.
Menhennet, Alan. *The Romantic Movement*, 206–208.
Pavlyshyn, Marko. "Gold, Guilt and Scholarship: Adelbert von Chamisso's 'Peter Schlemihl,'" *Germ Q*, 55 (1982), 49–63.
Walach, Dagmar. "Adelbert von Chamisso: 'Peter Schlemihls Wundersame Geschichte,'" in Lützeler, Paul M., Ed. *Romane und Erzählungen* . . . , 285–301.

JEFFERY PAUL CHAN

"Auntie Tsia Lays Dying"
Kim, Elaine H. *Asian American Literature* . . . , 191–193.

"Jackrabbit"
Kim, Elaine H. *Asian American Literature* . . . , 189–191.

RAYMOND CHANDLER

"Bay City Blues"
Speir, Jerry. *Raymond Chandler*, 86–89.

"Blackmailers Don't Shoot"
Speir, Jerry. *Raymond Chandler*, 91–92.

"The Lady in the Lake"
Speir, Jerry. *Raymond Chandler*, 88–89.

"Mandarin's Jade"
Speir, Jerry. *Raymond Chandler*, 97.

"No Crime in the Mountains"
Speir, Jerry. *Raymond Chandler*, 102–103.

"Pearls Are a Nuisance"
Speir, Jerry. *Raymond Chandler*, 101.

"Red Wind"
Speir, Jerry. *Raymond Chandler,* 98–100.

"Try the Girl"
Speir, Jerry. *Raymond Chandler,* 98–100.

FRANÇOIS-RENÉ de CHATEAUBRIAND

"Atala"
Kadish, Doris Y. "Symbolism of Exile: The Opening Description in 'Atala,'"
    French R, 55 (1982), 358–366.
Nemoianu, Virgil, *The Taming . . . ,* 113–114.

"René"
Call, Michael. "René in the Garden," *Constructions,* [n.v.] (1984), 43–53.
Garber, Frederick. *The Autonomy of the Self . . . ,* 168–170.
Nemoianu, Virgil. *The Taming . . . ,* 112–113.

JOHN CHEEVER

"The Angel of the Bridge"
Burhans, C[linton] S. "John Cheever and the Grave of Social Coherence," *Twentieth Century Lit,* 14 (1969), 193; rpt. Collins, R. G., Ed. *Critical Essays . . . ,*
    116–117.
Donaldson, Scott. "The Machine in Cheever's Garden," in Schwartz, Barry, Ed.
    The Changing Face . . . , 312–313; rpt. Collins, R. G., Ed. *Critical Essays . . . ,*
    142–143.
Hunt, George W. *John Cheever . . . ,* 259–261.
Miller, James E., and Bernice Slote. *Instructor's Manual . . . ,* 2nd ed., 19–20.
Rupp, Richard H. "Of That Time, of Those Places: The Short Stories of John
    Cheever," in Collins, R. G., Ed. *Critical Essays . . . ,* 235–236.

"Artemis, the Honest Well Digger"
Brown, John L. "Cheever's Expatriates," in Collins, R. G., Ed. *Critical Essays . . . ,*
    251–252.
Gerlach, John. "Closure in Modern Short Fiction: Cheever's 'The Enormous
    Radio' and 'Artemis, the Honest Well Digger,'" *Mod Fiction Stud,* 28 (1982),
    148–152.

"The Bella Lingua"
Burhans, C[linton] S. "John Cheever . . . ," 191; rpt. Collins, R. G., Ed. *Critical
    Essays . . . ,* 114.
Rupp, Richard H. "Of That Time . . . ," 234–235.

"Boy in Rome"
Hunt, George W. *John Cheever . . . ,* 284–285.

"The Brigadier and the Golf Widow"
Hunt, George W. *John Cheever . . . ,* 252–257.

"The Bus to St. James's"
Hunt, George W. *John Cheever* . . . , 240–241.

"Christmas Is a Sad Season for the Poor"
Rupp, Richard H. "Of That Time . . . ," 234–235.

"Clancy in the Tower of Babel"
Hunt, George W. *John Cheever* . . . , 235–238.

"Clementina"
Brown, John L. "Cheever's Expatriates," 256–257.
Burhans, C[linton] S. "John Cheever . . . ," 191–192; rpt. Collins, R. G., Ed. *Critical Essays* . . . , 114–115.

"The Country Husband"
Hunt, George W. *John Cheever* . . . , 273–280.

"The Day the Pig Fell into the Well"
Hunt, George W. *John Cheever* . . . , 241–243.

"The Death of Justina"
Chesnick, Eugene. "The Domesticated Stroke of John Cheever," *New England Q,* 44 (1971), 541–542; rpt. Collins, R. G., Ed. *Critical Essays* . . . , 131–132.
Coale, Samuel. *John Cheever,* 23–28.
———. "Cheever and Hawthorne: The American Romancer's Art," in Collins, R. G., Ed. *Critical Essays* . . . , 206–208.
Hunt, George W. *John Cheever* . . . , 23–28.

"The Embarkment for Cythera"
Bracher, Frederick. "John Cheever's Vision of the World," in Collins, R. G., Ed. *Critical Essays* . . . , 178–179.

"The Enormous Radio"
Chesnick, Eugene. "The Domesticated Stroke . . . ," 534–535; rpt. Collins, R. G., Ed. *Critical Essays* . . . , 126–127.
Donaldson, Scott. "The Machine . . . ," 309–310; rpt. Collins, R. G., Ed. *Critical Essays* . . . , 139–140.
Gerlach, John. "Closure in Modern Short Fiction . . . ," 146–148.
Hunt, George W. *John Cheever* . . . , 238–240.
Sheidley, William E., and Ann Charters. *Instructor's Manual* . . . , 136.

"The Five-Forty-Eight"
Hunt, George W. *John Cheever* . . . , 88–89.
Rupp, Richard H. "Of That Time . . . ," 239–240.

"The Fourth Alarm"
Madden, David. *Instructor's Manual* . . . , 5th ed., 20–21; Madden, David, and Virgil Scott. *Instructor's Manual* . . . , 6th ed., 122–124.
Rupp, Richard H. "Of That Time . . . ," 237–238.

"The Geometry of Love"
Hunt, George W. *John Cheever* . . . , 273.

"Goodbye, My Brother"
*Bracher, Frederick. "John Cheever's Vision . . . ," 170–171.
Coale, Samuel. *John Cheever,* 61–64.
———. "Cheever and Hawthorne . . . ," 197–198.
Kendle, Burton. "The Passion of Nostalgia in the Short Stories of John
    Cheever," in Collins, R. G., Ed. *Critical Essays . . . ,* 220–221.
Rupp, Richard H. "Of That Time . . . ," 247–248.

"The Housebreaker of Shady Hill"
Chesnick, Eugene. "The Domesticated Stroke . . . ," 539–540; rpt. Collins,
    R. G., Ed. *Critical Essays . . . ,* 129–130.
Hunt, George W. *John Cheever . . . ,* 271–273.
Rupp, Richard H. "Of That Time . . . ," 240–241.

"The Jewels of the Cabots"
Rupp, Richard H. "Of That Time . . . ," 248–249.

"Just Tell Me Who It Was"
Hunt, George W. *John Cheever . . . ,* 263–267.

"The Lowboy"
Coale, Samuel. "Cheever and Hawthorne . . . ," 196–197.
Hunt, George W. *John Cheever . . . ,* 89–90.

"Marito in Citta"
Hunt, George W. *John Cheever . . . ,* 73–74.

"Metamorphoses"
Rupp, Richard H. "Of That Time . . . ," 236–237.

"O City of Broken Dreams"
Hunt, George W. *John Cheever . . . ,* 232–233.

"O Youth and Beauty!"
Hunt, George W. *John Cheever . . . ,* 267–271.
Moore, Stephen C. "The Hero on the 5:42: John Cheever's Short Fiction,"
    Western Hum R, 30 (1976), 148–149; rpt. Collins, R. G., Ed. *Critical Es-
    says . . . ,* 34.
Oriard, Michael. *Dreaming of Heroes . . . ,* 157–159.
Rupp, Richard H. "Of That Time . . . ," 238–239.

"The Ocean"
Kendle, Burton. "The Passion . . . ," 221–222.

"The Pot of Gold"
Perrine, Laurence, and Thomas R. Arp. *Instructor's Manual . . . ,* 6th ed., 11–
    12.

"The Scarlet Moving Van"
Bracher, Frederick. "John Cheever's Vision . . . ," 174–175.
Hunt, George W. *John Cheever . . . ,* 261–263.
Moore, Stephen C. "The Hero on the 5:42 . . . ," 150–152; rpt. Collins, R. G.,
    Ed. *Critical Essays . . . ,* 36–37.

"The Seaside Houses"
Hunt, George W. *John Cheever* . . . , 92–93.

"The Sorrows of Gin"
Hunt, George W. *John Cheever* . . . , 248–249.

"The Summer Farmer"
Hunt, George W. *John Cheever* . . . , 44–45.

"The Superintendent"
Hunt, George W. *John Cheever* . . . , 51–52.

"The Swimmer"
Blythe, Hal, and Charlie Sweet. "Classical Allusion in John Cheever's 'The Swimmer,'" *Notes Mod Am Lit,* 8, i (1984), Item 1.
———. "Perverted Sacraments in John Cheever's 'The Swimmer,'" *Stud Short Fiction,* 21 (1984), 393–394.
———. "Ironic Nature Imagery in 'The Swimmer,'" *Notes Contemp Lit,* 14, iv (1984), 3–4.
Chesnick, Eugene. "The Domesticated Stroke . . . ," 546–547; rpt. Collins, R. G., Ed. *Critical Essays* . . . , 135–136.
Hunt, George W. *John Cheever* . . . , 280–283.
Moore, Stephen C. "The Hero on the 5:42 . . . ," 149–150; rpt. Collins, R. G., Ed. *Critical Essays* . . . , 34–36.
Sheidley, William E., and Ann Charters. *Instructor's Manual* . . . , 138–139.
Sirlin, Rhoda, and David H. Richter. *Instructor's Manual* . . . , 16–17.
Slabey, Robert M. "John Cheever: The 'Swimming' of America," in Collins, R. G., Ed. *Critical Essays* . . . , 180–193.

"The Trouble of Marcie Flint"
Hunt, George W. *John Cheever* . . . , 245–246.
Reilly, Edward C. "Cheever's 'The Trouble of Marcie Flint': A Refutation and an Insight," *Notes Contemp Lit,* 12, ii (1982), 7.

"A Vision of the World"
Hunt, George W. *John Cheever* . . . , 257–259.
Kendle, Burton. "The Passion . . . ," 224–225.

"The World of Apples"
Collins, Robert G. "Beyond Argument: Post-Marital Man in John Cheever's Late Fiction," *Mosaic,* 17 (1984), 266–268.
Hunt, George W. *John Cheever* . . . , 285–292.
Kendle, Burton. "The Passion . . . ," 228–229.
Wain, John. "Literary, Witty, Civilized," *New Republic,* 168 (May 26, 1973), 24–26; rpt. Collins, R. G., Ed. *Critical Essays* . . . , 28–31.

"The Wrysons"
Hunt, George W. *John Cheever* . . . , 249–251.

ANTON CHEKHOV

"At Sea—A Sailor's Story"
Vernon, John. *Money and Fiction* . . . , 90–91.

"The Bet"
Polakiewicz, Leonard A. "Crime and Punishment in Čexov," in Leighton, Lauren G., Ed. *Studies in Honor* . . . , 55–58.

"The Betrothed"
Jackson, Robert L. " 'The Betrothed': Čexov's Last Testament," in Nilsson, Nils A. . . . *Russian Prose*, 11–25.

"The Black Monk"
O'Toole, L. Michael. *Structure, Style and Interpretation* . . . , 161–179.

"The Head Gardener's Story"
Polakiewicz, Leonard A. "Crime and Punishment . . . ," 58–65.

"In Exile"
Miller, James E., and Bernice Slote. *Instructor's Manual* . . . , 9.
Perrine, Laurence, and Thomas R. Arp. *Instructor's Manual* . . . , 6th ed., 71–72.

"In the Ravine" [same as "In the Gully"]
Nabokov, Vladimir. *Lectures on Russian Literature*, 263–282.

"The Lady with the Lapdog" [same as "The Lady with the Dog" or "The Lady with the Pet Dog"]
Bergman, David, Joseph de Roche, and Daniel M. Epstein. *Instructor's Manual* . . . , 43–44.
Nabokov, Vladimir. *Lectures on Russian Literature*, 255–263; rpt. in part Charters, Ann, Ed. *The Story and Its Writer* . . . , 1158–1164.
Sheidley, William E., and Ann Charters. *Instructor's Manual* . . . , 41–42.
Sirlin, Rhoda, and David H. Richter. *Instructor's Manual* . . . , 17–18.

"The Lament" [same as "Misery"]
Madden, David. *Instructor's Manual* . . . , 5th ed., 69–71; Madden, David, and Virgil Scott. *Instructor's Manual* . . . , 6th ed., 70–72.

"A Nervous Breakdown"
Shugg, Wallace. "Chekhov's Use of Irony in 'A Nervous Breakdown,' " *Stud Short Fiction*, 21 (1984), 395–398.

"Peasants"
O'Toole, L. Michael. *Structure, Style and Interpretation* . . . , 204–220.

"A Trifle from Real Life"
Sheidley, William E., and Ann Charters. *Instructor's Manual* . . . , 39–40.

"Ward No. 6"
Becker, George J. *Master European Realists* . . . , 218–219.

CHARLES W. CHESNUTT

"The Conjurer's Revenge"
Ferguson, SallyAnn H. "Chesnutt's 'The Conjurer's Revenge': The Economics of Direct Confrontation," *Obsidian*, 7, ii–iii (1981), 37–42.
Terry, Eugene. "The Shadow of Slavery in Charles Chesnutt's *The Conjure Woman*," *Ethnic Groups*, 4, i–ii (1982), 116–117.

"The Goophered Grapevine"
Terry, Eugene. "The Shadow . . . ," 110–111.

"The Gray Wolf's Ha'nt"
Gidden, Nancy A. "'The Gray Wolf's Ha'nt': Charles W. Chesnutt's Instructive Failure," *Coll Lang Assoc J*, 27 (1984), 406–410.
Terry, Eugene. "The Shadow . . . ," 121–122.

"Hot-Foot Hannibal"
Terry, Eugene. "The Shadow . . . ," 123.

"Mars Jeem's Nightmare"
Terry, Eugene. "The Shadow . . . ," 115–116.

"A Matter of Principle"
Gibson, Donald B. *The Politics* . . . , 131–133.

"Po' Sandy"
Terry, Eugene. "The Shadow . . . ," 112–113.

"Sis' Becky's Pickaninny"
Terry, Eugene. "The Shadow . . . ," 117–121.

"The Web of Circumstance"
Gibson, Donald B. *The Politics* . . . , 127–128.

"The Wife of His Youth"
Gibson, Donald B. *The Politics* . . . , 130–133.

GILBERT KEITH CHESTERTON

"The Blast of the Book"
Porter, Thomas E. "Gilbert Keith Chesterton," in Bargainnier, Earl F., Ed. *Twelve Englishmen* . . . , 82–83.

"The Duel of Dr. Hirsch"
Porter, Thomas E. ". . . Chesterton," 75.

"The Ghost of Gideon Wise"
Porter, Thomas E. ". . . Chesterton," 78–79.

"The Miracle of Moon Crescent"
Porter, Thomas E. ". . . Chesterton," 78.

"The Mistake of the Machine"
Porter, Thomas E. ". . . Chesterton," 75.

"The Paradise of Thieves"
Porter, Thomas E. ". . . Chesterton," 74–75.

"The Resurrection of Father Brown"
Porter, Thomas E. ". . . Chesterton," 77.

"The Scandal of Father Brown"
Porter, Thomas E. ". . . Chesterton," 81.

"The Secret Garden"
Porter, Thomas E. ". . . Chesterton," 71–72.

FRANK CHIN

"Food for All His Dead"
Kim, Elaine H. *Asian American Literature* . . . , 183–185.

"Goong Hai Fot Choy"
Kim, Elaine H. *Asian American Literature* . . . , 182–183.

KATE CHOPIN

"Athénaïse"
Stein, Allen F. *After the Vows* . . . , 180–184.

"Desirée's Baby"
Fluck, Winfried. "Tentative Transgressions: Kate Chopin's Fiction as a Mode of Symbolic Action," *Stud Am Fiction*, 10 (1982), 160–161.

"A Dresden Lady in Dixie"
Bonner, Thomas. "Christianity and Catholicism in the Fiction of Kate Chopin," *Southern Q*, 20, ii (1982), 120.

"The Going Away of Liza"
Stein, Allen F. *After the Vows* . . . , 178–180.

"Her Letters"
Stein, Allen F. *After the Vows* . . . , 186–188.

"In Sabine"
Stein, Allen F. *After the Vows* . . . , 189–190.

"A Lady of Bayou St. John"
Stein, Allen F. *After the Vows* . . . , 188–189.

"Loka"
Dyer, Joyce C. "Epiphanies Through Nature in the Stories of Kate Chopin,"
    Univ Dayton R, 16, iii (1983–1984), 75–76.

"Love on the Bon-Dieu"
Bonner, Thomas. "Christianity . . . ," 123–124.

"The Maid of Saint Phillippe"
Fluck, Winfried. "Tentative Transgressions . . . ," 159–160.

"A Matter of Prejudice"
Bonner, Thomas. "Christianity . . . ," 124–125.

"A Morning Walk"
Bonner, Thomas. "Christianity . . . ," 123.
Dyer, Joyce C. "Epiphanies . . . ," 79–80.

"A Point at Issue"
Stein, Allen F. *After the Vows . . . ,* 167–170.

"Regret"
Sheidley, William E., and Ann Charters. *Instructor's Manual . . . ,* 32.

"A Respectable Woman"
Fluck, Winfried. "Tentative Transgressions . . . ," 162.

"Ripe Figs"
Gardiner, Elaine. " 'Ripe Figs': Kate Chopin in Miniature," *Mod Fiction Stud,* 28
    (1982), 379–382.

"A Shameful Affair"
Dyer, Joyce. "Symbolic Setting in Kate Chopin's 'A Shameful Affair,' " *Southern
    Stud,* 20 (1981), 447–452.
Fluck, Winfried. "Tentative Transgressions . . . ," 161–162.

"The Storm"
Abcarian, Richard, and Marvin Klotz. *Instructor's Manual . . . ,* 3rd ed., 3–4.
Stein, Allen F. *After the Vows . . . ,* 205–206.

"The Story of an Hour"
Dyer, Joyce C. "Epiphanies . . . ," 77–78.
Miner, Madonne M. "Veiled Hints: An Affective Stylist's Reading of Kate Cho-
    pin's 'Story of an Hour,' " *Markham R,* 11 (Winter, 1982), 29–31.
Sirlin, Rhoda, and David H. Richter. *Instructor's Manual . . . ,* 19–20.
Stein, Allen F. *After the Vows . . . ,* 184–186.

"The Unexpected"
Dyer, Joyce C. "Epiphanies . . . ," 78–79.

"A Visit to Avoyelles"
Stein, Allen F. *After the Vows . . . ,* 177–178.

"The White Eagle"
Dyer, Joyce C. "A Note on Kate Chopin's 'The White Eagle,'" *Arizona Q,* 40 (1984), 189–192.

"Wiser Than a God"
Fluck, Winfried. "Tentative Transgressions . . . ," 158–159.
Stein, Allen F. *After the Vows* . . . , 166–167.

CHOU CH'ÜAN-P'ING

"His Confession"
Doležalová, Anna. "The Short Stories in *Creation Daily,*" *Asian & African Stud,* 9 (1973), 59–60.

SADEQ CHUBAK

"A Bouquet"
Dorri, J. "The Satire of Sadeq Chubak," in Ricks, Thomas M., Ed. *Critical Perspectives* . . . , 324–325.

"The Burning of Omar"
Dorri, J. "The Satire . . . ," 326–327.

"The First Day in the Grave"
Dorri, J. "The Satire . . . ," 325–326.

"Flowers of Flesh"
Mostaghel, Deborah M. "The Second Sadeq: The Short Stories of Iranian Writer Sadeq Chubak," in Ricks, Thomas M., Ed. *Critical Perspectives* . . . , 314–315.

"The Glass Eye"
Mostaghel, Deborah M. "The Second Sadeq . . . ," 312.

"Gravediggers"
Mostaghel, Deborah M. "The Second Sadeq . . . ," 317.

"Impoliteness"
Dorri, J. "The Satire . . . ," 323.

"The Last Lamp"
Dorri, J. "The Satire . . . ," 326.

"The Maroon Dress"
Mostaghel, Deborah M. "The Second Sadeq . . . ," 314.

"The Monkey Whose Master Had Died"
Mostaghel, Deborah M. "The Second Sadeq . . . ," 313–314.

"Monsieur Ilyas"
Mostaghel, Deborah M. "The Second Sadeq . . . ," 319.

"The Purple Dress"
Dorri, J. "The Satire . . . ," 322–323.

"Under the Red Light"
Mostaghel, Deborah M. "The Second Sadeq . . . ," 316.

ARTHUR C. CLARKE

"Breaking Strain"
Hollow, John. *Against the Night* . . . , 31–33.

"Critical Mass"
Hollow, John. *Against the Night* . . . , 100–102.

"The Curse"
Hollow, John. *Against the Night* . . . , 25–26.

"The Defenestration of Erminstrude Inch"
Hollow, John. *Against the Night* . . . , 96–98.

"Encounter at Dawn"
Hollow, John. *Against the Night* . . . , 22–24.

"Hide and Seek"
Brigg, Peter. "Three Styles of Arthur C. Clarke: The Projector, the Wit, and
    the Mystic," in Olander, Joseph D., and Martin H. Greenberg, Eds.
    Arthur C. Clarke, 30.

"History Lesson"
Brigg, Peter. "Three Styles . . . ," 27–28.
Rabkin, Eric S. *Arthur C. Clarke*, 55.

"The Lion of Comarre"
Hollow, John. *Against the Night* . . . , 33–37.

"The Man Who Ploughed the Sea"
Hollow, John. *Against the Night* . . . , 98–99.

"A Meeting with Medusa"
Hollow, John. *Against the Night* . . . , 156–159.

"Moving Spirit"
Hollow, John. *Against the Night* . . . , 92–93.

"The Next Tenants"
Hollow, John. *Against the Night* . . . , 96.

"The Nine Billion Names of God"
Fredericks, Casey. *The Future of Eternity . . .* , 80–81.
Hartwell, David. *Age of Wonders . . .* , 51–52.
Hollow, John. *Against the Night . . .* , 128–129.
Rabkin, Eric S. *Arthur C. Clarke,* 59–60.
————. "Introduction: Why Destroy the World?" in Rabkin, Eric S., Martin H.
    Greenberg, and Joseph D. Olander, Eds. *The End . . .* , ix-x.
Samuelson, David N. "Arthur C. Clarke," in Bleiler, Everett F., Ed. *Science Fic-
    tion Writers . . .* , 317.

"The Pacifist"
Hollow, John. *Against the Night . . .* , 95–96.

"The Parasite"
Hollow, John. *Against the Night . . .* , 30–31.

"Patent Pending"
Hollow, John. *Against the Night . . .* , 90.

"The Reluctant Orchid"
Hollow, John. *Against the Night . . .* , 91–92.

"Rescue Party"
Hollow, John. *Against the Night . . .* , 46–47.
Rabkin, Eric S. *Arthur C. Clarke,* 58.

"The Road to the Sea" [originally titled "Seeker of the Sphynx"]
Hollow, John. *Against the Night . . .* , 10–14.

"Robin Hood, F.R.S."
Rabkin, Eric S. *Arthur C. Clarke,* 57–58.

"Saturn Rising"
Cary, Meredith. "Faustus Now," *Hartford Stud Lit,* 4 (1977), 170–173.

"The Sentinel"
Hartwell, David. *Age of Wonders . . .* , 39–41.
Hollow, John. *Against the Night . . .* , 151–154.

"Silence, Please"
Hollow, John. *Against the Night . . .* , 99–100.

"The Songs of Distant Earth"
Rabkin, Eric S. *Arthur C. Clarke,* 54–55.

"The Star"
Bergman, David, Joseph de Roche, and Daniel M. Epstein. *Instructor's Man-
    ual . . .* , 8–9.
Born, Daniel. "Character as Perception: Science Fiction and the Christian Man
    of Faith," *Extrapolation,* 24 (1983), 257–259.
Fredericks, Casey. *The Future of Eternity . . .* , 79–80.
Hollow, John. *Against the Night . . .* , 14–19.

"Summertime on Icarus"
Brigg, Peter. "Three Styles . . . ," 18–19.

"Superiority"
Rabkin, Eric S. *Arthur C. Clarke,* 59.

"Time's Arrow"
Hollow, John. *Against the Night . . . ,* 21–22.
Rabkin, Eric S. *Arthur C. Clarke,* 53–54.

"Trouble with Time"
Pierce, Hazel B. *A Literary Symbiosis . . . ,* 128–129.

"The Ultimate Melody"
Hollow, John. *Against the Night . . . ,* 90–91.

"What Goes Up"
Brigg, Peter. "Three Styles . . . ," 30–31.
Hollow, John. *Against the Night . . . ,* 94–95.

HAL CLEMENT

"Impediment"
Hassler, Donald M. *The Comic Tone . . . ,* 105–106.

MILDRED CLINGERMAN

"The Day of the Green Velvet Cloak"
King, Betty. *Women of the Future . . . ,* 81–83.

STANTON A. COBLENTZ

"Manna from Mars"
Cioffi, Frank. *Formula Fiction? . . . ,* 70–71.

MATT COHEN

"The Cure"
Woodcock, George. *The World . . . ,* 129.

"Johnny Crackle Sings"
Woodcock, George. *The World . . . ,* 131–132.

"Korsoniloff"
Woodcock, George. *The World . . . ,* 130–131.

"Vogel"
Woodcock, George. *The World . . . ,* 129–130.

JOHN REECE COLE

"It Was So Late"
Copland, R. A. "The Fictive Picture: Cole, Courage, Davin," in Hankin, Cherry,
    Ed. . . . *New Zealand Short Story,* 69.

"The Sixty-Nine Club"
Copland, R. A. "The Fictive Picture . . . ," 68.

"Up at the Mammoth"
Copland, R. A. "The Fictive Picture . . . ," 69.

SIDONIE-GABRIELLE COLETTE

"Bella-Vista"
Stewart, Joan H. *Colette,* 112–114.

"The Cat"
Stewart, Joan H. *Colette,* 69–72.

"Chance Acquaintances"
Stewart, Joan H. *Colette,* 114–117.

"Chéri"
Stewart, Joan H. *Colette,* 53–58.

"Duo"
Stewart, Joan H. *Colette,* 72–75.

"Gigi"
Stewart, Joan H. *Colette,* 85–90.

"The Kepi"
Stewart, Joan H. *Colette,* 124–128.

"The Last of Chéri"
Stewart, Joan H. *Colette,* 53–58.

"The Photographer's Missus"
Stewart, Joan H. *Colette,* 120–123.

"The Rainy Moon"
Stewart, Joan H. *Colette,* 117–120.

"The Secret Woman"
Sirlin, Rhoda, and David H. Richter. *Instructor's Manual . . . ,* 20–21.

"The Tender Shoot"
Stewart, Joan H. *Colette,* 128–133.

"Le Toutounier"
Stewart, Joan H. *Colette,* 75–79.

JOHN COLLIER

"After the Ball"
Richardson, Betty. *John Collier,* 96–97.

"Another American Tragedy"
Richardson, Betty. *John Collier,* 76–77.

"Back for Christmas"
Richardson, Betty. *John Collier,* 92–93.

"The Chaser"
Abcarian, Richard, and Marvin Klotz. *Instructor's Manual . . . ,* 3rd ed., 4.

"De Mortuis"
Richardson, Betty. *John Collier,* 93–94.

"The Devil George and Rosie"
Richardson, Betty. *John Collier,* 83–84.

"Evening Primrose"
Richardson, Betty. *John Collier,* 99–100.

"Fallen Star"
Richardson, Betty. *John Collier,* 88–89.

"The Frog Prince"
Richardson, Betty. *John Collier,* 81–82.

"Gavin O'Leary"
Richardson, Betty. *John Collier,* 85–86.

"The Invisible Dove of Strathpheen Island"
Richardson, Betty. *John Collier,* 101–102.

"Mary"
Richardson, Betty. *John Collier,* 86–87.

"A Matter of Taste"
Richardson, Betty. *John Collier,* 78–79.

"The Right Side"
Richardson, Betty. *John Collier,* 87–88.

"Romance Lingers, Adventure Lives"
Richardson, Betty. *John Collier,* 103–104.

"Sleeping Beauty"
Richardson, Betty. *John Collier*, 79–81.

"Special Delivery"
Richardson, Betty. *John Collier*, 104–105.

"Variation on a Theme"
Richardson, Betty. *John Collier*, 84–85.

"Wet Saturday"
Richardson, Betty. *John Collier*, 94–95.

"Witch's Money"
Richardson, Betty. *John Collier*, 100–101.

"Without Benefit of Galsworthy"
Richardson, Betty. *John Collier*, 77–78.

WILKIE COLLINS

"Anne Rodway"
Peterson, Audrey. *Victorian Masters . . .* , 36.

"The Biter Bit"
Peterson, Audrey. *Victorian Masters . . .* , 36–37.

"The Dream Woman"
Peterson, Audrey. *Victorian Masters . . .* , 35.

"Plot in Private Life"
Peterson, Audrey. *Victorian Masters . . .* , 38.

"The Spectre of Tappington"
Lonoff, Sue. *Wilkie Collins . . .* , 181–183.

JOSEPH CONRAD

"Amy Foster"
Gillon, Adam. *Joseph Conrad*, 54–60.

"Because of the Dollars"
Schwartz, Daniel R. *Conrad . . .* , 28–29.

"The Black Mate"
Kramer, Dale. "The Maturity of Conrad's First Tale," *Stud Short Fiction*, 20
     (1983), 45–49.
Schwartz, Daniel R. *Conrad . . .* , 97–98.

"The Brute"
Gillon, Adam. *Joseph Conrad*, 134–135.

"Il Conde"
Ghose, Zulfikar. *The Fiction of Reality,* 122–130.

"The End of the Tether"
Land, Stephen K. *Paradox and Polarity . . . ,* 99–104.
Lombard, F. "Rhétorique et symbole dans 'The End of the Tether' de Joseph Conrad," in Greven, Hubert, Ed. *Rhétorique . . . ,* 182–190.

"Falk"
DiGaetani, John L. *Richard Wagner . . . ,* 33–35.
Land, Stephen K. *Paradox and Polarity . . . ,* 94–97.

"Freya of the Seven Isles"
DiGaetani, John L. *Richard Wagner . . . ,* 43–45.
Land, Stephen K. *Paradox and Polarity . . . ,* 178–179.
Schwartz, Daniel R. *Conrad . . . ,* 18–21.

"Heart of Darkness"
Apter, T. E. *Fantasy Literature . . . ,* 13–19.
Ashour, Radwa. "Significant Incongruities in Conrad's 'Heart of Darkness,'" *Neohelicon,* 10 (1983), 183–201.
Batchelor, John. *The Edwardian Novelists,* 36–45.
Brooks, Peter. "Un Rapport illisible: 'Coeur des ténèbres,'" *Poétique,* 11, xliv (1980), 472–489.
Bruffee, Kenneth A. *Elegiac Romance . . . ,* 99–103.
Cleary, Thomas R., and Terry G. Sherwood. "Women in Conrad's Ironical Epic: Virgil, Dante and 'Heart of Darkness,'" *Conradiana,* 16 (1984), 183–194.
Darras, Jacques. *Joseph Conrad . . . ,* 37–96.
Dobrinsky, Joseph. "From Whisper to Voice: Marlow's 'Accursed Inheritance' in 'Heart of Darkness,'" *Cahiers Victoriens et Edouardiens,* 16 (October, 1982), 77–104.
Edel, Leon. "Symbolic Statement: A Psychological View," in Balakian, Anna, Ed. *The Symbolist Movement . . . ,* 663–668.
Fisch, Harold. *A Remembered Future . . . ,* 24–26.
Fogel, Aaron. "The Mood of Overhearing in Conrad's Fiction," *Conradiana,* 15 (1983), 133–135.
Gilbert, Sandra M. "Rider Haggard's Heart of Darkness," in Slusser, George E., Eric S. Rabkin, and Robert Scholes, Eds. *Coordinates . . . ,* 136–138.
Gillon, Adam. *Joseph Conrad,* 68–81.
Golden, Kenneth L. "Joseph Conrad's Mr. Kurtz and Jungian *Enantiodromia,*" *Interpretations,* 13 (Fall, 1981), 31–38.
Goonetilleke, D. C. R. A. "Conrad's African Tales: Ironies of Progress," *Ceylon J Hum,* 2, i (1971), 86–97.
Hawkins, Hunt. "The Issue of Racism in 'Heart of Darkness,'" *Conradiana,* 14 (1982), 163–171.
Kawin, Bruce F. *The Mind of the Novel . . . ,* 52–66.
Kelleher, Victor. "Conrad and Barth: Nihilism Revisited," *Unisa Engl Stud,* 21, i (1983), 19–22.
Kennedy, Alan. *Meaning and Sign . . . ,* 44–50.
Khan, M. Y. "Thriller in Conrad's 'Heart of Darkness,'" *Indian J Engl Stud,* 20 (1980), 117–123.

Krupat, Arnold. "Antonymy, Language and Value in Conrad's 'Heart of Dark-
    ness,'" *Missouri R*, 3, i (1979), 63–85.
Land, Stephen K. *Paradox and Polarity* . . . , 67–78.
Laskowski, Henry J. "'Heart of Darkness': A Primer for the Holocaust," *Virginia
    Q R*, 58 (1982), 93–110.
Lindenbaum, Peter. "Hulks with One and Two Anchors: The Frame, Geo-
    graphical Details, and Ritual Process in 'Heart of Darkness,'" *Mod Fiction
    Stud*, 30 (1984), 703–710.
Lord, George deF. *Trials of the Self* . . . , 192–216.
Lorsch, Susan E. *Where Nature Ends* . . . , 109–114.
McLauchlan, Juliet. "The 'Value' and 'Significance' of 'Heart of Darkness,'"
    Conradiana, 15 (1983), 3–21.
Meckier, Jerome. "The Truth About Marlow," *Stud Short Fiction*, 19 (1982), 373–
    379.
Nalbantian, Suzanne. *Seeds of Decadence* . . . , 104–112.
Otten, Terry. *After Innocence* . . . , 79–96.
Parr, Susan R. *The Moral* . . . , 79–87.
Parry, Benita. *Conrad and Imperialism* . . . , 20–39.
Pettersson, Torsten. *Consciousness and Time* . . . , 78–84.
Sheidley, William E., and Ann Charters. *Instructor's Manual* . . . , 36–37.
Simpson, David. *Fetishism* . . . , 97–99.
Steiner, Joan E. "Modern Pharisees and False Apostles: Ironic New Testament
    Parallels in Conrad's 'Heart of Darkness,'" *Nineteenth-Century Fiction*, 37
    (1982), 75–96.
Watts, Cedric. "Conrad's Covert Plots and Transtextual Narratives," *Critical Q*,
    24, iii (1982), 56–57.
————. *The Deceptive Text* . . . , 74–84.
Wilding, Michael. "'Heart of Darkness,'" *Sydney Stud Engl*, 10 (1984–1985),
    85–102.

"The Idiots"
Bruffee, Kenneth A. *Elegiac Romance* . . . , 74–76.

"The Inn of the Two Witches"
Schwartz, Daniel R. *Conrad* . . . , 26–28.

"Karain"
Bruffee, Kenneth A. *Elegiac Romance* . . . , 78–84.
Pettersson, Torsten. *Consciousness and Time* . . . , 74–75.
Simpson, David. *Fetishism* . . . , 101–102.

"The Lagoon"
Bruffee, Kenneth A. *Elegiac Romance* . . . , 76–79.
DiGaetani, John L. *Richard Wagner* . . . , 31–32.
Hulseberg, Richard A. "'The Lagoon,'" in Dietrich, R. F., and Roger H. Sun-
    dell. *Instructor's Manual* . . . , 3rd ed., 93–96; 4th ed., 85–89.

"An Outcast of the Islands"
Land, Stephen K. *Paradox and Polarity* . . . , 28–38.

"An Outpost of Progress"
Goonetilleke, D. C. R. A. "Conrad's African Tales . . . ," 64–72.
Land, Stephen K. *Paradox and Polarity* . . . , 40–43.
Sheidley, William E., and Ann Charters. *Instructor's Manual* . . . , 33–34.

"The Partner"
Schwartz, Daniel R. *Conrad* . . . , 28–29.

"The Planter of Malata"
Land, Stephen K. *Paradox and Polarity* . . . , 208–210.
Schwartz, Daniel R. *Conrad* . . . , 29–32.

"Prince Roman"
Gillon, Adam. *Joseph Conrad*, 81–83.
Schwartz, Daniel R. *Conrad* . . . , 94–97.

"The Return"
Bruffee, Kenneth A. *Elegiac Romance* . . . , 93–95.
D'Elia, Gaetano. " 'The Return' and Conrad's Umbrella," *Polish R*, 29, iii (1984), 35–41.
Land, Stephen K. *Paradox and Polarity* . . . , 65–66.
Pettersson, Torsten. *Consciousness and Time* . . . , 69–71.

"The Secret Sharer"
*Abcarian, Richard, and Marvin Klotz. *Instructor's Manual* . . . , 2nd ed., 5–6; 3rd ed., 4–5.
Bergman, David, Joseph de Roche, and Daniel M. Epstein. *Instructor's Manual* . . . , 46.
Coates, Paul. *The Realist Fantasy Fiction* . . . , 115–117.
Crawford, John W. " 'The Secret Sharer': A Touchstone for 'William Wilson,' " *J Evolutionary Psych*, 5, i–ii (1984), 81–85.
Gillon, Adam. *Joseph Conrad*, 153–156.
Hawthorn, Jeremy. *Multiple Personality* . . . , 84–90.
Hodges, Robert R. "Deep Fellowship: Homosexuality and Male Bonding in the Life and Fiction of Joseph Conrad," *J Homosexuality*, 4 (1979), 384–387.
Land, Stephen K. *Paradox and Polarity* . . . , 167–173.
Otten, Terry. *After Innocence* . . . , 42–51.
Ressler, Steve. "Conrad's 'The Secret Sharer': Affirmation of Action," *Conradiana*, 16 (1984), 195–214.
Schwartz, Daniel R. *Conrad* . . . , 1–10.
Watts, Cedric. *The Deceptive Text* . . . , 84–90.

"The Shadow Line"
Gillon, Adam. *Joseph Conrad*, 156–167.
Land, Stephen K. *Paradox and Polarity* . . . , 211–219.
Oshimoto, Toshimasa. "On 'The Shadow Line': A Fine Work with Narrow Perspective," *Doshisha Stud Engl*, 25 (1980), 75–94.
Pettersson, Torsten. *Consciousness and Time* . . . , 184–187.
Schwartz, Daniel R. *Conrad* . . . , 82–86.
Watts, Cedric. "Conrad's Covert Plots . . . ," 54–55.

"A Smile of Fortune"
Land, Stephen K. *Paradox and Polarity* . . . , 178.
Schwartz, Daniel R. *Conrad* . . . , 10–18.
Watts, Cedric. "Conrad's Covert Plots . . . ," 55–56.

"The Tale"
Hinchcliffe, Peter. "Fidelity and Complicity in Kipling and Conrad: 'Sea Constable' and 'The Tale,'" *Engl Stud Canada,* 9 (1983), 350–381.
Schwartz, Daniel R. *Conrad* . . . , 101–103.
Tarinayya, M. "Kipling's 'Sea Constable' and Conrad's 'The Tale,'" *Lit Criterion,* 16, iii (1981), 32–49.

"Typhoon"
Gillon, Adam. *Joseph Conrad,* 50–53.
Land, Stephen K. *Paradox and Polarity* . . . , 92–94.
Ray, Martin. "Language and Silence in the Novels of Joseph Conrad," *Conradiana,* 16 (1984), 30–32.
Schuster, Charles I. "Comedy and the Limits of Language in Conrad's 'Typhoon,'" *Conradiana,* 16 (1984), 55–71.

"The Warrior's Soul"
Schwartz, Daniel R. *Conrad* . . . , 98–101.

"Youth"
Batchelor, John. *The Edwardian Novelists,* 34–36.
Darras, Jacques. *Joseph Conrad* . . . , 11–21.
Gillon, Adam. *Joseph Conrad,* 63–68.
Land, Stephen K. *Paradox and Polarity* . . . , 66–67.
Miller, James E., and Bernice Slote. *Instructor's Manual* . . . , 2nd ed., 9–10.
Pettersson, Torsten. *Consciousness and Time* . . . , 75–78.
Sirlin, Rhoda, and David H. Richter. *Instructor's Manual* . . . , 22–23.

BENJAMIN CONSTANT

"Adolphe"
Coman, Colette. "Le Paradoxe de la maxime dans 'Adolphe,'" *Romanic R,* 73 (1982), 195–208.
Evans, Martha N. "'Adolphe''s Appeal to the Reader," *Romanic R,* 73 (1982), 302–313.
Jones, Grahame C. "The Para-Story in Constant's 'Adolphe,'" *Nineteenth-Century French Stud,* 11, i–ii (1982–1983), 23–31.
Niess, Robert J. "Disenchanted Narcissus: 'Adolphe,'" *Nineteenth-Century French Stud,* 11, i–ii (1982–1983), 16–22.
Peterson, Carla L. "Constant's 'Adolphe,' James's 'The Beast in the Jungle,' and the Quest for the Mother," *Essays Lit,* 9 (1982), 224–239.

ROSE TERRY COOKE

"Alcedema Sparks; or Old and New"
Donovan, Josephine. *New England Local Color* . . . , 80.

"Clary's Trial"
Donovan, Josephine. *New England Local Color* . . . , 76–77.

"Doom and Dan"
Kleitz, Katherine. "Essence of New England: The Portraits of Rose Terry
   Cooke," *Am Transcendental Q,* 47–48 (1982), 130–131.

"Freedom Wheeler's Controversy with Providence"
Donovan, Josephine. *New England Local Color* . . . , 73–74.
Kleitz, Katherine. "Essence . . . ," 131–134.

"How Celia Changed Her Mind"
Donovan, Josephine. *New England Local Color* . . . , 77–78.

"Love"
Donovan, Josephine. *New England Local Color* . . . , 70–71.

"Mrs. Flint's Marriage Experience"
Donovan, Josephine. *New England Local Color* . . . , 74–75.

"The Mormon's Wife"
Donovan, Josephine. *New England Local Color* . . . , 70.

"Polly Mariner, Tailoress"
Donovan, Josephine. *New England Local Color* . . . , 77.

"The Ring Fetter"
Donovan, Josephine. *New England Local Color* . . . , 72.

"Too Late"
Kleitz, Katherine. "Essence . . . ," 134–137.

ROBERT COOVER

"The Babysitter"
Gordon, Lois. *Robert Coover* . . . , 120.
Karl, Frederick R. *American Fictions* . . . , 367–368.
Klinkowitz, Jerome. *The Self-Apparent Word* . . . , 35–37.
Pearce, Richard. *The Novel in Motion* . . . , 115–117.
Waugh, Patricia. *Metafiction* . . . , 138–139.

"The Brother"
Gordon, Lois. *Robert Coover* . . . , 105–106.

"The Door"
Gordon, Lois. *Robert Coover* . . . , 94–95.

"The Elevator"
Gordon, Lois. *Robert Coover* . . . , 110–112.

"The Gingerbread House"
Sirlin, Rhoda, and David H. Richter. *Instructor's Manual* . . . , 23–24.

"The Hat Act"
Gordon, Lois. *Robert Coover* . . . , 120–121.

"In a Train Station"
Gordon, Lois. *Robert Coover* . . . , 106.

"J's Marriage"
Gordon, Lois. *Robert Coover* . . . , 108–109.

"Klee Dead"
Gordon, Lois. *Robert Coover* . . . , 106–108.

"The Leper's Helix"
Gordon, Lois. *Robert Coover* . . . , 118–119.
Wilde, Alan. *Horizons of Assent* . . . , 151–152.

"The Magic Poker"
Gordon, Lois. *Robert Coover* . . . , 96–99.
Waugh, Patricia. *Metafiction* . . . , 139.

"The Marker"
Gordon, Lois. *Robert Coover* . . . , 103–105.

"The Milkmaid of Samaniago"
Gordon, Lois. *Robert Coover* . . . , 116–118.

"Morris in Chains"
Gordon, Lois. *Robert Coover* . . . , 99–100.

"Panel Game"
Gordon, Lois. *Robert Coover* . . . , 102–103.

"A Pedestrian Accident"
Gordon, Lois. *Robert Coover* . . . , 119–120.

"Quenby and Ola, Swede and Carl"
Gordon, Lois. *Robert Coover* . . . , 113–115.

"Romance of the Thin Man and the Fat Woman"
Gordon, Lois. *Robert Coover* . . . , 112–113.
Wilde, Alan. *Horizons of Assent* . . . , 153–155.

"Scene for Winter"
Gordon, Lois. *Robert Coover* . . . , 115–116.

"Spanking the Maid"
Varsava, Jerry A. "Another Exemplary Fiction: Ambiguity in Robert Coover's 'Spanking the Maid,'" *Stud Short Fiction*, 21 (1984), 235–241.

"The Wayfarer"
Gordon, Lois. *Robert Coover.* . . , 110.

A. E. COPPARD

"The Field of Mustard"
Escuret, Annie. "'Le Champ de séneve': Un Récit exemplaire," *Les Cahiers de
la Nouvelle*, 1 (1983), 23–38.

"The Higgler"
Sheidley, William E., and Ann Charters. *Instructor's Manual* . . . , 67–68.

DANIEL CORKERY

"The Eyes of the Dead"
Kilroy, James F. "Setting the Standards: Writers of the 1920s and 1930s," in
Kilroy, James F., Ed. *The Irish Short Story* . . . , 139–140.

JULIO CORTÁZAR

"Axolotl"
Rosser, Harry L. "The Voice of the Salamander: Cortázar's 'Axolotl' and the
Transformation of Self," *Kentucky Romance Q*, 30 (1983), 419–427.
Sánchez, Marta E. "A View from Inside the Fishbowl: Julio Cortázar's 'Axo-
lotl,'" in Slusser, George E., Eric S. Rabkin, and Robert Scholes, Eds. *Bridges
to Fantasy*, 38–50.
Zamora, Lois P. "Voyeur/Voyant: Julio Cortázar's Spatial Esthetic," *Mosaic*, 14
(Fall, 1981), 48.

"The Band"
Morello-Frosch, Marta. "La Banda de los otros: Política fantástica en un cuento
de Julio Cortázar," in Schwartz Lerner, Lía, and Isaías Lerner, Eds. *Homenaje a Ana María Barrenechea*, 497–502.

"Bestiary"
Bockus Aponte, Barbara. "El niño como testigo: La visión infantil en el cuento
hispanoamericano contemporáneo," *Explicación de Textos Literarios*, 11, i
(1982), 12–19.
Concha, Jaime. "'Bestiary' de Julio Cortázar o el tigre en la biblioteca," *Hispamerica*, 11, xxxii (1982), 3–21.
Muñoz, Mario. "Realidad e intimidad en 'Bestiary,'" *Texto Crítico*, 7, xx (1981),
31–37.

"Blow-Up" [same as "Las babas del diablo"]
McMurray, George R. "The Spanish American Short Story from Borges to the
Present," in Peden, Margaret S., Ed. *The Latin American Short Story* . . . ,
113–114.
Madden, David, and Virgil Scott. *Instructor's Manual* . . . , 6th ed., 115–117.
Pérez, Genaro J. "Auto-Referential Elements in 'Blow-Up' and 'The Gates of
Heaven,'" *R Contemp Fiction*, 3, iii (1983), 48–51.
Zamora, Lois P. "Voyeur/Voyant . . . ," 48–53.

"Cambio de Luces"
Standish, Peter. "Cortázar's Latest Stories," *Revista de Estudios Hispánicos*, 16, i (1982), 57.

"La caras de medalla"
Standish, Peter. "Cortázar's Latest Stories," 55–56.

"Circe"
Lopes, Ruth S. B. "Circe: O Feitiço e o Enigma," *Cadernos de Lingüística*, 6 (December, 1981), 124–128.

"Clone"
Gyurko, Lanin A. "Art and the Demonic in Three Stories by Cortázar," *Symposium*, 37, i (1983), 22–25.

"Continuity of Parks"
Tittler, Jonathan. "La continuidad en 'Continuidad de los parques,'" *Critica Hispánica*, 6 (1984), 167–174.

"The Gates of Heaven"
Pérez, Genaro J. "Auto-Referential Elements . . . ," 48–51.

"Graffiti"
Villardi, Raquel. "'Graffiti': Leitura Refletida," *Revista Brasileira*, 5, xi (1983), 49–52.

"The Health of the Sick Ones"
Earle, Peter G. "Dreams of Creation: Short Fiction in Spanish America," *Denver Q*, 12 (1977), 76–77.

"Historia"
Johnston, Craig P. "Irony and the Double in Short Fiction of Julio Cortázar and Severo Sarduy," *J Spanish Stud: Twentieth Century*, 5, ii (1977), 112–113.

"House Taken Over"
Terramorsi, Bernard. "Maison occupée de Julio Cortázar: Le démon de la solitude," *Cahiers du Centre d'Études*, 9 (1984), 33–41.

"Junto al Río Cenizas de Rosa"
Johnston, Craig P. "Irony and the Double . . . ," 116–121.

"Letter to a Girl in Paris"
Muñoz, Willy O. "La alegoría de modernidad en 'Carta a una señorita en Paris,'" *Inti*, 15 (Spring, 1982), 33–40.

"The Maenads"
Gyurko, Lanin A. "Art and the Demonic . . . ," 36–46.

"The Night Face Up"
Daniel, Lee A. "*Realismo mágico*: True Realism with a Pinch of Magic," *So Central Bull*, 42 (1982), 129–130.
McMurray, George R. ". . . Borges to the Present," 112–113.
Zamora, Lois P. "Voyeur/Voyant . . . ," 47–48.

"Los pasos en las huellas"
Gyurko, Lanin A. "Artist and Critic as Self and Double in Cortázar's 'Los pasos
en las huellas,'" *Hispania*, 65, iii (1982), 352–364.
Standish, Peter. "Cortázar's Latest Stories," 57–58.

"The Pursuer"
Zamora, Lois P. "Voyeur/Voyant . . . ," 53–57.

"Queremos tanto a Glenda"
Gyurko, Lanin A. "Art and the Demonic . . . ," 25–28, 35.

"Reunión"
Standish, Peter. "Cortázar's Latest Stories," 44–46.

"Reunión con un cículo rojo"
Standish, Peter. "Cortázar's Latest Stories," 59.

"Segunda vez"
Standish, Peter. "Cortázar's Latest Stories," 59–60.

"The Southern Throughway"
McMurray, George R. ". . . Borges to the Present," 121–122.
Planells, Antonia. "'La autopista del sur' o la dinámica de la incomunicación
humana," *Explicación de Textos Literarios*, 12, i (1983–1984), 3–9.

"Summer"
McMurray, George R. ". . . Borges to the Present," 132–133.

"Usted se tendió a tu lado"
Standish, Peter. "Cortázar's Latest Stories," 60–61.

"Verana"
Standish, Peter. "Cortázar's Latest Stories," 51–52.

"Vientos alisios"
Standish, Peter. "Cortázar's Latest Stories," 46–51.

ODYLO COSTA FILHO

"A Faca e o Rio"
D'Amaral, Marcio T. "Meaning and Sense, Speech and Language: A Semiotic
and Philosophic Investigation," *Dispositio*, 6 (1981), 153–163.

JAMES COURAGE

"Flowers on the Table"
Copland, R. A. "The Fictive Picture: Cole, Courage, Davin," in Hankin, Cherry,
Ed. . . . *New Zealand Short Story*, 72.

PETER COWAN

"Drift"
Bennett, Bruce. "The Short Story," in Bennett, Bruce, Ed. . . . *Western Australia,*
    127–128.

"The Red-Backed Spider"
Bennett, Bruce. "The Short Story," 131.

"The Unploughed Land"
Bennett, Bruce. "The Short Story," 130–131.

DINAH MULOCK CRAIK

"Parson Garland's Daughter"
Mitchell, Sally. *The Fallen Angel* . . . , 117.

STEPHEN CRANE

"The Blue Hotel"
Cate, Hollis. "Seeing and Not Seeing in 'The Blue Hotel,'" *Coll Lit,* 9 (1982),
    150–152.
Colvert, James B. *Stephen Crane,* 125–126.
Conder, John J. *Naturalism* . . . , 30–42.
Miller, James E., and Bernice Slote. *Instructor's Manual* . . . , 2nd ed., 10.
Neglia, Erminio G. "Fictional Death in Stephen Crane's 'The Blue Hotel' and
    Jorge Luis Borges' 'El Sur,'" *Chasqui,* 10, ii–iii (1981), 20–25.
Proudfit, Charles L. "Parataxic Distortion and Group Process in Stephen
    Crane's 'The Blue Hotel,'" *Hartford Stud Lit,* 15, i (1984), 47–53.
Wolford, Chester L. *The Anger* . . . , 101–114.

"The Bride Comes to Yellow Sky"
*Abcarian, Richard, and Marvin Klotz. *Instructor's Manual* . . . , 2nd ed., 6–7;
    3rd ed., 4–5.
*Monteiro, George. "'The Bride Comes to Yellow Sky,'" in Dietrich, R. F., and
    Roger H. Sundell. *Instructor's Manual* . . . , 4th ed., 121–132.
Perrine, Laurence, and Thomas R. Arp. *Instructor's Manual* . . . , 6th ed., 52–
    53.
Petry, Alice H. "Crane's 'The Bride Comes to Yellow Sky,'" *Explicator,* 42, i
    (1983), 45–47.
Sheidley, William E., and Ann Charters. *Instructor's Manual* . . . , 52–53.
Wolford, Chester L. *The Anger* . . . , 94–101.

"Death and the Child"
Colvert, James B. *Stephen Crane,* 114–115.
Wolford, Chester L. *The Anger* . . . , 137–140.

"An Experiment in Luxury"
*Trachtenberg, Alan. "Experiments in Another Country: Stephen Crane's City
    Sketches," in Sundquist, Eric J., Ed. *American Realism* . . . , 149–153.

"An Experiment in Misery"
*Trachtenberg, Alan. "Experiments in Another Country...," 149–153.

"George's Mother"
Colvert, James B. *Stephen Crane,* 72–75.

"Killing His Bear"
Wolford, Chester L. *The Anger...,* 145–146.

"Maggie: A Girl of the Streets"
Colvert, James B. *Stephen Crane,* 49–53.
Conder, John J. *Naturalism...,* 42–52.
Fine, David M. "Abraham Cahan, Stephen Crane, and the Romantic Tenement
    Tale of the Nineties," *Am Stud,* 14, i (1973), 95–107.
Graff, Aida F. "Metaphor and Metonymy: The Two Worlds of Crane's 'Mag-
    gie,'" *Engl Stud Canada,* 8 (1982), 422–436.
Hapke, Laura. "The Alternate Fallen Woman in 'Maggie: A Girl of the
    Streets,'" *Markham R,* 12 (1983), 41–43.
Hussman, Lawrence E. "The Fate of the Fallen Woman in 'Maggie' and *Sister
    Carrie,*" in Horn, Pierre L., and Mary B. Pringle, Eds. *The Image of the
    Prostitute...,* 93–97.
Krause, Sydney J. "The Surrealism of Crane's Naturalism in 'Maggie,'" *Am Lit
    Realism,* 16 (1983), 253–261 [copyright 1984].
*Pizer, Donald. *Realism and Naturalism...,* 2nd ed., 143–153.
Westbrook, Perry D. *Free Will...,* 132–133.
Wolford, Chester L. *The Anger...,* 78–87.

"The Men in the Storm"
*Trachtenberg, Alan. "Experiments in Another Country...," 145–147.

"The Monster"
Wolford, Chester L. *The Anger...,* 87–93.

"Moonlight on the Snow"
Colvert, James B. *Stephen Crane,* 148–149.
Wolford, Chester L. *The Anger...,* 115–117.

"The Octopus"
Wolford, Chester L. *The Anger...,* 30–31.

"The Open Boat"
*Broer, Lawrence R. "'The Open Boat,'" in Dietrich, R. F., and Roger H. Sun-
    dell. *Instructor's Manual...,* 4th ed., 60–68.
Colvert, James B. *Stephen Crane,* 105–107.
Conder, John J. *Naturalism...,* 22–30.
Kennedy, X. J. *Instructor's Manual...,* 3rd ed., 36–38.
Schirmer, Gregory A. "Becoming Interpreters: The Importance of Tone in
    Crane's 'The Open Boat,'" *Am Lit Realism,* 15 (1982), 221–231.
Sheidley, William E., and Ann Charters. *Instructor's Manual...,* 48–50.
Sirlin, Rhoda, and David H. Richter. *Instructor's Manual...,* 25–26.
Wolford, Chester L. *The Anger...,* 129–134.

"The Reluctant Voyagers"
Wolford, Chester L. *The Anger...*, 25–28.

"Uncle Jake and the Bell Handle"
Wolford, Chester L. *The Anger...*, 24–25.

"The Upturned Face"
Christophersen, Bill. "Stephen Crane's 'The Upturned Face' as Expressionist
    Fiction," *Arizona Q,* 38 (1982), 147–161.

WILLIAM F. CRANE

"The Year 1899"
Wu, William F. *The Yellow Peril...*, 43–44.

CUBENA [CARLOS GUILLERMO WILSON]

"The Family"
Smart, Ian I. "The West Indian Presence in the Works of Three Central Amer-
    ican Writers," in Dorsey, David F., Phanuel A. Egejuru, and Stephen Ar-
    nold, Eds. *Design and Intent...*, 130.

RAY CUMMINGS

"The Girl in the Golden Atom"
Sampson, Robert. *Yesterday's Faces, II...*, 197–199.

"Tama of the Light Country"
Sampson, Robert. *Yesterday's Faces, II...*, 244–245.

ROBERT BONTINE CUNNINGHAME GRAHAM

"Animula Vagula"
Watts, Cedric, and Laurence Davies. *Cunninghame Graham...*, 284.

"Christie Christison"
Watts, Cedric, and Laurence Davies. *Cunninghame Graham...*, 202–205.

"The Gold Fish"
Watts, Cedric, and Laurence Davies. *Cunninghame Graham...*, 192–193.

"Snaekoll's Saga"
Watts, Cedric, and Laurence Davies. *Cunninghame Graham...*, 159–160.

DANIEL CURLEY

"Who, What, When, Where—Why?"
Robinson, James C. "1968–1980: Experiment and Tradition," in Weaver, Gordon, Ed. *The American Short Story, 1945–1980,* 101–102.

BERNARD DADIÉ

"The Confession"
Tollerson, Marie S. *Mythology . . . ,* 30–32.

"The Death of Men"
Tollerson, Marie S. *Mythology . . . ,* 22–23.

"The Light of the Setting Sun"
Tollerson, Marie S. *Mythology . . . ,* 30–32.

"The Pitcher"
Tollerson, Marie S. *Mythology . . . ,* 62–63.

"The Saltworks of the Old Woman of Amafi"
Tollerson, Marie S. *Mythology . . . ,* 20–22.

"Spider and His Son"
Tollerson, Marie S. *Mythology . . . ,* 42–43.

"Spider, Bad Father"
Tollerson, Marie S. *Mythology . . . ,* 95–100.

"Taweloro"
Tollerson, Marie S. *Mythology . . . ,* 12–13.

ULADZIMIR DADZIJONAU

"Bielaziersk Diary"
Rich, Vera. "Jewish Themes and Characters in Belorussian Texts," in Blum, Jakub, and Vera Rich. *The Image of the Jew . . . ,* 244.

STIG DAGERMAN

"The Hanging Tree"
Thompson, Laurie. *Stig Dagerman,* 63–64.

"The Man Condemned to Death"
Thompson, Laurie. *Stig Dagerman,* 67–68.

"Our Nocturnal Resort"
Thompson, Laurie. *Stig Dagerman,* 68–70.

"Where Is My Iceland Jumper?"
Thompson, Laurie. *Stig Dagerman,* 62–63.

HANS DAIBER

"It Is Written"
Koelb, Clayton. *The Incredulous Reader...*, 94–95.

VLADIMIR DAL [pseudonym: COSSACK LUGANSKY]

"The Gypsy Girl"
Mersereau, John. *Russian Romantic Fiction*, 297.

"Schlemiel"
Mersereau, John. *Russian Romantic Fiction*, 297–298.

ACHMED DANGOR

"Waiting for Leila"
Barnett, Ursula A. *A Vision of Order...*, 210–212.

GABRIELE D'ANNUNZIO

"The Idolators"
Sarkany, Stéphane. "'Gli idolatri' de Gabriele D'Annunzio," *Quaderni d'Italian-istica*, iii, i (1982), 44–50.

RUBÉN DARÍO

"The Case of Señorita Amelia"
Anderson-Imbert, Enrique. "Rubén Darío and the Fantastic Element in Liter-ature," trans. Anne Bonner, in González-Gerth, Miguel, and George D. Schade, Eds. *Rubén Darío...*, 110.

"Cuento de Noche Buena"
Anderson-Imbert, Enrique. "... Fantastic Element in Literature," 105–106.

"The Death of the Empress of China"
Lindstrom, Naomi. "The Spanish American Short Story from Echeverría to Quiroga," in Peden, Margaret S., Ed. *The Latin American Short Story...*, 60–61.

"La pesadilla de Honorio"
Anderson-Imbert, Enrique. "... Fantastic Element in Literature," 109–110.

"Thanathopía"
Anderson-Imbert, Enrique. "... Fantastic Element in Literature," 108.

"The Three Magian Queens"
Anderson-Imbert, Enrique. "... Fantastic Element in Literature," 105.

"Verónica"
Anderson-Imbert, Enrique. ". . . Fantastic Element in Literature," 106.

MANOJ DAS

"Birds in the Twilight"
Raja, P. "The Short Stories of Manoj Das," *Indian Lit,* 25, v (1982), 59–60.

"The Brothers"
Raja, P. "The Short Stories . . . ," 61–62.

"The Kite"
Raja, P. "The Short Stories . . . ," 60.

"Lakshmi's Adventure"
Raja, P. "The Short Stories . . . ," 60–61.

"Mystery of the Missing Cap"
Raja, P. "The Short Stories . . . ," 56–59.

RAI KRISHNA DAS

"Secrets of Ramani"
Pande, Trilochan. "Folk Elements in the Modern Hindi Short Story," *Folklore* (Calcutta), 231 (1979), 144.

GUY DAVENPORT

"Apples and Pears"
Bawer, Bruce. "The Stories of Guy Davenport: Fiction à la Fourier," *New Criterion,* 3, iv (1984), 11–14.

"The Bowmen of Shu"
Bawer, Bruce. "The Stories of Guy Davenport . . . ," 8–10.

"The Chair"
Bawer, Bruce. "The Stories of Guy Davenport . . . ," 11.

"Fifty-Seven Views of Fujiyama"
Bawer, Bruce. "The Stories of Guy Davenport . . . ," 10–11.

DAN DAVIN

"Below the Heavens"
Bertram, James. *Dan Davin,* 16–17.

"Growing Up"
Copland, R. A. "The Fictive Picture: Cole, Courage, Davin," in Hankin, Cherry,
    Ed. . . . *New Zealand Short Story,* 73–74.

"The Locksmith Laughs Last"
Copland, R. A. "The Fictive Picture . . . ," 79–80.

"Mortal"
Bertram, James. *Dan Davin,* 17–18.

"Not Substantial Things"
Bertram, James. *Dan Davin,* 19.

"Psychological Warfare at Cassino"
Copland, R. A. "The Fictive Picture . . . ," 79.

"The Quiet One"
Bertram, James. *Dan Davin,* 52–53.

"That Golden Time"
Copland, R. A. "The Fictive Picture . . . ," 75–76.

"The Wall of Doors"
Bertram, James. *Dan Davin,* 55–56.
Copland, R. A. "The Fictive Picture . . . ," 80.

REBECCA HARDING DAVIS

"John Lamar"
Cohn, Jan. "The Negro Character in Northern Magazine Fiction of the 1860's,"
    New England Q, 43 (1970), 582–584.

EMMA F. DAWSON

"The Dramatic in My Destiny"
Wu, William F. *The Yellow Peril . . . ,* 46–47.

L. SPRAGUE DE CAMP

"The Blue Giraffe"
Meyers, Walter E. *Aliens and Linguists . . . ,* 55–56.

"The Green Magician"
Fredericks, Casey. *The Future of Eternity . . . ,* 110–111.

"Hyperpilosity"
Cioffi, Frank. *Formula Fiction? . . . ,* 101–102.

"The Wall of Serpents"
Fredericks, Casey. *The Future of Eternity* . . . , 110–111.

L. SPRAGUE DE CAMP and ROBERT E. HOWARD

"The Road of Eagles"
Schweitzer, Darrell. *Conan's World* . . . , 24–25.

MIRIAM ALLEN DE FORD

"The Crib Circuit"
King, Betty. *Women of the Future* . . . , 116–117.

"The Eel"
Pierce, Hazel B. *A Literary Symbiosis* . . . , 153–154.

JOHN DE FOREST

"The Apotheosis of Ki"
Meyers, Walter E. *Aliens and Linguists* . . . , 89–90.

"A Gentleman of the Old South"
Cohn, Jan. "The Negro Character in Northern Magazine Fiction of the 1860's,"
   New England Q, 43 (1970), 581.

WALTER DE LA MARE

"All Hallows"
Reid, Forrest. *Walter de la Mare* . . . , 226–230.

"The Almond Tree"
Reid, Forrest. *Walter de la Mare* . . . , 73–78.

"Crossings"
Reid, Forrest. *Walter de la Mare* . . . , 237–238.

"The Dancing Princess"
Manlove, C. N. *The Impulse* . . . , 5–7.

"The Green Room"
Reid, Forrest. *Walter de la Mare* . . . , 230–232.

"An Ideal Craftsman"
Reid, Forrest. *Walter de la Mare* . . . , 78–86.

"Miss Duveen"
Reid, Forrest. *Walter de la Mare* . . . , 92–94.

"Miss Jemima"
Reid, Forrest. *Walter de la Mare* . . . , 236–237.

"Missing"
Reid, Forrest. *Walter de la Mare* . . . , 211–215.

"Out of the Deep" [originally titled "The Bell"]
Reid, Forrest. *Walter de la Mare* . . . , 224–226.

"A Recluse"
Reid, Forrest. *Walter de la Mare* . . . , 232–236.

"The Riddle"
Knieger, Bernard. "De la Mare's 'The Riddle,'" *Explicator,* 40 (1982), 43–44.
Reid, Forrest. *Walter de la Mare* . . . , 95–100.

"Seaton's Aunt"
Reid, Forrest. *Walter de la Mare* . . . , 217–224.

SAMUEL R. DELANY

"Cage of Brass"
Weedman, Jane B. *Samuel R. Delany,* 31–32.

"Corona"
Weedman, Jane B. *Samuel R. Delany,* 28–29.

"Dog in a Fisherman's Net"
Weedman, Jane B. *Samuel R. Delany,* 28.

"Driftglass"
Clareson, Thomas D. "Notes on 'Driftglass,'" in Clareson, Thomas D., Ed. *A
    Spectrum* . . . , 263–266.
Weedman, Jane B. *Samuel R. Delany,* 29.

"High Weir"
Weedman, Jane B. *Samuel R. Delany,* 32.

"Night and the Loves of Joe Dicostanzo"
Weedman, Jane B. *Samuel R. Delany,* 33.

"Power of the Nail"
Weedman, Jane B. *Samuel R. Delany,* 32.

"The Star Pit"
Weedman, Jane B. *Samuel R. Delany,* 26–27.

"We in Some Strange Power's Employ, Move on a Rigorous Line" [same as
    "Lines of Power"]
Weedman, Jane B. *Samuel R. Delany,* 31.

AUGUSTO MARIO DELFINO

"The Telephone"
Smyth, Philip. "Time and Memory in a Story by Augusto Mario Delfino," *Lang Q,* 21, iii–iv (1983), 17–18.

LESTER DEL REY

"The Day Is Done"
Cioffi, Frank. *Formula Fiction?* . . . , 125–126.

"Helen O'Loy"
King, Betty. *Women of the Future* . . . , 46–47.
Reilly, Robert. "How Machines Become Human: Process and Attribute," in Dunn, Thomas P., and Richard D. Erlich, Eds. *The Mechanical God* . . . , 154–164.

"Nerves"
Wolfe, Gary K. "Nuclear Rhetoric in Del Rey's 'Nerves,'" *Foundation,* 32 (November, 1984), 68–75.

MARCO DENEVI

"The Butterfly"
McMurray, George R. "The Spanish American Short Story from Borges to the Present," in Peden, Margaret S., Ed. *The Latin American Short Story* . . . , 119.

LESTER DENT

"Read 'Angelfish'"
Murray, Will. "Lester Dent: The Last of the Joe Shaw's *Black Mask* Boys," *Clues,* 2, ii (1981), 131–132.

"Sail"
Murray, Will. "Lester Dent . . . ," 131.

FEDERICO DE ROBERTO

"La 'Cocotte'"
Maugeri Salerno, Mirella. "Espressionismo e figuratività: Luce e colore nella novella derobertiana 'La "Cocotte,"'" in Zappulla Muscarà, Sarah, Ed. *Federico De Roberto,* 69–76.

CHARLES DE VET and KATHARINE MacLEAN

"Second Game"
Pierce, Hazel B. *A Literary Symbiosis* . . . , 187–188.

AUGUSTO D'HALMAR [AUGUSTO GEOMINE THOMPSON]

"In the Province"
Brushwood, John S. "The Spanish American Short Story from Quiroga to Borges," in Peden, Margaret S., Ed. *The Latin American Short Story* . . . , 74–75.

AHMADOU MAPADÉ DIAGNE

"Malic's Three Wishes"
Blair, Dorothy S. *Senegalese Literature* . . . , 40–42.

RAMÓN DÍAZ SÁNCHEZ

"La virgen no tiene cara"
Persico, Alan. "'La virgen no tiene cara': A Portrayal of Rebellion in Afro-Hispanic Narrative," *Afro-Hispanic R,* 3, iii (1984), 11–15.

PHILIP K. DICK

"A. Lincoln, Simulacra"
Robinson, Kim S. *The Novels of Philip K. Dick,* 105–106.

"The Days of Perky Pat"
Pierce, Hazel. *Philip K. Dick,* 23–24.

"The Defenders"
Abrash, Merritt. "Elusive Utopias: Societies as Mechanisms in the Early Fiction of Philip K. Dick," in Erlich, Richard D., and Thomas P. Dunn, Eds. *Clockwork Worlds* . . . , 116–117.
Warrick, Patricia S. "The Labyrinthian Process of the Artificial: Philip K. Dick's Androids and Mechanical Constructs," in Greenberg, Martin H., and Joseph D. Olander, Eds. *Philip Dick,* 193.
———, and Martin H. Greenberg, Eds. *Robots, Androids* . . . , 9.

"The Electric Ant"
Warrick, Patricia S. "The Labyrinthian Process . . . ," 212–213.

"Faith of Our Fathers"
Pierce, Hazel. *Philip K. Dick,* 44–45.
Warren, Eugene. "The Search for Absolutes," in Greenberg, Martin H., and Joseph D. Olander, Eds. *Philip Dick,* 182–187.

"The Father-Thing"
Warren, Eugene. "The Search . . . ," 162–163.

"If There Were No Benny Cemoli"
Warren, Eugene. "The Search . . . ," 164–165.

"The Imposter"
Warrick, Patricia S., and Martin H. Greenberg, Eds. *Robots, Androids* . . . , 77.

"The Little Movement"
Warrick, Patricia S., and Martin H. Greenberg, Eds. *Robots, Androids* . . . , 1.

"Man, Android and Machine"
Pierce, Hazel. *Philip K. Dick,* 49.

"Second Variety"
Warrick, Patricia S. "The Labyrinthian Process . . . ," 193.

"To Serve the Master"
Warrick, Patricia S., and Martin H. Greenberg, Eds. *Robots, Androids* . . . , 167.

CHARLES DICKENS

"The Black Veil"
Thomas, Deborah A. *Dickens and the Short Story,* 15–17.

"The Boarding-House"
Thomas, Deborah A. "Dickens's Mrs. Lirripet and the Evolution of a Feminine
    Stereotype," *Dickens Stud Annual,* 6 (1977), 157–159.

"The Bride's Chamber"
Thomas, Deborah A. *Dickens and the Short Story,* 110–112.

"The Drunkard's Death"
Thomas, Deborah A. *Dickens and the Short Story,* 17–19.

"George Silverman's Explanation"
Thomas, Deborah A. *Dickens and the Short Story,* 17–19.

"Mrs. Lirripet's Legacy"
Thomas, Deborah A. "Dickens's Mrs. Lirripet . . . ," 156.

"Mrs. Lirripet's Lodging"
Thomas, Deborah A. "Dickens's Mrs. Lirripet . . . ," 155–156.

"The Signalman"
Mengel, Ewald. "The Structure and Meaning of Dickens's 'The Signalman,'"
    Stud Short Fiction, 20 (1983), 271–280.

ISAK DINESEN [BARONESS KAREN BLIXEN]

"Babette's Feast"
Thurman, Judith. *Isak Dinesen* . . . , 329–330.

"The Blank Page"
Froula, Christine. "When Eve Reads Milton: Undoing the Canonical Economy,"
    Critical Inquiry, 10 (1983), 321–347.
Stambaugh, Sara. "Witch as Quintessential Woman: A Context for Isak Dine-
    sen's Fiction," *Mosaic*, 16, iii (1983), 88–89.

"The Cardinal's Third Tale"
Thurman, Judith. *Isak Dinesen* . . . , 363–365.

"Carnival"
Greene-Gantzberg, Vivian and Arthur R. "Karen Blixen's 'Carnival,'" *Scandi-
    navia*, 22 (1983), 159–170.

"Converse at Night in Copenhagen"
Thurman, Judith. *Isak Dinesen* . . . , 360–361.

"Copenhagen Season"
Thurman, Judith. *Isak Dinesen* . . . , 401–404.

"Grjotgard Alvesøn and Aud"
Thurman, Judith. *Isak Dinesen* . . . , 80–81.

"The Hermits"
Thurman, Judith. *Isak Dinesen* . . . , 81–82.

"The Monkey"
James, Sibyl. "Gothic Transformations: Isak Dinesen and the Gothic," in
    Fleenor, Julian E., Ed. *The Female Gothic*, 143–149.

"The Old Chevalier"
Sheidley, William E., and Ann Charters. *Instructor's Manual* . . . , 85–86.
Whissen, Thomas. "The Magic Circle: The Role of the Prostitute in Isak Di-
    nesen's Gothic Tales," in Horn, Pierre L., and Mary B. Pringle, Eds. *The
    Image of the Prostitute* . . . , 44–49.

"The Ploughman"
Thurman, Judith. *Isak Dinesen* . . . , 82–84.

"Sorrow-Acre"
Aiken, Susan H. "Dinesen's 'Sorrow-Acre': Tracing the Woman's Line," *Contemp
    Lit*, 25 (1984), 156–186.
Miller, James E., and Bernice Slote. *Instructor's Manual* . . . , 2nd ed., 15–16.
Sirlin, Rhoda, and David H. Richter. *Instructor's Manual* . . . , 27–28.

"Tempest"
Thurman, Judith. *Isak Dinesen* . . . , 410–415.

DING LING

"After He Left"
Feuerwerker, Yi-tsi Mei. *Ding Ling's Fiction* . . . , 34–35.

"A Certain Night"
Feuerwerker, Yi-tsi Mei. *Ding Ling's Fiction* . . . , 69–71.

"The Day Before New Year's Day"
Feuerwerker, Yi-tsi Mei. *Ding Ling's Fiction* . . . , 58–60.

"The Diary of Miss Sophie"
Feuerwerker, Yi-tsi Mei. *Ding Ling's Fiction* . . . , 42–51.

"Flight"
Feuerwerker, Yi-tsi Mei. *Ding Ling's Fiction* . . . , 64–66.

"Flood"
Feuerwerker, Yi-tsi Mei. *Ding Ling's Fiction* . . . , 66–68.

"From Night Till Daybreak"
Feuerwerker, Yi-tsi Mei. *Ding Ling's Fiction* . . . , 71–72.

"Mengke"
Feuerwerker, Yi-tsi Mei. *Ding Ling's Fiction* . . . , 25–26.

"Miss Amao"
Feuerwerker, Yi-tsi Mei. *Ding Ling's Fiction* . . . , 26–27.

"The Net of the Law"
Feuerwerker, Yi-tsi Mei. *Ding Ling's Fiction* . . . , 63–64.

"New Faith"
Feuerwerker, Yi-tsi Mei. *Ding Ling's Fiction* . . . , 107–108.

"New Year's Day"
Feuerwerker, Yi-tsi Mei. *Ding Ling's Fiction* . . . , 23–25.

"Night"
Feuerwerker, Yi-tsi Mei. *Ding Ling's Fiction* . . . , 109–110.

"On a Small Steamboat"
Feuerwerker, Yi-tsi Mei. *Ding Ling's Fiction* . . . , 32–33.

"One Day"
Feuerwerker, Yi-tsi Mei. *Ding Ling's Fiction* . . . , 81–88.

"The People's Artist Li Bu"
Feuerwerker, Yi-tsi Mei. *Ding Ling's Fiction* . . . , 115–121.

"A Secret Visitor on a Moonlit Night"
Feuerwerker, Yi-tsi Mei. *Ding Ling's Fiction* . . . , 22–23.

"A Small Room in Qingyun Lane"
Feuerwerker, Yi-tsi Mei. *Ding Ling's Fiction* . . . , 27–28.

"A Suicide's Diary"
Feuerwerker, Yi-tsi Mei. *Ding Ling's Fiction* . . . , 38–39.

"Tian Family Village"
Feuerwerker, Yi-tsi Mei. *Ding Ling's Fiction* . . . , 60–62.

"We Need *Zawen*"
Feuerwerker, Yi-tsi Mei. *Ding Ling's Fiction* . . . , 100–101.

"When I Was in Xia Village"
Feuerwerker, Yi-tsi Mei. *Ding Ling's Fiction* . . . , 112–114.

"Yecao"
Feuerwerker, Yi-tsi Mei. *Ding Ling's Fiction* . . . , 37–38.

"Yuan Guangfa"
Feuerwerker, Yi-tsi Mei. *Ding Ling's Fiction* . . . , 111–112.

BIRAGO DIOP

"Bouki and His Egg"
Tollerson, Marie S. *Mythology* . . . , 66–67.

"Bouki, Boarder"
Tollerson, Marie S. *Mythology* . . . , 105–110.

"The Breasts"
Tollerson, Marie S. *Mythology* . . . , 12.

"The Bull of Bouki"
Tollerson, Marie S. *Mythology* . . . , 66–67.

"The Calabashes of Kouss"
Tollerson, Marie S. *Mythology* . . . , 51–53.

"Dof Diop"
Tollerson, Marie S. *Mythology* . . . , 50–51.

"The Folly of the Dervish"
Tollerson, Marie S. *Mythology* . . . , 11–12.

"The Hind and the Two Hunters"
Tollerson, Marie S. *Mythology* . . . , 53–54.

"Khary Gaye"
Tollerson, Marie S. *Mythology* . . . , 5–7.

"Samba of the Night"
Tollerson, Marie S. *Mythology* . . . , 27–28.

"Sarzan"
Blair, Dorothy S. *Senegalese Literature* . . . , 59–60.

STEPHEN DIXON

"Fourteen Stories"
Klinkowitz, Jerome. *The Self-Apparent Word* . . . , 95–98.

"Goodbye to Goodbye"
Klinkowitz, Jerome. *The Self-Apparent Word* . . . , 136–137.

"Time to Go"
Klinkowitz, Jerome. *The Self-Apparent Word* . . . , 107–108.

ASSIA DJEBAR [FATIMA-ZOHRA IMALAYEN]

"Algerian Women in Their Quarters"
Monego, Joan P. *Maghrebian Literature* . . . , 140–141.

MARY DODGE

"Our Contraband"
Cohn, Jan. "The Negro Character in Northern Magazine Fiction in the 1860's,"
New England Q, 43 (1970), 580–581.

JOSÉ DONOSO

"The Güero"
Boschetto, Sandra M. "La inversión de la figura femenina en 'El güero' de José
Donoso," *Critica Hispánica,* 6, i (1984), 1–10.
Muñoz, Willy O. "El retorno a las fuentes primarias en 'El güero' de José
Donoso," in Paolini, Gilbert, Ed. *LA CHISPA '83* . . . , 187–194.

"A Lady"
Alonso, Carlos J. "Pathetic Falla-City: Donoso's 'Una señora,'" *Symposium,* 38
(1984), 267–277.

"Paseo"
Bockus Aponte, Barbara. "El niño como testigo: La visión infantil en el cuento
hispanoamericano contemporáneo," *Explicación de Textos Literarios,* 11, i
(1982), 12–19.

"Santelices"
Iñigo-Madrigal, Luis. "'Santelices,' capas medias, fascismo," *Texto Critico,* 7
(1981), 251–264.

SONDRA DORMAN

"Building Block"
Podojil, Catherine. "Sisters, Daughters, and Aliens," in Riley, Dick, Ed. *Critical Encounters [I]* . . . , 82–83.

FYODOR DOSTOEVSKY

"The Crocodile"
Miller, James E., and Bernice Slote. *Instructor's Manual* . . . , 2nd ed., 6.

"The Double"
Bakhtin, Mikhail M. "The Dismantled Consciousness: An Analysis of 'The Double,'" in Jackson, Robert L., Ed. . . . *New Perspectives*, 19–34.
———. *Problems* . . . , 224–227.
Hawthorn, Jeremy. *Multiple Personality* . . . , 48–59.
Jones, John. *Dostoevsky*, 175–195.
Katz, Michael R. *Dreams* . . . , 88–90.
Rosenthal, Richard J. "Dostoevsky's Use of Projection: Psychic Mechanism as Literary Form in 'The Double,'" *Dostoevsky Stud*, 3 (1982), 79–86.

"The Gambler"
*Savage, D. S. "Dostoevsky: The Idea of 'The Gambler,' in Jackson, Robert L., Ed. . . . *New Perspectives*, 111–125.

"The Grand Inquisitor"
Catteau, Jacques. "The Paradox of the Legend of the Grand Inquisitor in *The Brothers Karamazov*," in Jackson, Robert L., Ed. . . . *New Perspectives*, 243–254.
Weisberg, Richard H. *The Failure* . . . , 65–70.

"Mr. Prokharchin"
Katz, Michael R. *Dreams* . . . , 91–93.
Meyer, Priscilla. "Dostoevskij, Naturalist Poetics and 'Mr. Procharčin,'" *Russian Lit*, 10 (1981), 163–190.

"Notes from Underground"
Bakhtin, Mikhail. *Problems* . . . , 50–53.
Clardy, Jesse V. and Betty S. *The Superfluous Man* . . . , 37–39.
Edwards, T. R. N. *Three Russian Writers* . . . , 14–22.
Jackson, Robert L. *The Art of Dostoevsky* . . . , 171–188; rpt. Jackson, Robert L., Ed. . . . *New Perspectives*, 66–81.
Moravcevich, Nicholas. "The Romanticization of the Prostitute in Dostoevsky's Fiction," in Horn, Pierre L., and Mary B. Pringle, Eds. *The Image of the Prostitute* . . . , 56–58.
Nabokov, Vladimir. *Lectures on Russian Literature*, 115–121.
Palumbo, Donald. "The Paradoxical and Constructive Uses of Irony in Dostoyevsky's Novels," *Liberal & Fine Arts R*, 4, ii (1984), 30–33.
Rosenshield, Gary. "Artistic Consistency in 'Notes from Underground'—Part One," in Leighton, Lauren G., Ed. *Studies in Honor* . . . , 11–21.
Weisberg, Richard H. *The Failure* . . . , 65–70.

"Uncle's Dream"
Bakhtin, Mikhail. *Problems . . .* , 161–162.

ELLEN DOUGLAS

"Hold On"
Manning, Carol S. "Ellen Douglas: Moralist and Realist," in Prenshaw,
Peggy W., Ed. *Women Writers . . .* , 124–125.

"I Just Love Carrie Lee"
Manning, Carol S. "Ellen Douglas . . . ," 125–128.

"Jesse"
Manning, Carol S. "Ellen Douglas . . . ," 122–124.

FREDERICK DOUGLASS

"The Heroic Slave"
Stepto, Robert B. "Storytelling in Early Afro-American Fiction: Frederick
Douglass' 'The Heroic Slave,'" *Georgia R,* 36 (1982), 355–368.

COLEMAN DOWELL

"If Beggars Were Horses"
Fuchs, Miriam. "Coleman Dowell's Short Stories," *R Contemp Fiction,* 2, iii
(1982), 120–121.

"The Moon, the Owl, My Sister"
Fuchs, Miriam. ". . . Short Stories," 119–120.

"My Father Was a River"
Fuchs, Miriam. ". . . Short Stories," 118–119.

ARTHUR CONAN DOYLE

"The Adventure of the Speckled Band"
Bergman, David, Joseph de Roche, and Daniel M. Epstein. *Instructor's Man-
ual . . .* , 16–17.
Sirlin, Rhoda, and David H. Richter. *Instructor's Manual . . .* , 29–30.

"The Musgrave Ritual"
Brooks, Peter. *Reading for the Plot . . .* , 23–28.
Naugrette, Jean-Pierre. "Le Rituel du récit: Lecture d'une nouvelle de Conan
Doyle," *Littérature,* 53 (February, 1984), 46–58.

"The Noble Bachelor"
Foss, T. F. "The Bounder and the Bigamist," *Baker Street J,* 34, i (1984), 8–11.

"The Priory School"
Kamil, Irving. "The Priory School Map: A Re-Examination," *Baker Street J*, 34,
    i (1984), 12–16.

MARGARET DRABBLE

"Crossing the Alps"
Campbell, Jane. "Becoming Terrestrial: The Short Stories of Margaret Drab-
    ble," *Critique*, 25, i (1983), 31.
Mayer, Suzanne H. "Margaret Drabble's Short Stories: Worksheets for Her
    Novels," in Schmidt, Dorey, and Jan Seale, Eds. *Margaret Drabble . . .*, 82–
    83.
Moran, Mary H. *Margaret Drabble . . .*, 90–91.

"A Day in the Life of a Smiling Woman"
Campbell, Jane. "Becoming Terrestrial . . . ," 32–33.
Mayer, Suzanne H. "Margaret Drabble's Short Stories . . . ," 87–88.

"The Gifts of War"
Campbell, Jane. "Becoming Terrestrial . . . ," 31, 38–39.
Mayer, Suzanne H. "Margaret Drabble's Short Stories . . . ," 83–85.
Moran, Mary H. *Margaret Drabble . . .*, 99–100.

"Hassan's Tower"
Campbell, Jane. "Becoming Terrestrial . . . ," 28–29.
Mayer, Suzanne H. "Margaret Drabble's Short Stories . . . ," 77–79.

"A Pyrrhic Victory"
Campbell, Jane. "Becoming Terrestrial . . . ," 30–31.

"The Reunion" [same as "Faithful Lovers"]
Campbell, Jane. "Becoming Terrestrial . . . ," 29.
Moran, Mary H. *Margaret Drabble . . .*, 89–90.

"A Success Story"
Campbell, Jane. "Becoming Terrestrial . . . ," 31–32, 40–41.
Mayer, Suzanne H. "Margaret Drabble's Short Stories . . . ," 86–87.

"A Voyage to Cythera"
Campbell, Jane. "Becoming Terrestrial . . . ," 29, 37.
Mayer, Charles W. "Drabble and James: 'A Voyage to Cythera' and 'In the
    Cage,'" *Stud Short Fiction*, 21 (1984), 57–63.
Mayer, Suzanne H. "Margaret Drabble's Short Stories . . . ," 79–80.
Moran, Mary H. *Margaret Drabble . . .*, 91–93.

THEODORE DREISER

"Butcher Rogaum's Door"
Griffin, Joseph. "'Butcher Rogaum's Door': Dreiser's Early Tale of New York,"
    Am Lit Realism, 17 (1984), 24–31.

"Chains" [originally titled "Love"]
Hussman, Lawrence E. *Dreiser and His Fiction* . . . , 120–121.

"A Doer of the Word"
Hussman, Lawrence E. *Dreiser and His Fiction* . . . , 45–46.

"Free"
Hussman, Lawrence E. *Dreiser and His Fiction* . . . , 116–119.

"The Lost Phoebe"
Hussman, Lawrence E. *Dreiser and His Fiction* . . . , 119–120.
Kimbel, Ellen. "The American Short Story: 1900–1920," in Stevick, Philip, Ed. *The American Short Story, 1900–1945*, 59–60.

"McEwen of the Shining Slave Makers"
Singh, Brij M. "Dreiser's First Short Story, 'McEwen of the Shining Slave Makers': A Composite Study," *Panjab Univ Research Bull*, 13, i (1982), 21–29.

"Marriage—For One"
Hussman, Lawrence E. *Dreiser and His Fiction* . . . , 121–122.

"Married"
Hussman, Lawrence E. *Dreiser and His Fiction* . . . , 121–122.

"Nigger Jeff"
Kimbel, Ellen. "The American Short Story . . . ," 60–61.
Pizer, Donald. *Realism and Naturalism* . . . , 2nd ed., 187–188.

"The Second Choice"
Hussman, Lawrence E. *Dreiser and His Fiction* . . . , 115–116.

"The Shadow" [originally titled "Jealousy"]
Hussman, Lawrence E. *Dreiser and His Fiction* . . . , 122–123.

ANNETTE VON DROSTE-HÜLSHOFF

"Die Judenbuche"
Rölleke, Heinz. "Annette von Droste Hülshoff: 'Die Judenbuche,'" in Lützeler, Paul M., Ed. *Romane und Erzählungen* . . . , 335–353.

NIKOLAI DUBOV

"Escape"
Brown, Edward J. . . . *Since the Revolution*, 3rd ed., 333–334.

IHNAT DUBROUSKI

"The Komsomol Writer Solam Alejchem"
Rich, Vera. "Jewish Themes and Characters in Belorussian Texts," in Blum, Jakub, and Vera Rich. *The Image of the Jew . . .* , 248–251.

GUADALUPE DUEÑAS

"The Story of Mariquita"
Minc, Rose S. "Guadalupe Dueñas: Texto y contexto de la nueva alquimia del poder," *Discurso Literario,* 1 (1984), 231–241.

MAURICE DUGGAN

"Along Rideout Road"
Davin, Dan. "Maurice Duggan's *Summer in the Gravel Pit,*" in Hankin, Cherry, Ed. . . . *New Zealand Short Story,* 159–161.

"Blues for Miss Laverty"
Davin, Dan. ". . . *Summer in the Gravel Pit,*" 157–158.

"For the Love of Rupert"
Davin, Dan. ". . . *Summer in the Gravel Pit,*" 158–159.

"Salvation Sunday"
Davin, Dan. ". . . *Summer in the Gravel Pit,*" 154.

"The Wits of Willie Graves"
Davin, Dan. ". . . *Summer in the Gravel Pit,*" 156–157.

QUINCE DUNCAN

"Ancestral Myths"
Smart, Ian. *Central American Writers . . .* , 62–63.

"La luz del vigia"
Smart, Ian I. "The West Indian Presence in the Works of Three Central American Writers," in Dorsey, David F., Phanuel A. Egejuru, and Stephen Arnold, Eds. *Design and Intent . . .* , 126.

"La rebelión Pocomita"
Davis, Lisa E. "The World of the West Indian Black in Central America: The Recent Works of Quince Duncan," in Luis, William, Ed. *Voices from Under . . .* , 156–157.
Smart, Ian I. "The West Indian Presence . . . ," 126–127.

"The Signalman's Light"
Smart, Ian. *Central American Writers . . .* , 59.

SARA JEANNETTE DUNCAN

"The Hesitation of Miss Anderson"
Tausky, Thomas E. *Sara Jeannette Duncan* . . . , 227–228.

"An Impossible Ideal"
Tausky, Thomas E. *Sara Jeannette Duncan* . . . , 229–234.

"A Mother in India"
Tausky, Thomas E. *Sara Jeannette Duncan* . . . , 228–229.

"The Pool in the Desert"
Tausky, Thomas E. *Sara Jeannette Duncan* . . . , 226–227.

ASHLEY SHEUN DUNN

"No Man's Land"
Kim, Elaine H. *Asian American Literature* . . . , 223–224.

LORD DUNSANY [EDWARD JOHN MORETON DRAX PLUNKETT]

"Two Bottles of Relish"
*Dietrich, R. F. " 'Two Bottles of Relish,' " in Dietrich, R. F., and Roger H. Sundell. *Instructor's Manual* . . . , 4th ed., 92–94.

MARGUERITE DURAS

"Moderato cantabile"
Hirsch, Marianne. "Gender, Reading, and Desire in 'Moderato Cantabile,' " *Twentieth Century Lit*, 28 (Spring, 1982), 69–85.
Kauffmann, Judith. "Musique et matière romanesque dans 'Moderato cantabile' de Marguerite Duras," *Études Littéraires*, 15 (1982), 97–112.
Moskos, George. "Women and Fiction in Marguerite Duras's 'Moderato cantabile,' " *Contemp Lit*, 25 (1984), 28–52.
O'Callaghan, Raylene. "A Construction of Desire: *Le Voyeur* and 'Moderato cantabile,' " *New Zealand J French Stud*, 5, i (1984), 25–48.
Rava, Susan. "Marguerite Duras: Women's Language in Men's Cities," in Squier, Susan M., Ed. *Women Writers* . . . , 35–44.

WARREN EARLE

"In Re State vs. Forbes"
Pierce, Hazel B. *A Literary Symbiosis* . . . , 37–38.

EDITH EATON

"The Chinese Lily"
Ling, Amy. "Edith Eaton, Pioneer Chinamerican Writer and Feminist," *Am Lit Realism*, 16 (1983), 296–297 [copyright 1984].

"Her Chinese Husband"
Ling, Amy. "Edith Eaton . . . ," 295.

"The Inferior Woman"
Ling, Amy. "Edith Eaton . . . ," 296.

"Story of One White Woman Who Married a Chinese"
Ling, Amy. "Edith Eaton . . . ," 294–295.

ESTEBAN ECHEVERRÍA

"The Matador"
Lindstrom, Naomi. "The Spanish American Short Story from Echeverría to Quiroga," in Peden, Margaret S., Ed. *The Latin American Short Story . . . ,* 36–41.

MARIA EDGEWORTH

"Angelina; or l'Amie Inconnue"
Donovan, Josephine. *New England Local Color . . . ,* 21–22.

JOSEPH VON EICHENDORFF

"Die Entführung"
Menhennet, Alan. *The Romantic Movement,* 210.

"From the Life of a Good-for-Nothing"
Menhennet, Alan. *The Romantic Movement,* 211–212.

CYPRIAN O. D. EKWENSI

"African Alchemist"
Lindfors, Bernth. *Early Nigerian Literature,* 43–44.

"Death on the Bus"
Lindfors, Bernth. *Early Nigerian Literature,* 45–46.

"Loco Town"
Lindfors, Bernth. *Early Nigerian Literature,* 45.

ASGHAR ELAHI

"The Holy Day of Ashura"
[Anonymous]. "An Analysis of Modern Persian Engagé Literature," in Ricks, Thomas M., Ed. *Critical Perspectives . . .*, 98–99.

GEORGE ELIOT [MARY ANN EVANS]

"Amos Barton"
Ashton, Rosemary. *George Eliot,* 23–26.
Gilbert, Sandra M., and Susan Gubar. *The Madwoman . . .*, 485.
Jumeau, Alain. *"Scenes of Clerical Life*: George Eliot sur les chemins de les 'conversion,'" *Études Anglaises,* 33 (1980), 272–275.

"Brother Jacob"
Mann, Karen B. *The Language . . .*, 18–24.
Sziotny, J. S. "Two Confectioners the Reverse of Sweet: The Role of Metaphor in Determining George Eliot's Use of Experience," *Stud Short Fiction,* 21 (1984), 127–144.

"Janet's Repentance"
Ashton, Rosemary. *George Eliot,* 26–27.
Gilbert, Sandra M., and Susan Gubar. *The Madwoman . . .*, 487–490.
Jumeau, Alain. *"Scenes of Clerical Life . . . ,"* 271–272, 277–279.
Mann, Karen B. *The Language . . .*, 114–115.

"The Lifted Veil"
Gilbert, Sandra M., and Susan Gubar. *The Madwoman . . .*, 458–477.
Gray, B. M. "Pseudoscience and George Eliot's 'The Lifted Veil,'" *Nineteenth-Century Fiction,* 36 (1982), 407–423.
Handley, Graham. "'The Lifted Veil' and Its Relation to George Eliot's Fiction," *George Eliot Fellowship R,* 15 (1984), 64–69.
Mann, Karen B. *The Language . . .*, 115–117.
Miyoshi, Masao. *The Divided Self . . .*, 228–231.
Viera, Carroll. "'The Lifted Veil' and George Eliot's Aesthetic," *Stud Engl Lit,* 24 (1984), 749–767.

"Mr. Gilfil's Love Story"
Ashton, Rosemary. *George Eliot,* 26.
Gilbert, Sandra M., and Susan Gubar. *The Madwoman . . .*, 485–487.
Jumeau, Alain. *"Scenes of Clerical Life . . . ,"* 271, 275–277.
Mann, Karen B. *The Language . . .*, 152–154.

SALVADOR ELIZONDO

"History According to Pao Cheng"
McMurray, George R. "The Spanish American Short Story from Borges to the Present," in Peden, Margaret S., Ed. *The Latin American Short Story . . .*, 120.

STANLEY ELKIN

"The Bailbondsman"
Ditsky, John. "'Death Grotesque as Life': The Fiction of Stanley Elkin," *Hollins Critic,* 19, iii (1982), 8.

"The Conventional Wisdom"
Bargen, Doris G. *The Fiction . . . ,* 53.

"Fifty Dollars"
Bargen, Doris G. *The Fiction . . . ,* 92–97.

"I Look Out for Ed Wolfe"
Bargen, Doris G. *The Fiction . . . ,* 83–91.
Ditsky, John. "'Death Grotesque as Life' . . . ," 4–5.

"In the Alley"
Bargen, Doris G. *The Fiction . . . ,* 50–52.

"On a Field, Rampant"
Bargen, Doris G. *The Fiction . . . ,* 38–39.

"The Party"
Bargen, Doris G. *The Fiction . . . ,* 67–70.

"A Poetics for Bullies"
Bargen, Doris G. *The Fiction . . . ,* 46–50.

"A Sound of Distant Thunder"
Bargen, Doris G. *The Fiction . . . ,* 59–63.

HARLAN ELLISON

"A Boy and His Dog"
Slusser, George E. "Harlan Ellison," in Bleiler, Everett F., Ed. *Science Fiction Writers . . . ,* 365.

"Catman"
Slusser, George E. "Harlan Ellison," 366.

"Croatoan"
Slusser, George E. "Harlan Ellison," 366.

"Deathbird"
Slusser, George E. "Harlan Ellison," 366.

"I Have No Mouth and I Must Scream"
Cobb, Joann P. "Medium and Message in Ellison's 'I Have No Mouth and I Must Scream,'" in Myers, Robert E., Ed. *The Intersection . . . ,* 159–167.
Sullivan, Charles W. "Harlan Ellison and Robert A. Heinlein: The Paradigm Makers," in Erlich, Richard D., and Thomas P. Dunn, Eds. *Clockwork Worlds . . . ,* 98–102.

"The Place with No Name"
Fredericks, Casey. *The Future of Eternity* . . . , 26–28.

"Repent, Harlequin! Said the Ticktockman"
*Abcarian, Richard, and Marvin Klotz. *Instructor's Manual* . . . , 7–8; 3rd ed.,
    6–7.
Slusser, George E. "Harlan Ellison," 363–364.

"The Resurgence of Miss Ankle-Strap Wedgie"
Slusser, George E. "Harlan Ellison," 362–363.

"Run for the Stars"
Slusser, George E. "Harlan Ellison," 364.

"Santa Claus vs. S.P.I.D.E.R."
Pierce, Hazel B. *A Literary Symbiosis* . . . , 181–182.

"Silence in Gehenna"
Slusser, George E. "Harlan Ellison," 365–366.

"Worlds to Kill"
Slusser, George E. "Harlan Ellison," 364.

RALPH ELLISON

"Battle Royal"
Perrine, Laurence, and Thomas R. Arp. *Instructor's Manual* . . . , 6th ed., 59–
    61.
Sheidley, William E., and Ann Charters. *Instructor's Manual* . . . , 142–144.

"Flying Home"
Ogunyemi, Chikwenye O. " 'The Old Order Shall Pass': The Examples of
    'Flying Home' and 'Barbados,' " *Stud Short Fiction*, 20 (1983), 24–28.

"King of the Bingo Game"
Madden, David. *Instructor's Manual* . . . , 5th ed., 89; Madden, David, and Virgil
    Scott. *Instructor's Manual* . . . , 6th ed., 94–95.
Sirlin, Rhoda, and David H. Richter. *Instructor's Manual* . . . , 31–32.

PER OLOV ENQUIST

"After the Classical Highpoints"
Shideler, Ross. *Per Olov Enquist* . . . , 110–111.

"The Anxiety of the Loyal Souls"
Shideler, Ross. *Per Olov Enquist* . . . , 104–107.

"Balance in Santa Monica"
Shideler, Ross. *Per Olov Enquist* . . . , 111.

"From a Guinea Pig's Life"
Shideler, Ross. *Per Olov Enquist* . . . , 109–110.

"The Tracks in the Sea of Tranquillity"
Shideler, Ross. *Per Olov Enquist* . . . , 107–109.

AHMED ESSOP

"Film"
Barnett, Ursula A. *A Vision of Order* . . . , 207.

"Gerry's Brother"
Barnett, Ursula A. *A Vision of Order* . . . , 204.

"The Hajji"
Barnett, Ursula A. *A Vision of Order* . . . , 204–205.

"Mr. Moonreddy"
Barnett, Ursula A. *A Vision of Order* . . . , 207–208.

JOHN K. EWERS

"Carew's Place"
Bennett, Bruce. "The Short Story," in Bennett, Bruce, Ed. . . . *Western Australia,*
    125–126.

PHILIP JOSÉ FARMER

"Don't Wash the Carats"
Hasenberg, Peter. "Science Fiction als Rorschach-Test: Philip José Farmers
    'Don't Wash the Carats,'" *Anglistik & Englischunterricht,* 23 (1984), 141–
    157.

"Father"
Fredericks, Casey. *The Future of Eternity* . . . , 158–159.

"The Lovers"
Tweet, Roald D. "Philip José Farmer," in Bleiler, Everett F., Ed. *Science Fiction
    Writers* . . . , 370.

"The Öogenesis of Bird City"
Brizzi, Mary T. *Philip José Farmer,* 41.

"Prometheus"
Meyers, Walter E. *Aliens and Linguists* . . . , 35–36.

"Riders of the Purple Wage"
Brizzi, Mary T. *Philip José Farmer,* 40–47.

"Sketches Among the Ruins of My Mind"
Brizzi, Mary T. *Philip José Farmer,* 62–63.

"Son"
Fredericks, Casey. *The Future of Eternity . . . ,* 157–158.

JAMES T. FARRELL

"Studs"
Watson, James G. "The American Short Story: 1930–1945," in Stevick, Philip,
    Ed. *The American Short Story, 1900–1945,* 111–112.

"When Boyhood Dreams Come True"
Rohrberger, Mary. "The Question of Regionalism: Limitation and Transcen-
    dence," in Stevick, Philip, Ed. *The American Short Story, 1900–1945,* 172–
    173.

WILLIAM FAULKNER

"Ad Astra"
Bradford, M. E. "The Anomaly of Faulkner's World War I Stories," *Mississippi
    Q,* 36 (1983), 246–249.
Nordanberg, Thomas. *Cataclysm . . . ,* 37–40.

"All the Dead Pilots"
Nordanberg, Thomas. *Cataclysm . . . ,* 35–36.

"Barn Burning"
*Broer, Lawrence R. "'Barn Burning,'" in Dietrich, R. F., and Roger H. Sun-
    dell. *Instructor's Manual . . . ,* 4th ed., 45–51.
Brooks, Cleanth. . . . *First Encounters,* 16–19.
Comprone, Joseph. "Literature and the Writing Process: A Pedagogical Read-
    ing of William Faulkner's 'Barn Burning,'" *Coll Lit,* 9, i (1982), 1–21.
Kennedy, X. J. *Instructor's Manual . . . ,* 10–12; rpt. Kennedy, X. J. and
    Dorothy M. *Instructor's Manual . . . ,* 3rd ed., 28–30.
Parr, Susan R. *The Moral . . . ,* 131–136.

"The Bear"
Allen, Mary. *Animals . . . ,* 151–155.
Foster, Thomas C. "History, Private Consciousness, and Narrative Form in *Go
    Down, Moses,*" *Centennial R,* 28 (1984), 71–76.
Friedman, Alan W. *William Faulkner,* 128–136.
Green, Martin. *The Great American Adventure,* 185–198.
Hays, Peter L. "Exchange Between Rivals: Faulkner's Influence on 'The Old
    Man and the Sea,'" in Nagel, James, Ed. . . . *Writer in Context,* 152–157.
Kuyk, Dirk. *Threads Cable-Strong . . . ,* 93–150.
McFague, Sallie. "The Parabolic of Faulkner, O'Connor, and Percy," *J Religion
    & Lit,* 15, ii (1983), 52–55.
Matthews, John T. . . . *Faulkner's Language,* 250–265.
Mortimer, Gail L. *Faulkner's Rhetoric . . . ,* 102–103.

Pikoulis, John. *The Art . . .* , 208–215.
Sirlin, Rhoda, and David H. Richter. *Instructor's Manual . . .* , 32–36.
Zender, Karl F. "Reading in 'The Bear,'" *Faulkner Stud,* 1 (1980), 91–99.

"Black Music"
Watson, James G. "Short Story Fantasies and the Limits of Modernism," *Faulkner Stud,* 1 (1980), 82–83.

"Carcassonne"
Polk, Noel. "William Faulkner's 'Carcassonne,'" *Stud Am Fiction,* 12 (1984), 29–43.
Watson, James G. "Short Story Fantasies . . . ," 83–85.

"Crevasse"
Bradford, M. E. "The Anomaly . . . ," 258–260.
Nordanberg, Thomas. *Cataclysm . . .* , 28–29.

"Delta Autumn"
Grimwood, Michael. "'Delta Autumn': Stagnation and Sedimentation in Faulkner's Career," *Southern Lit J,* 16, ii (1984), 93–106.
Hays, Peter L. "Significant Names in 'Delta Autumn,'" *Notes Mod Am Lit,* 6, iii (1982), Item 19.
Kuyk, Dirk. *Threads Cable-Strong . . .* , 151–168.
Matthews, John T. . . . *Faulkner's Language,* 265–269.
Pikoulis, John. *The Art . . .* , 215–218.
Sirlin, Rhoda, and David H. Richter. *Instructor's Manual . . .* , 36–38.

"Dry September"
*Abcarian, Richard, and Marvin Klotz. *Instructor's Manual . . .* , 2nd ed., 8–9; 3rd ed., 7.
Dessner, Lawrence J. "William Faulkner's 'Dry September': Decadence Domesticated," *Coll Lit,* 11 (1984), 151–162.
Mortimer, Gail L. *Faulkner's Rhetoric . . .* , 54–57.
Parr, Susan R. *The Moral . . .* , 123–130.
Sheidley, William E., and Ann Charters. *Instructor's Manual . . .* , 107–108.
Vickery, John B. *Myths and Texts . . .* , 141–142.

"An Error in Chemistry"
Gidley, Mick. "Elements of the Detective Story in William Faulkner's Fiction," in Landrum, Larry N., Pat Browne, and Ray B. Browne, Eds. *Dimensions of Detective Fiction,* 238–239.

"The Fire and the Hearth"
Denniston, Dorothy L. "Faulkner's Image of Black in *Go Down, Moses,*" *Phylon,* 44 (1983), 34–37.
Kuyk, Dirk. *Threads Cable-Strong . . .* , 37–63.
Matthews, John T. . . . *Faulkner's Language,* 230–238.

"Go Down, Moses"
Kuyk, Dirk. *Threads Cable-Strong . . .* , 169–190.
Matthews, John T. . . . *Faulkner's Language,* 269–273.
Watson, James G. "The American Short Story: 1930–1945," in Stevick, Philip, Ed. *The American Short Story, 1900–1945,* 135–137.

"Golden Land"
Winchell, Mark R. "William Faulkner's 'Golden Land': Some Time in Hell,"
    Notes Mississippi Writers, 14 (1982), 12–17.

"Hand Upon the Waters"
Gidley, Mick. "Elements . . . ," 236.

"Honor"
Folks, Jeffrey J. "Honor in Faulkner's Short Fiction," *Southern R*, 18 (1982),
    511–515.

"A Justice"
Watson, James G. "The American Short Story . . . ," 131–133.

"Knight's Gambit"
Gidley, Mick. "Elements . . . ," 240–241.

"The Leg"
Carothers, James B. "Faulkner's Short Stories: 'And Now What's to Do,'" in
    Fowler, Doreen, and Ann J. Abadie, Eds. *New Directions . . .* , 219–223.
Nordanberg, Thomas. *Cataclysm . . .* , 17–21.
Watson, James G. "Short Story Fantasies . . . ," 81.

"Monk"
Gidley, Mick. "Elements . . . ," 234–235.

"Mountain Victory"
Howell, Elmo. "Southern Fiction and the Pattern of Failure: The Example of
    Faulkner," *Georgia R*, 36 (1982), 768.
Nordanberg, Thomas. *Cataclysm . . .* , 66–70.

"Mule in the Yard"
Perrine, Laurence, and Thomas R. Arp. *Instructor's Manual . . .* , 6th ed., 45–
    48.

"My Grandmother Millard"
Nordanberg, Thomas. *Cataclysm . . .* , 70–74.

"Old Man"
Brooks, Cleanth. . . . *First Encounters*, 22–23.
Cate, Hollis. "'Old Man': Faulkner's Absurd Comedy," *Coll Lit*, 11 (1984), 186–
    190.
Lee, Dorothy H. "Denial of Time and the Failure of Moral Choice: Camus'
    'The Stranger,' Faulkner's 'Old Man,' and Wright's 'The Man Who Lived
    Underground,'" *Coll Lang Assoc J*, 23 (1980), 368–370.

"The Old People"
Cabibbo, Paola. "'The Old People' di W. Faulkner: Un perenne ricominciare,"
    in Cabibbo, Paola, Ed. *Sigfrido . . .* , 237–249.
Duvall, John N. "Using Greimas' Narrative Semiotics: Signification in Faulk-
    ner's 'The Old People,'" *Coll Lit*, 9 (1982), 192–206.
Foster, Thomas C. "History . . . ," 66–67.

Kuyk, Dirk. *Threads Cable-Strong . . . ,"* 72–75.
Matthews, John T. *. . . Faulkner's Language,* 244–249.
Miller, James E., and Bernice Slote. *Instructor's Manual . . . ,* 2nd ed., 17–18.
Pikoulis, John. *The Art . . . ,* 205–208.

"Once Aboard the Lugger"
Carothers, James B. "Faulkner's Short Stories . . . ," 212–218.

"Pantaloon in Black"
Denniston, Dorothy L. "Faulkner's Image . . . ," 38–40.
Forkner, Ben. "The Titular Voice in Faulkner's 'Pantaloon in Black,'" *Les Cahiers de la Nouvelle,* 1 (1983), 39–48.
Foster, Thomas C. "History . . . ," 64–65.
Kuyk, Dirk. *Threads Cable-Strong . . . ,* 64–78.
Matthews, John T. *. . . Faulkner's Language,* 238–244.
Pikoulis, John. *The Art . . . ,* 203–204.
Sirlin, Rhoda, and David H. Richter. *Instructor's Manual . . . ,* 38–40.

"Raid"
Pikoulis, John. *The Art . . . ,* 119–121.

"Retreat"
Pikoulis, John. *The Art . . . ,* 112–114.

"A Rose for Emily"
Allen, Dennis W. "Horror and Perverse Delight: Faulkner's 'A Rose for Emily,'" *Mod Fiction Stud,* 30 (1984), 685–696.
Bergman, David, Joseph de Roche, and Daniel M. Epstein. *Instructor's Manual . . . ,* 17–18.
Jacobs, John T. "Ironic Allusions in 'A Rose for Emily,'" *Notes Mississippi Writers,* 14 (1982), 77–79.
Kennedy, X. J. *Instructor's Manual . . . ,* 3rd ed., 13–15.
Littler, Frank A. "The Tangled Thread of Time: Faulkner's 'A Rose for Emily,'" *Notes Mississippi Writers,* 14 (1982), 80–85.
Polk, Noel. "'The Dungeon Was Mother Herself': William Faulkner—1927–1931," in Fowler, Doreen, and Ann J. Abadie, Eds. *New Directions . . . ,* 84–86.
Sheidley, William E., and Ann Charters. *Instructor's Manual . . . ,* 104–105.
Weaks, Mary Louise. "The Meaning of Miss Emily's Rose," *Notes Contemp Lit,* 11 (November, 1981), 11–12.

"Shall Not Perish"
Nordanberg, Thomas. *Cataclysm . . . ,* 117–120.

"Shingles for the Lord"
Folks, Jeffrey J. "Honor . . . ," 507–511.
Pikoulis, John. *The Art . . . ,* 123–124.

"Smoke"
Gidley, Mick. "Elements . . . ," 232–234.

"Spotted Horses"
Eddins, Dwight. "Metahumour in Faulkner's 'Spotted Horses,'" *Ariel*, 13, i
  (1982), 23–31.
Perrine, Laurence, and Thomas R. Arp. *Instructor's Manual . . .* , 6th ed., 43–
  45.

"The Tall Men"
Nordanberg, Thomas. *Cataclysm . . .* , 112–115.

"That Evening Sun"
Momberger, Philip. "Faulkner's 'The Village' and 'That Evening Sun': The Tale
  in Context," *Southern Lit J*, 11, i (1978), 20–31.
Scott, Virgil, and David Madden. *Instructor's Manual . . .* , 4th ed., 17–18; Mad-
  den, David. *Instructor's Manual . . .* , 5th ed., 38–41; Madden, David, and
  Virgil Scott. *Instructor's Manual . . .* , 6th ed., 37–40.

"There Was a Queen"
Putzel, Max. "Faulkner's Memphis Stories," *Virginia Q R*, 59 (1983), 265–268.

"Thrift"
Nordanberg, Thomas. *Cataclysm . . .* , 30–33.

"Tomorrow"
Gidley, Mick. "Elements . . . ," 236–237.

"Turnabout"
Bradford, M. E. "The Anomaly . . . ," 251–253.
Nordanberg, Thomas. *Cataclysm . . .* , 21–26.

"Two Soldiers"
Nordanberg, Thomas. *Cataclysm . . .* , 116–117.

"Uncle Willy"
Bruffee, Kenneth A. *Elegiac Romance . . .* , 174–178.

"Vendee"
Pikoulis, John. *The Art . . .* , 121–122.

"Victory"
Nordanberg, Thomas. *Cataclysm . . .* , 26–28.

"Was"
Brooks, Cleanth. *. . . First Encounters*, 130–131.
Greenspan, Ezra. "Faulkner's 'Was,'" *Explicator*, 41, iv (1983), 42–43.
Kuyk, Dirk. *Threads Cable-Strong . . .* , 13–36.
Matthews, John T. *. . . Faulkner's Language*, 220–230.
Oriard, Michael. "The Lucid Vision of William Faulkner," *Mod Fiction Stud*, 28
  (1982), 171–172.
Yarup, Robert L. "Faulkner's 'Was,'" *Explicator*, 41, iv (1983), 43–45.

"With Caution and Dispatch"
Bradford, M. E. "The Anomaly . . . ," 260–261.
Nordanberg, Thomas. *Cataclysm . . .* , 33–35.

JOHN RUSSELL FEARN

"The Brain of Light"
Cioffi, Frank. *Formula Fiction?* . . . , 45–46.

KONSTANTIN FEDIN

"Transvaal"
Brown, Edward J. . . . *Since the Revolution,* 3rd ed., 98.

JESÚS FERNÁNDEZ SANTOS

"Although I Don't Know Your Name"
Herzberger, David K. *Jesús Fernández Santos,* 112–113.

"Apartment"
Herzberger, David K. *Jesús Fernández Santos,* 106–107.

"The Bicycle"
Herzberger, David K. *Jesús Fernández Santos,* 108–109.

"Climbing the Tower"
Herzberger, David K. *Jesús Fernández Santos,* 101–102.

"Interview"
Herzberger, David K. *Jesús Fernández Santos,* 107–108.

"The Long Journey of the Monstrance"
Herzberger, David K. *Jesús Fernández Santos,* 103–104.

"Pablo on the Threshold"
Herzberger, David K. *Jesús Fernández Santos,* 115–116.

"Premature Ruin"
Herzberger, David K. *Jesús Fernández Santos,* 104–105.

"The Shadow of the Horse"
Herzberger, David K. *Jesús Fernández Santos,* 114–115.

"The Snail"
Herzberger, David K. *Jesús Fernández Santos,* 109–110.

"Story of the Dean"
Herzberger, David K. *Jesús Fernández Santos,* 102–103.

"The Strike Child"
Herzberger, David K. *Jesús Fernández Santos,* 113–114.

"Within Sight of an Old Lady"
Herzberger, David K. *Jesús Fernández Santos,* 111–112.

ROSARIO FERRÉ

"In Defense of the White Bird"
Chaves, María J. "La Alegoría como Método en los Cuentos y Ensayos de Rosario Ferré," *Third Woman*, 2, ii (1984), 71–72.

"When Women Love Men"
Olmos, Margarite F. "From a Woman's Perspective: The Short Stories of Rosario Ferré and Ana Lydia Vega," in Meyer, Doris, and Margarite F. Olmos, Eds. *Contemporary Women . . .* , 82–84.

"The Youngest Doll"
Chaves, María J. "La Alegoría . . . ," 66–68.
Olmos, Margarite F. "From a Woman's Perspective . . . ," 80–82.

CLAY FISHER [HENRY W. ALLEN]

"Ghost Town"
Gale, Robert L. *Will Henry / Clay Fisher . . .* , 89–90.

"Pretty Face"
Gale, Robert L. *Will Henry / Clay Fisher . . .* , 87–88.

RUDOLPH FISHER

"The City of Refuge"
Ikonné, Chidi. *From Du Bois to Van Vechten . . .* , 181.

"High Yaller"
Ikonné, Chidi. *From Du Bois to Van Vechten . . .* , 180.

STEVE FISHER

"Shanghai Butterfly: A Short, Short Story"
Wu, William F. *The Yellow Peril . . .* , 59–60.

F. SCOTT FITZGERALD

"Absolution"
Brondell, William J. "Structural Metaphors in Fitzgerald's Short Fiction," *Kansas Q*, 14 (Spring, 1982), 97–102.
Malin, Irving. "'Absolution': Absolving Lies," in Bryer, Jackson R., Ed. *The Short Stories . . .* , 209–216.
Mellow, James R. *Invented Lives . . .* , 196–198.
Miller, James E., and Bernice Slote. *Instructor's Manual . . .* , 2nd ed., 16–17.
Scott, Virgil, and David Madden. *Instructor's Manual . . .* , 4th ed., 21–23; Madden, David. *Instructor's Manual . . .* , 5th ed., 75–77; Madden, David, and Virgil Scott. *Instructor's Manual . . .* , 6th ed., 84–86.

"The Adjuster"
Johnson, Christiane. "Freedom, Contingency, and Ethics in 'The Adjuster,'" in
    Bryer, Jackson R., Ed. *The Short Stories* . . . , 227–240.
Mellow, James R. *Invented Lives* . . . , 224–225.

"Babylon Revisited"
Baker, Carlos. "When the Party Ends: 'Babylon Revisited,'" in Bryer,
    Jackson R., Ed. *The Short Stories* . . . , 269–277.
Brondell, William J. "Structural Metaphors . . . ," 107–111.
Donaldson, Scott. "Money and Marriage in Fitzgerald's Stories," in Bryer,
    Jackson R., Ed. *The Short Stories* . . . , 87–88.
Nettels, Elsa. "Howells's 'A Circle in the Water' and Fitzgerald's 'Babylon Re-
    visited,'" *Stud Short Fiction*, 19 (1982), 261–267.
Sheidley, William E., and Ann Charters. *Instructor's Manual* . . . , 102.

"Berenice Bobs Her Hair"
Gullason, Thomas A. "The 'Lesser' Renaissance: The American Short Story in
    the 1920s," in Stevick, Philip, Ed. *The American Short Story, 1900–1945*, 79–
    80.

"The Bridal Party"
Donaldson, Scott. "Money and Marriage . . . ," 86–87.
Martine, James J. "Rich Boys and Rich Men: 'The Bridal Party,'" in Bryer,
    Jackson R., Ed. *The Short Stories* . . . , 264–268.

"Crazy Sunday"
Grebstein, Sheldon. "The Sane Method of 'Crazy Sunday,'" in Bryer,
    Jackson R., Ed. *The Short Stories* . . . , 279–289.
Martin, Robert A. "Hollywood in Fitzgerald: After Paradise," in Bryer,
    Jackson R., Ed. *The Short Stories* . . . , 143–146.

"The Diamond as Big as the Ritz"
Buell, Lawrence. "The Significance of Fantasy in Fitzgerald's Short Fiction," in
    Bryer, Jackson R., Ed. *The Short Stories* . . . , 30–34.
Lehan, Richard. "The Romantic Self and the Uses of Place in the Stories of
    F. Scott Fitzgerald," in Bryer, Jackson R., Ed. *The Short Stories* . . . , 7–8.
Martin, Robert A. "Hollywood in Fitzgerald . . . ," 132–133.

"Dice, Brass Knuckles & Guitar"
Margolies, Alan. "'Kissing, Shooting, and Sacrificing': F. Scott Fitzgerald and
    the Hollywood Market," in Bryer, Jackson R., Ed. *The Short Stories* . . . , 69–
    70.

"Family in the Wind"
Eble, Kenneth E. "Touches of Disaster: Alcoholism and Mental Illness in Fitz-
    gerald's Short Stories," in Bryer, Jackson R., Ed. *The Short Stories* . . . , 43–
    44.

"Financing Finnegan"
Monteiro, George. "Two Sets of Books, One Balance Sheet: 'Financing Finne-
    gan,'" in Bryer, Jackson R., Ed. *The Short Stories* . . . , 291–299.

"The Freshest Boy"
Brondell, William J. "Structural Metaphors . . . ," 103–107.

"The Ice Palace"
Holman, C. Hugh. "Fitzgerald's Changes on the Southern Belle: The Tarleton Trilogy," in Bryer, Jackson R., Ed. *The Short Stories* . . . , 57–58.
Kuehl, John. "Psychic Geography in 'The Ice Palace,'" in Bryer, Jackson R., Ed. *The Short Stories* . . . , 169–179.
Lehan, Richard. "The Romantic Self . . . ," 5–6.

"Jacob's Ladder"
Mellow, James R. *Invented Lives* . . . , 288–290.

"The Jelly-Bean"
Holman, C. Hugh. "Fitzgerald's Changes . . . ," 58–59.

"The Last Belle"
Holman, C. Hugh. "Fitzgerald's Changes . . . ," 59–60.
Lehan, Richard. "The Romantic Self . . . ," 13–14.

"The Lost Decade"
West, James L. W. "Fitzgerald and *Esquire*," in Bryer, Jackson R., Ed. *The Short Stories* . . . , 161–164.

"Magnetism"
Martin, Robert A. "Hollywood in Fitzgerald . . . ," 141–142.
Martine, James J. "Rich Boys . . . ," 263–264.
Mellow, James R. *Invented Lives* . . . , 290–291.

"May Day"
Martine, James J. "Rich Boys . . . ," 262–263.
Tuttleton, James W. "Seeing Slightly Red: Fitzgerald's 'May Day,'" in Bryer, Jackson R., Ed. *The Short Stories* . . . , 181–197.

"A New Leaf"
Eble, Kenneth E. "Touches of Disaster . . . ," 45–47.

"The Offshore Pirate"
Donaldson, Scott. "Money and Marriage . . . ," 78–79.

"One Trip Abroad"
Lehan, Richard. "The Romantic Self . . . ," 15–16.

"Our Own Movie Queen"
Martin, Robert A. "Hollywood in Fitzgerald . . . ," 134–136.

"Outside the Cabinet-Maker's"
Mellow, James R. *Invented Lives* . . . , 303–304.

"The Popular Girl"
Lehan, Richard. "The Romantic Self . . . ," 8–9.

"Presumption"
Donaldson, Scott. "Money and Marriage . . . ," 80–81.

"Rags Martin-Jones and the Pr-nce of W-les"
Doyno, Victor. "'No Americans Have Any Imagination': 'Rags Martin-Jones and the Pr-nce of W-les,'" in Bryer, Jackson R., Ed. *The Short Stories . . . ,* 217–225.

"The Rich Boy"
Wolfe, Peter. "Faces in a Dream: Innocence Perpetuated in 'The Rich Boy,'" in Bryer, Jackson R., Ed. *The Short Stories . . . ,* 241–249.

"The Sensible Thing"
Donaldson, Scott. "Money and Marriage . . . ," 84–85.

"The Spire and the Gargoyle"
Lehan, Richard. "The Romantic Self . . . ," 4–5.

"The Swimmers"
Friedman, Melvin J. "'The Swimmers': Paris and Virginia Reconciled," in Bryer, Jackson R., Ed. *The Short Stories . . . ,* 251–260.
Lehan, Richard. "The Romantic Self . . . ," 17–18.
Prigozy, Ruth. "Fitzgerald's Short Stories and the Depression: An Artistic Crisis," in Bryer, Jackson R., Ed. *The Short Stories . . . ,* 120–121.

"Three Acts of Music"
West, James L. W. "Fitzgerald and *Esquire*," 158–161.

"Winter Dreams"
Donaldson, Scott. "Money and Marriage . . . ," 83–84.
Isaacs, Neil D. "'Winter Dreams' and Summer Sports," in Bryer, Jackson R., Ed. *The Short Stories . . . ,* 199–207.
Sirlin, Rhoda, and David H. Richter. *Instructor's Manual . . . ,* 40–42.

GUSTAVE FLAUBERT

"Bouvard and Pécuchet"
Bernheimer, Charles. *Flaubert and Kafka . . . ,* 102–138.
———. "Fetishism and Allegory in 'Bouvard and Pécuchet,'" in Schor, Naomi, and Henry Majewski, Eds. *Flaubert and Postmodernism,* 160–176.
Smith, Peter. *Public and Private Value . . . ,* 104–109.

"Hérodias"
Debray-Genette, Raymonde. "Profane, Sacred: Disorder of Utterance in *Trois Contes*," in Schor, Naomi, and Henry Majewski, Eds. *Flaubert and Postmodernism,* 23–27.
Genette, Gerard. "Demotivation in 'Hérodias,'" in Schor, Naomi, and Henry Majewski, Eds. *Flaubert and Postmodernism,* 192–201.
Hubert, J. D. "Representations of Decapitation: Mallarmé's 'Herodiade' and Flaubert's 'Hérodias,'" *French Forum,* 7 (1982), 247–251.
Israel-Pelletier, Aimée. "Desire and Writing: An Allegorical Reading of Flau-

bert's 'Hérodias,'" in Martín, Gregorio C., Ed. *Selected Proceedings . . .* , 153–158.

Lytle, Andrew. "Three Ways of Making a Saint: A Reading of *Three Tales* by Flaubert," *Southern R,* 20 (1984), 496–508.

Selvin, Susan C. "Spatial Form in Flaubert's *Trois Contes," Romanic R,* 74 (1983), 212–214.

"St. Julien"
Debray-Genette, Raymonde. "Profane, Sacred . . . ," 15–19.

Felman, Shoshana. "Flaubert's Signature: 'The Legend of Saint Julian the Hospitable,'" in Schor, Naomi, and Henry Majewski, Eds. *Flaubert and Postmodernism,* 46–75.

Lytle, Andrew. "Three Ways . . . ," 508–519.

Selvin, Susan C. "Spatial Form . . . ," 205–209.

"A Simple Heart"
Debray-Genette, Raymonde. "Profane, Sacred . . . ," 19–23.

Lytle, Andrew. "Three Ways . . . ," 519–527.

Schulz-Buschhaus, Ulrich. "Die Sprachlosigkeit der Felicite: Interpretation von Flauberts Conte 'Un Coeur simple,'" *Zeitschrift für Französische Sprache und Literatur,* 93 (1983), 113–130.

Selvin, Susan C. "Spatial Form . . . ," 209–212.

Shaw, Valerie. *The Short Story . . . ,* 59–62.

RUBEM FONSECA

"The Exterminator"
Foster, David W. "Major Figures in the Brazilian Short Story," in Peden, Margaret S., Ed. *The Latin American Short Story . . . ,* 28–30.

THEODOR FONTANE

"Grete Minde"
Biener, Joachim. "Zur Diskussion," *Fontane Blätter,* 5 (1982), 80–82.

SHELBY FOOTE

"Child by Fever"
White, Helen, and Redding S. Sugg. *Shelby Foote,* 56–60.

"The Freedom Kick"
White, Helen, and Redding S. Sugg. *Shelby Foote,* 61.

"A Marriage Portion"
White, Helen, and Redding S. Sugg. *Shelby Foote,* 55–56.

"Pillar of Fire"
White, Helen, and Redding S. Sugg. *Shelby Foote,* 61–67.

"Rain Down Home"
Vauthier, Simone. "Fiction and Fictions in Shelby Foote's 'Rain Down Home,'" *Notes Mississippi Writers*, 8 (Fall, 1975), 35–50.
White, Helen, and Redding S. Sugg. *Shelby Foote*, 51–52.

"Ride Out"
White, Helen, and Redding S. Sugg. *Shelby Foote*, 54–55.

"The Sacred Mound"
White, Helen, and Redding S. Sugg. *Shelby Foote*, 67–69.

E. M. FORSTER

"Albergo Empedocle"
Summers, Claude J. *E. M. Forster*, 271–272.

"Ansell"
Summers, Claude J. *E. M. Forster*, 270–271.

"Arthur Snatchfold"
McDowell, Frederick P. *E. M. Forster*, 2nd ed., 97–98.
Summers, Claude J. *E. M. Forster*, 278–281.

"The Celestial Omnibus"
*Dietrich, R. F. "'The Celestial Omnibus,'" in Dietrich, R. F., and Roger H. Sundell. *Instructor's Manual . . .*, 4th ed., 1–5.
DiGaetani, John L. *Richard Wagner . . .*, 94–95.
Summers, Claude J. *E. M. Forster*, 244–248.

"Co-ordination" [originally titled "Cooperation"]
Summers, Claude J. *E. M. Forster*, 263–264.

"The Curate's Friend"
Hall, Susan G. "Among E. M. Forster's Idylls: 'The Curate's Friend,'" *Classical & Mod Lit*, 3 (1983), 99–105.
Summers, Claude J. *E. M. Forster*, 250–252.

"Dr. Woolacott"
Rosecrance, Barbara. *Forster's Narrative Vision*, 178–179.
Summers, Claude J. *E. M. Forster*, 276–278.
Wilde, Alan. *Horizons of Assent . . .*, 83–86.

"The Eternal Moment"
Gillie, Christopher. *A Preface . . .*, 44–46.
*McDowell, Frederick P. *E. M. Forster*, 2nd ed., 41–42.
Martin, Robert K. "The Paterian Mode in Forster's Fiction: *The Longest Journey* to *Pharos and Pharillon*," in Herz, Judith S., and Robert K. Martin, Eds. *E. M. Forster . . .*, 104–105.
Summers, Claude J. *E. M. Forster*, 266–268.

"The Life to Come"
Levine, June P. "The Tame in Pursuit of the Savage: The Posthumous Fiction
    of E. M. Forster," *PMLA*, 99 (1984), 84–85.
McDowell, Frederick P. *E. M. Forster,* 2nd ed., 98–99.
Rosecrance, Barbara. *Forster's Narrative Vision,* 177–178.
Summers, Claude J. *E. M. Forster,* 274–276.
Wilde, Alan. *Horizons of Assent . . . ,* 83–86.

"Little Imber"
Scott, P J. M. *E. M. Forster. . . ,* 145–146.

"The Machine Stops"
Gillie, Christopher. *A Preface . . . ,* 46–48.
King, Betty. *Women of the Future . . . ,* 22–23.

"Mr. Andrews"
Summers, Claude J. *E. M. Forster,* 262–263.

"The Obelisk"
McDowell, Frederick P. *E. M. Forster,* 2nd ed., 96–97.
Summers, Claude J. *E. M. Forster,* 282–283.

"The Other Boat"
Levine, June P. "The Tame in Pursuit . . . ," 85–87.
McDowell, Frederick P. *E. M. Forster,* 2nd ed., 99–100.
Rao, D. S. Kesava. "E. M. Forster's 'The Other Boat,'" *Lit Endeavor,* 4, iii–iv
    (1984), 15–21.
Rosecrance, Barbara. *Forster's Narrative Vision,* 180–182.
Scott, P. J. M. *E. M. Forster. . . ,* 14–16.
Summers, Claude J. *E. M. Forster,* 286–290.

"Other Kingdom"
*McDowell, Frederick P. *E. M. Forster,* 2nd ed., 40.
Summers, Claude J. *E. M. Forster,* 248–250.

"The Other Side of the Hedge"
Sirlin, Rhoda, and David H. Richter. *Instructor's Manual . . . ,* 42–44.
Summers, Claude J. *E. M. Forster,* 243–244.

"The Point of It"
*McDowell, Frederick P. *E. M. Forster,* 2nd ed., 44–45.
Summers, Claude J. *E. M. Forster,* 260–262.

"The Purple Envelope"
Summers, Claude J. *E. M. Forster,* 272–273.

"Ralph and Tony"
McDowell, Frederick P. *E. M. Forster,* 2nd ed., 42–43.
Scott, P. J. M. *E. M. Forster . . . ,* 109–110.

"The Road from Colonus"
Gillie, Christopher. *A Preface . . .* , 43–44.
*McDowell, Frederick P. *E. M. Forster,* 2nd ed., 41.
Scott, P. J. M. *E. M. Forster . . .* , 59–62.

"The Rock"
Summers, Claude J. *E. M. Forster,* 273–274.

"The Story of a Panic"
Gillie, Christopher. *A Preface . . .* , 40–43.
*McDowell, Frederick P. *E. M. Forster,* 2nd ed., 40.
Miller, James E., and Bernice Slote. *Instructor's Manual . . .* , 2nd ed., 12.
Summers, Claude J. *E. M. Forster,* 240–243.

"The Story of the Siren"
*McDowell, Frederick P. *E. M. Forster,* 2nd ed., 43–44.
Summers, Claude J. *E. M. Forster,* 264–266.

"The Torque"
McDowell, Frederick P. *E. M. Forster,* 2nd ed., 97.
Summers, Claude J. *E. M. Forster,* 284–286.

"What Does It Matter?"
Summers, Claude J. *E. M. Forster,* 283–285.

JOHN FOWLES

"The Cloud"
Conradi, Peter. *John Fowles,* 88–89.
Davidson, Arnold E. "The Barthesian Configuration of John Fowles's 'The
    Cloud,'" *Centennial R,* 28, iv–29, i (Fall-Winter, 1984–1985), 80–93.
McSweeney, Kerry. *Four Contemporary Novelists . . .* , 112–113.
Sollisch, James W. "The Passion of Existence: John Fowles's *The Ebony Tower,*"
    Critique, 25, i (1983), 7–8.
Wilson, Raymond J. "John Fowles's *The Ebony Tower*: Unity and Celtic Myth,"
    Twentieth Century Lit, 28 (1982), 305–314.
————. "Allusion and Implication in John Fowles's 'The Cloud,'" *Stud Short
    Fiction,* 20 (1983), 17–22.

"The Ebony Tower"
Conradi, Peter. *John Fowles,* 78–84.
Davidson, Arnold. "*Eliduc* and 'The Ebony Tower': John Fowles's Variation on
    a Medieval Lay," *Int'l Fiction R,* 11, i (1984), 31–36.
McSweeney, Kerry. *Four Contemporary Novelists . . .* , 118–121.
Wilson, Raymond J. "Ambiguity in John Fowles's 'The Ebony Tower,'" *Notes
    Contemp Lit,* 12, iv (1982), 6–8.
————. "John Fowles's *The Ebony Tower . . .* ," 302–304.

"Eliduc"
Davidson, Arnold. ". . . Medieval Lay," 31–36.

"The Enigma"
Conradi, Peter. *John Fowles*, 86–88.
McSweeney, Kerry. *Four Contemporary Novelists*, 113–116.
Sollisch, James W. "The Passion . . . ," 7.

"Poor Koko"
Conradi, Peter. *John Fowles*, 84–86.
McSweeney, Kerry. *Four Contemporary Novelists* . . . , 116–118.
Sollisch, James W. "The Passion . . . ," 6–7.

JOHN FOX

"A Cumberland Vendetta"
De Eulis, Marilyn. "Primitivism and Exoticism in John Fox's Early Works,"
   Appalachian J, 4 (Winter, 1977), 135–136.

"Grayson's Baby"
De Eulis, Marilyn. "Primitivism . . . ," 140–141.

"The Last Stetson"
De Eulis, Marilyn. "Primitivism . . . ," 135–137.

"A Message of Sand"
De Eulis, Marilyn. "Primitivism . . . ," 138–139.

"A Mountain Europa"
De Eulis, Marilyn. "Primitivism . . . ," 133–135.

"Preaching on Kingdom Come"
De Eulis, Marilyn. "Primitivism . . . ," 139–140.

"A Purple Rhododendron"
De Eulis, Marilyn. "Primitivism . . . ," 141–142.

"A Trick o' Trade"
De Eulis, Marilyn. "Primitivism . . . ," 138.

GEORGES FRADIER

"Empedocles in Bogota"
Achury Valenzuela, Dario. "Sombra de una sombra que pasa, Empedocles nom-
   brada," *Boletin Cultural y Bibliografia*, 18 (1981), 115–122.

JANET FRAME

"The Bedjacket"
Rhodes, H. Winston. "Janet Frame: A Way of Seeing in *The Lagoon and Other
   Stories*," in Hankin, Cherry, Ed. . . . *New Zealand Short Story*, 126–128.

"The Birds Began to Sing"
Rhodes, H. Winston. "Janet Frame . . . ," 129–130.

"Dossy"
Rhodes, H. Winston. "Janet Frame . . . ," 118–119.

"Keel and Kool"
Rhodes, H. Winston. "Janet Frame . . . ," 123–124.

"Miss Gibson"
Rhodes, H. Winston. "Janet Frame . . . ," 115–116.

"A Note on the Russian War"
Rhodes, H. Winston. "Janet Frame . . . ," 116–117.

"Summer"
Rhodes, H. Winston. "Janet Frame . . . ," 120–121.

"Swans"
Rhodes, H. Winston. "Janet Frame . . . ," 124–125.

MARY E. WILKINS FREEMAN

"Arethusa"
Donovan, Josephine. *New England Local Color. . .* , 129–130.

"Christmas Jenny"
Donovan, Josephine. *New England Local Color. . .* , 131–132.
Pryse, Marjorie, Ed. *Selected Stories . . .* , 330–331.

"A Church Mouse"
Pryse, Marjorie, Ed. *Selected Stories . . .* , 331–332.

"A Conflict Ended"
Pryse, Marjorie, Ed. *Selected Stories . . .* , 325.

"A Gala Dress"
Pryse, Marjorie, Ed. *Selected Stories . . .* , 321–322.

"A Gatherer of Simples"
Pryse, Marjorie, Ed. *Selected Stories . . .* , 319–320.

"Gentian"
Bader, Julia. "The Dissolving Vision: Realism in Jewett, Freeman, and Gilman,"
   in Sundquist, Eric J., Ed. *American Realism . . .* , 184–185.

"The Great Pine"
Donovan, Josephine. *New England Local Color. . .* , 138.

"An Honest Soul"
Pryse, Marjorie, Ed. *Selected Stories . . .* , 316–317.

"The Long Arm"
Donovan, Josephine. *New England Local Color*. . . , 130.

"The Love of Parson Lord"
Donovan, Josephine. *New England Local Color*. . . , 127–128.

"A Mistaken Charity"
Pryse, Marjorie, Ed. *Selected Stories* . . . , 326–327.

"A New England Nun"
Bader, Julia. "The Dissolving Vision . . . ," 187–189.
Pryse, Marjorie. "An Uncloistered 'New England Nun,'" *Stud Short Fiction*, 20
    (1983), 289–295.
———, Ed. *Selected Stories* . . . , 317–318.

"Old Woman Magoun"
Bader, Julia. "The 'Rooted' Landscape and the Woman Writer," in Hoffmann,
    Leonore, and Deborah Rosenfelt, Eds. *Teaching Women's Literature* . . . , 27–
    28.
———. "The Dissolving Vision . . . ," 189–191.
Donovan, Josephine. *New England Local Color*. . . , 130–131.

"On the Walpole Road"
Pryse, Marjorie, Ed. *Selected Stories* . . . , 320–321.

"One Good Time"
Donovan, Josephine. *New England Local Color*. . . , 134.

"A Patient Waiter"
Pryse, Marjorie, Ed. *Selected Stories* . . . , 318–319.

"A Poetess"
Donovan, Josephine. *New England Local Color*. . . , 135.
Pryse, Marjorie, Ed. *Selected Stories* . . . , 329–330.

"The Revolt of Mother"
Aarons, Victoria. "A Community of Women: Surviving Marriage in the Wil-
    derness," in Hargrove, Anne C., and Maurine Magliocco, Eds. *Portraits of
    Marriage* . . . , 142–145.
Pryse, Marjorie, Ed. *Selected Stories* . . . , 325–326.

"The Selfishness of Amelia"
Bader, Julia. "The Dissolving Vision . . . ," 186–187.

"Sister Liddy"
Pryse, Marjorie, Ed. *Selected Stories* . . . , 322.

"A Solitary"
Donovan, Josephine. *New England Local Color*. . . , 137–138.

"A Symphony in Lavender"
Donovan, Josephine. *New England Local Color*. . . , 132–133.

"Two Old Lovers"
Pryse, Marjorie, Ed. *Selected Stories* . . . , 315–316.

"Up Primrose Hill"
Pryse, Marjorie, Ed. *Selected Stories* . . . , 323–324.

"A Village Lear"
Pryse, Marjorie, Ed. *Selected Stories* . . . , 333–335.

"A Village Singer"
Pryse, Marjorie, Ed. *Selected Stories* . . . , 327–329.

HERMAN JAN FRIEDERICY

"The Counselor"
Beekman, E. M., Ed. *Two Tales* . . . , 118–121.

MAX FRISCH

"Antwort aus der Stille"
Stewart, Mary E. "Alpine Adventures: Some Thoughts on Max Frisch's 'Antwort aus der Stille,'" *Mod Lang R,* 78 (1983), 359–364.

DANIEL FUCHS

"Twilight in Southern California"
Greenspan, Ezra. *The "Schlemiel"* . . . , 78–79.

CARLOS FUENTES

"Aura"
Benevento, Joseph J. "An Introduction to the Realities of Fiction: Teaching
Magic Realism in Three Stories by Borges, Fuentes, and Márquez," *Kansas
Q,* 16, iii (1984), 128–129.

"Chac Mool"
Brushwood, John S. "*Los días enmascarados* and *Cantar de ciegos:* Reading the
Stories and Reading the Books," in Brody, Robert, and Charles Rossman,
Eds. *Carlos Fuentes* . . . , 19–20.
Leal, Luis. "History and Myth in the Narrative of Carlos Fuentes," in Brody,
Robert, and Charles Rossman, Eds. *Carlos Fuentes* . . . , 5–6.
McMurray, George R. "The Spanish American Short Story from Borges to the
Present," in Peden, Margaret S., Ed. *The Latin American Short Story* . . . ,
134–135.
Williams, Shirley A. "Prisoners of the Past: Three Fuentes Short Stories from
Los días enmascarados," *J Spanish Stud: Twentieth Century,* 6, i (1978), 40–43.

"The Cost of Life"
Brushwood, John S. *"Los días enmascarados . . . ,"* 29–30.

"The Doll Queen"
Brushwood, John S. *"Los días enmascarados . . . ,"* 27.
Duran, Gloria. "Dolls and Puppets as Wish-Fulfillment Symbols in Carlos
    Fuentes," in Brody, Robert, and Charles Rossman, Eds. *Carlos Fuentes . . . ,*
    174–176.
Larson, Ross. "Archetypal Patterns in Carlos Fuentes' 'La muñeca reina,'" *Mes-
    ter,* 11, i (1982), 41–46.

"The Gods Speak" [same as "By the Mouth of the Gods"]
Williams, Shirley A. "Prisoners . . . ," 48–51.

"In Defense of Trigolibia"
Brushwood, John S. *"Los días enmascarados . . . ,"* 20–21.

"Litany of the Orchids"
Brushwood, John S. *"Los días enmascarados . . . ,"* 23–24.

"The Man Who Invented Gunpowder"
Brushwood, John S. *"Los días enmascarados . . . ,"* 24–25.

"A Pure Soul"
Brushwood, John S. *"Los días enmascarados . . . ,"* 30.

"These Were Palaces"
McMurray, George R. ". . . Borges to the Present," 134–135.

"Tlactocatzine"
Brushwood, John S. *"Los días enmascarados . . . ,"* 21–22.
Williams, Shirley A. "Prisoners . . . ," 46–48.

"The Two Helens"
Brushwood, John S. *"Los días enmascarados . . . ,"* 26–27.

"What Fortune Brought"
Brushwood, John S. *"Los días enmascarados . . . ,"* 27–28.

NORBERTO FUENTES

"Captain Descalzo"
McMurray, George R. "The Spanish American Short Story from Borges to the
    Present," in Peden, Margaret S., Ed. *The Latin American Short Story . . . ,* 123.

HENRY BLAKE FULLER

"Dr. Gowdy and the Squash"
Smith, Carl S. *Chicago . . . ,* 31–33.

"The Downfall of Abner Joyce"
Smith, Carl S. *Chicago* . . . , 28–29.

"Little O'Grady vs. the Grindstone"
Smith, Carl S. *Chicago* . . . , 29–31.

ERNEST J. GAINES

"Bloodline"
Hicks, Jack. *In the Singer's Temple* . . . , 121.
Werner, Craig H. *Paradoxical Resolutions* . . . , 38–39.

"Just Like a Tree"
Hicks, Jack. *In the Singer's Temple* . . . , 121–124.
Madden, David, and Virgil Scott. *Instructor's Manual* . . . , 6th ed., 119–122.
Werner, Craig H. *Paradoxical Resolutions* . . . , 36–37.

"A Long Day in November"
Hicks, Jack. *In the Singer's Temple* . . . , 115–116.
Roberts, John W. "The Individual and the Community in Two Short Stories by
     Ernest Gaines," *Black Am Lit Forum*, 18 (1984), 110–111.

"The Sky Is Gray"
Hicks, Jack. *In the Singer's Temple* . . . , 116–121.
Roberts, John W. "The Individual . . . ," 111–112.

"Three Men"
Werner, Craig H. *Paradoxical Resolutions* . . . , 37–38.

MAVIS GALLANT

"Acceptance of Their Ways"
O'Rourke, David. "Exiles in Time: Gallant's *My Heart Is Broken*," *Canadian Lit*,
     93 (1982), 99.

"Bernadette"
O'Rourke, David. "Exiles in Time . . . ," 99–101.

"From the Fifteenth District"
Bergman, David, Joseph de Roche, and Daniel M. Epstein. *Instructor's Man-
     ual* . . . , 12.

"The Ice Wagon Going Down the Street"
O'Rourke, David. "Exiles in Time . . . ," 105–106.

"Irina"
Woodcock, George. *The World* . . . , 101–103.

"Its Image on the Mirror"
O'Rourke, David. "Exiles in Time . . . ," 102–104.

"The Moabites"
O'Rourke, David. "Exiles in Time . . . ," 101.

"My Heart Is Broken"
O'Rourke, David. "Exiles in Time . . . ," 104–105.

"The Pegnitz Junction"
Woodcock, George. *The World* . . . , 107–109.

"Sunday Afternoon"
O'Rourke, David. "Exiles in Time . . . ," 105.

"An Unmarried Man"
O'Rourke, David. "Exiles in Time . . . ," 101–102.

RAYMOND Z. GALLUN

"Hotel Cosmos"
Cioffi, Frank. *Formula Fiction?* . . . , 64–67.

"Old Faithful"
Meyers, Walter E. *Aliens and Linguists* . . . , 93–95.

JOHN GALSWORTHY

"Danäe"
Batchelor, John. *The Edwardian Novelists*, 202–204.

ELENA GAN [pseudonym: ZINAIDA R-VA]

"The Ideal"
Mersereau, John. *Russian Romantic Fiction*, 289–290.

SEVER GANSOVSKII

"The Day of Wrath"
Smyrniw, Walter. "Satirical Trends in Recent Soviet Science Fiction," in Bristol,
    Evelyn, Ed. *Russian Literature* . . . , 195–196.

GABRIEL GARCÍA MÁRQUEZ

"Baltazar's Wonderful Afternoon"
González, Eduardo. "Beware of Gift-Bearing Tales: Reading García Márquez
    According to Mauss," *Mod Lang Notes*, 97 (1982), 347–364.
McMurray, George R. "The Spanish American Short Story from Borges to the
    Present," in Peden, Margaret S., Ed. *The Latin American Short Story* . . . ,
    117–118.

"Big Mama's Funeral"
Williams, Raymond L. *Gabriel García Márquez*, 42–46.

"Bitterness for Three Sleepwalkers"
Williams, Raymond L. *Gabriel García Márquez*, 21.

"Blacamán the Good, Vendor of Miracles"
Tauzin, Jacqueline. "Un Exemple de réalisme magique: 'Blacamán le Bon mar-
chand de miracles,'" in Marotin, François, Ed. *Frontières du conte*, 137–144.
Williams, Raymond L. *Gabriel García Márquez*, 100–102.

"The Day After Saturday"
Williams, Raymond L. *Gabriel García Márquez*, 50–53.

"Death Constant Beyond Love"
Berroa, Rei. "Sobre 'Muerte constante más allá del amor,'" *Discorse Literario*, 1,
i (1983), 5–15.
Williams, Raymond L. *Gabriel García Márquez*, 108–109.

"Eyes of a Blue Dog"
Williams, Raymond L. *Gabriel García Márquez*, 19.

"The Handsomest Drowned Man in the World"
McMurray, George R. ". . . Borges to the Present," 130–131.
Williams, Raymond L. *Gabriel García Márquez*, 97–98.

"The Incredible and Sad Tale of Innocent Eréndira and Her Heartless Grandmother"
Beaty, Jerome. *The Norton Introduction . . .* , 576–578.
Benítez Rojo, Antonio, and Hilda O. Benítez. "Eréndira liberada: La subversión
del mito del macho occidental," *Revista Iberoamericana*, 50 (1984), 1057–
1075.
Burgos, Fernando. "Hacia el centro de la imaginación: 'La increíble y triste
historia de la cándida Eréndira y de su abuela desalmada,'" *Inti*, 16–17
(Fall–Spring, 1982–1983), 71–81.
Morello-Frosch, Marta. "Functión de lo fantástico en 'La increíble y triste historia de la cándida Eréndira y de su abuela desalmada,'" *Symposium*, 38
(1984), 321–330.
Williams, Raymond L. *Gabriel García Márquez*, 103–105.

"The Last Voyage of the Ghost Ship"
Williams, Raymond L. *Gabriel García Márquez*, 106–108.

"Monologue of Isabel Watching It Rain in Macondo"
Williams, Raymond L. *Gabriel García Márquez*, 23–27.

"Nabo, the Black Who Made the Angels Wait"
Williams, Raymond L. *Gabriel García Márquez*, 20–21.

"One of These Days"
Amoretti, H. María. "'Un día de estos' de García Márquez: Un desafortunado
proceso de venganza," *Káñina*, 7, i (1983), 35–42.

"The Sea of Lost Time"
Sirlin, Rhoda, and David H. Richter. *Instructor's Manual* . . . , 44–45.
Williams, Raymond L. *Gabriel García Márquez*, 98–100.

"Someone Has Been Disarranging These Roses"
Williams, Raymond L. *Gabriel García Márquez*, 19–20.

"Tale of a Castaway"
Williams, Raymond L. *Gabriel García Márquez*, 27–31.

"There Are No Thieves in This Town"
Williams, Raymond L. *Gabriel García Márquez*, 55–56.

"The Third Resignation"
Williams, Raymond L. *Gabriel García Márquez*, 14–16.

"Tuesday's Siesta"
Williams, Raymond L. *Gabriel García Márquez*, 54–55.

"A Very Old Man with Enormous Wings"
Benevento, Joseph J. "An Introduction to the Realities of Fiction: Teaching
    Magic Realism in Three Stories by Borges, Fuentes, and Márquez," *Kansas
    Q,* 16, iii (1984), 130–131.
Bergman, David, Joseph de Roche, and Daniel M. Epstein. *Instructor's Man-
    ual* . . . , 29.
Gerlach, John. "The Logic of Wings: García Márquez, Todorov, and the Endless
    Resources of Fantasy," in Slusser, George E., Eric S. Rabkin, and Robert
    Scholes, Eds. *Bridges to Fantasy*, 121–129.
Miller, James E., and Bernice Slote. *Instructor's Manual* . . . , 2nd ed., 23.
Sheidley, William E., and Ann Charters. *Instructor's Manual* . . . , 165–166.
Williams, Raymond L. *Gabriel García Márquez*, 93–97.

ERLE STANLEY GARDNER

"In Round Figures"
Van Dover, J. Kenneth. *Murder in the Millions* . . . , 29–30.

JOHN GARDNER

"The Art of Living"
Morris, Gregory L. *A World of Order* . . . , 203–205.

"Come on Back"
Morris, Gregory L. *A World of Order* . . . , 203–205.

"Dragon, Dragon"
Cowart, David. *Arches and Light* . . . , 130–131.

"The Griffin and the Wise Old Philosopher"
Cowart, David. *Arches and Light* . . . , 134–135.

"Gudgekin the Thistle Girl"
Cowart, David. *Arches and Light* . . . , 133–134.

"John Napper Sailing Through the Universe"
Cowart, David. *Arches and Light* . . . , 88–91.
Morris, Gregory L. *A World of Order* . . . , 131–132.

"The Joy of the Just"
Cowart, David. *Arches and Light* . . . , 176–178.
Morris, Gregory L. *A World of Order* . . . , 195–196.

"King Gregor and the Fool"
Cowart, David. *Arches and Light* . . . , 95–96.
Morris, Gregory L. *A World of Order* . . . , 134–135.

"The King's Indian"
Cowart, David. *Arches and Light* . . . , 99–109.
Morace, Robert A., and Kathryn VanSpanckeren, Eds. *John Gardner* . . . , 85–88.
Morris, Gregory L. *A World of Order* . . . , 137–142.

"The Library Horror"
Cowart, David. *Arches and Light* . . . , 174–176.
Morris, Gregory L. *A World of Order* . . . , 193–195.

"Muriel"
Cowart, David. *Arches and Light* . . . , 96–97.
Morris, Gregory L. *A World of Order* . . . , 135–137.

"The Music Lover"
Cowart, David. *Arches and Light* . . . , 172–174.
Morris, Gregory L. *A World of Order* . . . , 191–193.

"Nimram"
Morris, Gregory L. *A World of Order* . . . , 185–187.

"Pastoral Care"
Cowart, David. *Arches and Light* . . . , 78–80.
Morris, Gregory L. *A World of Order* . . . , 120–122.

"The Pear Tree"
Cowart, David. *Arches and Light* . . . , 137–138.

"Queen Louisa"
Cowart, David. *Arches and Light* . . . , 93–95.
Morris, Gregory L. *A World of Order* . . . , 132–134.

"The Ravages of Spring"
Cowart, David. *Arches and Light* . . . , 80–82.
Morace, Robert A., and Kathryn VanSpanckeren, Eds. *John Gardner* . . . , 83–84.
Morris, Gregory L. *A World of Order* . . . , 122–124.
Rout, Kay K. "The Ghoul-Haunted Woodland of Southern Illinois: John Gardner's 'The Ravages of Spring,'" *Stud Short Fiction*, 19 (1982), 27–33.

"Redemption"
Morris, Gregory L. *A World of Order* . . . , 187–190.

"Stillness"
Morris, Gregory L. *A World of Order* . . . , 190–191.

"The Tailor and the Giant"
Cowart, David. *Arches and Light* . . . , 131–132.

"The Temptation of St. Ivo"
Cowart, David. *Arches and Light* . . . , 82–85.
Morris, Gregory L. *A World of Order* . . . , 124–127.

"Trumpeter"
Cowart, David. *Arches and Light* . . . , 97–98.

"Vlemk the Box-Painter"
Cowart, David. *Arches and Light* . . . , 179–182.
Morris, Gregory L. *A World of Order* . . . , 196–201.

"The Warden"
Cowart, David. *Arches and Light* . . . , 85–88.
Morris, Gregory L. *A World of Order* . . . , 127–131.

HAMLIN GARLAND

"Under the Lion's Paw"
Walcutt, Charles C. *American Literary Naturalism* . . . , 56–57; rpt. Nagel, James,
    Ed. *Critical Essays* . . . , 202–203.

"Up the Coulé"
Pizer, Donald. *Realism and Naturalism* . . . , 2nd ed., 139–140.

A. B. GASKELL

"Holiday"
Jones, Lawrence. "Out from Under My Uncle's Hat: Gaskell, Middleton, and
    the Sargeson Tradition," in Hankin, Cherry, Ed. . . . *New Zealand Short Story*,
    92–93.

"Tell Me the Old Old Story"
Jones, Lawrence. "Out from Under . . . ," 95.

"Who Steals My Purse"
Jones, Lawrence. "Out from Under . . . ," 93–94.

ELIZABETH GASKELL

"The Crooked Branch"
Lansbury, Coral. *Elizabeth Gaskell*, 49–53.

"Crowley Castle"
Lansbury, Coral. *Elizabeth Gaskell*, 61–62.

"A Dark Night's Work"
Wright, Edgar. *Mrs. Gaskell* . . . , 191–192.

"The Grey Woman"
Lansbury, Coral. *Elizabeth Gaskell* . . . , 211–212.
————. *Elizabeth Gaskell*, 54–56.

"Half a Life-Time Ago"
Wright, Edgar. *Mrs. Gaskell* . . . , 45.

"The Heart of John Middleton"
Wright, Edgar. *Mrs. Gaskell* . . . , 42.

"Libbie Marsh's Three Eras"
Lansbury, Coral. *Elizabeth Gaskell* . . . , 42–43.
Walters, Anna, Ed. *Elizabeth Gaskell* . . . , 7–10.
Wright, Edgar. *Mrs. Gaskell* . . . , 90–91.

"Lizzie Leigh"
Mitchell, Sally. *The Fallen Angel* . . . , 39.
Walters, Anna, Ed. *Elizabeth Gaskell* . . . , 11–14.

"Lois the Witch"
Lansbury, Coral. *Elizabeth Gaskell* . . . , 157–158.
Wright, Edgar. *Mrs. Gaskell* . . . , 164–172.

"The Manchester Marriage"
Walters, Anna, Ed. *Elizabeth Gaskell* . . . , 16–20.

"Mr. Harrison's Confession"
Wright, Edgar. *Mrs. Gaskell* . . . , 109–111.

"The Moorland Cottage"
Wright, Edgar. *Mrs. Gaskell* . . . , 116–117.

"Morton Hall"
Lansbury, Coral. *Elizabeth Gaskell*, 56–58.

"My Lady Ludlow"
Lansbury, Coral. *Elizabeth Gaskell*, 70–71.

"The Old Nurse's Story"
Lansbury, Coral. *Elizabeth Gaskell* . . . , 82–83.

"The Poor Clare"
Reddy, Maureen T. "Female Sexuality in 'The Poor Clare': The Demon in the
    House," *Stud Short Fiction*, 21 (1984), 259–265.

"Six Weeks at Heppenheim"
Lansbury, Coral. *Elizabeth Gaskell*, 58–61.

"The Well of Pen-Morfa"
Walters, Anna, Ed. *Elizabeth Gaskell . . .* , 14–16.

WILLIAM GASS

"Icicles"
Bassoff, Bruce. *The Secret Sharers . . .* , 109–113.

"In the Heart of the Heart of the Country"
Bassoff, Bruce. *The Secret Sharers . . .* , 118–122.
Blake, Nancy. "'Out of time, out of body': An Erotic Map of the Heart of the
    Heart of the Country," *Revue Française d'Études Américaines*, 9 (1984), 265–
    274.

"Mrs. Mean"
Bassoff, Bruce. *The Secret Sharers . . .* , 113–118.

"Order of Insects"
Bassoff, Bruce. *The Secret Sharers . . .* , 107–109.

"The Pedersen Kid"
Bassoff, Bruce. *The Secret Sharers . . .* , 99–107.

"William Master's Lonesome Wife"
Blau, Marion. "'How I Would Brood Upon You': The Lonesome Wife of Wil-
    liam Gass," *Great Lakes R*, 2 (Summer, 1975), 40–50.

THÉOPHILE GAUTIER

"The Mummy's Foot"
Godfrey, Sima. "Mummy Dearest Cryptic Codes in Gautier's 'Pied de momie,'"
    Romanic R, 75 (1984), 302–311.

MAURICE GEE

"A Glorious Morning, Comrade"
Edmond, Lauris. "Definitions of New Zealanders: Stories of Maurice Shadbolt
    and Maurice Gee," in Hankin, Cherry, Ed. . . . *New Zealand Short Story*, 144–
    146.

"The Losers"
Edmond, Lauris. "Definitions . . . ," 141–144.

"Right Hand Man"
Edmond, Lauris. "Definitions . . . ," 148.

"A Sleeping Face"
Edmond, Lauris. "Definitions . . . ," 146–147.

IOSIF GERASIMOV

"The Nightingales"
Blum, Jakub. "Soviet Russian Literature," in Blum, Jakub, and Vera Rich. *The Image of the Jew . . .* , 46.

ANDRÉ GIDE

"The Immoralist"
Curry, Steven S. "Into the Shadow of Hesitation: Time and Identity in Gide's Middle Fiction," *Twentieth Century Lit,* 28 (1982), 237–240.

"Isabelle"
Curry, Steven S. "Into the Shadow . . . ," 242–243.

"The Pastoral Symphony"
Curry, Steven S. "Into the Shadow . . . ," 243–244.
Kingcaid, Renee A. "Retreat from Discovery: Symbol and Sign in 'La Symphonie pastorale,'" *Perspectives Contemp Lit,* 8 (1982), 34–41.

"Strait Is the Gate"
Curry, Steven S. "Into the Shadow . . . ," 240–242.

ELLEN GILCHRIST

"Revenge"
Thompson, Jeanie, and Anita M. Gardner. "The Miracle of Realism: The Bid for Self-Knowledge in the Fiction of Ellen Gilchrist," in Prenshaw, Peggy W., Ed. *Women Writers . . .* , 236–237.

"There's a Garden of Eden"
Thompson, Jeanie, and Anita M. Gardner. "The Miracle . . . ," 237.

"Traveler"
Thompson, Jeanie, and Anita M. Gardner. "The Miracle . . . ," 235–236.

CHARLOTTE PERKINS GILMAN

"The Giant Wistaria"
Fleenor, Julian E. "The Gothic Prism: Charlotte Perkins Gilman's Gothic Stories and Her Autobiography," in Fleenor, Julian E., Ed. *The Female Gothic,* 227–241.

"The Rocking Chair"
Fleenor, Julian E. "The Gothic Prism . . . ," 227–241.

"The Yellow Wallpaper"
Bader, Julia. "The Dissolving Vision: Realism in Jewett, Freeman, and Gilman,"
   in Sundquist, Eric J., Ed. *American Realism* . . . , 192–196.
Bergman, David, Joseph de Roche, and Daniel M. Epstein. *Instructor's Man-
   ual* . . . , 13–14.
Fleenor, Julian E. "The Gothic Prism . . . ," 227–241.
Gilbert, Sandra M., and Susan Gubar. *The Madwoman* . . . , 89–92.
Gubar, Susan. "*She* in *Herland*: Feminism as Fantasy," in Slusser, George E.,
   Eric S. Rabkin, and Robert Scholes, Eds. *Coordinates* . . . , 146–147.
Kawin, Bruce F. *The Mind of the Novel* . . . , 304–306.
MacPike, Lovales. "Environment as Psychopathological Symbolism in 'The Yel-
   low Wall-Paper,'" *Am Lit Realism*, 8 (1975), 286–288.
Parr, Susan R. *The Moral* . . . , 61–68.
Schöpp-Schilling, Beatte. " 'The Yellow Wall-Paper': A Rediscovered 'Realistic'
   Story," *Am Lit Realism*, 8 (1975), 284–286.
Sirlin, Rhoda, and David H. Richter. *Instructor's Manual* . . . , 46–47.

JEAN GIRAUDOUX

"Don Manuel the Lazy"
Reilly, John H. *Jean Giraudoux*, 31–33.

"Ice Palace"
Reilly, John H. *Jean Giraudoux*, 79–80.

"The Last Dream of Edmond About"
Reilly, John H. *Jean Giraudoux*, 27–28.

"Mirage of Bessines"
Lemaitre, Georges. *Jean Giraudoux* . . . , 75–76.
Reilly, John H. *Jean Giraudoux*, 80–81.

"The Sign"
Lemaitre, Georges. *Jean Giraudoux* . . . , 74–75.

GEORGE GISSING

"Comrades in Arms"
Bean, Lawless. "Gissing's 'Comrades in Arms': New Women, Old Attitudes,"
   Turn-of-the-Century Women, 1, ii (1984), 40–42.
Selig, Robert L. *George Gissing*, 116–118.

"The House of Cobwebs"
Selig, Robert L. *George Gissing*, 121–122.

"The Schoolmaster's Vision"
Selig, Robert L. *George Gissing*, 118–121.

"A Victim of Circumstances"
Selig, Robert L. *George Gissing,* 114–116.

ELLEN GLASGOW

"Between Two Shores"
Thiébaux, Marcelle. *Ellen Glasgow,* 178.

"Dare's Gift"
Carpenter, Lynette. "The Daring Gift in Ellen Glasgow's 'Dare's Gift,'" *Stud
    Short Fiction,* 21 (1984), 95–102.
Rohrberger, Mary. "The Question of Regionalism: Limitation and Transcen-
    dence," in Stevick, Philip, Ed. *The American Short Story, 1900–1945,* 166.
Thiébaux, Marcelle. *Ellen Glasgow,* 185–186.

"The Difference"
Rohrberger, Mary. "The Question . . . ," 167.
Thiébaux, Marcelle. *Ellen Glasgow,* 180.

"Jordan's End"
Thiébaux, Marcelle. *Ellen Glasgow,* 181.

"The Past"
Thiébaux, Marcelle. *Ellen Glasgow,* 186.

"A Point of Morals"
Thiébaux, Marcelle. *Ellen Glasgow,* 178–179.

"The Professional Instinct"
Thiébaux, Marcelle. *Ellen Glasgow,* 182–183.

"Romance and Sally Byrd"
Thiébaux, Marcelle. *Ellen Glasgow,* 182.

"The Shadowy Third"
Rohrberger, Mary. "The Question . . . ," 165–166.
Thiébaux, Marcelle. *Ellen Glasgow,* 184–185.

"Thinking Makes It So"
Thiébaux, Marcelle. *Ellen Glasgow,* 179–180.

"Whispering Leaves"
Rohrberger, Mary. "The Question . . . ," 166–167.
Thiébaux, Marcelle. *Ellen Glasgow,* 187.

"A Woman of Tomorrow"
Thiébaux, Marcelle. *Ellen Glasgow,* 177–178.

SUSAN GLASPELL

"A Jury of Her Peers"
Aarons, Victoria. "A Community of Women: Surviving Marriage in the Wilderness," in Hargrove, Anne C., and Maurine Magliocco, Eds. *Portraits of Marriage* . . . , 145–148.
Alkalay-Gut, Karen. "Jury of Her Peers: The Importance of Trifles," *Stud Short Fiction*, 21 (1984), 1–9.

JOHN GLASSCO

"The Black Helmet"
Woodcock, George. *The World* . . . , 118.

"The Fulfilled Destiny of Electra"
Woodcock, George. *The World* . . . , 118–119.

JACOB GLATSTEIN

"Abishag"
Baumgarten, Murray. *City Scriptures* . . . , 63–65.

TOM GODWIN

"The Cold Equations"
Hartwell, David. *Age of Wonders* . . . , 105–106.

NIKOLAI GOGOL

"The Diary of a Madman"
Apter, T. E. *Fantasy Literature* . . . , 81–83.
Bocharov, Sergei. "Petersburg Tales," *Soviet Lit*, [no vol.], iv (1984), 161–162.
Mersereau, John. *Russian Romantic Fiction*, 259–262.
Miller, James E., and Bernice Slote. *Instructor's Manual* . . . , 2nd ed., 6–7.
Penner, Dick, Ed. *Fiction of the Absurd* . . . , 30–31.

"Ivan Fyodorovich Shponka and His Aunt"
Apter, T. E. *Fantasy Literature* . . . , 76–78.
Katz, Michael R. *Dreams* . . . , 72–76.
Mersereau, John. *Russian Romantic Fiction*, 171.

"The Lost Letter"
Jamosky, Edward. "Gogol's *Evenings at a Farm Near Dikanka*: A Commentary," *Proceedings of the Kentucky Foreign Language Conference: Slavic Section*, 1, ii (1983), 77–78.

"May Night, or The Drowned Woman"
Mersereau, John. *Russian Romantic Fiction*, 169.

"The Nevsky Prospect"
Katz, Michael R. *Dreams* . . . , 76–79.
Mersereau, John. *Russian Romantic Fiction*, 255–259.

"The Nose"
Bocharov, Sergei. "Petersburg Tales," 160–161.
Penner, Dick, Ed. *Fiction of the Absurd* . . . , 31–37.
Sirlin, Rhoda, and David H. Richter. *Instructor's Manual* . . . , 48–49.

"The Overcoat"
Bocharov, Sergei. "Petersburg Tales," 162–164.
Clardy, Jesse V. and Betty S. *The Superfluous Man* . . . , 34–36.
Katz, Michael R. *Dreams* . . . , 79–80.
Mersereau, John. *Russian Romantic Fiction*, 301–306.
*Nabokov, Vladimir. *Lectures on Russian Literature*, 54–61; rpt. in part Charters,
     Ann, Ed. *The Story and Its Writer* . . . , 1147–1149.
O'Toole, L. Michael. *Structure, Style and Interpretation* . . . , 20–36.
Sheidley, William E., and Ann Charters. *Instructor's Manual* . . . , 7–8.
van der Eng, Jan. "Bashmachkin's Character: A Combination of Comic, Gro-
     tesque, Tragicomical and Tragic Elements," in Trahan, Elizabeth, Ed. *Go-
     gol's "Overcoat"* . . . , 73–85.
Wissemann, Heinz. "The Ideational Content of Gogol's 'Overcoat,'" in Trahan,
     Elizabeth, Ed. *Gogol's "Overcoat"* . . . , 86–105.

"The Portrait"
Bocharov, Sergei. "Petersburg Tales," 159–160.
Katz, Michael R. *Dreams* . . . , 81–83.
Mersereau, John. *Russian Romantic Fiction*, 263–265.

"The Quarrel Between Ivan Ivanovich and Ivan Nikiforovich"
Mersereau, John. *Russian Romantic Fiction*, 247–250.

"St. John's Eve"
Jamosky, Edward. ". . . A Commentary," 75–76.
Mersereau, John. *Russian Romantic Fiction*, 167–169.

"The Sorochinsty Fair"
Mersereau, John. *Russian Romantic Fiction*, 165–167.
Rancour-Laferriere, Daniel. "All the World's *Vertep*: The Personification/De-
     personification Complex in Gogol's 'Soročinskaja jarmarka,'" *Harvard
     Ukrainian Stud*, 6, iii (1982), 339–371.

"Taras Bulba"
Jamosky, Edward. "Romanticism or Realism: Which Predominates in Gogol's
     'Taras Bulba'?" *Proceedings of the Kentucky Foreign Language Conference: Slavic
     Section*, 2, i (1984), 53–63.
Mersereau, John. *Russian Romantic Fiction*, 250–253.
Pursglove, Michael. "A Note on the Bird Imagery of Gogol's 'Taras Bulba,'"
     Irish Slavonic Stud, 2 (1981), 16–21.

"A Terrible Vengeance"
Katz, Michael R. *Dreams* . . . , 71–72.

"Viy"
Mersereau, John. *Russian Romantic Fiction*, 253–255.

HERBERT GOLD

"A Selfish Story"
Robinson, James C. "1968–1980: Experiment and Tradition," in Weaver, Gordon, Ed. *The American Short Story, 1945–1980*, 84–85.

NADINE GORDIMER

"A Chip of Glass Ruby"
Sheidley, William E., and Ann Charters. *Instructor's Manual . . .* , 156.

"Is There Nowhere Else Where We Can Meet?"
JanMohamed, Abdul R. *Manichean Aesthetics . . .* , 87–88.
Sirlin, Rhoda, and David H. Richter. *Instructor's Manual . . .* , 50–51.

"The Termitary"
Madden, David, and Virgil Scott. *Instructor's Manual . . .* , 6th ed., 32–34.

CAROLINE GORDON

"The Last Day in the Field"
Scott, Virgil, and David Madden. *Instructor's Manual . . .* , 4th ed., 2–4; Madden, David. *Instructor's Manual . . .* , 5th ed., 3–4; Madden, David, and Virgil Scott. *Instructor's Manual . . .* , 6th ed., 10–12.

MAXIM GORKY

"Chelkash"
Clardy, Jesse V. and Betty S. *The Superfluous Man . . .* , 110–112.

"Makar Chudra"
Clardy, Jesse V. and Betty S. *The Superfluous Man . . .* , 108–110.

"Nilushka"
Kishtainy, Khalid. *The Prostitute . . .* , 96–97.

"On the Rafts"
Nabokov, Vladimir. *Lectures on Russian Literature*, 304–306.

"Twenty-Six Men and a Girl"
Clardy, Jesse V. and Betty S. *The Superfluous Man . . .* , 112–114.
Gutsche, George. "The Role of the 'One' in Gor'kij's 'Twenty-Six and One,'" in Leighton, Lauren G., Ed. *Studies in Honor . . .* , 145–154.
O'Toole, L. Michael. *Structure, Style and Interpretation . . .* , 128–141.

WILLIAM GOYEN

"Pore Perrie"
Vauthier, Simone. "The True Story: A Reading of William Goyen's 'Pore Perrie,'" *Les Cahiers de la Nouvelle*, 1 (1983), 139–158.

PATRICIA GRACE

"Letters from Whetu"
Beston, John B. "The Fiction of Patricia Grace," *Ariel*, 15, ii (1984), 45.

"Parade"
Pearson, Bill. "Witi Ihimaera and Patricia Grace," in Hankin, Cherry, Ed. ... *New Zealand Short Story*, 180.

"Valley"
Pearson, Bill. "Witi Ihimaera and Patricia Grace," 178–180.

DANIIL A. GRANIN

"Return Ticket"
Pankin, Boris. "The Past That Is Always with Us," *Soviet Stud Lit*, 18, i (1982), 44–48.

GORDON GRANT

"The Provocation of Ah Sing"
Wu, William F. *The Yellow Peril* ... , 51–52.

SHIRLEY ANN GRAU

"The Beach Party"
Rohrberger, Mary. "Shirley Ann Grau and the Short Story," in Prenshaw, Peggy W., Ed. *Women Writers* ... , 97.

"The Bright Day"
Rohrberger, Mary. "Shirley Ann Grau ... ," 92–93.

"Fever Flower"
Rohrberger, Mary. "Shirley Ann Grau ... ," 93–94.

"For a Place in the Sun"
Rohrberger, Mary. "Shirley Ann Grau ... ," 83–85.

"The Fragile Age"
Rohrberger, Mary. "Shirley Ann Grau ... ," 87–88.

"The Girl with the Flaxen Hair"
Rohrberger, Mary. "Shirley Ann Grau . . . ," 92.

"Letting Go"
Rohrberger, Mary. "Shirley Ann Grau . . . ," 100.

"The Lonely One"
Rohrberger, Mary. "Shirley Ann Grau . . . ," 86–87.

"Miss Yellow Eyes"
Rohrberger, Mary. "Shirley Ann Grau . . . ," 90–92.

"One Summer"
Rohrberger, Mary. "Shirley Ann Grau . . . ," 94.

"The Patriarch"
Rohrberger, Mary. "Shirley Ann Grau . . . ," 98–99.

"The Shadow Land"
Rohrberger, Mary. "Shirley Ann Grau . . . ," 86.

"So Many Worlds"
Rohrberger, Mary. "Shirley Ann Grau . . . ," 85–86.

"Stanley"
Rohrberger, Mary. "Shirley Ann Grau . . . ," 97–98.

"Summer Shore"
Rohrberger, Mary. "Shirley Ann Grau . . . ," 99–100.

"The Things You Keep"
Rohrberger, Mary. "Shirley Ann Grau . . . ," 87.

"White Girl, Fine Girl"
Rohrberger, Mary. "Shirley Ann Grau . . . ," 89–90.

"The Wind Shifting West"
Rohrberger, Mary. "Shirley Ann Grau . . . ," 95–97.

JOHN GRAY

"The Great Worm"
Cevasco, G. A. *John Gray,* 28–30.

"The Person in Question"
Cevasco, G. A. *John Gray,* 34–39.

JULIEN [JULIAN] GREEN

"Pilgrim on the Earth"
Dunaway, John M. *The Metamorphosis* . . . , 32–44.

GRAHAM GREENE

"The Basement Room"
Kelly, Richard. *Graham Greene,* 151–153.

"A Chance for Mr. Lever"
Kelly, Richard. *Graham Greene,* 154–155.

"Cheap in August"
Kelly, Richard. *Graham Greene,* 162–164.
Sharrock, Roger. *Saints* . . . , 211–212.

"The Destructors"
Feldmann, Hans. "The Idea of History in Graham Greene's 'The Destructors,' "
    Stud Short Fiction, 19 (1982), 241–245.
Kelly, Richard. *Graham Greene,* 145–147.

"Dream of a Strange Land"
Kelly, Richard. *Graham Greene,* 158–159.

"A Drive in the Country"
Kelly, Richard. *Graham Greene,* 147–148.

"The End of the Party"
Kelly, Richard. *Graham Greene,* 149–151.

"The Hint of an Explanation"
Kelly, Richard. *Graham Greene,* 153–154.

"I Spy"
Kelly, Richard. *Graham Greene,* 149–150.

"A Little Place Off the Edgeware Road"
Kelly, Richard. *Graham Greene,* 148–149.

"The Lottery Ticket"
Walker, Ronald G. *Infernal Paradise* . . . , 351–352.

"Under the Garden"
Kelly, Richard. *Graham Greene,* 156–158.
Sharrock, Roger. *Saints* . . . , 31–36.

"A Visit to Morin"
Sharrock, Roger. *Saints* . . . , 193–194.

LEE GREGOR

"Heavy Planet"
Cioffi, Frank. *Formula Fiction?* . . . , 121–122.

I. GREKOVA

"On Trial"
Blum, Jakub. "Soviet Russian Literature," in Blum, Jakub, and Vera Rich. *The Image of the Jew* . . . , 40–41.

GERALD GRIFFIN

"Half-Sir"
Schirmer, Gregory A. "Tales from Big House and Cabin: The Nineteenth Century," in Kilroy, James F., Ed. *The Irish Short Story* . . . , 31–32.

FRANZ GRILLPARZER

"The Poor Player"
Birrell, Gordon. "Time, Timelessness, and Music in Grillparzer's 'Spielmann,'" *Germ Q,* 57 (1984), 558–575.
Brandt, Helmut. "Grillparzers Erzählung 'Der arme Spielmann': Eine europäische Ortung der Kunst auf österreichischem Boden," in Zeman, Herbert, Ed. *Die österreichische Literatur* . . . , 343–346.
Seeba, Hinrich [sic] C. "Franz Grillparzer: 'Die arme Spielmann,'" in Lützeler, Paul M., Ed. *Romane und Erzählungen* . . . , 386–422.

HANS GRIMM

"The Life of John Neukwa"
Ridley, Hugh. *Images of Imperialism,* 106.

BEATRIZ GUIDO

"Diez vueltas a la manzana"
Lewald, H. Ernest. "Alienation and Eros in Three Stories by Beatriz Guido, Marta Lynch, and Amalia Jamilis," in Mora, Gabriela, and Karen S. Van Hooft, Eds. *Theory and Practice* . . . , 175–181.

A[LFRED] B[ERTRAM] GUTHRIE

"The Image"
Ford, Thomas W. *A. B. Guthrie,* 140.

"Loco"
Ford, Thomas W. *A. B. Guthrie,* 140–141.

MANUEL GUTÍERREZ NÁJERA

"After the Races"
Lindstrom, Naomi. "The Spanish American Short Story from Echeverría to
    Quiroga," in Peden, Margaret S., Ed. *The Latin American Short Story . . . ,*
    63–64.

"At the Hippodrome"
Lindstrom, Naomi. ". . . Echeverría to Quiroga," 63–64.

JOE HALDEMAN

"A Mind of His Own"
Gordon, Joan. *Joe Haldeman,* 55–56.

"Summer Lease"
Gordon, Joan. *Joe Haldeman,* 56–57.

"Tricentennial"
Gordon, Joan. *Joe Haldeman,* 53–54.

JAMES HALL

"The Dark Maid of Illinois"
Hallwas, John E. "James Hall's 'The Dark Maid of Illinois,'" *Old Northwest,* 5
    (1979), 141–147.

TAK HALLUS

"The Linguist"
Meyers, Walter E. *Aliens and Linguists . . . ,* 110–111.

EDMOND HAMILTON

"Devolution"
Hassler, Donald M. *The Comic Tone . . . ,* 88–89.

"The Island of Unreason"
Cioffi, Frank. *Formula Fiction? . . . ,* 114–116.

DASHIELL HAMMETT

"The Big Knock-Over"
Durham, Philip. "The 'Black Mask' School," in Madden, David, Ed. *Tough Guy Writers* . . . , 66–67.
Marling, William. *Dashiell Hammett,* 40–42.

"Corkscrew"
Durham, Philip. "The "Black Mask' School," 64–65.

"Dead Yellow Woman"
Marling, William. *Dashiell Hammett,* 38–40.
Wu, William F. *The Yellow Peril* . . . , 186–190.

"Fly Paper"
Sirlin, Rhoda, and David H. Richter. *Instructor's Manual* . . . , 51–52.

"The Girl with the Silver Eyes"
Marling, William. *Dashiell Hammett,* 33–35.

"The Golden Horseshoe"
Durham, Philip. "The 'Black Mask' School," 62.

"The House on Turk Street"
Wu, William F. *The Yellow Peril* . . . , 184–186.

"One Hour"
Wolfe, Peter. *Beams Falling* . . . , 60–61.

"This King Business"
Wolfe, Peter. *Beams Falling* . . . , 37–38, 68–69.

"Tom, Dick, or Harry"
Wolfe, Peter. *Beams Falling* . . . , 61.

KNUT HAMSUN

"Secret Suffering"
Buttry, Dolores. " 'Secret Suffering': Knut Hamsun's Allegory of the Creative Artist," *Stud Short Fiction,* 19 (1982), 1–7.

PETER HANDKE

"Der Chinese des Schmerzes"
Manthey, Jürgen. "Literatur: Eine Kolumne," *Merkur,* 38, i (1984), 80–86.

"Greeting the Board of Directors"
Klinkowitz, Jerome, and James Knowlton. *Peter Handke* . . . , 28.

"Der kurze Brief zum langen Abschied"
Pakendorf, Gunther. "Der Realismus der entfremdeten Welt: Peter Handke, 'Der kurze Brief zum langen Abschied,'" *Acta Germanica*, 14 (1981), 157–174.

"Martial Law"
Klinkowitz, Jerome, and James Knowlton. *Peter Handke . . .*, 29–31.

"The Peddler"
Klinkowitz, Jerome, and James Knowlton. *Peter Handke . . .*, 29.

"Wunschlose Unglück"
Mauser, Wolfgang. "Peter Handke: 'Wunschlose Unglück'—erwünschte Unglück?" *Der Deutschunterricht*, 34, v (1982), 73–89.

BARRY HANNAH

"Love Too Long"
Shepherd, Allen. "Outrage and Speculation: Barry Hannah's *Airships*," *Notes Mississippi Writers*, 14 (1982), 66–68.

"Testimony of Pilot"
Shepherd, Allen. "Outrage . . . ," 68–71.

"Water Liars"
Shepherd, Allen. "Outrage . . . ," 64–66.

CARL HANSEN

"Prosperity"
Mossberg, Christer L. *Scandinavian Immigrant Literature*, 25–26.

JAMES HANSON

"Behind the Devil Screen"
Wu, William F. *The Yellow Peril . . .*, 55–56.

YAHYA HAQQI

"Abu Fuda"
Cooke, Miriam. *. . . Yahya Haqqi*, 131–133.

"As Though"
Cooke, Miriam. *. . . Yahya Haqqi*, 75.

"Filla, Mishmish, Lulu"
Cooke, Miriam. *. . . Yahya Haqqi*, 135.

"The First Lesson"
Cooke, Miriam. . . . *Yahya Haqqi*, 130–131.

"A Glass House"
Cooke, Miriam. . . . *Yahya Haqqi*, 61.

"The Holy Man Is Not Confused"
Cooke, Miriam. . . . *Yahya Haqqi*, 77–78.

"Irony, or The Man with the Black Face"
Cooke, Miriam. . . . *Yahya Haqqi*, 136.

"The Mosque Mat"
Cooke, Miriam. . . . *Yahya Haqqi*, 39–40.

"People and People"
Cooke, Miriam. . . . *Yahya Haqqi*, 105–106.

"The Perfume Bottle"
Cooke, Miriam. . . . *Yahya Haqqi*, 75–76.

"A Photograph"
Cooke, Miriam. . . . *Yahya Haqqi*, 76–77.

"The Protest"
Cooke, Miriam. . . . *Yahya Haqqi*, 33–34.

"The Saint's Lamp"
Cooke, Miriam. . . . *Yahya Haqqi*, 70.

"Sale!!!"
Cooke, Miriam. . . . *Yahya Haqqi*, 74.

"The Spiral Staircase"
Cooke, Miriam. . . . *Yahya Haqqi*, 32–33.

"A Story from Prison"
Cooke, Miriam. . . . *Yahya Haqqi*, 110–112.

"The Ten Commandments for the Vegetable Market"
Cooke, Miriam. . . . *Yahya Haqqi*, 48–49.

"The Turkey"
Cooke, Miriam. . . . *Yahya Haqqi*, 112–113.

"The Vacant Bed"
Cooke, Miriam. . . . *Yahya Haqqi*, 121–123.

THOMAS HARDY

"Alicia's Diary"
Brady, Kristin. *The Short Stories* . . . , 173–175.

"Andrew Satchel and the Parson and Clerk"
Brady, Kristin. *The Short Stories* . . . , 146–147.

"Anna, Lady Baxby"
Brady, Kristin. *The Short Stories* . . . , 76–78.

"Barbara of the House of Grebe"
Brady, Kristin. *The Short Stories* . . . , 57–62.

"A Changed Man"
Brady, Kristin. *The Short Stories* . . . , 190–193.

"The Distracted Preacher"
Brady, Kristin. *The Short Stories* . . . , 37–40.

"The Duchess of Hamptonshire"
Brady, Kristin. *The Short Stories* . . . , 80–83.

"The Duke's Reappearance"
Brady, Kristin. *The Short Stories* . . . , 187–188.

"Enter a Dragoon"
Brady, Kristin. *The Short Stories* . . . , 189–190.

"Fellow-Townsmen"
Brady, Kristin. *The Short Stories* . . . , 28–33.
Herzog, Toby C. "Hardy's 'Fellow-Townsmen': A Primer for the Novels," *Colby Lib Q,* 18 (1982), 231–240.

"The Fiddler of the Reels"
Brady, Kristin. *The Short Stories* . . . , 132–141.

"The First Countess of Wessex"
Brady, Kristin. *The Short Stories* . . . , 54–57.

"For Conscience's Sake"
Brady, Kristin. *The Short Stories* . . . , 109–113.
Shaw, Valerie. *The Short Story* . . . , 220–221.

"The History of the Hardcomes"
Brady, Kristin. *The Short Stories* . . . , 144–145.

"The Honourable Laura"
Brady, Kristin. *The Short Stories* . . . , 83–84.

"An Imaginative Woman"
Brady, Kristin. *The Short Stories* . . . , 98–104.

"Interlopers at the Knap"
Brady, Kristin. *The Short Stories* . . . , 33–37.

"The Lady Icenway"
Brady, Kristin. *The Short Stories* . . . , 69–74.

"Lady Mottisfont"
Brady, Kristin. *The Short Stories* . . . , 66–69.

"The Lady Penelope"
Brady, Kristin. *The Short Stories* . . . , 78–80.

"A Legend of the Year Eighteen Hundred and Four"
Brady, Kristin. *The Short Stories* . . . , 12–16.

"The Marchioness of Stonehenge"
Brady, Kristin. *The Short Stories* . . . , 62–66.

"The Melancholy Hussar of the German Legion"
Brady, Kristin. *The Short Stories* . . . , 16–21.

"A Mere Interlude"
Brady, Kristin. *The Short Stories* . . . , 171–173.

"Netty Sargent's Copyhold"
Brady, Kristin. *The Short Stories* . . . , 149–150.

"On the Western Circuit"
Brady, Kristin. *The Short Stories* . . . , 120–128.

"Our Exploits at West Poley"
Brady, Kristin. *The Short Stories* . . . , 169–170.

"The Romantic Adventures of a Milkmaid"
Brady, Kristin. *The Short Stories* . . . , 166–169.

"Squire Petrick's Lady"
Brady, Kristin. *The Short Stories* . . . , 74–76.

"The Superstitious Man's Story"
Brady, Kristin. *The Short Stories* . . . , 145–146.

"The Three Strangers"
Brady, Kristin. *The Short Stories* . . . , 6–12.
Wilson, Keith. "Hardy and the Hangman: The Dramatic Appeal of 'The Three Strangers,'" *English Lit Transition*, 24 (1981), 155–160.

"To Please His Wife"
Brady, Kristin. *The Short Stories* . . . , 128–132.

"Tony Kytes, the Arch-Deceiver"
Brady, Kristin. *The Short Stories* . . . , 143–144.

WILSON HARRIS

HARRY HARRISON

"The Streets of Ashkelon"
Born, Daniel. "Character as Perception: Science Fiction and the Christian Man
    of Faith," *Extrapolation*, 24 (1983), 256–257.

WILLIAM HARRISON

"Roller Ball Murder"
Hull, Elizabeth A. "Merging Madness: *Rollerball* as a Cautionary Tale," in Erlich,
    Richard D., and Thomas P. Dunn, Eds. *Clockwork Worlds . . .* , 164–171.

BRET HARTE

"An Episode of Fiddletown"
Wu, William F. *The Yellow Peril . . .* , 19–20.

"The Queen of Pirate Isle"
Wu, William F. *The Yellow Peril . . .* , 15–16.

"See Yup"
Wu, William F. *The Yellow Peril . . .* , 16–17.

"Tennessee's Partner"
Shaw, Valerie. *The Short Story . . .* , 90–91.

"Three Vagabonds of Trinidad"
Wu, William F. *The Yellow Peril . . .* , 17–18.

"Wan Lee, the Pagan"
Wu, William F. *The Yellow Peril . . .* , 14–15.

L[ESLIE] P[OLES] HARTLEY

"A Beautiful Character"
Mulkeen, Anne. *Wild Thyme . . .* , 20–21.

"Conrad and the Dragon"
Mulkeen, Anne. *Wild Thyme . . .* , 31.

"The Crossways"
Mulkeen, Anne. *Wild Thyme . . .* , 36–37.

"Friends of the Bridegroom"
Mulkeen, Anne. *Wild Thyme . . .* , 22.

"The Island"
Mulkeen, Anne. *Wild Thyme . . .* , 21–22.

JAROSLAV HAŠEK

GERHART HAUPTMANN

"Carnival"
Maurer, Warren R. *Gerhart Hauptmann*, 13–15.

"Der Ketzer von Soana"
Maurer, Warren R. *Gerhart Hauptmann*, 112–113.

"The Miracle of the Sea"
Maurer, Warren R. *Gerhart Hauptmann*, 121–123.

"Signalman Thiel"
Hahn, Walther. "Zur Zeitstruktur in Gerhart Hauptmanns 'Bahnwärter Thiel,'" *Carleton Germ Papers*, 10 (1982), 35–49.
McLean, Sammy. "Wife as Mother and Double: The Origin and Importance of Bipolar Personality and Erotic Ambivalence in the Work of Gerhart Hauptmann," in Crook, Eugene J., Ed. *Fearful Symmetry* . . . , 84–99.
Maurer, Warren R. *Gerhart Hauptmann*, 15–25.
Post, Klaus D. *Gerhart Hauptmann* . . . , 55–63.

HAZEL H. HAVERMALE

"The Canton Shawl"
Wu, William F. *The Yellow Peril* . . . , 58.

JOHN HAWKES

"Charivari"
Berry, Eliot. *A Poetry of Love* . . . , 10–13.
Karl, Frederick R. *American Fictions* . . . , 217.
O'Donnell, Patrick. *John Hawkes*, 41–51.

"The Goose on the Grave"
Berry, Eliot. *A Poetry of Love* . . . , 13–15.
Frakes, James R. "The 'Undramatized Narrator' in John Hawkes: Who Says?" in Santore, Anthony C., and Michael Pocalyko, Eds. *A John Hawkes Symposium* . . . , 34–35.
Karl, Frederick R. *American Fictions* . . . , 216–217.
O'Donnell, Patrick. *John Hawkes*, 55–60.

"The Grandmother"
Steiner, Robert. "Form and the Bourgeois Traveler," in Santore, Anthony C., and Michael Pocalyko, Eds. *A John Hawkes Symposium* . . . , 117–118.

"The Nearest Cemetery"
Kuehl, John. *John Hawkes* . . . , 41–42.

"The Owl"
Berry, Eliot. *A Poetry of Love* . . . , 15–17.
Karl, Frederick R. *American Fictions* . . . , 215–216.
O'Donnell, Patrick. *John Hawkes*, 50–55.

"A Song Outside"
Sirlin, Rhoda, and David H. Richter. *Instructor's Manual . . .* , 53.

"The Traveler"
Steiner, Robert. "Form and the Bourgeois Traveler," 115–117.

NATHANIEL HAWTHORNE

"Alice Doane's Appeal"
Colacurcio, Michael J. *The Province of Piety . . .* , 78–93.
*Martin, Terence. *Nathaniel Hawthorne*, 2nd ed., 183–184.
Pandeya, Probhat K. "That Blasted Hilltop: Nature in 'Alice Doane's Appeal,'"
    J Dept Engl, 17, ii (1981–1982), 64–71.
Robinson, Douglas. "Metafiction and Heartfelt Memory: Narrative Balance in
    'Alice Doane's Appeal,'" *ESQ: J Am Renaissance*, 28, iv (1982), 213–219.
Thompson, G. R. "The Apparition of This World: Transcendentalism and the
    American 'Ghost' Story," in Slusser, George E., Eric S. Rabkin, and Robert
    Scholes, Eds. *Bridges to Fantasy*, 93–94.
Towers, Tom H. "Why Are Those Girls Laughing? The Unity and Failure of
    'Alice Doane's Appeal,'" in Johnson, Mary L., and Seraphia D. Leyda, Eds.
    Reconciliations . . . , 161–176.

"The Ambitious Guest"
Carlson, Patricia A. *Hawthorne's Functional Settings . . .* , 118–120.
Colacurcio, Michael J. *The Province of Piety . . .* , 509–510.
Sears, John F. "Hawthorne's 'The Ambitious Guest' and the Significance of the
    Willey Disaster," *Am Lit*, 54 (1982), 354–367.

"The Artist of the Beautiful"
Bassil, Veronica. "Eros and Psyche in 'The Artist of the Beautiful,'" *ESQ: J Am
    Renaissance*, 30 (1984), 1–21.
Erlich, Gloria C. *Family Themes . . .* , 135–138.
Howard, June. "The Watchmaker, the Artist and the Iron Accent of History:
    Notes on Hawthorne's 'Artist of the Beautiful,'" *ESQ: J Am Renaissance*, 28,
    i (1982), 1–10.
*Martin, Terence. *Nathaniel Hawthorne*, 2nd ed., 60–62.
Watts, Emily S. *The Businessman . . .* , 45–47.

"The Birthmark"
Abcarian, Richard, and Marvin Klotz. *Instructor's Manual . . .* , 3rd ed., 7–8.
Carlson, Patricia A. *Hawthorne's Functional Settings . . .* , 148–153.
Carvo, Nathan. "Hawthorne's 'The Birthmark,'" *Explicator*, 42, iv (1984), 19–
    21.
Herzog, Kristin. *Women, Ethnics, and Exotics . . .* , 3–7.
*Martin, Terence. *Nathaniel Hawthorne*, 2nd ed., 54–56.

"The Devil in Manuscript"
Colacurcio, Michael J. *The Province of Piety . . .* , 492–493.

"Edward Randolph's Portrait"
Colacurcio, Michael J. *The Province of Piety . . .* , 406–423.

"Endicott and the Red Cross"
Colacurcio, Michael J. *The Province of Piety* . . . , 221–238.
McWilliams, John P. *Hawthorne, Melville* . . . , 46–48.
*Martin, Terence. *Nathaniel Hawthorne*, 2nd ed., 49–51.

"Ethan Brand"
Butts, Leonard C. "Diorama, Spectroscope, or Peepshow: The Question of the
    Old German's Showbox in Nathaniel Hawthorne's 'Ethan Brand,'" *Stud
    Short Fiction*, 20 (1983), 320–322.
Klingel, Joan E. "'Ethan Brand' as Hawthorne's *Faust*," *Stud Short Fiction*, 19
    (1982), 74–76.
McWilliams, John P. *Hawthorne, Melville* . . . , 104–105.
*Martin, Terence. *Nathaniel Hawthorne*, 2nd ed., 92–98.
Ringe, Donald A. *American Gothic* . . . , 162–164.

"The Gentle Boy"
Colacurcio, Michael J. *The Province of Piety* . . . , 160–202.
Erlich, Gloria C. *Family Themes* . . . , 76–79.
McWilliams, John P. *Hawthorne, Melville* . . . , 52–54.
*Martin, Terence. *Nathaniel Hawthorne*, 2nd ed., 57–58.
Miller, Edwin H. "'Wounded Love': Nathaniel Hawthorne's 'The Gentle Boy,'"
    Nathaniel Hawthorne J, 8 (1978), 47–54.
Newberry, Frederick, "Hawthorne's 'Gentle Boy': Lost Mediators in Puritan
    History," *Stud Short Fiction*, 21 (1984), 363–373.

"The Gray Champion"
Kruse, Horst. "Hawthorne and the Matrix of History: The Andros Matter and
    'The Gray Champion,'" in Fluck, Winfried, Jürgen Peper, and Willi P.
    Adams, Eds. *Forms and Functions* . . . , 103–119.
Loughman, Celeste. "Hawthorne's Patriarchs and the American Revolution,"
    Am Transcendental Q, 40 (1978), 336–337.
McWilliams, John P. *Hawthorne, Melville* . . . , 55–58.

"The Hall of Fantasy"
*Martin, Terence. *Nathaniel Hawthorne*, 2nd ed., 53.

"The Haunted Mind"
Bergman, David, Joseph de Roche, and Daniel M. Epstein. *Instructor's Man-
    ual* . . . , 37.
Colacurcio, Michael J. *The Province of Piety* . . . , 487–489.
*Martin, Terence. *Nathaniel Hawthorne*, 2nd ed., 38–41.
Ringe, Donald A. *American Gothic* . . . , 166–167.
Thompson, G. R. "The Apparition . . . ," 103–104.

"The Hollow of the Three Hills"
Carlson, Patricia A. *Hawthorne's Functional Settings* . . . , 109–111.
Colacurcio, Michael J. *The Province of Piety* . . . , 41–46.
*Martin, Terence. *Nathaniel Hawthorne*, 2nd ed., 44–45.

"Howe's Masquerade"
Colacurcio, Michael J. *The Province of Piety* . . . , 397–405.
Loughman, Celeste. "Hawthorne's Patriarchs . . . ," 337–338.
McWilliams, John P. *Hawthorne, Melville* . . . , 81–82.

"Lady Eleanore's Mantle"
Colacurcio, Michael J. *The Province of Piety* . . . , 424–448.

"The Lily Quest"
Carlson, Patricia A. *Hawthorne's Functional Settings* . . . , 111–115.

"The Man of Adamant"
Carlson, Patricia A. *Hawthorne's Functional Settings* . . . , 121–124.
Colacurcio, Michael J. *The Province of Piety* . . . , 238–251.

"The Maypole of Merry Mount"
Carlson, Patricia A. *Hawthorne's Functional Settings* . . . , 147–148.
Colacurcio, Michael J. *The Province of Piety* . . . , 251–282.
Deamer, Robert G. "Hawthorne's Dream in the Forest," *Western Am Lit*, 13
    (1979), 334–336.
*Martin, Terence. *Nathaniel Hawthorne*, 2nd ed., 77–80.
Massa, Ann. *American Literature in Context, IV* . . . , 87–93.
Shurr, William H. *Rappaccini's Children* . . . , 89–90.

"The Minister's Black Veil"
Berkove, Lawrence I. " 'The Minister's Black Veil': The Gloomy Moses of Mil-
    ford," *Nathaniel Hawthorne J*, 8 (1978), 147–157.
Ducker, Dan. " 'The Minister's Black Veil': A Dissenting View," in Hayward,
    Malcolm, Ed. *Proceedings* . . . , 30–35.
*Martin, Terence. *Nathaniel Hawthorne*, 2nd ed., 72–77.

"Mr. Higginbotham's Catastrophe"
Colacurcio, Michael J. *The Province of Piety* . . . , 502–506.

"My Kinsman, Major Molineux"
Baker, Sheridan. "Hawthorne's Evidence," *Philol Q*, 61 (1982), 481–483.
Carlson, Patricia A. *Hawthorne's Functional Settings* . . . , 131–137.
Collins, Michael J. "Hawthorne's Use of Clothing in 'My Kinsman, Major Moli-
    neux,' " *Nathaniel Hawthorne J*, 8 (1978), 171–172.
England, Eugene. "Hawthorne and the Virtue of Sin," *Lit & Belief*, 3 (1983),
    109–120.
Freese, Peter. " 'Rising in the World' and 'Wanting to Know Why': The Social-
    ization Process as Theme of the American Short Story," *Archiv*, 218, ii
    (1981), 290–294.
Loughman, Celeste. "Hawthorne's Patriarchs . . . ," 339–340.
McWilliams, John P. *Hawthorne, Melville* . . . , 85–88.
*Martin, Terence. *Nathaniel Hawthorne*, 2nd ed., 98–104.
Miller, James E., and Bernice Slote. *Instructor's Manual* . . . , 2nd ed., 4–5.
Sirlin, Rhoda, and David H. Richter. *Instructor's Manual* . . . , 56–57.
Vickery, John B. *Myths and Texts* . . . , 138–139.
Way, Brian. "Art and the Spirit of Anarchy: A Reading of Hawthorne's Short
    Stories," in Lee, A. Robert, Ed. *Nathaniel Hawthorne* . . . , 23–25.
Zajkowski, Robert. "Renaissance Psychology and Hawthorne's 'My Kinsman,
    Major Molineux,' " *Nathaniel Hawthorne J*, 8 (1978), 159–168.

"Old Esther Dudley"
Colacurcio, Michael J. *The Province of Piety* . . . , 449–482.
Loughman, Celeste. "Hawthorne's Patriarchs . . . ," 342.
McWilliams, John P. *Hawthorne, Melville* . . . , 81–82.

"An Old Woman's Tale"
Colacurcio, Michael J. *The Province of Piety* . . . , 46–49.
Patterson, Amy. "Between the Walnut-Tree and the Fountain: Perspective of an Earthly Life in Hawthorne's 'An Old Woman's Tale,' " *RE: Artes Liberales*, 11, i (1984), 13–20.

"The Prophetic Pictures"
Richards, Sylvie L. F. "The Eye and the Portrait: The Fantastic in Poe, Hawthorne, and Gogol," *Stud Short Fiction*, 20 (1983), 310–312.
Smith, Allan G. *The Analysis* . . . , 90–91.

"Rappaccini's Daughter"
Carlson, Patricia A. *Hawthorne's Functional Settings* . . . , 137–141.
Garber, Frederick. *The Autonomy of the Self* . . . , 263–269.
Hallissy, Margaret. "Hawthorne's Venomous Beatrice," *Stud Short Fiction*, 19 (1982), 231–239.
Herzog, Kristin. *Women, Ethnics, and Exotics* . . . , 3–7.
Kennedy, X. J. *Instructor's Manual* . . . , 3rd ed., 41–43.
*Martin, Terence. *Nathaniel Hawthorne*, 2nd ed., 87–92.
Ringe, Donald A. *American Gothic* . . . , 167–168.
Shurr, William H. *Rappaccini's Children* . . . , 1–4.
Zamora, Lois P. " 'A Garden Enclosed': Fuentes' *Aura*, Hawthorne's and Paz's 'Rappaccini's Daughter,' and Uyeda's *Ugetsu Monogatari*," *Revista Canadiense de Estudios Hispánicos*, 8 (1984), 321–334.

"Roger Malvin's Burial"
Beaver, Harold. "Towards Romance: The Case of 'Roger Malvin's Burial,' " in Lee, A. Robert, Ed. *Nathaniel Hawthorne* . . . , 31–47.
Carlson, Patricia A. *Hawthorne's Functional Settings* . . . , 153–160.
Colacurcio, Michael J. *The Province of Piety* . . . , 107–130.
Erlich, Gloria C. *Family Themes* . . . , 113–116.
Josipovici, Gabriel. *The World and the Book* . . . , 159–160.

"A Select Party"
*Martin, Terence. *Nathaniel Hawthorne*, 2nd ed., 51–52.

"The Seven Vagabonds"
Colacurcio, Michael J. *The Province of Piety* . . . , 497–500.

"The Shaker Bridal"
*Martin, Terence. *Nathaniel Hawthorne*, 2nd ed., 56.

"The Snow Image"
Berthold, Dennis. "Anti-Idealism in Hawthorne's 'The Snow Image,' " *Arizona Q*, 38 (1982), 119–132.
Erlich, Gloria C. *Family Themes* . . . , 133–135.
Gilbert, Sandra M., and Susan Gubar. *The Madwoman* . . . , 618–619.

"Wakefield"

Apter, T. E. *Fantasy Literature* . . . , 75–76.

Chibka, Robert L. "Hawthorne's Tale Told Twice: A Reading of 'Wakefield,'" *ESQ: J Am Renaissance*, 28, iv (1982), 220–232.

Colacurcio, Michael J. *The Province of Piety* . . . , 490–492.

Erlich, Gloria C. *Family Themes* . . . , 81–82.

Madden, David. *Instructor's Manual* . . . , 5th ed., 67–69; Madden, David, and Virgil Scott. *Instructor's Manual* . . . , 6th ed., 65–67.

Manheim, Leonard F. "Outside Looking In: Evidence of Primal-Scene Fantasy in Hawthorne's Fiction," *Lit & Psych*, 31 (1981), 8–9.

Perluck, Herbert. "The Artist as 'Crafty Nincompoop': Hawthorne's 'Indescribable Obliquity of Gait' in 'Wakefield,'" *Nathaniel Hawthorne J*, 8 (1978), 181–194.

"The Wives of the Dead" [same as "The Two Widows"]

Carlson, Patricia A. *Hawthorne's Functional Settings* . . . , 115–118.

Christophersen, Bill. "Hawthorne's 'The Wives of the Dead': Bereavement and the 'Better Part,'" *Stud Short Fiction*, 20 (1983), 1–6.

Colacurcio, Michael J. *The Province of Piety* . . . , 100–107.

Erlich, Gloria C. *Family Themes* . . . , 106–108.

"Young Goodman Brown"

Apseloff, Stanford and Marilyn. "'Young Goodman Brown': The Goodman," *Am Notes & Queries*, 20 (1982), 103.

Bergman, David, Joseph de Roche, and Daniel M. Epstein. *Instructor's Manual* . . . , 37.

Carlson, Patricia A. *Hawthorne's Functional Settings* . . . , 128–131.

Colacurcio, Michael J. *The Province of Piety* . . . , 283–313.

Eberwein, Jane D. "'My Faith Is Gone!': 'Young Goodman Brown' and Puritan Conversion," *Christianity & Lit*, 32 (1982), 23–32.

*Fogle, Richard H. "'Young Goodman Brown,'" in Dietrich, R. F., and Roger H. Sundell. *Instructor's Manual* . . . , 4th ed., 31–44.

Hollinger, Karen. "'Young Goodman Brown': Hawthorne's 'Devil in Manuscript': A Rebuttal," *Stud Short Fiction*, 19 (1982), 381–384.

*Martin, Terence. *Nathaniel Hawthorne*, 2nd ed., 81–86.

Matheson, Terence J. "'Young Goodman Brown': Hawthorne's Condemnation of Conformity," *Nathaniel Hawthorne J*, 8 (1978), 137–145.

Perrine, Laurence, and Thomas R. Arp. *Instructor's Manual* . . . , 6th ed., 50–52.

Ringe, Donald A. *American Gothic* . . . , 160–163.

Sirlin, Rhoda, and David H. Richter. *Instructor's Manual* . . . , 54–55.

Wright, Elizabeth. "The New Psychoanalysis and Literary Criticism: A Reading of Hawthorne and Melville," *Poetics Today*, 3 (1982), 90–96.

HAYASHI FUMIKO

"Late Chrysanthemums"

Keene, Donald. *Dawn to the West* . . . , 1144–1145.

KATE HAYES

"An Episode at Clarke's Crossing"
Harrison, Dick. *Unnamed Country* . . . , 65.

HAIM [HAYIM] HAZAZ

"Harat Olam"
Yuter, Alan J. *The Holocaust* . . . , 111–112.

"The Sermon"
Ramras-Rauch, Gila. "Cultural Naturalism in Israeli Literature," in Lewald,
    H. Ernest, Ed. *The Cry of Home* . . . , 340–341.

BESSIE HEAD

"Heaven Is Not Closed"
Barnett, Ursula A. *A Vision of Order* . . . , 200–201.

ANNE HÉBERT

"The Coral Dress"
Benson, Renate. "Aspects of Love in Anne Hébert's Short Stories," *J Canadian
    Fiction*," 25/26 (1979), 161.
Russell, Delbert W. *Anne Hébert*, 20.

"The Death of Stella"
Benson, Renate. "Aspects of Love . . . ," 172–173.
Russell, Delbert W. *Anne Hébert*, 24–25.

"Dominique's Angel"
Benson, Renate. "Aspects of Love . . . ," 162–163.
Russell, Delbert W. *Anne Hébert*, 20–22.

"A Grand Marriage"
Benson, Renate. "Aspects of Love . . . ," 170–172.
Russell, Delbert W. *Anne Hébert*, 17–20.

"The House on the Esplanade"
Benson, Renate. "Aspects of Love . . . ," 163–164.
Russell, Delbert W. *Anne Hébert*, 15–17.

"The Spring Time of Catherine"
Benson, Renate. "Aspects of Love . . . ," 168–170.
Russell, Delbert W. *Anne Hébert*, 23–24.

"The Torrent"
Benson, Renate. "Aspects of Love . . . ," 164–167.
Lemieux, Pierre. "La Symbolique du 'Torrent' d'Anne Hébert," *Revue de l'U-
    niversité d'Ottawa*, 43 (1973), 114–127.
Russell, Delbert W. *Anne Hébert*, 25–31.

SADEQ HEDAYAT

"The Abyss"
Lashgari, Deirdre. "Absurdity and Creation in the Work of Sadeq Hedayat," *Iranian Stud,* 15, i–iv (1982), 40–41.

"The Antichrist's Donkey"
Dorri, J. "National Traditions in Contemporary Persian Satirical Prose, 1920's– 1960's," in Ricks, Thomas M., Ed. *Critical Perspectives . . . ,* 143–144.

"Dash Akul"
Kamshad, H. *Modern Persian Prose . . . ,* 153–154.

"David the Hunchback"
Kamshad, H. *Modern Persian Prose . . . ,* 151–152.
Lashgari, Deirdre. "Absurdity and Creation . . . ," 36.

"Dead End"
Kamshad, H. *Modern Persian Prose . . . ,* 185–187.
Lashgari, Deirdre. "Absurdity and Creation . . . ," 39–40.

"The Elder Sister"
Kamshad, H. *Modern Persian Prose . . . ,* 152–153.

"The Fire Worshipper"
Kamshad, H. *Modern Persian Prose . . . ,* 148.

"The Ghouls" [same as "Eaters of the Dead"]
Kamshad, H. *Modern Persian Prose . . . ,* 155–156.

"The Legalizer"
Kamshad, H. *Modern Persian Prose . . . ,* 157.

"The Man Who Killed His Passion"
Kamshad, H. *Modern Persian Prose . . . ,* 156–157.
Katouzian, Homayoun. "Sadeq Hedayat's 'The Man Who Killed His Passionate Self,'" *Iranian Stud,* 10 (1977), 196–200.

"The Patriot"
Kamshad, H. *Modern Persian Prose . . . ,* 188–189.

"The Stray Dog"
Kamshad, H. *Modern Persian Prose . . . ,* 184–185.
Lashgari, Deirdre. "Absurdity and Creation . . . ," 37–39.

"Tulip"
Lashgari, Deirdre. "Absurdity and Creation . . . ," 37.

"The Woman Who Lost Her Man"
Kamshad, H. *Modern Persian Prose . . . ,* 154.

ROBERT A. HEINLEIN

"All You Zombies"
Fredericks, Casey. *The Future of Eternity* . . . , 15–16.

"Gulf"
Meyers, Walter E. *Aliens and Linguists* . . . , 173–175.
Nicholls, Peter. "Robert A. Heinlein," in Bleiler, Everett F., Ed. *Science Fiction Writers* . . . , 188.

"They"
Nicholls, Peter. "Robert A. Heinlein," 194.

"Waldo"
Wolfe, Gary K. "Autoplastic and Alloplastic Adaptations in Science Fiction: 'Waldo' and 'Desertion,'" in Slusser, George E., Eric S. Rabkin, and Robert Scholes, Eds. *Coordinates* . . . , 69–75.

ERNEST HEMINGWAY

"An Alpine Idyll"
Flora, Joseph M. . . . *Nick Adams*, 200–212.

"The Battler"
Flora, Joseph M. . . . *Nick Adams*, 83–93.
Oriard, Michael. *Dreaming of Heroes* . . . , 100.
Scruggs, Charles. *The Sage in Harlem* . . . , 165–166.

"Big Two-Hearted River"
Allen, Mary. *Animals* . . . , 188–189.
Flora, Joseph M. . . . *Nick Adams*, 148–175.
Gullason, Thomas A. "The 'Lesser' Renaissance: The American Short Story in the 1920s," in Stevick, Philip, Ed. *The American Short Story, 1900–1945*, 88–90.
Hannum, Howard L. "Soldier's Home: Immersion Therapy and Lyric Pattern in 'Big Two-Hearted River,'" *Hemingway R*, 3, ii (1984), 2–13.
Hoffmann, Charles G., and A. C. Hoffmann. "'The Truest Sentence': Words as Equivalents of Time and Place in *In Our Time*," in Noble, Donald R., Ed. *Hemingway* . . . , 104–106.
Schwenger, Peter. *Phallic Critiques* . . . , 46–48.
Sirlin, Rhoda, and David H. Richter. *Instructor's Manual* . . . , 57–58.
Vijgen, Theo. "A Change of Point of View in Hemingway's 'Big Two-Hearted River,'" *Notes Mod Am Lit*, 6, i (1982), Item 5.

"Cat in the Rain"
Friberg, Ingegerd. "The Reflection in the Mirror: An Interpretation of Hemingway's Short Story 'Cat in the Rain,'" *Moderna Språk*, 76 (1982), 329–338.
Miller, James E., and Bernice Slote. *Instructor's Manual* . . . , 2nd ed., 17.

"A Clean, Well-Lighted Place"
Abcarian, Richard, and Marvin Klotz. *Instructor's Manual . . .*, 3rd ed., 8.
Bergman, David, Joseph de Roche, and Daniel M. Epstein. *Instructor's Manual . . .*, 46–47.
*Broer, Lawrence R. "'A Clean, Well-Lighted Place,'" in Dietrich, R. F., and Roger H. Sundell. *Instructor's Manual . . .*, 4th ed., 73–74.
Kennedy, X. J. and Dorothy M. *Instructor's Manual . . .*, 3rd ed., 26–28.

"Cross-Country Snow"
Flora, Joseph M. . . . *Nick Adams*, 191–200.
Whitlow, Roger. *Cassandra's Daughters . . .*, 91–92.

"A Day's Wait"
Flora, Joseph M. . . . *Nick Adams*, 218–223.

"The Doctor and the Doctor's Wife"
Flora, Joseph M. . . . *Nick Adams*, 34–44.
Westbrook, Max. "Grace under Pressure: Hemingway and the Summer of 1920," in Nagel, James, Ed. . . . *Writer in Context*, 95–97.
Whitlow, Roger. *Cassandra's Daughters . . .*, 96–99.

"The End of Something"
Flora, Joseph M. . . . *Nick Adams*, 54–58.
Whitlow, Roger. *Cassandra's Daughters . . .*, 86–88.

"Fathers and Sons"
Watson, James G. "The American Short Story: 1930–1945," in Stevick, Philip, Ed. *The American Short Story, 1900–1945*, 125–126.
Whitlow, Roger. *Cassandra's Daughters . . .*, 101–105.

"Fifty Grand"
Oriard, Michael. *Dreaming of Heroes . . .*, 100–101.
Weeks, Robert P. "Wise-Guy Narrator and Trickster Out-Tricked in Hemingway's 'Fifty Grand,'" *Stud Am Fiction*, 10 (1982), 83–91.

"The Gambler, the Nun, and the Radio"
Morton, Bruce. "Music and Distorted View in Hemingway's 'The Gambler, the Nun, and the Radio,'" *Stud Short Fiction*, 20 (1983), 79–85.
Murolo, Frederick L. "Another Look at the Nun and Her Prayers," *Hemingway R*, 4, i (1984), 52–53.
Nicholson, Colin E. "The Short Stories After *In Our Time*: A Profile," in Lee, A. Robert, Ed. *Ernest Hemingway . . .*, 39–41.

"Hills Like White Elephants"
Gillegan, Thomas M. "Topography in Hemingway's 'Hills Like White Elephants,'" *Notes Mod Am Lit*, 8, i (1984), Item 2.
Gilmour, David R. "Hemingway's 'Hills Like White Elephants,'" *Explicator*, 41, iv (1983), 47–49.
Johnston, Kenneth G. "'Hills Like White Elephants': Lean, Vintage Hemingway," *Stud Am Fiction*, 10 (1982), 233–238.
Sipiora, Phillip. "Hemingway's 'Hills Like White Elephants,'" *Explicator*, 42, iii (1984), 50.

Whitlow, Roger. *Cassandra's Daughters* . . . , 93–96.

"In Another Country"
Flora, Joseph M. . . . *Nick Adams*, 135–144.
Scott, Virgil, and David Madden. *Instructor's Manual* . . . , 4th ed., 19–21; Madden, David. *Instructor's Manual* . . . , 5th ed., 23–25; Madden, David, and Virgil Scott. *Instructor's Manual* . . . , 6th ed., 21–23.

"Indian Camp"
Flora, Joseph M. . . . *Nick Adams*, 22–30.
Hoffmann, Charles G., and A. C. Hoffmann. " 'The Truest Sentence' . . . ," 107–108.
Schwenger, Peter. *Phallic Critiques* . . . , 40–43.

"The Killers"
Fleming, Robert E. "Hemingway's 'The Killers': The Map and the Territory," *Hemingway R*, 4, i (1984), 40–43.
Houston, Neal B. "Hemingway's Nervous Killers," *RE: Artes Liberales*, 10, i (1983), 25–29.
Lafontaine, Cécile A. "Waiting in Hemingway's 'The Killers' and Borges' 'La espera,' " *Revue de Littérature Comparée*, 57 (1983), 67–80.

"The Last Good Country"
Flora, Joseph M. . . . *Nick Adams*, 262–273.

"The Mother of a Queen"
Stetler, Charles, and Gerald Locklin. "Beneath the Tip of the Iceberg in Hemingway's 'The Mother of a Queen,' " *Hemingway R*, 2, i (1982), 68–69.

"My Old Man"
Brenner, Gerry. *Concealments* . . . , 8–9.

"A Natural History of the Dead"
Brenner, Gerry. *Concealments* . . . , 74–75.

"Night Before Landing"
Flora, Joseph M. . . . *Nick Adams*, 110–113.

"Now I Lay Me"
Shaw, Valerie. *The Short Story* . . . , 234–236.
Whitlow, Roger. *Cassandra's Daughters* . . . , 99–101.

"The Old Man and the Sea"
Allen, Mary. *Animals* . . . , 190–193.
Brenner, Gerry. *Concealments* . . . , 179–183.
Liu, Lequn. "*The Enchanting Sea* and 'The Old Man and the Sea,' " *Foreign Lit Stud*, 25, iii (1984), 132–133.
Radeljković, Zvonimir. "A Long Journey to Hope: Hemingway's 'The Old Man and the Sea,' " in Thorson, James L., Ed. *Yugoslav Perspectives* . . . , 103–106.
Strauch, Edward H. " 'The Old Man and the Sea': An Anthropological View," *Aligarh J Engl Stud*, 9, i (1984), 56–63.
Taylor, Charles. " 'The Old Man and the Sea': A Nietzschean Tragic Vision," *Dalhousie R*, 61 (1982), 631–634.

"On the Quai at Smyrna"
Seed, David. "'The Picture of the Whole': *In Our Time*," in Lee, A. Robert, Ed. *Ernest Hemingway* . . . , 25–27.

"A Pursuit Race"
Fontana, Ernest. "Hemingway's 'A Pursuit Race,'" *Explicator,* 42, iv (1984), 43–45.

"The Short Happy Life of Francis Macomber"
Pullin, Faith. "Hemingway and the Secret Language of Hate," in Lee, A. Robert, Ed. *Ernest Hemingway* . . . , 190–191.
Whitlow, Roger. *Cassandra's Daughters* . . . , 59–68.

"The Snows of Kilimanjaro"
Johnston, Kenneth G. "'The Snows of Kilimanjaro': An African Purge," *Stud Short Fiction,* 21 (1984), 223–227.
Nicholson, Colin E. "The Short Stories After *In Our Time* . . . ," 45–47.
Pullin, Faith. "Hemingway and the Secret Language . . . ," 189–190.
Sheidley, William E., and Ann Charters. *Instructor's Manual* . . . , 109–110.
Watson, James G. "The American Short Story . . . ," 124–125.
Whitlow, Roger. *Cassandra's Daughters* . . . , 68–74.

"Soldier's Home"
Seed, David. "'The Picture of the Whole,'" 24–25.
Westbrook, Max. "Grace under Pressure . . . ," 98–99.

"Ten Indians"
Smith, Paul. "The Tenth Indian and the Thing Left Out," in Nagel, James E. . . . *Writer in Context,* 53–74.
Whitlow, Roger. *Cassandra's Daughters* . . . , 101–102.

"The Three-Day Blow"
Flora, Joseph M. . . . *Nick Adams,* 58–68.
Schwenger, Peter. *Phallic Critiques* . . . , 45–46.
Whitlow, Roger. *Cassandra's Daughters* . . . , 88–89.

"Up in Michigan"
Petry, Alice H. "Coming of Age in Hortons Bay: Hemingway's 'Up in Michigan,'" *Hemingway R,* 3, ii (1984), 23–28.
Whitlow, Roger. *Cassandra's Daughters* . . . , 83–86.

"A Way You'll Never Be"
Flora, Joseph M. . . . *Nick Adams,* 123–127.

"Wine of Wyoming"
Flora, Joseph M. . . . *Nick Adams,* 223–235.

ZENNA HENDERSON

"J-Line to Nowhere"
King, Betty. *Women of the Future* . . . , 121–122.

WILL HENRY [HENRY W. ALLEN]

"A Bullet for Billy the Kid"
Gale, Robert L. *Will Henry / Clay Fisher* . . . , 96–97.

"The Friendship of Red Fox"
Gale, Robert L. *Will Henry / Clay Fisher* . . . , 93–94.

"The Ghost Wolf of Thunder Mountain"
Gale, Robert L. *Will Henry / Clay Fisher* . . . , 95–96.

"The Pale Eyes"
Gale, Robert L. *Will Henry / Clay Fisher* . . . , 90–91.

"Peace of the Pony Soldiers"
Gale, Robert L. *Will Henry / Clay Fisher* . . . , 91–92.

"River of Decision"
Gale, Robert L. *Will Henry / Clay Fisher* . . . , 94–95.

"The Tallest Indian in Toltepec"
Gale, Robert L. *Will Henry / Clay Fisher* . . . , 97–98.

FRANK HERBERT

"Cease Fire"
O'Reilly, Timothy. *Frank Herbert*, 52–53.

"Operation Syndrome"
O'Reilly, Timothy. *Frank Herbert*, 21–23.

"The Priests of Psi"
O'Reilly, Timothy. *Frank Herbert*, 91–96.

"Seed Stock"
O'Reilly, Timothy. *Frank Herbert*, 190–191.

"Skylark"
O'Reilly, Timothy. *Frank Herbert*, 112.

"The Tactful Saboteur"
O'Reilly, Timothy. *Frank Herbert*, 179–180.

EFRÉM HERNÁNDEZ

"Crossouts"
Brushwood, John S. "The Spanish American Short Story from Quiroga to
    Borges," in Peden, Margaret S., Ed. *The Latin American Short Story* . . . , 79–
    80.

"Nicomaco Closed In"
Brushwood, John S. ". . . Quiroga to Borges," 91–92.

ALFONSO HERNÁNDEZ CATÁ

"Ninety Days"
Brushwood, John S. "The Spanish American Short Story from Quiroga to
Borges," in Peden, Margaret S., Ed. *The Latin American Short Story* . . . , 76.

JOHN HERSEY

"The Death of Buchan Walsh"
Huse, Nancy L. *The Survival Tales* . . . , 50–51.

"A Fable South of Cancer"
Huse, Nancy L. *The Survival Tales* . . . , 54–55.

"The Pen"
Huse, Nancy L. *The Survival Tales* . . . , 51–53.

"A Short Wait"
Huse, Nancy L. *The Survival Tales* . . . , 53.

"Why Were You Sent Out Here?"
Huse, Nancy L. *The Survival Tales* . . . , 53–54.

ALEXANDER HERZEN

"Dr. Krupov"
Rzhevsky, Nicholas. *Russian Literature* . . . , 61–64.

"Elena"
Rzhevsky, Nicholas. *Russian Literature* . . . , 37–41.

"The Legend"
Rzhevsky, Nicholas. *Russian Literature* . . . , 34–37.

"Notes of a Certain Young Man"
Rzhevsky, Nicholas. *Russian Literature* . . . , 42–43.

"Thieving Magpies"
Rzhevsky, Nicholas. *Russian Literature* . . . , 59–60.

HERMANN HESSE

"Bird"
Ziolkowski, Theodore, Ed. *"Pictor's Metamorphoses"* . . . , xiii–xiv.

"Pictor's Metamorphoses"
Ziolkowski, Theodore, Ed. *"Pictor's Metamorphoses"* . . . , xii–xiii.

"Report from Normalia"
Ziolkowski, Theodore, Ed. *"Pictor's Metamorphoses"* . . . , xxii–xxiii.

"Siddhartha"
Bischoff, Howard W. "Hesse's Philosophy of Timelessness and the Western
    Modus Vivendi," J Evolutionary Psych, 1, ii (1980), 69–74.
Grislis, Karen, and Adrian Hsia. "Siddhartha's Journey to Brahma/Tao," *Par
    Rapport,* [n.v.] (1982–1983), 5–6, 59–66.

GEORG HEYM

"An Afternoon"
Krispyn, Egbert. *Georg Heym* . . . , 120–121.

"The Fifth of October"
Krispyn, Egbert. *Georg Heym* . . . , 114–116.

"The Lunatic"
Krispyn, Egbert. *Georg Heym* . . . , 119–120.

"Shakleton's Diary"
Braungard, George and Wolfgang. "Golemisierung im Pol-Pardies: Zur Kritik
    des neuzeitlichen Zukunftsentwurfs in Georg Heyms Erzählung 'Das Tag-
    ebuch Shakletons,'" *Text & Kontext,* 12 (1984), 266–289.

"The Thief"
Krispyn, Egbert. *Georg Heym* . . . , 116–119.

HIGUCHI ICHIYŌ

"A Buried Life"
Keene, Donald. *Dawn to the West* . . . , 172–174.

"Growing Up"
Keene, Donald. *Dawn to the West* . . . , 179–182.

"Nightingale in the Grove"
Keene, Donald. *Dawn to the West* . . . , 167.

"On the Last Day of the Year"
Keene, Donald. *Dawn to the West* . . . , 176–177.

SUSAN HILL

"The Albatross"
Jackson, Rosemary. "Cold Enclosures: The Fiction of Susan Hill," in Staley, Thomas F., Ed. *Twentieth-Century Women Novelists*, 90–91.

"The Custodian"
Jackson, Rosemary. "Cold Enclosures . . . ," 97.

"The Peacock"
Jackson, Rosemary. "Cold Enclosures . . . ," 96–97.

"Somerville"
Jackson, Rosemary. "Cold Enclosures . . . ," 91–92.

ZINAIDA HIPPIUS

"All Is for the Worse"
Pachmuss, Temira. *Zinaida Hippius* . . . , 275.

"Born Too Early"
Pachmuss, Temira. *Zinaida Hippius* . . . , 88.

"He Is White"
Pachmuss, Temira. *Zinaida Hippius* . . . , 273–274.

HIRADE SHŪ

"The Plan"
Rubin, Jay. *Injurious to Public Morals* . . . , 162–163.

"The Rebels"
Rubin, Jay. *Injurious to Public Morals* . . . , 163–166.

"The Way of the Brutes"
Rubin, Jay. *Injurious to Public Morals* . . . , 162.

HIROTSU RYŪRŌ

"The Love Suicide at Imado"
Keene, Donald. *Dawn to the West* . . . , 145.

HO TAO-SHENG

"The Apprentice"
Doležalova, Anná. "The Short Stories in *Creation Daily*," *Asian & African Stud*, 9 (1973), 58.

WILLIAM HOPE HODGSON

"The Gateway of the Monster"
Sampson, Robert. *Yesterday's Faces, II* . . . , 77–78.

"The Hog"
Sampson, Robert. *Yesterday's Faces, II* . . . , 80–81.

"The Whistling Room"
Pierce, Hazel B. *A Literary Symbiosis* . . . , 208–209.
Sampson, Robert. *Yesterday's Faces, II* . . . , 78–79.

SIGURD HOEL

"The Dream"
Lyngstad, Sverre. *Sigurd Hoel's Fiction* . . . , 24–25.

"The Idiot"
Lyngstad, Sverre. *Sigurd Hoel's Fiction* . . . , 13–15.

"Love One Another"
Lyngstad, Sverre. *Sigurd Hoel's Fiction* . . . , 81–82.

"The Murderer"
Lyngstad, Sverre. *Sigurd Hoel's Fiction* . . . , 82.

"Nothing"
Lyngstad, Sverre. *Sigurd Hoel's Fiction* . . . , 25–26.

"The Old Ones on the Hill"
Lyngstad, Sverre. *Sigurd Hoel's Fiction* . . . , 82–83.

"Spleen"
Lyngstad, Sverre. *Sigurd Hoel's Fiction* . . . , 15–18.

"The Star"
Lyngstad, Sverre. *Sigurd Hoel's Fiction* . . . , 18–19.

E[RNST] T[HEODOR] A[MADEUS] HOFFMANN

"Adventure on New Year's Night"
Kayser, Wolfgang. *The Grotesque* . . . , 69–70.

"The Cremona Violin"
Schneiderman, Leo. "E. Th. A. Hoffmann's *Tales*: Ego Ideal and Parental Loss,"
    Am Imago, 40 (1983), 302–303.

"Datura Fastuosa"
Schneiderman, Leo. ". . . Parental Loss," 291–294.

"The Deserted House"
Ellis, John M. "Über einige scheinbare Widersprüche in Hoffmanns Erzählungen," *Mitteilungen der E. T. A. Hoffmann,* 29 (1983), 31–35.

"Doge and Dogaressa"
Menhennet, Alan. *The Romantic Movement,* 252–254.

"The Golden Pot"
Hunter-Lougheed, Rosemarie. "Ehrenrettung des Herrn Registrators Heer-
brand," *Mitteilungen der E. T. A. Hoffmann,* 28 (1982), 12–18.
Nygaard, L. C. "Anselmus as Amanuensis: The Motif of Copying in Hoff-
mann's 'Der goldne Topf,'" *Seminar,* 19 (1983), 79–104.
Schneiderman, Leo. ". . . Parental Loss," 296–297.

"Ignaz Denner"
Schmidt, Hans-Walter. "Der Kinderfresser: Ein Motiv in E. T. A. Hoffmanns
'Ignaz Denner' und sein Kontext," *Mitteilungen der E. T. A. Hoffmann,* 29
(1983), 17–30.

"The King's Bride"
Schneiderman, Leo. ". . . Parental Loss," 295–296.

"Knight Gluck"
Slusser, George E. "Death and the Mirror: Existential Fantasy," in Slusser,
George E., Eric S. Rabkin, and Robert Scholes, Eds. *Coordinates . . . ,* 166–
172.

"Mademoiselle de Scudery"
Menhennet, Alan. *The Romantic Movement,* 254–256.
Schneiderman, Leo. ". . . Parental Loss," 303–306.

"Master Floh"
Vitt-Maucher, Gisela. "E. T. A. Hoffmanns 'Meister Floh': Überwindung des
Inhalts durch die Sprache," *Aurora,* 42 (1982), 188–215.

"Princess Brambilla"
Menhennet, Alan. *The Romantic Movement,* 256–259.

"The Sandman"
Apter, T. E. *Fantasy Literature . . . ,* 33–40.
Billy, Ted. "Optics and Irony: Hoffmann's 'Sand-Man' and Joyce's *Portrait,*" in
Bowen, Zack, Ed. *Irish Renaissance Annual IV,* 110–117.
Brantly, Susan. "A Thermographic Reading of E. T. A. Hoffmann's 'Der Sand-
mann,'" *Germ Q,* 55 (1982), 324–335.
Ellis, John M. "Clara, Nathanael and Narrator: Interpreting Hoffmann's 'Der
Sandmann,'" *Germ Q,* 54 (1981), 1–18.
Kayser, Wolfgang. *The Grotesque . . . ,* 72–76.
Menhennet, Alan. *The Romantic Movement,* 249–252.
Schneiderman, Leo. ". . . Parental Loss," 298–301.

HUGO VON HOFMANNSTHAL

"The Tale of the 672nd Night"
Mathes, Jürg. "Überlegungen zur Verwendung der Zahlen in Hofmannsthals 'Die 672. Nacht,'" *Germanisch-Romanische Monatsschrift*, 32 (1982), 202–214.
Verhofstadt, Edward. "Hugo von Hofmannsthals 'Märchen der 672. Nacht': Eine soziopsychologische Interpretation," in Brinkmann, Richard, Karl-Heinz Habersetzer, Paul Raabe, Karl-Ludwig Selig, and Blake L. Spahr, Eds. *Theatrum Europaeum*, 559–575.

DESMOND HOGAN

"A Poet and an Englishman"
Hogan, Robert. "Old Boys, Young Bucks, and New Women: The Contemporary Irish Short Story," in Kilroy, James F., Ed. *The Irish Short Story* . . . , 195–196.

ROBERT J. HOGAN

"The Case of the Six Coffins"
Wu, William F. *The Yellow Peril* . . . , 196–199.

JAMES HOGG

"The Adventures of Basil Lee"
Simpson, Louis. *James Hogg* . . . , 138–141.
Smith, Nelson C. *James Hogg*, 100–103.

"The Adventures of Captain John Lochy"
Simpson, Louis. *James Hogg* . . . , 141–143.

"The Barber of Duncow"
Smith, Nelson C. *James Hogg*, 138–140.

"The Brownie of the Black Haggs"
Simpson, Louis. *James Hogg* . . . , 163–165.
Smith, Nelson C. *James Hogg*, 143–144.

"The Cameronian Preacher's Tale"
Simpson, Louis. *James Hogg* . . . , 160–163.

"Cousin Mattie"
Smith, Nelson C. *James Hogg*, 142–143.

"George Dobson's Expedition to Hell"
Smith, Nelson C. *James Hogg*, 129–130.

"The Mysterious Bride"
Smith, Nelson C. *James Hogg*, 166–167.

"Strange Letter of a Lunatic"
Smith, Nelson C. *James Hogg*, 144–145.

"The Surpassing Adventures of Allan Gordon"
Simpson, Louis. *James Hogg . . .* , 143–144.

"Tibby Johnston's Wraith"
Smith, Nelson C. *James Hogg*, 128–129.

GRO HOLM

"Life on the Løstøl Farm"
Hanson, Katherine, Ed. *An Everyday Story . . .* , 60.

HUGH HOOD

"An Allegory of Man's Fate"
Garebian, Keith. *Hugh Hood*, 37–38.

"Breaking Off"
Garebian, Keith. *Hugh Hood*, 43–44.

"Flying a Red Kite"
Garebian, Keith. *Hugh Hood*, 13–15.

"Going Out as a Ghost"
Garebian, Keith. *Hugh Hood*, 33–34.

"The Good Listeners"
Garebian, Keith. *Hugh Hood*, 44–46.

"The Hole"
Garebian, Keith. *Hugh Hood*, 35–37.

"Looking Down from Above"
Lecker, Robert. *On the Line . . .* , 99–120.

"None Genuine Without This Signature"
Garebian, Keith. *Hugh Hood*, 49–50.

"Thanksgiving: Between Junetown and Caintown"
Garebian, Keith. *Hugh Hood*, 34–35.

"Three Halves of a House"
Garebian, Keith. *Hugh Hood*, 18–20.

"The Woodcutter's Third Son"
Garebian, Keith. *Hugh Hood*, 47–49.

PAUL HORGAN

"The Candy Colonel"
Gish, Robert. *Paul Horgan*, 78–79.

"The Captain's Watch"
Gish, Robert. *Paul Horgan*, 77–78.

"National Honeymoon"
Gish, Robert. *Paul Horgan*, 82–83.

"The Peach Stone"
Gish, Robert. *Paul Horgan*, 80–81.

"The Surgeon and the Nun"
Gish, Robert. *Paul Horgan*, 79–80.

HORI TATSUO

"The Beautiful Village"
Keene, Donald. *Dawn to the West . . .* , 699–701.

"The Fake Rubens"
Keene, Donald. *Dawn to the West . . .* , 693–694.

"The Holy Family"
Keene, Donald. *Dawn to the West . . .* , 694–697.

BRANT HOUSE

"Curse of the Mandarin's Fan"
Wu, William F. *The Yellow Peril . . .* , 203–205.

JAMES HOWARD

"The Director"
Born, Daniel. "Character as Perception: Science Fiction and the Christian Man
   of Faith," *Extrapolation*, 24 (1983), 267–268.

ROBERT ERVIN HOWARD

"Beyond the Black River"
Leiber, Fritz. "Howard's Fantasy," in Herron, Don, Ed. *The Dark Barbarian . . .* ,
   14–15.
Schweitzer, Darrell. *Conan's World . . .* , 39–40.

"Black Canaan"
Rickard, Dennis. "Through Black Boughs: The Supernatural in Howard's Fiction," in Herron, Don, Ed. *The Dark Barbarian . . .* , 72–73.

"The Black Stone"
Rickard, Dennis. "Through Black Boughs . . . ," 73–74.

"The Blonde Goddess of Bal Sagoth"
Vasbinder, Samuel H. "Aspects of Fantasy in Literary Myth about Lost Civili-
    zations," in Schlobin, Roger C., Ed. *The Aesthetics* . . . , 200–204.

"The Devil in Iron"
Schweitzer, Darrell. *Conan's World* . . . , 28–29.

"The Frost Giant's Daughter" [originally titled "Gods of the North"]
Schweitzer, Darrell. *Conan's World* . . . , 15–18.

"The God in the Bowl"
Schweitzer, Darrell. *Conan's World* . . . , 12–14.

"Jewels of Gwahlur"
Schweitzer, Darrell. *Conan's World* . . . , 38–39.

"Kings of the Night"
Sampson, Robert. *Yesterday's Faces, II* . . . , 129–130.

"The Mansion of Unholy Magic"
Sampson, Robert. *Yesterday's Faces, II* . . . , 109–110.

"The People of the Black Circle"
Leiber, Fritz. "Howard's Fantasy," 8–9.
Schweitzer, Darrell. *Conan's World* . . . , 29–31.

"The Phoenix on the Sword" [revision of "By This Axe I Rule"]
Schweitzer, Darrell. *Conan's World* . . . , 43–45.

"Pigeons from Hell"
Rickard, Dennis. "Through Black Boughs . . . ," 70–72.

"The Pool of the Black One"
Leiber, Fritz. "Howard's Fantasy," 11–12.
Schweitzer, Darrell. *Conan's World* . . . , 34–36.

"Queen of the Black Coast"
Schweitzer, Darrell. *Conan's World* . . . , 18–20.

"Red Nails"
Leiber, Fritz. "Howard's Fantasy," 10–11.
Schweitzer, Darrell. *Conan's World* . . . , 36–38.

"Red Shadows"
Sampson, Robert. *Yesterday's Faces, II* . . . , 122–123.

"Rogues in the House"
Schweitzer, Darrell. *Conan's World* . . . , 14–15.

"The Scarlet Ruse"
Schweitzer, Darrell. *Conan's World* . . . , 45–46.

"The Shadow Kingdom"
Sampson, Robert. *Yesterday's Faces, II* . . . , 127–128.

"Shadows in the Moonlight"
Schweitzer, Darrell. *Conan's World* . . . , 23–24.

"Shadows in Zamboula"
Schweitzer, Darrell. *Conan's World* . . . , 26–28.

"The Slithering Shadow"
Leiber, Fritz. "Howard's Fantasy," 9–10.
Schweitzer, Darrell. *Conan's World* . . . , 31–34.
Vasbinder, Samuel H. "Aspects of Fantasy . . . ," 200.

"The Thunder-Rider"
Indick, Ben P. "The Western Fiction of Robert E. Howard," in Herron, Don,
   Ed. *The Dark Barbarian* . . . , 106–107.

"The Tower of the Elephant"
Schweitzer, Darrell. *Conan's World* . . . , 11–12.

"The Treasure of Tranicos"
Schweitzer, Darrell. *Conan's World* . . . , 40–43.

"The Vale of Lost Women"
Herron, Don. "The Dark Barbarian," in Herron, Don, Ed. *The Dark Barbar-
   ian* . . . , 170–173.
Schweitzer, Darrell. *Conan's World* . . . , 20–23.

"Wings in the Night"
Sampson, Robert. *Yesterday's Faces, II* . . . , 125–126.

"A Witch Shall Be Born"
Schweitzer, Darrell. *Conan's World* . . . , 25–26.

"Worms of the Earth"
Rickard, Dennis. "Through Black Boughs . . . ," 79–81.

ROBERT E[RVIN] HOWARD and L. SPRAGUE DE CAMP

"The Road of Eagles"
Schweitzer, Darrell. *Conan's World* . . . , 24–25.

WILLIAM DEAN HOWELLS

"A Circle in the Water"
Nettels, Elsa. "Howells's 'A Circle in the Water' and Fitzgerald's 'Babylon Revisited,'" *Stud Short Fiction,* 19 (1982), 261–267.

"The Pearl"
Prioleau, Elizabeth S. *The Circle of Eros . . . ,* 142–143.

"A Sleep and a Forgetting"
Crowley, John W., and Charles L. Crow. "Psychology and the Psychic in W. D. Howells' 'A Sleep and a Forgetting,'" in Kerr, Howard, John W. Crowley, and Charles L. Crow, Eds. *The Haunted Dusk . . . ,* 155–168.

HSÜ SHIH-HENG

"Punishment"
Doležalová, Anna. "The Short Stories in *Creation Daily,*" *Asian & African Stud,* 9 (1973), 57–58.

W[ILLIAM] H[ENRY] HUDSON

"Dead Man's Plack"
Haymaker, Richard E. *From Pampas . . . ,* 343–344.

"Marta Riquelme"
Haymaker, Richard E. *From Pampas . . . ,* 341–342.
Walker, John. "'Home Thoughts from Abroad': W. H. Hudson's Argentine Fiction," *Canadian R Contemp Lit,* 10 (1983), 364–370.

"Niño Diablo"
Walker, John. "'Home Thoughts . . . ,'" 356–359.

"An Old Thorn"
Haymaker, Richard E. *From Pampas . . . ,* 342–343.

"El Ombú"
Haymaker, Richard E. *From Pampas . . . ,* 340–341.
Walker, John. "'Home Thoughts . . . ,'" 359–364.

"Pelino Viera's Confession"
Haymaker, Richard E. *From Pampas . . . ,* 339–340.
Tomalin, Ruth. *W. H. Hudson . . . ,* 120.
Walker, John. "'Home Thoughts . . . ,'" 351–355.

"Story of a Piebald Horse"
Haymaker, Richard E. *From Pampas . . . ,* 338–339.

LANGSTON HUGHES

"The Blues I'm Playing"
Rohrberger, Mary. "The Question of Regionalism: Limitation and Transcendence," in Stevick, Philip, Ed. *The American Short Story, 1900–1945,* 159.

"Conversation on the Corner"
Sheidley, William E., and Ann Charters. *Instructor's Manual . . . ,* 121.

"Cora Unashamed"
Rohrberger, Mary. "The Question . . . ," 160.

"Father and Son"
Rohrberger, Mary. "The Question . . . ," 161.

"Jazz, Jive and Jam"
Tracy, Steven C. "Simple's Great African-American Joke, *Coll Lang Assoc J,* 27 (1984), 239–253.

"Little Dog"
Rohrberger, Mary. "The Question . . . ," 158–160.

"Luani of the Jungles"
Ikonné, Chidi. *From Du Bois to Van Vechten . . . ,* 167–168.

TED HUGHES

"The Rain Horse"
Devoize, Jeanne. " 'The Rain Horse': Approche psychanalytique," *Les Cahiers de la Nouvelle,* 1 (1983), 17–21.

WILLIAM HUMPHREYS

"A Job of the Plains"
Perrine, Laurence, and Thomas R. Arp. *Instructor's Manual . . . ,* 6th ed., 14–15.

ZORA NEALE HURSTON

"John Redding Goes to Sea"
Ikonné, Chidi. *From Du Bois to Van Vechten . . . ,* 185–186.

"Spunk"
Ikonné, Chidi. *From Du Bois to Van Vechten . . . ,* 184–185.

ALDOUS HUXLEY

"Two or Three Graces"
Walker, Ronald G. *Infernal Paradise . . . ,* 122–123.

"Young Archimedes"
Bruffee, Kenneth A. *Elegiac Romance* . . . , 197–199.

IBUSE MASUJI

"The Charcoal Bus"
Keene, Donald, *Dawn to the West* . . . , 948.

"The Far-Worshiping Commander"
Keene, Donald. *Dawn to the West* . . . , 947.

YŪSUF IDRĪS

"Addiction"
Kurpershoek, P. M. *The Short Stories* . . . , 97–98.

"An Affair of Honour"
Kurpershoek, P. M. *The Short Stories* . . . , 93–95.

"Ahmad of the Local Council"
Kurpershoek, P. M. *The Short Stories* . . . , 127–129.

"The Aorta"
Kurpershoek, P. M. *The Short Stories* . . . , 150–151.

"Bus Stop"
Kurpershoek, P. M. *The Short Stories* . . . , 133–134.

"Caught Red-Handed"
Kurpershoek, P. M. *The Short Stories* . . . , 134–136.

"The Chair Bearer"
Kurpershoek, P. M. *The Short Stories* . . . , 151–152.

"The Cheapest of Nights"
Kurpershoek, P. M. *The Short Stories* . . . , 79–80.

"The Concave Mattress"
Kurpershoek, P. M. *The Short Stories* . . . , 161–163.

"The Curtain"
Kurpershoek, P. M. *The Short Stories* . . . , 136–138.

"The Deception"
Kurpershoek, P. M. *The Short Stories* . . . , 157.

"A Dining Table"
Kurpershoek, P. M. *The Short Stories* . . . , 92.

"The Dromedary Riders"
Kurpershoek, P. M. *The Short Stories* . . . , 80–81.

"Old Age Without Madness"
Kurpershoek, P. M. *The Short Stories* . . . , 125–126.

"On Cellophane Paper"
Kurpershoek, P. M. *The Short Stories* . . . , 172–173.

"The Ow Ow Language"
Kurpershoek, P. M. *The Short Stories* . . . , 130–132.

"The People"
Kurpershoek, P. M. *The Short Stories* . . . , 86–87.

"The Point"
Kurpershoek, P. M. *The Short Stories* . . . , 152–153.

"She"
Kurpershoek, P. M. *The Short Stories* . . . , 167–168.

"The Sin"
Kurpershoek, P. M. *The Short Stories* . . . , 189.

"The Sphinx"
Kurpershoek, P. M. *The Short Stories* . . . , 84.

"A Story with a Thin Voice"
Kurpershoek, P. M. *The Short Stories* . . . , 145–146.

"A Summer Night"
Kurpershoek, P. M. *The Short Stories* . . . , 84–86.

"Sunset March"
Kurpershoek, P. M. *The Short Stories* . . . , 100–101.

"The Sweetness of the Soul"
Kurpershoek, P. M. *The Short Stories* . . . , 175–177.

"The Swing"
Kurpershoek, P. M. *The Short Stories* . . . , 79.

"The Syren"
Kurpershoek, P. M. *The Short Stories* . . . , 189–190.

"To Asyut"
Kurpershoek, P. M. *The Short Stories* . . . , 103–105.

"Upon My Word of Honour and My Honesty"
Kurpershoek, P. M. *The Short Stories* . . . , 101–102.

"Was It Really Necessary to Turn on the Light, Lili?"
Kurpershoek, P. M. *The Short Stories* . . . , 160–161, 164–165.

"The Wish"
Kurpershoek, P. M. *The Short Stories* . . . , 90–91, 105–106.

WITI IHIMAERA

The Greenstone Patu"
Pearson, Bill. "Witi Ihimaera and Patricia Grace," in Hankin, Cherry, Ed.
. . . *New Zealand Short Story*, 174–175.

"Halcyon"
Pearson, Bill. "Witi Ihimaera and Patricia Grace," 168.

"The Truth of the Matter"
Pearson, Bill. "Witi Ihimaera and Patricia Grace," 174.

"The Whale"
Pearson, Bill. "Witi Ihimaera and Patricia Grace," 169–170.

IKUTA KIZAN

"The City"
Rubin, Jay. *Injurious to Public Morals* . . . , 80–81.

NATALIYA ILYINA

"The Return"
Blum, Jakub. "Soviet Russian Literature," in Blum, Jakub, and Vera Rich. *The Image of the Jew* . . . , 71–72.

EUGÈNE IONESCO

"Oriflamme"
Penner, Dick, Ed. *Fiction of the Absurd* . . . , 194–196.

WASHINGTON IRVING

"The Adventure of My Aunt"
Thompson, G. R. "Washington Irving and the American Ghost Story," in Kerr, Howard, John W. Crowley, and Charles L. Crow, Eds. *The Haunted Dusk* . . . , 23–24.

"The Adventure of My Uncle"
Thompson, G. R. ". . . American Ghost Story," 19–23.

The Adventure of the German Student"
Lupack, Barbara T. "Irving's German Student," *Stud Short Fiction*, 21 (1984), 398–400.

Ringe, Donald A. *American Gothic . . .* , 96–97.
Thompson, G. R. ". . . American Ghost Story," 27–29.

"The Adventure of the Mysterious Picture"
Thompson, G. R. ". . . American Ghost Story," 29–30.

"The Bold Dragoon"
Thompson, G. R. ". . . American Ghost Story," 24–27.

"Dolph Heyliger"
Ringe, Donald A. *American Gothic . . .* , 94–95.

"The Legend of Sleepy Hollow"
Daigrepont, Lloyd M. "Ichabod Crane: Inglorious Man of Letters," *Early Am
    Lit,* 19 (1984), 68–81.
Ringe, Donald A. *American Gothic . . .* , 92–94.
Seelye, John. "Root and Branch: Washington Irving and American Humor,"
    Nineteenth-Century Fiction, 38 (1984), 415–425.

"Rip Van Winkle"
Nigro, August J. *The Diagonal Line . . .* , 85–87.

"The Spectre Bridegroom"
Ringe, Donald A. *American Gothic . . .* , 92.

"Wolfert Webber"
Ringe, Donald A. *American Gothic . . .* , 94.

ISHIKAWA JUN

"The Beautiful Woman"
Keene, Donald. *Dawn to the West . . .* , 1092–1093.

"Fugen"
Keene, Donald. *Dawn to the West . . .* , 1094–1095.

"The Golden Legend"
Keene, Donald. *Dawn to the West . . .* , 1098–1099.

"The Jesus of the Burned-Out Site"
Keene, Donald. *Dawn to the West . . .* , 1099–1101.

"The Song of Mars"
Keene, Donald. *Dawn to the West . . .* , 1095–1097.

FAZIL ABDULOVICH ISKANDER

"Constellation of the Goat-Buffalo"
Brown, Edward J. . . . *Since the Revolution*, 3rd ed., 331.

"My Uncle Had the Highest Principles"
Brown, Edward J. . . . *Since the Revolution*, 3rd ed., 331.

IZUMI KYŌKA

"Night Patrolman"
Keene, Donald. *Dawn to the West* . . . , 208–210.

"Noble Blood, Heroic Blood"
Keene, Donald. *Dawn to the West* . . . , 206–208.

"The Operating Room"
Keene, Donald. *Dawn to the West* . . . , 210–211.

"A Song Under Lanterns"
Keene, Donald. *Dawn to the West* . . . , 217.

SHIRLEY JACKSON

"The Lottery"
Bergman, David, Joseph de Roche, and Daniel M. Epstein. *Instructor's Manual* . . . , 26–27.
Kennedy, X. J. *Instructor's Manual* . . . , 3rd ed., 31–32.
Sheidley, William E., and Ann Charters. *Instructor's Manual* . . . , 151–152.
Sirlin, Rhoda, and David H. Richter. *Instructor's Manual* . . . , 59–60.

"The Tooth"
Pascal, Richard. "'Farther Than Samarkand': The Escape Theme in Shirley Jackson's 'The Tooth,'" *Stud Short Fiction*, 19 (1982), 133–139.

HENRY JAMES

"The Aspern Papers"
*Booth, Wayne C. "'The Purloining of the Aspern Papers' or 'The Evocation of Venice,'" in Wegelin, Christof, Ed. *Tales of Henry James*, 455–462.
*Hartsock, Mildred. "Unweeded Garden: A View of 'The Aspern Papers,'" in Wegelin, Christof, Ed. *Tales of Henry James*, 463–470.
Waldmeier, Joseph J. "Miss Tina Did It: A Fresh Look at 'The Aspern Papers,'" *Centennial R*, 26 (1982), 256–267.

"The Author of 'Beltraffio'"
Stein, Allen F. *After the Vows* . . . , 89–97.
Wirth-Nesher, Hana. "The Thematics of Interpretation: James's Artist Tales," *Henry James R*, 5 (1984), 118–120.

"The Beast in the Jungle"

Blake, Nancy. "Le Regard de l'autre: Double ou imposture: 'La Bête dans la Jungle' de James," in [La Cassagnère, Christian, Ed.]. *Le Double* . . . , 179–189.

Bleu, Patricia. "Fantastique et revelation dans 'The Beast in the Jungle,'" *Delta*, 15 (1982), 91–102.

*Cady, Edwin H. "'The Beast in the Jungle,'" in Wegelin, Christof, Ed. *Tales of Henry James*, 481–483.

Coates, Paul. *The Realist Fantasy Fiction* . . . , 134–139.

Hilfer, Anthony C. *The Ethics of Intensity* . . . , 71–79.

Kimbel, Ellen. "The American Short Story: 1900–1920," in Stevick, Philip, Ed. *The American Short Story, 1900–1945*, 37–38.

Miller, James E., and Bernice Slote. *Instructor's Manual* . . . , 2nd ed., 8.

Nalbantian, Suzanne. *Seeds of Decadence* . . . , 38–40.

Peterson, Carla L. "Constant's 'Adolphe,' James's 'The Beast in the Jungle,' and the Quest for the Mother," *Essays Lit*, 9 (1982), 224–239.

Sirlin, Rhoda, and David H. Richter. *Instructor's Manual* . . . , 65–66.

Terrie, Henry. "Introduction," in James, Henry. *Tales of Art and Life*, 13–14.

*Vaid, Krishna B. "'The Beast in the Jungle,'" in Wegelin, Christof, Ed. *Tales of Henry James*, 475–481.

"The Bench of Desolation"

Dyson, J. Peter. "Romance Elements in Three Late Tales of Henry James: 'Mora Montravers,' 'The Velvet Glove,' and 'The Bench of Desolation,'" *Engl Stud Canada*, 5 (1979), 72–76.

"The Birthplace"

Conn, Peter. *The Divided Mind* . . . , 25–26.

Stafford, William T. *Books Speaking* . . . , 114–119.

Stein, Allen F. *After the Vows* . . . , 101–106.

"A Bundle of Letters"

Kirschke, James J. *Henry James* . . . , 245–246.

"Covering End"

Moon, Heath. "More Royalist Than the King: The Governess, the Telegraphist, and Mrs. Gracedew," *Criterion*, 24 (1982), 28–31.

"Crawford's Consistency"

Stein, Allen F. *After the Vows* . . . , 80–84.

"Daisy Miller"

Allen, Elizabeth. *A Woman's Place* . . . , 49–57.

Beaty, Jerome. *The Norton Introduction* . . . , 42–45.

Newberry, Frederick. "A Note on Horror in James's Revision of 'Daisy Miller,'" *Henry James R*, 3 (1982), 229–232.

*Ohmann, Carol. "'Daisy Miller': A Study of Changing Intentions," in Wegelin, Christof, Ed. *Tales of Henry James*, 443–452.

*Rahv, Philip. "'Daisy Miller,'" in Wegelin, Christof, Ed. *Tales of Henry James*, 442–443.

Terrie, Henry. "Introduction," 5–6.

"The Figure in the Carpet"
Halter, Peter. "Is Henry James's 'The Figure in the Carpet' Unreadable?" in
    Mortimer, Anthony, Ed. *Contemporary Approaches . . .* , 25–37.
Rawlings, Peter, Ed. *Henry James's Short Masterpieces,* II, xii–xiv.
Sweeney, Gerald M. "The Deadly Figure in James's Carpet," *Mod Lang Stud,*
    13, iv (1983), 79–85.
Williams, M. A. "Reading 'The Figure in the Carpet': Henry James and Wolf-
    gang Iser," *Engl Stud Africa,* 27 (1984), 107–121.
Wirth-Nesher, Hana. "The Thematics . . . ," 123–125.

"The Friends of the Friends" [originally titled "The Way It Came"]
Rawlings, Peter, Ed. *Henry James's Short Masterpieces,* II, xvi–xviii.

"The Ghostly Rental"
Wolfe, Charles K. "Victorian Ghost Story Technique: The Case of Henry
    James," *Romantist,* 3 (1979), 69–70.

"The Great Condition"
Tintner, Adeline. "'The Great Condition': Henry James and Bergsonian Time,"
    Stud Short Fiction, 21 (1984), 111–115.

"The Great Good Place"
Conn, Peter. *The Divided Mind . . .* , 22–23.
Kimbel, Ellen. "The American Short Story . . . ," 36–37.
Rawlings, Peter, Ed. *Henry James's Short Masterpieces,* II, xxi–xxiv.
Terrie, Henry. "Introduction," 11–13.
Ward, J. A. "Silence, Realism, and 'The Great Good Place,'" *Henry James R,* 3
    (1982), 129–132.

"In the Cage"
Hutchinson, Stuart. "James's 'In the Cage': A New Interpretation," *Stud Short
    Fiction,* 19 (1982), 19–25.
Kaston, Carren. *Imagination and Desire . . .* , 108–120.
Mayer, Charles W. "Drabble and James: 'A Voyage to Cythera' and 'In the
    Cage,'" *Stud Short Fiction,* 21 (1984), 57–63.
Moon, Heath. "More Royalist . . . ," 31–35.

"An International Episode"
*Wegelin, Christof. "'An International Episode,'" in Wegelin, Christof, Ed.
    Tales of Henry James, 452–455.

"John Delavoy"
Rawlings, Peter, Ed. *Henry James's Short Masterpieces,* II, xviii–xx.

"The Jolly Corner"
Conn, Peter. *The Divided Mind . . .* , 46–47.
Esch, Deborah. "A Jamesian About-Face: Notes on 'The Jolly Corner,'" *Engl
    Lit Hist,* 50 (1983), 587–605.
Habegger, Alfred. *Gender, Fantasy . . .* , 265–267.
Kimbel, Ellen. "The American Short Story . . . ," 38–41.
Strout, Cushing. "Henry James' Dream of the Louvre, 'The Jolly Corner,' and
    Psychological Interpretation," *Psychohistory R,* 8, i–ii (1979), 47–52; rpt.

Kurzweil, Edith, and William Phillips, Eds. *Literature and Psychoanalysis*, 217–231.
Terrie, James. "Introduction," 14–16.
*Vaid, Krishna B. "'The Jolly Corner,'" in Wegelin, Christof, Ed. *Tales of Henry James*, 484–487.

"Lady Barberina"
Stein, Allen H. *After the Vows . . .* , 109–113.

"The Last of the Valerii"
Stein, Allen H. *After the Vows . . .* , 70–76.
Terrie, Henry. "Introduction," 4–5.

"The Lesson of the Master"
Stein, Allen H. *After the Vows . . .* , 106–108.
Wirth-Nesher, Hana. "The Thematics . . . ," 120–123.

"The Liar"
Kirschke, James J. *Henry James . . .* , 236–238.
Norrman, Ralf. *The Insecure World . . .* , 149–150.
Stein, Allen H. *After the Vows . . .* , 97–101.
Terrie, James. "Introduction," 6–8.

"Louisa Pallant"
Richard, Claude. "La Romance de Louisa Pallant," *Delta*, 15 (1982), 103–113.

"Madame de Mauves"
Fowler, Virginia C. *Henry James's American Girl . . .* , 34–35.
Kirschke, James J. *Henry James . . .* , 216–220.
Stein, Allen F. *After the Vows . . .* , 76–80.

"The Marriages"
Moon, Heath. "A Freudian Boondoggle: The Case of James's 'The Marriages,'" *Arizona Q*, 40 (1984), 35–48.

"Master Eustace"
Tintner, Adeline R. "Henry James's *Hamlets*: 'A Free Arrangement,'" *Colby Lib Q*, 18 (1982), 168–172.

"The Middle Years"
Ghose, Zulfikar. *The Fiction of Reality*, 26–33.
Rawlings, Peter, Ed. *Henry James's Short Masterpieces*, II, xiv–xvi.

"The Modern Warning" [originally titled "The Two Countries"]
Fowler, Virginia C. *Henry James's American Girl . . .* , 47–51.

"Mora Montravers"
Dyson, J. Peter. "Romance Elements . . . ," 68–70.
Martin, W. R., and Warren U. Ober. "'Superior to Oak': The Part of Mora Montravers in James's *The Finer Grain*," *Am Lit Realism*, 16 (1983), 121–128.
Stein, Allen H. *After the Vows . . .* , 115–118.

"My Friend Bingham"
Stein, Allen H. *After the Vows . . .* , 63–67.

"The Next Time"
Rawlings, Peter, Ed. *Henry James's Short Masterpieces,* II, x–xii.
Stein, Allen H. *After the Vows . . .* , 108–109.

"Owen Wingrave"
Evans, John. "'Owen Wingrave': A Case for Pacifism," in Palmer, Christopher,
    Ed. *The Britten Companion,* 227–237.

"The Papers"
Conn, Peter. *The Divided Mind . . .* , 21–22.

"Paste"
Rawlings, Peter, Ed. *Henry James's Short Masterpieces,* II, xx–xxi.
Scott, Virgil, and David Madden. *Instructor's Manual . . .* , 4th ed., 58–60; Mad-
    den, David. *Instructor's Manual . . .* , 5th ed., 15–17; Madden, David, and
    Virgil Scott. *Instructor's Manual . . .* , 6th ed., 76–79.
Terrie, Henry. "Introduction," 9–11.

"The Path of Duty"
Stein, Allen H. *After the Vows . . .* , 114–115.

"Professor Fargo"
Kerr, Howard. "James's Last Early Supernatural Tales: Hawthorne Demagne-
    tized, Poe Depoetized," in Kerr, Howard, John W. Crowley, and Charles L.
    Crow, Eds. *The Haunted Dusk . . .* , 135–139.

"The Pupil"
*Hartsock, Mildred. "'The Pupil,'" in Wegelin, Christof, Ed. *Tales of Henry
    James,* 470–472.
Sirlin, Rhoda, and David H. Richter. *Instructor's Manual . . .* , 63–64.
Stanzel, F. K. *A Theory of Narrative,* 95–97.

"The Real Thing"
Abcarian, Richard, and Marvin Klotz. *Instructor's Manual . . .* , 3rd ed., 9.
Bergman, David, Joseph de Roche, and Daniel M. Epstein. *Instructor's Man-
    ual . . .* , 47–48.
Kirschke, James J. *Henry James . . .* , 239–241.
*Labor, Earle. "James's 'The Real Thing': Three Levels of Meaning," in We-
    gelin, Christof, Ed. *Tales of Henry James,* 472–475.
Norrman, Ralf. *The Insecure World . . .* , 147–149.
Shaw, Valerie. *The Short Story . . .* , 69–75.
Sheidley, William E., and Ann Charters. *Instructor's Manual . . .* , 22–23.
Stein, Allen F. *After the Vows . . .* , 108–109.
*Sundell, Roger H. "'The Real Thing,'" in Dietrich, R. F., and Roger H. Sun-
    dell. *Instructor's Manual . . .* , 4th ed., 6–11.
Terrie, James. "Introduction," 8–9.
Wolpers, Theodor. "Sujet, Motive und Themen bei Henry James: Untersu-
    chungen zür seiner Literaturkritik und 'The Real Thing,'" in Wolpers,
    Theodor, Ed. *Motive und Themen . . .* , 88–141.

"A Romance of Old Clothes"
Wolfe, Charles K. "Victorian Ghost Story Technique . . . ," 69.

"The Siege of London"
Funston, Judith E. " 'The Siege of London': James's Dreadful Girl Grown Up,"
    Arizona Q, 40 (1984), 85–96.

"Sir Edmund Orme"
Ringe, Donald A. *American Gothic . . .* , 186–187.

"The Story in It"
Tintner, Adeline R. "Henry James's 'The Story in It' and Gabriele D'Annunzio,"
    Mod Fiction Stud, 28 (1982), 201–214.

"The Story of a Masterpiece"
Kirschke, James J. *Henry James . . .* , 213–214.

"A Tragedy of Error"
Stein, Allen F. *After the Vows . . .* , 61–63.

"Travelling Companions"
Habegger, Alfred. *Gender, Fantasy . . .* , 240–242.

"The Turn of the Screw"
Bell, Millicent. " 'The Turn of the Screw' and the *recherche de l'absolu*," *Delta*, 15
    (1982), 33–48.
Coates, Paul. *The Realist Fantasy Fiction . . .* , 130–134.
Kawin, Bruce F. *The Mind of the Novel . . .* , 182–186.
Kreischer, Edith. "Henry James' 'The Turn of the Screw,' " in Thomsen,
    Christian W., and Jens M. Fischer, Eds. *Phantastik . . .* , 219–236.
Matheson, Terence J. "Did the Governess Smother Miles? A Note on James's
    'The Turn of the Screw,' " *Stud Short Fiction*, 19 (1982), 172–175.
Miall, David S. "Designed Horror: James's Vision of Evil in 'The Turn of the
    Screw,' " *Nineteenth-Century Fiction*, 39 (1984), 305–327.
Moon, Heath. "More Royalist . . . ," 22–27.
Norrman, Ralf. *The Insecure World . . .* , 169–174.
Otten, Terry. *After Innocence . . .* , 53–67.
Parr, Susan R. *The Moral . . .* , 69–78.
Petry, Alice H. "Jamesian Parody, *Jane Eyre*, and 'The Turn of the Screw,' " *Mod
    Lang Stud*, 13, iv (1983), 61–78.
Prou, Suzanne. "Le Mal de l'innocence," *L'Arc*, 89 (1983), 72–73.
Ringe, Donald A. *American Gothic . . .* , 188–189.
Rowe, John C. "Screwball: The Use and Abuse of Uncertainty in Henry James's
    'The Turn of the Screw,' " *Delta*, 15 (1982), 1–31.
Sirlin, Rhoda, and David H. Richter. *Instructor's Manual . . .* , 61–63.

"The Velvet Glove"
Dyson, J. Peter. "Romance Elements . . . ," 70–72.
Stein, Allen F. "The Hack's Progress: A Reading of James's 'The Velvet Glove,' "
    Essays Lit, 1 (1974), 219–226.

"Washington Square"
Hovey, Richard B. " 'Washington Square': James and 'the Deeper Psychology,' "
    Hartford Stud Lit, 14, i (1982), 1–10.
Hutchinson, Stuart. *Henry James* . . . , 11–23.
Kaston, Carren. *Imagination and Desire* . . . , 31–39.
Long, Robert E. . . . *The Early Novels*, 89–101.

M[ONTAGUE] R[HODES] JAMES

"After the Dark in the Playing Field"
Butts, Mary. "The Art of Montague Rhodes James," *London Mercury*, 29 (1934),
    316–317.

"Casting the Runes"
Mason, Michael A. "On Not Letting Them Lie: Moral Significance in the Ghost
    Stories of M. R. James," *Stud Short Fiction*, 19 (1982), 257.

"The Diary of Mr. Poynter"
Manlove, C. N. *Modern Fantasy* . . . , 11–12; rpt. Schlobin, Roger C., Ed. *The
    Aesthetics* . . . , 25–26.

"An Episode of Cathedral History"
Mason, Michael A. "On Not Letting Them Lie . . . ," 254–255.

"The Mezzotint"
Butts, Mary. "The Art . . . ," 311–312.

"Number 13"
Mason, Michael A. "On Not Letting Them Lie . . . ," 258.

"The Rose Garden"
Mason, Michael A. "On Not Letting Them Lie . . . ," 259–260.

"The Uncommon Prayer Book"
Butts, Mary. "The Art . . . ," 312–315.

AMALIA JAMILIS

"Night Work"
Kaminsky, Amy K. "Women Writing About Prostitutes: Amalia Jamilis and
    Luisa Valenzuela," in Horn, Pierre L., and Mary B. Pringle, Eds. *The Image
    of the Prostitute* . . . , 124–131.

"Los trabajos nocturnos"
Lewald, H. Ernest. "Alienation and Eros in Three Stories by Beatriz Guido,
    Marta Lynch, and Amalia Jamilis," in Mora, Gabriela, and Karen S. Van
    Hooft, Eds. *Theory and Practice* . . . , 182–184.

KRISTOFER JANSON

"Wives Submit Yourselves Unto Your Husbands"
Mossberg, Christer L. *Scandinavian Immigrant Literature*, 17–18.

TOVE JANSSON

"Cedric"
Jones, W. Glyn. *Tove Jansson*, 76–77.

"The Doll's House"
Jones, W. Glyn. *Tove Jansson*, 150–151.

"The Fir Tree"
Jones, W. Glyn. *Tove Jansson*, 77–78.

"The Invisible Child"
Jones, W. Glyn. *Tove Jansson*, 74–75.

"The Listener"
Jones, W. Glyn. *Tove Jansson*, 117–118.

"Locomotive"
Jones, W. Glyn. *Tove Jansson*, 152–155.

"Wolves"
Jones, W. Glyn. *Tove Jansson*, 122–124.

JOHANNES V. JENSEN

"Dolores"
Rossel, Sven H. *Johannes V. Jensen*, 54–55.

"Louison"
Rossel, Sven H. *Johannes V. Jensen*, 56–57.

"Vanished Forests"
Rossel, Sven H. *Johannes V. Jensen*, 55–56.

"Wombwell"
Rossel, Sven H. *Johannes V. Jensen*, 62–63.

SARAH ORNE JEWETT

"The Confessions of a House-Breaker"
Renza, Louis A. . . . *Minor Literature*, 158–159.

"The Courting of Sister Wisby"
Crumpacker, Laurie. "The Art of the Healer: Women in the Fiction of Sarah Orne Jewett," *Colby Lib Q*, 19 (1983), 156–160.

"Cunner-Fishing"
Donovan, Josephine. *New England Local Color . . .* , 104.

"The Foreigner"
Donovan, Josephine. *New England Local Color . . .* , 117.
Pryse, Marjorie. "Women 'At Sea': Feminist Realism in Sarah Orne Jewett's
    'The Foreigner,'" *Am Lit Realism,* 15 (1982), 244–252.

"From a Mournful Village"
Renza, Louis A. . . . *Minor Literature,* 63–64.

"In Dark New England Days"
Donovan, Josephine. *New England Local Color . . .* , 112.

"An October Ride"
Renza, Louis A. . . . *Minor Literature,* 162–165.

"The Only Rose"
Shaw, Valerie. *The Short Story . . .* , 174–179.

"A White Heron"
Atkinson, Michael. "The Necessary Extravagance of Sarah Orne Jewett: Voices
    of Authority in 'A White Heron,'" *Stud Short Fiction,* 19 (1982), 71–74.
Donovan, Josephine. *New England Local Color . . .* , 107–109.
Held, George. "Heart of Hearts with Nature: Ways of Looking at 'A White
    Heron,'" *Colby Lib Q,* 18 (1982), 55–65.
Renza, Louis A. . . . *Minor Literature,* 64–72.
Shaw, Valerie. *The Short Story . . .* , 172–174.
Sheidley, William E., and Ann Charters. *Instructor's Manual . . .* , 25–26.

B. S. JOHNSON

"A Few Selected Sentences"
Waugh, Patricia. *Metafiction . . .* , 24.

DOROTHY JOHNSON

"The Hanging Tree"
Meldrum, Barbara H. "Dorothy Johnson's Short Fiction," *Western Am Lit,* 17
    (1982), 219–220.

"Laugh in the Face of Danger"
Meldrum, Barbara H. ". . . Short Fiction," 221–222.

"Lost Sister"
Meldrum, Barbara H. ". . . Short Fiction," 217–218, 224.

"A Man Called Horse"
Meldrum, Barbara H. ". . . Short Fiction," 216–217.

"Prairie Kid"
Meldrum, Barbara H. ". . . Short Fiction," 223–224.

"Scars of Honor"
Meldrum, Barbara H. ". . . Short Fiction," 222–223.

"A Time of Greatness"
Meldrum, Barbara H. ". . . Short Fiction," 224–225.

"The Unbeliever"
Meldrum, Barbara H. ". . . Short Fiction," 214–215.

"War Shirt"
Meldrum, Barbara H. ". . . Short Fiction," 215–216.

LESLIE T. JOHNSON

"Seeker of To-Morrow"
Cioffi, Frank. *Formula Fiction?* . . . , 63–64.

UWE JOHNSON

"Osterwasser"
Fickert, Kurt J. "Ambiguity in Style: A Study of Uwe Johnson's 'Osterwasser,' "
    Int'l Fiction R, 9, i (1982), 17–21.

GAYL JONES

"Return: A Fantasy"
Ward, Jerry W. "Escape from Trublem: The Fiction of Gayl Jones," in Evans,
    Mari, Ed. *Black Women* . . . , 252–253.

NEIL JONES

"The Jameson Satellite"
Hassler, Donald M. *The Comic Tone* . . . , 88–89.

WILLIAM JONES

"Anaska Mimiwina"
Littlefield, Daniel, and James W. Parins. "Short Fiction Writers of the Indian
    Territory," *Am Stud* (Kansas), 23, i (1982), 24–26.

"Lydie"
Littlefield, Daniel, and James W. Parins. "Short Fiction Writers . . . ," 26–28.

JAMES JOYCE

"After the Race"

Blayac, Alain. "'After the Race': A Study in Epiphanies," *Les Cahiers de la Nouvelle*, 2 (1984), 115–127.

Voelker, Joseph C. "'Chronicles of Disorder': Reading the Margins of *Dubliners*," *Colby Lib Q*, 18 (1982), 134–135.

"Araby"

*Abcarian, Richard, and Marvin Klotz, Eds. *Literature* . . . , 2nd ed., 1191–1195; 3rd ed., 1166–1169.

Bergman, David, Joseph de Roche, and Daniel M. Epstein. *Instructor's Manual* . . . , 23–24.

Bowen, Zack. "Joyce's Prophylactic Paralysis: Exposure in *Dubliners*," *James Joyce Q*, 19 (1982), 262–263.

Carens, James F. "In Quest of a New Impulse: George Moore's *The Untilled Fields* and James Joyce's *Dubliners*," in Kilroy, James F., Ed. *The Irish Short Story* . . . , 75–77.

Cronin, Edward. "James Joyce's Trilogy and Epilogue: 'The Sisters,' 'An Encounter,' 'Araby,' and 'The Dead,'" *Renascence*, 31 (1979), 235–238.

Morrissey, L. J. "Joyce's Narrative Strategies in 'Araby,'" *Mod Fiction Stud*, 28 (1982), 45–52.

Sirlin, Rhoda, and David H. Richter. *Instructor's Manual* . . . , 67–68.

Voelker, Joseph C. "'Chronicles of Disorder' . . . ," 131–133.

Walzl, Florence L. "*Dubliners*," in Bowen, Zack, and James F. Carens, Eds. *A Companion* . . . , 175–176.

"The Boarding House"

Bowen, Zack. ". . . Exposure in *Dubliners*," 264.

Garrison, Joseph M. "*Dubliners*: Portraits of the Artist as a Narrator," *Novel*, 8 (1975), 234–236.

Halper, Nathan. *Studies in Joyce*, 135–138.

Walzl, Florence L. "*Dubliners*," 176–177.

"Clay"

Bowen, Zack. ". . . Exposure in *Dubliners*," 265–266.

Breuer, Horst. "Verleugnung in James Joyces Erzählung 'Clay,'" *Literatur in Wissenschaft und Unterricht*, 16 (1983), 259–279.

Carens, James F. "In Quest . . . ," 82–84.

Parrinder, Patrick. *James Joyce*, 52–53.

Perrine, Laurence, and Thomas R. Arp. *Instructor's Manual* . . . , 6th ed., 65–66.

Sundell, Roger H. "'Clay,'" in Dietrich, R. F., and Roger H. Sundell. *Instructor's Manual* . . . , 3rd ed., 88–92; 4th ed., 69–72.

Walzl, Florence L. "Joyce's 'Clay': Fact and Fiction," *Renascence*, 35 (1983), 119–137.

———. "*Dubliners*," 177–178.

"Counterparts"

Bowen, Zack. ". . . Exposure in *Dubliners*," 265.

Carens, James F. "In Quest . . . ," 68–69.

Delany, Paul. "Joyce: Political Development and the Aesthetic of *Dubliners*," in Barber, Benjamin R., and Michael J. G. McGrath, Eds. *The Artist . . .* , 226–227.

Owens, Cóilín. "'A Man with Two Establishments to Keep Up': Joyce's Farrington," in Bowen, Zack, Ed. *Irish Renaissance Annual IV*, 128–156.

"The Dead"

Baker, Christopher P. "The Dead Art of 'The Dead,'" *Engl Stud*, 63 (1982), 531–534.

Bowen, Zack. ". . . Exposure in *Dubliners*," 269–273.

Carens, James F. "In Quest . . . ," 88–92.

Cronin, Edward. "James Joyce's Trilogy . . . ," 238–243.

Dunleavy, Gareth W. "Hyde's Crusade for the Language and the Case of the Embarrassing Packets," *Studies*, 21 (1984), 307–319.

Dunleavy, Janet E. "The Ectoplasmic Truthtellers of 'The Dead,'" *James Joyce Q*, 21 (1984), 307–319.

Halper, Nathan. *Studies in Joyce*, 151–155.

Lucente, Gregory L. "Encounters and Subtexts in 'The Dead': A Note on Joyce's Narrative Technique," *Stud Short Fiction*, 20 (1983), 281–287.

Munich, Adrienne A. "Form and Subtext in Joyce's 'The Dead,'" *Mod Philol*, 82 (1984), 173–184.

*O'Connor, Frank. "Elaboration of Style and Form in Joyce's 'The Dead,'" in Charters, Ann, Ed. *The Story . . .* , 1167–1168.

Parrinder, Patrick. *James Joyce*, 66–70.

Rabaté, Jean-Michel. "Silence in *Dubliners*," in MacCabe, Colin, Ed. *James Joyce . . .* , 64–68.

Sheidley, William E., and Ann Charters. *Instructor's Manual . . .* , 72–74.

Shurgot, Michael W. "Windows of Escape and the Death Wish in Man: Joyce's 'The Dead,'" *Éire*, 17, iv (1982), 58–71.

Sirlin, Rhoda, and David H. Richter. *Instructor's Manual . . .* , 70–71.

Splitter, Randolph. "Watery Words: Language, Sexuality, and Motherhood in Joyce's Fiction," *Engl Lit Hist*, 49 (1982), 191–194.

Voelker, Joseph C. "'Chronicles of Disorder' . . . ," 141–143.

Walzl, Florence L. "A Book of Signs and Symbols: The Protagonist," in Benstock, Bernard, Ed. *The Seventh of Joyce*, 122–123.

———. "*Dubliners*," 210–216.

Wright, David G. *Characters in Joyce*, 26–29.

Zasadimsky, Eugene. "Joyce's 'The Dead,'" *Explicator*, 40, ii (1982), 3–4.

"An Encounter"

Bowen, Zack. ". . . Exposure in *Dubliners*," 261–262.

Carens, James F. "In Quest . . . ," 74–75.

Cronin, Edward. "James Joyce's Trilogy . . . ," 232–235.

Sheidley, William E., and Ann Charters. *Instructor's Manual . . .* , 70–71.

Voelker, Joseph C. "'Chronicles of Disorder' . . . ," 129–131.

Walzl, Florence L. "*Dubliners*," 174–175.

"Eveline"

Carens, James F. "In Quest . . . ," 80–81.

Dumbleton, William A. *Ireland . . .* , 155–158.

Garrison, Joseph M. "*Dubliners* . . . ," 230–231.

Hrushovski, Benjamin. "Integrational Semantics: An Understander's Theory of Meaning in Context," *Georgetown Univ Round Table*, [n.v.] (1982), 156–190.
Voelker, Joseph C. "'Chronicles of Disorder' . . . ," 133–134.

"Grace"
Bowen, Zack. ". . . Exposure in *Dubliners*," 268–269.
Carens, James F. "In Quest . . . ," 86–88.
Dumbleton, William A. *Ireland* . . . , 158–161.
Parrinder, Patrick. *James Joyce*, 57–58.
Rabaté, Jean-Michel. "Silence . . . ," 63–64.
Voelker, Joseph C. "'Chronicles of Disorder' . . . ," 139–140.
Walzl, Florence L. "*Dubliners*," 187–192.

"Ivy Day in the Committee Room"
Bowen, Zack. ". . . Exposure in *Dubliners*," 266–267.
Carens, James F. "In Quest . . . ," 84–86.
Delany, Paul. "Joyce: Political Development . . . ," 227–228.
Garrison, Joseph M. "*Dubliners* . . . ," 237–238.
Horowitz, Sylvia H. "More Christian Allegory in 'Ivy Day in the Committee Room,'" *James Joyce Q*, 21 (1984), 145–154.
O'Brien, Richard. "From Joyce to Freud: Hero and Holocaust in 'Ivy Day in the Committee Room,'" *J Evolutionary Psych*, 5 (1984), 186–195.
Rabaté, Jean-Michel. "Silence . . . ," 61–63.
Walzl, Florence L. "*Dubliners*," 180–184.

"A Little Cloud"
Orth, Ghita. "Joyce's 'A Little Cloud,'" *Explicator*, 40, iv (1982), 35–36.
Scott, Virgil, and David Madden. *Instructor's Manual* . . . , 4th ed., 9–11; Madden, David. *Instructor's Manual* . . . , 5th ed., 21–23; Madden, David, and Virgil Scott. *Instructor's Manual* . . . , 6th ed., 18–20.
Sirlin, Rhoda, and David H. Richter. *Instructor's Manual* . . . , 69–70.
Voelker, Joseph C. "'Chronicles of Disorder' . . . ," 138–139.

"A Mother"
Bowen, Zack. ". . . Exposure in *Dubliners*," 267–268.
Rabaté, Jean-Michel. "Silence . . . ," 70–71.
Walzl, Florence L. "*Dubliners*," 184–187.

"A Painful Case"
Carens, James F. "In Quest . . . ," 79–80.
DiGaetani, John L. *Richard Wagner* . . . , 135–136.
Heumann, J. Mark. "Writing—and Not Writing—in Joyce's 'A Painful Case,'" *Éire*, 16, iii (1981), 81–97.
Hyman, Suzanne K. "'A Painful Case': The Movement of a Story Through a Switch in Voice," *James Joyce Q*, 19 (1982), 111–118.
Miller, James E., and Bernice Slote. *Instructor's Manual* . . . , 2nd ed., 13.
Parrinder, Patrick. *James Joyce*, 64–66.
Smith, Paul. "Crossing the Lines in 'A Painful Case,'" *Southern Hum R*, 17 (1983), 203–205.

Tucker, Lindsey. "Duffy's Last Supper: Food, Language, and the Failure of Integrative Processes in 'A Painful Case,'" in Bowen, Zack, Ed. *Irish Renaissance Annual IV,* 118–127.
Walzl, Florence L. *"Dubliners,"* 178–179.

"The Sisters"
Bowen, Zack. ". . . Exposure in *Dubliners,"* 259–261.
Bremer, Brian A. "'He Was Too Scrupulous Always': A Re-examination of Joyce's 'The Sisters,'" *James Joyce Q,* 22 (1984), 55–66.
Carens, James F. "In Quest . . . ," 72–74.
Chadwick, Joseph. "Silence in 'The Sisters,'" *James Joyce Q,* 21 (1984), 245–255.
Crawford, Claudia. "James Joyce's 'The Sisters,'" *Am Imago,* 41 (1984), 181–199.
Cronin, Edward. "James Joyce's Trilogy . . . ," 229–232.
Halper, Nathan. *Studies in Joyce,* 139–149.
Herring, Phillip. "Structure and Meaning in Joyce's 'The Sisters,'" in Benstock, Bernard, Ed. *The Seventh of Joyce,* 131–144.
Parrinder, Patrick. *James Joyce,* 55–56.
Rabaté, Jean-Michel. "Silence . . . ," 48–57.
Ruthrof, Horst. "The Problem of Inferred Modality in Narrative," *J Lit Semantics,* 13 (1984), 97–108.
Voelker, Joseph C. "'Chronicles of Disorder' . . . ," 128–129.
Walzl, Florence L. *"Dubliners,"* 174, 206–209.

"Two Gallants"
Bowen, Zack. ". . . Exposure in *Dubliners,"* 263–264.
Carens, James F. "In Quest . . . ," 81–82.
Garrison, Joseph M. *"Dubliners . . . ,"* 232–234.
Voelker, Joseph C. "'Chronicles of Disorder' . . . ," 135–137.

FRANZ KAFKA

"Before the Law"
Pascal, Roy. *Kafka's Narrators . . . ,* 148–153.
Penner, Dick, Ed. *Fiction of the Absurd . . . ,* 97–99.

"Blumfeld, an Elderly Bachelor"
Pascal, Roy. *Kafka's Narrators . . . ,* 91–104.
Sokel, Walter H. "Freud and the Magic of Kafka's Writing," in Stern, J. P., Ed. *The World of Franz Kafka,* 153–156.

"The Bridge"
Gross, Ruth V. "Fallen Bridge, Fallen Women, Fallen Text," *Newsletter Kafka Soc America,* 5, i (1981), 15–24; rpt. *Lit R,* 26 (1983), 577–587.

"The Burrow"
Boulby, Mark. "Kafka's End: A Reassessment of 'The Burrow,'" *Germ Q,* 55 (1982), 175–185.
Dinnage, Rosemary. "Under the Harrow," in Stern, J. P., Ed. *The World of Franz Kafka,* 77–78.

Gelus, Marjorie. "Notes on Kafka's 'Der Bau': Problems with Reality," *Colloquia Germanica*, 15 (1982), 98–110.
Kudszus, Winfried. "Verschüttungen in Kafkas 'Der Bau,'" in Bennett, Benjamin, Anton Kaes, and William J. Lillyman, Eds. *Probleme der Moderne . . . ,* 307–317.
Mache, Britta. "The Noise in the Burrow: Kafka's Final Dilemma," *Germ Q,* 55 (1982), 526–540.
Struc, Roman S. "Existence as Construct: Kafka's 'The Great Wall of China' and 'The Burrow,'" *Research Stud,* 50 (1982), 79–89.
Wehrli, Beatrice. "Monologische Kunst als Ausdruck moderner Weltenfahrung: Zu Kafkas Erzählung 'Der Bau,'" *Jahrbuch der Deutschen Schiller-Gesellschaft,* 25 (1981), 435–445.

"The Cares of a Family Man"
Strauss, Walter A. "A Spool of Thread and a Spinning Top: Two Fables by Kafka," *Newsletter Kafka Soc America,* [n.v.], ii (1979), 9–13.

"Conversation with a Supplicant" [same as "Conversation with a Praying Man"]
Penner, Dick, Ed. *Fiction of the Absurd . . . ,* 94–97.

"A Country Doctor"
Apter, T. E. *Fantasy Literature . . . ,* 83–85.
Kayser, Wolfgang. *The Grotesque . . . ,* 148–149.
McGlathery, James M. "Desire's Persecution in Kafka's 'Judgment,' 'Metamorphosis,' and 'A Country Doctor,'" *Perspectives Contemp Lit,* 7 (1981), 54–55.
McLean, Sammy. "Doubling and Sexual Identity in Stories by Franz Kafka," *Hartford Stud Lit,* 12 (1980), 9–11.
Strelka, [Joseph] P. "Les Eléments du moi littéraire dans 'Un médecin de campagne' de Kafka," *Études Germaniques,* 39 (1984), 205–214.

"Description of a Struggle"
Bernheimer, Charles. *Flaubert and Kafka . . . ,* 144–147.
Hayman, Ronald. *Kafka . . . ,* 44–48.

"A Dream"
Penner, Dick, Ed. *Fiction of the Absurd . . . ,* 99–100.

"First Sorrow"
Chatman, Seymour. "On the Notion of Theme in Narrative," in Fisher, John, Ed. *Essays on Aesthetics . . . ,* 161–179.
Fiedler, Leonhard M. "Zwischen 'Wahrheit' und 'Methode': Kafka-Rede in Mainz," *Neue Rundschau,* 94 (1983), 184–204.
Pascal, Roy. *Kafka's Narrators . . . ,* 177–179.
Ritter, Naomi. "Art as Spectacle: Kafka and the Circus," *Österreich in Amerikanischer Sicht,* 2 (1981), 65–70.

"The Giant Mole" [same as "The Village Schoolteacher"]
Pascal, Roy. *Kafka's Narrators . . . ,* 180–182.

"Give It Up!"
Pascal, Roy. *Kafka's Narrators . . . ,* 157–161.

"The Great Wall of China"
Hayman, Ronald. *Kafka* . . . , 220–221.
Kopper, John M. "Building Walls and Jumping over Them: Constructions in Franz Kafka's 'Beim Bau der chinesischen Mauer,'" *Mod Lang Notes*, 98 (1983), 351–365.
Struc, Roman S. "Existence as Construct . . . ," 79–89.

"Homecoming"
Pascal, Roy. *Kafka's Narrators* . . . , 167–170.

"A Hunger Artist"
*Abcarian, Richard, and Marvin Klotz. *Instructor's Manual* . . . , 3rd ed., 10.
Bergman, David, Joseph de Roche, and Daniel M. Epstein. *Instructor's Manual* . . . , 48.
Madden, David. *Instructor's Manual* . . . , 5th ed., 74–75; Madden, David, and Virgil Scott. *Instructor's Manual* . . . , 6th ed., 82–84.
Miller, James E., and Bernice Slote. *Instructor's Manual* . . . , 2nd ed., 14.
Pascal, Roy. *Kafka's Narrators* . . . , 105–135.
Ritter, Naomi. "Art as Spectacle . . . ," 65–70.

"The Hunter Gracchus"
Fisch, Harold. *A Remembered Future* . . . , 61–62.
Pascal, Roy. *Kafka's Narrators* . . . , 153–156.
Sirlin, Rhoda, and David H. Richter. *Instructor's Manual* . . . , 72–73.
Speirs, Ronald. "Where There's a Will There's No Way: A Reading of Kafka's 'Der Jäger Gracchus,'" *Oxford Germ Stud*, 14 (1983), 92–110.

"An Imperial Message"
Pascal, Roy. *Kafka's Narrators* . . . , 164–167.

"In the Gallery"
Hillmann, Heinz. "Fabel und Parabel in 20. Jahrhundert—Kafka und Brecht," in Hasubek, Peter, Ed. *Die Fabel* . . . , 223–224.
Ritter, Naomi. "Art as Spectacle . . . ," 65–70.
Schepers, Gerhard. "Masculine and Feminine Aspects of Creativity: With an Analysis of Kafka's 'Up in the Gallery,'" *Humanities*, 16 (1982), 105–124.

"In the Penal Colony"
Davey, E. R. "The Broken Engine: A Study of Franz Kafka's 'In der Strafkolonie,'" *J European Stud*, 14 (1984), 271–283.
Dekoven, Marianne. "History as Suppressed Referent in Modernist Fiction," *Engl Lit Hist*, 51 (1984), 137–152.
Pascal, Roy. *Kafka's Narrators* . . . , 60–89.
Thomas, J. D. "On the Penal Apparatus of Kafka," *Coll Lit*, 9, i (1982), 64–67.
Weinstein, Arnold. "Kafka's Writing Machine: Metamorphosis in the Penal Colony," *Stud Twentieth Century Lit*, 7 (Fall, 1982), 21–33.

"Investigations of a Dog"
Kudszus, Winfried. "Musik und Erkenntnis in Kafkas 'Forschungen eines Hundes,'" in Woodmansee, Martha, and Walter F. W. Lohnes, Eds. *Erkennen und Deuten* . . . , 79–90.
Pascal, Roy. "Kafka's Parables: Ways Out of the Dead End," in Stern, J. P., Ed. *The World of Franz Kafka*, 116–117.

"Josephine the Singer"
Beug, Joachim. "The Cunning of a Writer," in Stern, J. P., Ed. *The World of Franz Kafka*, 126–127.
Bruffee, Kenneth A. *Elegiac Romance* . . . , 205–206.
Hayman, Ronald. *Kafka* . . . , 298–299.
McLean, Sammy. "Doubling . . . ," 11–13.
Norris, Margot. "Kafka's Josefine: The Animal as the Negative Site of Narration," *Mod Lang Notes*, 98 (1983), 366–383.
Pascal, Roy. *Kafka's Narrators* . . . , 217–236.

"The Judgment"
Apter, T. E. *Fantasy Literature* . . . , 69–72.
Bartels, Martin. "Der Kampf um den Freund: Die psychoanalytische Sinneinheit in Kafkas Erzählung 'Das Urteil,'" *Deutsche Vierteljahrsschrift*, 56 (1982), 225–228.
Bernheimer, Charles. *Flaubert and Kafka* . . . , 167–187.
Corngold, Stanley. "Metaphor and Chiasmus in Kafka," *Newsletter Kafka Soc America*, 5, ii (1981), 23–31.
———. "Kafka's 'The Judgment' and Modern Rhetorical Theory," *Newsletter Kafka Soc America*, 7, i (1983), 15–21.
Kobligk, Helmut. "'. . . ohne dasser etwas Böses getan hätte . . .': Zum Verständnis der Schuld in Kafkas Erzählungen 'Die Verwandlung' und 'Das Urteil,'" *Wirkendes Wort*, 32 (1982), 397–401.
McGlathery, James M. "Desire's Persecution . . . ," 55–57.
McLean, Sammy. "Doubling . . . ," 1–5.
Yudkin, Leon I. *Jewish Writing* . . . , 49–51.

"A Little Fable"
Pascal, Roy. *Kafka's Narrators* . . . , 146–148.

"A Little Woman"
Pascal, Roy. *Kafka's Narrators* . . . , 183–186.

"Metamorphosis"
Beaty, Jerome. *The Norton Introduction* . . . , 367–369.
Clayton, David. "On Realistic and Fantastic Discourse," in Slusser, George E., Eric S. Rabkin, and Robert Scholes, Eds. *Bridges to Fantasy*, 76–77.
Hayman, Ronald. *Kafka* . . . , 150–153.
Kobligk, Helmut. "'. . . ohne dasser etwas . . . ,'" 392–397.
McGlathery, James M. "Desire's Persecution . . . ," 57–62.
McLean, Sammy. "Doubling . . . ," 5–9.
Mann, G. Thomas. "Kafka's 'Die Verwandlung' and Its Natural Model: An Alternative Reading," *Univ Dayton R*, 15, iii (1982), 65–74.
Nabokov, Vladimir. "Kafkas Erzählung 'Die Verwandlung,'" trans. Karl A. Klewer, *Neue Rundschau*, 93 (1982), 110–139.
Parr, Susan R. *The Moral* . . . , 105–110.
Pascal, Roy. *Kafka's Narrators* . . . , 47–59.
Sheidley, William E., and Ann Charters. *Instructor's Manual* . . . , 78–79.
Sokel, Walter H. "Freud and the Magic . . . ," 150–152.

Vietta, Silvio. "Franz Kafka, Expressionism, and Reification," in Bronner, Stephen E., and Douglas Kellner, Eds. *Passion and Rebellion* . . . , 201–216.

Winner, Thomas G. "Wortkunst als ein semiotisches System: Der Fall von Kafkas 'Verwandlung' als ein metasemiotischer Text," *Semiosis*, 34 (1984), 5–24.

"My Neighbor"
Pascal, Roy. *Kafka's Narrators* . . . , 182–183.

"A Report to an Academy"
Bridgwater, Patrick. "Rotpeters Ahnherren, oder: Der gelehrte Affe in der deutschen Dichtung," *Deutsche Vierteljahrsschrift*, 56 (1982), 447–462.

Nicolai, Ralf R. "Nietzschean Thought in Kafka's 'A Report to an Academy,'" *Lit R*, 26 (1983), 551–564.

Pascal, Roy. *Kafka's Narrators* . . . , 192–201.

"The Spinning Top"
Strauss, Walter A. ". . . Two Fables by Kafka," 13–15.

"Testimonials" [same as "Guarantors"]
Pascal, Roy. *Kafka's Narrators* . . . , 161–164.

"Wedding Preparations in the Country"
Hayman, Ronald. *Kafka* . . . , 53–55.

Möbus, Frank. "Kalmus: Zu einer Notiz aus dem Nachlass Franz Kafkas," *Jahrbuch des Freien Deutschen Hochstifts*, [n.v.] (1984), 295–305.

KAJII MOTOJIRO

"Lemon"
Keene, Donald. *Dawn to the West* . . . , 538–540.

KAMBAYASHI AKATSUKI

"At St. John's Hospital"
Keene, Donald. *Dawn to the West* . . . , 548.

"The Fields"
Keene, Donald. *Dawn to the West* . . . , 545–546.

KAMELESHWAR

"King Nirbansta"
Pande, Trilochan. "Folk Elements in the Modern Hindi Short Story," *Folklore* (Calcutta), 231 (1979), 147.

KAMURA ISOTA

"The Night of July 22nd"
Keene, Donald. *Dawn to the West* . . . , 526.

"The Torments of Karma"
Keene, Donald. *Dawn to the West* . . . , 525–526.

NIKOLAY KARAMZIN

"The Island of Bornholm"
Katz, Michael R. *Dreams* . . . , 22–24.

MUSTAI KARIM

"A Long, Long Childhood"
Pankin, Boris. "The Past That Is Always with Us," *Soviet Stud Lit,* 18, i (1982),
38–43.

KASAI ZENZŌ

"With Children on My Hands"
Keene, Donald. *Dawn to the West* . . . , 518.

"Young Oak Leaves"
Keene, Donald. *Dawn to the West* . . . , 519.

VALENTIN KATAEV

"At Night"
Russell, Robert. *Valentin Kataev,* 29–30.

"The Child"
Russell, Robert. *Valentin Kataev,* 47–48.

"The Drum"
Russell, Robert. *Valentin Kataev,* 30–31.

"The Father"
Russell, Robert. *Valentin Kataev,* 40–42.

"Fire"
Russell, Robert. *Valentin Kataev,* 44–45.

"The Flag"
Russell, Robert. *Valentin Kataev,* 97–98.

"The Gold Nib"
Russell, Robert. *Valentin Kataev,* 49–51.

"In Winter"
Russell, Robert. *Valentin Kataev*, 42–44.

"The Iron Ring"
Russell, Robert. *Valentin Kataev*, 36–38.

"Krants's Experiment"
Russell, Robert. *Valentin Kataev*, 34–36.

"Rodion Zhukov"
Russell, Robert. *Valentin Kataev*, 45–47.

"Sir Henry and the Devil"
Russell, Robert. *Valentin Kataev*, 38–40.

"Things"
Russell, Robert. *Valentin Kataev*, 57–58.

"Violet"
Russell, Robert. *Valentin Kataev*, 143–144.

IVAN KATAYEV

"Milk"
Brown, Edward J. . . . *Since the Revolution*, 3rd ed., 162–163.

NAIM KATTAN

"Les Bagages"
Greenstein, Michael. "The Desert, the River, and the Island: Naim Kattan's
    Short Stories," *Canadian Lit*, 103 (Winter, 1984), 45.

"L'Étude"
Greenstein, Michael. "The Desert . . . ," 46–47.

"La Fin du voyage"
Greenstein, Michael. "The Desert . . . ," 45.

"L'Hôtel"
Greenstein, Michael. "The Desert . . . ," 44.

"Rue Abou Nouas"
Greenstein, Michael. "The Desert . . . ," 42–43.

"Le Substitut"
Greenstein, Michael. "The Desert . . . ," 45–46.

"Sur le Balcon"
Greenstein, Michael. "The Desert . . . ," 43–44.

"Les Yeux fermés"
Greenstein, Michael. "The Desert . . . ," 47–48.

STEVE KATZ

"43"
Klinkowitz, Jerome. *The Self-Apparent Word* . . . , 13–14.

"Trip"
Klinkowitz, Jerome. *The Self-Apparent Word* . . . , 12–13.

VENIAMIN KAVERIN

"Engineer Shvarts"
Avins, Carol. *Border Crossings* . . . , 172–175.

KAWABATA YASUNARI

"Crystal Fantasies"
Keene, Donald. *Dawn to the West* . . . , 798–800.

"The Izu Dancer"
Keene, Donald. *Dawn to the West* . . . , 793–794.

"Lyric Poem"
Keene, Donald. *Dawn to the West* . . . , 805–808.

"The Moon in the Water"
Tsuruta, Kinya. "Kawabata's Use of Irony: An Analysis of 'The Moon in the
    Water,'" *Par Rapport*, 5–6 (1982–1983), 45–50.

"Of Birds and Beasts"
Keene, Donald. *Dawn to the West* . . . , 810–813.

EMMANUIL KAZAKEVICH

"The Blue Notebook"
Blum, Jakub. "Soviet Russian Literature," in Blum, Jakub, and Vera Rich. *The
    Image of the Jew* . . . , 32–33.

"Enemies"
Blum, Jakub. "Soviet Russian Literature," 33.

YURY KAZAKOV

"The Smell of Bread"
Brown, Edward J. . . . *Since the Revolution*, 3rd ed., 330.

DAVID H. KELLER

"The Feminine Metamorphosis"
Stableford, Brian M. "David H. Keller," in Bleiler, Everett F., Ed. *Science Fiction Writers* . . . , 121.

"The God Wheel"
Stableford, Brian M. "David H. Keller," 122.

"The Revolt of the Pedestrians"
Stableford, Brian M. "David H. Keller," 120.

"Tree of Evil"
Stableford, Brian M. "David H. Keller," 121.

"A Village Romeo and Juliet"
Kayser, Wolfgang. *The Grotesque* . . . , 107–108.

"The Yeast Men"
Stableford, Brian M. "David H. Keller," 120.

GOTTFRIED KELLER

"The Three Righteous Comb-Makers"
Kayser, Wolfgang. *The Grotesque* . . . , 13–16.

WILLIAM MELVIN KELLEY

"Cry for Me"
Ro, Sigmund. *Rage and Celebration* . . . , 27–39.

E. LINCOLN KELLOGG

"A Partly Celestial Tale"
Wu, William F. *The Yellow Peril* . . . , 52–53.

KEN ELTON KESEY

"Abdul and Ebenezer"
Tanner, Stephen L. *Ken Kesey*, 125–126.

"The Day After Superman Died"
Tanner, Stephen L. *Ken Kesey*, 126–130.

"Search for the Secret Pyramid"
Tanner, Stephen L. *Ken Kesey*, 130–133.

"Thrice-Thrown Tranny-Man or Ogre at Palo Alto High School"
Tanner, Stephen L. *Ken Kesey,* 122–125.

"Tools from My Chest"
Tanner, Stephen L. *Ken Kesey,* 116–118.

DANIIL KHARMS

"The Cashier"
Penner, Dick, Ed. *Fiction of the Absurd . . . ,* 63–64.

"The Old Woman"
Penner, Dick, Ed. *Fiction of the Absurd . . . ,* 64–67.

VIRGINIA KIDD and JAMES BLISH

"On the Wall of the Lodge"
Stableford, Brian M. *The Clash . . . ,* 43–44.

BENEDICT KIELY

"Blackbird in a Bramble Bough"
Dunleavy, Janet E. "Mary Lavin, Elizabeth Bowen, and a New Generation: The
    Irish Short Story at Midcentury," in Kilroy, James F., Ed. *The Irish Short
    Story . . . ,* 160–161.

"A Great God's Angel Standing"
Dunleavy, Janet E. "Mary Lavin . . . ," 161–162.

KIKUO ITAYA

"The Pilgrimage of the Curse"
Gardner, John, Ed. *Tengu Child . . . ,* xviii–xx.

"The Robber and the Flute"
Gardner, John, Ed. *Tengu Child . . . ,* xxi–xxiv.

LEE KILLOUGH

"The Existential Man"
Pierce, Hazel B. *A Literary Symbiosis . . . ,* 135–136.

"The Lying Ear"
Broege, Valerie. "Electric Eve: Images of Female Computers in Science Fiction,"
    in Erlich, Richard D., and Thomas P. Dunn, Eds. *Clockwork Worlds . . . ,*
    187–188.

KICHUNG KIM

"A Homecoming"
Kim, Elaine H. *Asian American Literature* . . . , 276–277.

GRACE KING

"Bayou L'Ombre"
Bush, Robert. *Grace King* . . . , 106–108.

"The Chevalier Alain de Triton"
Bush, Robert. *Grace King* . . . , 101–104.

"A Crippled Hope"
Bush, Robert. *Grace King* . . . , 147–149.

"A Domestic Interior"
Bush, Robert. *Grace King* . . . , 161–162.

"A Drama of Three"
Bush, Robert. *Grace King* . . . , 144–145.

"Earthlings"
Bush, Robert. *Grace King* . . . , 98–100.

"La Grande Demoiselle"
Bush, Robert. *Grace King* . . . , 145–146.

"Grandmother's Grandmother"
Bush, Robert. *Grace King* . . . , 156–157.

"Joe"
Bush, Robert. *Grace King* . . . , 157–158.

"The Story of a Day"
Bush, Robert. *Grace King* . . . , 154–155.

STEPHEN KING

"Children of the Corn"
Magistrale, Anthony S. "Stephen King's Vietnam Allegory: An Interpretation of 'Children of the Corn,'" *Cuyahoga R*, 2, i (1984), 61–66.

SUSAN PETIGRU KING

"The Best of Friends"
Scafidel, J. R. "Susan Petigru King: An Early South Carolina Realist," in Meriwether, James B., Ed. *South Carolina Women Writers*, 107–108.

"A Male Flirt"
Scafidel, J. R. "Susan Petigru King . . . ," 109.

"A Man of Honor"
Scafidel, J. R. "Susan Petigru King . . . ," 106–107.

"Old Maidism vs. Marriage"
Scafidel, J. R. "Susan Petigru King . . . ," 108.

"Sylvia's World"
Scafidel, J. R. "Susan Petigru King . . . ," 109–111.

MAXINE HONG KINGSTON

"On Mortality"
Bergman, David, Joseph de Roche, and Daniel M. Epstein. *Instructor's Manual . . .* , 8.

RUDYARD KIPLING

"As Easy as A. B. C."
Harrison, James. *Rudyard Kipling,* 93–95.

"At the End of the Passage"
Harrison, James. *Rudyard Kipling,* 31.
Ridley, Hugh. *Images of Imperialism,* 136–137.

"Beauty Spots"
Harrison, James. *Rudyard Kipling,* 104–105.

"Beyond the Pale"
Cornwell, Gareth. "'Beyond the Pale': A Preface," *Engl Stud Africa,* 27 (1984), 123–132.

"Black Jack"
Harrison, James. *Rudyard Kipling,* 37–38.

"The Bridge Builders"
Harrison, James. *Rudyard Kipling,* 31–34.

"The Brushwood Boy"
Henn, T. R. *Kipling,* 55–59.
Sullivan, Zohreh T. "Kipling the Nightwalker," *Mod Fiction Stud,* 30 (1984), 217–235.

"The Bull That Thought"
Harrison, James. *Rudyard Kipling,* 122–124.

"The Children of the Zodiac"
Harrison, James. *Rudyard Kipling,* 101–103.

"The Church That Was at Antioch"
Harrison, James. *Rudyard Kipling,* 112–114.

"The Courting of Dinah Shadd"
Harrison, James. *Rudyard Kipling*, 35–37.

"Dayspring Mishandled"
Harrison, James. *Rudyard Kipling*, 115–116.
Henn, T. R. *Kipling*, 48–49.
Shaw, Valerie. *The Short Story . . .* , 213–217.

"The Enemies to Each Other"
Harrison, James. *Rudyard Kipling*, 125–126.

"The Eye of Allah"
Harrison, James. *Rudyard Kipling*, 109–111.
Henn, T. R. *Kipling*, 50–52.

"The Gardener"
Harrison, James. *Rudyard Kipling*, 116–118.
Madden, David. *Instructor's Manual . . .* , 5th ed., 78–81; Madden, David, and
    Virgil Scott. *Instructor's Manual . . .* , 6th ed., 86–91.

"Georgie Porgie"
Belliappa, K. C. "Love and Racial Encounters in Kipling," in Gowda, H. H.
    Anniah, Ed. *The Colonial . . .* , 235–243.

"His Private Honour"
Ridley, Hugh. *Images of Imperialism*, 132.

"The Horse-Marines"
Harrison, James. *Rudyard Kipling*, 83–84.

"The Madness of Private Ortheris"
Paffard, Mark. "Ortheris: Private Stanley Ortheris, No. 22639, B Company,"
    Kipling J, 58 (June, 1984), 18–25.

"The Madonna of the Trenches"
Harrison, James. *Rudyard Kipling*, 105–106.

"The Man Who Would Be King"
Harrison, James. *Rudyard Kipling*, 40–41.
Sirlin, Rhoda, and David H. Richter. *Instructor's Manual . . .* , 73–74.

"The Manner of Men"
Harrison, James. *Rudyard Kipling*, 111–112.

"Marklake Witches"
Harrison, James. *Rudyard Kipling*, 72–73.

"Mary Postgate"
Harrison, James. *Rudyard Kipling*, 89–90.

"The Miracle of St. Jubanus"
Harrison, James. *Rudyard Kipling*, 107–108.

"Mrs. Bathurst"
Harrison, James. *Rudyard Kipling*, 84–86.
Shaw, Valerie. *The Short Story* . . . , 103–105.

"My Son's Wife"
Harrison, James. *Rudyard Kipling*, 98–99.

"On Greenhow Hill"
Harrison, James. *Rudyard Kipling*, 113–114.

"On the City Wall"
Harrison, James. *Rudyard Kipling*, 42–45.

"Sea Constable"
Harrison, James. *Rudyard Kipling*, 88–89.
Hinchcliffe, Peter. "Fidelity and Complicity in Kipling and Conrad: 'Sea Constable' and 'The Tale,'" *Engl Stud Canada*, 9 (1983), 350–381.
Tarinayya, M. "Kipling's 'Sea Constable' and Conrad's 'The Tale,'" *Lit Criterion*, 16, iii (1981), 32–49.

"They"
Batchelor, John. *The Edwardian Novelists*, 14–16.
Harrison, James. *Rudyard Kipling*, 96–98.
Henn, T. R. *Kipling*, 59–60.

"The Tomb of His Ancestors"
Harrison, James. *Rudyard Kipling*, 114–115.

"The Tree of Justice"
Harrison, James. *Rudyard Kipling*, 71–72.

"Uncovenanted Mercies"
Harrison, James. *Rudyard Kipling*, 124–125.

"Unprofessional"
Harrison, James. *Rudyard Kipling*, 108–109.

"The Wish House"
Harrison, James. *Rudyard Kipling*, 118–122.
Shaw, Valerie. *The Short Story* . . . , 180–186.
Sheidley, William E., and Ann Charters. *Instructor's Manual* . . . , 45–47.

"Without Benefit of Clergy"
Harrison, James. *Rudyard Kipling*, 45–47.
Ridley, Hugh. *Images of Imperialism*, 93–94.

SARAH KIRSCH

"Merkwürdiges Beispiel weiblicher Entschlossheit"
Armster, Charlotte E. "'Merkwürdiges Beispiel weiblicher Entschlossheit': A Woman's Story—by Sarah Kirsch," in Gerber, Margy, Ed. *Studies* . . . , 243–250.

HEINRICH VON KLEIST

"The Beggar Woman of Locarno"
Maass, Joachim. *Kleist* . . . , 227–228.

"The Duel"
Maass, Joachim. *Kleist* . . . , 253.
Sembdner, Helmut. "Heinrich von Kleists unbekannte Mitarbeit an einem
Hamburger Journal: Neientdeckte Prosatexte," *Jahrbuch der Deutschen
Schiller-Gesellschaft*, 25 (1981), 47–76.

"The Earthquake in Chile"
Clouser, Robin A. "Heroism in Kleist's 'Das Erdbeben in Chili,'" *Germ R*, 58
(1983), 129–140.
Fischer, Bernd. "Factum und Idee: Zu Kleists 'Erdbeben in Chili,'" *Deutsche
Vierteljahrsschrift*, 58 (1984), 414–427.
Maass, Joachim. *Kleist* . . . , 243–244.
Steinhauer, Harry. "Heinrich von Kleists 'Das Erdbeben in Chili,'" in Hoff-
meister, Gerhart, Ed. *Goethezeit* . . . , 281–300.

"The Engagement in Santo Domingo"
Maass, Joachim. *Kleist* . . . , 243–244.

"The Foundling"
Gelus, Marjorie. "Displacement of Meaning: Kleist's 'Der Findling,'" *Germ Q*,
55 (1982), 541–553.
Maass, Joachim. *Kleist* . . . , 252–253.

"The Marquise of O——"
Coates, Paul. *The Realist Fantasy Fiction* . . . , 53–57.
Huff, Steven R. "Kleist and Expectant Virgins: The Meaning of 'O' in 'Die
Marquise von O,'" *J Engl & Germ Philol*, 81 (1982), 367–375.
Rennert, Hal H. "Literary Revenge: Nabokov's 'Mademoiselle O' and Kleist's
'Die Marquise von O——,'" *Germano-Slavica*, 4 (1984), 331–337.

"Michael Kohlhaas"
Apter, T. E. *Fantasy Literature* . . . , 67–68.
Coates, Paul. *The Realist Fantasy Fiction* . . . , 220–221.
Horst, Falk. "Kleists 'Michael Kohlhaas,'" *Wirkendes Wort*, 33 (1983), 275–285.
Kuhns, Richard. "The Strangeness of Justice: Reading 'Michael Kohlhaas,'"
New Lit Hist, 15, i (1983), 73–91.
Maass, Joachim. *Kleist* . . . , 167–168.

"St. Cecilia or the Power of Music"
Laurs, Axel. "Narrative Strategy in Heinrich von Kleist's 'Die heilige Cäcilie
oder die Gewalt der Musik: Eine Legende,'" *J Australian Univs Lang & Lit
Assoc*, 60 (1983), 220–233.

ALEXANDER KLUGE

"Lernprozessen mit tödlichem Ausgang"
Stollman, Rainer. "Schwarzer Krieg, endlos: Erfahrung und Selbsterhaltung in

Alexander Kluges 'Lernprozessen mit tödlichem Ausgang,'" *Text & Kontext,*
12 (1984), 349–369.

DAMON FRANCIS KNIGHT

"The Earth Quarter"
Dozois, Gardner. "Damon Francis Knight," in Bleiler, Everett F., Ed. *Science
Fiction Writers . . . ,* 397.

"Masks"
Krulik, Ted. "Bounded by Metal," in Myers, Robert E., Ed. *The Intersection . . . ,*
122–125.

"Not with a Bang"
Plank, Robert. "The Lone Survivor," in Rabkin, Eric S., Martin H. Greenberg,
and Joseph D. Olander, Eds. *The End . . . ,* 29–30.

"Stranger Station"
Huntington, James. "Impossible Love in Science Fiction," *Raritan,* 14, ii (1984),
96–98.

"To Serve Man"
Dozois, Gardner. "Damon Francis Knight," 395–396.

KŌDA ROHAN

"Tarōbō"
Keene, Donald. *Dawn to the West . . . ,* 158–160.

L. A. KOELEWIJN [NIC BEETS]

"Best Forgotten"
Nieuwenhuys, Rob. *Mirror of the Indies . . . ,* 234–236.

CYRIL M. KORNBLUTH

"The Little Black Bag"
Edwards, Malcolm. "Cyril M. Kornbluth," in Bleiler, Everett F., Ed. *Science Fic-
tion Writers . . . ,* 402.
White, David E. "Medical Morals and Narrative Necessity," in Myers, Robert E.,
Ed. *The Intersection . . . ,* 188–189.

"The Marching Morons"
Edwards, Malcolm. "Cyril M. Kornbluth," 402–403.

"The Mindworm"
Pierce, Hazel. *A Literary Symbiosis . . . ,* 220–221.

VADIM KOZHEV

"Shield and Sword"
Blum, Jakub. "Soviet Russian Literature," in Blum, Jakub, and Vera Rich. *The Image of the Jew . . .* , 54.

TOM KRISTENSEN

"The Disaster"
Byram, Michael. *Tom Kristensen*, 9.

"What Is Death?"
Byram, Michael. *Tom Kristensen*, 95–96.

WILHELM KUCCHELBECKER

"Ado"
Mersereau, John. *Russian Romantic Fiction*, 64–66.

"The Land of the Headless"
Mersereau, John. *Russian Romantic Fiction*, 66–67.

MILAN KUNDERA

"The Hitchhiking Game"
Sheidley, William E., and Ann Charters. *Instructor's Manual . . .* , 167–168.

"Lost Letters"
Sirlin, Rhoda, and David H. Richter. *Instructor's Manual . . .* , 75–77.

KUNIKIDA DOPPO

"Beef and Potatoes"
Keene, Donald. *Dawn to the West . . .* , 235–236.

"Old Gen"
Chibbett, David G., Ed. *River Mist . . .* , xxviii.

"Unforgettable People"
Keene, Donald. *Dawn to the West . . .* , 233–234.

KUROSHINA DENJI

"A Flock of Circling Crows"
Keene, Donald. *Dawn to the West . . .* , 607–608.

"Siberia in the Snow"
Keene, Donald. *Dawn to the West* . . . , 606.

"The Sleigh"
Keene, Donald. *Dawn to the West* . . . , 606–607.

HENRY KUTTNER

"Mimsy Were the Borogoves"
Shroyer, Frederick. "Henry Kuttner," in Bleiler, Everett F., Ed. *Science Fiction Writers* . . . , 166.

SELMA LAGERLÖF

"The Changeling"
Edström, Vivi. *Selma Lagerlöf*, 74.

"Herr Arnes penningar"
Setterwall, Monica. "Two Sides to an Ending in 'Herr Arnes penningar,'" *Scandinavian Stud*, 55 (1983), 123–133.

"The Outcast"
Edström, Vivi. *Selma Lagerlöf*, 99–103.

"The Son of Ingemar"
Edström, Vivi. *Selma Lagerlöf*, 46–49.

"The Story of a Country House" [same as "From a Swedish Country House"]
Maule, Harry E. *Selma Lagerlöf* . . . , 43–44.

ENRIQUE A. LAGUERRE

"The Enemy"
Irizarry, Estelle. *Enrique A. Laguerre*, 133–134.

"Pacholí"
Irizarry, Estelle. *Enrique A. Laguerre*, 132–133.

"Roots"
Irizarry, Estelle. *Enrique A. Laguerre*, 131–132.

"Shipwreck"
Irizarry, Estelle. *Enrique A. Laguerre*, 134–135.

ALEX LA GUMA

"The Lemon Orchard"
Barnett, Ursula A. *A Vision of Order* . . . , 197.

"Tattoo Mark and Nails"
Barnett, Ursula A. *A Vision of Order* . . . , 197–198.

TOMMASO LANDOLFI

"Gogol's Wife"
Bruffee, Kenneth A. *Elegiac Romance* . . . , 207–208.
Madden, David. *Instructor's Manual* . . . , 5th ed., 103–107; Madden, David, and
     Virgil Scott. *Instructor's Manual* . . . , 6th ed., 57–62.
Penner, Dick, Ed. *Fiction of the Absurd* . . . , 206–208.

SPENCER LANE

"The Origin of Thought"
Cioffi, Frank. *Formula Fiction?* . . . , 48–54.

RING LARDNER

"Some Like Them Cold"
Gullason, Thomas A. "The 'Lesser' Renaissance: The American Short Story in
     the 1920s," in Stevick, Philip, Ed. *The American Short Story, 1900–1945*, 84–
     85.

MAHMUT TAHIR LASHIN

"The Talk of the Village"
Hafez, Sabry. "The Maturation of a New Literary Genre," *Int'l J Middle East
     Stud,* 16 (1984), 376–383.

KURD LASSWITZ

"Against the Law of the World: A Tale from the Year 3877"
Fischer, William B. *The Empire Strikes Out* . . . , 95–105.

"Aladdin's Magic Lamp"
Fischer, William B. *The Empire Strikes Out* . . . , 119–120.

"From the Diary of an Ant"
Fischer, William B. *The Empire Strikes Out* . . . , 114–117.

"How the Devil Fetched the Professor"
Fischer, William B. *The Empire Strikes Out* . . . , 118–119.

"On the Soap-Bubble"
Fischer, William B. *The Empire Strikes Out* . . . , 109–110.

"To the Zero-Point of Existence: A Tale from the Year 2371"
Fischer, William B. *The Empire Strikes Out* . . . , 84–95.

"The University Library"
Fischer, William B. *The Empire Strikes Out* . . . , 117–118.

MARGARET LAURENCE

"The Drummer of All the World"
Birbalsingh, Frank. "Margaret Laurence's Short Stories," *World Lit Today*, 56
     (Winter, 1982), 31.

"Godman's Master"
Birbalsingh, Frank. "Margaret Laurence's Short Stories," 32.
Woodcock, George. *The World* . . . , 50–51.

"The Perfumed Sea"
Woodcock, George. *The World* . . . , 49.

"To Set Our House in Order"
Darling, Michael. "'Undecipherable Signs': Margaret Laurence's 'To Set Our
     House in Order,'" *Essays Canadian Writers*, 29 (1984), 192–203.
Sirlin, Rhoda, and David H. Richter. *Instructor's Manual* . . . , 77–79.

"The Tomorrow Tamer"
Birbalsingh, Frank. "Margaret Laurence's Short Stories," 31–32.

"The Voice of Adamo"
Woodcock, George. *The World* . . . , 50.

MARY LAVIN

"An Akoulina of the Irish Midlands"
Burnham, Richard. "Mary Lavin's Short Stories in *The Dublin Magazine*," *Cahiers
     du Centre d'Études Irlandaises* (Université de Haute Bretagne), 2 (1977), 107–
     109.

"Assigh"
Caswell, Robert. "The Human Heart's Vagaries," *Kilkenny Mag*, 12–13 (Spring,
     1965), 86–88.

"At Sallygap"
Caswell, Robert. ". . . Heart's Vagaries," 75–82.

"The Becker Wives"
Koenig, Marianne. "Mary Lavin: The Novels and the Stories," *Irish Univ R*, 9
     (1979), 253–254.
Meszaros, Patricia K. "Woman as Artist: The Fiction of Mary Lavin," *Critique*,
     24, i (1982), 44–51.

"Brigid"
Burnham, Richard. "Mary Lavin's Short Stories . . . ," 105–107.

"The Convert"
Caswell, Robert. ". . . Heart's Vagaries," 73–75.

"The Cuckoo-Spit"
Murphy, Catherine A. "The Ironic Vision of Mary Lavin," *Mosaic,* 12, iii (1979), 74–76.

"Eterna"
Meszaros, Patricia K. "Woman as Artist . . . ," 51–52.

"A Fable"
Burnham, Richard. "Mary Lavin's Short Stories . . . ," 104.

"The Face of Hate"
Mahike, Regina. "Mary Lavin's 'The Patriot Son' and 'The Face of Hate,'" in Kosok, Heinz, Ed. . . . *Anglo-Irish Literature,* 333–337.

"The Great Wave"
Murphy, Catherine A. "The Ironic Vision . . . ," 77–79.

"In a Café"
Meszaros, Patricia K. "Woman as Artist . . . ," 42–44.
Murphy, Catherine A. "The Ironic Vision . . . ," 72–74.

"In the Middle of the Fields"
Koenig, Marianne. "Mary Lavin . . . ," 254–255.
Murphy, Catherine A. "The Ironic Vision . . . ," 76.

"The Lost Child"
Koenig, Marianne. "Mary Lavin . . . ," 258–259.

"The Lucky Pair"
Murphy, Catherine A. "The Ironic Vision . . . ," 76–77.

"A Memory"
Koenig, Marianne. "Mary Lavin . . . ," 258.

"Miss Holland"
Burnham, Richard. "Mary Lavin's Short Stories . . . ," 103.
Dunleavy, Janet E. "The Subtle Satire of Elizabeth Bowen and Mary Lavin," *Tulsa Stud Women's Lit,* 2, i (1983), 74–75.

"A Mug of Water"
Koenig, Marianne. "Mary Lavin . . . ," 256.

"The Pastor of Six Mile Bush"
Caswell, Robert. ". . . Heart's Vagaries," 82–85.

"The Patriot Son"
Mahike, Regina. "Mary Lavin's 'The Patriot Son' . . . ," 333–337.

"Posy"
Caswell, Robert. ". . . Heart's Vagaries," 71.

"Say Could That Lad Be I"
Burnham, Richard. "Mary Lavin's Short Stories . . . ," 105.

"The Shrine"
Koenig, Marianne. "Mary Lavin . . . ," 255–256.

"The Small Bequest"
Dunleavy, Janet E. "The Subtle Satire . . . ," 78–79.

"Villa Violetta"
Koenig, Marianne. "Mary Lavin . . . ," 260.

"A Wet Day"
Koenig, Marianne. "Mary Lavin . . . ," 250.

WARNER LAW

"The Harry Hastings Method"
Scott, Virgil, and David Madden. *Instructor's Manual . . .* , 4th ed., 49–51; Madden, David. *Instructor's Manual . . .* , 5th ed., 8–10; Madden, David, and Virgil Scott. *Instructor's Manual . . .* , 6th ed., 1–3.

D. H. LAWRENCE

"The Blind Man"
Harris, Janice H. *The Short Fiction . . .* , 129–134.
Ruderman, Judith. *D. H. Lawrence . . .* , 73–87.
Scott, Virgil, and David Madden. *Instructor's Manual . . .* , 4th ed., 6–9; Madden, David. *Instructor's Manual . . .* , 5th ed., 17–19; Madden, David, and Virgil Scott. *Instructor's Manual . . .* , 6th ed., 13–16.

"The Blue Moccasins"
Ruderman, Judith. *D. H. Lawrence . . .* , 166–167.

"The Border Line"
Harris, Janice H. *The Short Fiction . . .* , 178–184.
Temple, J. "The Definition of Innocence: A Consideration of the Short Stories of D. H. Lawrence," *Studia Germanica Gandensias,* 20 (1979), 111–114.

"The Captain's Doll"
Harris, Janice H. *The Short Fiction . . .* , 157–162.
Tallman, Warren. "Forest, Glacier, and Flood. The Moon. St. Mawr: A Canvas for Lawrence's Novellas," *Open Letter,* 3rd Series, 6 (Winter, 1976–1977), 84–86.

"The Christening"
Harris, Janice H. *The Short Fiction . . .* , 76–79.

"Daughters of the Vicar" [originally titled "Two Marriages"]
Harris, Janice H. *The Short Fiction . . .* , 54–60.

"Deliah and Mr. Bircumshaw"
Harris, Janice H. *The Short Fiction . . .* , 74–76.

"England, My England"
Harris, Janice H. *The Short Fiction . . .* , 116–123.
Ross, Charles L. "D. H. Lawrence and World War I or History and the 'Forms of Reality': The Case of 'England, My England,'" in Maybury, James F., and Marjorie A. Zerbel, Eds. *Franklin Pierce Studies . . .* , 11–21.
Tarinayya, M. "Lawrence's 'England, My England': An Analysis," *J School Langs,* 7, i–ii (1980–1981), 70–83.
Thornton, Weldon. "'The Flower or the Fruit': A Reading of D. H. Lawrence's 'England, My England,'" *D. H. Lawrence R,* 16 (1983), 247–258.
Vickery, John B. *Myths and Texts . . .* , 38–45.

"Fanny and Annie"
Harris, Janice H. *The Short Fiction . . .* , 135–137.

"The Fox"
Beaty, Jerome. *The Norton Introduction . . .* , 420–424.
Daalder, Joost. "Dogs and Foxes in D. H. Lawrence and W. H. Auden," *Zeitschrift für Anglistik und Amerikanistik,* 32 (1984), 330–334.
Greiff, Louis K. "Bittersweet Dreaming in Lawrence's 'The Fox': A Freudian Perspective," *Stud Short Fiction,* 20 (1983), 7–16.
Harris, Janice H. *The Short Fiction . . .* , 150–151.
Naugrette, J. P. "Le Renard et les rêves: Onirisme, écriture et inconscient dans 'The Fox,'" *Études Anglaises,* 37, ii (1984), 141–155.
Ruderman, Judith. *D. H. Lawrence . . .* , 48–70.
Simpson, Hilary. *. . . Feminism,* 70–73.
Sirlin, Rhoda, and David H. Richter. *Instructor's Manual . . .* , 79–81.
Vickery, John B. *Myths and Texts . . .* , 47–52.

"A Fragment of Stained Glass" [originally titled "Legend"]
Harris, Janice H. *The Short Fiction . . .* , 19–20.

"Her Turn"
Harris, Janice H. *The Short Fiction . . .* , 65–66.

"The Horse Dealer's Daughter" [originally "The Miracle"]
Abcarian, Richard, and Marvin Klotz. *Instructor's Manual . . .* , 2nd ed., 13–14; 3rd ed., 10–11.
Bergman, David, Joseph de Roche, and Daniel M. Epstein. *Instructor's Manual . . .* , 20.
Harris, Janice H. *The Short Fiction . . .* , 125–126.

"In Love"
Harris, Janice H. *The Short Fiction . . .* , 208–210.

"Jimmy and the Desperate Woman"
Harris, Janice H. *The Short Fiction . . .* , 177–178.

"The Ladybird" [originally titled "The Thimble"]
Harris, Janice H. *The Short Fiction . . .* , 123–124.
Humma, John B. "Lawrence's 'The Ladybird' and the Enabling Image," *D. H. Lawrence R*, 17 (1984), 219–232.
Ruderman, Judith. *D. H. Lawrence . . .* , 75–76.

"The Last Laugh"
Harris, Janice H. *The Short Fiction . . .* , 175–177.

"Love Among the Haystacks"
Harris, Janice H. *The Short Fiction . . .* , 70–73.

"The Lovely Lady"
Ruderman, Judith. *D. H. Lawrence . . .* , 157–158.

"The Man Who Died" [First part of story originally titled "The Escaped Cock"]
Derbin, Daniel. *A "Strange Sapience" . . .* , 120–121, 177–180.
Harris, Janice H. "The Many Faces of Lazarus: 'The Man Who Died' and Its Context," *D. H. Lawrence R*, 16 (1983), 291–311; rpt. in part in her *The Short Fiction . . .* , 237–249.
Larsen, Elizabeth. "Lawrence's 'The Man Who Died,'" *Explicator*, 40, iv (1982), 38–40.

"The Man Who Loved Islands"
Harris, Janice H. *The Short Fiction . . .* , 230–235.
Temple, J. "The Definition of Innocence . . . ," 114–116.
Turner, John F. "The Capacity To Be Alone and Its Failure in D. H. Lawrence's 'The Man Who Loved Islands,'" *D. H. Lawrence R*, 16 (1983), 259–289.

"The Miner at Home"
Harris, Janice H. *The Short Fiction . . .* , 63–65.

"A Modern Lover"
Harris, Janice H. *The Short Fiction . . .* , 38–39.

"Monkey Nuts"
Ruderman, Judith. *D. H. Lawrence . . .* , 87–88.
Simpson, Hilary. *. . . Feminism*, 69–70.

"Mother and Daughter"
Harris, Janice H. *The Short Fiction . . .* , 212–216.
Ruderman, Judith. *D. H. Lawrence . . .* , 168–171.

"New Eve and Old Adam"
Harris, Janice H. *The Short Fiction . . .* , 85–89.

"None of That"
Harris, Janice H. *The Short Fiction . . .* , 210–212.

"Odour of Chrysanthemums"
Harris, Janice H. *The Short Fiction* . . . , 48–51.
Stewart, Garrett. *Death Sentence* . . . , 246–247.

"Once"
Harris, Janice H. *The Short Fiction* . . . , 79–81.

"Prelude to a Happy Christmas"
Harris, Janice H. *The Short Fiction* . . . , 20–22.

"The Primrose Path"
DiGaetani, John L. *Richard Wagner* . . . , 65–66.
Sheidley, William E., and Ann Charters. *Instructor's Manual* . . . , 81–82.

"The Prussian Officer"
Harris, Janice H. *The Short Fiction* . . . , 93–99.
Sirlin, Rhoda, and David H. Richter. *Instructor's Manual* . . . , 81–84.

"The Rocking-Horse Winner"
Harris, Janice H. *The Short Fiction* . . . , 224–227.
Sheidley, William E., and Ann Charters. *Instructor's Manual* . . . , 83–84.
Sirlin, Rhoda, and David H. Richter. *Instructor's Manual* . . . , 84–86.
*Snodgrass, W. D. " 'The Rocking-Horse Winner,' " in Dietrich, R. F., and
    Roger H. Sundell. *Instructor's Manual* . . . , 4th ed., 110–119.

"St. Mawr"
Barker, Anne D. "The Fairy Tale and 'St. Mawr,' " *Forum Mod Lang Stud*, 20, i
    (1984), 76–83.
Brown, Keith. "Welsh Red Indians: D. H. Lawrence and 'St. Mawr,' " *Essays Crit*,
    32 (1982), 158–179.
Dervin, Daniel. *A "Strange Sapience"* . . . , 132–138.
Harris, Janice H. *The Short Fiction* . . . , 193–195.
Padhi, Bibhu. "Lawrence, 'St. Mawr,' and Irony," *So Dakota R*, 21, ii (1983), 5–
    13.
Ruderman, Judith. *D. H. Lawrence* . . . , 139–141.
Simpson, Hilary. . . . *Feminism*, 117–119.
Tallman, Warren. "Forest, Glacier . . . ," 90–92.

"Sun"
Ruderman, Judith. *D. H. Lawrence* . . . , 177–179.

"The Thorn in the Flesh" [same as "Vin Ordinaire"]
Harris, Janice H. *The Short Fiction* . . . , 113–116.

"Tickets, Please" [originally titled "The Eleventh Commandment"]
Harris, Janice H. *The Short Fiction* . . . , 137–139.
Simpson, Hilary. . . . *Feminism*, 67–69.

"Two Blue Birds"
Miller, James E., and Bernice Slote. *Instructor's Manual* . . . , 2nd ed., 15.

"The Virgin and the Gipsy"
Ruderman, Judith. *D. H. Lawrence* . . . , 154–158.
Tallman, Warren. "Forest, Glacier . . . ," 77–79.
Vickery, John B. *Myths and Texts* . . . , 45–47.

"The White Stocking"
Harris, Janice H. *The Short Fiction* . . . , 111–113.

"Witch à la Mode"
DiGaetani, John L. *Richard Wagner* . . . , 64–65.
Harris, Janice H. *The Short Fiction* . . . , 51–54.

"The Woman Who Rode Away"
Elsbree, Langdon. *The Rituals of Life*, 113–114.
Harris, Janice H. *The Short Fiction* . . . , 184–187.
Ruderman, Judith. *D. H. Lawrence* . . . , 134–135.
Steven, Laurence. "'The Woman Who Rode Away': D. H. Lawrence's Cul-de-Sac," *Engl Stud Canada*, 10 (1984), 209–220.

"You Touched Me"
Harris, Janice H. *The Short Fiction* . . . , 151–153.
Ruderman, Judith. *D. H. Lawrence* . . . , 81–83.
Temple, J. "The Definition of Innocence . . . ," 108–109.

HENRY LAWSON

"A Child in the Dark, and a Foreign Father"
Murray-Smith, Stephen. *Henry Lawson*, 9–10.

"Going Blind"
Kiernam, Brian. "Ways of Seeing: Henry Lawson's 'Going Blind,'" *Australian Lit Stud*, 9 (1980), 298–308.

"The Loaded Dog"
Stewart, Ken. "'The Loaded Dog': A Celebration," *Australian Lit Stud*, 11 (1983), 152–161.

CAMARA LAYE

"Groit's Tale"
Lee, Sonia. *Camara Laye*, 36–37.

JOSEPH SHERIDAN LE FANU

"The Evil Guest"
Peterson, Audrey. *Victorian Masters* . . . , 126.

"Green Tea"
Pierce, Hazel. *A Literary Symbiosis* . . . , 206–207.
Thompson, G. R. "Washington Irving and the American Ghost Story," in Kerr, Howard, John W. Crowley, and Charles L. Crow, Eds. *The Haunted Dusk* . . . , 14–16.

"Mr. Justice Harbottle"
Schirmer, Gregory A. "Tales from Big House and Cabin: The Nineteenth Century," in Kilroy, James F., Ed. *The Irish Short Story* . . . , 39–40.

"The Murdered Cousin"
Peterson, Audrey. *Victorian Masters* . . . , 143.

"The Room in the Dragon Volant"
Peterson, Audrey. *Victorian Masters* . . . , 154.

URSULA K. LE GUIN

"The Author of the Acacia Seeds and Other Extracts from the *Journal of the Association of Therolinguistics*"
Meyers, Walter E. *Aliens and Linguists* . . . , 59–60.

"The New Atlantis"
Bergman, David, Joseph de Roche, and Daniel M. Epstein. *Instructor's Manual* . . . , 31–32.

"Nine Lives"
Samuelson, David N. "Ursula Le Guin," in Bleiler, Everett F., Ed. *Science Fiction Writers* . . . , 414.

"A Trip to the Head"
Samuelson, David N. "Ursula Le Guin," 416.

"Vaster Than Empires and More Slow"
Sirlin, Rhoda, and David H. Richter. *Instructor's Manual* . . . , 87–89.

ROSAMOND LEHMANN

"A Dream of Winter"
LeStourgeon, Diana. *Rosamond Lehmann*, 132–134.

"The Gipsy's Baby"
LeStourgeon, Diana. *Rosamond Lehmann*, 122–127.

"The Red-Haired Miss Daintreys"
LeStourgeon, Diana. *Rosamond Lehmann*, 127–130.

"When the Waters Came"
LeStourgeon, Diana. *Rosamond Lehmann*, 131–132.

"Wonderful Holiday"
LeStourgeon, Diana. *Rosamond Lehmann,* 134–138.

FRITZ LEIBER

"Adept's Gambit"
De Camp, L. Sprague. *Literary Swordsmen . . . ,* 284–287.

"Belsen Express"
Staicar, Tom. *Fritz Leiber,* 102–103.

"Black Glass"
Staicar, Tom. *Fritz Leiber,* 104–106.

"The Button Moulder"
Staicar, Tom. *Fritz Leiber,* 106–109.

"Catch That Zeppelin"
Frane, Jeff. *Fritz Leiber,* 46.
Staicar, Tom. *Fritz Leiber,* 58–60.

"Crazy Wolf"
Staicar, Tom. *Fritz Leiber,* 46–47.

"The Girl with the Hungry Eyes"
Frane, Jeff. *Fritz Leiber,* 43–44.

"The Haunted Future"
Staicar, Tom. *Fritz Leiber,* 57–58.

"Ill Met in Lankhmar"
Frane, Jeff. *Fritz Leiber,* 39–40.

"No Great Magic"
Frane, Jeff. *Fritz Leiber,* 30.
Staicar, Tom. *Fritz Leiber,* 56–57.

"The Oldest Soldier"
Frane, Jeff. *Fritz Leiber,* 31.

"Smoke Ghost"
Frane, Jeff. *Fritz Leiber,* 42.

MURRAY LEINSTER

"First Contact"
Huntington, James. "Impossible Love in Science Fiction," *Raritan,* 14, ii (1984),
    90–93.

"The Runaway Skyscraper"
Clute, John. "Murray Leinster," in Bleiler, Everett F., Ed. *Science Fiction Writ-
    ers . . . ,* 113.

"Sidewise in Time"
Clute, John. "Murray Leinster," 114.

STANISLAW LEM

"Do You Exist, Mr. Johns?" [same as "Are You There, Mr. Johns?"]
Thomsen, Christian W. "Robot Ethics and Robot Parody: Remarks on Isaac Asimov's *I, Robot* and Some Critical Essays and Short Stories by Stanislaw Lem," in Dunn, Thomas P., and Richard D. Erlich, Eds. *The Mechanical God . . .*, 32.

"The Hammer"
Thomsen, Christian W. "Robot Ethics . . . ," 35–36.

"The Masque"
Thomsen, Christian W. "Robot Ethics . . . ," 36–37.

HENRY-RENÉ LENORMAND

"The Denizens of the Elite Bar"
Jones, Robert E. *Henry-René Lenormand*, 145–146.

CONSTANTINE LEONTIEV

"A Husband's Confession"
Rzhevsky, Nicholas. *Russian Literature . . .*, 112–113.

"A Summer in the Village"
Rzhevsky, Nicholas. *Russian Literature . . .*, 101–102.

DORIS LESSING

"The Black Madonna"
Perrine, Laurence, and Thomas R. Arp. *Instructor's Manual . . .*, 6th ed., 8–10.

"Eldorado"
Sage, Lorna. *Doris Lessing*, 20–21.

"Homage for Isaac Babel"
Bergman, David, Joseph de Roche, and Daniel M. Epstein. *Instructor's Manual . . .*, 38–39.

"Little Tembi"
Sage, Lorna. *Doris Lessing*, 28.

"A Man and Two Women"
Atack, Margaret. "Toward a Narrative Analysis of 'A Man and Two Women,'" in Taylor, Jenny, Ed. *Notebooks . . .*, 135–163.
Magliocco, Maurine. "Doris Lessing's 'A Man and Two Women': Is It Universal?" *Denver Q*, 17 (Winter, 1983), 29–39.

"My Father"
Sage, Lorna. *Doris Lessing*, 19–20.

"The Old Chief Mshlanga"
Sage, Lorna. *Doris Lessing*, 18–19.
Sirlin, Rhoda, and David H. Richter. *Instructor's Manual . . .* , 89–92.

"One Off the Short List"
Clements, Frances M. "Lessing's 'One Off the Short List' and the Definition of
    Self," *Frontiers*, 1 (Fall, 1975), 106–109.
Sirlin, Rhoda, and David H. Richter. *Instructor's Manual . . .* , 92–94.

"The Pig"
Sage, Lorna. *Doris Lessing*, 28–29.

"Sunrise on the Veldt"
Sage, Lorna. *Doris Lessing*, 19.

"The Temptation of Jack Orkney"
Sirlin, Rhoda, and David H. Richter. *Instructor's Manual . . .* , 95–97.

"To Room Nineteen"
Abcarian, Richard, and Marvin Klotz. *Instructor's Manual . . .* , 2nd ed., 14–15;
    3rd ed., 11–12.
Sheidley, William E., and Ann Charters. *Instructor's Manual . . .* , 148.

"An Unposted Love Letter"
Madden, David. *Instructor's Manual . . .* , 5th ed., 109–112; Madden, David, and
    Virgil Scott. *Instructor's Manual . . .* , 6th ed., 124–127.

"A Woman on the Roof"
Kennedy, X. J. *Instructor's Manual . . .* , 3rd ed., 16–18.

MEYER LEVIN

"Cheuing Gohm"
Rubin, Steven J. *Meyer Levin*, 7–8.

"Molasses Tide"
Rubin, Steven J. *Meyer Levin*, 6–7.

"A Seder"
Rubin, Steven J. *Meyer Levin*, 8.

ALUN LEWIS

"Acting Captain"
Pikoulis, John. *Alun Lewis . . .* , 156–157.

"The Children"
Pikoulis, John. *Alun Lewis . . .* , 157–158.

JANET LEWIS

SINCLAIR LEWIS

"Let's Play King"
Rohrberger, Mary. "The Question of Regionalism: Limitation and Transcendence," in Stevick, Philip, Ed. *The American Short Story, 1900–1945*, 168–169.

"Moths in the Arc Light"
Rohrberger, Mary. "The Question . . . ," 169–170.

"Virga Vay and Allan Cedar"
Bergman, David, Joseph de Roche, and Daniel M. Epstein. *Instructor's Manual . . .*, 42–43.

LUDWIG LEWISOHN

"Bolshevik"
Lainoff, Seymour. *Ludwig Lewisohn*, 57.

"The Saint"
Lainoff, Seymour. *Ludwig Lewisohn*, 57–58.

"Writ of Divorcement"
Lainoff, Seymour. *Ludwig Lewisohn*, 56–57.

BALDOMERO LILLO

"Gate Number 12"
Lindstrom, Naomi. "The Spanish American Short Story from Echeverría to Quiroga," in Peden, Margaret S., Ed. *The Latin American Short Story . . .*, 53.

"The Well"
Lindstrom, Naomi. ". . . Echeverría to Quiroga," 51–53.

LIN HWAI MIN

"Homecoming"
Kim, Elaine H. *Asian American Literature . . .*, 275–276.

CLARICE LISPECTOR

"The Crime of the Mathematics Professor"
Seniff, Dennis. "Self-Doubt in Clarice Lispector's *Laços de família*," *Luso-Brazilian R*, 14, ii (1977), 169–170.

"The Daydream of a Drunken Woman"
Foster, David W. "Major Figures in the Brazilian Short Story," in Peden, Margaret S., Ed. *The Latin American Short Story . . .*, 13–15.
Lindstrom, Naomi. "A Feminist Discourse Analysis of Clarice Lispector's 'Daydream of a Drunken Housewife,'" *Latin Am Lit R*, 9, xix (1981), 7–16.

Nunes, Maria L. "Narrative Modes in Clarice Lispector's *Laços de familia:* The Rendering of Consciousness," *Luso-Brazilian R,* 14, ii (1977), 176–177.
Seniff, Dennis. "Self-Doubt . . . ," 162–163.

"Happy Anniversary"
Seniff, Dennis. "Self-Doubt . . . ," 167–168.

"The Imitation of the Rose"
Nunes, Maria L. "Narrative Modes . . . ," 178.
Seniff, Dennis. "Self-Doubt . . . ," 166–167.

"Love"
Nunes, Maria L. "Narrative Modes . . . ," 177–178.
Seniff, Dennis. "Self-Doubt . . . ," 163–166.

"Preciousness"
Lindstrom, Naomi. "A Discourse Analysis of 'Preciosidade' by Clarice Lispector," *Luso-Brazilian R,* 19, ii (1982), 187–194.
Seniff, Dennis. "Self-Doubt . . . ," 168–169.

"The Smallest Woman in the World"
Seniff, Dennis. "Self-Doubt . . . ," 168.

JOSÉ BENTO MONTEIRO LOBATO

"Bracket Fungus"
Foster, David W. "Major Figures in the Brazilian Short Story," in Peden, Margaret S., Ed. *The Latin American Short Story . . . ,* 5–7.

JACK LONDON

"And 'Frisco Kid Came Back"
Johnston, Carolyn. *Jack London . . . ,* 18.

"The Apostate"
Hedrick, Joan D. *Solitary Comrade . . . ,* 171–176.

"The Call of the Wild"
Hedrick, Joan D. *Solitary Comrade . . . ,* 102–111.
Watson, Charles N. *The Novels of Jack London . . . ,* 33–52.

"Chun Ah Chun"
Wu, William F. *The Yellow Peril . . . ,* 119–120.

"A Curious Fragment"
Beauchamp, Gorman. *Jack London,* 64–65.

"Diable—A Dog"
Allen, Mary. *Animals . . . ,* 79–81.

"The Shadow and the Flash"
Beauchamp, Gorman. *Jack London,* 22–24.
Reich, Kenneth E. "Sport in Literature . . . ," 53–54.
Tavernier-Courbin, Jacqueline. ". . . Science-Fiction," 73–74.

"South of the Slot"
Conn, Peter. *The Divided Mind . . . ,* 106–107.
Hedrick, Joan D. *Solitary Comrade . . . ,* 176–185.
Johnston, Carolyn. *Jack London . . . ,* 132.

"The Strength of the Strong"
Beauchamp, Gorman. *Jack London,* 44–48.
Pizer, Donald. *Realism and Naturalism . . . ,* 2nd ed., 174–175.

"The Tears of Ah Kim"
Wu, William F. *The Yellow Peril . . . ,* 120–121.

"A Thousand Deaths"
Beauchamp, Gorman. *Jack London,* 19–21.
Tavernier-Courbin, Jacqueline. ". . . Science-Fiction," 72–73.

"To Build a Fire"
Allen, Mary. *Animals . . . ,* 93–95.
Hedrick, Joan D. *Solitary Comrade . . . ,* 53–54.
Pizer, Donald. *Realism and Naturalism . . . ,* 2nd ed., 172–173.
Sheidley, William E., and Ann Charters. *Instructor's Manual . . . ,* 60–61.
Sirlin, Rhoda, and David H. Richter. *Instructor's Manual . . . ,* 98–99.

"The Unparalleled Invasion"
Beauchamp, Gorman. *Jack London,* 28–31.
Wu, William F. *The Yellow Peril . . . ,* 118–119.

"When the World Was Young"
Beauchamp, Gorman. *Jack London,* 31–34.

"The White Silence"
Hedrick, Joan D. *Solitary Comrade . . . ,* 49–52.

AUGUSTUS BALDWIN LONGSTREET

"The Debating Society"
King, Kimball. *Augustus Baldwin Longstreet,* 80–83.

"The Fight"
King, Kimball. *Augustus Baldwin Longstreet,* 70–71.

"The Gnatville Gem"
King, Kimball. *Augustus Baldwin Longstreet,* 98–101.

"The Horse Swap"
King, Kimball. *Augustus Baldwin Longstreet,* 62–65.

LORELLE [unidentified]

"The Battle of Wabash"
Wu, William F. *The Yellow Peril* . . . , 42–43.

H. P. LOVECRAFT

"Arthur Jermyn" [same as "The White Ape"; originally titled "Facts Concerning
    Arthur Jermyn & His Family"]
Burleson, Donald R. *H. P. Lovecraft* . . . , 71–72.

"At the Mountains of Madness"
Wilson, Colin. "H. P. Lovecraft," in Bleiler, Everett F., Ed. *Science Fiction Writers* . . . , 135.

"Beyond the Wall of Sleep"
Burleson, Donald R. *H. P. Lovecraft* . . . , 31–32.

"The Call of Cthulhu"
Burleson, Donald R. *H. P. Lovecraft* . . . , 115–121.
De Camp, L. Sprague. *Literary Swordsmen* . . . , 98–101.
Joshi, S. T. *H. P. Lovecraft*, 33–34.
Wilson, Colin. "H. P. Lovecraft," 133.

"The Cats of Ulthar"
Burleson, Donald R. *H. P. Lovecraft* . . . , 47–48.

"Celephaïs"
Burleson, Donald R. *H. P. Lovecraft* . . . , 48–50.

"The Colour out of Space"
Burleson, Donald R. *H. P. Lovecraft* . . . , 135–140.
Joshi, S. T. *H. P. Lovecraft*, 34–35.
Wilson, Colin. "H. P. Lovecraft," 133–134.

"The Curse of Yig"
Burleson, Donald R. *H. P. Lovecraft* . . . , 153–154.

"Dagon"
Burleson, Donald R. *H. P. Lovecraft* . . . , 22–24.

"The Doom That Came to Sarnath"
Burleson, Donald R. *H. P. Lovecraft* . . . , 29–30.

"The Dream-Quest of Unknown Kadath"
De Camp, L. Sprague. *Literary Swordsmen* . . . , 102–103.

"The Dreams in the Witch House"
Burleson, Donald R. *H. P. Lovecraft* . . . , 177–180.

MALCOLM LOWRY

"The Bravest Boat"
Dahlie, Hallvard. "The New Land and Malcolm Lowry," in Chadbourne, Richard, and Hallvard Dahlie, Eds. *The New Land . . .* , 84–85.

"Bulls of the Resurrection"
Grace, Sherrill E. *The Voyage . . .* , 21–22.

"China"
Grace, Sherrill E. *The Voyage . . .* , 21.

"Elephant and Colosseum"
Rankin, Elizabeth D. "Malcolm Lowry's Comic Vision: 'Elephant and Colosseum,'" *Canadian Lit,* 101 (Summer, 1984), 167–171.

"The Forest Path to the Spring"
Dahlie, Hallvard. "The New Land . . . ," 88–91.

"Ghostkeeper"
Grace, Sherrill E. *The Voyage . . .* , 1–2.

"Gin and Goldenrod"
Dahlie, Hallvard. "The New Land . . . ," 88.

"June the 30th, 1934"
Grace, Sherrill E. *The Voyage . . .* , 22–24.

"Present Estate of Pompeii"
Dahlie, Hallvard. "The New Land . . . ," 86–87.

"Through the Panama"
Dahlie, Hallvard. "The New Land . . . ," 85–86.
Walker, Ronald G. *Infernal Paradise . . .* , 319–321.

"The Voyage That Never Ends"
Grace, Sherrill E. *The Voyage . . .* , 6–9.

LU HSÜN [LU XÜN or CHOU SHU-JEN]

"Divorce"
Hanan, Patrick. "The Technique of Lu Hsün's Fiction," *Harvard J Asiatic Stud,*
34 (1974), 86–87.

"Looking Backward to the Past"
Hanan, Patrick. "The Technique . . . ," 79–80.

"Medicine"
Hanan, Patrick. "The Technique . . . ," 61–65.

"Peking Street Scene"
Hanan, Patrick. "The Technique . . . ," 89.

"The True Story of Ah Q"
Li, Wallace. "History and Fiction: A New Interpretation of 'The True Story of Ah Q,'" *Fu Jen Stud,* 17 (1984), 69–89.

LEOPOLDO LUGONES

"The Pillar of Salt"
Lindstrom, Naomi. "The Spanish American Short Story from Echeverría to Quiroga," in Peden, Margaret S., Ed. *The Latin American Short Story . . . ,* 67–69.

MARTA LYNCH

"Campo de batalla"
Lewald, H. Ernest. "Alienation and Eros in Three Stories by Beatriz Guido, Marta Lynch, and Amalia Jamilis," in Mora, Gabriela, and Karen S. Van Hooft, Eds. *Theory and Practice . . . ,* 181–182.

MIKHAS' T. LYNKOŬ

"Giovanni"
Rich, Vera. "Jewish Themes and Characters in Belorussian Texts," in Blum, Jakub, and Vera Rich. *The Image of the Jew . . . ,* 244–245.

ANDREW LYTLE

"Alchemy"
Yow, John. "Alchemical Captains: Andrew Lytle's Tales of the Conquistadors," *Southern Lit J,* 14, ii (1982), 38–41.

"Jericho, Jericho, Jericho"
Hoy, Pat C. "The Wages of Sin: Terminal Considerations in Lytle's 'Jericho, Jericho, Jericho,'" *So Atlantic R,* 49, iv (1984), 107–118.

ANNE McCAFFREY

"Lady in the Tower"
King, Betty. *Women of the Future . . . ,* 87–89.

MARY McCARTHY

"Cruel and Barbarous Treatment"
Walker, Jeffrey. "1945—1956: Post-World War II Manners and Mores," in Weaver, Gordon, Ed. *The American Short Story, 1945–1980,* 7.

CARSON McCULLERS

"The Ballad of the Sad Café"
Gannon, Barbara C. "McCullers' 'The Ballad of the Sad Café,'" *Explicator,* 41,
    i (1982), 59–60.
Roberts, Mary. "Imperfect Androgyny and Imperfect Love in the Works of
    Carson McCullers," *Hartford Stud Lit,* 12 (1980), 93–95.
Westling, Louise. "Carson McCullers' Amazon Nightmare," *Mod Fiction Stud,*
    28 (1982), 365–373.

"A Tree, A Rock, A Cloud"
Scott, Virgil, and David Madden. *Instructor's Manual . . . ,* 4th ed., 4–6; Madden,
    David. *Instructor's Manual . . . ,* 5th ed., 4–5; Madden, David, and Virgil
    Scott. *Instructor's Manual . . . ,* 6th ed., 12–13.
Sundell, Roger H. "'A Tree, a Rock, a Cloud,'" in Dietrich, R. F., and Roger H.
    Sundell. *Instructor's Manual . . . ,* 4th ed., 20–22.

GEORGE MacDONALD

"The Golden Key"
Gifford, Douglas, Ed. *Scottish Short Stories . . . ,* 11–12.

JOAQUIM MARÍA MACHADO DE ASSIS

"Adam and Eve"
Gledson, John. *The Deceptive Realism . . . ,* 170–171.

"A Captain of Volunteers"
Gledson, John. *The Deceptive Realism . . . ,* 155–156.

"The Church of the Devil"
Gledson, John. *The Deceptive Realism . . . ,* 171.

"Midnight Mass"
Foster, David W. "Major Figures in the Brazilian Short Story," in Peden,
    Margaret S., Ed. *The Latin American Short Story . . . ,* 2–3.

"The Mockery of Dates"
Gledson, John. *The Deceptive Realism . . . ,* 151–153.

"O Caso de Vara"
Rassner, Ronald M. "Palmares and the Free Slave in Afro-Brazilian Literature,"
    in Luis, William, Ed. *Voices from Under . . . ,* 212–213.

"One Night"
Gledson, John. *The Deceptive Realism . . . ,* 153–155.

"The Opera"
Gledson, John. *The Deceptive Realism . . . ,* 171–172.

"Pai Contra Mae"
Rassner, Ronald M. "Palmares . . . ," 213.

"A Parasita Azul"
Gledson, John. "Machado de Assis Between Romance and Satire: 'A Parasita
    Azul,'" in Bacarisse, Salvador, Bernard Bentley, Mercedes Clarasó, and
    Douglas Gifford, Eds. *What's Past . . .* , 57–69.

"Singular Occurrence"
Foster, David W. "Major Figures . . . ," 3.

ARTHUR MACHEN

"The Great God Pan"
Fredericks, Casey. *The Future of Eternity . . .* , 151.

VONDA N. McINTYRE

"Aztecs"
Wendell, Carolyn. "Responsible Rebellion in Vonda N. McIntyre's *Fireflood,
    Dreamsnake,* and *Exile Waiting,*" in Staicar, Tom, Ed. *The Feminine Eye . . .* ,
    135–136.

"The Genius Freaks"
Wendell, Carolyn. "Responsible Rebellion . . . ," 134–135.

"The Mountains of Sunset, the Mountains of Dawn"
Wendell, Carolyn. "Responsible Rebellion . . . ," 134.

"Only at Night"
Wendell, Carolyn. "Responsible Rebellion . . . ," 133.

"Screwtop"
King, Betty. *Women of the Future . . .* , 163–165.
Wendell, Carolyn. "Responsible Rebellion . . . ," 130–132.

"Spectra"
Wendell, Carolyn. "Responsible Rebellion . . . ," 129.

"Wings"
Wendell, Carolyn. "Responsible Rebellion . . . ," 133–134.

RICHARD McKENNA

"The Secret Place"
Koelb, Clayton. *The Incredulous Reader . . .* , 98–100.

BERNARD MacLAVERTY

"A Schoolmaster"
Dunleavy, Janet E. "Mary Lavin, Elizabeth Bowen, and a New Generation: The
    Irish Short Story at Midcentury," in Kilroy, James F., Ed. *The Irish Short
    Story* . . . , 163.

"Stone"
Dunleavy, Janet E. "Mary Lavin . . . ," 164–165.

KATHERINE McLEAN

"And Be Merry"
King, Betty. *Women of the Future* . . . , 89–90.

"Contagion"
King, Betty. *Women of the Future* . . . , 90–91.

NORMAN MACLEAN

"A River Runs Through It"
Simonson, Harold P. "Norman Maclean's Two-Hearted River," *Western Am Lit*,
    17 (1982), 149–155.

JAMES ALAN McPHERSON

"Problems of Art"
Vauthier, Simone. "A Modern Version of the Confidence Game: James Alan
    McPherson's 'Problems of Art,'" *Am Stud*, 27 (1982), 141–155.

BERNARD MALAMUD

"Angel Levine"
Alter, Iska. *The Good Man's Dilemma* . . . , 64–68.
Bilik, Dorothy S. *Immigrant-Survivors* . . . , 68–69.
Peters, Carl. "'Angel Levine': A Sociolinguistic Analysis," *Linguistics in Lit*, 6
    (1981), 23–40.

"Black Is My Favorite Color"
Alter, Iska. *The Good Man's Dilemma* . . . , 68–73.
*Skaggs, Merrill M. "'Black Is My Favorite Color,'" in Dietrich, R. F., and
    Roger H. Sundell. *Instructor's Manual* . . . , 4th ed., 53–59.

"The German Refugee"
Blythe, Hal, and Charlie Sweet. "The Narrator in Malamud's 'The German
    Refugee,'" *Am Notes & Queries*, 22, iii–iv (1983), 47–49.

"Girl of My Dreams"
Alter, Iska. *The Good Man's Dilemma* . . . , 121–126.

"Idiots First"
*Abcarian, Richard, and Marvin Klotz. *Instructor's Manual* . . . , 2nd ed., 15; 3rd
    ed., 12–13.
Bryant, Earle V. "The Tree-Clock in Bernard Malamud's 'Idiots First,'" *Stud
    Short Fiction*, 20 (1983), 52–54.
Madden, David. *Instructor's Manual* . . . , 5th ed., 51–54; Madden, David, and
    Virgil Scott. *Instructor's Manual* . . . , 6th ed., 113–115.

"The Jewbird"
Baumgarten, Murray. *City Scriptures* . . . , 24–25.

"The Lady of the Lake"
Clayworth, Linda C. "Bernard Malamud's 'The Lady of the Lake': A Double
    Matrix," *Linguistics in Lit*, 6 (1981), 68–86.

"The Last Mohican"
Bilik, Dorothy S. *Immigrant-Survivors* . . . , 59–61.
Greenspan, Ezra. *The "Schlemiel"* . . . , 149–151.

"The Loan"
Bilik, Dorothy S. *Immigrant-Survivors* . . . , 61–63.
Greenspan, Ezra. *The "Schlemiel"* . . . , 152–153.

"The Magic Barrel"
Bargen, Doris G. *The Fiction* . . . , 73–74.
Bilik, Dorothy S. *Immigrant-Survivors* . . . , 58–59.
Karl, Frederick R. *American Fictions* . . . , 244.
Sirlin, Rhoda, and David H. Richter. *Instructor's Manual* . . . , 102–103.

"Man in the Drawer"
Greenspan, Ezra. *The "Schlemiel"* . . . , 190–191.

EDUARDO MALLEA

"La causa de Jacobo Uber, perdida"
Polt, John H. R. *The Writings* . . . , 54–55.

"Conversation"
Brushwood, John S. "The Spanish American Short Story from Quiroga to
    Borges," in Peden, Margaret S., Ed. *The Latin American Short Story* . . . , 88–
    89.

"Human Reason"
Earle, Peter G. "Dreams of Creation: Short Fiction in Spanish America," *Denver
    Q*, 12 (1977), 72.

McKNIGHT MALMAR

"The Storm"
Perrine, Laurence, Ed. *Story and Structure*, 6th ed., 237.

DAVID MALOUF

"Eustace"
Pierce, Peter. "David Malouf's Fiction," *Meanjin,* 41 (1982), 531.

"The Prowler"
Pierce, Peter. "David Malouf's Fiction," 531–533.

BARRY MALZBERG

"The Twentieth-Century Murder Case"
Pierce, Hazel. *A Literary Symbiosis . . . ,* 141–142.

NADEZHDA MANDELSTAM

"The Egyptian Stamp"
Yudkin, Leon I. *Jewish Writing . . . ,* 66.

"The Noise of Time"
Yudkin, Leon I. *Jewish Writing . . . ,* 65–66.

ANDRÉ PIEYRE DE MANDIARGUES

"The Archaeologist"
Bond, David J. "Jung and Pieyre de Mandiargues," *L'Esprit Créateur,* 22, ii
(1982), 53–62.
Habel, Angela. "'L'Archéologue' de Mandiargues entre le fantastique et la psy-
chanalyse," *Symposium,* 36 (1982), 129–148.

"The Diamond"
Bond, David L. *The Fiction . . . ,* 47–48.
McNerney, Kathleen, and John Martin. "Medieval Themes in André Pieyre de
Mandiargues' 'Le Diamant,'" *Stud Medievalism,* 2, ii (1983), 81–84.

"Le Marronnier"
Bond, David L. *The Fiction . . . ,* 58–59.

"Le Sang de l'agneau"
Bond, David L. *The Fiction . . . ,* 20–22.
Companini, Susan. "Blood Rites: Pieyre de Mandiargues' 'Le Sang de l'ag-
neau,'" *Romanic R,* 73 (1982), 364–372.

"Le Tombeau d'Aubrey Beardsley"
Bond, David L. *The Fiction . . . ,* 78–79.

"La Vision capitale"
Bond, David L. *The Fiction . . . ,* 79–80.

HEINRICH MANN

"Contessina"
Durzak, Manfred. "'Drei-Minuten-Romane' zu den novelistischen Anfängen
Heinrich Manns," in Koopmann, Helmut, and Peter-Paul Schneider, Eds.
Heinrich Mann . . . , 9–23.

THOMAS MANN

"Death in Venice"
Gullette, Margaret M. "The Exile of Adulthood: Pedophilia in the Midlife
Novel," *Novel*, 17 (1984), 215–232.
Hijiva-Kirschnereit, Irmela. "Thomas Mann's Short Novel 'Der Tod in Venedig'
and Mishima Yukio's Novel *Kinjiki*: A Comparison," in Nish, Ian, and
Charles Dunn, Eds. *European Studies* . . . , 711–724.
Kar, Prafulla C. "'Death in Venice': A Study in Symbolic Action," *Indian J Engl
Stud*, 20 (1980), 95–100.
McKeon, Zahava K. *Novels and Arguments* . . . , 87–88.
Rockwood, Heidi M. and Robert J. R. "The Psychological Reality of Myth in
'Der Tod in Venedig,'" *Germ R*, 59 (1984), 137–141.
Sirlin, Rhoda, and David H. Richter. *Instructor's Manual* . . . , 104–106.
Watts, Cedric. *The Deceptive Text* . . . , 167–175.

"Disorder and Early Sorrow"
Lehnert, Herbert. "Thomas Manns 'Unordnung und frühe Leid': Entstellte
Bürgerwelt und ästhetisches Reservat," *Text & Kontext*, 6 (1978), 239–256.

"Gladius Dei"
Frühwald, Wolfgang. "'Der christliche Müngling im Kunstladen': Milieu- und
Stilparodie in Thomas Manns Erzählung 'Gladius Dei,'" in Schnitzler,
Günter, Gerhard Neumann, and Jürgen Schröder, Eds. *Bild und Ge-
danke* . . . , 324–342.
Sirlin, Rhoda, and David H. Richter. *Instructor's Manual* . . . , 110–111.

"Mario and the Magician"
Emrich, Wilhelm. *Freiheit und Nihilismus* . . . , 1–17.
McIntyre, Allan J. "From Travemünde to Torre di Venere: Mannian Leitmotifs
in Political Transition," *Germ R*, 59 (1984), 26–31.
Müller-Salget, Klaus. "Der Tod in Torre di Venere: Spiegelung und Deutung
des italiensichen Faschismus in Thomas Manns 'Mario und der Zauberer,'"
Arcadia, 18, i (1983), 50–65.

"Railway Accident"
Sauer, Paul L. "Der 'hinkende Staat': Über einen 'Schmarten' Thomas Manns,
genannt 'Das Eisenbahnunglück,'" *Wirkendes Wort*, 30 (1980), 311–322.

"Tonio Kröger"
Sirlin, Rhoda, and David H. Richter. *Instructor's Manual* . . . , 108–110.

"The Transposed Heads"
Koelb, Clayton. *The Incredulous Reader. . .* , 21–22.
Stéphane, Nelly. "Les Têtes interverties," *Europe,* [n.v.] (June-July, 1982), 638–639, 172–174.

"Tristan"
Stanzel, F. K. *A Theory of Narrative . . .* , 180–184.

"The Wardrobe"
Koelb, Clayton. *The Incredulous Reader. . .* , 24–26.

"The Will to Happiness"
Vaget, Hans R. "Intertextualität im Frühwerk Thomas Manns 'Der Wille zun Glück' und Heinrich Manns *Das Wunderbare,*" *Zeitschrift für Deutsche Philologie,* 101 (1982), 193–216.

KATHERINE MANSFIELD [KATHERINE BEAUCHAMP]

"At Lehmann's"
Hankin, C. A. *Katherine Mansfield . . .* , 65–66.

"At the Bay"
Hankin, C. A. *Katherine Mansfield . . .* , 222–234.

"Bains Turcs"
Hankin, C. A. *Katherine Mansfield . . .* , 68–70.

"A Birthday"
Hankin, Cherry. "Katherine Mansfield and the Inner Life," in Hankin, Cherry, Ed. . . . *New Zealand Short Story,* 11–12.
———. *Katherine Mansfield . . .* , 109.

"Bliss"
Hankin, Cherry. "Katherine Mansfield . . . ," 21–23.
———. *Katherine Mansfield . . .* , 141–152.
Sheidley, William E., and Ann Charters. *Instructor's Manual . . .* , 88–89.

"Brave Love"
Hankin, C. A. *Katherine Mansfield . . .* , 95–96.

"The Daughters of the Late Colonel"
Hankin, Cherry. "Katherine Mansfield . . . ," 24–27.
———. *Katherine Mansfield . . .* , 200–205.

"A Dill Pickle"
Miller, James E., and Bernice Slote. *Instructor's Manual . . .* , 2nd ed., 16.

"The Doll's House"
Hankin, Cherry. "Katherine Mansfield . . . ," 17–18.
———. *Katherine Mansfield . . .* , 218–221.
Sheidley, William E., and Ann Charters. *Instructor's Manual . . .* , 90–91.

"Die Einsame"
Hankin, C. A. *Katherine Mansfield . . .* , 9–11.

"A Fairy Story"
Hankin, C. A. *Katherine Mansfield . . .* , 106–109.

"The Flower"
Gubar, Susan. "The Birth of the Artist as Heroine: (Re)production, the *Künstlerroman* Tradition, and the Fiction of Katherine Mansfield," in Heilbrun, Carolyn G., and Margaret R. Higonnet, Eds. . . . *Women in Fiction,* 30–33.

"The Fly"
Hankin, Cherry. "Katherine Mansfield . . . ," 15–16.
———. *Katherine Mansfield . . .* , 241–247.

"Frau Brechenmacher Attends a Wedding"
Hankin, C. A. *Katherine Mansfield . . .* , 63–65.

"The Garden Party"
Hankin, C. A. *Katherine Mansfield . . .* , 235–241.
Satterfield, Ben. "Irony in 'The Garden Party,'" *Ball State Univ Forum,* 23 (Winter, 1982), 68–70.
Sirlin, Rhoda, and David H. Richter. *Instructor's Manual . . .* , 112–113.
Stanzel, F. K. *A Theory of Narrative . . .* , 170–172.

"Germans at Meat"
Hankin, C. A. *Katherine Mansfield . . .* , 63–64.

"Her First Ball"
Franklin, Carol. "Mansfield and Richardson: A Short Story Dialectic," *Australian Lit Stud,* 11 (1983), 224–233.
Hankin, C. A. *Katherine Mansfield . . .* , 216–218.

"Je Ne Parle Pas Français"
Hankin, C. A. *Katherine Mansfield . . .* , 154–163.

"Lady's Maid"
Hankin, C. A. *Katherine Mansfield . . .* , 198–200.

"The Life of Ma Parker"
Hankin, Cherry. "Katherine Mansfield . . . ," 23–24.

"The Little Girl"
Hankin, C. A. *Katherine Mansfield . . .* , 82–84.

"The Little Governess"
Hankin, C. A. *Katherine Mansfield . . .* , 98–100.

"The Man Without a Temperament"
Hankin, C. A. *Katherine Mansfield . . .* , 184–188.

"A Married Man's Story"
Hankin, C. A. *Katherine Mansfield . . .* , 169–174.

"Millie"
Hankin, Cherry. "Katherine Mansfield . . . ," 8.
————. *Katherine Mansfield . . .* , 75–77.

"Miss Brill"
Madden, David, and Virgil Scott. *Instructor's Manual . . .* , 6th ed., 26–30.

"The Modern Soul"
Hankin, C. A. *Katherine Mansfield . . .* , 67–68.

"My Potplants"
Hankin, C. A. *Katherine Mansfield . . .* , 12–14.

"New Dresses"
Hankin, Cherry. "Katherine Mansfield . . . ," 16–17.
————. *Katherine Mansfield . . .* , 81–82.

"Ole Underwood"
Hankin, Cherry. "Katherine Mansfield . . . ," 4–6.

"Pictures" [originally titled "The Common Round"]
Kaplan, Sydney J. "'A Gigantic Mother': Katherine Mansfield's London," in
    Squier, Susan M., Ed. *Women Writers . . .* , 163–165.

"Prelude"
Gubar, Susan. "The Birth of the Artist . . . ," 36–39.
Hankin, Cherry. "Katherine Mansfield . . . ," 8–11.
————. *Katherine Mansfield . . .* , 116–135.

"The Stranger"
Hankin, Cherry. "Katherine Mansfield . . . ," 12–15.

"The Voyage"
Hankin, Cherry. "Katherine Mansfield . . . ," 18–20.
————. *Katherine Mansfield . . .* , 214–216.

"What You Please"
Hankin, C. A. *Katherine Mansfield . . .* , 22–24.

"The Woman at the Store"
Gubar, Susan. "The Birth of the Artist . . . ," 27–29.
Hankin, Cherry. "Katherine Mansfield . . . ," 6–8.
————. *Katherine Mansfield . . .* , 73–75.

SAADAT HASAN MANTO

"By God"
Flemming, Leslie A. "Riots and Refugees: The Post-Partition Stories of Saadat Hasan Manto," *J South Asian Lit,* 13, i–iv (1977–78), 105–106.

"Cold Meat"
Flemming, Leslie A. "Riots and Refugees . . . ," 101–102.

"Last Salute"
Flemming, Leslie A. "Riots and Refugees . . . ," 104.

"Mozel"
Flemming, Leslie A. "Riots and Refugees . . . ," 103.

"Open Up"
Flemming, Leslie A. "Riots and Refugees . . . ," 105.

"A Tetwal Dog"
Flemming, Leslie A. "Riots and Refugees . . . ," 104–105.

"Toba Tek Singh"
Flemming, Leslie A. "Riots and Refugees . . . ," 106–107.

HUMBERTO MARIOTTI

"Into the Deep, Into the Deep"
Urza, Carmelo. "Alienation and Symbol in Mariotti's 'No Fundo, No Fundo' and Bombal's *La última niebla,*" *Luso-Brazilian R,* 21, i (1984), 89–98.

MARKANDEYA

"The Loss of Karmnasha"
Pande, Trilochan. "Folk Elements in the Modern Hindi Short Story," *Folklore* (Calcutta), 231 (1979), 149.

VLADIMIR MARMARZIN

"Pushpull"
Brown, Edward J. . . . *Since the Revolution,* 386–387.

PAULE MARSHALL

"Barbados"

McCluskey, John. "Every Generation Blessed: Theme, Setting, and Ritual in the Works of Paule Marshall," in Evans, Mari, Ed. *Black Women . . .* , 321–322.

Ogunyemi, Chikwenye O. "'The Old Order Shall Pass': The Examples of 'Flying Home' and 'Barbados,'" *Stud Short Fiction*, 20 (1983), 28–32.

Waniek, Marilyn N. "Paltry Things: Immigrants and Marginal Men in Paule Marshall's Short Fiction," *Callaloo*, 6, ii (1983), 46–49.

"Brazil"

McCluskey, John. "Every Generation . . . ," 323–326.

Waniek, Marilyn N. "Paltry Things . . . ," 53–55.

"British Guiana"

McCluskey, John. "Every Generation . . . ," 324–325.

Waniek, Marilyn N. "Paltry Things . . . ," 51–53.

"Brooklyn"

McCluskey, John. "Every Generation . . . ," 322–324.

Waniek, Marilyn N. "Paltry Things . . . ," 49–51.

"Reena"

Denniston, Dorothy L. "Early Short Fiction by Paule Marshall," *Callaloo*, 6, ii (1983), 35–44.

"To Da-Duh in Memoriam"

Collier, Eugenia. "The Closing of the Circle: Movement from Division to Wholeness in Paule Marshall's Fiction," in Evans, Mari, Ed. *Black Women . . .* , 296–298.

"The Valley Between"

Denniston, Dorothy L. "Early Short Fiction . . . ," 31–35.

CLAIRE MARTIN

"C'est raté"

Brazeau, J. Raymond. . . . *French Canadian Literature*, 51–52.

"Femmes"

Brazeau, J. Raymond. . . . *French Canadian Literature*, 51.

MASAMUNE HAKUCHŌ

"A Dangerous Character"

Rubin, Jay. *Injurious to Public Morals . . .* , 187–188.

BOBBIE ANN MASON

"Gooseberry Winter"
Ryan, Maureen. "Stopping Places: Bobbie Ann Mason's Short Stories," in Prenshaw, Peggy W., Ed. *Women Writers . . .* , 289.

"Graveyard Day"
Ryan, Maureen. "Stopping Places . . . ," 290.

"A New-Wave Format"
Ryan, Maureen. "Stopping Places . . . ," 285.

"Offerings"
Ryan, Maureen. "Stopping Places . . . ," 290.

"Old Things"
Ryan, Maureen. "Stopping Places . . . ," 289, 292–293.

"Private Lies"
Ryan, Maureen. "Stopping Places . . . ," 286.

"Residents and Transients"
Ryan, Maureen. "Stopping Places . . . ," 293–294.

"The Retreat"
Ryan, Maureen. "Stopping Places . . . ," 287–288.

"The Rookers"
Ryan, Maureen. "Stopping Places . . . ," 286–287.

"Shiloh"
Ryan, Maureen. "Stopping Places . . . ," 286.

"Still Life with Watermelon"
Ryan, Maureen. "Stopping Places . . . ," 288.

RICHARD MATHESON

"Trespass" [originally titled "Mother by Protest"]
Nicholls, Peter. "Richard Matheson," in Bleiler, Everett F., Ed. *Science Fiction Writers . . .* , 429.

SHAILESH MATIYANI

"Married Women"
Pande, Trilochan. "Folk Elements in the Modern Hindi Short Story," *Folklore* (Calcutta), 231 (1979), 147–148.

MTUTUZELI MATSHOBA

"A Pilgrimage to the Isle of Makana"
Barnett, Ursula A. *A Vision of Order* . . . , 212–214.

JAMES MATTHEWS

"The Park"
Barnett, Ursula A. *A Vision of Order* . . . , 192.

W. SOMERSET MAUGHAM

"The Facts of Life"
Shaw, Valerie. *The Short Story* . . . , 83–84.

"Rain"
Davies, Horton. *Catching* . . . , 122–123.

MARIE K. MAULE

"A Week with a New Woman"
Harmon, Sandra D. "The Club Woman as New Woman: Late Nineteenth-
Century Androgynous Images," *Turn-of-the-Century Women*, 1, ii (1984), 27–
28.

GUY DE MAUPASSANT

"Le Baptême"
Swanepoel, Jaco. "*Die doop*: Guy de Maupassant," *Klasgids*, 17, ii (1982), 68–70.

"Boule de Suif"
Kishtainy, Khalid. *The Prostitute* . . . , 85–86.

"Epiphany"
Miller, James E., and Bernice Slote. *Instructor's Manual* . . . , 2nd ed., 8–9.

"The Horla"
Döning, Ulrich. "Die Bedeutung des Wahrnehmung in Maupassants phantas-
tique Erzählung 'Le Horla,'" *Zeitschrift für französische Sprache und Literatur*,
94 (1984), 49–65.

"Madame Tellier's House"
Kishtainy, Khalid. *The Prostitute* . . . , 62.

"Miss Harriet"
Sheidley, William E., and Ann Charters. *Instructor's Manual* . . . , 29–30.

"The Necklace"
Prince, Gerald. "Nom et destin dans 'La Parure,'" *French R,* 56 (1982), 267–271.
Scott, Virgil, and David Madden. *Instructor's Manual . . .* , 4th ed., 55–57; Madden, David. *Instructor's Manual . . .* , 5th ed., 13–15; Madden, David, and Virgil Scott. *Instructor's Manual . . .* , 6th ed., 67–70.
Sirlin, Rhoda, and David H. Richter. *Instructor's Manual . . .* , 113–115.

"The Olive Orchard"
Shaw, Valerie. *The Short Story . . .* , 62.

"A Piece of String"
Sheidley, William E., and Ann Charters. *Instructor's Manual . . .* , 27–28.

"A Trick"
Brooks, Peter. *Reading for the Plot . . .* , 217–218.

"Yvette"
Kishtainy, Khalid. *The Prostitute . . .* , 35.

FRANÇOIS MAURIAC

"Insomnia"
Canerot, Marie-Françoise. "La Nouvelle, lieu du meilleur théâtre mauriacen," *Licorne,* 7 (1983), 53–66.

KARL MAY

"Abdahn Effendi"
Sudhoff, Dieter. "Karl Mays 'Abdahn Effendi': Eine Werkanalyse," *Jahrbuch der Karl-May-Gesellschaft,* [n.v.] (1983), 197–244.

"Schamah"
Sudhoff, Dieter. "Karl Mays 'Schamah': Eine Werkanalyse," *Jahrbuch der Karl-May-Gesellschaft,* [n.v.] (1984), 175–230.

CHRISTOPHER MECKEL

"Drusch, the Happy Magician"
Rockwood, Heidi M. "Writing as a Magician's Game: The Strange Early World of Christopher Meckel," *Stud Twentieth-Century Lit,* 8 (1984), 198–204.

"A Man Came to Me"
Rockwood, Heidi M. "Writing . . . ," 198–204.

"Mr. Ucht"
Rockwood, Heidi M. "Writing . . . ," 198–204.

"The Shadow"
Rockwood, Heidi M. "Writing . . . ," 198–204.

AHARON MEGGED

"The Name"
Ramras-Rauch, Gila. "Cultural Naturalism in Israeli Literature," in Lewald,
    H. Ernest, Ed. *The Cry of Home . . .* , 340.

HERMAN MELVILLE

"The Apple-Tree Table"
Karcher, Carolyn L. "Philanthropy and the Occult in the Fiction of Hawthorne,
    Brownson, and Melville," in Kerr, Howard, John W. Crowley, and
    Charles L. Crow, Eds. *The Haunted Dusk . . .* , 77–79.
Senn, Werner. "Reading Melville's Mazes: An Aspect of the Short Stories," *Engl
    Stud*, 65, i (1984), 31.

"Bartleby the Scrivener"
*Abcarian, Richard, and Marvin Klotz. *Instructor's Manual . . .* , 3rd ed., 13–14.
Adams, Timothy D. "Architectural Imagery in Melville's Short Fiction," *Am
    Transcendental Q*, 44 (1979), 267–269.
Barbour, John D. *Tragedy as a Critique . . .* , 71–72.
Bergman, David, Joseph de Roche, and Daniel M. Epstein. *Instructor's Man-
    ual . . .* , 48–49.
Conkling, Chris. "Misery of Christian Joy: Conscience and Freedom in 'Bar-
    tleby the Scrivener,'" *Lit & Belief*, 1 (1981), 79–89.
Cornwell, Ethel F. "Bartleby the Absurd," *Int'l Fiction R*, 9, ii (1982), 93–99.
Craver, Donald H., and Patricia R. Plante. "Bartleby or, The Ambiguities," *Stud
    Short Fiction*, 20 (1983), 132–136.
Hoag, Gerald. "The Last Paragraph of 'Bartleby,'" in Johnson, Mary L., and
    Seraphia D. Leyda, Eds. *Reconciliations . . .* , 153–160.
Lewicki, Zbigniew. *The Bang . . .* ," 77–80.
McWilliams, John P. *Hawthorne, Melville . . .* , 179–181.
Meyer, William E. "'Bartleby': An American Story," *Ball State Univ Forum*, 24,
    iii (1983), 75–87.
Miller, James E., and Bernice Slote. *Instructor's Manual . . .* , 2nd ed., 7–8.
Rowe, John C. *Through the Custom-House . . .* , 118–124.
Schechter, Harold. "Bartleby the Chronometer," *Stud Short Fiction*, 19 (1982),
    359–366.
Schehr, Lawrence R. "Dead Letters: Theories of Writing in 'Bartleby the Scriv-
    ener,'" *Enclitic*, 7, i (1983), 96–103.
Thomas, Brook. "The Legal Fictions of Herman Melville and Lemuel Shaw,"
    Critical Inquiry, 11, i (1984), 34–39.
Wilson, James C. "The Significance of Petra in 'Bartleby,'" *Melville Soc Extracts*,
    57 (February, 1984), 10–12.

"Benito Cereno"
Adams, Timothy D. "Architectural Imagery . . . ," 273–274.
Baines, Barbara J. "Ritualized Cannibalism in 'Benito Cereno': Melville's 'Black
    Letter' Texts," *ESQ: J Am Renaissance*, 30, iii (1984), 163–169.

Barbour, John D. *Tragedy as a Critique . . .* , 70–71.
Emery, Allan M. "'Benito Cereno' and Manifest Destiny," *Nineteenth-Century Fiction*, 39 (1984), 48–68.
Herzog, Kristin. *Women, Ethnics, and Exotics . . .* , 94–97.
Hilfer, Anthony C. "The Philosophy of Clothes in Melville's 'Benito Cereno,'" *Philol Q*, 61 (1982), 220–225.
Horsley-Meacham, Gloria. "The Monastic Slaver: Images and Meaning in 'Benito Cereno,'" *New England Q*, 56 (1984), 261–266.
Kavanagh, James H. "'That Hive of Subtlety': 'Benito Cereno' as Critique of Ideology," *Bucknell R*, 29 (1984), 127–157.
McWilliams, John P. *Hawthorne, Melville . . .* , 181–183.
Senn, Werner. "Reading Melville's Mazes . . . ," 32–33.
Sirlin, Rhoda, and David H. Richter. *Instructor's Manual . . .* , 115–119.
Thomas, Brook. "The Legal Fictions . . . ," 26–34.
Wasserstrom, William. "Melville the Mannerist: Form in the Short Fiction," in Lee, A. Robert, Ed. *Herman Melville . . .* , 144–147.
Wright, Elizabeth. "The New Psychoanalysis and Literary Criticism: A Reading of Hawthorne and Melville," *Poetics Today*, 3 (1982), 96–104.

"Billy Budd"
Babin, James L. "Melville's 'Billy Budd,'" *Explicator*, 42, ii (1984), 14.
Barbour, John D. *Tragedy as a Critique . . .* , 75–92.
Beckmann, Peter. "'Billy Budd' und die Grundlagen der Zeichentheorie," *Semiosis*, 27, iii (1982), 21–31.
Coffler, Gail H. "Melville's 'Billy Budd,'" *Explicator*, 40, ii (1982), 2–3.
Cowan, S. A. "The Naming of Captain Vere in Melville's 'Billy Budd,'" *Stud Short Fiction*, 21 (1984), 41–46.
Davis, R. Evan. "An Allegory of America in Melville's 'Billy Budd,'" *J Narrative Technique*, 14 (1984), 172–181.
Durer, Christopher S. "Captain Vere and Upper-Class Mores in 'Billy Budd,'" *Stud Short Fiction*, 19 (1982), 9–18.
Evans, Lloyd. "'Too Good to Be True': Subverting Christian Hope in 'Billy Budd,'" *New England Q*, 55 (1982), 323–353.
Franklin, H. Bruce. "From Empire to Empire: 'Billy Budd, Sailor,'" in Lee, A. Robert, Ed. *Herman Melville . . .* , 199–216.
Georgoudaki, Ekaterini. "'Billy Budd, Sailor': An Affirmation of the Transforming and Synthesizing Power of Man's Mytho-Poetic Imagination," *Epistemonike*, 22 (1984), 123–141.
Hurtgen, James. "Melville: *Billy Budd* and the Context of Political Rule," in Barber, Benjamin R., and Michael J. G. McGrath, Eds. *The Artist . . .* , 245–262.
Kelley, Wyn. "Melville's Cain," *Am Lit*, 55 (1983), 35–40.
Lupack, Alan C. "The Merlin Allusion in 'Billy Budd,'" *Stud Short Fiction*, 19 (1982), 277–278.
Stafford, William T. *Books Speaking . . .* , 105–114.
Thomas, Brook. "'Billy Budd' and the Judgment of Silence," *Bucknell R*, 27 (1982), 51–78.
———. "The Legal Fictions . . . ," 39–50.
Wasserstrom, William. "Melville the Mannerist . . . ," 151–156.
Weisberg, Richard. "How Judges Speak: Some Lessons on Adjudication in 'Billy Budd, Sailor' with an Application to Justice Rehnquist," *NYU Law R*, 57 (1982), 1–69; rpt., with changes, in his *The Failure . . .* , 133–176.
Westbrook, Perry D. *Free Will . . .* , 38–40.

"Cock-A-Doodle-Doo!"
Emery, Allan M. "The Cocks in Melville's 'Cock-A-Doodle-Doo!'" *ESQ: J Am Renaissance,* 28 (1982), 89–111.

"The Encantadas"
Adams, Timothy D. "Architectural Imagery . . . ," 269–270.
Schricke, Gilbert. "Melville: 'The Encantadas' or the Deceitfulness of Appearance," *Les Cahiers de la Nouvelle,* 2 (1984), 147–154.
Senn, Werner. "Reading Melville's Mazes . . . ," 31–32, 34–35.

"I and My Chimney"
Emery, Allan M. "The Political Significance of Melville's Chimney," *New England Q,* 55 (1982), 201–228.
Senn, Werner. "Reading Melville's Mazes . . . ," 30–31.

"The Paradise of Bachelors and the Tartarus of Maids"
Herzog, Kristin. *Women, Ethnics, and Exotics . . . ,* 97–100.
Senn, Werner. "Reading Melville's Mazes . . . ," 29–30, 33.

"The Two Temples"
McWilliams, John P. *Hawthorne, Melville . . . ,* 177–178.

ALVARO MENÉNDEZ LEAL [same as ALVARO MENÉN DESLEAL]

"A Rope of Nylon and Gold"
McMurray, George R. "The Spanish American Short Story from Borges to the Present," in Peden, Margaret S., Ed. *The Latin American Short Story . . . ,* 125.

PROSPER MÉRIMÉE

"The Etruscan Vase"
Doran, Eva M. C. "Stratégies de discours et de silence dans 'Le Vase étrusque,'" *Mod Lang Stud,* 14, i (1984), 56–64.

JUDITH MERRIL

"Daughters of Earth"
King, Betty. *Women of the Future . . . ,* 91–93.
Morgan, Chris. "Judith Merril," in Bleiler, Everett F., Ed. *Science Fiction Writers . . . ,* 435.

"Peeping Tom"
Morgan, Chris. "Judith Merril," 435.

"Stormy Weather"
King, Betty. *Women of the Future . . . ,* 93–95.

"That Only a Mother"
King, Betty. *Women of the Future* ... , 68–69.
Law, Richard. "Science Fiction Women: Victims, Rebels, Heroes," in Hassler,
    Donald M., Ed. *Patterns* ... , 12.
Morgan, Chris. "Judith Merril," 434.

JAMES MERRILL

"Driver"
Labrie, Ross. *James Merrill*, 26–27.

"Peru: The Landscape Game"
Labrie, Ross. *James Merrill*, 27–29.

ABRAHAM MERRITT

"The Conquest of the Moon Pool"
Bleiler, Everett F. "A. Merritt," in Bleiler, Everett F., Ed. *Science Fiction Writ-
    ers* ... , 67.

"The Moon People"
Bleiler, Everett F. "A. Merritt," 67.

"The People of the Pit"
Bleiler, Everett F. "A. Merritt," 67.

"Three Lines of Old French"
Bleiler, Everett F. "A. Merritt," 67–68.

"Through the Dragon Glass"
Bleiler, Everett F. "A. Merritt," 66.

"The Woman of the Wood"
Bleiler, Everett F. "A. Merritt," 68.

JOHN METCALF

"Beryl"
Lecker, Robert. *On the Line* ... , 68–71.

"Early Morning Rabbits"
Lecker, Robert. *On the Line* ... , 62–64.

"Gentle As Flowers Make the Stones"
Lecker, Robert. *On the Line* ... , 77–80.

"The Girl in Gingham"
Lecker, Robert. *On the Line* ... , 74–77.

"Keys and Watercress"
Lecker, Robert. *On the Line* . . . , 66–68.

"The Lady Who Sold Furniture"
Lecker, Robert. *On the Line* . . . , 71–74.

"Private Parts"
Lecker, Robert. *On the Line* . . . , 88–96.

"The Teeth of My Father"
Lecker, Robert. *On the Line* . . . , 87–88.

"The Tide Line"
Lecker, Robert. *On the Line* . . . , 64–66.

"The Years in Exile"
Lecker, Robert. *On the Line* . . . , 80–86.

ELIZA METEYARD

"Lucy Dean, the Noble Needlewoman"
Mitchell, Sally. *The Fallen Angel* . . . , 29–30.

LEONARD MICHAELS

"City Boy"
Robinson, James C. "1968—1980: Experiment and Tradition," in Weaver, Gordon, Ed. *The American Short Story, 1945–1980,* 95–96.

O. E. MIDDLETON

"The Crows"
Jones, Lawrence. "Out from Under My Uncle's Hat: Gaskell, Middleton, and the Sargeson Tradition," in Hankin, Cherry, Ed. . . . *New Zealand Short Story,* 103.

"The Loners"
Jones, Lawrence. "Out from Under . . . ," 104–105.

"A Married Man"
Jones, Lawrence. "Out from Under . . . ," 100.

"A Means of Soaring"
Jones, Lawrence. "Out from Under . . . ," 106–107.

"The Will to Win"
Jones, Lawrence. "Out from Under . . . ," 106.

JOSÉ RODRIGUES MIGUÉIS

"The Accident"
Kerr, John A. "José Rodrigues Miguéis: Artist with a Commitment to Society,"
Lang Q, 21, i–ii (1982), 39–41.

"Beleza Orgulhosa"
Kerr, John A. "City Life: Two Miguéisian Views," *Lang Q,* 20, iii–iv (1982), 34–
36.

"Perdão, Frau Schwartz!"
Kerr, John A. "City Life . . . ," 36–38.

MIKHAIL MIKHAĬLOVICH ROSHCHIN

"Reminiscence"
Pankin, Boris. "The Past That Is Always with Us," *Soviet Stud Lit,* 18, i (1982),
31–38.

PIERRE MILLE

"The Hare"
Ridley, Hugh. *Images of Imperialism,* 88–89.

"Ramary and Kétaka"
Ridley, Hugh. *Images of Imperialism,* 82–83.

"The Victory"
Ridley, Hugh. *Images of Imperialism,* 117–119.

WALTER M. MILLER

"Anybody Else Like Me"
Ower, John B. "Walter M. Miller," in Bleiler, Everett F., Ed. *Science Fiction Writers . . . ,* 442.

"Big Joe and the Nth Generation"
Ower, John B. "Walter M. Miller," 445.

"Blood Bank"
Ower, John B. "Walter M. Miller," 442.

"Conditionally Human"
Ower, John B. "Walter M. Miller," 443.

"Crucifixus Etiam"
Ower, John B. "Walter M. Miller," 444–445.

"The Darfsteller"
Ower, John B. "Walter M. Miller," 444.

"Dark Benediction"
Ower, John B. "Walter M. Miller," 443–444.

"Dumb Waiter"
Ower, John B. "Walter M. Miller," 444.

MISHIMA YUKIO

"The Boy Who Wrote Poetry"
Keene, Donald. *Dawn to the West* . . . , 1170–1172.

"The Cigarette"
Keene, Donald. *Dawn to the West* . . . , 1176–1177.

"Patriotism"
*Abcarian, Richard, and Marvin Klotz. *Instructor's Manual* . . . , 2nd ed., 16–17; 3rd ed., 14–15.
Sirlin, Rhoda, and David H. Richter. *Instructor's Manual* . . . , 120–122.

WILLIAM ("BLOKE") MODISANE

"The Situation"
Barnett, Ursula A. *A Vision of Order* . . . , 185.

JOHN MONTAGUE

"A Ball of Fire"
Kersnowski, Frank. *John Montague*, 35–36.

"A Change of Management"
Kersnowski, Frank. *John Montague*, 32–33.

"The Cry"
Kersnowski, Frank. *John Montague*, 30–31.

"Death of a Chieftain"
Kersnowski, Frank. *John Montague*, 34–35.

"The New Enamel Bucket"
Kersnowski, Frank. *John Montague*, 32.

"An Occasion of Sin"
Kersnowski, Frank. *John Montague*, 33–34.

"The Oklahoma Kid"
Kersnowski, Frank. *John Montague*, 31.

"The Road Ahead"
Kersnowski, Frank. *John Montague*, 31–32.

"That Dark Accomplice"
Kersnowski, Frank. *John Montague*, 30.

AUGUSTO MONTERROSO

"Mr. Taylor"
McMurray, George R. "The Spanish American Short Story from Borges to the Present," in Peden, Margaret S., Ed. *The Latin American Short Story . . .* , 114–115.

BRIAN MOORE

"Catholics"
McSweeney, Kerry. *Four Contemporary Novelists . . .* , 71–73.

"Uncle T"
Stuart, Malcolm. "Moore Exiles: Joycean Counterparts in Brian Moore's 'Uncle T,'" *Recherches Anglaises et Américaines*, 16 (1983), 131–142.

C[ATHERINE] L. MOORE

"Black God's Kiss"
De Camp, L. Sprague. *Literary Swordsmen . . .* , 272–273.
King, Betty. *Women of the Future . . .* , 49–50.
Mathews, Patricia. "C. L. Moore's Classic Science Fiction," in Staicar, Tom, Ed. *The Feminine Eye . . . ,*" 18–19.

"Black God's Shadow"
Mathews, Patricia. ". . . Classic Science Fiction," 19.

"Greater Than Gods"
Franklin, H. Bruce. "America as Science Fiction: 1939," in Slusser, George E., Eric S. Rabkin, and Robert Scholes, Eds. *Coordinates . . .* , 112–113.

"Judgment Night"
King, Betty. *Women of the Future . . .* , 69–70.

"No Woman Born"
Mathews, Patricia. ". . . Classic Science Fiction," 16–17.

"Shambleau"
Shroyer, Frederick. "C. L. Moore," in Bleiler, Everett F., Ed. *Science Fiction Writers . . .* , 163–164.

GEORGE MOORE

"Almsgiving"
Welch, Robert. *The Way Back . . .* , 53–54.

"The Clerk's Quest"
Carens, James F. "In Quest of a New Impulse: George Moore's *The Untilled Fields* and James Joyce's *Dubliners,*" in Kilroy, James F., Ed. *The Irish Short Story . . .* , 68–69.

"The Exile"
Carens, James F. "In Quest . . . ," 52–53.
Welch, Robert. *The Way Back . . .* , 48–51.

"Home Sickness"
Carens, James F. "In Quest . . . ," 54–55.
Welch, Robert. *The Way Back . . .* , 60.

"In the Clay"
Carens, James F. "In Quest . . . ," 48–49.
Welch, Robert. *The Way Back . . .* , 35–39.

"Julie Cahill's Curse"
Carens, James F. "In Quest . . . ," 59–60.

"A Letter to Rome"
Carens, James F. "In Quest . . . ," 57–58.

"A Playhouse in the Waste"
Welch, Robert. *The Way Back . . .* , 61–63.

"So On He Fares"
Carens, James F. "In Quest . . . ," 63.

"Some Parishioners"
Carens, James F. "In Quest . . . ," 55–57.

"The Way Back"
Carens, James F. "In Quest . . . ," 49–50.

"The Wedding Gown"
Carens, James F. "In Quest . . . ," 60–62.

"The Window"
Welch, Robert. *The Way Back . . .* , 57–59.

ALBERTO MORAVIA

"The Chase"
Abcarian, Richard, and Marvin Klotz. *Instructor's Manual . . .* , 3rd ed., 15–16.

CARLOS MARTÍNEZ MORENO

"Biography"
McMurray, George R. "The Spanish American Short Story from Borges to the
Present," in Peden, Margaret S., Ed. *The Latin American Short Story* . . . ,
127.

MORI ŌGAI

"The Abe Clan"
Keene, Donald. *Dawn to the West* . . . , 372–374.

"The Dancing Girl"
Keene, Donald. *Dawn to the West* . . . , 189–190.

"Delusions"
Keene, Donald. *Dawn to the West* . . . , 361–363.

"Half a Day"
Keene, Donald. *Dawn to the West* . . . , 358–359.

"Hanako"
Keene, Donald. *Dawn to the West* . . . , 360.

"The Last Testament of Okitsu Yagoemon"
Keene, Donald. *Dawn to the West* . . . , 370–372.

"Tower of Silence"
Rubin, Jay. *Injurious to Public Morals* . . . , 153–154.

"Under Reconstruction"
Keene, Donald. *Dawn to the West* . . . , 360.

WILLIAM MORRIS

"Gertha's Lovers"
Silver, Carole. *The Romance* . . . , 93–94.

"The Hollow Land"
Manlove, C. N. *The Impulse* . . . , 129–130.
Silver, Carole. *The Romance* . . . , 6–7, 11–12.

"Lindenborg Pool"
Silver, Carole. *The Romance* . . . , 4–5.

WRIGHT MORRIS

"The Ram in the Thicket"
Scott, Virgil, and David Madden. *Instructor's Manual* . . . , 4th ed., 24–27; Madden, David. *Instructor's Manual* . . . , 5th ed., 28–31; Madden, David, and Virgil Scott. *Instructor's Manual* . . . , 6th ed., 100–104.

"Real Losses, Imaginary Gains"
Miller, James E., and Bernice Slote. *Instructor's Manual* . . . , 2nd ed., 19.

TONI MORRISON

"1919"
Madden, David, and Virgil Scott. *Instructor's Manual* . . . , 6th ed., 127–129.

"Sula"
Beaty, Jerome. *The Norton Introduction* . . . , 661–666.

MARY T. MOTT

"Poor Ah Toy"
Wu, William F. *The Yellow Peril* . . . , 61–63.

FRIEDRICH HEINRICH KARL DE LA MOTTE FOUQUÉ

"Undine"
Menhennet, Alan. *The Romantic Movement*, 191–92.

EZEKIEL MPHAHLELE

"The Master of Doornvlei"
Barnett, Ursula A. *A Vision of Order* . . . , 174–175.

"Mrs. Plum"
Barnett, Ursula A. *A Vision of Order* . . . , 176–177.

"We'll Have Dinner at Eight"
Barnett, Ursula A. *A Vision of Order* . . . , 174.

MANUEL MÚJICA LÁINEZ

"El ilustre amor"
Puente Guerra, Angel. "Manuel Mújica Láinez, o el lector cómplice," *Cuadernos Hispanoamericanos*, 409 (July, 1984), 106–111.

ROSA MULHOLLAND

"The Hungry Death"
Welch, Robert. *The Way Back* ... , 51–52.

CHARLES MUNGOSHI

"The Coming of the Dry Season"
Grandsaigne, Jean de, and Gary Spackey. "The African Short Story Written in English: A Survey," *Ariel*, 15, ii (1984), 75–76.

ALICE MUNRO

"At the Other Place"
Thacker, Robert. "'Clear Jelly': Alice Munro's Narrative Dialects," in MacKendrick, Louis K., Ed. *Probable Fictions* ... , 39–41.

"The Beggar Maid"
McMullen, Lorrain. "'Shameless, Marvellous, Shattering Absurdity': The Humour of Paradox in Alice Munro," in MacKendrick, Louis K., Ed. *Probable Fictions* ... , 150.

"Dance of the Happy Shades"
Osachoff, Margaret G. "'Treacheries of the Heart': Memoir, Confession, and Meditation in the Stories of Alice Munro," in MacKendrick, Louis K., Ed. *Probable Fictions* ... , 65–66.

"Day of the Butterfly"
Osachoff, Margaret G. "'Treacheries ... ,'" 64–65.

"The Edge of Town"
Thacker, Robert. "'Clear Jelly' ... ," 41–42.

"Forgiveness in Families"
Osachoff, Margaret G. "'Treacheries ... ,'" 71–73.

"Goodby, Myra"
Thacker, Robert. "'Clear Jelly' ... ," 43–48.

"Home"
Osachoff, Margaret G. "'Treacheries ... ,'" 79–81.

"How I Met My Husband"
Osachoff, Margaret G. "'Treacheries ... ,'" 67–68.
Sirlin, Rhoda, and David H. Richter. *Instructor's Manual* ... , 122–124.

"Images"
Osachoff, Margaret G. "'Treacheries ... ,'" 66–67.

"Marrakesh"
Orange, John. "Alice Munro and a Maze of Time," in MacKendrick, Louis K., Ed. *Probable Fictions* ... , 91–92.

"Who Do You Think You Are?"
Mathews, Lawrence. *"Who Do You Think You Are?:* Alice Munro's Art of Disarrangement," in MacKendrick, Louis K., Ed. *Probable Fictions . . .* , 190–192.

IRIS MURDOCH

"Venus, Cupid, Folly, and Time"
Ashworth, Ann M. "'Venus, Cupid, Folly, and Time': Bronzino's Allegory and Murdoch's Fiction," *Critique,* 23, i (1981), 18–24.

MARY NOAILLES MURFREE [pseudonym:
CHARLES EGBERT CRADDOCK]

"The Visitants from Yesterday"
Fisher, Benjamin F. "'The Visitants from Yesterday': An Atypical Previously Unpublished Story from the Pen of 'Charles Egbert Craddock,'" *Tennessee Stud Lit,* 26 (1981), 90–92.

ROBERT MUSIL

"Grigia"
Jennings, Michael W. "Mystical Selfhood, Self-Delusion, Self-Dissolution: Ethical and Narrative Experimentalism in Robert Musil's 'Grigia,'" *Mod Austrian Lit,* 17, i (1984), 59–77.
Paulson, Ronald M. "Myth and Fairy Tale in Robert Musil's 'Grigia,'" in Chapple, Gerald, and Hans H. Schulte, Eds. *The Turn of the Century . . .* , 135–148.

"The Perfection of Love"
Goltschnigg, Dietmar. "Die Rolle des geisteskranken Verbrechers in Robert Musils Erzählung 'Die Vollendung der Liebe' und im *Mann ohne Eigenschaften,*" in Brokoph-Mauch, Gudrun, Ed. *Beiträge zur Musil-Kritik,* 149–160.
Strelka, Joseph P. "Claudine und Veronika: Zur weiblichen Doppelfigur von Robert Musils *Vereingungen,*" in Bennett, Benjamin, Anton Kaes, and William J. Lillymann, Eds. *Probleme der Moderne . . .* , 133–142.
Willemsen, Robert. "Claudine und Gillis: Die Latenz des Verbrechens in Robert Musils Novelle 'Die Vollendung der Liebe,'" in Strutz, Josef, Ed. *Robert Musil . . .* , 29–58.

"The Portuguese Lady"
Heit, Siegfried E. "Supernatural Elements in Musil's 'The Portuguese Lady,'" *Christianity & Lit,* 31, iv (1982), 33–43.

MBULELO VIZIKHUNGO MZAMANE

"The Soweto Bride"
Barnett, Ursula A. *A Vision of Order . . .* , 208–209.

VLADIMIR NABOKOV

"An Affair of Honor" [originally titled "The Scoundrel"]
Apter, T. E. *Fantasy Literature* . . . , 94–98.

"Christmas"
Rowe, William W. *Nabokov's Spectral Dimension*, 126–127.

"First Love"
Sheidley, William E., and Ann Charters. *Instructor's Manual* . . . , 112–113.

"Krug"
Karlinsky, Simon. "Theme and Structure in Vladimir's 'Krug,'" in Brostrom, Kenneth N., Ed. *Russian Literature* . . . , 243–247.

"Lik"
Apter, T. E. *Fantasy Literature* . . . , 106–110.

"Mademoiselle O"
Rennert, Hal H. "Literary Revenge: Nabokov's 'Mademoiselle O' and Kleist's 'Die Marquise von O——,'" *Germano-Slavica*, 4 (1984), 331–337.

"The Potato Elf"
Evans, Walter. "The Conjuror in 'The Potato Elf,'" in Rivers, J. E., and Charles Nicol, Eds. *Nabokov's Fifth Arc* . . . , 75–81.

"Signs and Symbols"
Andrews, Larry R. "Deciphering 'Signs and Symbols,'" in Rivers, J. E., and Charles Nicol, Eds. *Nabokov's Fifth Arc* . . . , 139–152.
Tammi, Pekka. "Nabokov's Symbolic Cards and Pushkin's 'The Queen of Spades,'" *Nabokovian*, 13 (Fall, 1984), 31–32.

"Spring in Fialta"
Sirlin, Rhoda, and David H. Richter. *Instructor's Manual* . . . , 124–126.

"Terra Incognita"
Conolly, Julian W. "Nabokov's 'Terra Incognita' and *Invitation to a Beheading*: The Struggle for Imaginative Freedom," *Wiener Slawistischer Almanach*, 12 (1983), 55–65.

"Terror"
Bodenstein, Jürgen. *"The Excitement of Verbal Adventure"* . . . , I, 403–404.
Boyd, Michael. *The Reflexive Novel* . . . , 163–166.

"That in Aleppo Once . . ."
Maddox, Lucy. *Nabokov's Novels in English*, 7–9.

"Torpid Smoke"
Rowe, William W. *Nabokov's Spectral Dimension*, 127–129.

"Tyrants Destroyed"
Rampton, David. *Vladimir Nabokov* . . . , 48–49.

"Ultima Thule"
Rowe, William W. *Nabokov's Spectral Dimension,* 46–49.

"The Vane Sisters"
Miller, James E., and Bernice Slote. *Instructor's Manual . . .* , 2nd ed., 20.
Rowe, William W. *Nabokov's Spectral Dimension,* 17–29.
Walkiewicz, E. P. "1957–1968: Toward Diversity of Form," in Weaver, Gordon,
    Ed. *The American Short Story, 1945–1980,* 71–72.

"A Visit to the Museum"
Apter, T. E. *Fantasy Literature . . .* , 98–99.
Penner, Dick, Ed. *Fiction of the Absurd . . .* , 113–115.

"The Windows of the Mint"
McConkey, James. "Nabokov and 'The Windows of the Mint,'" in Gibian,
    George, and Stephen J. Parker, Eds. *The Adventures . . .* , 29–43.

NAGAI KAFŪ

"Behind the Prison"
Rubin, Jay. *Injurious to Public Morals . . .* , 123–124.

"The Bill Collector"
Seidensticker, Edward. *Kafū the Scribbler . . .* , 51.

"Clouds" [originally titled "Dissipation"]
Keene, Donald. *Dawn to the West . . .* , 408–409.
Seidensticker, Edward. *Kafū the Scribbler . . .* , 26.

"The Decoration"
Seidensticker, Edward. *Kafū the Scribbler . . .* , 160.

"Diary of One Who Returned to Japan"
Keene, Donald. *Dawn to the West . . .* , 404.

"Flower Basket"
Seidensticker, Edward. *Kafū the Scribbler . . .* , 10–11.

"Flower Vase"
Seidensticker, Edward. *Kafū the Scribbler . . .* , 82–83.

"Hydrangea"
Seidensticker, Edward. *Kafū the Scribbler . . .* , 125–126.

"Journey Alone"
Seidensticker, Edward. *Kafū the Scribbler . . .* , 28.

"Night Plovers"
Keene, Donald. *Dawn to the West . . .* , 392–393.

"The Peony Garden"
Seidensticker, Edward. *Kafū the Scribbler*. . . , 49–50.

"Pleasure"
Rubin, Jay. *Injurious to Public Morals* . . . , 121–122.

"Summer Dress"
Seidensticker, Edward. *Kafū the Scribbler*. . . , 75–76.

"A Swirl of Pine Needles"
Seidensticker, Edward. *Kafū the Scribbler*. . . , 50.

"A Tale of a Nettle Tree"
Seidensticker, Edward. *Kafū the Scribbler*. . . , 124.

"A Toast"
Rubin, Jay. *Injurious to Public Morals* . . . , 124–125.

AMRIT LAL NAGAR

"Problems of Truthfulness"
Pande, Trilochan. "Folk Elements in the Modern Hindi Short Story," *Folklore*
(Calcutta), 231 (1979), 146.

YURY NAGIBIN

"Echoes"
Brown, Edward J. . . . *Since the Revolution*, 333.

VIDIADHAR SURAJPRASAD NAIPAUL

"A Christmas Story"
Ramraj, Victor. "Sly Compassion: V. S. Naipaul's Ambivalence in 'A Christmas
Story,'" *Commonwealth* [Dijon], 6, i (1983), 61–70.
Sirlin, Rhoda, and David H. Richter. *Instructor's Manual* . . . , 126–129.

"The Night Watchman's Occurrence Book"
Bergman, David, Joseph de Roche, and Daniel M. Epstein. *Instructor's Manual* . . . , 12.

NAKAJIMA ATSUSHI

"The Disciple"
Keene, Donald. *Dawn to the West* . . . , 942–944.

NAKAYAMA GISHŪ

"The Last Days of Tinian"
Keene, Donald. *Dawn to the West* . . . , 952–953.

LILIKA NAKOS

"And the Child Lied"
Tannen, Deborah. *Lilika Nakos*, 29–30.

"The Cat"
Tannen, Deborah. *Lilika Nakos*, 38–39.

"Elenitsa"
Tannen, Deborah. *Lilika Nakos*, 40–41.

"God's Garden"
Tannen, Deborah. *Lilika Nakos*, 43–44.

"The Little Servant"
Tannen, Deborah. *Lilika Nakos*, 27–28.

"Love"
Tannen, Deborah. *Lilika Nakos*, 32–33.

"Maternity"
Tannen, Deborah. *Lilika Nakos*, 26–27.

"The Story of the Virginity of Miss Tade"
Tannen, Deborah. *Lilika Nakos*, 31–32.

R. K. NARAYAN

"Annamalai"
Walsh, William. *R. K. Narayan* . . . , 106–109.

"Another Community"
David, P. C., and S. Z. H. Abidi. "Levels of Irony in the Short Stories of R. K.
    Narayan," *Lit Endeavor*, 3, iii–iv (1982), 43–44.

"A Breath of Lucifer"
Walsh, William. *R. K. Narayan* . . . , 110–112.

"Gateman's Gift"
Sah, Prajapati P. "R. K. Narayan's 'Gateman's Gift': The Central Theme," *Lit
    Criterion*, 15, i (1980), 37–46.

"Half-a-Rupee Worth"
David, P. C., and S. Z. H. Abidi. "Levels of Irony . . . ," 41.

"A Horse and Two Goats"
Walsh, William. *R. K. Narayan* . . . , 100–103.

"The Martyr's Corner"
David, P. C., and S. Z. H. Abidi. "Levels of Irony . . . ," 39–41.

"The Seventh House"
Walsh, William. *R. K. Narayan* . . . , 99–100.

"Trail of the Green Blazer"
David, P. C., and S. Z. H. Abidi. "Levels of Irony . . . ," 43–44.

"Uncle"
Walsh, William. *R. K. Narayan* . . . , 103–106.

"Wife's Holiday"
David, P. C., and S. Z. H. Abidi. "Levels of Irony . . . ," 42.

NJABULO NDEBELE

"The Music of the Violin"
Barnett, Ursula A. *A Vision of Order* . . . , 190.

JOHN G. NEIHARDT

"The Alien"
Deloria, Vine. *A Sender of Words* . . . , 82–83.
Whitney, Blair. *John G. Neihardt,* 61.

"Beyond the Spectrum"
Whitney, Blair. *John G. Neihardt,* 65–66.

"The End of a Dream"
Deloria, Vine. *A Sender of Words* . . . , 75–76.

"The Fading of a Shadow Flower"
Deloria, Vine. *A Sender of Words* . . . , 78.

"The Heart of a Woman"
Deloria, Vine. *A Sender of Words* . . . , 81.

"The Look in the Face"
Whitney, Blair. *John G. Neihardt,* 62–63.

"Mignon"
Whitney, Blair. *John G. Neihardt,* 64.

"A Prairie Borgia"
Deloria, Vine. *A Sender of Words* . . . , 76–77.

"The Red Roan Mare"
Deloria, Vine. *A Sender of Words* . . . , 80–81.

"The Scars"
Whitney, Blair. *John G. Neihardt*, 63.

"The Singer of the Ache"
Deloria, Vine. *A Sender of Words* . . . , 76.
Whitney, Blair. *John G. Neihardt*, 76.

"Vylin"
Whitney, Blair. *John G. Neihardt*, 64.

"The White Wakunda"
Deloria, Vine. *A Sender of Words* . . . , 82.

GÉRARD DE NERVAL [GÉRARD LABRUNIE]

"Sylvie"
Gordon, Rae B. "Dentelle: Metaphore du texte dans 'Sylvie,'" *Romanic R*, 73
(1982), 45–66.
———. "Eros et Thanatos dans 'Sylvie,'" *Nineteenth-Century French Stud*, 10, iii–
iv (1982), 278–290.

EDITH NESBIT

"The Cockatoucan"
Manlove, C. N. *The Impulse* . . . , 67–68.

"Melisande"
Manlove, C. N. *The Impulse* . . . , 65–66.

"Whereyouwantogoto"
Manlove, C. N. *The Impulse* . . . , 55–56.

JAY NEUGEBOREN

"Something Is Rotten in the Borough of Brooklyn"
Oriard, Michael. *Dreaming of Heroes* . . . , 201–202.

NI I-TE

"On the Bank of the River"
Doležalová, Anna. "The Short Stories in *Creation Daily*," *Asian & African Stud*,
9 (1973), 56–57.

"A Poor Scholar"
Doležalová, Anna. "The Short Stories . . . ," 58–59.

DJIBRIL TAMSIR NIANE

"Kakandé"
Blair, Dorothy S. *Senegalese Literature* . . . , 129–130.

ANAÏS NIN

"Birth"
Scholar, Nancy. *Anaïs Nin,* 99–101.

"Hejda"
Scholar, Nancy. *Anaïs Nin,* 105–107.

"Houseboat"
Scholar, Nancy. *Anaïs Nin,* 101–103.

"The Labyrinth"
Scholar, Nancy. *Anaïs Nin,* 103–105.

"Lilith"
Schwichtenberg, Cathy. "Erotica: The Semey [sic] Side of Semiotics," *Sub-Stance,*
    32 (1981), 26–38.

"The Maya"
Kamboureli, Smaro. "Discourse and Intercourse, Design and Desire in the
    Erotica of Anaïs Nin," *J Mod Lit,* 11 (1984), 156–157.

"Ragtime"
Madden, David. *Instructor's Manual* . . . , 5th ed., 57–59; Madden, David, and
    Virgil Scott. *Instructor's Manual* . . . , 6th ed., 48–51.

"Stella"
Scholar, Nancy. *Anaïs Nin,* 90–93.

"Under a Glass Bell"
Scholar, Nancy. *Anaïs Nin,* 107.

"The Voice"
Scholar, Nancy. *Anaïs Nin,* 96–97.

"Waste of Timelessness"
Scholar, Nancy. *Anaïs Nin,* 12–13.

"Winter of Artifice"
Scholar, Nancy. *Anaïs Nin,* 93–97.

LARRY NIVEN

"Rammer"
Meyers, Walter E. *Aliens and Linguists* . . . , 113–114.

"Three Vignettes: Grammar Lesson"
Meyers, Walter E. *Aliens and Linguists* . . . , 165–166.

LARRY NIXON

"Inconstant Moon"
Hartwell, David. *Age of Wonders* . . . , 49–50.

LEWIS NKOSI

"The Prisoner"
Barnett, Ursula A. *A Vision of Order* . . . , 182–183.

CHARLES NODIER

"Ines de Las Sierras"
Kelly, Dorothy. "The Ghost of Meaning: Language in the Fantastic," *Sub-Stance*,
    11, ii (1982), 46–55.

FRANK NORRIS

"After Strange Gods"
Wu, William F. *The Yellow Peril* . . . , 57–58.

"'As Long As Ye Both Shall Live'"
Leitz, Robert G., and Joseph R. McElrath. "A New Short Story by Frank
    Norris," *Am Lit Realism,* 17 (1984), 10–11.

"Dying Fires"
Pizer, Donald. *Realism and Naturalism* . . . , 2nd ed., 116–118.

LINO NOVÁS CALVO

"'Allies' and 'Germans'"
Brushwood, John S. "The Spanish American Short Story from Quiroga to
    Borges," in Peden, Margaret S., Ed. *The Latin American Short Story* . . . , 93–
    94.

"I Don't Know What to Say"
Brushwood, John S. ". . . Quiroga to Borges," 93.

PHILLIP FRANCIS NOWLAN

"The Air Lords of Han"
Sampson, Robert. *Yesterday's Faces, II* . . . , 228–229.

JOYCE CAROL OATES

"At the Seminary"
Fowler, Doreen. "Oates's 'At the Seminary,'" *Explicator,* 41, i (1982), 62–64.

"How I Contemplated the World from the Detroit House of Correction and Began My Life Over Again"
Madden, David. *Instructor's Manual . . . ,* 5th ed., 54–57; Madden, David, and Virgil Scott. *Instructor's Manual . . . ,* 6th ed., 45–48.

"In the Region of Ice"
Sirlin, Rhoda, and David H. Richter. *Instructor's Manual . . . ,* 129–131.

"The Lady with the Pet Dog"
Sheidley, William E., and Ann Charters. *Instructor's Manual . . . ,* 188–189.

"Pastoral Blood"
Robinson, James C. "1968–1980: Experiment and Tradition," in Weaver, Gordon, Ed. *The American Short Story, 1945–1980,* 86–87.

"Where Are You Going, Where Have You Been?"
Healey, James. "Pop Music and Joyce Carol Oates' 'Where Are You Going, Where Have You Been?'" *Notes Mod Am Lit,* 7, i (1983), Item 5.
Robson, Mark. "Oates's 'Where Are You Going, Where Have You Been?'" *Explicator,* 40, iv (1982), 59–60.
Rubin, Larry. "Oates's 'Where Are You Going, Where Have You Been?'" *Explicator,* 42, iv (1984), 57–60.
Schulz, Gretchen, and R. J. R. Rockwood. "In Fairyland, Without a Map: Connie's Exploration Inward in Joyce Carol Oates's 'Where Are You Going, Where Have You Been?'" *Lit & Psych,* 30 (1980), 155–167.
Sheidley, William E., and Ann Charters. *Instructor's Manual . . . ,* 184–185.

FLANN O'BRIEN

"John Duffy's Brother"
Penner, Dick, Ed. *Fiction of the Absurd . . . ,* 126–128.

SIGBJØRN OBSTFELDER

"Autumn"
Norseng, Mary K. *Sigbjørn Obstfelder,* 101–102.

"Liv"
Norseng, Mary K. *Sigbjørn Obstfelder,* 97–101.

"The Plain"
Norseng, Mary K. *Sigbjørn Obstfelder,* 102–107.

"The Unknown One"
Norseng, Mary K. *Sigbjørn Obstfelder,* 112–113.

FLANNERY O'CONNOR

"The Artificial Nigger"
Allen, William A. "Mr. Head and Hawthorne: Allusion and Conversion in Flannery O'Connor's 'The Artificial Nigger,'" *Stud Short Fiction,* 21 (1984), 17–23.
Asals, Frederick. *Flannery O'Connor...,* 79–92.
Coulthard, A. R. "From Sermon to Parable: Four Conversion Stories from Flannery O'Connor," *Am Lit,* 55 (1983), 58–63.
Hawkins, Peter S. *The Language of Grace...,* 36–39.
Monroe, W. F. "Flannery O'Connor's Sacramental Icon: 'The Artificial Nigger,'" *So Central R,* 1, iv (1984), 64–81.
Okeke-Ezigbo, Emeka. "Three Artificial Blacks: A Reexamination of Flannery O'Connor's 'The Artificial Nigger,'" *Coll Lang Assoc J,* 27 (1984), 371–382.
Rubin, Louis D. *A Gallery...,* 115–134.
Sheidley, William E., and Ann Charters. *Instructor's Manual...,* 161–163.
Walker, Jeffrey. "1945–1956: Post-World War II Manners and Mores," in Weaver, Gordon, Ed. *The American Short Story, 1945–1980,* 21.

"The Comforts of Home"
Asals, Frederick. *Flannery O'Connor...,* 108–115.
Magistrale, Anthony S. "O'Connor's 'The Comforts of Home,'" *Explicator,* 42, iv (1984), 52–54; rpt. *Explicator,* 43, i (1984), 57–59.
*Quinn, Sister M. Bernetta. "Flannery O'Connor, a Realist of Distances," in McClave, Heather, Ed. *Women Writers...,* 139–140.

"The Cross"
Asals, Frederick. *Flannery O'Connor...,* 15–17.

"The Displaced Person"
Hawkins, Peter S. *The Language of Grace...,* 39–40.
Herrscher, Walter. "O'Connor's 'The Displaced Person': The Problem of Doing Good," *Notes Contemp Lit,* 14, i (1984), 5–7.
Karl, Frederick R. *American Fictions...,* 233–234.
Napierkowski, Thomas J. "The Image of Polish Americans in American Literature," *Polish Am Stud,* 40 (1983), 30–42.

"Everything That Rises Must Converge"
Avila, Carmen. "'Everything That Rises Must Converge,'" in Dietrich, R. F., and Roger H. Sundell. *Instructor's Manual...,* 3rd ed., 42–45; 4th ed., 22–25.
Sirlin, Rhoda, and David H. Richter. *Instructor's Manual...,* 135–137.

"The Geranium"
Asals, Frederick. *Flannery O'Connor...,* 11–13.

"Good Country People"
Abcarian, Richard, and Marvin Klotz. *Instructor's Manual . . .* , 2nd ed., 17–18;
    3rd ed., 16.
Asals, Frederick. *Flannery O'Connor . . .* , 102–108.
Halsen, Ruth M. "O'Connor's 'Good Country People,'" *Explicator,* 42, iii (1984),
    59.
Scott, Virgil, and David Madden. *Instructor's Manual . . .* , 4th ed., 29–31; Mad-
    den, David. *Instructor's Manual . . .* , 5th ed., 31–33; Madden, David, and
    Virgil Scott. *Instructor's Manual . . .* , 6th ed., 34–37.

"A Good Man Is Hard to Find"
Asals, Frederick. *Flannery O'Connor . . .* , 142–154.
Bergman, David, Joseph de Roche, and Daniel M. Epstein. *Instructor's Man-
    ual . . .* , 49–50.
Hawkins, Peter S. *The Language of Grace . . .* , 40–50.
Jones, Madison. "A Good Man's Predicament," *Southern R,* 20 (1984), 836–841.
Lasseter, Victor. "The Children's Names in Flannery O'Connor's 'A Good Man
    Is Hard to Find,'" *Notes Mod Am Lit,* 6, i (1982), Item 6.
Renner, Stanley. "Secular Meaning in 'A Good Man Is Hard to Find,'" *Coll Lit,*
    9 (1982), 123–132.
Sheidley, William E., and Ann Charters. *Instructor's Manual . . .* , 158–159.
Sirlin, Rhoda, and David H. Richter. *Instructor's Manual . . .* , 132–134.
Sweet-Hurd, Evelyn. "Finding O'Connor's Good Man," *Notes Contemp Lit,* 14, iii
    (1984), 9–10.

"Greenleaf"
Davies, Horton. "Anagogical Signals in Flannery O'Connor's Fiction," *Thought,*
    55 (1980), 434–435.
———. *Catching . . .* , 143.
McDermott, John V. "Listening and Speaking: Byways to Action—Human and
    Divine—in O'Connor's 'Greenleaf,'" *Notes Mod Am Lit,* 7, i (1983), Item 2.
Marston, Jane. "Epistemology and the Solipsistic Consciousness in Flannery
    O'Connor's 'Greenleaf,'" *Stud Short Fiction,* 21 (1984), 375–382.

"Judgement Day"
Asals, Frederick. *Flannery O'Connor . . .* , 141–142.
Napier, James J. "Flannery O'Connor's Last Three: 'The Sense of an Ending,'"
    Southern Lit J, 14, ii (1982), 22–23.

"The Lame Shall Enter First"
Asals, Frederick. *Flannery O'Connor . . .* , 155–159.
McKeon, Zahava K. *Novels and Arguments . . .* , 192–213.

"Parker's Back"
Asals, Frederick. *Flannery O'Connor . . .* , 126–127.
Bleikasten, André. "Writing on the Flesh: Tattoos and Taboos in 'Parker's
    Back,'" *Southern Lit J,* 14 (Spring, 1982), 8–18.
Coulthard, A. R. "From Sermon to Parable . . .," 67–71.
Jorgenson, Eric. "A Note on the Jonah Motif in 'Parker's Back,'" *Stud Short
    Fiction,* 21 (1984), 400–402.
McKeon, Zahava K. *Novels and Arguments . . .* , 213–225.

*Quinn, Sister M. Bernetta. ". . . Realist of Distances," 142–144.
Werner, Craig H. *Paradoxical Resolutions . . .* , 44–45.

"Revelation"
Coulthard, A. R. "From Sermon to Parable . . . ," 63–67.
Kennedy, X. J. and Dorothy M. *Instructor's Manual . . .* , 3rd ed., 33–35.
McDonald, Russ. "Comedy and Flannery O'Connor," *So Atlantic Q,* 81 (1982),
    194–196.
Napier, James J. "Flannery O'Connor's Last Three . . . ," 24–26.
Phillips, D. Z. "Mystery and Meditation: Reflections on Flannery O'Connor and
    Joan Didion," in Jasper, David, Ed. *Images of Belief . . .* , 36–39.

"The River"
Chapin, John D. "Flannery O'Connor and the Rich Red River of Jesus' Blood,"
    Christianity & Lit, 25, iii (1976), 30–35.
Miller, James E., and Bernice Slote. *Instructor's Manual . . .* , 2nd ed., 21.

"A Temple of the Holy Ghost"
Coulthard, A. R. "From Sermon to Parable . . . ," 56–58.
Kahane, Claire. "The Maternal Legacy: The Grotesque Tradition in Flannery
    O'Connor's Female Gothic," in Fleenor, Julian E., Ed. *The Female Gothic,*
    248–255.

"The Train"
Asals, Frederick. *Flannery O'Connor . . .* , 17–22.

"The Turkey"
Asals, Frederick. *Flannery O'Connor . . .* , 13–15.

"A View of the Woods"
Asals, Frederick. *Flannery O'Connor . . .* , 99–102.
Davies, Horton. *Catching . . .* , 142–143.

FRANK O'CONNOR [MICHAEL O'DONOVAN]

"After Fourteen Years"
Bordewyk, Gordon. "Quest for Meaning: The Stories of Frank O'Connor,"
    Illinois Q, 41, ii (1978), 46.

"The Cheat"
Kilroy, James F. "Setting the Standards: Writers of the 1920s and 1930s," in
    Kilroy, James F., Ed. *The Irish Short Story . . .* , 119–120.
Matthews, James. *Voices . . .* , 362–363.

"The Conversion"
Matthews, James. *Voices . . .* , 261–262.

"The Custom of the Country"
Bordewyk, Gordon. "Quest for Meaning . . . ," 46.
Thompson, Richard. "A Kingdom of Commoners: The Moral Art of Frank
    O'Connor," *Eiré,* 13 (1978), 79–80.

"Don Juan's Temptation"
Kilroy, James F. "Setting the Standards . . . ," 112.

"The Drunkard"
Kilroy, James F. "Setting the Standards . . . ," 114–115.

"The Duke's Children"
Kilroy, James F. "Setting the Standards . . . ," 117.

"Expectation of Life"
Kilroy, James F. "Setting the Standards . . . ," 117–118.
Matthews, James. *Voices . . .* , 306–307.

"First Confession"
Bordewyk, Gordon. "Quest for Meaning . . . ," 43–44.
Kennedy, X. J. *Instructor's Manual . . .* , 3rd ed., 15–16.
Scott, Virgil, and David Madden. *Instructor's Manual . . .* , 4th ed., 36–38; Madden, David. *Instructor's Manual . . .* , 5th ed., 41–42; Madden, David, and Virgil Scott. *Instructor's Manual . . .* , 6th ed., 16–18.

"The Frying Pan"
Kilroy, James F. "Setting the Standards . . . ," 112.

"Guests of the Nation"
Bordewyk, Gordon. "Quest for Meaning . . . ," 38–39.
Kilroy, James F. "Setting the Standards . . . ," 106–107.
Matthews, James H. "Women, War, and Words: Frank O'Connor's First Confession," *Irish Renaissance Annual,* 1 (1980), 73–112.
Sheidley, William E., and Ann Charters. *Instructor's Manual . . .* , 122–123.
Sirlin, Rhoda, and David H. Richter. *Instructor's Manual . . .* , 138–139.
Thompson, Richard. "A Kingdom of Commoners . . . ," 70–72.

"The Holy Door"
Kilroy, James F. "Setting the Standards . . . ," 113–114.

"The Idealist"
Bordewyk, Gordon. "Quest for Meaning . . . ," 44.

"In the Train"
Matthews, James. *Voices . . .* , 112–113.
Thompson, Richard. "A Kingdom of Commoners . . . ," 73–74.

"Jerome"
Bordewyk, Gordon. "Quest for Meaning . . . ," 47.

"Jo"
Bordewyk, Gordon. "Quest for Meaning . . . ," 40.

"Jumbo's Wife"
Kilroy, James F. "Setting the Standards . . . ," 107–108.

"The Luceys"
Thompson, Richard. "A Kingdom of Commoners . . . ," 77.

"Mac's Masterpiece"
Matthews, James. *Voices* . . . , 150–152.

"The Mad Lomasneys"
Kilroy, James F. "Setting the Standards . . . ," 110–111.
Matthews, James. *Voices* . . . , 204–205.

"The Majesty of the Law"
Kilroy, James F. "Setting the Standards . . . ," 108–109.

"The Man of the World"
Bordewyk, Gordon. "Quest for Meaning . . . ," 44.

"The Masculine Principle"
Kilroy, James F. "Setting the Standards . . . ," 115–116.

"Masculine Protest"
Bordewyk, Gordon. "Quest for Meaning . . . ," 45.

"The Mass Island"
Bonaccorso, Richard. "Irish Elegies: Three Tales of Gougane Barra," *Stud Short
     Fiction,* 19 (1982), 166–167.

"A Minority"
Kilroy, James F. "Setting the Standards . . . ," 119.

"My First Protestant"
Bordewyk, Gordon. "Quest for Meaning . . . ," 42–43.

"My Oedipus Complex"
*Abcarian, Richard, and Marvin Klotz. *Instructor's Manual* . . . , 2nd ed., 18–
     19; 3rd ed., 17.
Sheidley, William E., and Ann Charters. *Instructor's Manual* . . . , 124–125.

"News for the Church"
Bordewyk, Gordon. "Quest for Meaning . . . ," 42.
Thompson, Richard. "A Kingdom of Commoners . . . ," 78–79.

"Nightpiece with Figures"
Bordewyk, Gordon. "Quest for Meaning . . . ," 39.

"The Old Faith"
Bordewyk, Gordon. "Quest for Meaning . . . ," 40–41.

"September Dawn"
Bordewyk, Gordon. "Quest for Meaning . . . ," 39–40.

"The Star That Bids the Shepherd Fold"
Bordewyk, Gordon. "Quest for Meaning . . . ," 41–42.

"The Thief"
Bordewyk, Gordon. "Quest for Meaning . . . ," 44–45.

"A Torrent Damned"
Bordewyk, Gordon. "Quest for Meaning . . . ," 46.
Matthews, James. *Voices* . . . , 275–276.

"Uprooted"
Kilroy, James F. "Setting the Standards . . . ," 109–110.

ODA SAKUNOSUKE

"The State of the Times"
Keene, Donald. *Dawn to the West* . . . , 1084–1087.

VLADIMIR ODOEVSKY

"Princess Mimi"
Mersereau, John. *Russian Romantic Fiction*, 229–230.

"Sebastian Bach"
Mersereau, John. *Russian Romantic Fiction*, 177–179.

"The Sylph"
Mersereau, John. *Russian Romantic Fiction*, 179–181.

SEAN O'FAOLAIN

"The Bosom of the Country"
Kilroy, James F. "Setting the Standards: Writers of the 1920s and 1930s," in
    Kilroy, James F., Ed. *The Irish Short Story* . . . , 132–133.

"The Broken World"
Kilroy, James F. "Setting the Standards . . . ," 124–125.

"Fugue"
Kilroy, James F. "Setting the Standards . . . ," 122–123.

"The Heat of the Sun"
Kilroy, James F. "Setting the Standards . . . ," 131–132.

"How to Write a Short Story"
Sheidley, William E., and Ann Charters. *Instructor's Manual* . . . , 118–119.

"I Remember! I Remember!"
Kilroy, James F. "Setting the Standards . . . ," 130.

"An Inside Outside Complex"
Tessiera, Thérèsa, Simone Lavabre, and Maurice Pergnier. "Lecture plurielle
    de la nouvelle 'An Inside Outside Complex' de Sean O'Faolain," *Les Cahiers
    de la Nouvelle,* 1 (1983), 127–138.

"Lady Lucifer"
Kilroy, James F. "Setting the Standards . . . ," 125–126.

"Lovers of the Lake"
Kilroy, James F. "Setting the Standards . . . ," 128–129.

"The Man Who Invented Sin"
Bonaccorso, Richard. "Irish Elegies: Three Tales of Gougane Barra," *Stud Short
    Fiction,* 19 (1982), 164–165.
Kilroy, James F. "Setting the Standards . . . ," 125.

"Midsummer Night Madness"
Kilroy, James F. "Setting the Standards . . . ," 123.

"One Night in Turin"
Kilroy, James F. "Setting the Standards . . . ," 131.

"Our Fearful Innocence"
Kilroy, James F. "Setting the Standards . . . ," 133–134.

"The Patriot"
Kilroy, James F. "Setting the Standards . . . ," 123–124.

"The Silence of the Valley"
Bonaccorso, Richard. "Irish Elegies . . . ," 165–166.
Kilroy, James F. "Setting the Standards . . . ," 126–127.

"The Time of Their Lives"
Kilroy, James F. "Setting the Standards . . . ," 133.

"A Touch of Autumn in the Air"
Kilroy, James F. "Setting the Standards . . . ," 130–131.

LIAM O'FLAHERTY

"Blood Lust"
Kilroy, James F. "Setting the Standards: Writers of the 1920s and 1930s," in
    Kilroy, James F., Ed. *The Irish Short Story . . . ,* 98.

"The Blow"
Thompson, Richard J. "The Sage Who Deep in Central Nature Delves: Liam
    O'Flaherty's Short Stories," *Eiré,* 18, i (1983), 96–97.

"Galway Bay"
Thompson, Richard J. "The Sage . . . ," 96.

"Going into Exile"
Dumbleton, William A. *Ireland* . . . , 108–113.

"The Mountain Tavern"
Kilroy, James F. "Setting the Standards . . . ," 100–101.

"The Outcast"
Kilroy, James F. "Setting the Standards . . . ," 99–100.

"The Tent"
Thompson, Richard J. "The Sage . . . ," 95.

"Two Lovely Beasts"
Kilroy, James F. "Setting the Standards . . . ," 102–103.
Thompson, Richard J. "The Sage . . . ," 95–96.

OGURI FŪYŌ

"Big Sister's Little Sister"
Rubin, Jay. *Injurious to Public Morals* . . . , 126–127.

"Cold and Flaming"
Rubin, Jay. *Injurious to Public Morals* . . . , 74.

"Lazy Woman"
Rubin, Jay. *Injurious to Public Morals* . . . , 74–76.

"Making Up for Bed"
Rubin, Jay. *Injurious to Public Morals* . . . , 42–43.

JOHN O'HARA

"Agatha"
Long, Robert E. *John O'Hara*, 111–112.

"Alone"
Bassett, Charles W. "John O'Hara's 'Alone': Previews of Coming Attractions,"
     John O'Hara J, 5, i–ii (1982–1983), 18–24.

"Appearances"
Molloy, Francis C. "The Suburban Vision in John O'Hara's Short Stories," *Critique*, 25, ii (1984), 109.

"Assistant"
Long, Robert E. *John O'Hara*, 119–120.

"The Bucket of Blood"
Long, Robert E. *John O'Hara*, 107–108.

"The Clear Track"
Molloy, Francis C. "The Suburban Vision . . . ," 105.

"Days"
Long, Robert E. *John O'Hara*, 27–29.

"The Doctor's Son"
Long, Robert E. *John O'Hara*, 16–20.

"Ella and the Chinee"
Long, Robert E. *John O'Hara*, 22–23.

"Family Evening"
Molloy, Francis C. "The Suburban Vision . . . ," 109–110.

"The Father"
Molloy, Francis C. "The Suburban Vision . . . ," 108.

"A Few Trips and Some Poetry"
Long, Robert E. *John O'Hara*, 122–123.

"The General"
Long, Robert E. *John O'Hara*, 120–121.

"The Gunboat and Madge"
Long, Robert E. *John O'Hara*, 121–122.

"How Can I Tell You?"
Molloy, Francis C. "The Suburban Vision . . . ," 110–111.

"James Francis and the Star"
Long, Robert E. *John O'Hara*, 118–119.

"The Lesson"
Molloy, Francis C. "The Suburban Vision . . . ," 108–109.

"The Madeline Wherry Case"
Molloy, Francis C. "The Suburban Vision . . . ," 103.

"Most Gorgeous Thing"
Long, Robert E. *John O'Hara*, 25–26.

"Natica Jackson"
Long, Robert E. *John O'Hara*, 117–118.

"Nothing Missing"
Long, Robert E. *John O'Hara*, 31–32.

"Over the River and Through the Woods"
Long, Robert E. *John O'Hara*, 23–24.
Rohrberger, Mary. "The Question of Regionalism: Limitation and Transcendence," in Stevick, Philip, Ed. *The American Short Story, 1900–1945*, 176–177.

"The Pig"
Molloy, Francis C. "The Suburban Vision . . . ," 111.

"The Pioneer Hep-Cat"
Long, Robert E. *John O'Hara,* 102–103.

"Saturday Lunch"
Molloy, Francis C. "The Suburban Vision . . . ," 104–105.

"The Sharks"
Long, Robert E. *John O'Hara,* 103–104.

"Sterling Silver"
Long, Robert E. *John O'Hara,* 104–105.

"Sunday Morning"
Molloy, Francis C. "The Suburban Vision . . . ," 106–107.

"The Time Element"
Molloy, Francis C. "The Suburban Vision . . . ," 105–106.

"The Twinkle in His Eye"
Molloy, Francis C. "The Suburban Vision . . . ," 102–103.

"Yostie"
Long, Robert E. *John O'Hara,* 114–115.

O. HENRY [WILLIAM SYDNEY PORTER]

"The Enchanted Profile"
Stevick, Philip. "Introduction," in Stevick, Philip, Ed. *The American Short Story,*
    1900–1945, 24–25.

"The Gift of the Magi"
Shaw, Valerie. *The Short Story . . . ,* 53–55.

OKAMOTO KANOKO

"Mother and Son, a Lyric"
Keene, Donald. *Dawn to the West . . . ,* 1126–1128.

SEAMUS O'KELLY

"The Weaver's Grave"
Kilroy, James F. "Setting the Standards: Writers of the 1920s and 1930s," in
    Kilroy, James F., Ed. *The Irish Short Story . . . ,* 142–143.

IURII [YURY] KARLOVICH OLESHA

"The Cherry Pit"
Brown, Edward J. . . . *Since the Revolution*, 3rd ed., 62–63, 69.

"Liompa"
Björling, Fiona. "Verbal Aspect and Narrative Perspective in Olesha's 'Liompa,'" *Russian Lit*, 9 (1981), 133–162.
Brown, Edward J. . . . *Since the Revolution*, 3rd ed., 63–64.
Ingdahl, Kazimiera. "The Life/Death Dichotomy in Jurij Oleša's Short Story 'Liompa,'" in Nilsson, Nils A., Ed. . . . *Russian Prose*, 156–185.

MARGARET OLIPHANT

"Earthbound"
Colby, Vineta and Robert A. *The Equivocal Virtue* . . . , 101–103.

"The Library Window"
Colby, Vineta and Robert A. *The Equivocal Virtue* . . . , 227–228.
Gifford, Douglas, Ed. *Scottish Short Stories* . . . , 12–13.

"Old Lady Mary"
Colby, Vineta and Robert A. *The Equivocal Virtue* . . . , 96–101.

"The Open Door"
Colby, Vineta and Robert A. *The Equivocal Virtue* . . . , 95–97.

"Queen Eleanor and Fair Rosamond"
Colby, Vineta and Robert A. *The Equivocal Virtue* . . . , 126–127.

CHAD OLIVER

"Rite of Passage"
Allen, L. David. "Chad Oliver," in Bleiler, Everett F., Ed. *Science Fiction Writers* . . . , 469.

TILLIE OLSEN

"I Stand Here Ironing"
Sheidley, William E., and Ann Charters. *Instructor's Manual* . . . , 140–141.
Sirlin, Rhoda, and David H. Richter. *Instructor's Manual* . . . , 140–141.

"Requa"
Gelfant, Blanche H. "After Long Silence: Tillie Olsen's 'Requa,'" *Stud Am Fiction*, 12 (1984), 61–69; rpt. in her *Women Writing* . . . , 61–70.

"Tell Me a Riddle"
Nilsen, Helge N. "Tillie Olsen's 'Tell Me a Riddle': The Political Theme," *Études Anglaises*, 37 (1984), 163–169.

JUAN CARLOS ONETTI

"El album"
Boschetto, Sandra M. "El canto de la sirena en dos relatos de Juan Carlos
    Onetti," in Paolini, Gilbert, Ed. *LA CHISPA '83* . . . , 45–52.

"As Sad as She"
Benso, Silvia. "Una comunicazione impossibile: 'Triste come lei' de Juan Carlos
    Onetti," *Studi di Letteratura*, 13–14 (1983), 193–198.

"A Dream Come True"
McMurray, George R. "The Spanish American Short Story from Borges to the
    Present," in Peden, Margaret S., Ed. *The Latin American Short Story* . . . , 102.
Penner, Dick, Ed. *Fiction of the Absurd* . . . , 222–224.

"Esbjerg, en la costa"
Turton, Peter. "Las permutaciones de desgracia o 'Esbjerg, en la costa' de Juan
    Carlos Onetti," *Revista Canadiense de Estudios Hispanicos*, 8, i (1983), 75–87.

"El infierno tan temido"
Boschetto, Sandra M. "El canto de la sirena . . . ," 45–52.

"The Knight of the Rose"
Sotomayor, Aurea María. "'El caballero de la rose' o los inventos del prejuicio,"
    Inti, 12 (1980), 47–64.

GEORGE ORWELL

"Animal Farm"
Elkins, Charles L. "George Orwell," in Bleiler, Everett F., Ed. *Science Fiction
    Writers* . . . , 237–238.

JOHN A. OSKINSON

"Only the Master Shall Praise"
Littlefield, Daniel, and James W. Parins. "Short Fiction Writers of the Indian
    Territory," *Am Stud* (Kansas), 23, i (1982), 33–34.

WAYNE D. OVERHOLSER

"Book L'arnin' and the Equalizer"
Overholser, Stephen. "Introduction: A Critical Memoir," in *The Best Western
    Stories* . . . , xv–xvi.

"The Steadfast"
Overholser, Stephen. "Introduction . . . ," xvi–xvii.

AMOS OZ

"Crusade"
Baumgarten, Murray. *City Scriptures* . . . , 134–135.

OZAKI KAZUO

"Various Kinds of Bugs"
Keene, Donald. *Dawn to the West* . . . , 522–523.

OZAKI KŌYŌ

"The Erotic Confessions of Two Nuns"
Rubin, Jay. *Injurious to Public Morals* . . . , 40–41.

CYNTHIA OZICK

"Bloodshed"
Gitenstein, R. Barbara. "The Temptation of Apollo and the Loss of Yiddish in
    Cynthia Ozick's Fiction," *Stud Am Jewish Lit,* 3 (1983), 197–199.

"Envy; or, Yiddish in America"
Baumgarten, Murray. *City Scriptures* . . . , 133.
Gitenstein, R. Barbara. "The Temptation . . . ," 195–196.
Weiner, Deborah H. "Cynthia Ozick, Pagan vs Jew (1966–1976)," *Stud Am Jewish
    Lit,* 3 (1983), 187–188.

"Puttermesser and Xhanthippe"
Fisch, Harold. *A Remembered Future* . . . , 157–158.

"Usurpation"
Gitenstein, R. Barbara. "The Temptation . . . ," 196–197.

PA CHIN [LI FEI-KAN]

"The Cross of Love"
Mao, Nathan K. *Pa Chin,* 77.

"The Days When the Snow Melts"
Mao, Nathan K. *Pa Chin,* 64–65.

"Dog"
Mao, Nathan K. *Pa Chin,* 67–69.

"Father and Son"
Mao, Nathan K. *Pa Chin,* 79–80.

"First Love"
Mao, Nathan K. *Pa Chin*, 74–75.

"The General "
Mao, Nathan K. *Pa Chin*, 66–67.

"A Girl and Her Cat"
Mao, Nathan K. *Pa Chin*, 110–111.

"A Good Man"
Mao, Nathan K. *Pa Chin*, 77–79.

"Man"
Mao, Nathan K. *Pa Chin*, 71–72.

"Mrs. Landlady"
Mao, Nathan K. *Pa Chin*, 82–83.

"Mona Lisa",
Mao, Nathan K. *Pa Chin*, 104–105.

"Monsieur Robert"
Mao, Nathan K. *Pa Chin*, 75–77.

"Piglet and Chickens"
Mao, Nathan K. *Pa Chin*, 109–110.

"Revenge"
Mao, Nathan K. *Pa Chin*, 80–82.

"Sinking Down"
Mao, Nathan K. *Pa Chin*, 70–71.

"Star"
Lang, Olga. *Pa Chin . . .* , 167–168.

"A Woman"
Mao, Nathan K. *Pa Chin*, 63–64.

"Yuliana"
Lang, Olga. *Pa Chin . . .* , 119–120.

JOSÉ EMILIO PACHECO

"Civilization and Barbarism"
Cluff, Russell M. "Immutable Humanity Within the Hands of Time: Two Short Stories by José Emilio Pacheco," *Latin Am Lit R,* 10 (Spring-Summer, 1982), 49–56.

"The Fierce Sport of Bullfighting"
McMurray, George R. "The Spanish American Short Story from Borges to the Present," in Peden, Margaret S., Ed. *The Latin American Short Story . . .*, 129–130.

"The Night of the Immortal"
Cluff, Russell M. "Immutable Humanity . . . ," 42–49.

LEWIS PADGETT [CATHERINE L. MOORE and HENRY KUTTNER]

"The Proud Robot"
Schuyler, William M. "Mechanisms of Morality: Philosophical Implications of Selected (A)moral Science Fiction Machines," in Dunn, Thomas P., and Richard D. Erlich, Eds. *The Mechanical God . . . ,*" 184–185.

"When the Bough Breaks"
King, Betty. *Women of the Future . . .* , 72–74.

GRACE PALEY

"A Conversation with My Father"
Bergman, David, Joseph de Roche, and Daniel M. Epstein. *Instructor's Manual . . .* , 25–26.
Neff, D. S. "'Extraordinary Means': Healers and Healing in 'A Conversation with my Father,'" *Lit & Med,* 2 (1983), 118–124.
Sheidley, William E., and Ann Charters. *Instructor's Manual . . .* , 154–155.

"Distance"
Sirlin, Rhoda, and David H. Richter. *Instructor's Manual . . .* , 142–143.

"Faith in a Tree"
Mandel, Dena. "Keeping Up with Faith: Grace Paley's Sturdy American Jewess," *Stud Am Jewish Lit,* 3 (1983), 92–93.

"Friends"
Gelfant, Blanche H. *Women Writing . . .* , 18–19.

"In Time Which Made Monkeys of Us All"
Sorkin, Adam J. "What Are We, Animals? Grace Paley's World of Talk and Laughter," *Stud Am Jewish Lit,* 2 (1982), 148–153.

"The Long-Distance Runner"
Gelfant, Blanche H. *Women Writing . . .* , 16–17.
Mandel, Dena. "Keeping Up with Faith . . . ," 93–95.

"A Subject of Childhood"
Mandel, Dena. "Keeping Up with Faith . . . ," 89–91.

"The Used-Boy Raisers"
Mandel, Dena. "Keeping Up with Faith . . . ," 88.

CLEMENTE PALMA

"Lina's Eyes"
Earle, Peter G. "Dreams of Creation: Short Fiction in Spanish America," *Denver Q,* 12 (1977), 70.

"White Farm"
Earle, Peter G. "Dreams of Creation . . . ," 70.

RICARDO PALMA

"Broadside and Counter-Broadside"
Lindstrom, Naomi. "The Spanish American Short Story from Echeverría to Quiroga," in Peden, Margaret S., Ed. *The Latin American Short Story . . . ,* 45–47.

CHARLES H. PALMER

"Citizen 505"
King, Betty. *Women of the Future . . . ,* 19–20.

W. H. PALMER

"A Woman"
Cohn, Jan. "The Negro Character in Northern Magazine Fiction of the 1860's," *New England Q,* 43 (1970), 585.

I. I. PANAEV

"The Boudoir of a Fashionable Lady"
Mersereau, John. *Russian Romantic Fiction,* 226–227.

"She Will Be Happy"
Mersereau, John. *Russian Romantic Fiction,* 227.

DOROTHY PARKER

"Big Blonde"
Gullason, Thomas A. "The 'Lesser' Renaissance: The American Short Story in the 1920s," in Stevick, Philip, Ed. *The American Short Story, 1900–1945,* 94.

"Mr. Durant"
Gullason, Thomas A. "The 'Lesser' Renaissance . . . ," 92–93.

"Too Bad"
Gullason, Thomas A. "The 'Lesser' Renaissance . . . ," 92–93.

"Wonderful Old Gentleman"
Gullason, Thomas A. "The 'Lesser' Renaissance . . . ," 93–94.

BORIS PASTERNAK

"The Childhood of Luvers"
Björling, Fiona. "Child Perspective: Tradition and Experience: An Analysis of
  'Detstvo Ljuvers' by Boris Pasternak," in Nilsson, Nils A., Ed. . . . *Russian
  Prose*, 130–154.

JAMES KIRKE PAULDING

"Cobus Yerks"
Reynolds, Larry J. *James Kirke Paulding*, 106–108.

"The Dumb Girl"
Reynolds, Larry J. *James Kirke Paulding*, 108–109.

"The Little Dutch Sentinel of the Manhadoes"
Reynolds, Larry J. *James Kirke Paulding*, 104–106.

NIKOLAY PAVLOV

"The Demon"
Mersereau, John. *Russian Romantic Fiction*, 244–245.

"The Name Day Party"
Mersereau, John. *Russian Romantic Fiction*, 240–241.

"Yataghan"
Mersereau, John. *Russian Romantic Fiction*, 241–243.

ROBERTO J. PAYRÓ

"The Devil in Pago Chico"
Lindstrom, Naomi. "The Spanish American Short Story from Echeverría to
  Quiroga," in Peden, Margaret S., Ed. *The Latin American Short Story* . . . ,
  55–57.

R. J. PEARSALL

"Revelation"
Wu, William F. *The Yellow Peril* . . . , 44–46.

Y. L. PERETZ [ITZHAK L. PERETZ]

"Between Two Mountains"
Liptzin, Sol. *The Flowering* . . . , 105–106.

"Bontsie Shvayg"
Liptzin, Sol. *The Flowering* . . . , 107–110.

"The Magician"
Liptzin, Sol. *The Flowering* . . . , 110–111.

"Seven Years of Plenty"
Liptzin, Sol. *The Flowering* . . . , 106–107.

BENITO PÉREZ GALDÓS

"The Streetcar Novel"
Spires, Robert C. *Beyond the Metafictional* . . . , 27–32.

ALEXEY PEROVSKY [pseudonym: ANTONY POGORELSKY]

"Isadore and Anyuta"
Mersereau, John. *Russian Romantic Fiction*, 94–95.

"A Journey by Diligence"
Mersereau, John. *Russian Romantic Fiction*, 97–100.

"The Lafertov District Poppyseed-Cake Vendor"
Mersereau, John. *Russian Romantic Fiction*, 75–77.

"The Pernicious Consequences of an Uncontrolled Imagination"
Mersereau, John. *Russian Romantic Fiction*, 95–96.

JULIA PETERKIN

"Ashes"
Polk, Noel. "Julia Peterkin's *Green Thursday*," in Meriwether, James B., Ed. *South Carolina Women Writers*, 180–181.

"Finding Peace"
Polk, Noel. "Julia Peterkin's *Green Thursday*," 184.

"Green Thursday"
Polk, Noel. "Julia Peterkin's *Green Thursday*," 181–183.

"Missie"
Polk, Noel. "Julia Peterkin's *Green Thursday*," 183–184.

"Son"
Polk, Noel. "Julia Peterkin's *Green Thursday*," 185–186.

"A Sunday"
Polk, Noel. "Julia Peterkin's *Green Thursday*," 186–189.

ANTHONY PHELPS

"Hier, hier encore . . ."
Ferdinand, Joseph. "The New Political Statement in Haitian Fiction," in Luis,
  William, Ed. *Voices from Under . . .* , 131.

ELIZABETH STUART PHELPS

"At Bay"
Donovan, Josephine. *New England Local Color . . .* , 85–86.

"A Brave Girl"
Kessler, Carol F. *Elizabeth Stuart Phelps*, 56–57.

"Comrades"
Kessler, Carol F. *Elizabeth Stuart Phelps*, 118–119.

"The Girl Who Could Not Write a Composition"
Kelly, Lori D. *The Life and Works . . .* , 73–74.

"Hannah Colby's Chance"
Kessler, Carol F. *Elizabeth Stuart Phelps*, 55–56.

"His Soul to Keep"
Kelly, Lori D. *The Life and Works . . .* , 85–86.

"Margaret Bronson"
Donovan, Josephine. *New England Local Color . . .* , 91.

"No News"
Donovan, Josephine. *New England Local Color . . .* , 95–96.

"The Sacred Fire"
Kelly, Lori D. *The Life and Works . . .* , 97–98.

"Sweet Home Road"
Donovan, Josephine. *New England Local Color . . .* , 90.

"The True Woman"
Donovan, Josephine. *New England Local Color . . .* , 91–92.

"Twenty-Four: Four"
Kelly, Lori D. *The Life and Works . . .* , 84–85.

"What Was the Matter?" [originally titled "What Did She See With?"]
Donovan, Josephine. *New England Local Color . . .* , 85.

"A Woman's Pulpit"
Kelly, Lori D. *The Life and Works . . .* , 74–76.

PETER PHILLIPS

"Lost Memory"
Krulik, Ted. "Bounded by Metal," in Myers, Robert E., Ed. *The Intersection . . .* ,
122–123.

HELEN W. PIERSON

"Chips"
Cohn, Jan. "The Negro Character in Northern Magazine Fiction of the 1860's,"
New England Q, 43 (1970), 577–578.

"In Bonds"
Cohn, Jan. "The Negro Character . . . ," 576–577.

"My Heart"
Cohn, Jan. "The Negro Character . . . ," 576.

"Queen's Good Work"
Cohn, Jan. "The Negro Character . . . ," 578–579.

BORIS PIL'NYAK

"The Bridegroom Cometh"
Edwards, T. R. N. *Three Russian Writers . . .* , 123–127.

"A Story of the Unextinguished Moon"
Brown, Edward J. . . . *Since the Revolution,* 3rd ed., 82.

"The Third Capital"
Avins, Carol. *Border Crossings . . .* , 38–47.

"A Whole Lifetime"
Edwards, T. R. N. *Three Russian Writers . . .* , 87–90.

"A Year in Their Life"
Edwards, T. R. N. *Three Russian Writers . . .* , 90–92.

VIRGILIO PIÑERA

"The Great Baro"
Schwartz, Kessel. . . . *Spanish and Spanish-American Literature,* 246–247.

"The Puppet"
Schwartz, Kessel. . . . *Spanish and Spanish-American Literature*, 247.

NÉLIDA PIÑON

"Trophy Room"
Foster, David W. "Major Figures in the Brazilian Short Story," in Peden,
   Margaret S., Ed. *The Latin American Short Story . . .* , 19–22.

LUIGI PIRANDELLO

"The Captive"
Finch, Mark S. "Life and Form in Pirandello's Short Prose: An Existential
   Atmosphere," *Revista/Review Interamericana*, 9 (1979), 620–621.

"The Husband's Revenge"
Finch, Mark S. "Life and Form . . . ," 619–620.

"It's Nothing Serious"
Finch, Mark S. "Life and Form . . . ," 618–619.

"The Jar"
Finch, Mark S. "Life and Form . . . ," 617–618.

"Sicilian Honor"
Finch, Mark S. "Life and Form . . . ," 619.

ANDREI PLATONOV

"The Epifan Locks"
Avins, Carol. *Border Crossings . . .* , 175–179.

JAMES PLUNKETT

"A Walk Through the Summer"
Hogan, Robert. "Old Boys, Young Bucks, and New Woman: The Contemporary Irish Short Story," in Kilroy, James F., Ed. *The Irish Short Story . . .* ,
   179–180.

ERNEST M. POATE

"Phantom Footsteps"
Sampson, Robert. *Yesterday's Faces, II . . .* , 55–57.

EDGAR ALLAN POE

"The Angel of the Odd"
*Richard, Claude. "Arrant Bubbles: Poe's 'The Angel of the Odd,' " in Eddings, Dennis W., Ed. *The Naiad Voice* . . . , 66–72.

"The Assignation"
*Benton, Richard P. "Is Poe's 'The Assignation' a Hoax?" in Eddings, Dennis W., Ed. *The Naiad Voice* . . . ," 18–21.
Saliba, David R. *A Psychology of Fear* . . . , 62–65.

"Berenice"
Dayan, Joan. "The Identity of Berenice, Poe's Idol of the Mind," *Stud Romanticism*, 23 (1984), 491–513.
Saliba, David R. *A Psychology of Fear* . . . , 119–130.
Smith, Allan G. *The Analysis* . . . , 42–44.

"The Black Cat"
Crisman, William. " 'Mere Household Events' in Poe's 'The Black Cat,' " *Stud Am Fiction*, 12 (1984), 87–90.
*Gargano, James W. "The Question of Poe's Narrators," in Eddings, Dennis W., Ed. *The Naiad Voice* . . . , 26–27.
*Martin, Terence. "The Imagination at Play: Edgar Allan Poe," in Eddings, Dennis W., Ed. *The Naiad Voice* . . . , 30–31.
Sadlier, Darlene J. "Compreendendo o Medo de Gatos no Narrador de 'Sardanapalo,' " *Minas Gerais*, 14 (Nov. 14, 1981), 6–7.
Smith, Allan G. *The Analysis* . . . , 38–41.

"Bon-Bon"
Kemp, Anthony. "The Greek Joke in Poe's 'Bon-Bon,' " *Am Lit*, 56 (1984), 580–583.

"The Business Man"
Lemay, J. A. Leo. "Poe's 'The Business Man': Its Context and Satire of Franklin's *Autobiography*," *Poe Stud*, 15, ii (1982), 29–37.

"The Cask of Amontillado"
Bergman, David, Joseph de Roche, and Daniel M. Epstein. *Instructor's Manual* . . . , 14–15.
Garber, Frederick. *The Autonomy of the Self* . . . , 237–241.
*Gargano, James W. " . . . Poe's Narrators," 25–26.
———. *The Masquerade Vision* . . . , [9]–[11].
Knox, Helene. "Poe's 'The Cask of Amontillado,' " *Explicator*, 41, i (1982), 30–31.
Levine, Stuart. "Masonry, Impunity, and Revolution," *Poe Stud*, 17, i (1984), 22.
*Martin, Terence. "The Imagination at Play . . . ," 30–31.

"The Colloquy of Monos and Una"
Bleiler, Everett F. "Edgar Allan Poe," in Bleiler, Everett F., Ed. *Science Fiction Writers* . . . , 14–15.

"The Conversation of Eiros and Charmion"
Bleiler, Everett F. "Edgar Allan Poe," 14.
Robinson, Douglas. "Poe's Mini-Apocalypse: 'The Conversation of Eiros and Charmion,'" *Stud Short Fiction*, 19 (1982), 329–337.

"A Descent into the Maelström"
Egan, Kenneth V. "Descent to an Ascent: Poe's Use of Perspective in 'A Descent into the Maelström,'" *Stud Short Fiction*, 19 (1982), 157–162.

"The Devil in the Belfry"
Forbes, Christopher J. "Satire of Irving's *History of New York* in Poe's 'The Devil in the Belfry,'" *Stud Am Fiction*, 10 (1982), 93–100.

"The Domain of Arnheim"
Garber, Frederick. *The Autonomy of the Self* . . . , 245–255.
Zanger, Jules. "Poe's American Garden: 'The Domain of Arnheim,'" *Am Transcendental Q,* 50 (1981), 93–103.

"Eleonora"
Garber, Frederick. *The Autonomy of the Self* . . . , 225–229.

"The Facts in the Case of M. Valdemar"
Bleiler, Everett F. "Edgar Allan Poe," 15.
Kennedy, J. Gerald. "Phantasms of Death in Poe's Fiction," in Kerr, Howard, John W. Crowley, and Charles L. Crow, Eds. *The Haunted Dusk* . . . , 61–63.

"The Fall of the House of Usher"
Clayton, David. "On Realistic and Fantastic Discourse," in Slusser, George E., Eric S. Rabkin, and Robert Scholes, Eds. *Bridges to Fantasy*, 72–73.
*Cox, James M. "Edgar Poe: Style as Pose," in Eddings, Dennis W., Ed. *The Naiad Voice* . . . , 50.
Gargano, James W. " 'The Fall of the House of Usher': An Apocalyptic Vision," *Univ Mississippi Stud Engl*, 3 (1982), 53–63.
Hoffman, Gerhard. "Space and Symbol in the Tales of Edgar Allan Poe," *Poe Stud*, 12 (1979), 3–8.
Jefferson, Ann. "*Mise en abyme* and the Prophetic," *Style*, 17 (1983), 203–206.
Kerr, Howard. "James's Last Early Supernatural Tales: Hawthorne Demagnetized, Poe Depoetized," in Kerr, Howard, John W. Crowley, and Charles L. Crow, Eds. *The Haunted Dusk* . . . , 140–143.
Massa, Ann. *American Literature in Context, IV* . . . , 48–54.
Nigro, August J. *The Diagonal Line* . . . , 62–65.
Ressmeyer, Karl-Heinz. "Interieur und Symbol: Zum Phantasyischen im Werk E. A. Poes," in Thomsen, Christian W., and Jens M. Fischer, Eds. *Phantastik* . . . , 162–165.
Ringe, Donald A. *American Gothic* . . . , 146–148.
Saliba, David R. *A Psychology of Fear* . . . , 162–190.
Sirlin, Rhoda, and David H. Richter. *Instructor's Manual* . . . , 144–146.
Smith, Allan G. *The Analysis* . . . , 45–49.
Stahlberg, Lawrence. "The Source of Usher's Fear," *Interpretations*, 13 (1981), 10–17.
Tani, Stefano. *The Doomed Detective* . . . , 12–13.

"The Gold Bug"
Williams, Michael. "'The *Language* of the Cipher': Interpretation in 'The Gold Bug,'" *Am Lit*, 53 (1982), 646–660.

"Hop-Frog"
Gargano, James W. *The Masquerade Vision* . . . , [6]–[8].

"How to Write a Blackwood Article"
Weiner, Bruce I. "Poe's Subversion of Verisimilitude," *Am Transcendental Q*, 24 (Supplement) (Fall, 1974), 2; rpt. Eddings, Dennis W., Ed. *The Naiad Voice* . . . , 112–113.

"The Imp of the Perverse"
*Kanjo, Eugene R. "'The Imp of the Perverse': Poe's Dark Comedy of Art and Death," in Eddings, Dennis W., Ed. *The Naiad Voice* . . . , 57–65.

"The Island of the Fay"
Garber, Frederick. *The Autonomy of the Self* . . . , 220–226.
Ljungquist, Kent. "Poe's 'The Island of the Fay': The Passing of Fairyland," *Stud Short Fiction*, 14 (1977), 265–271; rpt. Eddings, Dennis W., Ed. *The Naiad Voice* . . . , 148–154.

"King Pest"
Gargano, James W. *The Masquerade Vision* . . . , [8]–[9].

"Landor's Cottage"
Dayan, Joan. "The Road to Landor's Cottage: Poe's Landscape of Effect," *Univ Mississippi Stud Engl*, 3 (1982), 136–154.

"The Landscape Garden"
Garber, Frederick. *The Autonomy of the Self* . . . , 245–249.

"Ligeia"
*Cox, James M. ". . . Style as Pose," 48–50.
Engel, Leonard W. "Obsession, Madness and Enclosure in Poe's 'Ligeia' and 'Morella,'" *Coll Lit*, 9 (1982), 141–143.
Garber, Frederick. *The Autonomy of the Self* . . . , 238–240.
*Griffith, Clark. "Poe's 'Ligeia' and the English Romantics," in Eddings, Dennis W., Ed. *The Naiad Voice* . . . , 1–17.
Jones, Daryl E. "Poe's Siren: Character and Meaning in 'Ligeia,'" *Stud Short Fiction*, 20 (1983), 33–37.
Kennedy, J. Gerald. "Phantasms of Death . . . ," 54–57.
Matheson, Terence J. "The Multiple Murders in 'Ligeia': A New Look at Poe's Narrator," *Canadian R Am Stud*, 13 (1982), 279–289.
Nigro, August J. *The Diagonal Line* . . . , 59–62.
Obuchowski, Peter A. "A Case Against 'Ligeia,'" *J Nassau Community Coll*, 3, v (1979), 59–63.
Ressmeyer, Karl-Heinz. "Interieur und Symbol . . . ," 155–161.
Richard, Claude. "Edgar A. Poe et l'esthétique du double," in [La Cassagnère, Christian, Ed.]. *Le Double* . . . , 155–164.
Ringe, Donald A. *American Gothic* . . . , 135–136.
Saliba, David R. *A Psychology of Fear* . . . , 145–162.

Smith, Allan G. *The Analysis* . . . , 51–53.
Tani, Stefano. *The Doomed Detective* . . . , 11–12.

"The Man of the Crowd"
Keogh, J. G. "The Crowd as No-Man's Land: Gas-Light and Poe's Symbolist Effects," *Antigonish R*, 58 (1984), 19–31.
Miller, James E., and Bernice Slote. *Instructor's Manual* . . . , 2nd ed., 5.

"MS. Found in a Bottle"
Bleiler, Everett F. "Edgar Allan Poe," 13.
Kennedy, J. Gerald. "Phantasms of Death . . . ," 52–53.
Saliba, David R. *A Psychology of Fear* . . . , 106–119.

"The Masque of the Red Death"
Abcarian, Richard, and Marvin Klotz. *Instructor's Manual* . . . , 2nd ed., 19–20; 3rd ed., 17–18.
Garber, Frederick. *The Autonomy of the Self* . . . , 233–235.
Gargano, James W. *The Masquerade Vision* . . . , [4]–[6].
Hoffman, Gerhard. "Space and Symbol . . . ," 8–10.
Kayser, Wolfgang. *The Grotesque* . . . , 78–79.
Ressmeyer, Karl-Heinz. "Interieur und Symbol . . . ," 165–167.
Roth, Martin. "Inside 'The Masque of the Red Death,'" *SubStance*, 13, ii (1984), 50–53.
Wheat, Patricia H. "The Mask of Indifference in 'The Masque of the Red Death,'" *Stud Short Fiction*, 19 (1982), 51–56.

"Mellonta Tauta"
Bleiler, Everett F. "Edgar Allan Poe," 15.

"Mesmeric Revelation"
Kennedy, J. Gerald. "Phantasms of Death . . . ," 58–59.

"Metzengerstein"
Hirsch, David H. "Poe's 'Metzengerstein' as a Tale of the Subconscious," *Univ Mississippi Stud Engl*, 3 (1982), 40–52.
Kennedy, J. Gerald. "Phantasms of Death . . . ," 51–52.

"Morella"
Engel, Leonard W. "Obsession . . . ," 143–145.
Kennedy, J. Gerald. "Phantasms of Death . . . ," 54–56.
Ringe, Donald A. *American Gothic* . . . , 142–143.

"The Murders in the Rue Morgue"
Eddings, Dennis W. "Poe, Dupin, and the Reader," *Univ Mississippi Stud Engl*, 3 (1982), 129–131.
Lemay, J. A. Leo. "The Psychology of 'The Murders in the Rue Morgue,'" *Am Lit*, 54 (1982), 165–188.

"The Mystery of Marie Roget"
Eddings, Dennis W. "Poe, Dupin . . . ," 131–132.

"The Narrative of Arthur Gordon Pym"
Bleiler, Everett F. "Edgar Allan Poe," 16–17.
*Cox, James M. ". . . Style as Pose," 44–48.
Holländer, Hans. "Das Bild in der Theorie des Phantastischen," in Thomsen, Christian W., and Jens M. Fischer, Eds. *Phantastik . . .* , 66–69.
Kennedy, J. Gerald. "'The Infernal Twosome' in 'Arthur Gordon Pym,'" *Topic*, 16, xxx (1976), 41–53; rpt., retitled "The Invisible Message: The Problem of Truth in 'Pym,'" in Eddings, Dennis W., Ed. *The Naiad Voice . . .* , 124–135.
Kopley, Richard. "The Hidden Journey of 'Arthur Gordon Pym,'" in Myerson, Joel, Ed. *Studies in the American Renaissance, 1982*, 29–51.
Massa, Ann. *American Literature in Context, IV . . .* , 59–63.
Montgomery, Marion. *Why Poe Drank Liquor*, 389–392.
Peden, William. "Prologue to the Dark Journey: The 'Opening' to Poe's 'Pym,'" in Veler, Richard P., Ed. *Papers on Poe . . .* , 84–91.
Ridgely, J. V. "The End of Pym and the Ending of *Pym*," in Veler, Richard P., Ed. *Papers on Poe . . .* , 104–112.
Rowe, John C. *Through the Custom-House . . .* , 91–110.
Stout, Janis P. *The Journey Narrative . . .* , 93–95.

"The Pit and the Pendulum"
Saliba, David R. *A Psychology of Fear . . .* , 190–205.

"A Predicament"
Weiner, Bruce I. "Poe's Subversion . . . ," 2; rpt. Eddings, Dennis W., Ed. *The Naiad Voice . . .* , 113.

"The Premature Burial"
Weiner, Bruce I. "Poe's Subversion . . . ," 2–5; rpt. Eddings, Dennis W., Ed. *The Naiad Voice . . .* , 113–118.

"The Purloined Letter"
*Cox, James M. ". . . Style as Pose," 52–54.
Eddings, Dennis W. "Poe, Dupin . . . ," 132–134.
Gavrelli, Kenneth. "The Problem of Poe's Purloined Letter," *Armchair Detective*, 15 (1982), 381–382.
Tani, Stefano. *The Doomed Detective . . .* , 7–9.

"Shadow—A Parable"
Kennedy, J. Gerald. "Phantasms of Death . . . ," 47–48.

"The System of Dr. Tarr and Professor Fether"
Fisher, Benjamin F. "Poe's 'Tarr and Fether': Hoaxing in the Blackwood Mode," *Topic*, 31 (1977), 29–40; rpt. Eddings, Dennis W., Ed. *The Naiad Voice . . .* , 136–147.

"A Tale of the Ragged Mountains"
Friederich, Reinhard H. "Necessary Inadequacies: Poe's 'Tale of the Ragged Mountains' and Borges's 'South,'" *J Narrative Technique*, 12, i (1982), 155–166.

"The Tell-Tale Heart"
*Gargano, James W. ". . . Poe's Narrators," 24.

"The Unparalleled Adventures of One Hans Pfaall"
Bennett, Maurice J. "Edgar Allan Poe and the Literary Tradition of Lunar
    Speculation," *Sci-Fiction Stud*, 10 (1983), 137–147.
Bleiler, Everett F. "Edgar Allan Poe," 13–14.
*Ketterer, David. "Poe's Usage of the Hoax and the Unity of 'Hans Pfaal,'" in
    Eddings, Dennis W., Ed. *The Naiad Voice . . .* , 88–96.

"Von Kemperlen and His Discovery"
Weiner, Bruce I. "Poe's Subversion . . . ," 5–6; rpt. Eddings, Dennis W., Ed.
    The Naiad Voice . . . , 118–120.

"William Wilson"
Coates, Paul. *The Realist Fantasy Fiction . . .* , 118–120.
*Cox, James M. ". . . Style as Pose," 50–52.
Crawford, John W. "'The Secret Sharer': A Touchstone for 'William Wilson,'"
    J Evolutionary Psych, 5, i–ii (1984), 81–85.
*Gargano, James W. ". . . Poe's Narrators," 24–25.
————. *The Masquerade Vision . . .* , [3]–[4].
Montgomery, Marion. *Why Poe Drank Liquor*, 291–294.
Ringe, Donald A. *American Gothic . . .* , 139–141.
Tani, Stefano. *The Doomed Detective . . .* , 13–14.

MIKHAIL POGODIN

"The Deacon-Wizard"
Mersereau, John. *Russian Romantic Fiction*, 200.

"Happiness in Misfortune"
Mersereau, John. *Russian Romantic Fiction*, 203–204.

"Sokolnitsky Park"
Mersereau, John. *Russian Romantic Fiction*, 201–203.

FREDERIK POHL

"The Gold at the Starbow's End"
Samuelson, David N. "Frederik Pohl," in Bleiler, Frederick F., Ed. *Science Fiction
    Writers . . .* , 479.

"Gravy Planet"
Samuelson, David N. "Frederik Pohl," 476.

"The Mapmakers"
Samuelson, David N. "Frederik Pohl," 479.

"The Midas Plague"
Pierce, Hazel B. *A Literary Symbiosis . . .* , 114.

BORIS POLEVOY

"Doctor Vera"
Blum, Jakub. "Soviet Russian Literature," in Blum, Jakub, and Vera Rich. *The Image of the Jew* . . . , 41.

NIKOLAY POLEVOY

"The Artist"
Mersereau, John. *Russian Romantic Fiction,* 206–207.

WILLIAM T. POLK

"Golden Eagle Ordinary"
Nolan, Charles J. *Aaron Burr* . . . , 113–115.

FRANK LILLIE POLLACK

"Finis"
King, Betty. *Women of the Future* . . . , 21–22.

ELENA PONIATOWSKA

"The House in Sololoi"
Flori, Mónica. "Visions of Women: Symbolic Physical Portrayal as Social Commentary in the Short Fiction of Elena Poniatowska," *Third Woman,* 2, ii (1984), 81–82.

"Limbo"
Flori, Mónica. "Visions of Women . . . ," 80–81.

"Place Yourself, My Lovely, Between the Tie and the Whistle"
Flori, Mónica. "Visions of Women . . . ," 77–80.

KATHERINE ANNE PORTER

"The Circus"
DeMouy, Jane K. . . . *Porter's Women* . . . , 129–133.

"The Cracked Looking-Glass"
DeMouy, Jane K. . . . *Porter's Women* . . . , 61–72.
*Warren, Robert P. "Irony with a Center: Katherine Anne Porter," in McClave, Heather, Ed. *Women Writers* . . . , 79.

"The Fig Tree"
DeMouy, Jane K. . . . *Porter's Women* . . . , 136–139.

"Flowering Judas"
Scott, Virgil, and David Madden. *Instructor's Manual* . . . , 4th ed., 32–34; Madden, David. *Instructor's Manual* . . . , 5th ed., 82–83; Madden, David, and Virgil Scott. *Instructor's Manual* . . . , 6th ed., 40–45.
Sheidley, William E., and Ann Charters. *Instructor's Manual* . . . , 94–95.
Sirlin, Rhoda, and David H. Richter. *Instructor's Manual* . . . , 146–149.
Walsh, Thomas F. "Braggioni's Jockey Club in Porter's 'Flowering Judas,'" *Stud Short Fiction*, 20 (1983), 136–138.
*Warren, Robert P. "Irony with a Center . . . ," 72–74.

"The Grave"
DeMouy, Jane K. . . . *Porter's Women* . . . , 139–144.
Gardiner, Judith K. "'The Grave,' 'On Not Shooting Sitting Birds,' and the Female Esthetic," *Stud Short Fiction*, 20 (1984), 266–268, 269–270.
Miller, James E., and Bernice Slote. *Instructor's Manual* . . . , 2nd ed., 18.

"Hacienda"
Camati, Anne S. "Violence and Death: Their Interpretation by K. A. Porter and Eudora Welty," *Revista Letras*, 32 (1983), 45–49.
DeMouy, Jane K. . . . *Porter's Women* . . . , 93–111.

"He"
DeMouy, Jane K. . . . *Porter's Women* . . . , 36–38.
Jorgensen, Bruce W. "'The Other Side of Silence': Katherine Anne Porter's 'He,'" *Mod Fiction Stud*, 28 (1982), 395–404.
Moddelmog, Debra A. "Narrative Irony and Hidden Motivations in Katherine Anne Porter's 'He,'" *Mod Fiction Stud*, 28 (1982), 405–413.

"Holiday"
DeMouy, Jane K. . . . *Porter's Women* . . . , 166–176.

"The Jilting of Granny Weatherall"
*Abcarian, Richard, and Marvin Klotz. *Instructor's Manual* . . . , 2nd ed., 20–21; 3rd ed., 18–19.
Bergman, David, Joseph de Roche, and Daniel M. Epstein. *Instructor's Manual* . . . , , 20–21.
DeMouy, Jane K. . . . *Porter's Women* . . . , 45–54.
Gullason, Thomas A. "The 'Lesser' Renaissance: The American Short Story in the 1920s," in Stevick, Philip, Ed. *The American Short Story, 1900–1945*, 96–97.
Kennedy, X. J. *Instructor's Manual* . . . , 3rd ed., 20–23.

"The Last Leaf"
DeMouy, Jane K. . . . *Porter's Women* . . . , 133–136.

"María Concepción"
Camati, Anne S. "Violence and Death . . . ," 42–45.
DeMouy, Jane K. . . . *Porter's Women* . . . , 21–27.
Sheidley, William E., and Ann Charters. *Instructor's Manual* . . . , 92.

"The Martyr"
DeMouy, Jane K. . . . *Porter's Women* . . . , 27–30.

"Noon Wine"
*Warren, Robert P. "Irony with a Center . . . ," 75–79.

"Old Mortality"
Beaty, Jerome. *The Norton Introduction* . . . , 461–464.
DeMouy, Jane K. . . . *Porter's Women* . . . , 154–157.
*Warren, Robert P. "Irony with a Center . . . ," 79–84.

"The Old Order"
DeMouy, Jane K. . . . *Porter's Women* . . . , 115–120.

"Pale Horse, Pale Rider"
DeMouy, Jane K. . . . *Porter's Women* . . . , 157–166.

"Rope"
DeMouy, Jane K. . . . *Porter's Women* . . . , 40–44.
Perrine, Laurence, and Thomas R. Arp. *Instructor's Manual* . . . , 6th ed., 54–56.

"The Source"
DeMouy, Jane K. . . . *Porter's Women* . . . , 120–122.

"That Tree"
DeMouy, Jane K. . . . *Porter's Women* . . . , 73–75.

"Theft"
DeMouy, Jane K. . . . *Porter's Women* . . . , 55–61.

"Virgin Violeta"
DeMouy, Jane K. . . . *Porter's Women* . . . , 30–36.

"The Witness"
DeMouy, Jane K. . . . *Porter's Women* . . . , 127–129.

ALEXANDER A. POSEY

"Jes 'Bout a Mid'lin', Sah"
Littlefield, Daniel, and James W. Parins. "Short Fiction Writers of the Indian Territory," *Am Stud* (Kansas), 23, i (1982), 29–30.

"Moses and Richard"
Littlefield, Daniel, and James W. Parins. "Short Fiction Writers . . . ," 29.

J. F. POWERS

"The Valiant Woman"
Sirlin, Rhoda, and David H. Richter. *Instructor's Manual* . . . , 150.

JOHN C. POWYS

"The Mountains of the Moon"
Hopkins, Kenneth. *The Powys Brothers* . . . , 251–252.

"Up and Out"
Hopkins, Kenneth. *The Powys Brothers* . . . , 250–251.

T[HEODORE] F[RANCIS] POWYS

"Abraham Men"
Hopkins, Kenneth. *The Powys Brothers* . . . , 80–82.

"The Baked Mole"
Coombes, H. *T. F. Powys,* 91–92.

"The Barometer"
Coombes, H. *T. F. Powys,* 92.

"The Blind Hen and the Earthworm"
Coombes, H. *T. F. Powys,* 88.

"The Bucket and the Rope"
Coombes, H. *T. F. Powys,* 84–86.

"The Corpse and the Flea"
Coombes, H. *T. F. Powys,* 70–78.

"Hester Dominy"
Cavaliero, Glen. *The Rural Tradition* . . . , 176–177.

"Jane Moller's Box"
Coombes, H. *T. F. Powys,* 89–90.

"John Pardy and the Waves"
Coombes, H. *T. F. Powys,* 78–79.

"The Left Leg"
Hopkins, Kenneth. *The Powys Brothers* . . . , 78–80.

"Mr. Pim and the Holy Crumb"
Coombes, H. *T. F. Powys,* 81–84.
Hopkins, Kenneth. *The Powys Brothers* . . . , 163–165.

"The Only Penitent"
Coombes, H. *T. F. Powys,* 93–96.

"The Spittoon and the Slate"
Coombes, H. *T. F. Powys,* 86–87.

"The Stone and Mr. Thomas"
Coombes, H. *T. F. Powys,* 80–81.

JAISHANKAR PRASAD

"Ashoka"
Singh, Rajendra. *Jaishankar Prasad*, 24–25.

"The Beggar Woman"
Singh, Rajendra. *Jaishankar Prasad*, 55–56.

"A Broken Vow"
Singh, Rajendra. *Jaishankar Prasad*, 61–63.

"The Chariot of the Gods"
Singh, Rajendra. *Jaishankar Prasad*, 106.

"Doubt"
Singh, Rajendra. *Jaishankar Prasad*, 106–107.

"Echo"
Singh, Rajendra. *Jaishankar Prasad*, 56–57.

"Gangster"
Singh, Rajendra. *Jaishankar Prasad*, 105–106.

"Jahanara"
Singh, Rajendra. *Jaishankar Prasad*, 25.

"The Liberation of Chittor"
Singh, Rajendra. *Jaishankar Prasad*, 25.

"The Lighthouse"
Singh, Rajendra. *Jaishankar Prasad*, 51–54.

"Madhua"
Singh, Rajendra. *Jaishankar Prasad*, 59–61.

"Mamata"
Singh, Rajendra. *Jaishankar Prasad*, 54–55.

"The Moon"
Singh, Rajendra. *Jaishankar Prasad*, 20.

"The Recluse"
Singh, Rajendra. *Jaishankar Prasad*, 57–59.

"Tansen"
Singh, Rajendra. *Jaishankar Prasad*, 20–21.

MUNSHI PREM CHAND [DHANPAT RAI SHRIVASTAV]

"Battle Journey"
Swan, Robert O. *Munshi Premchand . . .*, 88.

"Man's Highest Duty"
Swan, Robert O. *Munshi Premchand* . . . , 80–81.

"Miss Padma"
Swan, Robert O. *Munshi Premchand* . . . , 117.

"A Mother's Heart"
Madan, Indar Nath. *Premchand* . . . , 134–135.

"The New Marriage"
Swan, Robert O. *Munshi Premchand* . . . , 131–133.

"The Plaything of Pride"
Swan, Robert O. *Munshi Premchand* . . . , 74–75.

"The Price of Milk"
Swan, Robert O. *Munshi Premchand* . . . , 126–127.

"Rani Sarandha"
Swan, Robert O. *Munshi Premchand* . . . , 66–68.

"Reconciliation"
Swan, Robert O. *Munshi Premchand* . . . , 58–59.

"Sacrifice"
Swan, Robert O. *Munshi Premchand* . . . , 78–79.

"The Shroud"
Madan, Indar Nath. *Premchand* . . . , 141–142.
Swan, Robert O. *Munshi Premchand* . . . , 124–126.

"Temple and Mosque"
Swan, Robert O. *Munshi Premchand* . . . , 93–95.

"The Thakur's Well"
Swan, Robert O. *Munshi Premchand* . . . , 126–127.

"This Is My Country"
Swan, Robert O. *Munshi Premchand* . . . , 61–63.

"A Winter Night"
Madan, Indar Nath. *Premchand* . . . , 134–135.

HARRIET E. PRESCOTT

"Down the River"
Cohn, Jan. "The Negro Character in Northern Magazine Fiction of the 1860's,"
    New England Q, 43 (1970), 584–585.

REYNOLDS PRICE

"The Anniversary"
Rooke, Constance. *Reynolds Price*, 46–48.

"A Chain of Love"
Rooke, Constance. *Reynolds Price*, 40–42.

"A Dog's Death"
Rooke, Constance. *Reynolds Price*, 90–91.

"Elegies"
Rooke, Constance. *Reynolds Price*, 100–101.

"Good and Bad Dreams"
Rooke, Constance. *Reynolds Price*, 104–105.

"The Happiness of Others"
Rooke, Constance. *Reynolds Price*, 88–90.

"Michael Egerton"
Rooke, Constance. *Reynolds Price*, 44–46.

"The Names and Faces of Heroes"
Rooke, Constance. *Reynolds Price*, 52–55.

"Scars"
Rooke, Constance. *Reynolds Price*, 91–93.

"Troubled Sleep"
Rooke, Constance. *Reynolds Price*, 48–50.

"Truth and Lies"
Rooke, Constance. *Reynolds Price*, 101–103.

"Uncle Grant"
Rooke, Constance. *Reynolds Price*, 50–51.

"Waiting at Dachau"
Rooke, Constance. *Reynolds Price*, 93–100.

"Walking Lessons"
Rooke, Constance. *Reynolds Price*, 105–110.

"The Warrior Princess Ozimba"
Rooke, Constance. *Reynolds Price*, 42–44.

J. B. PRIESTLEY

"The Pavilion of Masks"
DeVitis, A. A., and Albert E. Kalson. *J. B. Priestley*, 114–115.

MARIYA PRILEZHAEVA

"The Pushkin Waltz"
Blum, Jakub. "Soviet Russian Literature," in Blum, Jakub, and Vera Rich. *The Image of the Jew* . . . , 46.

MARÍA LUISA PUGA

"Secret, Immobile Sun"
McMurray, George R. "The Spanish American Short Story from Borges to the Present," in Peden, Margaret S., Ed. *The Latin American Short Story* . . . , 133–134.

JAMES PURDY

"63: Dream Palace"
Karl, Frederick R. *American Fictions* . . . , 164–165.

ALEXANDER PUSHKIN

"The Blizzard"
Debreczeny, Paul. *The Other Pushkin* . . . , 80–95.

"The Coffinmaker"
Katz, Michael R. *Dreams* . . . , 22–24.

"Egyptian Nights"
Todd, William M. "*Eugene Onegin*: 'Life's Novel,'" in Todd, William M., Ed. *Literature and Society* . . . , 204–205.

"The Guests Were Arriving at the Dacha"
Debreczeny, Paul. *The Other Pushkin* . . . , 41–51.

"Kirdzhali"
Debreczeny, Paul. *The Other Pushkin* . . . , 278–280.

"Mistress into Maid"
Mersereau, John. *Russian Romantic Fiction,* 139–140.

"The Queen of Spades"
Barker, Adele. "Pushkin's 'Queen of Spades': A Displaced Mother Figure," *Am Imago,* 41 (1984), 201–209.
Debreczeny, Paul. *The Other Pushkin* . . . , 209–226.
Katz, Michael R. *Dreams* . . . , 49–51.
Leighton, Lauren G. "Puškin and Freemasonry: 'The Queen of Spades,'" in Gutsche, George J., and Lauren G. Leighton, Eds. *New Perspectives* . . . , 15–25.
Mersereau, John. *Russian Romantic Fiction,* 221–226.
Reeder, Roberta. "'The Queen of Spades': A Parody of Hoffmann's Tale," in

Gutsche, George J., and Lauren G. Leighton, Eds. *New Perspectives* . . . , 73–98.

Tammi, Pekka. "Nabokov's Symbolic Cards and Pushkin's 'The Queen of Spades,'" *Nabokovian*, 13 (1984), 31–32.

"The Shot" [same as "The Pistol Shot"]
Debreczeny, Paul. *The Other Pushkin* . . . , 102–119.
Mersereau, John. *Russian Romantic Fiction*, 129–132.
O'Toole, L. Michael. *Structure, Style and Interpretation* . . . , 117–128.

"The Snowstorm"
Katz, Michael R. *Dreams* . . . , 46–47.
Mersereau, John. *Russian Romantic Fiction*, 132–134.

"The Squire's Daughter"
Debreczeny, Paul. *The Other Pushkin* . . . , 80–95.

"The Stationmaster" [same as "The Post-Stage Master"]
Debreczeny, Paul. *The Other Pushkin* . . . , 119–137.
Mersereau, John. *Russian Romantic Fiction*, 136–139.
O'Toole, L. Michael. *Structure, Style and Interpretation* . . . , 99–111.

"The Undertaker"
Debreczeny, Paul. *The Other Pushkin* . . . , 95–101.
Mersereau, John. *Russian Romantic Fiction*, 134–136.

THOMAS PYNCHON

"Entropy"
Cooper, Peter L. *Signs and Symptoms* . . . , 65–67.
Karl, Frederick R. *American Fictions* . . . , 307–308.
Lewicki, Zbigniew. *The Bang* . . . , 85–86.
Tabbi, Joseph. "Pynchon's 'Entropy,'" *Explicator*, 43, i (1984), 61–63.
Tanner, Tony. *Thomas Pynchon*, 32–35.

"Low-Lands"
Karl, Frederick R. *American Fictions* . . . , 308–309.
Tanner, Tony. *Thomas Pynchon*, 29–32.

"Mortality and Mercy in Vienna"
Karl, Frederick R. *American Fictions* . . . , 309.
Tanner, Tony. *Thomas Pynchon*, 26–29.

"The Secret Integration"
Tanner, Tony. *Thomas Pynchon*, 37–39.

"The Small Rain"
Tanner, Tony. *Thomas Pynchon*, 23–25.

"Under the Rose"
Tanner, Tony. *Thomas Pynchon*, 35–37.

QIAN ZHONGSHU

"The Cat"
Huters, Theodore. *Qian Zhongshu,* 111–117.

"God's Dream"
Huters, Theodore. *Qian Zhongshu,* 98–104.

"Inspiration"
Huters, Theodore. *Qian Zhongshu,* 104–105.

"Satan Pays an Evening Visit to Mr. Qian Zhongshu"
Huters, Theodore. *Qian Zhongshu,* 96–98.

"Souvenir"
Huters, Theodore. *Qian Zhongshu,* 105–110.

SEABURY GRANDIN QUINN

"The Jest of Warburg Tantaval"
Sampson, Robert. *Yesterday's Faces, II . . . ,* 111–112.

HORACIO QUIROGA

"A la deriva"
Arango, Manuel A. "Sobre dos cuentos de Horacio Quiroga: Correlación en el tema de la muerte, el ambiente y la estructura narrativa en 'A la deriva' y 'El hombre muerto,'" *Thesaurus,* 37, i (1982), 153–161.

"The Dead Man"
Arango, Manuel A. "Sobre dos cuentos . . . ," 153–161.
Brushwood, John S. "The Spanish American Short Story from Quiroga to Borges," in Peden, Margaret S., Ed. *The Latin American Short Story . . . ,* 73–74.
Earle, Peter G. "Dreams of Creation: Short Fiction in Spanish America," *Denver Q,* 12 (1977), 71.
Videla de Rivero, Gloria. "Sobre 'El hombre muerto' de Horacio Quiroga," *Explicación de Textos Literarios,* 12, i (1983–1984), 11–18.

"The Decapitated Chicken"
Brushwood, John S. ". . . Quiroga to Borges," 72–73.

"Juan Daríen"
Brushwood, John S. ". . . Quiroga to Borges," 73.

WILHELM RAABE

"Pfister's Mill"
Denkler, Horst. "Die Antwort literarischer Phantasie auf eine der 'grösseren Fragen der Zeit': Zu Wilhelm Raabe Erzähltext 'Pfisters Mühle,'" in Lensing, Leo A., and Peter Hans-Werner, Eds. *Wilhelm Raabe* . . . , 234–254.

THOMAS H. RADDALL

"Resurrection"
Young, Alan R. *Thomas H. Raddall*, 84–85.

"Triangle in Steel"
Young, Alan R. *Thomas H. Raddall*, 72–74.

VALENTIN GRIGOREVICH RASPUTIN

"Parting with Matera"
Dunlop, John B. "Valentin Rasputin's 'Proshchanie s materoĭ,'" in Bristol, Evelyn, Ed. *Russian Literature* . . . , 63–68.
Kluge, Rolf-Dieter. "Rasputin: 'Abschied von Matjora,'" in Zelinsky, Bodo, Ed. *Die russische Novelle*, 274–284.

TOM REAMY

"The Detweiler Boy"
Pierce, Hazel B. *A Literary Symbiosis* . . . , 224–225.

JOSÉ REVUELTAS

"The Abyss"
Slick, Sam L. *José Revueltas*, 108–109.

"Dream Matter"
Slick, Sam L. *José Revueltas*, 123–124.

"The Escape Plan"
Slick, Sam L. *José Revueltas*, 103–104.

"Ezekiel, or The Massacre of the Innocents"
Slick, Sam L. *José Revueltas*, 129–131.

"The Fall"
Slick, Sam L. *José Revueltas*, 110.

"God on This Earth"
Brushwood, John S. "The Spanish American Short Story from Quiroga to Borges," in Peden, Margaret S., Ed. *The Latin American Short Story* . . . , 95.
Slick, Sam L. *José Revueltas*, 100–101.

"The Green Heart"
Slick, Sam L. *José Revueltas*, 105–106.

"Green Is the Color of Hope"
Slick, Sam L. *José Revueltas*, 106.

"Hegel and I"
Slick, Sam L. *José Revueltas*, 131–133.

"The Hostile Sister"
Slick, Sam L. *José Revueltas*, 116–117.

"How Great Is That Darkness?"
Slick, Sam L. *José Revueltas*, 101–103.

"The Idiot"
Slick, Sam L. *José Revueltas*, 109.

"The Language of the Dispossessed"
Slick, Sam L. *José Revueltas*, 119–120.

"The Living God"
Slick, Sam L. *José Revueltas*, 104–105.

"The Men in the Swamp"
Slick, Sam L. *José Revueltas*, 114–115.

"Night of Epiphany"
Slick, Sam L. *José Revueltas*, 115–116.

"Pastoral Symphony"
Slick, Sam L. *José Revueltas*, 125–126.

"Preferences"
Slick, Sam L. *José Revueltas*, 107.

"Resurrection Without Life"
Slick, Sam L. *José Revueltas*, 126–127.

"The Sacred Word"
Slick, Sam L. *José Revueltas*, 117–119.

"Self-Spying"
Slick, Sam L. *José Revueltas*, 129.

"The Surrender"
Slick, Sam L. *José Revueltas*, 103.

"To Sleep on Earth"
Slick, Sam L. *José Revueltas*, 120–122.

"A Woman on Earth"
Slick, Sam L. *José Revueltas*, 107.

JEAN RHYS

"I Used to Live Here Once"
Bergman, David, Joseph de Roche, and Daniel M. Epstein. *Instructor's Manual . . .* , 7–8.

"On Not Shooting Sitting Birds"
Gardiner, Judith K. "'The Grave,' 'On Not Shooting Sitting Birds,' and the Female Esthetic," *Stud Short Fiction*, 20 (1983), 268–270.

JULIO RAMÓN RIBEYRO

"The Featherless Buzzards"
McMurray, George R. "The Spanish American Short Story from Borges to the Present," in Peden, Margaret S., Ed. *The Latin American Short Story . . .* , 109–110.

HENRY HANDEL RICHARDSON
[ETHEL FLORENCE LINDESAY RICHARDSON]

"And Women Must Weep"
Franklin, Carol. "Mansfield and Richardson: A Short Story Dialectic," *Australian Lit Stud*, 11 (1983), 227–233.

"The Coat"
Green, Dorothy. *Ulysses Bound . . .* , 467–477.

"Life and Death of Peterle Luthy"
Green, Dorothy. *Ulysses Bound . . .* , 409–410.

"Mary Christina" [originally titled "Death"]
Green, Dorothy. *Ulysses Bound . . .* , 418–422.

"The Professor's Experiment"
Green, Dorothy. *Ulysses Bound . . .* , 411–412.

"Succedaneum"
Green, Dorothy. *Ulysses Bound . . .* , 412–418.

"Two Hanged Women"
Green, Dorothy. *Ulysses Bound . . .* , 407–409.

"The Wrong Turning"
Green, Dorothy. *Ulysses Bound . . .* , 406–407.

TOMÁS RIVERA

"... and the earth did not part"
Rocard, Marcienne. "The Cycle of Chicano Experience in '... and the earth did not part' by Tomás Rivera," *Annales de l'Université,* [n.v.] (1973), 149–150.
Sommers, Joseph. "Interpreting Tomás Rivera," in Sommers, Joseph, and Tomás Ybarra-Frausto, Eds. *Modern Chicano Writers* . . . , 104–106.

"Christmas Eve"
Rocard, Marcienne. "The Cycle . . . ," 147–148.

"It Is Painful"
Rocard, Marcienne. "The Cycle . . . ," 146.
Testa, Daniel P. "Narrative Technique and Human Experience in Tomás Rivera," in Sommers, Joseph, and Tomás Ybarra-Frausto, Eds. *Modern Chicano Writers* . . . , 90.

"It Was a Silvery Night"
Rocard, Marcienne. "The Cycle . . . ," 148–149.

"The Lost Year"
Testa, Daniel P. "Narrative Technique . . . ," 90–91.

"The Portrait"
Rocard, Marcienne. "The Cycle . . . ," 147.

"A Prayer"
Testa, Daniel P. "Narrative Technique . . . ," 88.

"Under the House"
Rocard, Marcienne. "The Cycle . . . ," 150–151.
Testa, Daniel P. "Narrative Technique . . . ," 91–93.

"When We Arrive"
Rocard, Marcienne. "The Cycle . . . ," 145.
Testa, Daniel P. "Narrative Technique . . . ," 87–88.

RICHARD RIVES

"Rain"
Barnett, Ursula A. *A Vision of Order* . . . , 195–196.

AUGUSTO ROA BASTOS

"Encounter with the Traitor"
Saad, Gabriel. "Vacío semántico, relato, mutilación: Del cuento como encuentro con un traidor," *Revista de Crítica,* 10 (1984), 101–108.

"The Excavation"
McMurray, George R. "The Spanish American Short Story from Borges to the
Present," in Peden, Margaret S., Ed. *The Latin American Short Story* . . . ,
108–109.

"Lucha hasta el alba"
Esquerro, Milagros. "El cuento último-primero de Augusto Roa Bastos," *Revista
de Crítica*, 10 (1984), 117–124.

"To Tell a Story"
Horl, Sabine. "La forma como portador de significado: Acerca de 'Contar un
cuento' de Augusto Roa Bastos," *Revista de Crítica*, 10 (1984), 109–115.

ALAIN ROBBE-GRILLET

"The Secret Room"
Bogue, Ronald L. "A Generative Phantasy: Robbe-Grillet's 'La chambre se-
crete,'" *So Atlantic R*, 46 (November, 1981), 1–16.
Dietrich, R. F. "The Secret of Robbe-Grillet's 'The Secret Room,'" *Notes Contemp
Lit*, 12, ii (1982), 8–9; rpt. Dietrich, R. F., and Roger H. Sundell. *Instructor's
Manual* . . . , 4th ed., 140–141.
Madden, David. *Instructor's Manual* . . . , 5th ed., 59–62; Madden, David, and
Virgil Scott. *Instructor's Manual* . . . , 6th ed., 51–54.
Sirlin, Rhoda, and David H. Richter. *Instructor's Manual* . . . , 151–152.

MANUEL ROJAS

"The Glass of Milk"
Brushwood, John S. "The Spanish American Short Story from Quiroga to
Borges," in Peden, Margaret S., Ed. *The Latin American Short Story* . . . , 83.

LEON ROOKE

"Mama Tuddi Done Over"
Hancock, Geoff. "The Hi-Tech World of Leon Rooke," *Canadian Fiction Mag*,
38 (1981), 144.

JOÃO GUIMARÃES ROSA

"The Aldacious [sic] Navigator"
Vincent, Jon. *João Guimarães Rosa*, 92–93.

"Altar Piece of St. Never"
Vincent, Jon. *João Guimarães Rosa*, 136–137.

"The Appearance of the Shiny Stones"
Vincent, Jon. *João Guimarães Rosa*, 137–139.

"Augusto Matraga's Hour and Turn"
Vincent, Jon. *João Guimarães Rosa*, 34–37.

"Conversation Among Oxen"
Vincent, Jon. *João Guimarães Rosa*, 31–34.

"The Dagobé Brothers"
Vincent, Jon. *João Guimarães Rosa*, 100–101.

"Duel"
Vincent, Jon. *João Guimarães Rosa*, 22–24.

"Evil Beast"
Vincent, Jon. *João Guimarães Rosa*, 139–140.

"The Little Dust-Brown Donkey"
Vincent, Jon. *João Guimarães Rosa*, 17–19.

"The Man with the Snake"
Vincent, Jon. *João Guimarães Rosa*, 131–133.

"Mine Own People"
Vincent, Jon. *João Guimarães Rosa*, 24–26.

"The Mirror"
Vincent, Jon. *João Guimarães Rosa*, 102–103.

"Much Ado"
Vincent, Jon. *João Guimarães Rosa*, 97–99.

"My Friend the Fatalist"
Vincent, Jon. *João Guimarães Rosa*, 100–101.

"My Uncle the Jaguar"
Vincent, Jon. *João Guimarães Rosa*, 140–141.

"No Man, No Woman"
Vincent, Jon. *João Guimarães Rosa*, 96–97.

"Nothingness and the Human Condition"
Vincent, Jon. *João Guimarães Rosa*, 98–99.

"Notorious"
Vincent, Jon. *João Guimarães Rosa*, 100–101.

"Páramo"
Vincent, Jon. *João Guimarães Rosa*, 133–135.

"The Return of the Prodigal Husband"
Vincent, Jon. *João Guimarães Rosa*, 19–21.

"The Simple and Exact Story of the Captain's Donkey"
Vincent, Jon. *João Guimarães Rosa*, 127–129.

"The Straw Spinners"
Vincent, Jon. *João Guimarães Rosa*, 21–22.

"Tantarum, My Boss"
Vincent, Jon. *João Guimarães Rosa*, 98–99.

"The Thin Edge of Happiness"
Foster, David W. "Major Figures in the Brazilian Short Story," in Peden, Margaret S., Ed. *The Latin American Short Story . . .* , 16–17.

"The Third Bank of the River"
Foster, David W. "Major Figures . . . ," 17–19.
Vincent, Jon. *João Guimarães Rosa*, 98–99.

"The Transient Hats"
Vincent, Jon. *João Guimarães Rosa*, 129–131.

"Treetops"
Vincent, Jon. *João Guimarães Rosa*, 95–96.

"With Cowboy Mariano"
Vincent, Jon. *João Guimarães Rosa*, 141–143.

"Woodland Witchery"
Vincent, Jon. *João Guimarães Rosa*, 26–29.

"A Young Man, Gleaming, White"
Vincent, Jon. *João Guimarães Rosa*, 101–102.

ISAAC ROSENFELD

"The Hand That Fed Me"
Greenspan, Ezra. *The "Schlemiel" . . .* , 128–130.

"Joe the Janitor"
Greenspan, Ezra. *The "Schlemiel" . . .* , 124–126.

"King Solomon"
Greenspan, Ezra. *The "Schlemiel" . . .* , 134–136.

"My Landlady"
Greenspan, Ezra. *The "Schlemiel" . . .* , 126–128.

SINCLAIR ROSS

"Cornet at Night"
Harrison, Dick. *Unnamed Country . . .* , 143–144.

"A Day with Pegasus"
McMullen, Lorraine, Ed. . . . *Stories by Sinclair Ross*, 18–19.

"The Flowers That Killed Him"
McMullen, Lorraine, Ed. . . . *Stories by Sinclair Ross*, 20–21.

"Nell"
McMullen, Lorraine, Ed. . . . *Stories by Sinclair Ross*, 17–18.

"No Other Way"
McMullen, Lorraine, Ed. . . . *Stories by Sinclair Ross*, 15–17.

"One's a Heifer"
Whitman, F. H. "The Case of Ross's Mysterious Barn," *Canadian Lit*, 94 (1982),
    168–169.

"The Race"
McMullen, Lorraine, Ed. . . . *Stories by Sinclair Ross*, 19–20.

DANTE GABRIEL ROSSETTI

"Hand and Soul"
Pfordresher, John. "Dante Gabriel Rossetti's 'Hand and Soul': Sources and Sig-
    nificance," *Stud Short Fiction*, 19 (1982), 103–132.

EVDOKIA ROSTOPCHINA [pseudonym: CLAIRVOYANT]

"The Duel"
Mersereau, John. *Russian Romantic Fiction*, 280–282.

"Rank and Money"
Mersereau, John. *Russian Romantic Fiction*, 279–280.

PHILIP ROTH

"The Conversion of the Jews"
Greenspan, Ezra. *The "Schlemiel"* . . . , 201–202.
Guttmann, Allen. *The Jewish Writer* . . . , 65–66; rpt. Lewald, H. Ernest, Ed. *The
    Cry of Home* . . . , 252–253; Pinsker, Sanford, Ed. *Critical Essays* . . . , 172–
    173.
McDaniel, John N. *The Fiction* . . . , 51–58.
Madden, David. *Instructor's Manual* . . . , 5th ed., 101–102; Madden, David, and
    Virgil Scott. *Instructor's Manual* . . . , 6th ed., 111–113.

"Courting Disaster"
McDaniel, John N. *The Fiction* . . . , 180–189.

"Defender of the Faith"
Greenspan, Ezra. *The "Schlemiel"* . . . , 202–203.
Guttmann, Allen. *The Jewish Writer* . . . , 66–67; rpt. Pinsker, Sanford, Ed. *Critical Essays* . . . , 173–174.
Isaac, Dan. "In Defense of Philip Roth," *Chicago R*, 17, ii–iii (1964), 91–92; rpt. Pinsker, Sanford, Ed. *Critical Essays* . . . , 188–189.
Sirlin, Rhoda, and David H. Richter. *Instructor's Manual* . . . , 153–154.

"Eli the Fanatic"
Baumgarten, Murray. *City Scriptures* . . . , 43–44.
Bilik, Dorothy S. *Immigrant-Survivors* . . . , 46–47.
Greenspan, Ezra. *The "Schlemiel"* . . . , 206–210.
Guttmann, Allen. *The Jewish Writer* . . . , 70–72; rpt. Pinsker, Sanford, Ed. *Critical Essays* . . . , 176–178.
Isaac, Dan. "In Defense . . . ," 92–94; rpt. Pinsker, Sanford, Ed. *Critical Essays* . . . , 189–191.
McDaniel, John N. *The Fiction* . . . , 58–68.

"Epstein"
Isaac, Dan. "In Defense . . . ," 95; rpt. Pinsker, Sanford, Ed. *Critical Essays* . . . , 191–192.
McDaniel, John N. *The Fiction* . . . , 103–111.

"Ferdinand"
Morse, J. Mitchell. "Brand Names and Others," *Hudson R*, 22 (1969), 319; rpt. Pinsker, Sanford, Ed. *Critical Essays* . . . , 50.

"Goodbye, Columbus"
Beaty, Jerome. *The Norton Introduction* . . . , 538–541.
Greenspan, Ezra. *The "Schlemiel"* . . . , 203–206.
Guttmann, Allen. *The Jewish Writer* . . . , 67–70; rpt. Pinsker, Sanford, Ed. *Critical Essays* . . . , 174–175.
Isaac, Dan. "In Defense . . . ," 87–90; rpt. Pinsker, Sanford, Ed. *Critical Essays* . . . , 185–188.
McDaniel, John N. *The Fiction* . . . , 68–76.

"I Always Wanted You to Admire My Fasting"
Sheidley, William E., and Ann Charters. *Instructor's Manual* . . . , 179–180.

"It Was"
Morse, J. Mitchell. "Brand Names . . . ," 319–320; rpt. Pinsker, Sanford, Ed. *Critical Essays* . . . , 50–51.

"Letting Go"
McDaniel, John N. *The Fiction* . . . , 76–89, 116–120.

"Marriage à la Mode"
McDaniel, John N. *The Fiction* . . . , 191–195.

"Novotny's Pain"
McDaniel, John N. *The Fiction* . . . , 111–116.

"On the Air"
McDaniel, John N. *The Fiction . . .* , 150–160.

GABRIELLE ROY

"A Garden at the End of the World"
Chadbourne, Richard. "Two Visions of the Prairie: Willa Cather and Gabrielle Roy," in Chadbourne, Richard, and Hallvard Dahlie, Eds. *The New Land . . .* , 111.

"Ma grandmère tout-puissante"
Brazeau, J. Raymond. . . . *French Canadian Literature,* 12–13.

"La Route d'Altamont"
Brazeau, J. Raymond. . . . *French Canadian Literature,* 14.

"La Vallée Houdou"
Chadbourne, Richard. "Two Visions . . . ," 110–111.

"Le Vieillard et l'enfant"
Brazeau, J. Raymond. . . . *French Canadian Literature,* 13.

HUGHES RUDD

"Miss Euayla Is the Sweetest *Thang!*"
Klinkowitz, Jerome. *The Self-Apparent Word . . .* , 29–30.

JUAN RULFO

"Anacleto Morones"
Leal, Luis. *Juan Rulfo,* 57–58.

"At Daybreak"
Leal, Luis. *Juan Rulfo,* 46–49.

"The Burning Plain"
Leal, Luis. *Juan Rulfo,* 38–40.

"The Day of the Landslide"
Leal, Luis. *Juan Rulfo,* 58–60.

"Es que somos muy pobres"
Bockus Aponte, Barbara. "El niño como testigo: La visión infantil en el cuento hispanoamericano contemporáneo," *Explicación de Textos Literarios,* 11, i (1982), 19–23.
Minc, Rose S. "La contra-dicción como ley: Notas sobre 'Es que somos muy pobres,'" *Inti,* 13–14 (Spring-Fall, 1981), 83–91.

"The Heritage of Matilde Archangel"
Leal, Luis. *Juan Rulfo*, 60–62.
Lichtblau, Myron L. "El papel del narrador en 'La herencia de Matilda Arcángel,'" *Inti*, 13–14 (Spring-Fall, 1981), 92–102.

"The Hill of the *Comadres*"
Leal, Luis. *Juan Rulfo*, 32–33.

"Life Is Not Very Serious About Things"
Leal, Luis. *Juan Rulfo*, 23–25.

"Luvina"
Leal, Luis. *Juan Rulfo*, 49–50.

"Macario"
Bastos, María Luisa. "El discurso subversivo de Rulfo o la autoridad de la palabra alienda," *Inti*, 13–14 (Spring-Fall, 1981), 34–43.
Cantú, Roberto. "El relato como articulación infinita: 'Macario' y el arte de Juan Rulfo," *Palabra*, 4–5, i–ii (1982–1983), 107–126.
Leal, Luis. *Juan Rulfo*, 27–28.

"The Man"
Leal, Luis. *Juan Rulfo*, 44–46.

"The Night They Left Him Alone"
Leal, Luis. *Juan Rulfo*, 50–52.

"A Night's Fragment"
Leal, Luis. *Juan Rulfo*, 21–23.

"No Dogs Bark"
Leal, Luis. *Juan Rulfo*, 54–55.

"Nos han dado la tierra"
Ellis, Keith. "La función de la dualidad en 'Nos han dado la tierra' de Rulfo," trans. Robert Aulet, *Casa de las Americas*, 23 (March-April, 1983), 40–45.

"Paso del Norte"
Leal, Luis. *Juan Rulfo*, 55–-56.

"Remember"
Leal, Luis. *Juan Rulfo*, 52–53.

"Talpa"
Leal, Luis. *Juan Rulfo*, 36–38.

"'Tell Them Not to Kill Me!'"
Leal, Luis. *Juan Rulfo*, 40–42.

"They Gave Us the Land"
Leal, Luis. *Juan Rulfo*, 29–32.

340

"We're Very Poor"
Leal, Luis. *Juan Rulfo*, 34–36.
McMurray, George R. "The Spanish American Short Story from Borges to the
Present," in Peden, Margaret S., Ed. *The Latin American Short Story . . .* ,
107–108.

PHILIPP RUNGE

"Von dem Fischer un syner Fru"
Bichel, Ulf. "Philipp Otto Runges Märchen 'Von dem Fischer un syner Fru':
Sein Aufbau und seine Farbsymbolik," *Niederdeutsches Jahrbuch*, 105 (1982),
71–87.

JOANNA RUSS

When It Changed"
King, Betty. *Women of the Future . . .* , 174–175.
Podojil, Catherine. "Sisters, Daughters, and Aliens," in Riley, Dick, Ed. *Critical
Encounters [I] . . .* , 81–82.

BERTRAND RUSSELL

"The Corsican Ordeal of Miss X"
Shusterman, Richard. "Russell's Fiction and the Vanity of Human Knowledge,"
Mod Fiction Stud, 29 (1983), 680–681, 684. [Copyright 1984]

"The Infra-redioscope"
Shusterman, Richard. "Russell's Fiction . . . ," 682, 684–685.

"Satan in the Suburbs or Horrors Manufactured Here"
Shusterman, Richard. "Russell's Fiction . . . ," 681–682, 684, 685.

ERIC FRANK RUSSELL

". . . And Then There Were None"
Edwards, Malcolm. "Eric Frank Russell," in Bleiler, Everett F., Ed. *Science Fiction
Writers . . .* , 199–200.

"Design for Great-Day"
Edwards, Malcolm. "Eric Frank Russell," 199.

"Fast Falls the Eventide"
King, Betty. *Women of the Future . . .* , 96–97.

"Metamorphosis"
Edwards, Malcolm. "Eric Frank Russell," 198–199.

"Sole Solution"
Fabry, Heinz-Wilhelm, and Peter Wenzel. "Mythisch-religöse Themen in der
    Very Short Science Fiction Story: Eric Frank Russells 'Sole Solution' und
    Frederic Browns 'Answer,'" [sic] *Anglistik & Englishunterricht*, 23 (1984),
    129–140.

RAMAN SABALENKA

"Always on the Road"
Rich, Vera. "Jewish Themes and Characters in Belorussian Texts," in Blum,
    Jakub, and Vera Rich. *The Image of the Jew . . .* , 245–247.

FRED SABERHAGEN

"The Face of the Deep"
Stewart, A. D. "Fred Saberhagen, Cybernetic Psychologist: A Study of the Ber-
    serker Stories," *Extrapolation*, 18, i (1976), 44–45.

"Goodlife"
Stewart, A. D. "Fred Saberhagen . . . ," 45–46.

"In the Temple of Mars"
Stewart, A. D. "Fred Saberhagen . . . ," 45.

"Patron of the Arts"
Stewart, A. D. "Fred Saberhagen . . . ," 47–49.

"The Peacemaker"
Stewart, A. D. "Fred Saberhagen . . . ," 46–47.

"Starsong"
Stewart, A. D. "Fred Saberhagen . . . ," 48.

GHOLAMHOSAYN SA'EDI

"The Mourners of Bayal"
Komissarov, D. S. "Realistic Features of the Persian Novel and Story in the
    '60's," in Ricks, Thomas M., Ed. *Critical Perspectives . . .* , 156–158.

BHISHAM SAHNI

"Chief ki Davat"
Sinha, Raghuvir. "Bhisham Sahni: His Short Stories," *Indian Lit*, 22, v (1979),
    36–40.

SAKARUCHI ANGO

"Under the Forest of Cherry Trees in Full Bloom"
Keene, Donald. *Dawn to the West* . . . , 1079–1080.

SALVADOR SALAZAR ARRUÉ [same as SALVADOR SALARRUÉ]

"Buried Treasure"
Brushwood, John S. "The Spanish American Short Story from Quiroga to
Borges," in Peden, Margaret S., Ed. *The Latin American Short Story* . . . , 84.

J. D. SALINGER

"De Daumier-Smith's Blue Period"
Tierce, Mike. "Salinger's 'De Daumier-Smith's Blue Period,'" *Explicator,* 42, i
(1983), 56–57.

"For Esmé—With Love and Squalor"
Tierce, Mike. "Salinger's 'For Esmé—With Love and Squalor,'" *Explicator,* 42,
iii (1984), 56–57.

"Franny"
Karl, Frederick R. *American Fictions* . . . , 138–139.
Rose-Werle, Kordula. *Harlekinade* . . . , 111–114.

"Raise High the Roof Beam, Carpenters"
Karl, Frederick R. *American Fictions* . . . , 139–140.

"Seymour: An Introduction"
Bruffee, Kenneth A. *Elegiac Romance* . . . , 183–188.
Karl, Frederick R. *American Fictions* . . . , 140.
Yu, Beonggheon. *The Great Circle* . . . , 211–213.

"Teddy"
Yu, Beonggheon. *The Great Circle* . . . , 210–211.

"Zooey"
Karl, Frederick R. *American Fictions* . . . , 138–139.
Rose-Werle, Kordula. *Harlekinade* . . . , 94–111.

MIKHAIL EVGRAFOVICH SALTYKOV

"Glava"
Woldan, Alois. "Liebe als Lebensaporie: Eine Untersuchung zur poetischen
Welt von M. Saltykov-Ščedrins Erzälung 'Glava,'" *Wiener Slawistischer Al-
manach,* 12 (1983), 211–227.

IVAN SAMIAKIN

"The Bridge"
Rich, Vera. "Jewish Themes and Characters in Belorussian Texts," in Blum,
  Jakub, and Vera Rich. *The Image of the Jew . . . ,* 247–248.

"The Market Woman and the Poet"
Rich, Vera. "Jewish Themes . . . ," 210–212.

SCOTT SANDERS

"Touch the Earth"
King, Betty. *Women of the Future . . . ,* 222–224.

MARI SANDOZ

"Peachstone Basket"
Oehlschlaeger, Fritz. "Passion and Denial in Mari Sandoz's 'Peachstone Basket,'" *Great Plains Q,* 2 (1982), 106–113.

BIENVENIDO N. SANTOS

"Be American"
San Juan, E. *Toward a People's Literature . . . ,* 128–133.

"The Day the Dancers Came"
Kim, Elaine H. *Asian American Literature . . . ,* 269–271.
San Juan, E. *Toward a People's Literature . . . ,* 172–173.

"Scent of Apples"
San Juan, E. *Toward a People's Literature . . . ,* 172.

PAMELA SARGENT

"IMT"
King, Betty. *Women of the Future . . . ,* 175–176.

FRANK SARGESON

"An Attempt at an Explanation"
Norton, David [joint author]. "Two Views of Frank Sargeson's Short Stories,"
  in Hankin, Cherry, Ed. . . . *New Zealand Short Story,* 46–47.
Shaw, Helen [joint author]. "Two Views of Frank Sargeson's Short Stories," in
  Hankin, Cherry, Ed. . . . *New Zealand Short Story,* 32–33.

"The Colonel's Daughter"
Norton, David [joint author]. "Two Views . . . ," 56.

"A Great Day"
Norton, David [joint author]. "Two Views . . . ," 48–49.

"The Hole That Jack Dug"
Norton, David [joint author]. "Two Views . . . ," 54–55.

"I've Lost My Pal"
Norton, David [joint author]. "Two Views . . . ," 47–48.

"Just Trespassing, Thanks"
Norton, David [joint author]. "Two Views . . . ," 57–59.
Shaw, Helen [joint author]. "Two Views . . . ," 34.

"Old Man's Story"
Norton, David [joint author]. "Two Views . . . ," 52–53.

"A Pair of Socks"
Norton, David [joint author]. "Two Views . . . ," 50–52.

WILLIAM SAROYAN

"Baby"
Calonne, David S. *William Saroyan* . . . , 31–33.

"Citizens of the Third Grade"
Calonne, David S. *William Saroyan* . . . , 61–62.

"Countryman, How Do You Like America?"
Calonne, David S. *William Saroyan* . . . , 54–56.

"The Daring Young Man on the Flying Trapeze"
Calonne, David S. *William Saroyan* . . . , 15–17.

"The Journey and the Dream"
Calonne, David S. *William Saroyan* . . . , 45–46.

"The Man with the Heart in the Highlands"
Calonne, David S. *William Saroyan* . . . , 76–77.

"The Trains"
Calonne, David S. *William Saroyan* . . . , 38–40.

JEAN-PAUL SARTRE

"L'Ange du morbide"
Contat, Michel. "'L'Ange du morbide' ou le mystère de la femme qui crache,"
    in Issacharoff, Michael, and Jean-Claude Vilquin, Eds. *Sartre* . . . , 114–
    126.

"The Childhood of a Leader"
Brosman, Catharine S. *Jean-Paul Sartre*, 52–54.
Harvey, C. J. "Jean-Paul Sartre's 'L'Enfance d'un chef': The Longing for Obscenity," *Romance Notes*, 23 (1983), 204–209.

"Erostratus"
Brosman, Catharine S. *Jean-Paul Sartre*, 50–51.

"Intimacy"
Brosman, Catharine S. *Jean-Paul Sartre*, 51.

"The Room"
Brosman, Catharine S. *Jean-Paul Sartre*, 49–50.

"Strange Friendship"
Brosman, Catharine S. *Jean-Paul Sartre*, 69–70.

"The Wall"
Sirlin, Rhoda, and David H. Richter. *Instructor's Manual . . .* , 155–157.

SATOMI TON

"Early Summer in a Certain Year"
Keene, Donald. *Dawn to the West . . .* , 494–495.

JOSEPHINE SAXTON

"Elouise and the Doctors of Planet Pergamon"
White, David E. "Medical Morals and Narrative Necessity," in Myers, Robert E., Ed. *The Intersection . . .* , 189–190.

DOROTHY SAYERS

"The Abominable History of the Man with Copper Fingers"
Durkin, Mary B. *Dorothy Sayers*, 84–85.
Gaillard, Dawson. *Dorothy Sayers*, 18–20.

"The Adventurous Exploit of the Cave of Ali Baba"
Durkin, Mary B. *Dorothy Sayers*, 85–86.

"An Arrow O'er the House"
Gaillard, Dawson. *Dorothy Sayers*, 23–24.

"Bitter Almonds"
Durkin, Mary B. *Dorothy Sayers*, 93.

"Blood-Sacrifice"
Durkin, Mary B. *Dorothy Sayers*, 94–95.

NAT SCHACHNER

ARNO SCHMIDT

"Leviathan oder die Beste der Welten"
Kühlmann, Wilhelm. "Prekäre Positionen: Zu Arno Schmidts 'Leviathan oder die Beste der Welten,'" *Der Deutschunterricht*, 33, iii (1981), 62–71.
Thomé, Horst. "Wissenschaft und Spekulation in Arno Schmidts 'Leviathan,'" in Drew, Jörg, Ed. *Gebirgslandschaft mit Arno Schmidt . . .*, 9–29.

"Seascape with Pocahontas"
Ott, F. Peter. "Tradition and Innovation: An Introduction to the Prose Theory and Practice of Arno Schmidt," *Germ Q,* 51 (1978), 23–24.
Scheel, Kurt. "Wir zeigen uns den papierenen Mond: Die Mondmetaphern in Arno Schmidts 'Seelandschaft mit Pocahontas,'" in Drew, Jörg, Ed. *Gebirgslandschaft mit Arno Schmidt . . .*, 41–45.

"Die Umsiedler"
Minden, M. R. *Arno Schmidt . . .*, 45–48.

JAMES H. SCHMITZ

"The Witches of Karres"
King, Betty. *Women of the Future . . .*, 74–75.

A. J. SCHNEIDERS

"The Cannons"
Nieuwenhuys, Rob. *Mirror of the Indies . . .*," 245–246.

ARTHUR SCHNITZLER

"An Author's Last Letter"
Lawson, Richard H. "Poets and Physicians in Arthur Schnitzler's 'The Bachelor's Death' and 'An Author's Last Letter,'" in Peschel, Enid R., Ed. *Medicine . . .*, 51–54.

"The Bachelor's Death"
Lawson, Richard H. "Poets and Physicians . . .," 49–51.

OLIVE SCHREINER

"The Sunlight Lay Across My Bed"
Blake, Kathleen. *Love and the Woman Question . . .*, 220–221.

"Three Dreams in a Desert"
Blake, Kathleen. *Love and the Woman Question . . .*, 222–223.

GEORGE S. SCHUYLER

"Seldom Seen"
Peplow, Michael W. *George S. Schuyler*, 49–50.

LEONARDO SCIASCIA

"The American Aunt"
Jones, Verina R. "Leonardo Sciascia," in Caesar, Michael, and Peter Hainsworth, Eds. *Writers and Society . . .* , 241–242.

"The Death of Stalin"
Jones, Verina R. "Leonardo Sciascia," 239–240.

MOACYR SCLIAR

"A Balada do Falso Massias"
Lindstrom, Naomi. "Oracular Jewish Tradition in Two Works by Moacyr Scliar," *Luso-Brazilian R*, 21, ii (1984), 23–33.

"Os Profetas de Benjamin Bok"
Lindstrom, Naomi. "Oracular Jewish Tradition . . . ," 23–33.

ROBIN S. SCOTT

"Who Needs Insurance?"
Meyers, Walter E. *Aliens and Linguists . . .* , 34–35.

WALTER SCOTT

"The Two Drovers"
Gifford, Douglas, Ed. *Scottish Short Stories . . .* , 10.

ALLAN SEAGER

"The Street"
Connelly, Stephen E. *Allan Seager*, 23–27.

"This Town and Salamanca"
Connelly, Stephen E. *Allan Seager*, 26–29.

"The Unicorn"
Connelly, Stephen E. *Allan Seager*, 34–36.

G. EMMERSON SEARS

"Baxter's Beat"
Wu, William F. *The Yellow Peril . . .* , 50–51.

RICHARD SELZER

"An Act of Faith"
Peschel, Enid R. "Eroticism, Mysticism, and Surgery in the Writing of Richard
  Selzer," *Denver Q,* 16, i (1981), 90–91.

"The Harbinger"
Peschel, Enid R. "Eroticism . . . ," 88–90.

"Korea"
Peschel, Enid R. "'A Terrible Beauty Is Born': Richard Selzer's 'Korea,'" in
  Lévy, Angélique, Ed. *Le Mythe d'Etiemble . . . ,* 209–217.

OUSMANE SEMBÈNE

"Le Noire de . . . "
Blair, Dorothy S. *Senegalese Literature . . . ,* 83–84.

MAURICE SHADBOLT

"After the Depression"
Edmond, Lauris. "Definitions of New Zealanders: Stories of Maurice Shadbolt
  and Maurice Gee," in Hankin, Cherry, Ed. . . . *New Zealand Short Story,* 134–
  135.

"Knock on Yesterday's Door"
Edmond, Lauris. "Definitions . . . ," 135–136.

"Love Story"
Edmond, Lauris. "Definitions . . . ," 136–137.

"Maria"
Edmond, Lauris. "Definitions . . . ," 138–139.

"The Paua Gatherers"
Edmond, Lauris. "Definitions . . . ," 136.

KHOSROW SHAHANI

"The Hurricane"
Dorri, J. "National Traditions in Contemporary Persian Satirical Prose,
  1920's—1960's," in Ricks, Thomas M., Ed. *Critical Perspectives . . . ,* 141.

"Plastic Surgery"
Dorri, J. "National Traditions . . . ," 141.

LAMED SHAPIRO

"The Cross"
Roskies, David G. *Against the Apocalypse* . . . , 148–149.

"The Dead Town"
Roskies, David G. *Against the Apocalypse* . . . , 147–148.

"The Jewish State"
Roskies, David G. *Against the Apocalypse* . . . , 150–153.

"White Chalah"
Roskies, David G. *Against the Apocalypse* . . . , 153–155.

IRWIN SHAW

"Act of Faith"
Giles, James R. *Irwin Shaw*, 60–61.

"Circle of Light"
Giles, James R. *Irwin Shaw*, 41–42.

"The City Was in Total Darkness"
Giles, James R. *Irwin Shaw*, 50–51.

"The Climate of Insomnia"
Giles, James R. *Irwin Shaw*, 67–68.

"Dinner in a Good Restaurant"
Giles, James R. *Irwin Shaw*, 36–37.

"The Eighty-Yard Run"
Giles, James R. *Irwin Shaw*, 38–40.
Oriard, Michael. *Dreaming of Heroes* . . . , 155–157.

"Faith at Sea"
Giles, James R. *Irwin Shaw*, 55–56.

"Free Conscience, Void of Offense"
Giles, James R. *Irwin Shaw*, 51.

"Full Many a Flower"
Giles, James R. *Irwin Shaw*, 73–74.

"The Girls in Their Summer Dresses"
Abcarian, Richard, and Marvin Klotz. *Instructor's Manual* . . . , 3rd ed., 19–20.
Giles, James R. *Irwin Shaw*, 35–36.

"God Was Here, But He Left Early"
Giles, James R. *Irwin Shaw*, 76–78.

"Second Mortgage"
Giles, James R. *Irwin Shaw*, 46.

"The Sunny Banks of the River Lethe"
Giles, James R. *Irwin Shaw*, 40–41.

"Then We Were Three"
Giles, James R. *Irwin Shaw*, 69–70.

"Tip on a Dead Jockey"
Giles, James R. *Irwin Shaw*, 70–71.

"Walking Wounded"
Giles, James R. *Irwin Shaw*, 54–55.

"Weep in Years to Come"
Giles, James R. *Irwin Shaw*, 53–54.

"Welcome to the City"
Giles, James R. *Irwin Shaw*, 47–48.

"Where All Things Wise and Fair Descend"
Giles, James R. *Irwin Shaw*, 42–44.

"Whispers in Bedlam"
Giles, James R. *Irwin Shaw*, 73–74.

"A Year to Learn the Language"
Giles, James R. *Irwin Shaw*, 68–69.

ROBERT SHAW

"Appointment on Prila"
Madden, David, and Virgil Scott. *Instructor's Manual . . .* , 6th ed., 6–8.

ROBERT SHECKLEY

"Can You Feel Anything When I Do This?"
Morgan, Chris. "Robert Sheckley," in Bleiler, Everett F., Ed. *Science Fiction Writers . . .* , 498–499.

"The Cruel Equations"
Morgan, Chris. "Robert Sheckley," 499.

"Hands Off!"
Morgan, Chris. "Robert Sheckley," 498.

"A Thief in Time"
Morgan, Chris. "Robert Sheckley," 498.

"Watchbird"
Morgan, Chris. "Robert Sheckley," 501.

CHARLES SHEFFIELD

"Transition Team"
White, David E. "Medical Morals and Narrative Necessity," in Myers, Robert E.,
Ed. *The Intersection* . . . , 190.

SHEN TUAN-HSIEN [pseudonyms: SHEN TSAI-PAI and HSIA YENG]

"On Board a Ship"
Doležalová, Anna. "The Short Stories of *Creation Daily*," *Asian & African Stud*,
9 (1973), 61.

LEV SHEYNIN

"The Semenchuk Affair"
Blum, Jakub. "Soviet Russian Literature," in Blum, Jakub, and Vera Rich. *The
Image of the Jew* . . . , 70.

BORIS SHIBAEV

"Can This Be?"
Mersereau, John. *Russian Romantic Fiction,* 228.

SHIGA NAOYA

"All the Way to Abashiri"
Keene, Donald. *Dawn to the West* . . . , 460–461.

SHIMA RINZŌ

"In the Heavy Flow"
Keene, Donald. *Dawn to the West* . . . , 992–993.

"Midnight Feast"
Keene, Donald. *Dawn to the West* . . . , 989–991.

MIKHAIL SHOLOKOV

"The Science of Hatred"
Ermolaev, Herman. *Mikhail Sholokov* . . . , 129–130.

"The Wind"
Ermolaev, Herman. *Mikhail Sholokov* . . . , 15–16.

J[OSEPH] H[ENRY] SHORTHOUSE

"An Apologue"
Wagner, F. J. *J. H. Shorthouse*, 113–114.

"The Baroness Helena von Saarfeld"
Wagner, F. J. *J. H. Shorthouse*, 111–112.

"Ellie: A Story of a Boy and Girl"
Wagner, F. J. *J. H. Shorthouse*, 113.

"The Marquis Jeanne Hyacinthe de St. Palaye"
Wagner, F. J. *J. H. Shorthouse*, 110–111.

"A Teacher of the Violin"
Wagner, F. J. *J. H. Shorthouse*, 107–108.

WILLIAM WIRT SIKES

"Absalom Mather"
Cohn, Jan. "The Negro Character in Northern Magazine Fiction of the 1860's,"
    New England Q, 43 (1970), 579.

LESLIE SILKO

"Yellow Woman"
Madden, David. *Instructor's Manual* . . . , 5th ed., 113–114; Madden, David, and
    Virgil Scott. *Instructor's Manual* . . . , 6th ed., 129–131.

ROBERT SILVERBERG

"After the Myths Went Home"
Fredericks, Casey. *The Future of Eternity* . . . , 1–4.

"Breckenridge and the Continuum"
Clareson, Thomas D. *Robert Silverberg*, 81–82.

"Caliban"
Clareson, Thomas D. *Robert Silverberg*, 77–78.

"A Happy Day in 2381"
Clareson, Thomas D. *Robert Silverberg*, 60–62.

"In Entropy's Jaws"
Clareson, Thomas D. *Robert Silverberg*, 80–81.

"Mind for Business"
Clareson, Thomas D. *Robert Silverberg*, 18–19.

"New Men for Mars"
Clareson, Thomas D. *Robert Silverberg*, 17.

"Nightwings"
Edwards, Malcolm. "Robert Silverberg," in Bleiler, Everett F., Ed. *Science Fiction Writers . . .* , 507–508.

"Passengers"
Clareson, Thomas D. *Robert Silverberg*, 33–34.

"Road to Nightfall"
Clareson, Thomas D. *Robert Silverberg*, 15–16.

"Sundance"
Clareson, Thomas D. *Robert Silverberg*, 76–77.
Edwards, Malcolm. "Robert Silverberg," 507.

"Translation Error"
Clareson, Thomas D. *Robert Silverberg*, 19–20.

"Warm Man"
Clareson, Thomas D. *Robert Silverberg*, 31–32.

CLIFFORD D. SIMAK

"The Big Front Yard"
Tweet, Roald D. "Clifford D. Simak," in Bleiler, Everett F., Ed. *Science Fiction Writers . . .* , 517.

"City"
Tweet, Roald D. "Clifford D. Simak," 515.

"A Death in the House"
Tweet, Roald D. "Clifford D. Simak," 517.

"Desertion"
Wolfe, Gary K. "Autoplastic and Alloplastic Adaptations in Science Fiction: 'Waldo' and 'Desertion,'" in Slusser, George E., Eric S. Rabkin, and Robert Scholes, Eds. *Coordinates . . .* , 74–77.

"Huddling Place"
White, David E. "Medical Morals and Narrative Necessity," in Myers, Robert E., Ed. *The Intersection . . .* , 190–191.

WILLIAM GILMORE SIMMS

"Grayling"
Ringe, Donald A. *American Gothic* . . . , 7–8.

MAY SINCLAIR

"The Flaw in the Crystal"
Kinnamon, Rebecca. "May Sinclair's *Uncanny Stories,*" *Engl Lit Transition,* 26 (1983), 187–189.

ISAAC BASHEVIS SINGER

"The Admirer"
Fisch, Harold. *A Remembered Future* . . . , 158–159.

"Blood"
Sheridan, Judith R. "Isaac Bashevis Singer: Sex as Cosmic Metaphor," *Midwest Q,* 23 (1982), 375–376.

"A Crown of Feathers"
Sheidley, William E., and Ann Charters. *Instructor's Manual* . . . , 126–127.

"The Gentleman from Cracow"
Sinclair, Clive. *The Brothers* . . . , 31–33.

"Gimpel the Fool"
Kennedy, X. J. *Instructor's Manual* . . . , 3rd ed., 23–25.
Madden, David. *Instructor's Manual* . . . , 5th ed., 94; Madden, David, and Virgil Scott. *Instructor's Manual* . . . , 6th ed., 104–105.
Siegel, Paul N. "Gimpel and the Archetype of the Wise Fool," in Allentuck, Marcia, Ed. *The Achievement* . . . , 159–173.
Sinclair, Clive. *The Brothers* . . . , 45–46.
Sirlin, Rhoda, and David H. Richter. *Instructor's Manual* . . . , 158–159.

"Grandfather and Grandson"
Sinclair, Clive. *The Brothers* . . . , 100.

"The Last Demon"
Roskies, David G. *Against the Apocalypse* . . . , 192–195.

"The Little Shoemaker"
Baumgarten, Murray. *City Scriptures* . . . , 47–52.

"Short Friday"
Sheridan, Judith R. ". . . Sex as Cosmic Metaphor," 370–371.

"The Spinoza of Market Street"
Baumgarten, Murray. *City Scriptures* . . . , 26–27.
Sheridan, Judith R. ". . . Sex as Cosmic Metaphor," 372–373.

"The Third One"
Collins, Robert G. "Beyond Argument: Post-Marital Man in John Cheever's Late Fiction," *Mosaic*, 17 (1984), 261–263.

"Zlateh the Goat"
Wolf, H. R. "Universalism and the Rankian Hero," in Allentuck, Marcia, Ed. *The Achievement . . .* , 151–152.

IQBAL SINGH

"When One Is in It"
Kishtainy, Khalid. *The Prostitute . . .* , 67.

ANDREY SINYAVSKY [ABRAM TERTZ]

"At the Circus"
Durkin, Andrew R. "Narrator, Metaphor, and Theme in Sinjavskij's *Fantastic Tales*," *Slavic & East European J*, 24 (1980), 141–142.

"Graphomaniacs"
Clardy, Jesse V. and Betty S. *The Superfluous Man . . .* , 153–157.
Durkin, Andrew R. "Narrator . . . ," 137–138.

"The Icicle"
Clardy, Jesse V. and Betty S. *The Superfluous Man . . .* , 150–153.
Durkin, Andrew R. "Narrator . . . ," 138–140.

"Pxenc"
Brown, Edward J. . . . *Since the Revolution*, 3rd ed., 245–246.
Durkin, Andrew R. "Narrator . . . ," 133–135.
Kolonosky, Walter F. "Inherent and Ulterior Design in Sinjavskij's 'Pxenc,'" *Slavic & East European J*, 26 (1982), 329–337.

"Tenants"
Durkin, Andrew R. "Narrator . . . ," 135–137.

"Tiny Tsores"
Brown, Edward J. . . . *Since the Revolution*, 3rd ed., 246–247.

"You and I"
Brown, Edward J. . . . *Since the Revolution*, 3rd ed., 248.
Durkin, Andrew R. "Narrator . . . ," 140–141.

ANTONIO SKARMETA

"First Grade"
McMurray, George R. "The Spanish American Short Story from Borges to the Present," in Peden, Margaret S., Ed. *The Latin American Short Story . . .* , 131, 132.

"The Phone Call"
McMurray, George R. ". . . Borges to the Present," 131, 132.

IOAN SLAVICI

"Zina Zorilor"
Simms, Norman. "Ioan Slavici's 'Zina Zorilor': Boundaries and Blindness and
    the Ambiguities of Moral Determination," *Miorita*, 8, i–ii (1983), 51–76.

HENRY SLESAR

"After"
Pierce, Hazel B. *A Literary Symbiosis . . .* , 118.

CLARK ASHTON SMITH

"The City of the Singing Flame"
Stableford, Brian M. "Clark Ashton Smith," in Bleiler, Everett F., Ed. *Science
    Fiction Writers . . .* , 141.

CORDWAINER SMITH [PAUL MYRON ANTHONY LINEBARGER]

"The Game of Rats and Dragons"
Elms, Alan C. "The Creation of Cordwainer Smith," *Sci-Fiction Stud,* 11 (1984),
    276–278.

"Scanners Live in Vain"
Elms, Alan C. "The Creation . . . ," 274–276.
Wolfe, Gary K. "Instrumentalities of the Body: The Mechanization of Human
    Form in Science Fiction," in Dunn, Thomas P., and Richard D. Erlich, Eds.
    The Mechanical God . . . , 213–216.

CORDWAINER SMITH [PAUL MYRON ANTHONY LINEBARGER]
and GENEVIEVE LINEBARGER

"The Lady Who Sailed the *Soul*"
King, Betty. *Women of the Future . . .* , 130–131.

LEE SMITH

"All the Days of Our Lives"
Goodwyn, Anne J. "The World of Lee Smith," in Prenshaw, Peggy W., Ed.
    Women Writers . . . , 246.

"Artists"
Goodwyn, Anne J. "The World . . . ," 263.

"Between the Lines"
Goodwyn, Anne J. "The World . . . ," 263–264.

"Cakewalk"
Goodwyn, Anne J. "The World . . . ," 250–251.

"Mrs. Darcy Meets the Blue-Eyed Stranger at the Beach"
Goodwyn, Anne J. "The World . . . ," 250.

"Saint Paul"
Goodwyn, Anne J. "The World . . . ," 249.

FËDOR SOLOGUB [FËDOR KUZ'MICH TETERNIKOV]

"Dream on the Rocks"
Ivanits, Linda J. "Fairy Tale Motifs in Sologub's 'Dream on the Rocks,'" in
    Leighton, Lauren G., Ed. *Studies in Honor . . .* , 81–87.

"In Bondage"
Hart, Pierre R. "Functions of the Fairy Tale in Sologub's Prose," in Leighton,
    Lauren G., Ed. *Studies in Honor . . .* , 72–77.

"Turandina"
Hart, Pierre R. "Functions of the Fairy Tale . . . ," 77–79.

ALEXANDER SOLZHENITSYN

"The Right Hand"
Sirlin, Rhoda, and David H. Richter. *Instructor's Manual . . .* , 160–162.

"Zakhar the Pouch"
Sheidley, William E., and Ann Charters. *Instructor's Manual . . .* , 145–146.

EDITH SOMERVILLE

"The Finger of Mrs. Knox"
Schirmer, Gregory A. "Tales from Big House and Cabin: The Nineteenth Cen-
    tury," in Kilroy, James F., Ed. *The Irish Short Story . . .* , 41–42.

"The Last Day of Shraft"
Schirmer, Gregory A. "Tales from Big House . . . ," 42–43.

OREST SOMOV

"A Command from the Other World"
Mersereau, John. *Russian Romantic Fiction*, 88–90.

"An Epigraph in Place of a Title"
Mersereau, John. *Russian Romantic Fiction*, 194–198.

"The Fearful Guest"
Mersereau, John. *Russian Romantic Fiction*, 115.

"Kikimora—The Story of a Russian Peasant on the Highroad"
Mersereau, John. *Russian Romantic Fiction*, 118–120.

"Matchmaking"
Mersereau, John. *Russian Romantic Fiction*, 188–190.

"Mommy and Sonny"
Mersereau, John. *Russian Romantic Fiction*, 190–194.

"The Suicide"
Mersereau, John. *Russian Romantic Fiction*, 115–118.

FERNANDO SORRENTINO

"The Fetid Tale of Antulin"
McMurray, George R. "The Spanish American Short Story from Borges to the
    Present," in Peden, Margaret S., Ed. *The Latin American Short Story . . . ,*
    128.

PEDRO JUAN SOTO

"Scribbles"
McMurray, George R. "The Spanish American Short Story from Borges to the
    Present," in Peden, Margaret S., Ed. *The Latin American Short Story . . . ,*
    110–111.

WOLE SOYINKA

"Egbe's Sworn Enemy"
Lindfors, Bernth. *Early Nigerian Literature*, 143–153.

"A Tale of Two Cities" [in *Gryphon*]
Lindfors, Bernth. *Early Nigerian Literature*, 125–126.

"A Tale of Two Cities" [in *New Nigeria Forum*]
Lindfors, Bernth. *Early Nigerian Literature*, 126.

MURIEL SPARK

"Bang, Bang—You're Dead"
Hubbard, Tom. "The Liberated Instant: Muriel Spark and the Short Story," in
    Bold, Alan, Ed. *Muriel Spark . . . ,* 177.

"Black Madonna"
Whittaker, Ruth. *The Faith and Fiction* . . . , 46–48.

"The Go-Away Bird"
Hubbard, Tom. "The Liberated Instant . . . ," 176–177.
Richmond, Velma B. *Muriel Spark*, 62.
Whittaker, Ruth. *The Faith and Fiction* . . . , 134–137.

"A Member of the Family"
Hubbard, Tom. "The Liberated Instant . . . ," 178.

"The Ormolu Clock"
Hubbard, Tom. "The Liberated Instant . . . ," 171–173.

"You Should Have Seen the Mess"
Hubbard, Tom. "The Liberated Instant . . . ," 174.

ELIZABETH SPENCER

"Ship Island: The Story of a Mermaid"
Prenshaw, Peggy W. "Mermaids, Angels and Free Women: The Heroines of
Elizabeth Spencer's Fiction," in Prenshaw, Peggy W., Ed. *Women Writers* . . . ,
152–154.

MICKEY SPILLANE

"The Bastard Bannerman"
Van Dover, J. Kenneth. *Murder in the Millions* . . . , 144.

"The Flier"
Banks, R. Jeff. "Spillane's Anti-Establishment Heroes," in Landrum, Larry N.,
Pat Browne, and Ray B. Browne, Eds. *Dimensions of Detective Fiction*, 138.

"Kick It or Kill!"
Banks, R. Jeff. "Spillane's . . . Heroes," 135–136.

"Killer Mine"
Banks, R. Jeff. "Spillane's . . . Heroes," 134–135.
Van Dover, J. Kenneth. *Murder in the Millions* . . . , 143.

"The Seven-Year Kill"
Banks, R. Jeff. "Spillane's . . . Heroes," 139.

HARRIET PRESCOTT SPOFFORD

"The Amber Gods"
St. Armand, Barton Levi. " 'I Must Have Died at Ten Minutes Past One': Post-
humous Reverie in Harriet Prescott Spofford's 'The Amber Gods,' " in
Kerr, Howard, John W. Crowley, and Charles L. Crow, Eds. *The Haunted
Dusk* . . . , 103–116.

MARGUERITE STABLER

"The Sale of Sooy Yet"
Wu, William F. *The Yellow Peril* . . . , 54–55.

JEAN STAFFORD

"The Darkening Moon"
Walsh, Mary E. W. "The Young Girl in the West: Disenchantment in Jean
    Stafford's Short Fiction," in Stauffer, Helen W., and Susan J. Rosowski,
    Eds. . . . *Western American Literature,* 240–241.

"The Interior Castle"
Leary, William G. "Through Caverns Measureless to Man: Jean Stafford's 'The
    Interior Castle,'" *Shenandoah,* 34, iv (1983), 79–95.

"The Mountain Day"
Walsh, Mary E. W. "The Young Girl . . . ," 239–240.

"A Summer Day"
Walsh, Mary E. W. "The Young Girl . . . ," 239.

OLAF STAPLEDON

"Arms Out of Hand"
McCarthy, Patrick A. *Olaf Stapledon,* 132–133.

"The Man Who Became a Tree"
McCarthy, Patrick A. *Olaf Stapledon,* 131–132.

WALLACE STEGNER

"The Blue-Winged Teal"
*Canzoneri, Robert. "Wallace Stegner: Trial by Existence," in Arthur, Anthony,
    Ed. *Critical Essays* . . . , 72.

"The City of the Living"
*Canzoneri, Robert. "Wallace Stegner . . . ," 72–73.

"The Double Corner"
*Canzoneri, Robert. "Wallace Stegner . . . ," 70.

"Two Rivers"
*Canzoneri, Robert. "Wallace Stegner . . . ," 69–70.

"The View from the Balcony"
*Canzoneri, Robert. "Wallace Stegner . . . ," 71.

"The Women on the Wall"
*Canzoneri, Robert. "Wallace Stegner . . . ," 70–71.

GERTRUDE STEIN

"As a Wife Has a Cow"
Sheidley, William E., and Ann Charters. *Instructor's Manual . . .* , 57–58.

"The Gentle Lena"
Walker, Jayne L. *The Making . . .* , 24–27.

"The Good Anna"
Walker, Jayne L. *The Making . . .* , 19–23.

"Melanctha"
Cohen, Milton A. "Black Brutes and Mulatto Saints: The Racial Hierarchy of
    Stein's 'Melanctha,'" *Black Am Lit Forum*, 18 (1984), 119–121.
Hilfer, Anthony C. *The Ethics of Intensity . . .* , 143–162.
Ikonné, Chidi. *From Du Bois to Van Vechten . . .* , 19–22.
Walker, Jayne L. *The Making . . .* , 29–41.

"Miss Furr and Miss Skeene"
Walker, Jayne L. *The Making . . .* , 80–81.

"Nadelman"
Walker, Jayne L. *The Making . . .* , 85–87.

"*Q.E.D.*"
Walker, Jayne L. *The Making . . .* , 34–38.

"A Water-fall and a Piano"
Bassoff, Bruce. *The Secret Sharers . . .* , 134–136.

JOHN STEINBECK

"The Chrysanthemums"
Bergman, David, Joseph de Roche, and Daniel M. Epstein. *Instructor's Man-
    ual . . .* , 50.
*Dietrich, R. F. "'The Chrysanthemums,'" in Dietrich, R. F., and Roger H.
    Sundell. *Instructor's Manual . . .* , 80–84.
Kennedy, X. J. and Dorothy M. *Instructor's Manual . . .* , 3rd ed., 39–41.
Rohrberger, Mary. "The Question of Regionalism: Limitation and Transcen-
    dence," in Stevick, Philip, Ed. *The American Short Story, 1900–1945*, 179–
    180.

"Flight"
Allen, Mary. *Animals . . .* , 128–129.

"The Leader of the People"
Work, James C. "Coordinate Forces in 'The Leader of the People,'" *Western Am
    Lit*, 16 (1982), 278–289.

"The Murder"
Owens, Louis. "Steinbeck's 'The Murder': Illusions of Chivalry," *Steinbeck Q,* 17
(1984), 10–14.

"The Snake"
Rohrberger, Mary. "The Question . . . ," 180–182.

"The White Quail"
Renner, Stanley. "Sexual Idealism and Violence in 'The White Quail,'" *Steinbeck
Q,* 17 (1984), 76–87.
Rohrberger, Mary. "The Question . . . ," 180.

CARL STERNHEIM

"Busekow"
Dedner, Burghard. *Carl Sternheim,* 103–104.

"Heidenstam"
Dedner, Burghard. *Carl Sternheim,* 118–120.

"Meta"
Dedner, Burghard. *Carl Sternheim,* 116.

"Schuhlin"
Dedner, Burghard. *Carl Sternheim,* 105–106.

"Vanderbilt"
Dedner, Burghard. *Carl Sternheim,* 102–103.

ROBERT LOUIS STEVENSON

"The Beach of Falesá"
Mulholland, Honor. "Robert Louis Stevenson and the Romance Form," in Noble, Andrew, Ed. *Robert Louis Stevenson,* 112–114.

"Edifying Letters of the Rutherford Family"
Swearingen, Roger G., Ed. *A Newly Discovered Long Story . . . ,* 22–23.

"The House of Eld"
Mulholland, Honor. ". . . Romance Form," 110–111.

"A Lodging for the Night"
Shaw, Valerie. *The Short Story . . . ,* 37–38.

"Markheim"
Miyoshi, Masao. *The Divided Self . . . ,* 294–296.

"The Merry Men"
Block, Ed. "James Sully, Evolutionist Psychology, and Late Victorian Gothic
Fiction," *Victorian Stud,* 25 (1982), 458–459.
Gifford, Douglas, Ed. *Scottish Short Stories . . . ,* 13–15.

"Olalla"

Block, Ed. "James Sully . . . ," 459–460.
Graham, Kenneth. "Stevenson and Henry James: A Crossing," in Noble, Andrew, Ed. *Robert Louis Stevenson*, 37–46.

"An Old Song"

Swearingen, Roger G., Ed. *A Newly Discovered Long Story . . .* , 13–16.

"The Strange Case of Dr. Jekyll and Mr. Hyde"

Apter, T. E. *Fantasy Literature . . .* , 48–49.
Beaty, Jerome. *The Norton Introduction . . .* , 137–140.
Block, Ed. "James Sully . . . ," 452–458.
Fraustino, Daniel V. " 'Dr. Jekyll and Mr. Hyde': Anatomy of Misperception," *Arizona Q,* 38 (1982), 235–240.
Good, Graham. "Rereading Robert Louis Stevenson," *Dalhousie R,* 62 (1982), 56–57.
Hawthorn, Jeremy. *Multiple Personality . . .* , 63–65.
Jefford, Andrew. "Dr. Jekyll and Professor Nabokov: Reading a Reading," in Noble, Andrew, Ed. *Robert Louis Stevenson,* 47–71.
Miyoshi, Masao. *The Divided Self . . .* , 296–301.
*Saposnik, Irving S. "The Anatomy of 'Dr. Jekyll and Mr. Hyde,' " in Geduld, Harry M., Ed. *The Definitive . . . Companion,* 108–117.

THE STEVENSONS [no further identification]

"Chinatown: My Land of Dreams"

Wu, William F. *The Yellow Peril . . .* , 66–67.

ADALBERT STIFTER

"Abdias"

Swales, Martin and Erika. *Adalbert Stifter . . .* , 57–67.

"Brigitta"

Hunter-Loughed, Rosemarie. "Adalbert Stifter: 'Brigitta,' " in Lützeler, Paul M., Ed. *Romane und Erzählungen . . .* , 354–385.
Meier, Albert. "Diskretes Erzählen: Über den Zusammenhang von Dichtung, Wissenschaft und Didaktik in Adalbert Stifters Erzählung 'Brigitta,' " *Aurora,* 44 (1984), 213–223.
Sjögren, Christine O. "The Allure of Beauty in Stifter's 'Brigitta,' " *J Engl & Germ Philol,* 81 (1982), 47–54.
Swales, Martin and Erika. *Adalbert Stifter . . .* , 97–107.

"Confidence"

Swales, Martin and Erika. *Adalbert Stifter . . .* , 171–172.

"The Elderly Bachelor"

Swales, Martin and Erika. *Adalbert Stifter . . .* , 86–95.

"Fools' Castle"
Domandl, Sepp. "Wiedegeburt aus der Schönheit: Der 'Kern' in Adalbert Stifters 'Nachsommer,'" *Adalbert Stifter Institut*, 32, i–ii (1983), 45–60.
Hohendahl, Peter U. "Die gebildete Gemeinschaft: Stifters 'Nachsommer' als Utopie der ästhetischen Erziehung," in Vosskamp, Wilhelm, Ed. *Utopieforschung* . . . , 333–356.

"Der fromme Spruch"
Swales, Martin and Erika. *Adalbert Stifter* . . . , 165–171.

"Granite"
Swales, Martin and Erika. *Adalbert Stifter* . . . , 142–155.

"The Kiss of Sentze"
Swales, Martin and Erika. *Adalbert Stifter* . . . , 161–165.

"Limestone"
Swales, Martin and Erika. *Adalbert Stifter* . . . , 205–217.

"Mica"
Swales, Martin and Erika. *Adalbert Stifter* . . . , 183–191.

"The Old Seal"
Angress, R[uth] K. "Das Ehebruchmotiv in Stifters 'Das alte Siegel': Ein Beitrag zur Literaturgeschichte der bürgerlichen Erotik," *Zeitschrift für Deutsche Philologie*, 103 (1984), 481–502.
Swales, Martin and Erika. *Adalbert Stifter* . . . , 75–86.

"The Primeval Forest"
Swales, Martin and Erika. *Adalbert Stifter* . . . , 49–57.

"Prokopus"
Swales, Martin and Erika. *Adalbert Stifter* . . . , 67–69.

"Rock Crystal"
Sinka, Margrit M. "Unappreciated Symbol: The *Unglückssäule* in Stifter's 'Bergkristall,'" *Mod Austrian Lit*, 16, ii (1983), 1–17.

"Turmaline"
Swales, Martin and Erika. *Adalbert Stifter* . . . , 173–183.

"The Wanderer in the Forest"
Swales, Martin and Erika. *Adalbert Stifter* . . . , 69–75.

GRANT STOCKBRIDGE [NORVELL W. PAGE?]

"Dragon Lord of the Underworld"
Wu, William F. *The Yellow Peril* . . . , 192–196.

LESLIE F. STONE

"The Conquest of Gola"
Cioffi, Frank. *Formula Fiction?* . . . , 128–131.

THEODOR STORM

"Ein Bekenntnis"
Terpstra, Jan U. "Die Motivik des Visionären und Märchenhaften in Storms Novelle 'Ein Bekenntnis' als archetypischer Ausdruck des Unbewussten," in Schönau, Walter, Ed. *Literaturpsychologische Studien* . . . , 131–168.

"Marthe and Her Clock"
Jackson, David. "Theodor Storm's 'Marthe und ihr Uhr,'" *Trivium*, 19 (May, 1984), 39–53.

RANDOLPH STOW

"Dokónikan"
Willbanks, Ray. *Randolph Stow*, 136.

"Magic"
Willbanks, Ray. *Randolph Stow*, 135.

HARRIET BEECHER STOWE

"The Deacon's Dilemma; or The Use of the Beautiful"
Donovan, Josephine. *New England Local Color* . . . , 54.

"The Yankee Girl"
Donovan, Josephine. *New England Local Color* . . . , 55–56.

T. S. STRIBLING

"Passage to Benares"
Pierce, Hazel B. *A Literary Symbiosis* . . . , 38–39.

AUGUST STRINDBERG

"Bad Luck"
Lamm, Martin. *August Strindberg*, 143–144.

"Battle of the Brains"
Lagercrantz, Olof. *August Strindberg*, 156–157.

"The Breadwinner"
Lamm, Martin. *August Strindberg*, 158–159.

ARKADY and BORIS STRUGATSKY

"Almost the Same"
McGuire, Patrick L. "Future History, Soviet Style: The Work of the Strugatsky
    Brothers," in Staicar, Tom, Ed. *Critical Encounters II . . .* , 107–108.

"The Conspirators"
McGuire, Patrick L. "Future History . . . ," 110–111.

"The Fellow from Hell"
McGuire, Patrick L. "Future History . . . ," 119.

"The Kid"
McGuire, Patrick L. "Future History . . . ," 117–119.

DON A. STUART [pseudonym of JOHN W. CAMPBELL]

"Night"
Bleiler, Everett F. "John W. Campbell," in Bleiler, Everett F., Ed. *Science Fiction
    Writers . . .* , 155.

"Twilight"
Bleiler, Everett F. "John W. Campbell," 154–155.

"Who Goes There?"
Bleiler, Everett F. "John W. Campbell," 155.

JESSE STUART

"Another Hanging"
Rohrberger, Mary. "The Question of Regionalism: Limitation and Transcen-
    dence," in Stevick, Philip, Ed. *The American Short Story, 1900–1945*, 157–
    158.

"Frog Trouncin' Contest"
Sundell, Roger H. " 'Frog Trouncin' Contest,' " in Dietrich, R. F., and Roger H.
    Sundell. *Instructor's Manual . . .* , 4th ed., 25–29.

"My Father Is an Educated Man"
Rohrberger, Mary. "The Question . . . ," 155–156.

THEODORE STURGEON

"Affair with a Great Monkey"
Diskin, Lahna F. *Theodore Sturgeon*, 46–47.

"Bright Segment"
Menger, Lucy. *Theodore Sturgeon*, 113–114.

"Brownshoes" [originally titled "The Man Who Learned Loving"]
Diskin, Lahna F. *Theodore Sturgeon*, 49–50.
Menger, Lucy. *Theodore Sturgeon*, 95–97.

"Dazed"
Menger, Lucy. *Theodore Sturgeon*, 99–102.

"The Education of Drusilla Strange"
Menger, Lucy. *Theodore Sturgeon*, 57–58.

"Extrapolation"
Sackmary, Regina. "An Ideal of Three: The Art of Theodore Sturgeon," in
    Riley, Dick, Ed. *Critical Encounters [I]* . . . , 137–138.

"Fear Is a Business"
Menger, Lucy. *Theodore Sturgeon*, 56–57.

"The Hurkle Is a Happy Beast"
Diskin, Lahna F. *Theodore Sturgeon*, 55.

"Hurricane Trio"
Diskin, Lahna F. *Theodore Sturgeon*, 50–51.

"It"
Menger, Lucy. *Theodore Sturgeon*, 22–24.

"Make Room for Me"
Menger, Lucy. *Theodore Sturgeon*, 53–54.

"Maturity"
Hassler, Donald M. *The Comic Tone* . . . , 82–83.
Menger, Lucy. *Theodore Sturgeon*, 34–39.
Stableford, Brian M. "Theodore Sturgeon," in Bleiler, Everett F., Ed. *Science
    Fiction Writers* . . . , 204.

"Memorial"
Diskin, Lahna F. *Theodore Sturgeon*, 52.
Menger, Lucy. *Theodore Sturgeon*, 30–31.

"Microcosmic God"
Diskin, Lahna F. *Theodore Sturgeon*, 52–53.
Hassler, Donald M. *The Comic Tone* . . . , 70–71.
Menger, Lucy. *Theodore Sturgeon*, 18–21.

"Mr. Costello, Hero"
Menger, Lucy. *Theodore Sturgeon*, 57.

"Morality"
Menger, Lucy. *Theodore Sturgeon*, 70–71.

"Never Underestimate"
Menger, Lucy. *Theodore Sturgeon*, 47–48.

"The Other Celia"
Diskin, Lahna F. *Theodore Sturgeon*, 51.

"When You Care, When You Love"
Diskin, Lahna F. *Theodore Sturgeon,* 47.

"The World Well Lost"
Diskin, Lahna F. *Theodore Sturgeon,* 47, 54–55.
Menger, Lucy. *Theodore Sturgeon,* 48–49.

WILLIAM STYRON

"The Long March"
Crane, John K. *The Root . . . ,* 70–76.

"Marriott the Marine"
Crane, John K. *The Root . . . ,* 60–70.

RUTH SUCKOW

"Eltha"
Hamblen, Abigail A. *Ruth Suckow,* 39–40.

"Four Generations"
Hamblen, Abigail A. *Ruth Suckow,* 17.
Rohrberger, Mary. "The Question of Regionalism: Limitation and Transcen-
    dence," in Stevick, Philip, Ed. *The American Short Story, 1900–1945,* 150–
    151.

"Mrs. Vogel and Ollie"
Hamblen, Abigail A. *Ruth Suckow,* 27–28.

"Retired"
Hamblen, Abigail A. *Ruth Suckow,* 16–17.

"A Rural Community"
Rohrberger, Mary, "The Question . . . ," 151–153.

"Uprooted"
Rohrberger, Mary. "The Question . . . ," 153–154.

SUI SIN FAR [EDITH EATON]

"A Chinese Ishmael"
Wu, William F. *The Yellow Peril . . . ,* 53–54.

RONALD SUKENICK

"Momentum"
Klinkowitz, Jerome. *The Self-Apparent Word . . . ,* 38–39.

PYOTR SUMAROKOV

"Coquetry and Love"
Mersereau, John. *Russian Romantic Fiction,* 105–107.

PER OLOF SUNDMAN

"The Controller"
Warme, Lars G. *Per Olof Sundman . . .* , 38–39.

"The Drummer"
Warme, Lars G. *Per Olof Sundman . . .* , 46–47.

"The Hunters II"
Warme, Lars G. *Per Olof Sundman . . .* , 94–97.

"Ivory"
Warme, Lars G. *Per Olof Sundman . . .* , 51–53.

"Negotiation"
Warme, Lars G. *Per Olof Sundman . . .* , 58–59.

"The Observer"
Warme, Lars G. *Per Olof Sundman . . .* , 36–37.

"The Rooster"
Warme, Lars G. *Per Olof Sundman . . .* , 37–38.

"The Seekers"
Warme, Lars G. *Per Olof Sundman . . .* , 49–51.

"Seeking a Road"
Warme, Lars G. *Per Olof Sundman . . .* , 25–27.

"The Skier"
Warme, Lars G. *Per Olof Sundman . . .* , 40–41.

"The Sports Fisherman"
Warme, Lars G. *Per Olof Sundman . . .* , 56–58.

"The Strangers"
Warme, Lars G. *Per Olof Sundman . . .* , 59–61.

"The Stylite"
Warme, Lars G. *Per Olof Sundman . . .* , 44–46.

"Summer Night"
Warme, Lars G. *Per Olof Sundman . . .* , 53–54.

SUNG-YEH

"The Hound Yung-nu"
Doležalová, Anna. "The Short Stories in *Creation Daily*," *Asian & African Stud*,
   9 (1973), 57.

ABRAHAM SUTZKEVER

"Green Aquarium"
Roskies, David G. *Against the Apocalypse* . . . , 255–256.

JOHN TAINE [ERIC TEMPLE BELL]

"The Ultimate Catalyst"
King, Betty. *Women of the Future* . . . , 51–52.

TAKEDA RINTARŌ

"The Tune of Treason"
Keene, Donald. *Dawn to the West* . . . , 865–866.

"Violence"
Keene, Donald. *Dawn to the West* . . . , 862–865.

TANIZAKI JUN'ICHIRŌ

"Account of Spring Breeze and Autumn Rain"
Keene, Donald. *Dawn to the West* . . . , 724–725.

"The Bridge of Dreams"
Rimer, J. Thomas. *Modern Japanese Fiction* . . . , 31–37.

"The Kylin"
Keene, Donald. *Dawn to the West* . . . , 729–731.

"Sorrow of a Heretic"
Rubin, Jay. *Injurious to Public Morals* . . . , 139–141.

"The Story of Tomoda and Matsunaga"
Rubin, Jay. *Injurious to Public Morals* . . . , 236–238.

TAYAMA KATAI

"Perpetual Calendar"
Rubin, Jay. *Injurious to Public Morals* . . . , 189–190.

PETER TAYLOR

"Their Losses"
Walker, Jeffrey. "1945–1956: Post-World War II Manners and Mores," in
    Weaver, Gordon, Ed. *The American Short Story, 1945–1980*, 17–18.

"Venus, Cupid, Folly and Time"
Malina, Marilyn. "An Analysis of Peter Taylor's 'Venus, Cupid, Folly and
    Time,'" *Stud Short Fiction*, 20 (1983), 249–254.

HERNANDO TÉLLEZ

"Just Lather, That's All"
Abcarian, Richard, and Marvin Klotz. *Instructor's Manual . . .* , 3rd ed., 20.
McMurray, George R. "The Spanish American Short Story from Borges to the
    Present," in Peden, Margaret S., Ed. *The Latin American Short Story . . .* ,
    105–106.

VLADIMIR FËDOROVICH TENDRIAKOV

"Three, Seven, Ace"
Brown, Edward J. . . . *Since the Revolution*, 3rd ed., 323.

"The Trial"
Brown, Edward J. . . . *Since the Revolution*, 3rd ed., 323–324.

WILLIAM TENN

"Betelgeuse Bridge"
Edwards, Malcolm. "William Tenn," in Bleiler, Everett F., Ed. *Science Fiction
    Writers . . .* , 527.

"The Discovery of Morniel Mathaway"
Edwards, Malcolm. "William Tenn," 526.

"Down Among the Dead Men"
Edwards, Malcolm. "William Tenn," 528.

"It Ends with a Flicker"
Edwards, Malcolm. "William Tenn," 526.

"The Liberation of Earth"
Edwards, Malcolm. "William Tenn," 527–528.

"Medusa Was a Lady!"
Fredericks, Casey. *The Future of Eternity . . .* , 12–15.

"Null-P"
Edwards, Malcolm. "William Tenn," 528.

"Venus and the Seven Sexes"
Edwards, Malcolm. "William Tenn," 526–527.

"Winthrop Was Stubborn" [originally titled "Time Waits for Winthrop"]
Edwards, Malcolm. "William Tenn," 528.

CAN THEMBA

"The Suit"
Barnett, Ursula A. *A Vision of Order . . .* , 186–187.

DYLAN THOMAS

"A Map of Love"
Tinkler, Valeria. "Dylan Thomas as Poet and Story-Teller," *Dutch Q R*, 11
    (1981), 228–229.

"A Visit to Grandpa"
Tinkler, Valeria. "Dylan Thomas . . . ," 229–230.

JAMES THURBER

"The Beast in the Dingle"
Kenney, Catherine M. *Thurber's Anatomy . . .* , 157–158.

"The Black Magic of Barney Haller"
Kenney, Catherine M. *Thurber's Anatomy . . .* , 116–117.

"The Breaking Up of the Winships"
Kenney, Catherine M. *Thurber's Anatomy . . .* , 58–59.

"A Call on Mrs. Forrester"
Kenney, Catherine M. *Thurber's Anatomy . . .* , 117–120.

"The Car We Had to Push"
Kenney, Catherine M. *Thurber's Anatomy . . .* , 96.

"The Catbird Seat"
Kennedy, X. J. and Dorothy M. *Instructor's Manual . . .* , 3rd ed., 19–20.
Kenney, Catherine M. *Thurber's Anatomy . . .* , 60–62.
Underwood, Marylyn. "Thurber's 'The Catbird Seat,'" *Explicator,* 40, iv (1982),
    49–50.

"A Couple of Hamburgers"
Kenney, Catherine M. *Thurber's Anatomy . . .* , 59–60.

"The Fairly Intelligent Fly"
Kenney, Catherine M. *Thurber's Anatomy . . .* , 102–103.

JOHANN LUDWIG TIECK

"Der Runenberg"
Knight, Victor. "The Perceptive Non-Artist: A Study of Tieck's 'Der Runenberg,'" *New Germ Stud*, 10, i (1982), 21–31.
Mecklenburg, Norbert. "'Die Gesellschaft der verwilderten Steine': Interpretationsprobleme von Ludwig Tiecks Erzählung 'Der Runenberg,'" *Der Deutschunterricht*, 34, vi (1982), 62–76.

TILUMANYA

"Rice from the Beards"
Senkoro, F. E. M. K. "*Ng'ombe Akivundika Guu:* Preliminary Remarks on the Proverb Story in Written Swahili Literature," in Dorsey, David F., Phanuel A. Egejuru, and Stephen Arnold, Eds. *Design and Intent . . .* , 66–67.

JAMES TIPTREE, JR. [ALICE HASTINGS SHELDON]

"Afternoon"
Dozois, Gardner. *The Fiction . . .* , [19–20].

"And I Awoke"
Dozois, Gardner. *The Fiction . . .* , [16].
Wood, Susan. "James Tiptree, Jr.," in Bleiler, Everett F., Ed. *Science Fiction Writers . . .* , 534–535.

"Beam Us Home"
Dozois, Gardner. *The Fiction . . .* , [10–12].

"Birth of a Salesman"
Dozois, Gardner. *The Fiction . . .* , [6–7].

"Faith"
Dozois, Gardner. *The Fiction . . .* , [8–9].

"Forever to a Hudson's Bay Blanket"
Dozois, Gardner. *The Fiction . . .* , [20].

"Help" [originally titled "Pupa Knows Best"]
Dozois, Gardner. *The Fiction . . .* , [7–8].

"Houston, Houston, Do You Read?"
Frisch, Adam J. "Toward New Sexual Identities: James Tiptree, Jr.," in Staicar, Tom, Ed. *The Feminine Eye . . .* , 49–50.
Podojil, Catherine. "Sisters, Daughters, and Aliens," in Riley, Dick, Ed. *Critical Encounters [I] . . .* , 76–80.
Wood, Susan. "James Tiptree, Jr.," 537.

"I'll Be Waiting for You When the Swimming Pool Is Empty"
Dozois, Gardner. *The Fiction* . . . , [16–17].

"I'm Too Big"
Dozois, Gardner. *The Fiction* . . . , [14–15].

"The Last Flight of Dr. Ain"
Dozois, Gardner. *The Fiction* . . . , [9–10].
Wood, Susan. "James Tiptree, Jr.," 535.

"Lirois"
Frisch, Adam J. "Toward New Sexual Identities . . . ," 53.

"Mamma Come Home"
Dozois, Gardner. *The Fiction* . . . , [7].

"A Momentary Taste of Being"
Frisch, Adam J. "Toward New Sexual Identities . . . ," 52–53.

"Mother in the Sky"
Dozois, Gardner. *The Fiction* . . . , [17–18].

"The Peacefulness of Vivyan"
Wood, Susan. "James Tiptree, Jr.," 534.

"The Psychologist Who Wouldn't Do Awful Things to Rats"
Frisch, Adam J. "Toward New Sexual Identities . . . ," 50.

"She Waits for All Men Born"
Frisch, Adam J. "Toward New Sexual Identities . . . ," 52.

"The Snows Are Melted, the Snows Are Gone"
King, Betty. *Women of the Future* . . . , 132–133.

"With Delicate Mad Hands"
King, Betty. *Women of the Future* . . . , 226–227.

"The Women Men Don't See"
Dozois, Gardner. *The Fiction* . . . , [22–23].
Frisch, Adam J. "Toward New Sexual Identities . . . ," 52.
King, Betty. *Women of the Future* . . . , 177–178.
Podojil, Catherine. "Sisters, Daughters, and Aliens," 80–81.

"Your Haploid Heart"
Dozois, Gardner. *The Fiction* . . . , [12–13].

VLADIMIR TITOV [pseudonym: TIT KOSMOKRATOV]

"The Isolated Little House of Vasilievsky Island"
Mersereau, John. *Russian Romantic Fiction*, 100–101.

J[OHN] R[ONALD] R[EUEL] TOLKIEN

"Farmer Giles of Ham"
Doxey, William S. "Culture as an Aspect of Style in Fantasy," *West Georgia Coll R*, 13 (May, 1981), 5–7.

"Leaf by Niggle"
Purtill, Richard L. *J. R. R. Tolkien . . .* , 16–27.
Shippey, T. A. *The Road . . .* , 33–36.
Timmerman, John H. *Other Worlds . . .* , 9–12.

"Of Beren and Lúthien"
Shippey, T. A. *The Road . . .* , 192–195.

"Quenta Silmarillion"
Purtill, Richard L. *J. R. R. Tolkien . . .* , 98–101.

LEO TOLSTOY

"After the Ball"
Fodor, Alexander. *Tolstoy and the Russians . . .* ," 111.

"The Death of Ivan Ilych"
*Abcarian, Richard, and Marvin Klotz. *Instructor's Manual . . .* , 2nd ed., 22–23; 3rd ed., 20–21.
Beaty, Jerome. *The Norton Introduction . . .* , 88–91.
Bergman, David, Joseph de Roche, and Daniel M. Epstein. *Instructor's Manual . . .* , 40–41.
Clardy, Jesse V. and Betty S. *The Superfluous Man . . .* , 76–79.
Jahn, Gary R. "The Role of the Ending in Lev Tolstoi's 'The Death of Ivan Il'ich,'" *Canadian Slavonic Papers*, 24 (1982), 229–234.
———. "'The Death of Ivan Il'ič'—Chapter One," in Leighton, Lauren G., Ed. *Studies in Honor . . .* , 37–43.
Nabokov, Vladimir. *Lectures on Russian Literature*, 236–241.
Napier, James J. "The Stages of Dying and 'The Death of Ivan Ilyich,'" *Coll Lit*, 10, ii (1983), 147–157.
Painter, Rebecca M. "From Death to Self-Knowledge: An Essay on Works by Tolstoy and Rilke," *Coll Lang Assoc J*, 26, ii (1982), 174–181.
Parr, Susan R. *The Moral . . .* , 53–60.
Perrine, Laurence, and Thomas R. Arp. *Instructor's Manual . . .* , 6th ed., 73–75.
Sheidley, William E., and Ann Charters. *Instructor's Manual . . .* , 16–18.
Sirlin, Rhoda, and David H. Richter. *Instructor's Manual . . .* , 164–167.
Spanos, William V. "Leo Tolstoy's 'The Death of Ivan Ilych': A Temporal Interpretation," in Orr, Leonard, Ed. *De-Structing the Novel . . .* , 1–64.
Williams, Michael V. "Tolstoy's 'The Death of Ivan Ilych': After the Fall," *Stud Short Fiction*, 21 (1984), 229–234.
Wilshire, John. "The Argument of Ivan Ilych's Death," *Critical R*, 24 (1982), 46–54.

"Father Sergius"
Ziolkowski, Margaret. "Hagiographical Motifs in Tolstoy's 'Father Sergius,'" *So Atlantic R*, 47, ii (1982), 63–80.

"Polikushka"
Fodor, Alexander. *Tolstoy and the Russians . . .* , 108–109.
MacMaster, Robert E. "Tsarism Right Side Up in Tolstoj's 'Polikuška,'" in Debreczeny, Paul, Ed. *American Contributions . . .* , 285–304.

"The Snowstorm"
Katz, Michael R. *Dreams . . .* , 119–120.

"Three Deaths"
Bakhtin, Mikhail. *Problems . . .* , 69–73.

FEREYDOUN TONKABONI

"The Sultan's Six Sons"
Dorri, J. "National Traditions in Contemporary Persian Satirical Prose, 1920's—1960's," in Ricks, Thomas M., Ed. *Critical Perspectives . . .* , 142–143.

JEAN TOOMER

"Avey"
Gibson, Donald B. *The Politics . . .* , 164–165.
McKay, Nellie Y. *Jean Toomer . . .* , 132–138.

"Becky"
Durham, Frank. "Jean Toomer's Vision of the Southern Negro," *Southern Hum R*, 6 (Winter, 1972), 19.
Gibson, Donald B. *The Politics . . .* , 157–158.
McKay, Nellie Y. *Jean Toomer . . .* , 97–101.

"Blood-Burning Moon"
Bowen, Barbara E. "Untroubled Voice: Call-and-Response in *Cane*," *Black Am Lit Forum*, 16 (Spring, 1982), 16–17; rpt. Gates, Henry L., Ed. *Black Literature . . .* , 196–198.
Durham, Frank. "Jean Toomer's Vision . . . ," 19–20.
Gibson, Donald B. *The Politics . . .* , 163–164.
McKay, Nellie Y. *Jean Toomer . . .* , 118–124.
Miller, James E., and Bernice Slote. *Instructor's Manual . . .* , 2nd ed., 11–12.

"Bona and Paul"
Bowen, Barbara E. "Untroubled Voice . . . ," 200–201.
Cooke, Michael G. *Afro-American Literature . . .* , 179–186.
Gibson, Donald B. *The Politics . . .* , 168–170.
McKay, Nellie Y. *Jean Toomer . . .* , 145–148.

GONZALO TORRENTE BALLESTER

"The Bastard Farruco"
Pérez, Janet. *Gonzalo Torrente Ballester*, 124–125.

"The Inn of the Amiable Deities"
Pérez, Janet. *Gonzalo Torrente Ballester*, 130–132.

"The Tale of the Siren"
Benítez, Margarita. "The Self-Conscious Narrative as Vehicle for a Fantastic Tale: A Study of *Cuento de Sirena* by Gonzalo Torrente Ballester," in *Homenaje a Gonzalo Torrente Ballester*, 19–28.
Pérez, Janet. *Gonzalo Torrente Ballester*, 119–121.

JAIME TORRES BODET

"Venus Rising from the Sea"
Brushwood, John S. "The Spanish American Short Story from Quiroga to Borges," in Peden, Margaret S., Ed. *The Latin American Short Story . . .* , 81.

BRUNO TRAVEN

"The Night Visitor"
Walker, Ronald G. *Infernal Paradise . . .* , 14–15.

F. ORLIN TREMAINE

"The Upper-Level Road"
Cioffi, Frank. *Formula Fiction? . . .* , 98–99.

NELSON TREMAINE

"Vibratory"
Cioffi, Frank. *Formula Fiction? . . .* , 99–100.

DALTON TREVISAN

"Train"
Foster, David W. "Major Figures in the Brazilian Short Story," in Peden, Margaret S., Ed. *The Latin American Short Story . . .* , 24–25.

WILLIAM TREVOR [TREVOR COX]

"Another Christmas"
Rhodes, Robert E. "William Trevor's Stories of the Troubles," in Brophy, James D., and Raymond J. Porter, Eds. *Contemporary Irish Writing*, 110–113.

"Attracta"
Rhodes, Robert E. ". . . Stories of the Troubles," 103–106.

"Autumn Sunshine"
Rhodes, Robert E. ". . . Stories of the Troubles," 106–109.

"The Distant Past"
Rhodes, Robert E. ". . . Stories of the Troubles," 98–100.

"The Raising of Elvira Tremlett"
Hogan, Robert. "Old Boys, Young Bucks, and New Women: The Contemporary
    Irish Short Story," in Kilroy, James F., Ed. *The Irish Short Story* . . . , 182–
    183.

"Saints"
Rhodes, Robert E. ". . . Stories of the Troubles," 101–103.

IURII TRIFONOV

"Another Life"
De Maegd-Soëp, Caroline. "The Theme of 'Byt'—Everyday Life—in the Stories
    of Iurii Trifonov," in Bristol, Evelyn, Ed. *Russian Literature* . . . , 56.

"The Exchange"
De Maegd-Soëp, Caroline. "The Theme of 'Byt' . . . ," 54–55.

LIONEL TRILLING

"Of This Time, Of That Place"
Elledge, W. Paul. "The Profaning of Romanticism in Trilling's 'Of This Time,
    Of That Place,'" *Mod Fiction Stud*, 29 (1983), 213–226.

ANTHONY TROLLOPE

"Mrs. General Talboys"
Shaw, Valerie. *The Short Story* . . . , 222–223.

HENRI TROYAT

"La Clef de voûte"
Hewitt, Nicholas. *Henri Troyat*, 114–116.

"Erratum"
Hewitt, Nicholas. *Henri Troyat*, 120–121.

"The Guinea-Pig"
Hewitt, Nicholas. *Henri Troyat*, 122–123.

"The Judgment of God"
Hewitt, Nicholas. *Henri Troyat*, 124–125.

"The Lady in Black"
Hewitt, Nicholas. *Henri Troyat*, 121.

"The Marvellous Journey of Jacques Mazeyrat"
Hewitt, Nicholas. *Henri Troyat*, 126–127.

"Mr. Breadborough"
Hewitt, Nicholas. *Henri Troyat*, 123.

"Monsieur Citrine"
Hewitt, Nicholas. *Henri Troyat*, 116–117.

"The Murderer"
Hewitt, Nicholas. *Henri Troyat*, 118–119.

"The Portrait"
Hewitt, Nicholas. *Henri Troyat*, 129–130.

"Le Puy Saint-Clair"
Hewitt, Nicholas. *Henri Troyat*, 125–126.

"Le Ratuset"
Hewitt, Nicholas. *Henri Troyat*, 121–122.

"The Son of Heaven"
Hewitt, Nicholas. *Henri Troyat*, 129.

"The Tandem"
Hewitt, Nicholas. *Henri Troyat*, 121.

"The Undertow"
Hewitt, Nicholas. *Henri Troyat*, 119–120.

"Vertigo"
Hewitt, Nicholas. *Henri Troyat*, 118.

KONSTANTIN TSIOLKOVSKY

"Island of Ether"
Starchild, Adam, Ed. *The Science Fiction . . .* , 6–7.

TSUBOUCHI SHŌVŌ

"The Wife"
Keene, Donald. *Dawn to the West . . .* , 107–108.

IVAN SERGEEVICH TURGENEV

"Asya"
Freeborn, Richard. "Introduction," in Freeborn, Richard, Ed. *Love and Death* . . . , 18–19.

"Bezhin Meadow"
Miller, James E., and Bernice Slote. *Instructor's Manual* . . . , 2nd ed., 7.
*O'Connor, Frank. "Narrative in Turgenev's 'Byezhin Prairie,'" in Charters, Ann, Ed. *The Story* . . . , 1150–1152.
O'Toole, L. Michael. *Structure, Style and Interpretation* . . . , 193–203.
Sheidley, William E., and Ann Charters. *Instructor's Manual* . . . , 10–11.

"Death"
Perschel, Richard E. and Enid R. "'Am I in Heaven Now?' Case History, Literary Histories," *Soundings*, 66 (1983), 469–480.

"The Diary of a Superfluous Man"
Freeborn, Richard. "Introduction," 12–14.

"First Love"
Freeborn, Richard. "Introduction," 21–22.

"King Lear of the Steppes"
Freeborn, Richard. "Introduction," 22–24.

"Klara Milich"
Harvie, J. A. "Turgenev's Swan-Song, 'Klara Milich,'" *New Zealand Slavonic J*, [n.v.] (1983), 105–121.

"Kor and Kalinch"
Clardy, Jesse V. and Betty S. *The Superfluous Man* . . . , 25–28.

"The Living Relic"
Welch, Robert. *The Way Back* . . . , 55–56.

"The Song of Triumphant Love"
Freeborn, Richard. "Introduction," 24–25.

"The Tryst"
Welch, Robert. *The Way Back* . . . , 52–53.

"Yermolai and the Miller's Wife"
Welch, Robert. *The Way Back* . . . , 46–48.

AMOS TUTUOLA

"The Wild Hunter in the Bush of the Ghosts"
Lindfors, Bernth. *Early Nigerian Literature*, 25–34.

MARK TWAIN [SAMUEL L. CLEMENS]

"Baker's Blue-Jay Yarn"
Emerson, Everett. *The Authentic Mark Twain . . .* , 105–106.
Gervais, Ronald J. "What Remains When Everything Is Left Out: The Joke of 'Baker's Blue-Jay Yarn,'" *Mark Twain J*, 21, iv (1983), 14–17.

"Captain Stormfield's Visit to Heaven"
Emerson, Everett. *The Authentic Mark Twain . . .* , 111–114.

"The Celebrated Jumping Frog of Calaveras County"
Allen, Mary. *Animals . . .* , 64–65.
Miller, Robert K. *Mark Twain*, 161–164.
Sirlin, Rhoda, and David H. Richter. *Instructor's Manual . . .* , 167–168.

"The Facts Concerning the Recent Carnival of Crime in Connecticut"
Johnson, James L. *Mark Twain . . .* , 71–73.
Miller, Robert K. *Mark Twain*, 162–165.

"The Great Dark"
Emerson, Everett. *The Authentic Mark Twain . . .* , 221–222.

"The Holy Children"
Johnson, James L. *Mark Twain . . .* , 76–79.

"The Man That Corrupted Hadleyburg"
Bennett, Fordyce R. "The Moral Obliquity of 'The Man That Corrupted Hadleyburg,'" *Mark Twain J*, 21, iii (1983), 10–11.
Briden, Earl F., and Mary Prescott. "The Lie That I Am I: Paradoxes of Identity in Mark Twain's 'Hadleyburg,'" *Stud Short Fiction*, 21 (1984), 383–391.
Harris, Susan K. "'Hadleyburg': Mark Twain's Dual Attack on Banal Theology and Banal Literature," *Am Lit Realism*, 16 (1983), 240–252 [copyright 1984].
Kennedy, X. J. *Instructor's Manual . . .* , 3rd ed., 52–53.
Miller, Robert K. *Mark Twain*, 172–174.

"A Murder, a Mystery, and a Marriage"
Ketterer, David. "Power Fantasy in the 'Science Fiction' of Mark Twain," in Slusser, George E., Eric S. Rabkin, and Robert Scholes, Eds. *Bridges to Fantasy*, 134–136; rpt. in part in Ketterer, David, Ed. *The Science Fiction . . .* , xvii.

"The Mysterious Stranger"
Johnson, James L. *Mark Twain . . .* , 168–182.
Lewicki, Zbigniew. *The Bang . . .* , 40–45.
Matheson, Terence. "The Devil and Philip Traum: Twain's Satiric Purpose in 'The Mysterious Stranger,'" *Markham R*, 12 (1982), 5–11.

"A Story Without an End"
Sheidley, William E., and Ann Charters. *Instructor's Manual . . .* , 19–20.

"The $30,000 Bequest"
McMahan, Elizabeth. "Finance and Fantasy as Destroyers in Twain's 'The
  $30,000 Bequest,'" *Mark Twain J*, 21, ii (1982), 23–26.

UCHIDA ROAN

"Broken Fence"
Rubin, Jay. *Injurious to Public Morals . . .* , 45–49.

UEDA AKINARI

"The Bloodstained Robe"
Young, Blake M. *Ueda Akinari*, 129.

"The Cauldron of Kibitsu"
Kato, Shuichi. . . . *Japanese Literature*, II, 196.

"The Celestial Maidens"
Young, Blake M. *Ueda Akinari*, 129–130.

"The Chrysanthemum Pledge"
Kato, Shuichi. . . . *Japanese Literature*, II, 195–196.

"The Destiny That Spanned Two Lifetimes"
Young, Blake M. *Ueda Akinari*, 131–132.

"The Grave of Miyagi"
Young, Blake M. *Ueda Akinari*, 135–136.

"Hankai"
Young, Blake M. *Ueda Akinari*, 136–138.

"The Lust of the White Serpent"
Rimer, J. Thomas. *Modern Japanese Fiction . . .* , 132–133.

"The One-Eyed God"
Young, Blake M. *Ueda Akinari*, 132.

"The Pirate"
Young, Blake M. *Ueda Akinari*, 131.

"The Smiling Death's-Head"
Young, Blake M. *Ueda Akinari*, 133–135.

BECHAN SARMA UGRA

"Ganga Gandatta and Gangi"
Pande, Trilochan. "Folk Elements in the Modern Hindi Short Story," *Folklore*
  (Calcutta), 231 (1979), 144.

MIGUEL DE UNAMUNO

"Saint Manuel the Good, Martyr"
Spires, Robert C. *Beyond the Metafictional* . . . , 43–44.
Tejerina, Arsenio R. "San Manuel Bueno no cree en la immortalidad del alma,"
    in Finke, Wayne H., and Enrique Ledesma, Eds. *Homenaje a Humberto*
    Piñera . . . , 209–219.

JOHN UPDIKE

"A & P"
Bergman, David, Joseph de Roche, and Daniel M. Epstein. *Instructor's Man-*
    ual . . . , 22–23.
*Detweiler, Robert. *John Updike*, 2nd ed., 52–53.
Greiner, Donald J. *The Other John Updike* . . . , 117–119.
Kennedy, X. J. *Instructor's Manual* . . . , 3rd ed., 11–12.
McFarland, Ronald E. "Updike and the Critics: Reflections on 'A & P,'" *Stud*
    Short Fiction, 20 (1983), 95–100.
Miller, James E., and Bernice Slote. *Instructor's Manual* . . . , 2nd ed., 22.
Sirlin, Rhoda, and David H. Richter. *Instructor's Manual* . . . , 169–170.

"Ace in the Hole"
*Detweiler, Robert. *John Updike*, 2nd ed., 10–12.
Greiner, Donald J. *The Other John Updike* . . . , 67–68.

"The Astronomer"
Detweiler, Robert. *John Updike*, 2nd ed., 57–58.

"At a Bar in Charlotte Amalie"
Detweiler, Robert. *John Updike*, 2nd ed., 103–104.

"Australia and Canada"
Detweiler, Robert. *John Updike*, 2nd ed., 181–182.

"Avec la Bébé-sitter"
Greiner, Donald J. *The Other John Updike* . . . , 145–146.

"Bech in Rumania"
Detweiler, Robert. *John Updike*, 2nd ed., 119–120.

"Bech Panics"
Detweiler, Robert. *John Updike*, 2nd ed., 121–123.

"Bech Third-Worlds It"
Detweiler, Robert. *John Updike*, 2nd ed., 180–181.

"Bech Wed"
Detweiler, Robert. *John Updike*, 2nd ed., 183–184.

"The Blessed Man of Boston, My Grandmother's Thimble, and Fanning Is-
    land"
Greiner, Donald J. *The Other John Updike* . . . , 123–124.

"A Madman"
Greiner, Donald J. *The Other John Updike* . . . , 140–141.

"Marching Through Boston"
Greiner, Donald J. *The Other John Updike* . . . , 188–189.

"The Morning"
*Detweiler, Robert. *John Updike,* 2nd ed., 100–101.
Greiner, Donald J. *The Other John Updike* . . . , 149–151.

"Museums and Women"
Detweiler, Robert. *John Updike,* 2nd ed., 140–142.
Greiner, Donald J. *The Other John Updike* . . . , 165–167.

"The Music School"
*Detweiler, Robert. *John Updike,* 2nd ed., 93–96.
Greiner, Donald J. *The Other John Updike* . . . , 153–157.
Tracy, Bruce H. "The Habit of Confession: Recovery of the Self in Updike's
    'The Music School,'" *Stud Short Fiction,* 21 (1984), 339–355.

"My Love Has Dirty Fingernails"
*Detweiler, Robert. *John Updike,* 2nd ed., 97–98.

"The Orphaned Swimming Pool"
Detweiler, Robert. *John Updike,* 2nd ed., 143.

"Other Modes"
Greiner, Donald J. *The Other John Updike* . . . , 181–186.

"Packed Dirt, Churchgoing, A Dying Cat, A Traded Car"
*Detweiler, Robert. *John Updike,* 2nd ed., 60.
Greiner, Donald J. *The Other John Updike* . . . , 114–116.

"The Persistence of Desire"
*Detweiler, Robert. *John Updike,* 2nd ed., 47–48.
Greiner, Donald J. *The Other John Updike* . . . , 99–101.

"Pigeon Feathers"
*Detweiler, Robert. *John Updike,* 2nd ed., 48–51.
Greiner, Donald J. *The Other John Updike* . . . , 111–114.

"Plumbing"
Greiner, Donald J. *The Other John Updike* . . . , 180–181.

"The Pro"
Greiner, Donald J. *The Other John Updike* . . . , 185.

"The Rescue"
*Detweiler, Robert. *John Updike,* 2nd ed., 96–97.

"The Sea's Green Sameness"
Greiner, Donald J. *The Other John Updike* . . . , 182–183.

"Who Made Yellow Roses Yellow?"
Greiner, Donald J. *The Other John Updike* . . . , 75–77.
Scott, Virgil, and David Madden. *Instructor's Manual* . . . , 4th ed., 94–97; Madden, David. *Instructor's Manual* . . . , 5th ed., 99–101; Madden, David, and Virgil Scott. *Instructor's Manual* . . . , 6th ed., 106–109.

"Wife-Wooing"
Detweiler, Robert. *John Updike*, 2nd ed., 56–57.
Greiner, Donald J. *The Other John Updike* . . . , 109–111.
Sheidley, William E., and Ann Charters. *Instructor's Manual* . . . , 177.

"The Witnesses"
Greiner, Donald J. *The Other John Updike* . . . , 172–173.

ARTURO USLAR PIETRI

"Rain"
Brushwood, John S. "The Spanish American Short Story from Quiroga to Borges," in Peden, Margaret S., Ed. *The Latin American Short Story* . . . , 88.

GLEB USPENSKY

"Coachman with a Device"
Prutskov, Nikita I. *Gleb Uspensky*, 143.

"He Got Angry!"
Prutskov, Nikita I. *Gleb Uspensky*, 142–143.

"Incubator Chick"
Prutskov, Nikita I. *Gleb Uspensky*, 139–140.

"Sentry Box"
Prutskov, Nikita I. *Gleb Uspensky*, 32–34.

"Something Went to His Head"
Prutskov, Nikita I. *Gleb Uspensky*, 143–144.

JACK VANCE

"Abercrombie Station"
Tiedman, Richard. "Jack Vance: Science Fiction Stylist," in Underwood, Tim, and Chuck Miller, Eds. *Jack Vance*, 195–196.

"Cholwell's Chickens"
Tiedman, Richard. "Jack Vance . . . ," 195–196.

"Coup de Grâce"
Pierce, Hazel B. *A Literary Symbiosis* . . . , 147–148.

"Dodkin's Job"
Tiedman, Richard. "Jack Vance . . . ," 199–200.

"The Five Gold Bands"
Close, Peter. "Fantasms, Magics, and Unfamiliar Sciences: The Early Fiction of
    Jack Vance, 1945–50," in Underwood, Tim, and Chuck Miller, Eds. *Jack
    Vance*, 52–55.

"Guyal the Sfere"
Close, Peter. "Fantasms . . . ," 63–64.

"Hard-Luck Diggings"
Close, Peter. "Fantasms . . . ," 35–36.

"The House of Iszm"
Cox, Arthur J. "Jack Vance—The World Thinker," in Underwood, Tim, and
    Chuck Miller, Eds. *Jack Vance*, 74–75.

"The Howling Bounders"
Close, Peter. "Fantasms . . . ," 41–43.

"I'll Build Your Dream Castle"
Close, Peter. "Fantasms . . . ," 32–34.

"The King of Thieves"
Close, Peter. "Fantasms . . . ," 43–45.

"Liane the Wayfarer"
Close, Peter. "Fantasms . . . ," 61–62.

"The Men Return"
Cox, Arthur J. ". . . World Thinker," 75–76.

"The Miracle Workers"
Tiedman, Richard. "Jack Vance . . . ," 208–211.

"The Moon Moth"
Edwards, Malcolm. "Jack Vance," in Bleiler, Everett F., Ed. *Science Fiction Writ-
    ers . . . ,* 545–546.

"New Bodies for Old"
Close, Peter. "Fantasms . . . ," 48–50.

"Parapsyche"
Tiedman, Richard. "Jack Vance . . . ," 206–208.

"Phalid's Fate"
Close, Peter. "Fantasms . . . ," 31–32.

"Planet of the Black Dust"
Close, Peter. "Fantasms . . . ," 28–30.

"The Potter of Firsk"
Close, Peter. "Fantasms . . . ," 45–47.

"Sanatoris Short-Cut"
Close, Peter. "Fantasms . . . ," 36–38.

"Son of the Tree"
Tiedman, Richard. "Jack Vance . . . ," 194–195.

"The Substandard Sardines"
Close, Peter. "Fantasms . . . ," 40–41.

"T'sais"
Close, Peter. "Fantasms . . . ," 61.

"Ulan Dhor Ends a Dream"
Close, Peter. "Fantasms . . . ," 62–63.

"Ullward's Retreat"
Tiedman, Richard. "Jack Vance . . . ," 200–201.

"Ultimate Quest"
Close, Peter. "Fantasms . . . ," 50–52.

"The Unspeakable McInch"
Close, Peter. "Fantasms . . . ," 38–40.

"The World-Thinker"
Cox, Arthur J. ". . . World Thinker," 71–72.
Tiedman, Richard. "Jack Vance . . . ," 190–191.

CHARLES E. VAN LOAN

"Easy Picking"
Oriard, Michael. *Dreaming of Heroes* . . . , 81–82.

"Excess Baggage"
Oriard, Michael. *Dreaming of Heroes* . . . , 180–181.

SYDNEY J[OYCE] VAN SCYOC

"When Petals Fall"
King, Betty. *Women of the Future* . . . , 180–182.

A. E. VAN VOGT

"Black Destroyer"
Cioffi, Frank. *Formula Fiction?* . . . , 57–59.
Sussex, Lucy. "Long Versus Short SF: The Examination of a Fix-Up," *Foundation*, 26 (1983), 29–31.

"Discord in Scarlet"
Wilson, Colin. "A. E. van Vogt," in Bleiler, Everett F., Ed. *Science Fiction Writers* . . . , 211.

"Resurrection"
Meyers, Walter E. *Aliens and Linguists* . . . , 40–41.

"The Rulers"
Wilson, Colin. "A. E. van Vogt," 213.

"Vault of the Beast"
Wilson, Colin. "A. E. van Vogt," 210–211.

MARIO VARGAS LLOSA

"The Cubs"
Ortega, Julio. "Sobre *Los cachorros*," in Giacoman, Helmy, and José Miguel Oviedo, Eds. *Homenaje a Mario Vargas Llosa*, 265–273.

JOHN VARLEY

"The Persistence of Vision"
Cioffi, Frank. *Formula Fiction?* . . . , 102–109.
Koelb, Clayton. "The Language of Presence in Varley's 'The Persistence of Vision,'" *Sci-Fiction Stud*, 11, ii (1984), 154–165.

"The Phantom of Kansas"
Hartwell, David. *Age of Wonders* . . . , 97–103.

ANA LYDIA VEGA

"Pollito chicken"
Olmos, Margarite F. "From a Woman's Perspective: The Short Stories of Rosario Ferré and Ana Lydia Vega," in Meyer, Doris, and Margarite F. Olmos, Eds. *Contemporary Women* . . . , 86–87.

"Salsa Rhymes and Three Short-Order Tunes"
Olmos, Margarite F. "From a Woman's Perspective . . . ," 88–89.

JOSÉ J. VEIGA

"The Misplaced Machine"
Foster, David W. "Major Figures in the Brazilian Short Story," in Peden,
Margaret S., Ed. *The Latin American Short Story* . . . , 30–31.

ALEXANDER VELTMAN

"Erotica"
Mersereau, John. *Russian Romantic Fiction,* 230–232.

ELENA SERGEEVNA VENTZEL

"Ladies' Hairdresser"
Brown, Edward J. . . . *Since the Revolution,* 3rd ed., 321–322.

GIOVANNI VERGA

"Black Bread"
Savoca, Giuseppe. "'Pane nero,'" in Musumarra, Carmelo, Ed. *Novelle rusticane* . . . , 121–133.

"Cos'è il re"
Tropea, Mario. "'Cos'è il re,'" in Musumarra, Carmelo, Ed. *Novelle rusticane* . . . , 19–30.

"Libertà"
Sipala, Paolo M. "'Libertà,'" in Musumarra, Carmelo, Ed. *Novelle rusticane* . . . ,
151–161.

"Malaria"
Reina, Luigi. "'Malaria,'" in Musumarra, Carmelo, Ed. *Novelle rusticane* . . . ,
57–74.

"The Mystery"
Lo Nigro, Sebastiano. "'Il mistero,'" in Musumarra, Carmelo, Ed. *Novelle rusticane* . . . , 47–56.

"The Orphans"
Finocchiaro Chimirri, Giovanna. "'Gli orfani,'" in Musumarra, Carmelo, Ed.
Novelle rusticane . . . , 75–88.

"The She-Wolf"
Jehenson, Yvonne. "Verga's 'La Lupa': A Study in Archetypal Symbolism,"
Forum Italicum, 17 (1983), 196–206.

"A Story of St. Joseph's Donkey"
Gioviale, Fernando. "'Storia dell'asino di S. Giuseppe,'" in Musumarra, Carmelo, Ed. *Novelle rusticane* . . . , 101–119.

JULES VERNE

"The Eternal Adam"
Fredericks, Casey. *The Future of Eternity . . .* , 71–73.

JAVIER DE VIANA

"Andean Legend"
Garganigo, John F. *Javier de Viana,* 146–147.

"Bitter Triumph"
Garganigo, John F. *Javier de Viana,* 123–124.

"Black Abdón's Raffle"
Garganigo, John F. *Javier de Viana,* 90–91.

"The Black Man's Way of Doing Things"
Garganigo, John F. *Javier de Viana,* 127–128.

"Brothers"
Garganigo, John F. *Javier de Viana,* 109–110.

"Chaqueña"
Garganigo, John F. *Javier de Viana,* 96–97.

"The Consumptive"
Garganigo, John F. *Javier de Viana,* 86–87.
Lindstrom, Naomi. "The Spanish American Short Story from Echeverría to
    Quiroga," in Peden, Margaret S., Ed. *The Latin American Short Story . . .* ,
    48–50.

"Contradiction"
Garganigo, John F. *Javier de Viana,* 107–108.

"The Crow's Nest"
Garganigo, John F. *Javier de Viana,* 100–103.

"The Cure"
Garganigo, John F. *Javier de Viana,* 54–55.

"Do You Understand?"
Garganigo, John F. *Javier de Viana,* 105–106.

"Don Liborio's Tale"
Garganigo, John F. *Javier de Viana,* 144–145.

"Doña Melitona"
Garganigo, John F. *Javier de Viana,* 80–81.

"The Duty to Live"
Garganigo, John F. *Javier de Viana,* 106–107.

"Just for Killing the Bird"
Garganigo, John F. *Javier de Viana*, 79–80.

"The Land Is Small"
Garganigo, John F. *Javier de Viana*, 148–149.

"The Last Campaign"
Garganigo, John F. *Javier de Viana*, 55–56.

"Leopoldo Almeida"
Barros-Lémez, Alvaro. "'Leopoldo Almeida': Un relato clave para la comprensión de la obra de Javier de Viana," *Hispamerica*, 10 (August, 1981), 63–69.

"Like Real Folks"
Garganigo, John F. *Javier de Viana*, 91–92.

"Like the Good Old Times"
Garganigo, John F. *Javier de Viana*, 122–123.

"The Loves of Bentos Sagrera"
Garganigo, John F. *Javier de Viana*, 58–61.

"The Making of a Caudillo"
Garganigo, John F. *Javier de Viana*, 155–156.

"Manduca's Place"
Garganigo, John F. *Javier de Viana*, 81–82.

"The Pair from Urubolí"
Garganigo, John F. *Javier de Viana*, 78–79.

"Pals and Godfathers"
Garganigo, John F. *Javier de Viana*, 125–126.

"Persecution"
Garganigo, John F. *Javier de Viana*, 56–57.

"Playing Wolf"
Garganigo, John F. *Javier de Viana*, 117–119.

"The Rascal Ant"
Garganigo, John F. *Javier de Viana*, 142–143.

"The Recalcitrant Dead Man"
Garganigo, John F. *Javier de Viana*, 160–162.

"The Return to the Village"
Garganigo, John F. *Javier de Viana*, 126–127.

"Rounding-Up Calves"
Garganigo, John F. *Javier de Viana*, 112–113.

"The Rustic"
Garganigo, John F. *Javier de Viana*, 108–109.

"The Shame of the Family"
Garganigo, John F. *Javier de Viana*, 139–140.

"A Static Life"
Garganigo, John F. *Javier de Viana*, 147–148.

"The Storm"
Garganigo, John F. *Javier de Viana*, 121–122.

"The Thistle"
Garganigo, John F. *Javier de Viana*, 131–132.

"Through the Land of Arachanes"
Garganigo, John F. *Javier de Viana*, 92–94.

"A Tie"
Garganigo, John F. *Javier de Viana*, 133–134.

"Tiger vs. Tiger"
Garganigo, John F. *Javier de Viana*, 87–88.

"The Useless Ones"
Garganigo, John F. *Javier de Viana*, 154–155.

"A Useless Trip"
Garganigo, John F. *Javier de Viana*, 141–142.

"Yellow Field"
Garganigo, John F. *Javier de Viana*, 157–158.

GORE VIDAL

"The Ladies in the Library"
Kiernan, Robert F. *Gore Vidal*, 135–136.
Phillips, Robert. "Gore Vidal's Greek Revival: 'The Ladies in the Library,'"
    Notes Mod Am Lit, 6, i (1982), Item 3.

"A Moment of Green Laurel"
Kiernan, Robert F. *Gore Vidal*, 133–134.

"Three Stratagems"
Kiernan, Robert F. *Gore Vidal*, 132–133.

[COUNT] VILLIERS DE L'ISLE-ADAM
[JEAN MARIE MATTHIAS PHILIPPE AUGUSTE]

"Véra"
Watthée-Delmotte, Myriam. "Villiers de l'Isle-Adam et l'hégelianisme: Étude textuelle de 'Véra,'" *Les Lettres Romanes*, 38, i–ii (1984), 3–47.

HARL VINCENT

"Rex"
Cioffi, Frank. *Formula Fiction?* . . . , 119–120.

JOAN D. VINGE

"The Crystal Ship"
Yoke, Carl. "From Alienation to Personal Triumph: The Science Fiction of Joan D. Vinge," in Staicar, Tom, Ed. *The Feminine Eye* . . . , 109–110, 117.

"Eyes of Amber"
King, Betty. *Women of the Future* . . . , 183–185.
Yoke, Carl. "From Alienation . . . ," 114–115, 118–119.

"Legacy"
Yoke, Carl. "From Alienation . . . ," 108–109, 116–117.

"Mother and Child"
Yoke, Carl. "From Alienation . . . ," 111–112, 117–118.

"Phoenix in the Ashes"
Yoke, Carl. "From Alienation . . . ," 110–111.

VLADIMIR VOINOVICH

"I Want to Be Honest"
Brown, Edward J. . . . *Since the Revolution*, 3rd ed., 367.

"We Live Here"
Brown, Edward J. . . . *Since the Revolution*, 3rd ed., 365–366.

KURT VONNEGUT

"The Foster Portfolio"
Klinkowitz, Jerome. *Kurt Vonnegut*, 23–24.

"Harrison Bergeron"
Kennedy, X. J. *Instructor's Manual* . . . , 3rd ed., 35–36.

"The Hyannis Port Story"
Klinkowitz, Jerome. *Kurt Vonnegut*, 25–27.
————. *The Self-Apparent Word . . .* , 24–29.

"Tomorrow and Tomorrow and Tomorrow"
Sirlin, Rhoda, and David H. Richter. *Instructor's Manual . . .* , 171–172.

"Unready to Wear"
Broer, Lawrence R. "'Unready to Wear,'" in Dietrich, R. F., and Roger H. Sundell. *Instructor's Manual . . .* , 3rd ed., 38–41; 4th ed., 98–101.

"Who Am I This Time?"
Woodward, Robert H. "Dramatic License in Vonnegut's 'Who Am I This Time?'" *Notes Contemp Lit*, 12, i (1982), 8–9.

BEB VUYK

"The Last House in the World"
Beekman, E. M., Ed. *Two Tales . . .* , 6–18.

"A Spectator's Story"
Nieuwenhuys, Rob. *Mirror of the Indies . . .* , 275–276.

"Villa Sonja"
Nieuwenhuys, Rob. *Mirror of the Indies . . .* , 276–277.

OLIVE WADSWORTH

"Our Phil"
Cohn, Jan. "The Negro Character in Northern Magazine Fiction of the 1860's," *New England Q*, 43 (1970), 585–588.

F. N. WALDROP and POUL ANDERSON

"Tomorrow's Children"
Miesel, Sandra. *Against Time's Arrow . . .* , 43–44.

ALICE WALKER

"The Abortion"
Cooke, Michael G. *Afro-American Literature . . .* , 173–174.

"The Child Who Favored Daughter"
Harris, Trudier. "Tiptoeing Through Taboo: Incest in 'The Child Who Favored Daughter,'" *Mod Fiction Stud*, 28 (1982), 495–505.

"Elethia"
Davis, Thadious M. "Alice Walker's Celebration of Self in Southern Generations," in Prenshaw, Peggy W., Ed. *Women Writers . . .* , 43.

"Everyday Use"
Christian, Barbara. "Alice Walker: The Black Woman Artist as Wayward," in
    Evans, Mari, Ed. *Black Women . . .* , 462–463.

"Luna Advancing"
Christian, Barbara. "Alice Walker . . . ," 468–469.

"Petunias"
Davis, Thadious M. "Alice Walker's Celebration . . . ," 46–47.

"To Hell with Dying"
Perrine, Laurence, and Thomas R. Arp. *Instructor's Manual . . .* , 6th ed., 61–
    62.

ERIC WALROND

"Panama Gold"
Ikonné, Chidi. *From Du Bois to Van Vechten . . .* , 176–177.

"The Vampire Bat"
Ikonné, Chidi. *From Du Bois to Van Vechten . . .* , 178–179.

"The Wharf Rats"
Ikonné, Chidi. *From Du Bois to Van Vechten . . .* , 177–178.

EUNICE WARD

"Ah Gin"
Wu, William F. *The Yellow Peril . . .* , 64–65.

ROBERT PENN WARREN

"Blackberry Winter"
Tucker, Kenneth. "The Pied Piper—A Key to Understanding Robert Penn War-
    ren's 'Blackberry Winter,' " *Stud Short Fiction*, 19 (1982), 339–342.

"Goodwood Comes Back"
Oriard, Michael. *Dreaming of Heroes . . .* , 96–97.

"The Patented Gate and the Mean Hamburger"
Scott, Virgil, and David Madden. *Instructor's Manual . . .* , 4th ed., 88–90; Mad-
    den, David. *Instructor's Manual . . .* , 5th ed., 90–93; Madden, David, and
    Virgil Scott. *Instructor's Manual . . .* , 6th ed., 97–99.

GRANT WATSON

"Man and Brute"
Bennett, Bruce. "The Short Story,"in Bennett, Bruce, Ed. . . . *Western Australia,*
114–115.

"Out There"
Bennett, Bruce. "The Short Story,"114.

EVELYN WAUGH

"The Balance"
Heath, Jeffrey. *The Picturesque Prison* . . . , 22–23.

"The Tutor's Tale"
Heath, Jeffrey. *The Picturesque Prison* . . . , 24–25.

MASON LOCKE WEEMS

"Good News for the Devil"
Leary, Lewis. " 'Good News for the Devil': An Early Southern Admonitory
Tale," *Southern Lit J,* 17, i (1984), 96–97.

STANLEY G. WEINBAUM

"Dawn of Flame"
King, Betty. *Women of the Future* . . . , 52–53.
Stableford, Brian M. "Stanley G. Weinbaum," in Bleiler, Everett F., Ed. *Science
Fiction Writers* . . . , 146.

"Flight on Titan"
King, Betty. *Women of the Future* . . . , 53–55.

"A Martian Odyssey"
Arbur, Rosemarie. "Teleology of Human Nature for Mentality," in Myers,
Robert E., Ed. *The Intersection* . . . , 75–77.
Fredericks, Casey. *The Future of Eternity* . . . , 29–31.
Stableford, Brian M. "Stanley G. Weinbaum," 145–146.

"Parasite Planet"
Cioffi, Frank. *Formula Fiction?* . . . , 60–61.

"Pygmalion's Spectacles"
Stableford, Brian M. "Stanley G. Weinbaum," 146.

STANLEY G. WEINBAUM and RALPH MILNE FARLEY

"Smothered Seas"
King, Betty. *Women of the Future* . . . , 59–60.

H. G. WELLS

"Aepyornis Island"
Huntington, John. *The Logic of Fantasy* . . . , 60–61.

"The Cone"
Kemp, Peter H. *H. G. Wells* . . . , 102–103.

"The Country of the Blind"
Huntington, John. *The Logic of Fantasy* . . . , 126–129.
Stanzel, F. K. *A Theory of Literature* . . . , 134–136.

"A Deal in Ostriches"
Huntington, John. *The Logic of Fantasy* . . . , 27–28.

"The Flowering of the Strange Orchid"
Huntington, John. *The Logic of Fantasy* . . . , 34–35.

"The Flying Man"
Huntington, John. *The Logic of Fantasy* . . . , 37–40.

"In the Avu Observatory"
Huntington, John. *The Logic of Fantasy* . . . , 72.

"The Lord of the Dynamos"
Huntington, John. *The Logic of Fantasy* . . . , 36–37.

"The Star"
Hollow, John. *Against the Night* . . . , 14–19.

"The Stolen Bacillus"
Huntington, John. *The Logic of Fantasy* . . . , 32–35.

"A Story of the Days to Come"
Bailey, J. O. *Pilgrims Through Space* . . . , 81–83.
Huntington, John. *The Logic of Fantasy* . . . , 97–107.
Morton, Peter. *The Vital Science* . . . , 104–105.

"The Time Machine"
Begiebing, Robert J. "The Mythic Hero in H. G. Wells's 'The Time Machine,'"
    Essays Lit, 11 (1984), 201–210.
Bellamy, William. *The Novels* . . . , 51–70.
Cioffi, Frank. *Formula Fiction?* . . . , 83–84.
Fredericks, Casey. *The Future of Eternity* . . . , 69–71.
Huntington, John. *The Logic of Fantasy* . . . , 41–55.
Kemp, Peter H. *H. G. Wells* . . . , 12–15.
Morton, Peter. *The Vital Science* . . . , 106–112.
Peer, Willie van. "Pulp and Purpose: Stylistic Analysis As an Aid to a Theory
    of Texts," *Dutch Q R*, 14 (1984), 229–248.
Seeber, Hans Ulrich. "Utopien und Biologen: Zu H. G. Wells' 'The Time Ma-
    chine' und *A Modern Utopia*," in Berghahn, Klaus L., and Hans Ulrich
    Seeber, Eds. *Literarische Utopien* . . . , 172–190.

"The Triumphs of a Taxidermist"
Huntington, John. *The Logic of Fantasy* . . . , 28–30.

EUDORA WELTY

"Asphodel"
Camati, Anne S. "Violence and Death: Their Interpretation by K. A. Porter
and Eudora Welty," *Revista Letras,* 32 (1983), 53–57.

"At the Landing"
Carson, Barbara H. "Eudora Welty's Tangled Bank," *So Atlantic R,* 48, iv (1983),
8–10.
*Warren, Robert P. "Love and Separateness in Eudora Welty," in McClave,
Heather, Ed. *Women Writers* . . . , 119–121.

"The Bride of Innisfallen"
Liscio, Lorraine. "The Female Voice of Poetry in 'The Bride of Innisfallen,'"
Stud Short Fiction, 21 (1984), 357–362.

"Clytie"
Camati, Anne S. "Violence and Death . . . ," 51–52.
*Jones, Alun R. "The World of Love: The Fiction of Eudora Welty," in McClave,
Heather, Ed. *Women Writers* . . . , 99–100.

"A Curtain of Green"
Carson, Barbara H. ". . . Tangled Bank," 2–4.

"Death of a Traveling Salesman"
Carson, Barbara H. ". . . Tangled Bank," 12–13.
Kreyling, Michael. "Modernism in Welty's *A Curtain of Green and Other Stories,*"
Southern Q, 20, iv (1982), 44–45.
Perrine, Laurence, and Thomas R. Arp. *Instructor's Manual* . . . , 6th ed., 56–
58.
Sederberg, Nancy B. "Welty's 'Death of a Traveling Salesman,'" *Explicator,* 42,
i (1983), 52–54.

"First Love"
Arnold, St. George T. "Eudora Welty's 'First Love' and the Personalizing of
Southern Regional History," *J Regional Cultures,* 1, ii (1981), 97–105.
*Jones, Alun R. "The World of Love . . . ," 102–103.
Nolan, Charles J. *Aaron Burr* . . . , 111–113.

"Flowers for Marjorie"
Gretlund, Jan N. "Out of Life into Fiction," *Notes Mississippi Writers,* 14 (1982),
55–57.
Kreyling, Michael. "Modernism . . . ," 45–46.

"The Hitchhikers"
*Jones, Alun R. "The World of Love . . . ," 98–99.
Kreyling, Michael. "Modernism . . . ," 42–44.

"June Recital"
Demmin, Julia, and Daniel Curley. "Golden Apples and Silver Apples," in Pren-
    shaw, Peggy W., Ed. *Eudora Welty . . .* , 250; rpt. Prenshaw, Peggy W., Ed.
    Eudora Welty: Thirteen Essays . . . , 138–139.
*Jones, Alun R. "The World of Love . . . ," 105–106.

"Keela, the Outcast Indian Maiden"
Cooley, John R. *Savages and Naturals . . .* , 125–129.

"The Key"
Kreyling, Michael. "Modernism . . . ," 47–49.

"Lily Daw and the Three Ladies"
Watson, James G. "The American Short Story: 1930–1945," in Stevick, Philip,
    Ed. *The American Short Story, 1900–1945,* 144–145.

"Livvie"
*Warren, Robert P. "Love and Separateness . . . ," 119.

"A Memory"
*Warren, Robert P. "Love and Separateness . . . ," 117–118.

"Moon Lake"
Allen, John A. "The Other Way to Live: Demigods in Eudora Welty's Fiction,"
    in Prenshaw, Peggy W., Ed. *Eudora Welty . . .* , 32–35; rpt. Prenshaw,
    Peggy W., Ed. *Eudora Welty: Thirteen Essays . . .* , 32–35 [sic].
Carson, Barbara H. ". . . Tangled Bank," 4–8.
Demmin, Julia, and Daniel Curley. "Golden Apples and Silver Apples," in Pren-
    shaw, Peggy W., Ed. *Eudora Welty . . .* , 245–247; rpt. Prenshaw, Peggy W.,
    Ed. *Eudora Welty: Thirteen Essays . . .* , 133–135.
Pei, Lowry. "Dreaming the Other in *The Golden Apples,*" *Mod Fiction Stud,* 28
    (1982), 423–427.

"Music from Spain"
Carson, Barbara H. ". . . Tangled Bank," 13–15.
Pei, Lowry. "Dreaming the Other . . . ," 427–428.

"No Place for You, My Love"
Carson, Barbara H. ". . . Tangled Bank," 10–11.
*Jones, Alun R. "The World of Love . . . ," 109–110.

"Petrified Man"
Deer, Harriet A. "'Petrified Man,'" in Dietrich, R. F., and Roger H. Sundell.
    Instructor's Manual . . . , 3rd ed., 51–54; 4th ed., 95–97.
*Jones, Alun R. "The World of Love . . . ," 100–101.
Kennedy, X. J. and Dorothy M. *Instructor's Manual . . .* , 3rd ed., 67–68.
Scott, Virgil, and David Madden. *Instructor's Manual . . .* , 4th ed., 78–81; Mad-
    den, David. *Instructor's Manual . . .* , 5th ed., 84–86; Madden, David, and
    Virgil Scott. *Instructor's Manual . . .* , 6th ed., 91–94.
Sheidley, William E., and Ann Charters. *Instructor's Manual . . .* , 130–132.

"Powerhouse"
Cooley, John R. *Savages and Naturals* . . . , 132–136.
Kreyling, Michael. "Modernism . . . ," 46–47.
Lampkin, Loretta M. "Musical Movement and Harmony in Eudora Welty's 'Powerhouse,'" *Coll Engl Assoc Critic*, 45, i (1982), 24–28.

"Sir Rabbit"
Yaeger, Patrick S. "'Because a Fire Was in My Head': Eudora Welty and the Dialogic Imagination," *PMLA*, 99 (1984), 960–962.

"A Still Moment"
*Warren, Robert P. "Love and Separateness . . . ," 116–117.

"A Visit of Charity"
Kelly, Edward E. "Eudora Welty's Hollow Women," *Notes Mod Am Lit*, 6, ii (1982), Item 15.

"The Wanderers"
Demmin, Julia, and Daniel Curley. "Golden Apples and Silver Apples," in Prenshaw, Peggy W., Ed. *Eudora Welty* . . . , 254–257; rpt. Prenshaw, Peggy W., Ed. *Eudora Welty: Thirteen Essays* . . . , 142–145.

"The Whole World Knows"
*Jones, Alun R. "The World of Love . . . ," 106.
Pei, Lowry. "Dreaming the Other . . . ," 419–420.

"Why I Live at the P.O."
Bergman, David, Joseph de Roche, and Daniel M. Epstein. *Instructor's Manual* . . . , 15.
Du Priest, Travis. "'Why I Live at the P. O.': Eudora Welty's Epic Question," *Christianity & Lit*, 31, iv (1982), 45–54.
*Jones, Alun R. "The World of Love . . . ," 101.
Miller, James E., and Bernice Slote. *Instructor's Manual* . . . , 2nd ed., 18–19.

"The Wide Net"
Allen, John A. "The Other Way . . . ," in Prenshaw, Peggy W., Ed. *Eudora Welty* . . . , 46–47; rpt. Prenshaw, Peggy W., Ed. *Eudora Welty: Thirteen Essays* . . . , 46–47 [sic].
Carson, Barbara H. ". . . Tangled Bank," 15–17.
*Warren, Robert P. "Love and Separateness . . . ," 118–119.

"A Worn Path"
Cooley, John R. *Savages and Naturals* . . . , 129–132.
Sheidley, William E., and Ann Charters. *Instructor's Manual* . . . , 133–134.
Sirlin, Rhoda, and David H. Richter. *Instructor's Manual* . . . , 173–174.
*Welty, Eudora. "'Is Phoenix Jackson's Grandson Really Dead?'" in Charters, Ann, Ed. *The Story* . . . , 1187–1189.

NATHANAEL WEST

"A Cool Million"
Greenspan, Ezra. *The "Schlemiel"* . . . , 89–91.
Widmer, Kingsley. *Nathanael West,* 51–63.

"The Dream Life of Balso Snell"
Greenspan, Ezra. *The "Schlemiel"* . . . , 81–83.
Sherry, Charles. "Keeping One's Balance: Nathanael West's Equillabrist," *Amerikastudien,* 21, i (1976), 75–78.
Widmer, Kingsley. *Nathanael West,* 16–25.

"Miss Lonelyhearts"
Greenspan, Ezra. *The "Schlemiel"* . . . , 83–89.
Sherry, Charles. "Keeping One's Balance . . . ," 78–81.
Walsh, Joy. "'Miss Lonelyhearts': The Problem of Touching and the Primary Need for Fictions," *Notes Mod Am Lit,* 6, i (1982), Item 4.
Widmer, Kingsley. *Nathanael West,* 26–50.

REBECCA WEST

"The Salt of the Earth"
Beauman, Nicola. *A Very Great Profession* . . . , 168–169.

WALLACE WEST

"Sculptors of Life"
Franklin, H. Bruce. "America as Science Fiction: 1939," in Slusser, George E., Eric S. Rabkin, and Robert Scholes, Eds. *Coordinates* . . . , 113–114.

EDITH WHARTON

"Autre Temps"
Kimbel, Ellen. "The American Short Story: 1900–1920," in Stevick, Philip, Ed. *The American Short Story, 1900–1945,* 49–51.

"Ethan Frome"
Blackall, Jean F. "The Sledding Accident in 'Ethan Frome,'" *Stud Short Fiction,* 21 (1984), 145–146.
Gimbel, Wendy. *Edith Wharton* . . . , 61–92.
Murad, Orlene. "Edith Wharton and Ethan Frome," *Mod Lang Stud,* 13, iii (1983), 90–103.
Stein, Allen F. *After the Vows* . . . , 225–230.
Wershoven, Carol. *The Female Intruder* . . . , 20–22.

"The Eyes"
Kimbel, Ellen. "The American Short Story . . . ," 42–45.
Lewis, R. W. B. "Introduction," in Lewis, R. W. B., Ed. *The Collected Short Stories* . . . , xix–xxi; rpt. McClave, Heather, Ed. *Women Writers* . . . , 47–48.

"The Fulness of Life"
Stein, Allen F. *After the Vows* . . . , 210–211.

"The Hermit and the Wild Woman"
Lewis, R. W. B. "Introduction," xviii–xix; rpt. McClave, Heather, Ed. *Women Writers* . . . , 45–47.

"Joy in the House"
Stein, Allen F. *After the Vows* . . . , 222–224.

"The Lamp of Psyche"
Stein, Allen F. *After the Vows* . . . , 213–214.

"The Letters"
Stein, Allen F. *After the Vows* . . . , 263–265.

"The Line of Least Resistance"
Stein, Allen F. *After the Vows* . . . , 219–220.

"The Long Run"
Lewis, R. W. B. "Introduction," xii; rpt. McClave, Heather, Ed. *Women Writers* . . . , 38–39.

"The Mission of Jane"
Stein, Allen F. *After the Vows* . . . , 259–260.

"The Other Two"
Kimbel, Ellen. "The American Short Story . . . ," 47–49.
Lewis, R. W. B. "Introduction," xiv–xv; rpt. McClave, Heather, Ed. *Women Writers* . . . , 41–42.

"Pomegranate Seeds"
Lewis, R. W. B. "Introduction," xvi; rpt. McClave, Heather, Ed. *Women Writers* . . . , 43.

"The Quicksand"
Stein, Allen F. *After the Vows* . . . , 220–221.

"The Reckoning"
Stein, Allen F. *After the Vows* . . . , 221–222.

"Roman Fever"
Lewis, R. W. B. "Introduction," xxiv.
O'Neal, Michael J. "Point of View and Narrative Technique in the Fiction of Edith Wharton," *Style,* 17 (1983), 270–272.
Sheidley, William E., and Ann Charters. *Instructor's Manual* . . . , 42–44.
Sirlin, Rhoda, and David H. Richter. *Instructor's Manual* . . . , 175–177.

"Souls Belated"
Conn, Peter. *The Divided Mind* . . . , 177–181.
Kimbel, Ellen. "The American Short Story . . . ," 45–47.
Lewis, R. W. B. "Introduction," x–xi; rpt. McClave, Heather, Ed. *Women Writers* . . . , 36.

"The Valley of Childish Things"
Wershoven, Carol. *The Female Intruder*..., 75–77.

"Xingu"
Funston, Judith. "'Xingu': Edith Wharton's Velvet Gauntlet," *Stud Am Fiction*, 12 (1984), 227–234.

CECIL B. WHITE

"The Retreat to Mars"
Meyers, Walter E. *Aliens and Linguists*..., 41–42.

E. B. WHITE

"Child's Play"
Elledge, Scott. *E. B. White*..., 106–107.

"The Morning of the Day They Did It"
Elledge, Scott. *E. B. White*..., 308–309.

"The Second Tree from the Corner"
Abcarian, Richard, and Marvin Klotz. *Instructor's Manual*..., 3rd ed., 22–23.
Elledge, Scott. *E. B. White*..., 269–270.

PATRICK WHITE

"Being Kind to Titina"
Weigel, John A. *Patrick White*, 90.

"A Cheery Soul"
Weigel, John A. *Patrick White*, 91.

"The Cockatoos"
Weigel, John A. *Patrick White*, 94–95.

"Dead Roses"
Nelson, Timothy G. A. "Proserpine and Pluto, Ariadne and Bacchus," *Australian Lit Stud*, 10 (1981), 111–114.
Weigel, John A. *Patrick White*, 90.

"Down at the Dump"
Brady, Veronica. "'Down at the Dump' and Lacan's Mirror Stage," *Australian Lit Stud*, 11 (1983), 233–237.
Weigel, John A. *Patrick White*, 91–92.

"The Evening at Sissy Kamara's"
Weigel, John A. *Patrick White*, 89–90.

"Five-Twenty"
Weigel, John A. *Patrick White*, 95–96.

"The Full Belly"
Weigel, John A. *Patrick White*, 96.

"The Night the Prowler"
Weigel, John A. *Patrick White*, 92–93.

"Sicilian Vespers"
Weigel, John A. *Patrick White*, 93–94.

"The Twitching Colonel"
Weigel, John A. *Patrick White*, 17–18.

"The Woman Who Wasn't Allowed to Keep Cats"
Weigel, John A. *Patrick White*, 89.

"A Woman's Hand"
Weigel, John A. *Patrick White*, 94.

WILLIAM ALLEN WHITE

"The Mercy of Death"
Jernigan, E. Jay. *William Allen White*, 85.

"A Most Lamentable Comedy"
Jernigan, E. Jay. *William Allen White*, 84–85.

"A Social Rectangle"
Jernigan, E. Jay. *William Allen White*, 97.

"The Tremolo Stop"
Jernigan, E. Jay. *William Allen White*, 86.

"A Victory of the People"
Jernigan, E. Jay. *William Allen White*, 84.

RUDY WIEBE

"Bluecoats on the Sacred Hill of the Wild Peas"
Howells, Coral A. "'If I Had a Reliable Interpreter Who Would Make a Reliable
    Interpretation': Language, Screams, and Silence in Rudy Wiebe's *Where Is
    the Voice Coming From?*" *Recherches Anglaises et Américaines*, 16 (1983), 99–
    100.

"The Naming of Albert Johnson"
Howells, Coral A. "'If I Had a Reliable Interpreter . . . ,'" 102–103.

"Where Is the Voice Coming From?"
Howells, Coral A. "'If I Had a Reliable Interpreter...,'" 100–102.

ALLEN WIER

"Things About to Disappear"
Madden, David. *Instructor's Manual* . . . , 5th ed., 114–116; Madden, David, and
    Virgil Scott. *Instructor's Manual* . . . , 6th ed., 131–134.

ELIE WIESEL

"The Wandering Jew"
Fisch, Harold. *A Remembered Future* . . . , 77–78.

OSCAR WILDE

"Lord Arthur Savile's Crime"
Klein, Alfons. "Motive und Themen in Oscar Wildes 'Lord Arthur Savile's
    Crime,'" in Wolpers, Theodor, Ed. *Motive und Themen* . . . , 66–87.

MICHAEL WILDING

"Hector and Freddie"
Ross, Bruce C. "A New Version of Pastoral: Development in Michael Wilding's
    Fiction," *Australian Lit Stud*, 11 (1983), 185.

"The Phallic Forest"
Ross, Bruce C. "A New Version of Pastoral . . . , 185.

HUGH WILEY

"In Chinatown"
Wu, William F. *The Yellow Peril* . . . , 144–145.

KATE WILHELM

"April Fools' Day Forever"
Law, Richard. "Science Fiction Women: Victims, Rebels, Heroes," in Hassler,
    Donald M., Ed. *Patterns* . . . , 14.

JOHN A. WILLIAMS

"Son in the Afternoon"
Harris, Trudier. *From Mammies to Militants* . . . , 136–143.
Muller, Gilbert H. *John A. Williams*, 12–13.

WILLIAM CARLOS WILLIAMS

"A Face of Stone"
Watson, James G. "The American Short Story: 1930–1945," in Stevick, Philip,
    Ed. *The American Short Story, 1900–1945,* 120–121.

"Jean Beicke"
Monteiro, George. "The Doctor's Black Bag: William Carlos Williams' Passaic
    River Stories," *Mod Lang Stud,* 13, i (1983), 79–81.
Watson, James G. "The American Short Story . . . ," 120–121.

"The Knife of the Times"
Sorrentino, Gilbert. "Polish Mothers and 'The Knife of the Times,'" in Terrell,
    Carroll F., Ed. *William Carlos Williams . . . ,* 391–395.

"A Night in June"
Monteiro, George. "The Doctor's Black Bag . . . ," 81–84.

"The Use of Force"
*Dietrich, R. F. "'The Use of Force,'" in Dietrich, R. F., and Roger H. Sundell.
    Instructor's Manual . . . , 4th ed., 12–17.
McKeon, Zahava K. *Novels and Arguments . . . ,* 60–61.
Madden, David. *Instructor's Manual . . . ,* 5th ed., 1–2; Madden, David, and Vir-
    gil Scott. *Instructor's Manual . . . ,* 6th ed., 8–10.
Monteiro, George. "The Doctor's Black Bag . . . ," 78–79.
Watson, James G. "The American Short Story . . . ," 120–121.

JACK WILLIAMSON

"Breakdown"
Born, Daniel. "Character as Perception: Science Fiction and the Christian Man
    of Faith," *Extrapolation,* 24 (1983), 255–256.
Myers, Robert E. "Jack Williamson," in Bleiler, Everett F., Ed. *Science Fiction
    Writers . . . ,* 229.

"Guinevere for Everybody"
Myers, Robert E. "Jack Williamson," 228–229.

"Jamboree"
Meyers, Walter E. *Aliens and Linguists . . . ,* 46–47.

ANGUS WILSON

"Fresh Air Fiend"
Swinden, Patrick. *The English Novel . . . ,* 132–133.

"Raspberry Jam"
Fletcher, Mary D. "Wilson's 'Raspberry Jam,'" *Explicator,* 40 (1982), 49–51.
Swinden, Patrick. *The English Novel . . . ,* 136–138.

"Realpolitik"
Monod, Sylvere. "A Bit Off the Darling Set: The World of Sir Angus Wilson's
    Short Stories," *Les Cahiers de la Nouvelle*, 1 (1983), 97–100.

EDMUND WILSON

"Ellen Terhune"
Douglas, George H. *Edmund Wilson's America*, 132–134.

"Glimpses of Wilbur Flick"
Douglas, George H. *Edmund Wilson's America*, 134–137.

"The Man Who Shot Snapping Turtles"
Douglas, George H. *Edmund Wilson's America*, 129–132.

"Mr. and Mrs. Blackburn at Home"
Douglas, George H. *Edmund Wilson's America*, 144–146.

"The Princess with the Golden Hair"
Douglas, George H. *Edmund Wilson's America*, 137–144.

OWEN WISTER

"Absalom and Moulting Pelican"
Cobbs, John L. *Owen Wister*, 94–95.

"Bad Medicine"
Cobbs, John L. *Owen Wister*, 93–94.

"Balaam and Pedro"
Cobbs, John L. *Owen Wister*, 77.

"Captain Quid"
Cobbs, John L. *Owen Wister*, 95.

"The Drake Who Had Means of His Own"
Cobbs, John L. *Owen Wister*, 92.

"Extra Dry"
Cobbs, John L. *Owen Wister*, 91.

"The General's Bluff"
Cobbs, John L. *Owen Wister*, 43.

"Hank's Woman"
Cobbs, John L. *Owen Wister*, 49.

"Happy-Teeth"
Cobbs, John L. *Owen Wister*, 88–89.

P. G. WODEHOUSE

"Bill the Bloodhound"
Green, Benny. *P. G. Wodehouse* . . . , 140–142.

"Chester Forgets Himself"
Green, Benny. *P. G. Wodehouse* . . . , 89–90.

"Extricating Young Gussie"
Green, Benny. *P. G. Wodehouse* . . . , 138–140.

"It's a Long Way Back to Mother's Knee"
Green, Benny. *P. G. Wodehouse* . . . , 135–136.

"Rodney Has a Relapse"
Green, Benny. *P. G. Wodehouse* . . . , 210–212.

CHRISTA WOLF

"Selbstversuch"
Pegoraro, Anna C. "'Mann' versus 'Mensch': Zur Christa Wolfs Erzählung 'Selbstversuch,'" *Colloquia Germanica*, 15 (1982), 239–252.

"Unter den Linden"
Bradley, Brigitte L. "Christa Wolfs Erzählung 'Unter den Linden': Unerwünschtes und erwünschtes 'Glück,'" *Germ Q*, 57 (1984), 231–249.

THOMAS WOLFE

"An Angel on the Porch"
Madden, David, and Virgil Scott. *Instructor's Manual* . . . , 6th ed., 23–26.

"The Bums at Sunset"
Evans, Elizabeth. *Thomas Wolfe*, 103–104.

"Chickamauga"
Evans, Elizabeth. *Thomas Wolfe*, 121–122.

"Death the Proud Brother"
Evans, Elizabeth. *Thomas Wolfe*, 111–114.

"The Face of War"
Evans, Elizabeth. *Thomas Wolfe*, 108–111.

"The Lost Boy"
Evans, Elizabeth. *Thomas Wolfe*, 118–121.

"No Door"
Evans, Elizabeth. *Thomas Wolfe*, 105–108.

"The Party at Jack's"
Evans, Elizabeth. *Thomas Wolfe*, 132–133.

"The Sun and the Rain"
Boyer, James. "The Metaphoric Level in Wolfe's 'The Sun and the Rain,'" *Stud Short Fiction*, 19 (1982), 384–387.

BARBARA WOODS

"The Final Supper"
Harris, Trudier. *From Mammies to Militants . . .* , 156–160.

DOUGLAS WOOLF

"Bank Days"
Bowering, George. "Douglas Woolf's 'Bank Days,'" *R Contemp Fiction*, 2, i (1982), 83–87.

VIRGINIA WOOLF

"Kew Gardens"
Bishop, Edward L. "Pursuing 'It' Through 'Kew Gardens,'" *Stud Short Fiction*, 19 (1982), 269–275.
Madden, David, and Virgil Scott. *Instructor's Manual . . .* , 6th ed., 62–65.

"Moments of Being"
Sheidley, William E., and Ann Charters. *Instructor's Manual . . .* , 76.

"Monday or Tuesday"
Wilde, Alan. *Horizons of Assent . . .* , 34–35.

"The New Dress"
Miller, James E., and Bernice Slote. *Instructor's Manual . . .* , 2nd ed., 12–13.
Sirlin, Rhoda, and David H. Richter. *Instructor's Manual . . .* , 178–180.

LAN WRIGHT

"And Earthly Power . . ."
Aldiss, Brian. "British Science Fiction Now: Studies of Three Writers," *SF Horizons*, 2 (Winter, 1965), 14–16; rpt. Aldiss, Brian, and Harry Harrison, Eds. *SF Horizons 1 and 2*, 14–16.

RICHARD WRIGHT

"Big Boy Leaves Home"
Allen, Mary. *Animals . . .* , 140–141.
Baker, Houston A. *Blues, Ideology . . .* , 155–157.

Gibson, Donald B. *The Politics* . . . , 25–26.
Kent, George E. "Richard Wright: Blackness and the Adventure of Western Culture," *Coll Lang Assoc J*, 12 (1969), 330–331; rpt. Macksey, Richard, and Frank E. Moorer, Eds. *Richard Wright* . . . , 44–45.
*Margolies, Edward. "The Short Stories: *Uncle Tom's Children: Eight Men*," in Hakutani, Yoshinobu, Ed. *Critical Essays* . . . , 130–132.
Watson, James G. "The American Short Story: 1930–1945," in Stevick, Philip, Ed. *The American Short Story, 1900–1945*, 113.

"Bright and Morning Star"
*Burgum, Edwin B. "The Art of Richard Wright's Short Stories," in Macksey, Richard, and Frank E. Moorer, Eds. *Richard Wright* . . . , 204–205.
Gibson, Donald B. *The Politics* . . . , 34–35.
*Margolies, Edward. "The Short Stories . . . ," 136–137.

"Down by the Riverside"
Gibson, Donald B. *The Politics* . . . , 26–27.
*Margolies, Edward. "The Short Stories . . . ," 132–133.

"Fire and Cloud"
*Margolies, Edward. "The Short Stories . . . ," 135–137.

"Long Black Song"
*Burgum, Edwin B. "The Art . . . ," 201–204.
Gibson, Donald B. *The Politics* . . . , 27–31.
Kent, George E. "Richard Wright . . . ," 332–333; rpt. Macksey, Richard, and Frank E. Moorer, Eds. *Richard Wright* . . . , 45–46.
*Margolies, Edward. "The Short Stories . . . ," 129–130.

"Man, God Ain't Like That"
*Margolies, Edward. "The Short Stories . . . ," 146–147.

"Man of All Work"
Harris, Trudier. *From Mammies to Militants* . . . , 71–86.
*Margolies, Edward. "The Short Stories . . . ," 145–146.

"The Man Who Killed a Shadow"
Bryant, Earle V. "The Sexualization of Racism in Richard Wright's 'The Man Who Killed a Shadow,'" *Black Am Lit Forum*, 16 (1982), 119–121.
*Margolies, Edward. "The Short Stories . . . ," 144–145.
Miller, Eugene E. "Folkloric Aspects of Wright's 'The Man Who Killed a Shadow,'" *Coll Lang Assoc J*, 22 (1983), 210–223.

"The Man Who Lived Underground"
*Abcarian, Richard, and Marvin Klotz. *Instructor's Manual* . . . , 2nd ed., 24–26; 3rd ed., 23–25.
Baker, Houston A. *Blues, Ideology* . . . , 157–172.
Gibson, Donald B. *The Politics* . . . , 38–40.
Lee, A. Robert. "Richard Wright's Inside Narratives," in Gray, Richard, Ed. *American Fiction* . . . , 212–213.

Lee, Dorothy H. "Denial of Time and the Failure of Moral Choice: Camus' 'The Stranger,' Faulkner's 'Old Man,' and Wright's 'The Man Who Lived Underground,'" *Coll Lang Assoc J*, 23 (1980), 370–371.
*Margolies, Edward. "The Short Stories . . . ," 147.
Mitchell, Carolyn. "'A Laying on of Hands': Transcending the City in Ntozake Shange's 'for colored girls who have considered suicide / when the rainbow is enuf,'" in Squier, Susan M., Ed. *Women Writers* . . . , 236–237.

"The Man Who Was Almost a Man"
Allen, Mary. *Animals* . . . , 139–140.
Sheidley, William E., and Ann Charters. *Instructor's Manual* . . . , 129.
Sirlin, Rhoda, and David H. Richter. *Instructor's Manual* . . . , 180–182.

"The Man Who Went to Chicago"
Allen, Mary. *Animals* . . . , 145–147.

S. FOWLER WRIGHT

"Automata"
Stableford, Brian. "Against the New Gods: The Speculative Fiction of S. Fowler Wright," *Foundation*, 29 (November, 1983), 32–33.

"The Choice"
Stableford, Brian. "Against the New Gods . . . ," 34.

"The Rat"
Stableford, Brian. "Against the New Gods . . . ," 33.

"Rule"
Stableford, Brian. "Against the New Gods . . . ," 33–34.

JOHN WYNDHAM [JOHN BEYNON HARRIS]

"Consider Her Ways"
King, Betty. *Women of the Future* . . . , 100–102.

YAMADA BIMYŌ

"The Butterfly"
Keene, Donald. *Dawn to the West* . . . , 125–126.

HISAYE YAMAMOTO

"Yoneko's Earthquake"
Crow, Charles L. "Home and Transcendence in Los Angeles Fiction," in Fine, David, Ed. *Los Angeles in Fiction*, 200–202.

AUGUSTÍN YÁÑEZ

"Baralipton"
Brushwood, John S. "The Spanish American Short Story from Quiroga to Borges," in Peden, Margaret S., Ed. *The Latin American Short Story . . . ,*" 80.

CHELSEA QUINN YARBRO

"False Dawn"
King, Betty. *Women of the Future . . . ,* 186–187.

YASHPAL

"One Cigarette"
Weir, Ann L. "Courtesans and Prostitutes in South Asian Literature," in Horn, Pierre L., and Mary B. Pringle, Eds. *The Image of the Prostitute . . . ,* 86–87.

WILLIAM BUTLER YEATS

"The Adoration of the Magi"
O'Donnell, William H. *A Guide . . . ,* 122–129.

"The Binding of the Hair"
O'Donnell, William H. *A Guide . . . ,* 70–73.

"Costello the Proud"
O'Donnell, William H. *A Guide . . . ,* 84–87.

"The Cradles of Gold"
O'Donnell, William H. *A Guide . . . ,* 79–81.

"The Crucifixion of the Outcast"
O'Donnell, William H. *A Guide . . . ,* 55–59.

"The Curse of the Fires and the Shadows"
O'Donnell, William H. *A Guide . . . ,* 52–54.

"The Death of Hanrahan"
O'Donnell, William H. *A Guide . . . ,* 81–84.

"Dhoya"
O'Donnell, William H. *A Guide . . . ,* 31–33.

"Hanrahan and Cathleen, the Daughter of Houlihan" [originally titled "Kathleen-ny-Hoolihan"]
O'Donnell, William H. *A Guide . . . ,* 61–62.

ABRAHAM B. YEHOSHUA

ANZIA YEZIERSKA

"A Bed for the Night"
Schoen, Carol B. *Anzia Yezierska,* 52–53.

"A Chair in Heaven"
Schoen, Carol B. *Anzia Yezierska,* 119–121.

"Children of Loneliness"
Schoen, Carol B. *Anzia Yezierska,* 50–51.

"Dreams and Dollars"
Schoen, Carol B. *Anzia Yezierska,* 53.

"The Fat of the Land"
Schoen, Carol B. *Anzia Yezierska,* 29–31.

"The Free Vacation House"
Schoen, Carol B. *Anzia Yezierska,* 18–19.

"How I Found America"
Schoen, Carol B. *Anzia Yezierska,* 27–29.

"Hunger"
Schoen, Carol B. *Anzia Yezierska,* 21–22.

"The Lord Giveth"
Schoen, Carol B. *Anzia Yezierska,* 54.

"The Lost Beautifulness"
Schoen, Carol B. *Anzia Yezierska,* 24–25.

"The Lower Depths of Upper Broadway"
Schoen, Carol B. *Anzia Yezierska,* 119.

"The Miracle"
Schoen, Carol B. *Anzia Yezierska,* 22–24.

"Mostly About Myself"
Schoen, Carol B. *Anzia Yezierska,* 57–59.

"My Own People"
Schoen, Carol B. *Anzia Yezierska,* 25–27.

"The Open Cage"
Schoen, Carol B. *Anzia Yezierska,* 124–125.

"Soap and Water"
Schoen, Carol B. *Anzia Yezierska,* 17.

"Take Up Your Bed and Walk"
Schoen, Carol B. *Anzia Yezierska,* 123–124.

"To the Stars"
Schoen, Carol B. *Anzia Yezierska,* 54.

"Where Lovers Dream"
Schoen, Carol B. *Anzia Yezierska,* 22.

"Wings"
Schoen, Carol B. *Anzia Yezierska,* 20–21.

YOKOMITSU RIICHI

"The Bridegroom's Reflections, or The Man Who Pursued Current Fashions"
Keene, Donald. *Dawn to the West . . . ,* 654–655.

"The Fly"
Keene, Donald. *Dawn to the West . . . ,* 646–647.

"The Machine"
Keene, Donald. *Dawn to the West . . . ,* 658–661.

MATILDA YUFIT

"Husband and Wife"
Blum, Jakub. "Soviet Russian Literature," in Blum, Jakub, and Vera Rich. *The Image of the Jew . . . ,* 64.

EVGENIZ ZAMJATIN [same as EVGENIJ or EVGENIĬ ZAMIATIN]

"Africa"
Shane, Alex M. . . . *Evgeniz Zamjatin,* 111–112.

"Alatyr"
Shane, Alex M. . . . *Evgeniz Zamjatin,* 105–106.

"The Cave"
Barratt, Andrew. "Adam and the Ark of Ice: Man and Revolution in Zamiatin's 'The Cave,'" *Irish Slavonic Stud,* 4 (1983), 20–37.
Shane, Alex M. . . . *Evgeniz Zamjatin,* 44–45.

"Comrade Čurygin Has the Floor"
Shane, Alex M. . . . *Evgeniz Zamjatin,* 177–178.

"The Eyes"
Shane, Alex M. . . . *Evgeniz Zamjatin,* 149–150.

"The Fisher of Men"
Shane, Alex M. . . . *Evgeniz Zamjatin,* 136–137.

"God"
Shane, Alex M. . . . *Evgeniz Zamjatin*, 114–115.

"The Islanders"
Shane, Alex M. . . . *Evgeniz Zamjatin*, 132–137.

"Mamaj"
Shane, Alex M. . . . *Evgeniz Zamjatin*, 148–149.

"The Nursery"
Shane, Alex M. . . . *Evgeniz Zamjatin*, 146–147.

"Old Russia"
Shane, Alex M. . . . *Evgeniz Zamjatin*, 167–171.

"Out in the Sticks"
Shane, Alex M. . . . *Evgeniz Zamjatin*, 102–104.

"The Provinces"
Shane, Alex M. . . . *Evgeniz Zamjatin*, 99–102.

"Scythians?"
Shane, Alex M. . . . *Evgeniz Zamjatin*, 18–19.

"A Story About the Most Important Thing"
Shane, Alex M. . . . *Evgeniz Zamjatin*, 173–175.

"X"
Shane, Alex M. . . . *Evgeniz Zamjatin*, 175–176.

ROGER ZELAZNY

"And Call Me Conrad"
Yoke, Carl B. *Roger Zelazny*, 30.
——. "Roger Zelazny's Bold New Mythologies," in Staicar, Tom, Ed. *Critical Encounters II* . . . , 76–78.

"The Doors of His Face, the Lamps of His Mouth"
Nicholls, Peter. "Roger Zelazny," in Bleiler, Everett F., Ed. *Science Fiction Writers* . . . , 564–565.
Yoke, Carl. ". . . Bold New Mythologies," 75–76.

"The Engine at Heartspring's Center"
Yoke, Carl B. *Roger Zelazny*, 95–96.
——. "What a Piece of Work Is a Man: Mechanical Gods in the Fiction of Roger Zelazny," in Dunn, Thomas P., and Richard D. Erlich, Eds. *The Mechanical God* . . . , 64–65.

"The Eve of RUMOKO"
Yoke, Carl B. *Roger Zelazny*, 72–74.

"For a Breath I Tarry"
Reilly, Robert. "How Machines Become Human: Process and Attribute," in Dunn, Thomas P., and Richard D. Erlich, Eds. *The Mechanical God . . .*, 154–164.

"Home Is the Hangman"
Yoke, Carl B. *Roger Zelazny*, 76–79.

"Kjwalll'Kje'k'koothaill'kje'k"
Yoke, Carl B. *Roger Zelazny*, 74–76.

"The Man Who Loved the Faioli"
Yoke, Carl B. *Roger Zelazny*, 96.

"A Rose for Ecclesiastes"
Nicholls, Peter. "Roger Zelazny," 546.
Yoke, Carl B. *Roger Zelazny*, 31.

"This Moment of the Storm"
Yoke, Carl B. *Roger Zelazny*, 94.

R. ZERNOVA

"The Sunny Side"
Blum, Jakub. "Soviet Russian Literature," in Blum, Jakub, and Vera Rich. *The Image of the Jew . . .*, 44.

MARIYA ZHUKOVA

"Judgment of the Heart"
Mersereau, John. *Russian Romantic Fiction*, 286–287.

"Self-Sacrifice"
Mersereau, John. *Russian Romantic Fiction*, 287–288.

PAMELA ZOLINE

"The Heat Death of the Universe"
Law, Richard. "Science Fiction Women: Victims, Rebels, Heroes," in Hassler, Donald M., Ed. *Patterns . . .*, 12.

A CHECKLIST OF BOOKS USED

Abcarian, Richard, and Marvin Klotz. *Instructor's Manual to Accompany "Literature: The Human Experience, Third Edition."* New York: St. Martin's Press, 1982.

Accad, Évelyne. *Veil of Shame: The Role of Women in the Contemporary Fiction of North Africa and the Arab World.* Sherbrooke, Quebec: Éditions Naaman, 1978.

Aldiss, Brian, and Harry Harrison, Eds. *SF Horizons 1 and 2.* New York: Arno Press, 1975.

Allen, Elizabeth. *A Woman's Place in the Novels of Henry James.* New York: St. Martin's Press, 1984.

Allen, Mary. *Animals in American Literature.* Urbana: Univ. of Illinois Press, 1983.

Allentuck, Marcia, Ed. *The Achievement of Isaac Bashevis Singer.* Carbondale: Southern Illinois Univ. Press, 1969.

Alter, Iska. *The Good Man's Dilemma: Social Criticism in the Fiction of Bernard Malamud.* New York: AMS Press, 1981.

Anderer, Paul. *Other Worlds: Arishima Takeo and the Bounds of Modern Japanese Fiction.* New York: Columbia Univ. Press, 1984.

Anderson, David D. *Louis Bromfield.* New York: Twayne, 1964.

Apter, T. E. *Fantasy Literature: An Approach to Reality.* Bloomington: Indiana Univ. Press, 1982.

Arnold, Marilyn. *Willa Cather's Short Fiction.* Athens: Ohio Univ. Press, 1984.

Arthur, Anthony, Ed. *Critical Essays on Wallace Stegner.* Boston: G. K. Hall, 1982.

Asals, Frederick. *Flannery O'Connor: The Imagination of Extremity.* Athens: Univ. of Georgia Press, 1982.

Ashton, Rosemary. *George Eliot.* New York: Oxford Univ. Press, 1983.

Avins, Carol. *Border Crossings: The West and Russian Identity in Soviet Literature, 1917–1934.* Berkeley: Univ. of California Press, 1983.

Awwad, Hanan A. *Arab Causes in the Fiction of Ghadah Al-Samman (1961–1975).* Sherbrooke, Quebec: Naaman, 1983.

Axelrod, Alan. *Charles Brockden Brown: An American Tale.* Austin: Univ. of Texas Press, 1983.

Bacarisse, Salvador, Bernard Bentley, Mercedes Clarasó, and Douglas Gifford, Eds. *What's Past Is Prologue: A Collection of Essays in Honour of L. J. Woodward.* Edinburgh: Scottish Academic Publishers, 1984.

Bailey, J. O. *Pilgrims Through Space and Time: Trends and Patterns in Scientific and Utopian Fiction.* New York: Argus, 1974.

Baker, Houston A. *Blues, Ideology, and Afro-American Literature: A Vernacular Theory.* Chicago: Univ. of Chicago Press, 1984.

Bakhtin, Mikhail. *Problems of Dostoevsky's Poetics,* trans. Caryl Emerson. Minneapolis: Univ. of Minnesota Press, 1984.

Balakian, Anna, Ed. *The Symbolist Movement in Literature of European Languages.* Budapest: Akadémiai Kiadó, 1982.

Barber, Benjamin R., and Michael J. G. McGrath, Eds. *The Artist and Political Vision.* New Brunswick, N.J.: Transaction, 1982.

Barbour, John D. *Tragedy as a Critique of Virtue: The Novel and Ethical Reflection.* Chico, Calif.: Scholars Press, 1984.

Bargainnier, Earl F., Ed. *Twelve Englishmen of Mystery.* Bowling Green: Bowling Green State Univ. Popular Press, 1984.

Bargen, Doris G. *The Fiction of Stanley Elkin.* Frankfurt: Peter Lang, 1980.

Barnett, Ursula A. *A Vision of Order: A Study of Black South African Literature in English (1914–1980).* London: Sinclair Browne, 1983; Am. ed. Amherst: Univ. of Massachusetts Press, 1983.

Bassoff, Bruce. *The Secret Sharers: Studies in Contemporary Fictions.* New York: AMS Press, 1983.

Batchelor, John. *The Edwardian Novelists.* New York: St. Martin's Press, 1982.

Baumgarten, Murray. *City Scriptures: Modern Jewish Writing.* Cambridge: Harvard Univ. Press, 1982.

Beaty, Jerome. *The Norton Introduction to the Short Novel.* New York: Norton, 1982; Canadian ed. Toronto: McLeod, 1982.

Beauchamp, Gorman. *Jack London.* Mercer Island, Wash.: Starmont, 1984.

Beauman, Nicola. *A Very Great Profession: The Woman's Novel 1914–39.* London: Virago Press, 1983.

Becker, George J. *Master European Realists of the Nineteenth Century.* New York: Ungar, 1982.

Bedell, R. Meredith. *Stella Benson.* Boston: Twayne, 1983.

Beekman, E. M., Ed. *Two Tales of the Indies.* Amherst: Univ. of Massachusetts Press, 1983.

Bellamy, William. *The Novels of Wells, Bennett and Galsworthy: 1890–1910.* London: Routledge & Kegan Paul, 1971.

Bennett, Benjamin, Anton Kaes, and William J. Lillyman, Eds. *Probleme der Moderne: Studien zur deutschen Literatur von Nietzsche bis Brecht.* Tübingen: Niemeyer, 1983.

Bennett, Bruce, Ed. *The Literature of Western Australia.* Perth: Univ. of Western Australia Press, 1979.

Benstock, Bernard, Ed. *The Seventh of Joyce.* Bloomington: Indiana Univ. Press, 1982; Brt. ed. Brighton, Sussex: Harvester Press, 1982.

Berghahn, Klaus L., and Hans Ulrich Seeber, Eds. *Literarische Utopien von Morus bis zu Gegenwart.* Königstein: Athenäum, 1983.

Bergman, David, Joseph de Roche, and Daniel M. Epstein. *Instructor's Manual for "The Heath Guide to Literature."* Lexington, Mass.: D. C. Heath, 1984.

Bernheimer, Charles. *Flaubert and Kafka: Studies in Psychopoetic Structure.* New Haven: Yale Univ. Press, 1982.

Berry, Eliot. *A Poetry of Love and Darkness: The Fiction of John Hawkes.* San Bernardino, Calif.: Borgo, 1979.

Bertens, Johannes W. *The Fiction of Paul Bowles: The Soul Is the Weariest Part of the Body.* Amsterdam: Rodopi, 1979; Am. ed. Atlantic Highlands, N.J.: Humanities Press, 1979.

Bertram, James. *Dan Davin.* Auckland: Oxford Univ. Press, 1983.

Bickley, R. Bruce. *Joel Chandler Harris.* Boston: Twayne, 1978.

Bilik, Dorothy S. *Immigrant-Survivors: Post-Holocaust Consciousness in Recent Jewish American Fiction.* Middletown, Conn.: Wesleyan Univ. Press, 1981.

Blair, Dorothy S. *Senegalese Literature: A Critical History.* Boston: Twayne, 1984.

Blake, Kathleen. *Love and the Woman Question in Victorian Literature: The Art of Self-Postponement.* Brighton, Sussex: Harvester Press, 1983; Am. ed. Totowa, N.J.: Barnes & Noble, 1983.

Bleiler, Everett F., Ed. *Science Fiction Writers: Critical Studies of the Major Authors from the Early Nineteenth Century to the Present Day.* New York: Scribner, 1982.

Blinkin, Meir. *Stories by Meir Blinkin,* trans. Max Rosenfeld, introd. Ruth R. Wisse. Albany: State Univ. of New York Press, 1984.

Blum, Jakub, and Vera Rich. *The Image of the Jew in Soviet Literature: The Post-Stalin Period.* New York: Ktav Publishing House [for Institute of Jewish Affairs], 1984.

Bodenstein, Jürgen. *"The Excitement of Verbal Adventure": A Study of Vladimir Nabokov's English Prose,* I. Heidelberg: Ruprecht-Karl Univ., 1977.

Bold, Alan, Ed. *Muriel Spark: The Odd Capacity for Vision.* London: Vision, 1984; Am. ed. Totowa, N.J.: Barnes & Noble, 1984.

Bond, David L. *The Fiction of André Pieyre de Mandiargues.* Syracuse: Syracuse Univ. Press, 1982.

Bowen, Zack, Ed. *Irish Renaissance Annual IV.* East Brunswick, N.J.: Associated Univ. Presses [for Univ. of Delaware Press], 1983.

Bowen, Zack, and James F. Carens, Eds. *A Companion to Joyce Studies.* Westport, Conn.: Greenwood Press, 1984.

Boyd, Michael. *The Reflexive Novel: Fiction as Critique.* East Brunswick, N.J.: Associated Univ. Presses [for Bucknell Univ. Press], 1983.

Bradbury, Malcolm. *Saul Bellow.* London: Methuen, 1982.

Brady, Kristin. *The Short Stories of Thomas Hardy.* New York: St. Martin's Press, 1982.

Braham, Jeanne. *A Sort of Columbus: The American Voyages of Saul Bellow's Fiction.* Athens: Univ. of Georgia Press, 1984.

Brazeau, J. Raymond. *An Outline of Contemporary French Canadian Literature.* Toronto: Forum House, 1972.

Brenner, Gerry. *Concealments in Hemingway's Works.* Columbus: Ohio State Univ. Press, 1983.

Brinkmann, Richard, Karl-Heinz Habersetzer, Paul Raabe, Karl-Ludwig Selig, and Blake L. Spahr, Eds. *Theatrum Europaeum.* Munich: Fink, 1982.

Bristol, Evelyn, Ed. *Russian Literature and Criticism.* Berkeley: Berkeley Slavic Specialties, 1982.

Brizzi, Mary T. *Philip José Farmer.* Mercer Island, Wash.: Starmont House, 1980.

Brodwin, Stanley, and Michael D'Innocenzo, Eds. *William Cullen Bryant and His America: Centennial Conference Proceedings 1878–1978.* New York: AMS Press, 1983.

Brody, Robert, and Charles Rossman, Eds. *Carlos Fuentes: A Critical View.* Austin: Univ. of Texas Press, 1982.

Brokoph-Mauch, Gudrun, Ed. *Beiträge zur Musil-Kritik.* Berne: Lang, 1983.

Bronner, Stephen E., and Douglas Kellner, Eds. *Passion and Rebellion: The Expressionist Heritage.* South Hadley, Mass.: Bergin, 1983.

Brooks, Cleanth. *William Faulkner: First Encounters.* New Haven: Yale Univ. Press, 1983.

Brooks, Peter. *Reading for the Plot: Design and Intention in Narrative.* New York: Knopf, 1984.

Brophy, James D., and Raymond J. Porter, Eds. *Contemporary Irish Writing.* New Rochelle, N.Y.: Iona College Press, 1983.

Brosman, Catharine S. *Jean-Paul Sartre.* Boston: Twayne, 1983.

Brostrom, Kenneth N., Ed. *Russian Literature and American Critics: In Honor of Deming B. Brown.* Ann Arbor: Univ. of Michigan Press, 1984.

Brown, Edward J. *Russian Literature Since the Revolution,* 3rd ed. Cambridge: Harvard Univ. Press, 1982.

Bruffee, Kenneth A. *Elegiac Romance: Cultural Change and Loss of the Hero in Modern Fiction.* Ithaca: Cornell Univ. Press, 1983.

Bryer, Jackson R., Ed. *The Short Stories of F. Scott Fitzgerald.* Madison: Univ. of Wisconsin Press, 1982.

Burleson, Donald R. *H. P. Lovecraft: A Critical Study.* Westport, Conn.: Greenwood Press, 1983.

Bush, Robert. *Grace King: A Southern Destiny.* Baton Rouge: Louisiana State Univ. Press, 1983.

Butler, Lance S. *Samuel Beckett and the Meaning of Being: A Study of Ontological Parable*. New York: St. Martin's Press, 1984.

Byram, Michael. *Tom Kristensen*. Boston: Twayne, 1982.

Cabibbo, Paola, Ed. *Sigfrido nel nuovo mondo: Studi sulla narrativa d'inizazione*. Rome: Goliardica, 1983.

Cabrera, Vicente. *Juan Benet*. Boston: Twayne, 1983.

Caesar, Michael, and Peter Hainsworth, Eds. *Writers and Society in Contemporary Italy: A Collection of Essays*. New York: St. Martin's Press, 1984.

Calonne, David S. *William Saroyan: My Real Work Is Being*. Chapel Hill: Univ. of North Carolina Press, 1983.

Carlson, Patricia A. *Hawthorne's Functional Settings: A Study of Artistic Method*. Amsterdam: Rodopi, 1977.

Cavaliero, Glen. *The Rural Tradition in the English Novel 1900–1939*. London: Macmillan, 1977.

Cevasco, G. A. *John Gray*. Boston: Twayne, 1982.

Chadbourne, Richard, and Hallvard Dahlie, Eds. *The New Land: Studies in a Literary Theme*. Waterloo, Ont.: Wilfrid Laurier Univ. Press, 1978.

Chapple, Gerald, and Hans H. Schulte, Eds. *The Turn of the Century: German Literature and Art 1890–1915*. Bonn: Bouvier, 1981.

Charters, Ann, Ed. *The Story and Its Writer: An Introduction to Short Fiction*. New York: St. Martin's Press, 1983.

Chesnutt, Margaret. *Studies in the Short Stories of William Carleton*. Göteborg: Acta Universitatis Gotheburgensis, 1976.

Chibbett, David G., Ed. *River Mist and Other Stories by Kunikida Doppo*, trans. David G. Chibbett. Tokyo: Kodansha, 1982; Am. ed. New York: Kodansha, 1983.

Cioffi, Frank. *Formula Fiction? An Anatomy of American Science Fiction, 1930–1940*. Westport, Conn.: Greenwood Press, 1982.

Clardy, Jesse V. and Betty S. *The Superfluous Man in Russian Letters*. Washington: Univ. Press of America, 1980.

Clareson, Thomas D., Ed. *A Spectrum of Worlds*. New York: Doubleday, 1972.

———. *Robert Silverberg*. Mercer Island, Wash.: Starmont House, 1983.

Coates, Paul. *The Realist Fantasy Fiction and Reality Since "Clarissa."* New York: St. Martin's Press, 1983.

Cobbs, John L. *Owen Wister*. Boston: Twayne, 1984.

Colacurcio, Michael J. *The Province of Piety: Moral History in Hawthorne's Early Tales*. Cambridge: Harvard Univ. Press, 1984.

Colby, Vineta and Robert A. *The Equivocal Virtue: Mrs. Oliphant and the Victorian Literary Market Place*. Hamden, Conn.: Archon, 1966.

Collins, R. G., Ed. *Critical Essays on John Cheever*. Boston: Hall, 1982.

Colvert, James B. *Stephen Crane*. New York: Harcourt Brace Jovanovich, 1984.

Conard, Robert C. *Heinrich Böll*. Boston: Twayne, 1981.

Conder, John J. *Naturalism in American Fiction: The Classic Phase*. Lexington: Univ. Press of Kentucky, 1984.

Conn, Peter. *The Divided Mind: Ideology and Imagination in America, 1898–1917*. Cambridge: Cambridge Univ. Press, 1983.

Connelly, Stephen E. *Allan Seager*. Boston: Twayne, 1983.

Connolly, Julian W. *Ivan Bunin*. Boston: Twayne, 1982.

Conradi, Peter. *John Fowles*. London: Methuen, 1982.

Cooke, Michael G. *Afro-American Literature in the Twentieth Century: The Achievement of Intimacy*. New Haven: Yale Univ. Press, 1984.

Cooke, Miriam. *The Anatomy of an Egyptian Intellectual, Yahya Haqqi.* Washington: Three Continents Press, 1984.

Cooley, John R. *Savages and Naturals: Black Portraits by White Writers in Modern American Literature.* East Brunswick, N.J.: Associated Univ. Presses [for Univ. of Delaware Press], 1982.

Coombes, H. T. F. *Powys.* London: Barrie & Rockliff, 1960.

Cooper, Peter L. *Signs and Symptoms: Thomas Pynchon and the Contemporary World.* Berkeley: Univ. of California Press, 1983.

Cowart, David. *Arches and Light: The Fiction of John Gardner.* Carbondale: Southern Illinois Univ. Press, 1983.

Crane, John K. *The Root of All Evil: The Thematic Unity of William Styron's Fiction.* Columbia: Univ. of South Carolina Press, 1984.

Crook, Eugene J., Ed. *Fearful Symmetry: Doubles and Doubling in Literature and Film.* Tallahassee: Univ. Press of Florida, 1982.

Crow, Charles L. *Janet Lewis.* Boise: Boise State Univ., 1980.

Darras, Jacques. *Joseph Conrad and the West: Signs of Empire,* trans. Anne Luyat and Jacques Darras. Totowa, N.J.: Barnes & Noble, 1982.

Davidson, Cathy N., Ed. *Critical Essays on Ambrose Bierce.* Boston: Hall, 1982.

———. *The Experimental Fiction of Ambrose Bierce: Structuring the Ineffable.* Lincoln: Univ. of Nebraska Press, 1984.

Davies, Horton. *Catching the Conscience.* Cambridge, Mass.: Cowley, 1984.

Dearlove, J. E. *Accommodating the Chaos: Samuel Beckett's Nonrelational Art.* Durham: Duke Univ. Press, 1982.

Debreczeny, Paul. *The Other Pushkin: A Study of Alexander Pushkin's Prose Fiction.* Stanford Univ. Press, 1983.

———, Ed. *American Contributions to the Ninth International Congress of Slavists, Kiev, September, 1983, II: Literature, Poetics, History.* Columbus: Slavica, 1983.

De Camp, L. Sprague. *Literary Swordsmen and Sorcerers: The Makers of Heroic Fantasy.* Sauk City, Wis.: Arkham House, 1976.

Dedner, Burghard. *Carl Sternheim.* Boston: Twayne, 1982.

Deloria, Vine. *A Sender of Words: Essays in Memory of John G. Neihardt.* Salt Lake City: Howe, 1984.

DeMouy, Jane K. *Katherine Anne Porter's Women: The Eye of Her Fiction.* Austin: Univ. of Texas Press, 1983.

Dervin, Daniel. *A "Strange Sapience": The Creative Imagination of D. H. Lawrence.* Amherst: Univ. of Massachusetts Press, 1984.

Detweiler, Robert. *John Updike,* 2nd ed. Boston: Twayne, 1984.

DeVitis, A. A., and Albert E. Kalson. *J. B. Priestley.* Boston: Twayne, 1980.

Devlin, James E. *Erskine Caldwell.* Boston: Twayne, 1984.

Dietrich, R. F., and Roger H. Sundell. *Instructor's Manual for "The Art of Fiction, Fourth Edition."* New York: Holt, Rinehart & Winston, 1983.

DiGaetani, John L. *Richard Wagner and the Modern British Novel.* Cranbury, N.J.: Associated Univ. Presses [for Fairleigh Dickinson Univ. Press], 1978.

Diskin, Lahna F. *Theodore Sturgeon.* Mercer Island, Wash.: Starmont House, 1981.

Donovan, Josephine. *New England Local Color Literature: A Women's Tradition.* New York: Ungar, 1983.

Dorsey, David F., Phanuel A. Egejuru, and Stephen Arnold, Eds. *Design and Intent in African Literature.* Washington: Three Continents Press, 1982.

Douglas, George H. *Edmund Wilson's America.* Lexington: Univ. Press of Kentucky, 1983.

Dozois, Gardner. *The Fiction of James Tiptree, Jr.* New York: Argol Press, 1977.

Drew, Jörg, Ed. *Gebirgslandschaft mit Arno Schmidt: Grazer Symposion 1980*. Munich: Text und Kritik, 1982.

Dumbleton, William A. *Ireland: Life and Land in Literature*. Albany: State Univ. of New York Press, 1984.

Dunn, Thomas P., and Richard D. Erlich, Eds. *The Mechanical God: Machines in Science Fiction*. Westport, Conn.: Greenwood, 1982.

Durkin, Mary B. *Dorothy Sayers*. Boston: Twayne, 1980.

Eddings, Dennis W., Ed. *The Naiad Voice: Essays on Poe's Satiric Hoaxing*. Port Washington, N.Y.: Associated Faculty Press, 1983.

Edström, Vivi. *Selma Lagerlöf*, trans. Barbara Lide. Boston: Twayne, 1984.

Edwards, T. R. N. *Three Russian Writers and the Irrational: Zamyatin, Pil'nyak, and Bulgakov*. Cambridge: Cambridge Univ. Press, 1982.

Elledge, Scott. *E. B. White: A Biography*. New York: Norton, 1984.

Elsbree, Langdon. *The Rituals of Life*. Port Washington, N.Y.: Kennikat, 1982.

Emerson, Everett. *The Authentic Mark Twain: A Literary Biography of Samuel L. Clemens*. Philadelphia: Univ. of Pennsylvania Press, 1984.

Emrich, Wilhelm. *Freiheit und Nihilismus in der Literatur des 20. Jahrhunderts*. Mainz: Akademie der Wissenschaften, 1981.

Erlich, Gloria C. *Family Themes and Hawthorne's Fiction: The Tenacious Web*. New Brunswick: Rutgers Univ. Press, 1984.

Erlich, Richard D., and Thomas P. Dunn, Eds. *Clockwork Worlds: Mechanized Environments in SF.* Westport, Conn.: Greenwood Press, 1983.

Ermolaev, Herman. *Mikhail Sholokov and His Art*. Princeton: Princeton Univ. Press, 1982.

Evans, Elizabeth. *Thomas Wolfe*. New York: Ungar, 1984.

Evans, Mari, Ed. *Black Women Writers (1950–1980): A Critical Evaluation*. New York: Doubleday, 1983.

Faik, Sait. *A Dot on the Map: Selected Stories and Poems*, ed. Talat S. Halman. Bloomington: Indiana Univ. Turkish Studies, 1983.

Feuerwerker, Yi-tsi Mei. *Ding Ling's Fiction: Ideology and Narrative in Modern Chinese Literature*. Cambridge: Harvard Univ. Press, 1982.

Fiedler, Jean, and Jim Mele. *Isaac Asimov*. New York: Ungar, 1982.

Fine, David, Ed. *Los Angeles in Fiction*. Albuquerque: Univ. of New Mexico Press, 1984.

Finke, Wayne H., and Enrique Ledesma, Eds. *Homenaje a Humberto Piñera: Estudios de literatura, arte e historia*. Madrid: Editorial Playor, 1979.

Fisch, Harold. *A Remembered Future: A Study in Literary Mythology*. Bloomington: Indiana Univ. Press, 1984.

Fischer, William B. *The Empire Strikes Out: Kurd Lasswitz, Hans Dominik, and the Development of German Science Fiction*. Bowling Green: Bowling Green State Univ. Popular Press, 1984.

Fisher, John, Ed. *Essays on Aesthetics: Perspectives on the Work of Monroe C. Beardsley*. Philadelphia: Temple Univ. Press, 1983.

Fitch, Brian T. *The Narcissistic Text: A Reading of Camus' Fiction*. Toronto: Univ. of Toronto Press, 1982.

Fleenor, Julian E., Ed. *The Female Gothic*. Montreal: Eden, 1983.

Flora, Joseph M. *Hemingway's Nick Adams*. Baton Rouge: Louisiana State Univ. Press, 1982.

Fluck, Winfried, Jürgen Peper, and Willi P. Adams, Eds. *Forms and Functions of History in American Literature: Essays in Honor of Ursula Brumm*. Berlin: Schmidt, 1981.

Fodor, Alexander. *Tolstoy and the Russians: Reflections on a Relationship.* Ann Arbor: Ardis, 1984.

Ford, Thomas W. *A. B. Guthrie.* Boston: Twayne, 1981.

Fowler, Doreen, and Ann J. Abadie, Eds. *New Directions in Faulkner Studies: Faulkner and Yoknapatawpha, 1983.* Jackson: Univ. Press of Mississippi, 1984.

Fowler, Virginia C. *Henry James's American Girl: the Embroidery on the Canvas.* Madison: Univ. of Wisconsin Press, 1984.

Frane, Jeff. *Fritz Leiber.* Mercer Island, Wash.: Starmont House, 1980.

Fredericks, Casey. *The Future of Eternity: Mythologies of Science Fiction.* Bloomington: Indiana Univ. Press, 1982.

Freeborn, Richard, Ed. *Love and Death: Six Stories by Ivan Turgenev.* London: Folio Society, 1983.

Friedman, Alan W. *William Faulkner.* New York: Ungar, 1984.

Fuchs, Daniel. *Saul Bellow: Vision and Revision.* Durham: Duke Univ. Press, 1984.

Gado, Frank, Ed. *Sherwood Anderson: The Teller's Tales.* Schenectady: Union College Press, 1983.

Gaillard, Dawson. *Dorothy Sayers.* New York: Ungar, 1981.

Gale, Robert L. *Will Henry / Clay Fisher (Henry W. Allen).* Boston: Twayne, 1984.

Garber, Frederick. *The Autonomy of the Self from Richardson to Huysmans.* Princeton: Princeton Univ. Press, 1982.

Gardner, John, Ed. *Tengu Child: Stories by Kikuo Itaya.* Carbondale: Southern Illinois Univ. Press, 1983.

Garebian, Keith. *Hugh Hood.* Boston: Twayne, 1983.

Garganigo, John F. *Javier de Viana.* New York: Twayne, 1972.

Gargano, James W. *The Masquerade Vision in Poe's Short Stories.* Baltimore: Enoch Pratt Free Library, Edgar Allan Poe Society, and Library of the Univ. of Baltimore, 1977.

Gates, Henry L., Ed. *Black Literature and Literary Theory.* New York: Methuen, 1984.

Geduld, Harry M., Ed. *The Definitive "Dr. Jekyll and Mr. Hyde" Companion.* New York: Garland, 1983.

Gelfant, Blanche H. *Women Writing in America: Voices in Collage.* Hanover, N.H.: Univ. Press of New England [for Dartmouth College], 1984.

Gerber, Margy, Ed. *Studies in GDR Culture and Society, II.* Washington: Univ. Press of America, 1982.

Ghose, Zulfikar. *The Fiction of Reality.* London: Macmillan, 1983.

Giacoman, Helmy, and José Miguel Oviedo, Eds. *Homenaje a Mario Vargas Llosa.* Long Island City, N.Y.: Las Américas, 1971.

Gibian, George, and Stephen J. Parker, Eds. *The Adventures of Vladimir Nabokov: Essays, Studies, Reminiscences, and Stories from the Cornell Nabokov Festival.* Ithaca: Center for International Studies, Cornell Univ., 1984.

Gibson, Donald B. *The Politics of Literary Expression: A Study of Major Black Writers.* Westport, Conn.: Greenwood Press, 1981.

Gifford, Douglas, Ed. *Scottish Short Stories 1800–1900.* London: Calder & Boyars, 1971.

Gilbert, Sandra M., and Susan Gubar. *The Madwoman in the Attic: A Study of Women and the Literary Imagination in the Nineteenth Century.* New Haven: Yale Univ. Press, 1979.

Giles, James R. *Irwin Shaw.* Boston: Twayne, 1983.

Gillie, Christopher. *A Preface to Forster.* London: Longman, 1983.

Gillon, Adam. *Joseph Conrad.* Boston: Twayne, 1982.

Gimbel, Wendy. *Edith Wharton: Orphancy and Survival.* New York: Praeger, 1984.

Gish, Robert. *Paul Horgan*. Boston: Twayne, 1983.

Gledson, John. *The Deceptive Realism of Machado de Assis*. Liverpool: Francis Cairns, 1984.

González-Gerth, Miguel, and George D. Schade, Eds. *Rubén Darío Centennial Studies*. Austin: Institute of Latin American Studies, Univ. of Texas, 1970.

Gordon, Joan. *Joe Haldeman*. Mercer Island, Wash.: Starmont House, 1980.

Gordon, Lois. *Robert Coover: The Universal Fictionmaking Process*. Carbondale: Southern Illinois Univ. Press, 1983.

Gowda, H. H. Anniah, Ed. *The Colonial and Neo-Colonial Encounters in Commonwealth Literature*. Mysore: Prasaragana Univ., 1983.

Grace, Sherrill E. *The Voyage That Never Ends: Malcolm Lowry's Fiction*. Vancouver: Univ. of British Columbia Press, 1982.

Gray, Richard, Ed. *American Fictions: New Readings*. London: Vision Press, 1983; Am. ed. Totowa, N.J.: Barnes & Noble, 1983.

Green, Benny. *P. G. Wodehouse: A Literary Biography*. New York: Rutledge, 1981.

Green, Dorothy. *Ulysses Bound: Henry Handel Richardson and Her Fiction*. Canberra: Australian National Univ. Press, 1973.

Green, Martin. *The Great American Adventure*. Boston: Beacon, 1984.

Greenberg, Martin H., and Joseph D. Olander, Eds. *Philip Dick*. New York: Taplinger, 1983.

Greenspan, Ezra. *The "Schlemiel" Comes to America*. Metuchen, N.J.: Scarecrow Press, 1983.

Greiner, Donald J. *The Other John Updike: Poems/Short Stories/Prose/Play*. Athens: Ohio Univ. Press, 1981.

Greven, Hubert, Ed. *Rhétorique et communication*. Paris: Didier, 1979.

Griffin, Brian, and David Wingrove. *Apertures: A Study of the Writings of Brian W. Aldiss*. Westport, Conn.: Greenwood Press, 1984.

Gunn, James. *Isaac Asimov: The Foundations of Science Fiction*. New York: Oxford Univ. Press, 1982.

Gutsche, George J., and Lauren G. Leighton, Eds. *New Perspectives on Nineteenth-Century Russian Prose*. Columbus: Slavica, 1982.

Guttmann, Allen. *The Jewish Writer in America: Assimilation and the Crisis of Identity*. New York: Oxford Univ. Press, 1971.

Habegger, Alfred. *Gender, Fantasy, and Realism in American Literature*. New York: Columbia Univ. Press, 1982.

Hakutani, Yoshinobu, Ed. *Critical Essays on Richard Wright*. Boston: G. K. Hall, 1982.

Halper, Nathan. *Studies in Joyce*. Ann Arbor: Univ. Microfilms International Research Press, 1983.

Hamblen, Abigail A. *Ruth Suckow*. Boise: Boise State Univ., 1978.

Hankin, C[herry]. *Katherine Mansfield and Her Confessional Stories*. New York: St. Martin's Press, 1983.

———, Ed. *Critical Essays on the New Zealand Short Story*. Auckland: Heinemann, 1982.

Hanson, Katherine, Ed. *An Everyday Story: Norwegian Women's Fiction*. Seattle: Seal Press, 1984.

Hargrove, Anne C., and Maurine Magliocco, Eds. *Portraits of Marriage in Literature*. Macomb: Western Illinois Univ., 1984.

Harris, Charles B. *Passionate Virtuosity: The Fiction of John Barth*. Urbana: Univ. of Illinois Press, 1983.

Harris, Janice H. *The Short Fiction of D. H. Lawrence*. New Brunswick: Rutgers Univ. Press, 1984.

Harris, Trudier. *From Mammies to Militants: Domestics in Black American Literature.* Philadelphia: Temple Univ. Press, 1982.

Harrison, Dick. *Unnamed Country: The Struggle for a Canadian Prairie Fiction.* Edmonton: Univ. of Alberta Press, 1977.

Harrison, James. *Rudyard Kipling.* Boston: Twayne, 1982.

Hartwell, David. *Age of Wonders: Exploring the World of Science Fiction.* New York: Walker, 1984; Canadian ed. Rexdale, Ont.: Wiley, 1984.

Hassler, Donald M. *The Comic Tone in Science Fiction: The Art of Compromise with Nature.* Westport, Conn.: Greenwood Press, 1982.

———, Ed. *Patterns of the Fantastic.* Mercer Island, Wash.: Starmont House, 1983.

Hasubek, Peter, Ed. *Die Fabel: Theorie, Geschichte und Rezeption einer Gattung.* Berlin: Schmidt, 1982.

Hawkins, Peter S. *The Language of Grace: Flannery O'Connor, Walker Percy, and Iris Murdoch.* Cambridge, Mass.: Cowley, 1983.

Hawthorn, Jeremy. *Multiple Personality and the Disintegration of Literary Character: From Oliver Goldsmith to Sylvia Plath.* New York: St. Martin's Press, 1983.

Hayles, N. Katherine. *The Cosmic Web: Scientific Field Models and Literary Strategies in the Twentieth Century.* Ithaca: Cornell Univ. Press, 1984.

Hayley, Barbara. *Carleton's "Traits and Stories" and the 19th-Century Anglo-Irish Tradition.* Gerrards Cross, Bucks: Colin Smythe, 1983; Am. ed. Totowa, N.J.: Barnes & Noble, 1983.

Haymaker, Richard E. *From Pampas to Hedgerows and Downs: A Study of W. H. Hudson.* New York: Bookman Associates, 1954.

Hayman, Ronald. *K: A Biography.* London: George Weidenfeld and Nicolson, 1981; Am. ed., retitled *Kafka: A Biography.* New York: Oxford Univ. Press, 1982.

Hayward, Malcolm, Ed. *Proceedings of the Second Annual Conference of EAPSCU.* [n.p.]: English Assoc. of Pennsylvania State Colls. & Univs., 1984.

Heath, Jeffrey. *The Picturesque Prison: Evelyn Waugh and His Writing.* Montreal: McGill-Queen's Univ. Press, 1982.

Hedrick, Joan D. *Solitary Comrade: Jack London and His Work.* Chapel Hill: Univ. of North Carolina Press, 1982.

Heilbrun, Carolyn G., and Margaret R. Higonnet, Eds. *The Representation of Women in Fiction.* Baltimore: Johns Hopkins Univ. Press, 1983.

Henn, T. R. *Kipling.* New York: Barnes & Noble, 1967; Brt. ed. Edinburgh: Oliver & Boyd, 1967.

Herron, Don, Ed. *The Dark Barbarian: The Writings of Robert E. Howard.* Westport, Conn.: Greenwood Press, 1984.

Herz, Judith S., and Robert K. Martin, Eds. *E. M. Forster: Centenary Revaluations.* Toronto: Univ. of Toronto Press, 1982.

Herzberger, David K. *Jesús Fernández Santos.* Boston: Twayne, 1983.

Herzog, Kristin. *Women, Ethnics, and Exotics: Images of Power in Mid-Nineteenth-Century American Fiction.* Knoxville: Univ. of Tennessee Press, 1983.

Hewitt, Nicholas. *Henri Troyat.* Boston: Twayne, 1984.

Hicks, Jack. *In the Singer's Temple: Prose Fictions of Barthelme, Gaines, Brautigan, Piercey, Kesey, and Kosinski.* Chapel Hill: Univ. of North Carolina Press, 1981.

Hilfer, Anthony C. *The Ethics of Intensity in American Fiction.* Austin: Univ. of Texas Press, 1981.

Hipkiss, Robert A. *The American Absurd: Pynchon, Vonnegut, and Barth.* Port Washington: Associated Faculty Press, 1984.

Hoermann, Roland. *Achim von Arnim.* Boston: Twayne, 1984.

Hoffmann, Leonore, and Deborah Rosenfelt, Eds. *Teaching Women's Literature from a Regional Perspective.* New York: Modern Language Association of America, 1982.

Hoffmeister, Gerhart, Ed. *Goethezeit: Studien zur Erkenntnis und Rezeption Goethes und seiner Zeitgenossen.* Bern: Francke, 1981.

Höller, Hans, Ed. *Der dunkle Schatten dem ich schon seit Anfang folge: Ingeborg Bachmann—Vorschläge zu einer neuen Lektüre des Werks.* Vienna: Löcker, 1982.

Hollow, John. *Against the Night, the Stars: The Science Fiction of Arthur C. Clarke.* New York: Harcourt Brace Jovanovich, 1983.

Hopkins, Kenneth. *The Powys Brothers: A Biographical Appreciation.* Cranbury, N.J.: Associated Univ. Presses [for Fairleigh Dickinson Univ. Press], 1967.

Horn, Pierre L., and Mary B. Pringle, Eds. *The Image of the Prostitute in Modern Literature.* New York: Ungar, 1984.

Hunt, George W. *John Updike and the Three Great Secret Things: Sex, Religion, and Art.* Grand Rapids: Eerdmans, 1980.

————. *John Cheever: The Hobgoblin Company of Love.* Grand Rapids: Eerdmans, 1983.

Hunter, Jefferson. *Edwardian Fiction.* Cambridge: Harvard Univ. Press, 1982.

Huntington, John. *The Logic of Fantasy: H. G. Wells and Science Fiction.* New York: Columbia Univ. Press, 1982.

Huse, Nancy L. *The Survival Tales of John Hersey.* Troy, N.Y.: Whitston, 1983.

Hussman, Lawrence E. *Dreiser and His Fiction: A Twentieth-Century Quest.* Philadelphia: Univ. of Pennsylvania Press, 1983.

Hutchinson, Stuart. *Henry James: An American As Modernist.* London: Vision Press, 1982; Am. ed. Totowa, N.J.: Barnes & Noble, 1983.

Huters, Theodore. *Qian Zhongshu.* Boston: Twayne, 1982.

Ikonné, Chidi. *From Du Bois to Van Vechten: The Early New Negro Literature, 1903–1926.* Westport, Conn.: Greenwood Press, 1981.

Irizarry, Estelle. *Enrique A. Laguerre.* Boston: Twayne, 1982.

Issacharoff, Michael, and Jean-Claude Vilquin, Eds. *Sartre et la mise en signe.* Paris: Klincksieck, 1982.

Jackson, Robert L. *The Art of Dostoevsky: Deliriums and Nocturnes.* Princeton: Princeton Univ. Press, 1981.

————, Ed. *Dostoevsky: New Perspectives.* Englewood Cliffs: Prentice-Hall, 1984.

James, Henry. *Tales of Art and Life,* introd. Henry Terrie. Schenectady: Union College Press, 1984.

JanMohamed, Abdul R. *Manichean Aesthetics: The Politics of Literature in Colonial Africa.* Amherst: Univ. of Massachusetts Press, 1983.

Jasper, David, Ed. *Images of Belief in Literature.* New York: St. Martin's Press, 1984.

Jernigan, E. Jay. *William Allen White.* Boston: Twayne, 1983.

Johannesson, Eric O. *The Novels of August Strindberg: A Study in Theme and Structure.* Berkeley: Univ. of California Press, 1968.

Johnson, James L. *Mark Twain and the Limits of Power.* Knoxville: Univ. of Tennessee Press, 1982.

Johnson, Mary L., and Seraphia D. Leyda, Eds. *Reconciliations: Studies in Honor of Richard Harter Fogle.* Salzburg: Institut für Anglistik & Amerikanistik, Univ. Salzburg, 1983.

Johnson, Walter. *August Strindberg.* Boston: Twayne, 1976.

Johnson, Wayne L. *Ray Bradbury.* New York: Ungar, 1980.

Johnston, Carolyn. *Jack London—An American Radical?* Westport, Conn.: Greenwood Press, 1984.

Jones, John. *Dostoevsky.* Oxford: Clarendon Press, 1983.

Jones, Robert E. *Henry-René Lenormand.* Boston: Twayne, 1984.

Jones, W. Glyn. *Tove Jansson.* Boston: Twayne, 1984.

Joshi, S. T. *H. P. Lovecraft.* Mercer Island, Wash.: Starmont House, 1982.

Josipovici, Gabriel. *The World and the Book: A Study of Modern Fiction.* Stanford: Stanford Univ. Press, 1971.

Kamshad, H[assan]. *Modern Persian Prose Literature.* Cambridge: Cambridge Univ. Press, 1966.

Karl, Frederick R. *American Fictions, 1940–1980.* New York: Harper & Row, 1983.

Kaston, Carren. *Imagination and Desire in the Novels of Henry James.* New Brunswick: Rutgers Univ. Press, 1984.

Kato, Shuichi. *A History of Japanese Literature,* II. London: Macmillan, 1983; Am. ed. New York: Kodansha International/USA Ltd., 1983; Jap. ed. Tokyo: Kodansha International Ltd., 1983.

Katz, Michael R. *Dreams and the Unconscious in Nineteenth-Century Russian Fiction.* Hanover, N.H.: Univ. Press of New England, 1984.

Kawin, Bruce F. *The Mind of the Novel: Reflexive Fiction and the Ineffable.* Princeton: Princeton Univ. Press, 1982.

Kayser, Wolfgang. *The Grotesque in Art and Literature,* trans. Ulrich Weisstein. Bloomington: Indiana Univ. Press, 1983.

Keene, Donald. *Dawn to the West: Japanese Literature of the Modern Era—Fiction.* New York: Holt, Rinehart & Winston, 1984.

Kelly, Lori D. *The Life and Works of Elizabeth Stuart Phelps, Victorian Feminist Writer.* Troy, N.Y.: Whitston, 1983.

Kelly, Richard. *Graham Greene.* New York: Ungar, 1984.

Kemp, Peter H. *H. G. Wells and the Culminating Ape.* New York: St. Martin's Press, 1982.

Kennedy, Alan. *Meaning and Sign in Fiction.* New York: St. Martin's Press, 1979.

Kennedy, Catherine M. *Thurber's Anatomy of Confusion.* Hamden, Conn.: Archon Books, 1984.

Kennedy, X. J. and Dorothy M. *Instructor's Manual to Accompany "An Introduction to Fiction, Third Edition."* Boston: Little, Brown, 1983.

Kerr, Howard, John W. Crowley, and Charles L. Crow, Eds. *The Haunted Dusk: American Supernatural Fiction, 1820–1920.* Athens: Univ. of Georgia Press, 1983.

Kersnowski, Frank. *John Montague.* Cranbury, N.J.: Associated Univ. Presses [for Bucknell Univ. Press], 1975.

Kessler, Carol F. *Elizabeth Stuart Phelps.* Boston: Twayne, 1982.

Ketterer, David, Ed. *The Science Fiction of Mark Twain.* Hamden, Conn.: Archon Books, 1984.

Kiernan, Robert F. *Gore Vidal.* New York: Ungar, 1982.

Kilroy, James F., Ed. *The Irish Short Story: A Critical History.* Boston: Twayne, 1984.

Kim, Elaine H. *Asian American Literature: An Introduction to the Writings and Their Social Context.* Philadelphia: Temple Univ. Press, 1982.

King, Betty. *Women of the Future: The Female Main Character in Science Fiction.* Metuchen, N.J.: Scarecrow Press, 1984.

King, Kimball. *Augustus Baldwin Longstreet.* Boston: Twayne, 1984.

Kirschke, James J. *Henry James and Impressionism.* Troy, N.Y.: Whitston, 1981.

Kishtainy, Khalid. *The Prostitute in Progressive Literature.* London: Allison & Busby, 1982.

Klinkowitz, Jerome. *Kurt Vonnegut*. London: Methuen, 1982.

———. *The Self-Apparent Word: Fiction as Language / Language as Fiction*. Carbondale: Southern Illinois Univ. Press, 1984.

———, and James Knowlton. *Peter Handke and the Postmodern Transformation: The Goalie's Journey Home*. Columbia: Univ. of Missouri Press, 1983.

Knabe, Peter-Eckhard, Jürgen Rolshoven, and Margarethe Stracke, Eds. *Le Sacré: Aspects et manifestations: Études publiées in memoriam Horst Baader*. Tübingen: Narr, 1982; French ed. Paris: Place, 1982.

Koelb, Clayton. *The Incredulous Reader: Literature and the Function of Disbelief*. Ithaca: Cornell Univ. Press, 1984.

Koopmann, Helmut, and Peter-Paul Schneider, Eds. *Heinrich Mann: Sein Werk in der Weimare Republik*. Frankfurt: Klostermann, 1983.

Kosok, Heinz, Ed. *Studies in Anglo-Irish Literature*. Bonn: Bouvier, 1982.

Kreuziger, Frederick A. *Apocalypse and Science Fiction: A Dialectic of Religious and Secular Soteriologies*. Chico: Scholars Press, 1982.

Krispyn, Egbert. *Georg Heym: A Reluctant Rebel*. Gainesville: Univ. of Florida Press, 1968.

Kuehl, John. *John Hawkes and the Craft of Conflict*. New Brunswick: Rutgers Univ. Press, 1975.

Kurpershoek, P. M. *The Short Stories of Yūsuf Idrīs, A Modern Egyptian Author*. Leiden: Brill, 1981.

Kurzweil, Edith, and William Phillips, Eds. *Literature and Psychoanalysis*. New York: Columbia Univ. Press, 1983.

Kuyk, Dirk. *Threads Cable-Strong: William Faulkner's "Go Down, Moses."* East Brunswick, N.J.: Associated Univ. Presses [for Bucknell Univ. Press], 1983.

Labrie, Ross. *James Merrill*. Boston: Twayne, 1982.

[La Cassagnère, Christian, Ed.]. *Le Double dans le Romanticisme anglo-américain*. Clermont-Ferrand: Univ. of Clermont-Ferrand, 1984.

Lagercrantz, Olof. *August Strindberg*, trans. Anselm Hollo. New York: Farrar Straus Giroux, 1984.

Lainoff, Seymour. *Ludwig Lewisohn*. Boston: Twayne, 1982.

Lamm, Martin. *August Strindberg*, trans. Harry G. Carlson. New York: Blom, 1971.

Land, Stephen K. *Paradox and Polarity in the Fiction of Joseph Conrad*. New York: St. Martin's Press, 1984; Brt. ed. London: Macmillan, 1984.

Landrum, Larry N., Pat Browne, and Ray B. Browne, Eds. *Dimensions of Detective Fiction*. Bowling Green: Popular Press, 1976.

Lang, Olga. *Pa Chin and His Writings: Chinese Youth Between the Two Revolutions*. Cambridge: Harvard Univ. Press, 1967.

Langer, Lawrence L. *Versions of Survival: The Holocaust and the Human Spirit*. Albany: State Univ. of New York Press, 1982.

Lansbury, Coral. *Elizabeth Gaskell: The Novel of Social Crisis*. London: Elek, 1975; Am. ed. New York: Barnes & Noble, 1975.

———. *Elizabeth Gaskell*. Boston: Twayne, 1984.

Leal, Luis. *Juan Rulfo*. Boston: Twayne, 1983.

Lecker, Robert. *On the Line: Readings in the Short Fiction of Clark Blaise, John Metcalf, and Hugh Hood*. Downsview, Ont.: ECW Press, 1982.

Lee, A. Robert, Ed. *Nathaniel Hawthorne: New Critical Essays*. London: Vision Press, 1982; Am. ed. Totowa, N.J.: Barnes & Noble, 1982.

———. *Ernest Hemingway: New Critical Essays*. London: Vision Press, 1983; Am. ed. Totowa, N.J.: Barnes & Noble, 1983.

————. *Herman Melville: Reassessments*. London: Vision Press, 1984; Am. ed. Totowa, N.J.: Barnes & Noble, 1984.

Lee, Sonia. *Camara Laye*. Boston: Twayne, 1984.

Leighton, Lauren, Ed. *Studies in Honor of Xenia Gasiorowska*. Columbus: Slavica, 1982.

Lemaitre, Georges. *Jean Giraudoux: The Writer and His Work*. New York: Ungar, 1971.

Lensing, Leo A., and Peter Hans-Werner, Eds. *Wilhelm Raabe: Studien zu seinem Leben und Werk*. Braunschweig: pp. Verlag, 1984.

LeStourgeon, Diana. *Rosamond Lehmann*. New York: Twayne, 1965.

Lévy, Angélique, Ed. *Le Mythe d'Etiemble: Hommages, études et recherches; Inédits*. Paris: Didier Erudition, 1979.

Lewald, H. Ernest, Ed. *The Cry of Home: Cultural Nationalism and the Modern Writer*. Knoxville: Univ. of Tennessee Press, 1972.

Lewicki, Zbigniew. *The Bang and the Whimper: Apocalypse and Entropy in American Literature*. Westport, Conn.: Greenwood Press, 1984.

Lewis, R. W. B., Ed. *The Collected Short Stories of Edith Wharton*, Vol. I. New York: Scribner, 1968.

Lindfors, Bernth. *Early Nigerian Literature*. New York: Africana, 1982.

Liptzin, Sol. *The Flowering of Yiddish Literature*. New York: Yoseloff, 1983.

Long, Robert E. *Henry James: The Early Novels*. Boston: Twayne, 1983.

————. *John O'Hara*. New York: Ungar, 1983.

Lonoff, Sue. *Wilkie Collins and His Victorian Readers*. New York: AMS Press, 1982.

Lord, George deF. *Trials of the Self: Heroic Ordeals in the Epic Tradition*. Hamden, Conn.: Archon, 1983.

Lorsch, Susan E. *Where Nature Ends: Literary Responses to the Designification of Landscape*. Cranbury, N.J.: Associated Univ. Presses [for Fairleigh Dickinson Univ. Press], 1983.

Luis, William, Ed. *Voices from Under: Black Narrative in Latin America and the Caribbean*. Westport, Conn.: Greenwood Press, 1984.

Lützeler, Paul M., Ed. *Romane und Erzählungen der deutschen Romantik: Neue Interpretationen*. Stuttgart: Reclam, 1983.

Lyngstad, Sverre. *Sigurd Hoel's Fiction: Cultural Criticism and Tragic Vision*. Westport, Conn.: Greenwood Press, 1984.

Maass, Joachim. *Kleist: A Biography*, trans. Ralph Manheim. New York: Farrar, Straus & Giroux, 1983.

MacAloon, John J., Ed. *Rite, Drama, Festival, Spectacle: Rehearsals Toward a Theory of Cultural Performance*. Philadelphia: Institute for the Study of Human Issues, 1984.

MacCabe, Colin, Ed. *James Joyce: New Perspectives*. Sussex: Harvester Press, 1982; Am. ed. Bloomington: Indiana Univ. Press, 1982.

McCarthy, Mary S. *Balzac and His Reader: A Study of the Creation of Meaning in "La comédie humaine."* Columbia: Univ. of Missouri Press, 1982.

McCarthy, Patrick. *Camus*. New York: Random House, 1982.

McCarthy, Patrick A. *Olaf Stapledon*. Boston: Twayne, 1982.

McClave, Heather, Ed. *Women Writers of the Short Story: A Collection of Critical Essays*. Englewood Cliffs: Prentice-Hall, 1980.

McDaniel, John N. *The Fiction of Philip Roth*. Haddonfield, N.J.: Haddonfield House, 1974.

McDowell, Frederick P. *E. M. Forster*, 2nd ed. Boston: Twayne, 1982.

McKay, Nellie Y. *Jean Toomer, Artist: A Study of His Literary Life and Work, 1894–1936.* Chapel Hill: Univ. of North Carolina Press, 1984.

MacKendrick, Louis K., Ed. *Probable Fictions: Alice Munro's Narrative Acts.* Downsville, Ont.: ECW Press, York Univ., 1983.

McKeon, Zahava K. *Novels and Arguments: Inventing Rhetorical Criticism.* Chicago: Univ. of Chicago Press, 1982.

Macksey, Richard, and Frank E. Moorer, Eds. *Richard Wright: A Collection of Critical Essays.* Englewood Cliffs: Prentice-Hall, 1984.

McMullen, Lorraine, Ed. *"The Race" and Other Stories by Sinclair Ross.* Ottawa: Univ. of Ottawa Press, 1982.

Macnaughton, William R., Ed. *Critical Essays on John Updike.* Boston: Hall, 1982.

McSweeney, Kerry. *Four Contemporary Novelists: Angus Wilson, Brian Moore, John Fowles, V. S. Naipaul.* Montreal: McGill-Queen's Univ. Press, 1983.

McWilliams, John P. *Hawthorne, Melville, and the American Character: A Looking-Glass Business.* Cambridge: Cambridge Univ. Press, 1984.

Madan, Indar Nath. *Premchand: An Interpretation.* Lahore: Miniver Book Shop, 1946.

Madden, David. *Instructor's Manual for "Studies in the Short Story, Fifth Edition,"* 5th ed. New York: Holt, Rinehart & Winston, 1980.

———, and Virgil Scott. *Instructor's Manual for "Studies in the Short Story,"* 6th ed. New York: Holt, Rinehart & Winston, 1984.

———, Ed. *Tough Guy Writers of the Thirties.* Carbondale: Southern Illinois Univ. Press, 1968.

Maddox, Lucy. *Nabokov's Novels in English.* Athens: Univ. of Georgia Press, 1983.

Maes-Jelinek, Hena. *Wilson Harris.* Boston: Twayne, 1982.

Manlove, C. N. *Modern Fantasy: Five Studies.* Cambridge: Cambridge Univ. Press, 1975.

———. *The Impulse of Fantasy Literature.* Kent: Kent State Univ. Press, 1983.

Mann, Karen B. *The Language That Makes George Eliot's Fiction.* Baltimore: Johns Hopkins Univ. Press, 1983.

Manteiga, Roberto C., David K. Herzberger, and Malcolm A. Compitello, Eds. *Critical Approaches to the Writings of Juan Benet.* Hanover, N.H.: Univ. Press of New England [for Univ. of Rhode Island], 1984.

Mao, Nathan K. *Pa Chin.* Boston: Twayne, 1978.

Marling, William. *Dashiell Hammett.* Boston: Twayne, 1983.

Marotin, François, Ed. *Frontières du conte.* Paris: CNRS, 1982.

Marsella, Joy A. *The Promise of Destiny: Children and Women in the Short Stories of Louisa May Alcott.* Westport, Conn.: Greenwood Press, 1983.

Martín, Gregorio C., Ed. *Selected Proceedings: 32nd Mountain Interstate Foreign Language Conference.* Winston-Salem: Wake Forest Univ., 1984.

Martin, Terence. *Nathaniel Hawthorne,* 2nd ed. Boston: Twayne, 1983.

Marx, Leonie. *Benny Andersen: A Critical Study.* Westport, Conn.: Greenwood Press, 1983.

Massa, Ann. *American Literature in Context, IV: 1900–1930.* London: Methuen, 1982.

Matthews, James. *Voices: A Life of Frank O'Connor.* New York: Atheneum, 1983.

Matthews, John T. *The Play of Faulkner's Language.* Ithaca: Cornell Univ. Press, 1982.

Maule, Harry E. *Selma Lagerlöf: The Woman, Her Work, Her Message.* Garden City, N.Y.: Doubleday, Doran, 1928.

Maurer, Warren R. *Gerhart Hauptmann.* Boston: Twayne, 1982.

Maybury, James F., and Marjorie A. Zerbel, Eds. *Franklin Pierce Studies in Literature 1981*. Rindge, N.H.: Franklin Pierce College, 1982.

Mélanges à la mémoire de Franco Simone: France et Italie dans la culture européenne, III: XIXᵉ et XXᵉ siècles. Geneva: Slatkine, 1984.

Mellow, James R. *Invented Lives: F. Scott and Zelda Fitzgerald*. Boston: Houghton Mifflin, 1984.

Mendelson, Danuta. *Metaphor in Babel's Short Stories*. Ann Arbor: Ardis, 1982.

Menger, Lucy. *Theodore Sturgeon*. New York: Ungar, 1981.

Menhennet, Alan. *The Romantic Movement*. London: Croom Held, 1981; Am. ed. Totowa, N.J.: Barnes & Noble, 1981.

Meriwether, James B., Ed. *South Carolina Women Writers*. Spartansburg, S.C.: Reprint Company, Publishers, 1979.

Mersereau, John. *Russian Romantic Fiction*. Ann Arbor: Ardis, 1983.

Meyer, Doris, and Margarite F. Olmos, Eds. *Contemporary Women Authors of Latin America*. Brooklyn: Brooklyn College Press, 1983.

Meyers, Walter E. *Aliens and Linguists: Language Studies and Science Fiction*. Athens: Univ. of Georgia Press, 1980.

Miesel, Sandra. *Against Time's Arrow: The High Crusade of Poul Anderson*. San Bernardino: Borgo Press, 1978.

Miller, James E., and Bernice Slote. *Instructor's Manual to Accompany "The Dimensions of the Short Story: A Critical Anthology,"* 2nd ed. New York: Harper & Row, 1981.

Miller, Robert K. *Mark Twain*. New York: Ungar, 1983.

Miller, Yvette E., and Charles M. Tatum, Eds. *Latin American Women Writers: Yesterday and Today*. Pittsburgh: Carnegie-Mellon Univ., 1977.

Minden, M. R. *Arno Schmidt: A Critical Study of His Prose*. Cambridge: Cambridge Univ. Press, 1982.

Mintz, Alan. *Hurban: Responses to Catastrophe in Hebrew Literature*. New York: Columbia Univ. Press, 1984.

Mitchell, Sally. *The Fallen Angel: Chastity, Class and Women's Reading, 1835–1880*. Bowling Green: Bowling Green Univ. Popular Press, 1981.

Miyoshi, Masao. *The Divided Self: A Perspective on the Literature of the Victorians*. New York: New York Univ. Press, 1969.

Molesworth, Charles. *Donald Barthelme's Fiction: The Ironist Saved from Drowning*. Columbia: Univ. of Missouri Press, 1982.

Monego, Joan P. *Maghrebian Literature in French*. Boston: Twayne, 1984.

Montgomery, Marion. *Why Poe Drank Liquor*. La Salle, Ill.: Sherwood Sugden, 1983.

Mora, Gabriela, and Karen S. Van Hooft, Eds. *Theory and Practice of Feminist Literary Criticism*. Ypsilanti, Mich.: Bilingual Press, 1982.

Morace, Robert A., and Kathryn VanSpanckeren, Eds. *John Gardner: Critical Perspectives*. Carbondale: Southern Illinois Univ. Press, 1982.

Moran, Mary H. *Margaret Drabble: Existing Within Structures*. Carbondale: Southern Illinois Univ. Press, 1983.

Morris, Gregory L. *A World of Order and Light: The Fiction of John Gardner*. Athens: Univ. of Georgia Press, 1984.

Mortimer, Anthony, Ed. *Contemporary Approaches to Narrative*. Tübingen: Narr, 1984.

Mortimer, Gail L. *Faulkner's Rhetoric of Loss: A Study in Perception and Meaning*. Austin: Univ. of Texas Press, 1983.

Morton, Peter. *The Vital Science: Biology and the Literary Imagination, 1860–1900*. London: Allen & Unwin, 1984.

Mossberg, Christer L. *Scandinavian Immigrant Literature*. Boise: Boise State Univ., 1981.

Mulkeen, Anne. *Wild Thyme, Winter Lightning: The Symbolic Novels of L. P. Hartley*. Detroit: Wayne State Univ. Press, 1974.

Muller, Gilbert H. *John A. Williams*. Boston: Twayne, 1984.

Murray-Smith, Stephen. *Henry Lawson*. Melbourne: Oxford Univ. Press, 1975.

Musumarra, Carmelo, Ed. *Novelle rusticane di Giovanni Verga, 1883–1983: Letture critiche*. Palermo: Palumbo, 1984.

Myers, Robert E., Ed. *The Intersection of Science Fiction and Philosophy: Critical Studies*. Westport, Conn.: Greenwood Press, 1983.

Myerson, Joel, Ed. *Studies in the American Renaissance, 1982*. Boston: Twayne, 1982.

Nabokov, Vladimir. *Lectures on Russian Literature*, ed. Fredson Bowers. New York: Harcourt Brace Jovanovich, 1981.

Nagel, James, Ed. *Critical Essays on Hamlin Garland*. Boston: Hall, 1982.

———. *Ernest Hemingway: The Writer in Context*. Madison: Univ. of Wisconsin Press, 1984.

Nalbantian, Suzanne. *Seeds of Decadence in the Late Nineteenth-Century Novel: A Crisis in Values*. New York: St. Martin's Press, 1983.

Nemoianu, Virgil. *The Taming of Romanticism: European Literature and the Age of Biedermeier*. Cambridge: Harvard Univ. Press, 1984.

Nieuwenhuys, Rob. *Mirror of the Indies: A History of Dutch Colonial Literature*, trans. Frans van Rosevelt. Amherst: Univ. of Massachusetts Press, 1982.

Nigro, August J. *The Diagonal Line: Separation and Reparation in American Literature*. Cranbury, N.J.: Associated Univ. Presses [for Susquehanna Univ. Press], 1984.

Nilsson, Nils A., Ed. *Studies in Twentieth-Century Russian Prose*. Stockholm: Almqvist & Wiksell, 1982.

Nish, Ian, and Charles Dunn, Eds. *European Studies on Japan*. Tenterden, Kent: Norbury, 1979.

Noble, Andrew, Ed. *Robert Louis Stevenson*. London: Vision Press, 1983; Am. ed. Totowa, N.J.: Barnes & Noble, 1983.

Noble, Donald R., Ed. *Hemingway: A Revaluation*. Troy, N.Y.: Whitston, 1983.

Nolan, Charles J. *Aaron Burr and the American Literary Imagination*. Westport, Conn.: Greenwood Press, 1980.

Nordanberg, Thomas. *Cataclysm as Catalyst: The Theme of War in William Faulkner's Fiction*. Uppsala: Acta Universitatis Upsaliensis, 1983.

Norrman, Ralf. *The Insecure World of Henry James's Fiction: Intensity and Ambiguity*. New York: St. Martin's Press, 1982.

Norseng, Mary K. *Sigbjørn Obstfelder*. Boston: Twayne, 1982.

O'Donnell, Patrick. *John Hawkes*. Boston: Twayne, 1982.

O'Donnell, William H. *A Guide to the Prose Fiction of W. B. Yeats*. Ann Arbor: Univ. Microfilms International Research Press, 1983.

Olander, Joseph D., and Martin H. Greenberg, Eds. *Arthur C. Clarke*. New York: Taplinger, 1977.

O'Reilly, Timothy. *Frank Herbert*. New York: Ungar, 1981.

Oriard, Michael. *Dreaming of Heroes: American Sports Fiction, 1868–1980*. Chicago: Nelson-Hall, 1982.

Orr, Leonard, Ed. *De-Structing the Novel: Essays in Applied Postmodern Hermeneutics*. Troy, N.Y.: Whitston, 1982.

Ortega, Julio. *Poetics of Change: The New Spanish-American Narrative*, trans. Galen D. Greaser. Austin: Univ. of Texas Press, 1984.

O'Toole, L. Michael. *Structure, Style and Interpretation in the Russian Short Story.* New Haven: Yale Univ. Press, 1982.

Otten, Terry. *After Innocence: Visions of the Fall in Modern Literature.* Pittsburgh: Univ. of Pittsburgh Press, 1982.

Overholser, Wayne D. *The Best Western Stories of Wayne D. Overholser,* ed. Bill Pronzini and Martin H. Greenberg. Carbondale: Southern Illinois Univ. Press, 1984.

Pachmuss, Temira. *Zinaida Hippius: An Intellectual Profile.* Carbondale: Southern Illinois Univ. Press, 1971.

Palmer, Christopher, Ed. *The Britten Companion.* Cambridge: Cambridge Univ. Press, 1984.

Paolini, Gilbert, Ed. *LA CHISPA '83: Selected Proceedings.* New Orleans: Tulane Univ., 1983.

Parr, Susan R. *The Moral of the Story: Literature, Values, and American Education.* New York: Teachers College Press [Columbia Univ.], 1982.

Parrinder, Patrick. *James Joyce.* Cambridge: Cambridge Univ. Press, 1984.

Parrott, Cecil. *Jaroslav Hašek: A Study of "Švejk" and the Short Stories.* Cambridge: Cambridge Univ. Press, 1982.

Parry, Benita. *Conrad and Imperialism: Ideological Boundaries and Visionary Frontiers.* Salem, N.H.: Salem House, 1984.

Pascal, Roy. *Kafka's Narrators: A Study of His Stories and Sketches.* Cambridge: Cambridge Univ. Press, 1982.

Pearce, Richard. *The Novel in Motion: An Approach to Modern Fiction.* Columbus: Ohio State Univ. Press, 1983.

Peden, Margaret S., Ed. *The Latin American Short Story: A Critical History.* Boston: Twayne, 1983.

Penner, Dick, Ed. *Fiction of the Absurd: Pratfalls in the Void.* New York: New American Library, 1980.

Peplow, Michael W. *George S. Schuyler.* Boston: Twayne, 1980.

Pérez, Janet. *Gonzalo Torrente Ballester.* Boston: Twayne, 1984.

Perrine, Laurence, Ed. *Story and Structure,* 6th ed. New York: Harcourt Brace Jovanovich, 1983.

————, and Thomas R. Arp. *Instructor's Manual to Accompany "Story and Structure, Sixth Edition."* New York: Harcourt Brace Jovanovich, 1983.

Peschel, Dietmar, Ed. *Germanistik in Erlangen: Hundert Jahre nach der Gründung des Deutschen Seminars.* Erlangen: Universitätsbund Erlangen-Nürnberg, 1983.

Peschel, Enid R., Ed. *Medicine and Literature.* New York: Neale Watson Academic Publications, 1980.

Peterson, Audrey. *Victorian Masters of Mystery from Wilkie Collins to Conan Doyle.* New York: Ungar, 1984.

Pettersson, Torsten. *Consciousness and Time: A Study of the Philosophy and Narrative Technique of Joseph Conrad.* Abo, Finland: Abo Akademi, 1982.

Pickford, Cedric, Ed. *Mélanges de littérature française moderne offerts à Garnet Rees par ses collègues et amis.* Paris: Minard, 1980.

Pierce, Hazel. *Philip K. Dick.* Mercer Island, Wash.: Starmont House, 1982.

————. *A Literary Symbiosis: Science Fiction / Fantasy Mystery.* Westport, Conn.: Greenwood Press, 1983.

Pikoulis, John. *The Art of William Faulkner.* Totowa, N.J.: Barnes & Noble, 1982.

————. *Alun Lewis—A Life.* Bridgend, Mid Glamourgan: Poetry Wales Press, 1984.

Pinsker, Sanford, Ed. *Critical Essays on Philip Roth.* Boston: Hall, 1982.

Pizer, Donald. *Realism and Naturalism in Nineteenth-Century American Literature,* 2nd ed. Carbondale: Southern Illinois Univ. Press, 1984.

Polt, John H. R. *The Writings of Eduardo Mallea.* Berkeley: Univ. of California Press, 1959.

Post, Klaus D. *Gerhart Hauptmann: "Bahnwärter Thiel"—Text, Materialien, Kommentar.* Munich: Hanser, 1979.

Prenshaw, Peggy W., Ed. *Eudora Welty: Critical Essays.* Jackson: Univ. Press of Mississippi, 1979.

————. *Eudora Welty: Thirteen Essays Selected from "Eudora Welty: Critical Essays."* Jackson: Univ. Press of Mississippi, 1983.

————. *Women Writers of the Contemporary South.* Jackson: Univ. Press of Mississippi, 1984.

Pringle, David. *Earth Is the Alien Planet: J. G. Ballard's Four-Dimensional Nightmare.* San Bernardino: Borgo Press, 1979.

Prioleau, Elizabeth S. *The Circle of Eros: Sexuality in the Works of William Dean Howells.* Durham: Duke Univ. Press, 1983.

Proffer, Ellendea. *Bulgakov: Life and Work.* Ann Arbor: Ardis, 1984.

Prutskov, Nikita I. *Gleb Uspensky.* New York: Twayne, 1972.

Pryse, Marjorie, Ed. *Selected Stories of Mary E. Wilkins Freeman.* New York: Norton, 1983.

Purtill, Richard L. *J. R. R. Tolkien: Myth, Morality, and Religion.* San Francisco: Harper & Row, 1984; Canadian ed. Toronto: Fitzhenry & Whiteside, 1984.

Rabinovitz, Rubin. *The Development of Samuel Beckett's Fiction.* Urbana: Univ. of Illinois Press, 1984.

Rabkin, Eric S. *Arthur C. Clarke.* West Linn, Ore.: Starmont House, 1979.

————, Martin H. Greenberg, and Joseph D. Olander, Eds. *The End of the World.* Carbondale: Southern Illinois Univ. Press, 1983.

Rampton, David. *Vladimir Nabokov: A Critical Study of the Novels.* Cambridge: Cambridge Univ. Press, 1984.

Rawlings, Peter, Ed. *Henry James's Short Masterpieces,* II. Brighton, Sussex: Harvester Press, 1984; Am. ed. Totowa, N.J.: Barnes & Noble, 1984.

Rawson, Claude, Ed. *English Satire and the Satiric Tradition.* Oxford: Blackwell, 1984.

Reid, Forrest. *Walter de la Mare: A Critical Study.* London: Faber & Faber, 1929; Am. ed. New York: Holt, 1929; rpt. St. Clair Shores, Mich.: Scholarly Press, 1970.

Reilly, John H. *Jean Giraudoux.* Boston: Twayne, 1978.

Renza, Louis A. *"A White Heron" and the Question of Minor Literature.* Madison: Univ. of Wisconsin Press, 1984.

Reynolds, Larry J. *James Kirke Paulding.* Boston: Twayne, 1984.

Richardson, Betty. *John Collier.* Boston: Twayne, 1983.

Richmond, Velma B. *Muriel Spark.* New York: Ungar, 1984.

Ricks, Thomas M., Ed. *Critical Perspectives on Modern Persian Literature.* Washington: Three Continents Press, 1984.

Ridgeway, Jaqueline. *Louise Bogan.* Boston: Twayne, 1984.

Ridley, Hugh. *Images of Imperialism.* London: Croom Helm, 1983; Am. ed. New York: St. Martin's Press, 1983.

Riley, Dick, Ed. *Critical Encounters [I]: Writers and Themes in Science Fiction.* New York: Ungar, 1978.

Rimer, J. Thomas. *Modern Japanese Fiction and Tradition: An Introduction.* Princeton: Princeton Univ. Press, 1978.

Ringe, Donald A. *American Gothic: Imagination and Realism in Nineteenth-Century Fiction.* Lexington: Univ. Press of Kentucky, 1982.

Rivers, J. E., and Charles Nicol, Eds. *Nabokov's Fifth Arc: Nabokov and Others on His Life's Work.* Austin: Univ. of Texas Press, 1982.

Ro, Sigmund. *Rage and Celebration: Essays on Contemporary Afro-American Writing.* Oslo: Solum Forlag A. S., 1984; Am. ed. Atlantic Highlands, N.J.: Humanities Press, 1984.

Robinson, Kim S. *The Novels of Philip K. Dick.* Ann Arbor: UMI Research Press, 1984.

Rodrigues, Eusebio L. *Quest for the Human: An Exploration of Saul Bellow's Fiction.* East Brunswick, N.J.: Associated Univ. Presses [for Bucknell Univ. Press], 1981.

Rooke, Constance. *Reynolds Price.* Boston: Twayne, 1983.

Rosecrance, Barbara. *Forster's Narrative Vision.* Ithaca: Cornell Univ. Press, 1982.

Rosenberg, Israel. *Shay Agnon's World of Mystery and Allegory: An Analysis of "Iddo and Aynam."* Philadelphia: Dorrance, 1978.

Rosenberg, Jerome H. *Margaret Atwood.* Boston: Twayne, 1984.

Rose-Werle, Kordula. *Harlekinade—Genealogie und Metamorphose: Struktur und Deutung des Motivs bei J. D. Salinger und V. Nabokov.* Frankfurt: Peter D. Lang, 1979.

Roskies, David G. *Against the Apocalypse: Responses to Catastrophe in Modern Jewish Culture.* Cambridge: Harvard Univ. Press, 1984.

Rossel, Sven H. *Johannes V. Jensen.* Boston: Twayne, 1984.

Rowe, John C. *Through the Custom-House: Nineteenth-Century American Fiction and Modern Theory.* Baltimore: Johns Hopkins Univ. Press, 1982.

Rowe, William W. *Nabokov's Spectral Dimension.* Ann Arbor: Ardis, 1981.

Rubin, Jay. *Injurious to Public Morals: Writers and the Meiji State.* Seattle: Univ. of Washington Press, 1984.

Rubin, Louis D. *A Gallery of Southerners.* Baton Rouge: Louisiana State Univ. Press, 1982.

Rubin, Steven J. *Meyer Levin.* Boston: Twayne, 1982.

Ruderman, Judith. *D. H. Lawrence and the Devouring Mother: The Search for a Patriarchal Ideal of Leadership.* Durham: Duke Univ. Press, 1984.

Russell, Delbert W. *Anne Hébert.* Boston: Twayne, 1983.

Russell, Robert. *Valentin Kataev.* Boston: Twayne, 1981.

Rzhevsky, Nicholas. *Russian Literature and Ideology: Herzen, Dostoevsky, Leontiev, Tolstoy, Fadeyev.* Urbana: Univ. of Illinois Press, 1983.

Sage, Lorna. *Doris Lessing.* London: Methuen, 1983.

Saliba, David R. *A Psychology of Fear: The Nightmare Formula of Edgar Allan Poe.* Washington, D.C.: Univ. Press of America, 1980.

Sampson, Robert. *Yesterday's Faces, II—Strange Days.* Bowling Green: Bowling Green Univ. Press, 1984.

San Juan, E. *Toward a People's Literature: Essays in the Dialectics of Praxis and Contradiction in Philippine Writing.* Quezon City: Univ. of Philippines Press, 1984.

Santore, Anthony C., and Michael Pocalyko, Eds. *A John Hawkes Symposium: Design and Debris.* New York: New Directions, 1977.

Schlobin, Roger C., Ed. *The Aesthetics of Fantasy Literature and Art.* London: Harvester Press, 1982; Am ed. Notre Dame, Ind.: Univ. of Notre Dame Press, 1982.

Schmidt, Dorey, and Jan Seale, Eds. *Margaret Drabble: Golden Realms.* Edinburg, Tx.: Pan American Univ., 1982.

Schnitzler, Günter, Gerhard Neumann, and Jürgen Schröder, Eds. *Bild und Gedanke: Festschrift Gerhard Baumann zum 60. Geburtstag.* Munich: Fink, 1980.

Schoen, Carol B. *Anzia Yezierska.* Boston: Twayne, 1982.

Scholar, Nancy. *Anaïs Nin.* Boston: Twayne, 1984.

Schönau, Walter, Ed. *Literaturpsychologische Studien und Analysen.* Amsterdam: Rodopi, 1983.

Schor, Naomi, and Henry Majewski, Eds. *Flaubert and Postmodernism.* Lincoln: Univ. of Nebraska Press, 1984.

Schwartz, Barry, Ed. *The Changing Face of the Suburbs.* Chicago: Univ. of Chicago Press, 1976.

Schwartz, Daniel R. *Conrad: The Later Fiction.* London: Macmillan, 1982.

Schwartz, Kessel. *Studies in Twentieth-Century Spanish and Spanish-American Literature.* Lanham, Md.: Univ. Press of America, 1983.

Schwartz Lerner, Lía, and Isaías Lerner, Eds. *Homenaje a Ana María Barrenechea.* Madrid: Castalia, 1984.

Schwarz, Wilhelm J. *Heinrich Böll, Teller of Tales: A Study of His Works and Characters,* trans. Alexander and Elizabeth Henderson. New York: Ungar, 1969.

Schweitzer, Darrell. *Conan's World and Robert E. Howard.* San Bernardino, Calif.: Borgo Press, 1978.

Schwenger, Peter. *Phallic Critiques: Masculinity and Twentieth-Century Literature.* Boston: Routledge & Kegan Paul, 1984.

Scott, P. J. M. *E. M. Forster: Our Permanent Contemporary.* London: Vision Press, 1984; Am. ed. Totowa, N.J.: Barnes & Noble, 1984.

Scott, Virgil, and David Madden. *Instructor's Manual to Accompany "Studies in Short Fiction, Fourth Edition,"* 4th ed. New York: Holt, Rinehart & Winston, 1976.

Scruggs, Charles. *The Sage in Harlem: H. L. Mencken and the Black Writers of the 1920s.* Baltimore: Johns Hopkins Univ. Press, 1984.

Seidensticker, Edward. *Kafū the Scribbler: The Life and Writings of Nagai Kafū, 1879–1959.* Stanford: Stanford Univ. Press, 1965.

Selig, Robert L. *George Gissing.* Boston: Twayne, 1983.

Shane, Alex M. *The Life and Works of Evgeniz Zamjatin.* Berkeley: Univ. of California Press, 1980.

Sharrock, Roger. *Saints, Sinners and Comedians: The Novels of Graham Greene.* Tunbridge Wells, Kent: Burns & Oates, 1984; Am. ed. Notre Dame, Ind.: Univ. of Notre Dame Press, 1984.

Shaw, Valerie. *The Short Story: A Critical Introduction.* London: Longman, 1983.

Sheidley, William E., and Ann Charters. *Instructor's Manual to Accompany "The Story and Its Writer: An Introduction to Short Fiction."* New York: St. Martin's Press, 1983.

Shideler, Ross. *Per Olov Enquist: A Critical Study.* Westport, Conn.: Greenwood Press, 1984.

Shippey, T. A. *The Road to Middle-Earth.* Boston: Houghton Mifflin, 1983.

Showalter, English. *Exiles and Strangers: A Reading of Camus's "Exile and the Kingdom."* Columbus: Ohio State Univ. Press, 1984.

Shurr, William H. *Rappaccini's Children: American Writers in a Calvinistic World.* Lexington: Univ. Press of Kentucky, 1981.

Silver, Carole. *The Romance of William Morris.* Athens: Ohio Univ. Press, 1982.

Simpson, David. *Fetishism and Imagination: Dickens, Melville, Conrad.* Baltimore: Johns Hopkins Univ. Press, 1982.

Simpson, Hilary. *D. H. Lawrence and Feminism.* DeKalb: Northern Illinois Univ. Press, 1982.

Simpson, Louis. *James Hogg: A Critical Study.* Edinburgh: Oliver & Boyd, 1962.

Sinclair, Clive. *The Brothers Singer.* London: Allison & Busby, 1983.

Singh, Rajendra. *Jaishankar Prasad.* Boston: Twayne, 1982.

Sirlin, Rhoda, and David H. Richter. *Instructor's Manual for "The Borzoi Book of Short Fiction,"* ed. David H. Richter. New York: Knopf, 1983.

Slick, Sam L. *José Revueltas.* Boston: Twayne, 1983.

Slusser, George E., Eric S. Rabkin, and Robert Scholes, Eds. *Bridges to Fantasy.* Carbondale: Southern Illinois Univ. Press, 1982.

———. *Coordinates: Placing Science Fiction and Fantasy.* Carbondale: Southern Illinois Univ. Press, 1983.

Smart, Ian. *Central American Writers of West Indian Origin: A New Hispanic Literature.* Washington: Three Continents Press, 1984.

Smith, Allan G. *The Analysis of Motives: Early American Psychology and Fiction.* Amsterdam: Rodopi, 1980.

Smith, Carl S. *Chicago and the American Literary Imagination 1880–1920.* Chicago: Univ. of Chicago Press, 1984.

Smith, Nelson C. *James Hogg.* Boston: Twayne, 1980.

Smith, Peter. *Public and Private Value: Studies in the Nineteenth-Century Novel.* Cambridge: Cambridge Univ. Press, 1984.

Sommers, Joseph, and Tomas Ybarra-Frausto, Eds. *Modern Chicano Writers: A Collection of Critical Essays.* Englewood Cliffs: Prentice-Hall, 1979.

Speir, Jerry. *Raymond Chandler.* New York: Ungar, 1981.

Spires, Robert C. *Beyond the Metafictional Mode: Directions in the Modern Spanish Novel.* Lexington: Univ. Press of Kentucky, 1984.

Squier, Susan M., Ed. *Women Writers and the City: Essays in Feminist Literary Criticism.* Knoxville: Univ. of Tennessee Press, 1984.

Stableford, Brian M. *The Clash of Symbols: The Triumph of James Blish.* San Bernardino: Borgo Press, 1979.

Stafford, William T. *Books Speaking to Books: A Contextual Approach to American Fiction.* Chapel Hill: Univ. of North Carolina Press, 1981.

Staicar, Tom. *Fritz Leiber.* New York: Ungar, 1983.

———, Ed. *The Feminine Eye: Science Fiction and the Women Who Write It.* New York: Ungar, 1982.

———. *Critical Encounters II: Writers and Themes in Science Fiction.* New York: Ungar, 1982.

Staines, David, Ed. *The Callaghan Symposium.* Ottawa: Univ. of Ottawa Press, 1981.

Staley, Thomas F., Ed. *Twentieth-Century Women Novelists.* Totowa, N.J.: Barnes & Noble, 1982.

Stanzel, F. K. *A Theory of Narrative,* trans. Charlotte Goedsche. Cambridge: Cambridge Univ. Press, 1984.

Starchild, Adam, Ed. *The Science Fiction of Konstantin Tsiolkovsky.* Seattle: Univ. Press of the Pacific, 1979.

Stauffer, Helen W., and Susan J. Rosowski, Eds. *Women and Western American Literature.* Troy, N.Y.: Whitston, 1982.

Stein, Allen F. *After the Vows Were Spoken: Marriage in American Literary Realism.* Columbus: Ohio State Univ. Press, 1984.

Steiner, P[eter], M[iroslav] Červenka, and R[onald] Vroom, Eds. *The Structure of the Literary Process: Studies Dedicated to the Memory of Felix Vodička.* Amsterdam: Benjamins, 1982.

Stern, J. P., Ed. *The World of Franz Kafka.* London: Weidenfeld & Nicolson, 1980; Am. ed. New York: Holt, Rinehart & Winston, 1980.

Stern, Madeleine B., Ed. *Behind a Mask: The Unknown Thrillers of Louisa May Alcott*. New York: Morrow, 1975.

———. *Critical Essays on Louisa May Alcott*. Boston: Hall, 1984.

Stevick, Philip, Ed. *The American Short Story, 1900–1945*. Boston: Twayne, 1984.

Stewart, Garrett. *Death Sentence: Styles of Dying in British Fiction*. Cambridge: Harvard Univ. Press, 1984.

Stewart, Joan H. *Colette*. Boston: Twayne, 1983.

Stout, Janis P. *The Journey Narrative in American Literature: Patterns and Departures*. Westport, Conn.: Greenwood Press, 1983.

Strutz, Josef, Ed. *Robert Musil und die kulturellen Tendenzen seiner Zeit*. Munich: Fink, 1983.

Sullivan, Eileen A. *William Carleton*. Boston: Twayne, 1983.

Summers, Claude J. *E. M. Forster*. New York: Ungar, 1983.

Sundquist, Eric J., Ed. *American Realism: New Essays*. Baltimore: Johns Hopkins Univ. Press, 1982.

Swales, Martin and Erika. *Adalbert Stifter: A Critical Study*. Cambridge: Cambridge Univ. Press, 1984.

Swan, Robert O. *Munshi Premchand of Lamhi Village*. Durham: Duke Univ. Press, 1969.

Swearingen, Roger G., Ed. *A Newly Discovered Long Story, "An Old Song" and a Previously Unpublished Short Story, "Edifying Letters of the Rutherford Family," by Robert Louis Stevenson*. Hamden, Conn.: Archon, 1982; Brt. ed. Paisley, Scotland: Wilfion, 1982.

Swinden, Patrick. *The English Novel of History and Society, 1940–1980*. New York: St. Martin's Press, 1984.

Tani, Stefano. *The Doomed Detective: The Contribution of the Detective Novel to Post-Modern American and Italian Fiction*. Carbondale: Southern Illinois Univ. Press, 1984.

Tannen, Deborah. *Lilika Nakos*. Boston: Twayne, 1983.

Tanner, Stephen L. *Ken Kesey*. Boston: Twayne, 1983.

Tanner, Tony. *Thomas Pynchon*. London: Methuen, 1982.

Tausky, Thomas E. *Sara Jeannette Duncan: Novelist of Empire*. Port Credit, Ont.: P. D. Meany, 1980.

Taylor, Jenny, Ed. *Notebooks/Memoirs/Archives: Reading and Rereading Doris Lessing*. Boston: Routledge, 1982.

Terrell, Carroll F., Ed. *William Carlos Williams: Man and Poet*. Orono: Univ. of Maine, 1983.

Thiébaux, Marcelle. *Ellen Glasgow*. New York: Ungar, 1982.

Thomas, Deborah A. *Dickens and the Short Story*. Philadelphia: Univ. of Pennsylvania Press, 1982.

Thompson, Laurie. *Stig Dagerman*. Boston: Twayne, 1983.

Thomsen, Christian W., and Jens M. Fischer, Eds. *Phantastik in Literatur und Kunst*. Darmstadt: Wissenschaftliche Buchgesellschaft, 1980.

Thorson, James L., Ed. *Yugoslav Perspectives on American Literature: An Anthology*. Ann Arbor: Ardis, 1980.

Thurman, Judith. *Isak Dinesen: The Life of a Storyteller*. New York: St. Martin's Press, 1982.

Timmerman, John H. *Other Worlds: The Fantasy Genre*. Bowling Green: Bowling Green Univ. Popular Press, 1983.

Todd, William M., Ed. *Literature and Society in Imperial Russia, 1800–1914*. Stanford: Stanford Univ. Press, 1978.

Tollerson, Marie S. *Mythology and Cosmology in the Narratives of Bernard Dadié and Birago Diop.* Washington: Three Continents Press, 1984.

Tomalin, Ruth. *W. H. Hudson: A Biography.* London: Faber & Faber, 1982.

Trahan, Elizabeth, Ed. *Gogol's "Overcoat": An Anthology of Critical Essays.* Ann Arbor: Ardis, 1982.

Underwood, Tim, and Chuck Miller, Eds. *Jack Vance.* New York: Taplinger, 1980.

Van Dover, J. Kenneth. *Murder in the Millions: Erle Stanley Gardner, Mickey Spillane, Ian Fleming.* New York: Ungar, 1984.

Vannatta, Dennis. *H. E. Bates.* Boston: Twayne, 1983.

Veler, Richard P., Ed. *Papers on Poe: Essays in Honor of John Ward Ostrom.* Springfield, Ohio: Chantry Music Press, Wittenberg Univ. Press, 1972.

Vernon, John. *Money and Fiction: Literary Realism in the Nineteenth and Early Twentieth Centuries.* Ithaca: Cornell Univ. Press, 1984.

Vickery, John B. *Myths and Texts: Strategies of Incorporation and Displacement.* Baton Rouge: Louisiana State Univ. Press, 1983.

Vincent, Jon. *João Guimarães Rosa.* Boston: Twayne, 1978.

Vosskamp, Wilhelm, Ed. *Utopieforschung: Interdisziplinäre Studien zur neuzeitlichen Utopie, III.* Stuttgart: Metzler, 1982.

Wagar, W. Warren. *Terminal Visions: The Literature of Last Things.* Bloomington: Indiana Univ. Press, 1982.

Wagner, F. J. *J. H. Shorthouse.* Boston: Twayne, 1979.

Walcutt, Charles C. *American Literary Naturalism: A Divided Stream.* Minneapolis: Univ. of Minnesota Press, 1956.

Walker, Jayne L. *The Making of a Modernist: Gertrude Stein from "Three Lives" to "Tender Buttons."* Amherst: Univ. of Massachusetts Press, 1984.

Walker, Ronald G. *Infernal Paradise: Mexico and the Modern English Novel.* Berkeley: Univ. of California Press, 1978.

Walsh, William. *R. K. Narayan: A Critical Appreciation.* Chicago: Univ. of Chicago Press, 1982.

Walters, Anna, Ed. *Elizabeth Gaskell: Four Short Stories.* London: Routledge & Kegan Paul, 1983.

Warme, Lars G. *Per Olof Sundman: Writer of the North.* Westport, Conn.: Greenwood Press, 1984.

Warrick, Patricia, and Martin H. Greenberg, Eds. *Robots, Androids and Mechanical Oddities: The Science Fiction of Philip K. Dick.* Carbondale: Southern Illinois Univ. Press, 1984.

Washburn, Yulan M. *Juan José Arreola.* Boston: Twayne, 1983.

Waters, Maureen. *The Comic Irishman.* Albany: State Univ. of New York Press, 1984.

Watson, Charles N. *The Novels of Jack London: A Reappraisal.* Madison: Univ. of Wisconsin Press, 1983.

Watts, Cedric. *The Deceptive Text: An Introduction to Covert Plots.* Brighton, Sussex: Harvester Press, 1984; Am. ed. Totowa, N.J.: Barnes & Noble, 1984.

———, and Laurence Davies. *Cunninghame Graham: A Critical Biography.* Cambridge: Cambridge Univ. Press, 1979.

Watts, Emily S. *The Businessman in American Literature.* Athens: Univ. of Georgia Press, 1982.

Waugh, Patricia. *Metafiction: The Theory and Practice of Self-Conscious Fiction.* London: Methuen, 1984.

Weaver, Gordon, Ed. *The American Short Story, 1945–1980.* Boston: Twayne, 1983.

Weedman, Jane B. *Samuel R. Delany.* Mercer Island, Wash.: Starmont House, 1982.

Wegelin, Christof, Ed. *Tales of Henry James.* New York: Norton, 1984; Canadian ed. Don Mills, Ont.: Stoddard, 1984.

Weigel, John A. *Patrick White.* Boston: Twayne, 1983.

Weisberg, Richard H. *The Failure of the Word: The Protagonist as Lawyer in Modern Fiction.* New Haven: Yale Univ. Press, 1984.

Welch, Robert. *The Way Back: George Moore's "The Untilled Fields" and "The Lark."* Dublin: Wolfhound Press, 1982; Am. ed. Totowa, N.J.: Barnes & Noble, 1982.

Wendell, Carolyn. *Alfred Bester.* Mercer Island, Wash.: Starmont House, 1982.

Werner, Craig H. *Paradoxical Resolutions: American Fiction Since James Joyce.* Urbana: Univ. of Illinois Press, 1982.

Wershoven, Carol. *The Female Intruder in the Novels of Edith Wharton.* East Brunswick, N.J.: Associated Univ. Presses [for Fairleigh Dickinson Univ. Press], 1982.

West, James L. W. *Gyascutus: Studies in Antebellum Southern Humorous and Sporting Writing.* Atlantic Highlands, N.J.: Humanities Press, 1978.

Westbrook, Perry D. *Free Will and Determinism in American Literature.* Cranbury, N.J.: Associated Univ. Presses [for Fairleigh Dickinson Univ. Press], 1979.

White, Helen, and Redding S. Sugg. *Shelby Foote.* Boston: Twayne, 1982.

Whitlow, Roger. *Cassandra's Daughters: The Women in Hemingway.* Westport, Conn.: Greenwood Press, 1984.

Whitney, Blair. *John G. Neihardt.* Boston: Twayne, 1976.

Whittaker, Ruth. *The Faith and Fiction of Muriel Spark.* New York: St. Martin's Press, 1982.

Widmer, Kingsley. *Nathanael West.* Boston: Twayne, 1982.

Wilde, Alan. *Horizons of Assent: Modernism, Postmodernism, and the Ironic Imagination.* Baltimore: Johns Hopkins Univ. Press, 1981.

Willbanks, Ray. *Randolph Stow.* Boston: Twayne, 1978.

Williams, Raymond L. *Gabriel García Márquez.* Boston: Twayne, 1984.

Wolfe, Peter. *Beams Falling: The Art of Dashiell Hammett.* Bowling Green: Bowling Green Univ. Popular Press, 1980.

Wolford, Chester L. *The Anger of Stephen Crane: Fiction and the Epic Tradition.* Lincoln: Univ. of Nebraska Press, 1983.

Wolpers, Theodor, Ed. *Motive und Themen in Erzählungen des später 19. Jahrhunderts: Bericht über Kolloquiem der Kommission für literatürwissenschaftliche Motiv- und Themenforschung, 1978–1979,* I. Göttingen: Vandenhoeck & Ruprecht, 1982.

Woodcock, George. *The World of Canadian Writing.* Vancouver: Douglas & McIntyre, 1980; Am. ed. Seattle: Univ. of Washington Press, 1980.

Woodmansee, Martha, and Walter F. W. Lohnes, Eds. *Erkennen und Deuten: Essays zur Literatur und Literaturtheorie—Edgar Lohner in Memoriam.* Berlin: Schmidt, 1983.

Wright, David G. *Characters in Joyce.* Dublin: Gill & Macmillan, 1983; Am. ed. Totowa, N.J.: Barnes & Noble, 1983.

Wright, Edgar. *Mrs. Gaskell: The Basis for Reassessment.* London: Oxford Univ. Press, 1965.

Wu, William F. *The Yellow Peril: Chinese Americans in American Fiction, 1850–1940.* Hamden, Conn.: Shoe String Press, 1982.

Yoke, Carl B. *Roger Zelazny.* West Linn, Ore.: Starmont House, 1979.

Young, Alan R. *Thomas H. Raddall.* Boston: Twayne, 1983.

Young, Blake M. *Ueda Akinari.* Vancouver: Univ. of British Columbia Press, 1982.

Yu, Beonggheon. *The Great Circle: American Writers and the Orient.* Detroit: Wayne State Univ. Press, 1983.

Yudkin, Leon I. *Jewish Writing and Identity in the Twentieth Century.* New York: St. Martin's Press, 1982.

Yuter, Alan J. *The Holocaust in Hebrew Literature.* Port Washington, N.Y.: Associated Faculty Press, 1983.

Zappulla Muscarà, Sarah, Ed. *Federico De Roberto.* Palermo: Palumbo, 1984.

Zelinsky, Bodo, Ed. *Die russische Novelle.* Düsseldorf: Bagel, 1982.

Zeman, Herbert, Ed. *Die österreichische Literatur: Ihr Profil im 19. Jahrhundert (1830–1880).* Graz: Akad. Druck & Verlagsanstalt, 1982.

Ziolkowski, Theodore, Ed. *"Pictor's Metamorphoses" and Other Fantasies.* New York: Farrar, Straus & Giroux, 1982.

A CHECKLIST OF JOURNALS USED

Acta Germanica	*Acta Germanica: Jahrbuch des Südafrikanischen Germanistenverbandes*
Adalbert Stifter Institut	*Adalbert Stifter Institut des Landes Oberösterreich: Vierteljahrsschrift*
	Africa Today
Afro-Hispanic R	*Afro-Hispanic Review*
	Algol
Aligarh J Engl Stud	*The Aligarh Journal of English Studies*
Am Hispanist	*The American Hispanist*
Am Imago	*American Imago: A Psychoanalytic Journal for Culture, Science, and the Arts*
Am Lit	*American Literature: A Journal of Literary History, Criticism, and Bibliography*
Am Lit Realism	*American Literary Realism, 1870–1910*
Am Notes & Queries	*American Notes and Queries*
Am Stud (Kansas)	*American Studies* (Kansas)
Am Stud	*Amerikastudien/American Studies*
Am Transcendental Q	*American Transcendental Quarterly: A Journal of New England Writers*
	Anales Ştiinţifice ale Universităţii Iaşi
Anglia	*Anglia: Zeitschrift für Englische Philologie*
	Anglistik & Englischunterricht
Anglo-Welsh R	*The Anglo-Welsh Review*
Annales de l'Université	*Annales de l'Université de Toulouse-le-Murail*
Annali della Facultà	*Annali della Facultà di Lingua e Letterature Straniere di Ca'Foscari*
Annali Sezione Slava (Naples)	*Annali Instituto Universitario Orientale. Sezione Slava* (Napoli)
	L'Année Balzacienne

Antigonish R	*The Antigonish Review*
Anuario del Departamento de Inglés	*Anuario del Departamento de Inglés* (Barcelona, Spain)
Appalachian Stud	*Appalachian Studies*
	Arbeiten aus Anglistik und Amerikanistik
	L'Arc
Arcadia	*Arcadia: Zeitschrift für Vergleichende Literaturwissenschaft*
Archiv	*Archiv für das Studium der Neueren Sprachen und Literaturen*
Ariel	*Ariel: A Review of International English Literature*
Arizona Q	*Arizona Quarterly*
Armchair Detective	*Armchair Detective: A Quarterly Journal Devoted to the Appreciation of Mystery, Detective, and Suspense Fiction*
	Arquipélago
Asian & African Stud	*Asian and African Studies*
Asian Folklore Stud	*Asian Folklore Studies*
Atlantic	*The Atlantic Monthly*
Aurora	*Aurora: Jahrbuch der Eichendorff Gesellschaft*
Australian J French Stud	*Australian Journal of French Studies*
Australian Lit Stud	*Australian Literary Studies*
Baker Street J	*The Baker Street Journal: An Irregular Quarterly of Sherlockiana*
Ball State Univ Forum	*Ball State University Forum*
Black Am Lit Forum	*Black American Literature Forum* [formerly *Negro American Literature Forum*]
	Boletin Cultural y Bibliografia (Bogota, Colombia)
Boletín de la Academia Norteamericana	*Boletín de la Academia Norteamericana de la Lengua Española*

Bucknell R	*Bucknell Review: A Scholarly Journal of Letters, Arts and Sciences*
Bull Hispanic Stud	*Bulletin of Hispanic Studies*
Bull Hispanique	*Bulletin Hispanique*
Bull West Virginia Assoc Coll Engl Teachers	*Bulletin of the West Virginia Association of College English Teachers*
Cadernos de Lingüística	*Cadernos de Lingüística e Teoria da Literatura*
	Cahiers Algériens de Littérature Comparée
Cahiers de l'Association Internationale	*Cahiers de l'Association Internationale des Études Françaises*
Les Cahiers de la Nouvelle	*Les Cahiers de la Nouvelle: Journal of the Short Story*
Cahiers du Centre d'Études	*Cahiers du Centre d'Études et de Recherches sur les Littéraires de l'Imaginaire*
	Cahiers du Centre d'Études Irlandaises (Université de Haute Bretagne)
	Cahiers Universitaires Catholiques
Cahiers Victoriens et Edouardiens	*Cahiers Victoriens et Edouardiens: Revue du Centre d'Études et de Recherches Victoriennes et Edouardiennes de l'Université Paul Valéry, Montpellier*
Callaloo	*Callaloo: A Black South Journal of Arts and Letters*
Canadian Fiction Mag	*Canadian Fiction Magazine*
Canadian J Irish Stud	*Canadian Journal of Irish Studies*
Canadian J Italian Stud	*Canadian Journal of Italian Studies*
Canadian-Am Slavic Stud	*Canadian-American Slavic Studies*
Canadian Lit	*Canadian Literature*
Canadian R Am Stud	*Canadian Review of American Studies*
Canadian R Contemp Lit	*Canadian Review of Contemporary Literature*
Canadian Slavonic Papers	*Canadian Slavonic Papers: An Inter-Disciplinary Quarterly Devoted to the Soviet Union and Eastern Europe*
Carleton Germ Papers	*Carleton Germanic Papers*

	Casa de las Americas
	Catholic World
Centennial R	*Centennial Review*
Centerpoint	*Centerpoint: A Journal of Interdisciplinary Studies*
Ceylon J Hum	*Ceylon Journal of the Humanities*
Chasqui	*Chasqui: Revista de Literatura Latinoamericana*
Chicago R	*Chicago Review*
Chimères	*Chimères: A Journal of French and Italian Literature*
Chinese Lit	*Chinese Literature*
	Chiricú
Christianity & Lit	*Christianity and Literature*
Chu-Shikoku Stud Am Lit	*Chu-Shikoku Studies in American Literature*
Cithara	*Cithara: Essays in the Judaeo-Christian Tradition*
Claflin Coll R	*Claflin College Review*
Classical & Mod Lit	*Classical and Modern Literature*
Clues	*Clues: A Journal of Detection*
Colby Lib Q	*Colby Library Quarterly*
Coll Engl Assoc Critic	*CEA Critic: An Official Journal of the College English Association*
Coll Lang Assoc J	*College Language Association Journal*
Coll Lit	*College Literature*
Colloquia Germanica	*Colloquia Germanica, Internationale Zeitschrift für Germanische Sprach- und Literaturwissenschaft*
	Commonwealth [Dijon]
Commonwealth Q	*Commonwealth Quarterly*
Comparatist	*The Comparatist: Journal of the Southern Comparative Literature Association*
Comp Lit	*Comparative Literature*

Comp Lit Stud	Comparative Literature Studies
	Confluents
Conradiana	Conradiana: A Journal of Joseph Conrad
	Constructions
Contemp Lit	Contemporary Literature
	Critica Hispánica
Critical I	Critical Inquiry
Critical Q	Critical Quarterly
Critical R	The Critical Review
Criticism	Criticism: A Quarterly for Literature and the Arts
Critique	Critique: Revue Générale des Publications Françaises et Étrangères
Critique	Critique: Studies in Modern Fiction
Cuaderno de Norte	Cuaderno de Norte: Revista Hispanica de Amsterdam
	Cuadernos Americanos
Cuadernos Hispanoamericanos	Cuadernos Hispanoamericanos: Revista Mensual de Cultura Hispanica
Cuyahoga R	Cuyahoga Review
D. H. Lawrence R	The D. H. Lawrence Review
Delta	Delta: Revue du Centre d'Études et de Recherche sur les Écrivains du Sud aux États-Unis
Denver Q	Denver Quarterly
Deutsche Vierteljahrsschrift	Deutsche Virteljahrsschrift für Literaturwissenschaft und Geistesgeschichte
Der Deutschunterricht	Der Deutschunterricht: Beiträge zu seiner Praxis und wissenschaftlichen Grundlegung
	Deutschunterricht in Südafrika
Diacritics	Diactritics: A Review of Contemporary Criticism
Diálogos	Diálogos Hispánicos de Amsterdam

Dickens Stud Annual	Dickens Studies Annual: Essays on Victorian Fiction
Discorso Literario	Discorso Literario: Revista de Temas Hispánicos
Dispositio	Dispositio: Revista Hispánica de Semiótica Literaria
	Doris Lessing Newsletter
Doshisha Stud Engl	Doshisha Studies in English
Dostoevsky Stud	Dostoevsky Studies: Journal of the International Dostoevsky Society [formerly International Dostoevsky Society Bulletin]
	Drab
Durham Univ J	Durham University Journal
Dutch Q R	Dutch Quarterly Review of Anglo-American Letters
Early Am Lit	Early American Literature
	Eco
	Edda: Nordisk Tidsskrift for Litteraturforskning
Edebiyat: J Middle Eastern Lit	Edebiyat: A Journal of Middle Eastern Literatures
Éire	Éire-Ireland: A Journal of Irish Studies
Emerson Soc Q	Emerson Society Quarterly—now ESQ: Journal of the American Renaissance
	Enclitic
Encyclia	Encyclia: The Journal of the Utah Academy of Sciences, Arts, and Letters
Engl Lang Notes	English Language Notes
Engl Lit Hist	English Literary History [formerly Journal of English Literary History]
Engl Lit Transition	English Literature in Transition
Engl Stud	English Studies: A Journal of English Language and Literature
Engl Stud Africa	English Studies in Africa: A Journal of the Humanities

Engl Stud Canada	*English Studies in Canada*
Epistemonike	*Epistemonike Epeterida Philosophikes Scholes Aristoteleiou Panepistemiou Thessalonikes*
L'Epoque Conradienne	*L'Epoque Conradienne: Bulletin annuel de la Société Conradienne*
Escritura	*Escritura: Teoría y Crítica Literarias*
	L'Esprit Créateur
ESQ: J Am Renaissance	*Emerson Society Quarterly: Journal of the American Renaissance*
Essays Arts & Sciences	*Essays in Arts & Sciences*
Essays Canadian Writing	*Essays on Canadian Writing*
Essays Crit	*Essays in Criticism: A Quarterly Journal of Literary Criticism*
Essays French Lit	*Essays in French Literature*
Essays Lit	*Essays in Literature* (Western Illinois)
	Estudos Anglo-Americanos
	Estudios Filológicos
Études Anglaises	*Études Anglaises: Grande Bretagne, États-Unis*
Études de Lettres	*Études de Lettres* (Lausanne)
	Études Germaniques
	Études Irlandaises
	Études Littéraires
Euphorion	*Euphorion: Zeitschrift für Literaturgeschichte*
Europe	*Europe: Revue Littéraire Mensuelle*
	Explicación de Textos Literarios
	Explicator
	Extrapolation
	Fabula

Faulkner Stud — *Faulkner Studies: An Annual of Research, Criticism, and Reviews*

Fiction Int'l — *Fiction International*

Fitzgerald/Hemingway Annual 1974

Fitzgerald/Hemingway Annual 1975

Fitzgerald/Hemingway Annual 1979

Folio — *Folio: Papers on Foreign Languages and Literature*

Folklore

Folklore (Calcutta) — *Folklore: India's Only English Monthly on the Subject* (Calcutta)

Fontane Blätter

Forum Italicum

Forum Mod Lang Stud — *Forum for Modern Language Studies*

Foundation — *Foundation: Review of Science Fiction*

Francofonia — *Francofonia: Studi e Ricerche Sulle Letterature di Lingua Francese*

Französische Heute

French Forum

French R — *French Review: Journal of the American Association of Teachers of French*

Frontiers — *Frontiers: A Journal of Women Studies*

Fu Jen Stud — *Fu Jen Studies: Literature & Linguistics* (Taipei)

Genre

Geographical R — *The Geographical Review*

George Eliot Fellowship R — *The George Eliot Fellowship Review*

Georgetown Univ Round Table — *Georgetown University Round Table on Languages and Linguistics*

Georgia R — *Georgia Review*

Germ Life & Letters	*German Life and Letters*
Germ Notes	*Germanic Notes*
Germ Q	*German Quarterly*
German R	*Germanic Review*
Germanisch-Romanische Monatsschrift	*Germanisch-Romanische Monatsschrift*, Neue Folge
Germano-Slavica	*Germano-Slavica: A Canadian Journal of Germanic and Slavic Comparative Studies*
Glyph	*Glyph: Johns Hopkins Textual Studies*
	Gothic
Great Plains Q	*Great Plains Quarterly*
Gypsy Scholar	*Gypsy Scholar: A Graduate Forum for Literary Criticism*
Hartford Stud Lit	*University of Hartford Studies in Literature: A Journal of Interdisciplinary Criticism*
Harvard J Asiatic Stud	*Harvard Journal of Asiatic Studies*
Harvard Ukrainian Stud	*Harvard Ukrainian Studies*
	Haunted
Hebrew Univ Stud Lit	*Hebrew University Studies in Literature*
Heine J	*Heine Jahrbuch*
Hemingway R	*Hemingway Review* [formerly *Hemingway Notes*]
Henry James R	*Henry James Review*
Hispamerica	*Hispamerica: Revista de Literatura*
Hispania	*Hispania: A Journal Devoted to the Interests of the Teaching of Spanish and Portuguese*
Hispanic J	*Hispanic Journal*
Hitotsubashi	*Hitotsubashi Journal of Arts & Sciences*
	Hollins Critic

Horizontes	*Horizontes: Revista de la Universidad Católica de Puerto Rico*
Hudson R	*Hudson Review*
Humanitas	*Humanitas: Revista di Cultura* (Brescia, Italy)
Humanities	*Humanities: Christianity & Culture*
	Ibero-Amerikanisches Archiv
	Imprévue
Indian J Engl Stud	*Indian Journal of English Studies*
Indian Lit	*Indian Literature*
Inti	*Inti: Revista de literatura Hispánica*
Int'l Dostoevsky Soc Bull	*International Dostoevsky Society Bulletin*
Int'l Fiction R	*International Fiction Review*
Int'l Folklore R	*International Folklore Review*
Int'l J Middle East Stud	*International Journal of Middle East Studies*
Int'l R Psycho-Analysis	*International Review of Psycho-Analysis*
Interpretations	*Interpretations: Studies in Language and Literature*
Iowa R	*Iowa Review*
	Irish Renaissance Annual
Irish Slavonic Stud	*Irish Slavonic Studies*
Irish Univ R	*Irish University Review: A Journal of Irish Studies*
	Irish Writing
	Italianist
	Italica
	Jack London Newsletter
	Jahrbuch der Deutschen Schiller-Gesellschaft
	Jahrbuch der Karl-May-Gesellschaft

Jahrbuch des Freien Deutschen Hochstifts

Jahrbuch für Internationale Germanistik

James Joyce Q	*James Joyce Quarterly*
John O'Hara J	*John O'Hara Journal*
	Joseph Conrad Today
J Am Oriental Soc	*Journal of the American Oriental Society*
J Australasian Univs Lang & Lit Assoc	*Journal of the Australasian Universities Language and Literature Association: A Journal of Literary Criticism, Philology & Linguistics*
J Beckett Stud	*Journal of Beckett Studies*
J Commonwealth Lit	*The Journal of Commonwealth Literature*
J Dept Engl	*Journal of the Department of English* (Calcutta University)
J Engl	*Journal of English* (Sana'a Univ.)
J Engl & Germ Philol	*Journal of English and Germanic Philology*
J Evolutionary Psych	*Journal of Evolutionary Psychology*
J Gen Ed	*Journal of General Education*
J Homosexuality	*Journal of Homosexuality*
J Illinois State Hist Soc	*Journal of the Illinois State Historical Society*
J Joseph Conrad Soc	*Journal of the Joseph Conrad Society*
J Karnatak Univ	*Journal of the Karnatak University—Humanities*
J Lit Semantics	*Journal of Literary Semantics*
J Mod Lit	*Journal of Modern Literature*
J Narrative Technique	*Journal of Narrative Technique*
J Nassau Community Coll	*Journal of the Nassau Community College Devoted to Art, Letters, and Science*
J Pop Culture	*Journal of Popular Culture*

J Regional Cultures	*Journal of Regional Cultures*
J Religion Lit	*Journal of Religion in Literature*
J School Langs	*Journal of the School of Languages*
J Semitic Stud	*Journal of Semitic Studies*
J So Asian Lit	*Journal of South Asian Literature*
J Spanish Stud: Twentieth Century	*Journal of Spanish Studies: Twentieth Century*
J Ukrainian Stud	*Journal of Ukrainian Studies*
Káñina	*Káñina: Revista de Artes y Letras de la Universidad de Costa Rica*
Kansas Q	*Kansas Quarterly*
	Kate Chopin Newsletter
Kentucky Folklore Record	*Kentucky Folklore Record: A Regional Journal of Folklore and Folklife*
Kentucky Romance Q	*Kentucky Romance Quarterly*
Kilkenny Mag	*Kilkenny Magazine*
Kipling J	*The Kipling Journal*
Klasgids	*Klasgids: By die Studie van die Afrikaanse Taal en Letterkunde*
	Kunapipi
Kyushu Am Lit	*Kyushu American Literature*
Lagos R Engl Stud	*Lagos Review of English Studies*
Lang & Style	*Language and Style: An International Journal*
Lang Q	*The University of Southern Florida Language Quarterly*
	Les Langues Modernes
Latin Am Lit R	*Latin American Literary Review*
	Letteratura

	Les Lettres Romanes
Lib Chronicle	*Library Chronicle*
Liberal & Fine Arts R	*Liberal & Fine Arts Review*
Licorne	*La Licorne*
Linguistics in Lit	*Linguistics in Literature*
Lit & Hist	*Literature and History: A New Journal for the Humanities*
Lit & Med	*Literature and Medicine*
Lit & Psych	*Literature and Psychology*
Lit Criterion	*Literary Criterion*
Lit East & West	*Literature East and West*
Lit Endeavor	*The Literary Endeavor: A Quarterly Devoted to English Literature*
Lit/Film Q	*Literature/Film Quarterly*
Lit North Queensland	*Literature in North Queensland*
	Literatur in Wissenschaft und Unterricht
	Literatur und Kritik
Lit Onomastics Stud	*Literary Onomastics Studies*
Lit R	*Literary Review: An International Journal of Contemporary Writing*
Littérature	*Littérature* (Paris)
Lost Generation J	*Lost Generation Journal*
Luso-Brazilian R	*Luso-Brazilian Review*
Mark Twain J	*Mark Twain Journal*
Markham R	*Markham Review*
Massachusetts R	*Massachusetts Review: A Quarterly of Literature, the Arts and Public Affairs*
Massachusetts Stud Engl	*Massachusetts Studies in English*

	Meanjin
MELUS	*MELUS: Multi-Ethnic Literature in the United States*
	Mester
Michigan Academician	*Michigan Academician: Papers of the Michigan Academy of Science, Arts, and Letters*
Midamerica	*Midamerica: The Yearbook of the Society for the Study of Midwestern Literature*
Mid-Hudson Lang Stud	*Mid-Hudson Language Studies* (Bulletin of the Mid-Hudson Modern Language Association)
Minas Gerais	*Minas Gerais, Suplemento Literário*
Minnesota R	*Minnesota Review*
Miorita	*Miorita: A Journal of Romanian Studies*
Mississippi Q	*Mississippi Quarterly: The Journal of Southern Culture*
Missouri R	*Missouri Review*
Mitteilungen der E. T. A. Hoffmann	*Mitteilungen der E. T. A. Hoffmann-Gesellschaft-Bamberg*
Mod Austrian Lit	*Modern Austrian Literature: Journal of the International Arthur Schnitzler Research Association*
Mod Fiction Stud	*Modern Fiction Studies*
Mod Lang Notes	*Modern Language Notes* [retitled *MLN*]
Mod Lang Q	*Modern Language Quarterly*
Mod Lang R	*Modern Language Review*
Mod Lang Stud	*Modern Language Studies*
Mod Langs	*Modern Languages: Journal of the Modern Language Association* (London)
Mod Philol	*Modern Philology: A Journal Devoted to Research in Medieval and Modern Literature*
	Moderna Sprak

Monatshefte	*Monatshefte: Für Deutschen Unterricht, Deutsche Sprache und Literatur*
Mosaic	*Mosaic: A Journal for the Comparative Study of Literature and Ideas for the Interdisciplinary Study of Literature*
Mundus Artium	*Mundus Artium: A Journal of International Literature and the Arts*
Nabokovian	*The Nabokovian* [formerly *Vladimir Nabokov Research Newsletter*]
Names	*Names: Journal of the American Names Society*
Nassau R	*The Nassau Review: The Journal of Nassau Community College Devoted to Arts, Letters, and Sciences*
Nathaniel Hawthorne J	*Nathaniel Hawthorne Journal*
	Nation
Neohelicon	*Neohelicon: Acta Comparationis Litterarum Universatum*
	Neophilologus
	Neue Rundschau
Neue Sammlung	*Neue Sammlung: Zeitschrift für Erziehung und Gesellschaft*
	Die Neueren Sprachen
Neuphilologische Mitteilungen	*Neuphilologische Mitteilungen: Bulletin de la Société Néophilologique/Bulletin of the Modern Language Society*
Neusprachliche Mitteilungen	*Neusprachliche Mitteilungen aus Wissenschaft und Praxis*
	New Criterion
New England Q	*New England Quarterly: A Historical Review of New England Life and Letters*
New Germ Stud	*New German Studies*
New Lit Hist	*New Literary History*

New Orleans R	*New Orleans Review*
	New Republic
New York R Books	*The New York Review of Books*
New Zealand J French Stud	*New Zealand Journal of French Studies*
New Zealand Slavonic J	*New Zealand Slavonic Journal*
Newsletter Kafka Soc America	*Newsletter of the Kafka Society of America*
Niederdeutsches Jahrbuch	*Niederdeutches Jahrbuch: Jahrbuch des Vereins für Niederdeutsche Sprachforschung*
	Nineteenth-Century Fiction
Nineteenth-Century French Stud	*Nineteenth-Century French Studies*
Notes & Queries	*Notes and Queries*
Notes Contemp Lit	*Notes on Contemporary Literature*
Notes Mississippi Writers	*Notes on Mississippi Writers*
Notes Mod Am Lit	*NMAL: Notes on Modern American Literature*
Nottingham French Stud	*Nottingham French Studies*
	Nouvelle Revue Française
Novel	*Novel: A Forum on Fiction*
	Nueva Dimensión
	Nueva Revista del Pacifico
Nuova Corrente	*Nuova Corrente: Rivista di Letteratura*
	Nyctalops
NYU Law R	*N.Y.U. Law Review*
Obsidian	*Obsidian: Black Literature in Review*
Odyssey	*Odyssey: A Journal of the Humanities*
Okike	*Okike: An African Journal of New Writing*

Old Northwest	*The Old Northwest: A Journal of Regional Life and Letters*
	Open Letter
Orbis Litterarum	*Orbis Litterarum: International Review of Literary Studies*
Österreich in Amerikanischer Sicht	*Österreich in Amerikanischer Sicht: Das Österreichbild Amerikanischen Schulunterricht*
Österreich in Geschichte und Literatur	*Österreich in Geschichte und Literatur (mit Geographie)*
Oxford Germ Stud	*Oxford German Studies*
Pacific Q	*Pacific Quarterly (Moana): An International Review of Arts and Ideas*
Paideia	*Paideia: Journal of Foundational Studies in Education*
Palabra	*La Palabra: Revista de Literatura Chicana* (Tempe, Ariz.)
Panjab Univ Research Bull	*Panjab University Research Bulletin (Arts)*
	Papers in Romance
Papers Lang & Lit	*Papers on Language and Literature: A Journal for Scholars and Critics of Language and Literature*
Par Rapport	*Par Rapport: A Journal of the Humanities*
Paragone	*Paragone: Rivista Mensile di Arte Figurativa e Letteratura*
Partisan R	*Partisan Review*
Pembroke Mag	*The Pembroke Magazine*
Pennsylvania Engl	*Pennsylvania English*
Perspectives Contemp Lit	*Perspectives on Contemporary Literature*
Philol Q	*Philological Quarterly*
Philosophy & Lit	*Philosophy and Literature*
	Phoenix (Korea)

Phylon	*Phylon: The Atlanta University Review of Race and Culture*
Platte Valley R	*Platte Valley Review*
PMLA	*PMLA: Publications of the Modern Language Association of America*
Poe Stud	*Poe Studies*
Poetics Today	*Poetics Today: Theory and Analysis of Literature and Communication* (Tel Aviv, Israel)
Poétique	*Poétique: Revue de Théorie et d'Analyse Littéraires*
Polish Am Stud	*Polish American Studies*
Polish R	*The Polish Review*
	Prairie Schooner
Présence Africaine	*Présence Africaine: Revue Culturelle du Monde Noir/Cultural Review of the Negro World*
Présence Francophone	*Présence Francophone: Revue Littéraire*
	Proceedings of the Kentucky Foreign Language Conference: Slavic Section
Proceedings Pacific Northwest Conference Foreign Langs	*Proceedings of the Pacific Northwest Conference on Foreign Languages*
Prospects	*Prospects: An Annual Journal of American Cultural Studies*
Psychocultural R	*Psychocultural Review: Interpretations in the Psychology of Art, Literature and Society*
Psychohistory R	*The Psychohistory Review*
PTL: J Descriptive Poetics and Theory Lit	*PTL: A Journal for Descriptive Poetics and Theory of Literature*
Pubs Missouri Philol Assoc	*Publications of the Missouri Philological Association*
Quaderni die Filologia Germanica	*Quaderni di Filologia Germanica della Facultà di Lettere e Filosofia dell'Università di Bologna*
Quaderni d'Italianistica	*Quaderni d'Italianistica: Official Journal of the Canadian Society for Italian Studies*

Quarber Merkur

Quimera   *Quimera: Revista de Literatura*

Raritan   *Raritan: A Quarterly Review*

                                  RE: Artes Liberales

                                  Il Re in Giallo

                                  Recherches Anglaises et Américaines

Recherches et Études   *Recherches et Études Comparatistes Ibéro-Françaises
                                  de la Sorbonne*

                                  Recherches Germanique

Renascence   *Renascence: Essays on Value in Literature*

Rendezvous   *Rendezvous: Journal of Arts and Letters*

Research Stud   *Washington State University Research Studies*

R (New York)   *Review* (New York)

R Contemp Fiction   *Review of Contemporary Fiction*

R Engl Lit   *Review of English Literature*

                                  Revista Canadiense de Estudios Hispánicos

Revista de Critica   *Revista de Critica Literaria Latinoamericana*

                                  Revista de Estudios Hispánicos (Puerto Rico)

                                  Revista Iberoamericanas

                                  Revista Letras

                                  Revista Nacional de Cultura

                                  Revista/Review Interamericana

Revue Belge   *Revue Belge de Philologie et d'Histoire*

                                  Revue de Littérature Comparée

                                  Revue de l'Université d'Ottawa

R Lettres Modernes   *La Revue des Lettres Modernes Histoire des Idées des
                                  Littératures*

Revue Française d'Études Américaines

Revue Romane

Revue Roumaine de Linguistique

Riverside Q — *Riverside Quarterly*

Rivista di Letterature — *Rivista di Letterature Moderne e Comparate (Florence)*

Rocky Mt R — *Rocky Mountain Review* [formerly *Bulletin of the Rocky Mountain Modern Language Association*]

Romance Notes

Romanic R — *Romanic Review*

Romantisme — *Romantisme: Revue du Dix-Neuvième Siècle*

Romantist — *The Romantist*

Russian Lang J — *Russian Language Journal*

Russian Lit Tri-Q — *Russian Literature Triquarterly*

Russian R — *Russian Review: An American Quarterly Devoted to Russia Past and Present*

Saul Bellow J — *Saul Bellow Journal* [formerly *Saul Bellow Newsletter*]

Scandinavian Stud — *Scandinavian Studies*

Scandinavica — *Scandinavica: An International Journal of Scandinavian Studies*

Schriften der Theodor-Storm-Gesellschaft

Sci Fiction R Monthly — *Science Fiction Review Monthly*

Sci-Fiction Stud — *Science-Fiction Studies*

Selecta — *Selecta: Journal of the Pacific Northwest Council on Foreign Languages* [formerly *Proceedings of the Pacific Northwest Conference on Foreign Languages*]

Seminar — *Seminar: A Journal of Germanic Studies*

Semiosis — *Semiosis: Cuadernos del Seminario de Semiótica Literaria*

	SF Horizons
	Sin Nombre
Slavic & East European J	*Slavic and East European Journal*
Slavic R	*Slavic Review: American Quarterly of Soviet and East European Studies*
So Asian R	*South Asian Review*
So Atlantic Bull	*South Atlantic Bulletin: A Quarterly Journal Devoted to Research and Teaching in the Modern Languages and Literatures*
So Atlantic Q	*South Atlantic Quarterly*
So Carolina Bull	*South Carolina Bulletin*
So Carolina R	*South Carolina Review*
So Central Bull	*South Central Bulletin*
So Central R	*South Central Review*
So Dakota R	*South Dakota Review*
Southern Hum R	*Southern Humanities Review*
Southern Lit J	*Southern Literary Journal*
Southern Q	*The Southern Quarterly: A Journal of the Arts in the South*
Southern R	*Southern Review* (Baton Rouge)
Southern Stud	*Southern Studies: An Interdisciplinary Journal of the South*
Soviet Lit	*Soviet Literature*
Soviet Stud Lit	*Soviet Studies in Literature*
Sphinx	*The Sphinx: A Magazine of Literature and Society*
Sprachkunst	*Sprachkunst: Beiträge zur Literaturwissenschaft*
Stanford French R	*Stanford French Review*
Steinbeck Q	*Steinbeck Quarterly*
Studies	*Studies: An Irish Quarterly Review*

Stud Am Fiction	*Studies in American Fiction*
Stud Am Humor	*Studies in American Humor*
Stud Am Jewish Lit	*Studies in American Jewish Literature*
Stud Black Lit	*Studies in Black Literature*
Stud Engl Lit	*Studies in English Literature, 1500–1900*
Stud Hum	*Studies in the Humanities*
Stud Medievalism	*Studies in Medievalism*
Stud Novel	*Studies in the Novel*
Stud Romanticism	*Studies in Romanticism*
Stud Scottish Lit	*Studies in Scottish Literature*
Stud Short Fiction	*Studies in Short Fiction*
Stud Twentieth Century Lit	*Studies in Twentieth Century Literature*
Studi di Letteratura	*Studi di Letteratura Ispano-Americana*
	Studi Francesi
	Studia Germanica Gandensias
	Studia Romanica et Anglica Zagrabiensia
	Studii şi Cercetări Lingvistice
	Style
SubStance	*SubStance: A Review of Theory and Literary Criticism*
Sur	*Revista Sur*
Swiss-French Stud	*Swiss-French Studies/Études Romandes* (Wolfville, Canada)
Sydney Stud Engl	*Sydney Studies in English*
Symposium	*Symposium: A Quarterly Journal of Modern Literatures*
Tennessee Folklore Soc Bull	*Tennessee Folklore Society Bulletin*

Tennessee Stud Lit	*Tennessee Studies in Literature*
Texas Stud Lit & Lang	*Texas Studies in Literature and Language: A Journal of the Humanities*
	Text & Kontext
	Texto Crítico
Thalia	*Thalia: Studies in Literary Humor*
Thesaurus	*Thesaurus: Boletín del Instituto Caro y Cuevo*
	Third Woman
Thomas Wolfe R	*The Thomas Wolfe Review*
	Thought
Travaux de Linguistique et de Littérature	*Travaux de Linguistique et de Littérature Publiés par le Centre de Philologie et de Littératures Romanes de l'Université de Strasbourg*
Tristania	*Tristania: A Journal Devoted to Tristan Studies*
Tulsa Stud Women's Lit	*Tulsa Studies in Women's Literature*
Turkish Stud Assoc Bull	*Turkish Studies Association Bulletin*
	Turn-of-the-Century Women
Twentieth Century Lit	*Twentieth Century Literature: A Scholarly and Critical Journal*
Ukrainian Q	*Ukrainian Quarterly: Journal of East European and Asian Affairs*
Ulbandus R	*Ulbandus Review: A Journal of Slavic Languages and Literatures*
Unisa Engl Stud	*Unisa English Studies: Journal of the Department of English, University of South Africa*
Universidad	*Universidad de La Habana*
Univ Dayton R	*University of Dayton Review*
Univ Mississippi Stud Engl	*University of Mississippi Studies in English*
	Vermont History

Virginia Q R	*Virginia Quarterly Review: A National Journal of Literature and Discussion*
	Virginia Woolf Miscellany
Virginia Woolf Q	*Virginia Woolf Quarterly*
Walt Whitman R	*Walt Whitman Review*
Wascana R	*Wascana Review*
West Georgia Coll R	*West Georgia College Review*
West Virginia Univ Philol Papers	*West Virginia University Philological Papers*
Western Am Lit	*Western American Literature*
Western Hum R	*Western Humanities Review*
	Whisper
	Wiener Slawistischer Almanach
Wirkendes Wort	*Wirkendes Wort: Deutsche Sprache in Forschung und Lehre*
Women & Lit	*Women & Literature*
Women's Stud	*Women's Studies: An Interdisciplinary Journal*
World Lit Today	*World Literature Today: A Literary Quarterly of the University of Oklahoma*
World Lit Written Engl	*World Literature Written in English*
Xavier R	*Xavier Review* [formerly *Xavier University Studies*]
Yale French Stud	*Yale French Studies*
Yale R	*The Yale Review: A National Quarterly*
Yale Univ Lib Gazette	*Yale University Library Gazette*
	Zeitschrift für Anglistik und Amerikanistik
	Zeitschrift für Deutsche Philologie
	Zeitschrift für französische Sprache und Literatur
Zona Franca	*Zona Franca: Revista de Literatura*

INDEX OF SHORT STORY WRITERS

DATE DUE			